MARK LEVINE

DEMOCRAT FOR CONGRESS

TheAggressiveProgressive.com

Paid for by Mark Levine for Congress

BARNEY FRANK

Barney Frank

THE STORY OF AMERICA'S ONLY LEFT-HANDED, GAY, JEWISH CONGRESSMAN

Stuart E. Weisberg

University of Massachusetts Press
Amherst & Boston

LC 2009022362
ISBN 978-1-55849-721-4

Designed by Jack Harrison
Set in ITC Galliard
Printed and bound by Sheridan Books, Inc.

Library of Congress Cataloging-in-Publication Data
Weisberg, Stuart E., 1949–
Barney Frank : the story of America's only left-handed, gay, Jewish congressman /
Stuart E. Weisberg.
p. cm.
Includes index.
ISBN 978-1-55849-721-4 (cloth : alk. paper)
1. Frank, Barney, 1940– 2. Legislators—United States—Biography.
3. United States. Congress. House—Biography.
4. United States—Politics and government—1945–1989.
5. United States—Politics and government—1989– I. Title.
E840.8.F695W45 2009
328.73'092—dc22
[B]
2009022362

British Library Cataloguing in Publication data are available.

To Beth, the best thing that ever happened to me, and to Andrew and Eric, who prove each day that wishes really do come true.

In memory of Elsie Frank (1912–2005), the matriarch of the Frank family, a caring, energetic, and remarkable woman who at age seventy began a new career as an advocate for senior citizens. She acted with conviction, humility, and charm and is sorely missed by all who came in contact with her.

Contents

Illustrations follow page 214

Preface

This is a biography of perhaps the most fascinating and certainly the most entertaining political figure in Washington. It is a portrait of the complex life and career of Barney Frank, an outspoken liberal, Jewish, fifteen-term Democratic congressman from Massachusetts by way of Bayonne, New Jersey, a colorful, pragmatic, and effective legislator whose political career has been defined by depth of intellect and sharpness of wit, and who happens to be gay. As the chairman of the House Financial Services Committee since 2007, he has been a pivotal figure and at the center of the debate on how to deal with the unprecedented economic crisis and challenge facing the nation and the world.

I am deeply indebted to so many people who helped make my idea for a book a reality. Barney Frank's cooperation was invaluable on the project. Without it this book would be but a shell.

When I first mentioned to Barney the idea of writing a book about him, he was intrigued by the project and suggested that we get together to discuss it. In early February 2004, we met for breakfast. I handed him a ten-page introduction to the book that I had prepared. As he began to read the document, with startling speed, I glanced down at the single-page breakfast menu. He finished reading the document before I got through the juices. He told me it was well written and pointed out two minor inaccuracies.

"Start asking your questions," he said.

Thus began the first in a series of nearly twenty interviews with him over a five-year period. These sessions generally lasted between one and two hours, depending on his schedule and attention span on a particular day. There were clearly some subjects that he enjoyed talking about more than others. Delving into his personal life was not something he relished doing, because he is essentially a private person, but he did so with characteristic candor and openness. He answered all of my questions, many of which were highly personal or potentially embarrassing. Either there was no area out of bounds or I didn't cross that line. I am grateful to Barney Frank for generously giving me his time, a very precious commodity to him, and for sharing with me his intimate thoughts, feelings, and recollections.

Although putting together this book has proved to be a formidable task, it has also been enjoyable and rewarding. It has been a great adventure for me, discovering and learning about somebody I thought I knew. My friendship with Barney spans almost four decades. I first met him during the summer of 1971 when I was an intern for Massachusetts congressman Michael J. Harrington and he was the chief of staff. We soon developed a friendship based on a common interest in politics and sports, as well as a propensity to rely on movies and television shows for purposes of analogy. I had the opportunity to observe Barney from close up as he chaired the House Government Operations Subcommittee on Employment and Housing in the mid-1980s when I was the panel's staff director and chief counsel.

The nonfiction author extraordinaire Gay Talese, during a book-tour stop in Washington in May 2006 to promote his memoir, *A Writer's Life*, explained that before he starts to write, he always spends a lot of time really getting to know his subject, whether it is the baseball great Joe DiMaggio or the mafia chieftain Joseph Bonanno. Asked how he could be objective after spending so much time with that person, Talese replied that he writes only about people whom he respects. Talese's answer rings true for me as well.

In the seventeenth century, when the English military commander and political leader Oliver Cromwell was asked to have his portrait painted, he told the artist, "Use all your skill to paint your picture truly like me" and include "roughness, pimples, warts and everything as you see me." Although this book is an admiring biography of Barney Frank, it shows warts and everything. It does not skirt any issue or controversy and there is no airbrushing of events. The story is not always told as Barney might like it.

My wonderful wife, Beth, and our two sons, Andrew and Eric, deserve special thanks not just for putting up with me but for giving me their understanding, continued encouragement, and support throughout the lengthy process of researching and writing.

One of the joys of doing this book was the afternoon I spent with Elsie Frank in May 2004 at her apartment in Boston. Barney's ninety-one-year-old mother regaled me with Frank family stories. A fascinating and extraordinary woman, Elsie was alert and sharp. I continued to communicate with her by e-mail. In January 2005, after interviewing the journalist Steven V. Roberts, a Bayonne native, I shared with her Steve's comment that his father, Will, used to describe her as "one of the most beautiful young women [he knew] in Bayonne." Elsie replied, "Thanks for the compliment but for heaven's sake do not include that in Barney's biography! Better to say that he was only twenty years old when my husband died suddenly and I challenge anyone to match the sacrifices he made in his personal life to help me get my affairs in order." Sadly, Elsie Frank passed away in August 2005 and did not live to read this book.

My sincere thanks go to Barney's siblings, Ann, Doris, and David, for spending time with me relating family stories, offering insights, and answering questions.

I am beholden to more than 150 people, a group too numerous to list by name here, who gave generously of their time and shared their personal and political recollections. They graciously invited me into their homes and offices, the historic Hawthorne Inn in Salem (Michael J. Harrington), a Columbia Law School classroom (Lance Liebman), a small faculty office at Northeastern University in Boston (Michael Dukakis), and even the West Wing of the White House (Andrew Card), to talk about Barney Frank and permitted me, a notoriously slow note-taker, to record those interviews on tape. One person asked whether Barney would be listening to the interview tape. "I couldn't get him to listen to these tapes at gunpoint," I replied. Others agreed to interviews on the telephone or by e-mail. The overwhelming majority of those interviewed are cited and quoted by name in the book. There are a few, however, who asked not to be identified by name, and I have respected their wishes.

A special note of gratitude goes to Dorothy "Dottie" Reichard, a delightful woman who has been the director of Barney Frank's district office since his election to Congress in 1980. Dottie provided me with access to all of the congressman's records stored at the Federal Archives in Waltham, Massachusetts, and assisted me in tracking down several former legislators.

A similar notice of appreciation goes to Peter Kovar, the longtime chief of staff in Barney Frank's Washington office, for among other things, venturing down to the dusty catacombs in the subbasement of the Rayburn House Office Building, to the storage area, a place where even OSHA inspectors fear to venture, to find, dust off, and provide me with access to several large boxes containing audio and video tapes, many unlabeled, of interviews, speeches, debates, and radio and television appearances dating to the early 1980s. I would also like to recognize Daniel McGlinchey, a professional staff member of the House Financial Services Committee, who was instrumental in helping me track down several photos that appear in the book, and Jim Ready, Barney's partner, for providing several photos.

I deeply appreciate the constructive suggestions of my friends Bill Gainer, Deborah Katz, and David Lowe, who took the time to read my initial draft and made it better. I am indebted to my friend Charles Tiefer, who has written several books, for his thoughtful and useful advice. Another pal, Eileen Jones, kindly proofread the page proofs, for which I am grateful. Special thanks to my literary agent, Ronald Goldfarb, for helping a rookie author navigate the maze of the publishing world and for performing so admirably. Finally, I would like to express my gratitude to director Bruce Wilcox, copy editors Deborah Smith and Mary Bellino, managing editor Carol Betsch, production manager Jack Harrison, associate production manager Sally Nichols, who designed the book jacket, and the others on the exceptional team at the University of Massachusetts Press for their invaluable assistance and their enthusiasm and excitement about this project.

BARNEY FRANK

Introduction

IN MOST CONGRESSIONAL OFFICES, television sets are tuned to C-SPAN and play continuously when the House is in session so that members and staff can keep abreast of the proceedings on the floor. The volume on the television set is either muted or turned down so low it is barely audible. When Barney Frank's face appears on the television screen, however, people in offices across the Capitol reach for the remote to turn up the volume and hear what he is saying. Staff and legislators, Democrats and Republicans, often stop what they are doing and crowd in front of the television monitor. They stand, eyes riveted to the screen as they listen to Barney, often howling with laughter at one of the trademark one-liners he puts forward effortlessly.

Barney has a remarkable ability to simplify the issue at hand in a clever and witty way. On July 29, 1982, he labeled a proposal before the House that millions of Americans could commute their way out of a nuclear war as the "Traffic Jam and False Expectation Creation Act of 1982." "This plan simply will not work," he declared. He pointed out that every major city is faced with traffic problems that reduce car travel to a standstill during rush hours. "When the people in the town of Brookline, which I represent, are told that they have to all go to New Hampshire, at once, when they could not get to Copley Square in Boston if the Red Sox were playing, we have left the realm of reality," he said. "Perhaps this would work if we could get the Russian military to coordinate their schedule with the Red Sox."

During a debate on an appropriations bill for the Department of Housing and Urban Development in the 1980s, Barney decried the stinginess of the Republican-supported funding for housing programs: "There is hardly an aspect of this important appropriations bill which comes close to being adequately funded. We are reduced not even to robbing Peter to pay Paul but to mugging Peter to pay Paul's burial expenses."

Barney's stage is the floor of the House of Representatives chamber. When he approaches the microphone to speak, members conversing in the rear of the chamber tend to stop their chatter to hear what he has to say. "Barney Frank's voice is unlike any other. People listen when he speaks," Rep. William Delahunt commented. "It's like that old television commercial—'When E. F. Hutton speaks, people listen.' They listen to the rest of us on occasion." "When Barney Frank talks on the House floor, even the Republicans tend to start repeating what he says. The Republicans may not agree with him but they need to know what he is saying because there is a high likelihood that when they come off the House floor they are going to be forced by reporters to respond to what he said," his colleague Edward Markey said. "That's why many times Republicans come over to ask him to slow down so they can understand what it is that he said."

During debate on the House floor, some members appear wooden as they read scripted speeches prepared by staff or by interest groups whose agendas they are advancing. They can be seen glancing down at note cards and when asked a question during a debate, they occasionally look bewildered. You can almost hear them thinking, trying to come up with a response. Not Barney Frank. He is a master of thinking on his feet and speaking extemporaneously. Many consider him to be without peer in Congress as a debater, whether engaging in ideological combat or in skirmishes on narrowly defined issues. "It is Frank's wit that commands attention and his mind that commands respect," Richard Gaines wrote in the *Boston Phoenix* in 1980.

Barney sometimes moves quickly from one idea to another without transition and often speaks in long, run-on sentences. Yet his arguments are well reasoned and logical. He listens to arguments by other members, quickly dissects them, peels away the disingenuous statements, and homes in on the weakest, most absurd part of the argument. Then, with his rapid-fire delivery, he engages the speaker in legitimate intellectual dialogue. He is the last person GOP members want to see getting up to speak on the House floor. "Every time Barney steps up to the microphone on the floor of the House, there is a Republican on another microphone who takes half a step back," Markey said.

"Barney Frank is a brilliant debater and a good spokesman for liberal causes," the late Rep. Henry Hyde said. "Barney usually initiates the debate in the House. He will leap into a discussion with some controversial remarks delivered with considerable emphasis and punch. His remarks are always provocative and invite a reply in kind." "You don't want to get into a debate with Barney because you've lost before you begin," the late Jack Valenti, former president of the Motion Picture Association of America, observed. "He can be brutal in debate and suddenly you realize that you've been cut up into pieces."

The words never flow slowly from Barney's lips. He seems incapable of talking at a deliberate pace. When he served in the state legislature, he kept an old cartoon taped on the wall in his office with a caption that read: "He either thinks faster than he talks or talks faster than he thinks. But whichever it is, I can't understand a word he says." On a radio program on Boston station WEEI on election night, when asked by the host to comment on a particular election, state representative Barney Frank responded knowledgeably for about four minutes at a rapid pace without taking a breath. Finally, when he stopped, the other guest, John Sears, a venerable, moderate Republican politician from Boston, remarked, "Five hundred words a minute with gusts up to a thousand." At a Judiciary Committee hearing in 1998 on the impeachment of President Bill Clinton, when the conservative Republican Bob Barr of Georgia complained about members on the other side who "talk too fast for those of us from the South to understand what they are saying," Barney said that he would try to talk slowly. During the ensuing debate, Barr exclaimed, "[Those present] have heard something very historical—Barney Frank and Bob Barr agree on something." Chairman Henry Hyde interrupted, "I don't think that was the historical aspect of that. I think it was Mr. Frank speaking slowly." On another occasion, Hyde referred to Barney's "predilection to talking like a tobacco auctioneer on Benzedrine."

A Boston newspaper columnist once described Barney's speech pattern as one that "combines the worst of two cultures: the slurred vowels of New Jersey and the unintelligible staccato of New England." Mark Rose, a friend and classmate at Bayonne High School in the mid-1950s and later when they were graduate students at Harvard in the mid-1960s, insists it is a Bayonne, New Jersey, accent: "He spoke fast with that same accent back in high school. It's a Bayonne, not a Boston accent." Barney concurred: "When people in the South say they can't understand me because I have a Massachusetts accent, I tell them no, I have a Jersey accent." He once joked that he and Rep. Jamie Whitten, an elderly Democrat who spoke in a semi-audible Mississippi drawl, "would be the two biggest beneficiaries of bilingual education." After meeting Barney for the first time, the South Korean ambassador was overheard asking an aide, "What is Congressman Frank's native tongue?"

Yet his rapid-fire speech is matched by his intellect. "What stands out overall is Barney Frank's ability, with no notes, to listen to the debate, especially on bills in which he has not been on the committee [reporting the measure], assimilate it, and then summarize it in the most concise, articulate way possible, crafting a summarizing comment that is often devastating and usually makes a good political point in terms of fairness and hypocrisy. He does it better than any other member I have ever seen in the House," Charles Johnson, a retired

House parliamentarian who has listened to virtually every House debate over the past forty years, remarked. Former attorney general Janet Reno declared his command of the issues "really extraordinary." "To me," she said, "it is what a legislator is all about."

Although Barney is one of the fastest talkers in Washington, his tongue still can't keep up with his mind. Markey, who sat next to him in the state legislature, said that Barney has "a nuclear power plant for a brain." The *Boston Globe* reporter Tom Oliphant observed, "Barney Frank is not somebody whose mouth races ahead of his thought processes. His mind and his mouth are both sprinting and I have never seen him get tangled." Former New York representative Tom Downey remarked, "Barney has the fastest political mind in Washington. Everyone else is fighting for second or third place. If you remember the old record speeds, Barney is operating at seventy-eight while the rest of us are still at thirty-three and a third."

Barney is naturally funny in a business where there are few comedians. "Barney is one of the great natural wits of all time," the journalist Steven V. Roberts remarked. "Barney's ability to find the bon mot that is the exact right thing to say, in real time, is probably one of the most impressive things about him," Robert Kaiser, a longtime friend and associate editor of the *Washington Post*, observed. Commenting on the New Right's opposition to abortion and to child nutrition programs, Barney made the classic remark: "Sure, they're pro-life. They believe that life begins at conception and ends at birth."

Barney uses humor to entertain, to educate, to make people think, and to win debates. The late *Washington Post* columnist Mary McGrory described him this way in 1985: "He is probably the sharpest member of the House, an ultra-vocal liberal and expert needler, who pricks the pompous with much-quoted aphorisms. He knows the rules of the House and the rules of the game. As befits a former member of the [Massachusetts legislature], he has little reverence for the established order, and no prejudice against having fun in politics."

In the mid-1980s, during a House–Senate conference committee meeting on a housing bill, Utah Senator Jake Garn, the chairman of the Senate Banking Committee, and Chick Hecht, a freshman from Nevada, were the only two GOP senators present. Garn would regularly turn to Hecht and ask, "Don't you agree with me, Senator Hecht?" and Hecht would reply, "You are absolutely right." Finally, Barney wrote a note and passed it to Gerry McMurray, the Housing subcommittee staff director. It was December, and the note read: "This is what I want for Chanukah—a Chick Hecht doll. It answers yes to everything that I say."

In a 2008 *Washingtonian* magazine poll of top aides on Capitol Hill, Barney was rated best in the House in two categories—Brainiest and Funniest—second in Most Eloquent, and third in the category Workhorse.

John Kenneth Galbraith referred to Barney in 1986 as "the most relentlessly diligent, effectively articulate, and uniformly commendable politician of our time." Senator John Kerry observed, "He is so bright, so capable, and so quick that it almost intimidates some people but he is funny and pulls it all [off]. It is a gift and he is a very gifted public person."

With Barney, one never knows what's coming next. During a House debate in March 1988 on aid to the Contras in Nicaragua, Barney remarked that Assistant Secretary of State Elliott Abrams admitted that he had lied to Congress, explaining that he was not authorized to tell the truth. That, Barney acknowledged, is "a new concept for me." Then he said: "There was a king in the dim recesses of English history, known as Ethelred the Unready. We now have his nomenclature equal, Elliott the Unauthorized, as assistant secretary, who apparently does not as a matter of course tell Congress the truth but has to be authorized."

On another occasion, in February 2007, Patrick McHenry, the diminutive deputy Republican whip from North Carolina, had lambasted the new Speaker, Nancy Pelosi, for seeking carte blanche access to one of the most extravagant planes in the military fleet for travel to her district in San Francisco. Barney stepped to the microphone and, invoking the signature line that the three-foot-eleven-inch character Tattoo would shout on the old television series *Fantasy Island*, he commented, "As I was walking by I thought I heard someone yelling, 'De plane, boss! De plane!'"

Barney has a reputation for saying exactly what he believes, regardless of the political consequences or criticism from others. "I have this rule," he explained, "when I am in my own congressional district within three months of an election, it is very important to make sure that I am agreeable in what I say, but on other occasions it is okay if people don't like what I say. What's going to happen? Is someone going to hit me?"

One of the attributes that distinguishes Barney from many other legislators is how he examines policy issues. He thinks through issues in a way that many other liberals do not. For example, he differs with most liberals on crime issues because he believes "it's important to catch criminals." He wants criminals off the streets and thinks that "prison is a good form of crime prevention." He opposes the death penalty, explaining, "We are human beings and we make mistakes. I don't think that a fallible group of people ought to do something that is irrevocable. But then again, I've never read about anybody executed that I'm gonna miss." He favors imprisoning those who cross the border illegally. "The problem has been that you catch people, you release them, [and] they go back and come back again. It's just a game of merry-go-round," he explained to Larry Kudlow in a television interview. "I think we need to make a short-term increase in penal facilities at the border."

Barney has a well-deserved reputation for being abrupt, impatient, rude, and sometimes infuriating. He believes that patience is a great time waster rather than a virtue. He gets annoyed with people who don't know what they are talking about or who speak too slowly. He has a short attention span that often puts people on edge. He does not suffer fools gladly, unless, as he points out, "they happen to be constituents." "He would be even more effective if he were a little more patient with people," a former aide commented. He constantly tells people, especially staff, to get to the point. A former legislative assistant suggested that "Get to the Point" would be a good title for a biography of him. He has been known to publicly chastise an activist for making a ridiculous argument, and, from the stage, to berate a person in the audience for asking a stupid question.

One man who witnessed Barney Frank's ill-temper and abrasiveness was so taken aback that he looked up the name of Barney's secretary, Patty Hamel, in the *Congressional Directory* and sent her a letter. The letter read simply: "I just want to tell you how sorry I am that you have to work for that guy." "I received several of those 'how could you work for that guy' letters," Hamel recalled. "However, the majority of the letters were of the 'that guy is so entertaining it must be fun working for him' type."

"You think he's rude until you've been with him long enough and you realize that he's actually giving 100 percent to everything he's doing," Robert Raben, Barney's legislative counsel from 1993 to 1999, observed. "He is both reading the newspaper and talking to you, which infuriates most people. Yet he's listening to you. His mind processes things a little differently than yours or mine."

Friends recount telephoning him and learning that there is no room for pleasantries in the conversation. "Hi Barney, how are you?" the caller begins. "Get to the point, I'm very busy," he responds. Sometimes his restlessness and impatience come across as arrogance. Barney offered a partial explanation: "I read a wonderful biography of Sherman Adams. Adams didn't say hello or goodbye on the telephone. As White House chief of staff [for President Dwight Eisenhower], Adams would have maybe eighty-seven phone conversations a day, and he calculated that if he engaged in pleasantries and small talk it would take an extra [hour or two a day]. So I don't do that." It is largely a time management issue with him. "People think that I shouldn't be impatient or rude at any given moment, but they have three things they want me to do and I [wouldn't have the time to] do them all."

In May 2007, Barney ruptured a tendon in his left arm using a curling machine in the gym and had to have it surgically repaired. As a result, his arm was in a sling for a few weeks. Growing impatient at having to explain to colleagues why his arm was in a sling and wasting time by having to repeat the same conversation, he sent out a "Dear Colleague" letter (a communication that is distributed to every member of the House) explaining what happened. He ended the letter with "Thank you for not asking."

About a dozen people interviewed for this book each commented independently that Barney is not someone they would call up at the end of the day to say to let's go have a beer. One person went so far as to call him "socially handicapped." Barney often pokes fun at his own grumpy personality. In a letter to campaign contributors a few years back, he wrote, "I'm not quite at the point where I can win entirely on my charm, so I solicit you again for money."

Barney's crankiness and gruff exterior often mask his natural compassion. William Cowin, now a justice on the Massachusetts Appeals Court, who worked closely with Barney in 1968–69 in Boston City Hall, remembered: "[At the time] my wife and I had an infant die of SIDS. People were all very supportive but Barney's response was extraordinary. The feeling that he communicated was not just sympathy with what I felt. He really felt pain over the event himself. That has stayed with me forever."

At times Barney can be charming. In the mid-1980s, the director of his district office, Dottie Reichard, a veteran of many political campaigns on tight budgets who has a reputation for being thrifty, decided to save money by not upgrading the telephones in the district office. One day, Barney, who regularly places his own phone calls, gently inquired, "Dottie, do you think we can afford to get some touchtone phones? The problem with the rotary phone is that by the time I finish dialing the number, I forget who I am calling."

"The bottom line is that Barney is a lot nicer than anyone gives him credit for in his own abrupt way," Mary Beth Cahill, a campaign strategist who has known him almost thirty years, observed. Thaleia Schlesinger, the late senator Paul Tsongas's twin sister, who was Barney's press secretary in his first race for Congress in 1980 and is now a Boston-based consultant, said, "Barney is not one of God's easy creatures, but he is one of God's better ones."

Barney believes that government is what we do when we come together and pool our resources to achieve common values. In his view, the purpose of government is not to interfere with the free enterprise system but to work alongside it to reduce inequality. Government has to take on the responsibility of helping those less fortunate. "Hungry three-year-old children in America bother me a great deal," he asserts. "We don't solve problems in government. It is not mathematics homework. The federal budget is not Rubik's cube. What we do is to alleviate problems. We mitigate them. We diminish them. We make improvements. We are talking about lessening human misery and improving the quality of human life. People say government programs don't work. Some government programs work badly, but I've never seen an elderly housing project built either directly by the government or with substantial government subsidy that didn't have a waiting list longer than your arm."

Barney's roots in the blue-collar city of Bayonne, New Jersey, where he grew up and later worked at his father's truck stop, taught him respect for working people and nurtured an instinct for treating people fairly. It is the source of his Hubert Humphrey brand of liberalism, which Humphrey described as "an attitude toward life characterized by a warm heart, an open mind, and willing hands." "Barney is a serious legislator with a sense of history and a feel for the New Deal, a lot like Hubert Humphrey," David Cohen, a liberal activist who served as president of Common Cause from 1975 to 1981, observed.

Barney once said, of his job in Congress, "If there weren't poor people in this world, and if we didn't have discrimination, I wouldn't be here." He fights for racial equality and social and economic justice and has championed the interests of the poor, the jobless, the underprivileged, and the vulnerable, people low on the economic spectrum who don't have political action committees or high-powered lobbyists and don't otherwise get a fair shake. Joe Martin, a former legislative assistant, recalled a meeting in the mid-1980s with a lobbyist seeking Barney's support for an amendment to the Savings and Loan bill. Barney glanced at the amendment and remarked, "It looks like the poor people are going to get screwed by this amendment." The lobbyist replied, "But poor people always get screwed." Barney slammed his fist on the desk and shouted, "Damn it, poor people don't have to get screwed. It is because of attitudes from—expletive deleted—people like you that they get screwed. Those are the people I want to go to bat for, people who cannot afford to spend four hundred dollars an hour to hire someone to lobby for them."

Although passionate about his causes and notwithstanding his reputation as a partisan, Barney is pragmatic. He is an open-minded, astute, and practical deal-maker who works across party lines to craft compromises and build bridges, coalitions, and consensus. "If you're not able to work with people you despise you have to find another line of work. That doesn't mean when the time comes, you don't whack them," he explained on NPR's *Wait, Wait . . . Don't Tell Me* in November 2008. As a legislator, he understands the virtues of compromise and focuses on what is attainable based on political reality. In 1993 he told the *Boston Globe*, "It's always been a mistake to think that because I have strong ideological commitments, therefore I must be uncompromising." He is passionate about ideals but compellingly pragmatic as well, a lesson he learned from Allard Lowenstein, the iconoclastic civil rights, peace, and human rights activist. John F. Kennedy once characterized himself as "an idealist without illusions." That description might apply equally to Barney.

"It makes me crazy when people claim you have to choose one or the other, idealism or pragmatism. I would make it a misdemeanor to use idealism and pragmatism as if they are opposites," Barney said. "People tell me, 'You can say that because you are pragmatic but I am an idealist.' That doesn't make sense. This is not a chicken-and-egg problem. The idealism comes first. But once you have your ideals, to argue that you are then relieved of any obligation to be pragmatic is totally irresponsible. The more idealistic you are, the more morally obligated you are to be pragmatic. No unrealized ideal ever fed a hungry child, cleaned up a polluted river, gave shelter for homeless people, or provided medical care for people in need. Unrealized ideals play no role except to make you feel morally superior. There is nothing wrong," he insists, "with wanting to care about your effectiveness. There is nothing as easy as idealism unrelated to results." Barney has advised liberals, "Recognizing reality doesn't mean you love it." His philosophy is "I will take anything better that doesn't make things worse."

Former New York representative Stephen Solarz likened Barney's pragmatism and incrementalism to that displayed by the fictional Texas governor Arthur Fenstemaker, a character modeled after Senator Lyndon Johnson in William Brammer's 1961 novel *The Gay Place*. An aide asks Governor Fenstemaker whether he would settle for a part-way measure, a half a loaf on an education bill, and the governor replies, "A goddamned slice even."

Other colleagues have also attested to Barney's pragmatism. Treasury secretary Henry Paulson Jr. said in a statement to the *Boston Globe*: "When we're faced with a tough situation and a real need for immediate action, Barney approaches the discussion in a pragmatic way and doesn't let the perfect be the enemy of the good." "Barney has a great instinct for being able pragmatically to weave together a working relationship with colleagues," ex–Massachusetts representative Mike Harrington said about his former administrative assistant. "He is result-oriented. Using me as a totally invidious comparison, I was at the opposite end of the spectrum in that I couldn't care less."

Barney is able through intellect, energy, and hard work to be successful in an institution where he can't just will his way to get what he wants. Joe Early said about his colleague, "He's not just a liberal. He's a doer. He's a liberal with common sense." And, Markey said, "If you want to deal, he'll deal and try to out negotiate you. If you want to go to war, he'll go to war with you."

"It is being responsible for the outcome that is really the toughest thing," Barney said. "I know how to win. If I don't care about the outcome I can win a lot more than I do. The hard decisions are how far you push, when do you stop and when do you go forward. There are no easy answers."

Barney attended college, graduate school, and later law school at Harvard.

Yet he is as much Bayonne as he is Harvard. The clash between Bayonne and Harvard may be the essence of Barney Frank, and this contrast punctuates his public life. "The Harvard in him is able to conceive of programs. The Bayonne in him is utterly unafraid of what it takes to move a bill," his friend Tom Oliphant observed.

1

An Outspoken Voice at the White House Table

IT WAS THE BEGINNING of an extraordinary period of economic turbulence as Americans witnessed a series of financial failures that had seemed unimaginable. On Sunday, September 7, 2008, Treasury secretary Henry M. Paulson Jr., exercising the stand-by authority he had been given by Congress only six weeks earlier, seized control of Fannie Mae and Freddie Mac, the mortgage-finance giants who together owned or guaranteed half of the nation's mortgage debt. That same week, Lehman Brothers, the venerable 158-year-old Wall Street investment banking company, came to the federal government seeking the kind of help given six months earlier to the ailing investment firm Bear Stearns when the government had orchestrated and provided guarantees for the sale of that company to J. P. Morgan Chase. The federal government rejected the rescue plea from Lehman Brothers, letting the free market take its course and forcing the firm to file for bankruptcy on Monday, September 15. That same day, the iconic Merrill Lynch, another victim of overleveraging and underestimating risk, was acquired by the Bank of America in a shotgun wedding arranged and financed by the federal government.

Then, on Tuesday evening, September 16, at a meeting in the U.S. Capitol with a dozen or so congressional leaders, Secretary Paulson and Federal Reserve chairman Ben Bernanke announced that American International Group (AIG), the world's largest insurance company, was on the brink of collapse and was being rescued by the government. AIG through unregulated credit default swaps had guaranteed or insured almost $450 billion in investments by other firms in mortgage-backed securities, many of them tied to risky subprime mortgages. In a deal put together on the fly, without any input from Congress, the Federal Reserve Board, using emergency lending power that it had been delegated during the Great Depression, extended an eighty-five-billion-dollar line of credit to AIG in exchange for 80 percent of the company's stock. The president's two chief economic officials explained that the federal government was under tremendous pressure to intervene by foreign ministers and the European Central Bank, who feared that the collapse of AIG, which operated in 130 countries, could trigger a tidal wave of losses by foreign banks. Barney Frank, the brainy and feisty chairman of the House Financial Services Committee, asked how much the other countries were contributing to the rescue effort. The answer was zero. "Why don't they kick in some money?" he exclaimed. "We can't wait. We have to do it now," Bernanke replied. At one point, Barney asked whether Bernanke had eighty-five billion dollars to lend to AIG. "I have eight hundred billion," Bernanke said.

The most terrifying economic news, however, was yet to come. Two days later, on Thursday evening, September 18, at about seven o'clock, Secretary Paulson and Chairman Bernanke met with the bipartisan congressional leadership and key lawmakers on the Financial Services Committee and the Banking Committee in an emergency session in Speaker Nancy Pelosi's office on the second floor of the Capitol. They revealed that the U.S. economy was facing its most drastic financial crisis since the Great Depression. Paulson explained that the U.S. financial system was unsound because it had accumulated too much bad debt, in the form of mortgage-backed securities, which was clogging the nation's financial arteries and stopping the flow of credit. The Treasury secretary warned of dire consequences, declaring that the United States could face a financial meltdown, an economic disaster, if Congress did not act quickly to pass the administration's bailout plan. Paulson contended that a massive government intervention in the markets was needed to stave off a global economic collapse. The heart of Paulson's proposed financial rescue plan involved Congress's giving the Treasury Department immediate authorization to buy up and remove troubled mortgage assets from the books of the floundering banks and other financial institutions. It was clear to the assembled congressional leaders that the plan would involve hundreds of billions of dollars. Paulson deflected questions about the exact cost of the bailout plan.

Barney sat in the room listening to the Treasury secretary and the Federal Reserve chairman, two economic officials who in his judgment were not known for excessive pessimism and who, if anything, could be accused of being too optimistic. He agreed with the premise of their call for action, recognizing that bold action was needed to shore up the financial system, steady the distressed capital markets, restore public confidence, and prevent a global economic disaster. As the flow of money stops, loans of all kinds become more difficult to get. Students would find it difficult to borrow money. People who are trying to buy or sell automobiles, furniture, and housing would be hurt and the effect would be cumulative. All of which would lead to job losses. Average Americans, not the top bankers and top corporate executives, would feel the pain. Frozen credit markets would also prevent the economy from growing. Intervention by the president's two top economic officials in the case of AIG and nonintervention with respect to Lehman Brothers had failed to calm the financial markets. The situation was at a point where confidence in the market was plummeting, businesses were failing, and people were losing jobs.

In Barney's view, the only available solution to restore economic stability and remove the sludge from the financial system was for the federal government to tackle the crisis by intervening. The federal government was the only entity that could buy up toxic assets, hold them, and sell them as they regained their value. "The costs of doing nothing are enormous. The alternative to doing something now and putting American taxpayer dollars at risk is to allow the economy to continue to deteriorate, which we know in the long run will cost us more in taxpayer dollars," he said. Yet he acknowledged some doubts. "We know how to prevent a recurrence but we don't know how to get out of the mess."

Barney also favored establishing a federal entity to make those important decisions systematically rather than having the Federal Reserve chairman and the Treasury secretary continue with ad hoc intervention. Although he regards Bernanke and Paulson as men of high integrity and total commitment to the national interest, he did not like the process and referred to the two men as "the Loan Arranger and his faithful companion Paulson."

Barney recognized that a massive taxpayer bailout of the U.S. financial system would be widely unpopular with voters and difficult politically to shepherd through the Congress. "It is hard to get political credit for avoiding [a catastrophe] that hasn't yet happened but you think is going to happen. That is not something people are going to stand up and cheer about. You don't get any credit for disaster averted," he said. Yet he realized that the national interest required Congress to act to prevent something worse from happening. He therefore lined up on the side of an unpopular lame-duck Republican president, George W. Bush, and in support of a bill that he expected would be received unfavorably by the public.

The root of the problem, according to Barney, was that the financial community had been left on its own to engage in innovative ways to make money, such as derivatives and credit default swaps, at a time when a right-wing philosophy of unregulation prevailed in Washington. He cited the remark by the "noted economist" and former House Republican leader Dick Armey, who said, "The markets are smart and the government is dumb." The government's failure to regulate resulted in a series of irresponsible financial decisions by the private sector. Lenders' ability to package mortgage loans into securities (lend money and sell the loans to passive investors) took away from lenders the incentive to be more careful in making loans. This was exacerbated by rating agencies that were being paid by the very companies that benefited from their securities being graded as low risk. Insurance companies such as AIG then insured these mortgage-backed securities against default through credit default swaps. According to Barney, some financial companies insured so much money that they now owe others more money than there is money.

On Saturday, September 18, the Bush administration transmitted to Congress a three-page bill that gave the secretary of the Treasury sweeping authority, with no oversight or judicial review, to spend up to seven hundred billion dollars to rescue the financial markets. Barney saw the White House proposal as a kind of Dick Cheney wish list: "I'm in charge, I'll do what I want, and nobody can stop me." Secretary Paulson said that Congress needed to act on the measure quickly—by Monday. Barney responded that Congress would do it as quickly as they could but that it was not going to happen by Monday.

There followed several long days of intense negotiations between the Bush economic team and congressional negotiators. These four-party negotiations involved House Democrats, Senate Democrats, Senate Republicans, and the Treasury Department. The House Republicans never got their act together.

Speaker Pelosi named Barney as the point person for House Democrats in the effort to hammer out an agreement with the administration. On one side of the bargaining table sat Henry Paulson, the calm and humorless sixty-two-year-old Treasury secretary. He is a Christian Scientist, a former All-Ivy-League football star at Dartmouth, and a former CEO of Goldman Sacks with a net worth of about $500 million. He lives in a $4.5 million mansion in the Massachusetts Avenue Heights area in the District of Columbia. On the other side sat Barney Frank, the gay, Jewish, wisecracking sixty-eight-year-old Financial Services Committee chairman. Barney once described himself as, at Harvard Law School, "the oldest member of my class and the slowest member of my touch football team." Early in his congressional career he had been hesitant about publicly releasing a net-worth statement for fear voters would not support a Harvard-educated lawyer whose only asset at the time was half of a beaten-up old car. He lives in a one-bedroom apartment that he rents on Capitol Hill, a short distance from the Cannon House Office Building.

At first glance the two men appeared to be very different, but in many significant ways they are the same. Both men have a reputation for being brilliant and for being workaholics. Because they like to focus on the business at hand, they have little patience with small talk and at times can be brusque. They are both old school in that they don't like to use e-mail and prefer to communicate by telephone. Above all, they are pragmatists who in an effort to get something done search for areas of agreement, and they recognize the value of reaching a compromise. Also, neither is trying to score political points.

Barney was basically supportive of the rescue effort and Paulson was grateful. But during the intense negotiations, disagreements arose and things began to fray. A major sticking point was the Democrats' insistence on placing limits on executive compensation and preventing companies that would benefit from the financial bailout plan from awarding "golden parachutes" to their departing executives. Paulson was enormously resistant to placing any such limits, maintaining that they would kill the program. "Paulson reacted as if I had told the chief rabbi in Jerusalem to eat pork on Yom Kippur," Barney said. He had said, "Hank, I'll put this to a vote but I don't think you have many Republican votes against placing limitations on executive compensation." Ultimately, Paulson bowed to bipartisan pressure and recognized that it would be a serious error to use taxpayer funds to buy up the bad debt that resulted from irresponsible decisions by company executives and then allow these same executives to get millions of dollars on their way out.

Both the Treasury secretary and the Financial Services Committee chairman recognized that neither side gets everything they want in negotiations. Paulson agreed to an oversight board to monitor the Treasury's actions and pledged to use added leverage in the mortgage market to assist homeowners facing foreclosure, two provisions important to the Democrats. The two sides came to an agreement also on safeguards to protect taxpayers.

According to Barney, the negotiators were working together in a bipartisan fashion and getting close to a deal when Senator John McCain, the Republican presidential candidate, announced on Wednesday, September 24, that he was suspending his campaign to return to Washington to fix the economy. His gesture reminded Barney of the comedian Andy Kaufman, who used to do the Mighty Mouse impression, "Here I come to save the day!" "We're trying to rescue the economy, not the McCain campaign," he told reporters. Many observers viewed Senator McCain's entry into the negotiations late in the fourth quarter as the quarterback as a "long shot." "It's the longest Hail Mary pass in the history of either football or Marys," Barney observed.

At a climactic meeting on Thursday morning, September 25, to try to work out a deal, Spencer Bachus, the top Republican on the House Financial Services Committee, entered the negotiating room and observed but did not participate. "I'm not authorized to negotiate," he said. At a midday press conference, the lawmakers announced that a tentative deal had been reached. According to Barney, there really was not much of a deadlock to break at a meeting at the White House later that afternoon. But then, shortly after the press conference, Barney heard that the House Republicans were trashing the deal. Angry and upset, he phoned Secretary Paulson and asked what the hell was going on. "First the House Republicans say they can't take a position and then they come out against the deal we reached," he said. "I know. I just heard the news. I understand why you are upset. I'm going to try to fix it," Paulson replied.

John McCain was coming to the White House to discuss the economic crisis, and therefore the Bush administration felt obliged to invite the Democratic candidate, Barack Obama, as well. The White House asked Speaker Pelosi, Senate majority leader Harry Reid, Senate Republican leader Mitch McConnell, and House Republican leader John Boehner to attend the meeting. Pelosi and Reid said they were bringing along Barney Frank and Christopher Dodd, who were the experts and to whom they had delegated the task of hammering out a bill. The White House objected but Pelosi and Reid stood firm and said that they would not come to the meeting without the two committee chairmen. Bachus and Richard Shelby, the ranking Republicans on the Financial Services and Banking Committees, both from Alabama, were then added to the White House meeting list. Treasury secretary Paulson and Federal Reserve chairman Bernanke were also there.

Although Barney had been to several events at the White House during his twenty-eight-year congressional career, he had never before been to a meeting in the Cabinet Room presided over by the president. That Thursday afternoon, he found himself attending a dramatic, high-stakes summit meeting convened by President Bush to close a deal. As Barney sat in a leather chair at the striking oval mahogany table, donated by President Richard Nixon, in the stately Cabinet Room, he was in many ways at the pinnacle of his power.

President Bush sat in the center on one side of the table, flanked by Speaker Pelosi and Senate leader Reid and across from Vice President Dick Cheney. Presidential candidates John McCain and Barack Obama sat on opposite ends of the table. At the start of the meeting, Senator McCain was asked about his position on the legislation, but he deferred, saying that he wanted to sit and listen to the discussion. The president then called on Pelosi and Reid, who both deferred to Senator Obama. According to Barney, Obama presented the Democrats' position skillfully and knowledgeably. His performance at the meeting, Barney said, was "masterful." Barney had been under some pressure from House Democratic Caucus liberals during the negotiations to include in the bailout bill a provision to change the bankruptcy law to allow bankruptcy judges to restructure mortgage repayment terms for people facing foreclosures. But it had proven to be a hard sell. Obama began by stating that the Democrats were willing to give up their efforts to change the bankruptcy law as part of the bill.

The House and Senate Democrats, the Senate Republicans, and the Treasury Department all supported the legislation. Senate Republican leader McConnell promised to deliver forty votes. "My caucus is united on this from the conservatives to the moderates to the liberals," he said. Harry Reid wasn't so sure about those Republican liberals. "Yes, Mitch," he said, "both of them." "I wish there were only two," McConnell retorted.

Only House minority leader Boehner raised objections to the bailout bill. A week earlier, when Treasury Secretary Paulson had urged congressional leaders to act immediately on the financial rescue plan, Boehner was most enthusiastic about the measure, arguing that members of Congress had a patriotic duty to pass the bill. Several days later, however, under pressure from conservatives in the Republican Caucus, he withdrew his support for the measure. Boehner proposed an alternative plan that centered on a government-backed insurance program in combination with capital-gains-tax relief. Under the plan put on the table by Boehner, the distressed financial institutions would not sell their toxic mortgage-secured debt to the federal government. Instead, the companies would hold them and they would be insured by the federal government, with the cost of that insurance coming from premiums assessed against the financial firms who own those assets. The House GOP plan would have eliminated the need for a seven-hundred-billion-dollar taxpayer funded bailout. Secretary Paulson had previously rejected that idea as unworkable and irrelevant to the current crisis.

A heated and at times rancorous discussion followed. Obama and Barney, in particular, began peppering Boehner with questions about the alternative plan. Barney asked, "How does that insurance proposal do anything to solve the credit liquidity crisis?" Boehner accused the group of ganging up on him.

Barney then pressed McCain about whether he supported Boehner's plan. "John, what do you think?" he said. "Do you agree with the House Republicans or with the president, the Treasury secretary, and the rest of the congressional leadership?"

McCain said he sided with the House Republicans, arguing that they shouldn't be pushed into doing something they object to.

"So you agree with that position?" Barney asked.

"No, I think they have a right to their position," McCain said.

McCain was asked what his plan was to address the economic crisis but he wouldn't say.

Obama then attempted to put Paulson on the spot. "Mr. Secretary," he said, "what do you think of the plan proposed by Representative Boehner?" Paulson gingerly avoided giving a direct response to the question. Obama then pressed the Treasury secretary and Barney tried to help. At this point, President Bush, who had been sitting quietly, looking bemused, concluded that the meeting, which had been going on for about an hour, had deteriorated and probably accomplished as much as it could. He abruptly ended the meeting, saving Paulson from having to answer the follow-up questions. A Republican later commented to Barney on the president's performance at the meeting. Referring to the president's ranch in Texas, he said, "I think the president was in Crawford."

Someone mentioned to Barney that President Bush thought he had violated White House protocol because, at a meeting in the Cabinet Room, one is not supposed to speak or ask questions unless recognized by the president. "I didn't know that," Barney, who has never been on anybody's short list for chief of protocol, responded.

After the meeting, the Democrats caucused in the nearby Roosevelt Room to discuss what statement to make to the press corps camped out in the White House driveway. They agreed that Senator Obama would speak to the press and they would all just stand behind him. Then they learned that Senator McCain had left the building, exiting through a side door onto West Executive Avenue between the White House and the Eisenhower Executive Office, without making a statement to the press. At that point, Obama decided he should not make a statement to the White House press if McCain was not there, and that he would speak with the press elsewhere.

Among themselves the Democrats expressed some exasperation at what had happened in the Cabinet Room and how they had found themselves defending President Bush's position against conservative members of his own party. Barney likened it to being in the middle of a Republican civil war. When Secretary Paulson entered the room, several lawmakers attacked him. "What's the matter with you? We came here to try to help you with this bill and this is what happens," one Democrat said. "I know how frustrated you are by what happened," Paulson replied. At that point, Paulson suddenly bent down on one knee and begged Speaker Pelosi not to blow up the bailout package. She looked down at him and said, "Oh, Hank, I didn't know you were Catholic." The Democrats agreed not to walk away from the deal and to restart negotiations.

Barney had been looking forward to spending a relaxing weekend in his district with his partner, thirty-nine-year-old Jim Ready, the owner of an awning company in Maine. He had planned to attend the running race named in memory of his mother, Elsie, on Saturday morning. That evening he was scheduled to be the keynote speaker at the twenty-fifth anniversary of the Harvard Gay and Lesbian Caucus. But he had to cancel those appearances to participate in further negotiations on the financial bailout bill. On Friday, the negotiations resumed. House Republican whip Roy Blunt of Missouri, whom the Republican leadership had appointed to represent them, entered the talks. Barney brought House Democratic Caucus chairman Rahm Emanuel into the negotiations, because, he said, "I didn't feel comfortable making all the decisions by myself and Rahm has some financial business experience." Democratic Senators Chris Dodd, Charles

Schumer, and Max Baucus and GOP Senators Judd Gregg and Robert Bennett participated in the talks with the Treasury Department. The negotiations continued as lawmakers and their staffs worked late into Saturday night. The parties went back and forth on the issues and finally agreed on the contentious issue of how much money the Treasury would get in the Troubled Asset Relief Program and when. The agreement provided that the Treasury Department would be given the funds in two installments, $350 billion initially, and Treasury would have to notify Congress to request the additional $350 billion when it was needed.

On Sunday morning, the parties announced that they had reached an agreement. The 3-page financial bailout bill submitted by the Bush administration eight days earlier had been reshaped into a 110-page bill. The House Republican leadership signed off on the deal reluctantly because it included their insurance plan as a component of the bailout measure, not as a replacement for the seven-hundred-billion-dollar rescue plan. Barney had agreed to the insurance plan because he knew it wasn't going to happen and he said so publicly, driving the Republican whip Roy Blunt to say, "I'm trying to get Republicans to vote for the bill. Can you please stop saying publicly that you went along with it because you knew it wasn't going to happen?" "Fine," Barney replied. "I won't say it anymore."

The expectation was that the leadership from each party would try to produce a majority of their caucus in support of the bailout bill—120 Democratic votes and about 100 Republican votes for the measure.

The Democratic leadership held a series of caucuses to discuss, defend, and build support for the bill among their members. At one of these caucuses, Jerrold Nadler, a liberal from New York City, told his colleagues, "I am not sure this plan will work but maybe it will work. I am convinced that if we do nothing it will be a disaster. Therefore, based on this maybe I am going to support the plan." Barney commented, "Yes sir, that's my maybe."

On Monday, September 29, the seven-hundred-billion-dollar bill to provide a historic rescue of the nation's financial markets was brought to a vote in the House and was unexpectedly rejected by a margin of 228 to 205. At that point, the House Democratic and Republican floor leaders, Steny Hoyer and Roy Blunt, held the vote open for a few minutes to see whether they could switch a few votes. Barney waded into the sidebar discussion taking place on the House floor. "You have to call this as a no and we need to go back to work on it," he insisted. "The whole world is watching. This is not the usual inside baseball. This is too important an issue for the country to strong arm it through." George Miller of California supported his argument. Finally Hoyer agreed and the vote was gaveled closed.

Republican leader John Boehner blamed the bill's defeat on Speaker Pelosi's partisan floor speech denouncing President Bush's "reckless economic policies" and "a right-wing ideology of anything goes—no supervision, no discipline, no regulation." Boehner maintained that a dozen Republicans went south and voted against the bill because they were offended by Pelosi's remarks. "Because somebody hurt their feelings, they decide to punish the country," Barney said. "Give me those twelve people's names and I will talk uncharacteristically nicely to them, and tell them what wonderful people they are, and maybe they'll think about the country," he added. The Democrats produced more votes than expected—141. However, over two-thirds of the Republicans and about 40 percent of the Democrats had voted against the bailout measure.

After the vote, the stock market plummeted 778 points, the largest ever one-day drop in the Dow Jones industrial average. Later that day, as it became clear that opinions were changing, Barney said to Paulson, "Sometimes, Hank, you have to let the kid run away from home and get cold, hungry, and frightened and come back a few hours later." Paulson thought it was a good analogy.

That evening, two middle-aged men, recognizing Barney, approached him at Reagan National Airport, where he was waiting for a flight to go home to Massachusetts to observe the Jewish holiday of Rosh Hashanah. One of them said, "You can't allow this to happen. It is terrible." "We will try to change it," Barney replied. Then, learning that they were represented in Congress by Howard Coble of North Carolina, he told them to call their congressman and urge him to support the bill.

The negative consequences of the bill's defeat in the House had an impact. About 95 percent of the letters, e-mail messages, and telephone calls to the offices of House members had been against the bill. After the bill lost, although a majority of the public was still against the bill, a significant number of people now voiced their support for it. "There were many members who wanted to vote for the bill but were afraid to. The negative consequences changed it," Barney said, noting that when former British Prime Minister Harold Macmillan was once asked what has the most important influence on political decisions, he had replied, "Events, dear boy, events."

Three of the ten members of the Massachusetts delegation, Bill Delahunt, John Tierney, and Steven Lynch, voted against the bill. Among their reasons were that working people should not have to foot the bill for rescuing Wall Street firms and other financial institutions and the bill did not do enough to assist homeowners. Shortly thereafter, the treasurer of Massachusetts announced that he could not roll over his short-term notes and was having trouble making payroll.

On Wednesday, October 1, the Senate proceeded to vote on a bailout bill. Had the House passed the measure, the Senate could not have easily changed it. The Senate took advantage of the situation and added $150 billion of tax breaks, earmarks, and other legislative sweeteners to the financial rescue bill, everything from money for rural schools, businesses, and middle-class tax breaks to $172 million for rum importers, and even a tax break for the manufacturers of wooden arrows for children at the behest of Senator Gordon Smith of Oregon, who was in a close race for reelection. "The Senate may have taken us hostage," Barney acknowledged. "They might have us at arrow point." The Senate overwhelmingly approved the financial rescue bill by a vote of 74 to 25.

Barney returned to Washington on Thursday to prepare for the vote on Friday on the Senate bill. By then, it was clear to him that because of the negative public reaction to the bill's defeat in the House earlier that week, there was now an "informed opinion" for it. In response both to the carnage on Wall Street and to the tax breaks and other sweeteners, the House passed the revised bill 263 to 171 and President Bush signed the Emergency Economic Stabilization Act, establishing the Troubled Asset Relief Program.

2

Bayonne Born and Bred

BARNEY FRANK'S JOURNEY to Washington began about 225 miles to the north in Bayonne, New Jersey, a petrochemical industrial working-class city just across the Hudson River from Manhattan. He was born March 31, 1940 BT (that's eleven years Before the Turnpike opened). Named Barnett after his paternal grandfather, he was called Barney by everyone. In the mid-1960s, he went to court and changed his name legally from Barnett to Barney. "It was complicated having things in both names," he explained. "Besides, with Barney Frank, I had a fifty-fifty chance of people getting it right. With Barnett Frank, people would inevitably call me Frank Barnett."

He was the second of four children born to Samuel and Elsie Frank, the offspring of Eastern European immigrants. Their first child, Ann, was born two years earlier. Doris was born three and a half years later, and David, the youngest, was born in 1950.

Bayonne is a small peninsula, shaped somewhat like a boot and located south of Jersey City on the west side of New York harbor. According to tradition, Bayonne ("bay-on" or "on the bays") got its name from its location on the shores of two bays, Newark and New York. To anyone flying between Washington and LaGuardia Airport in New York, other than Manhattan, Bayonne is the most conspicuous geographical entity in the whole New York area. Unlike most cities and towns in New Jersey, which give no indication where one ends and another begins, making them indistinguishable from the air, Bayonne stands out because it is surrounded on three sides by water.

The advent of oil refineries, first Prentice Refining Company in 1875, then Standard Oil in 1877, stimulated Bayonne as a shipping center and created industry and jobs. The prospect of employment attracted many immigrants, including Barney's grandparents, who settled in Bayonne soon after arriving from Eastern Europe.

In the 1940s and 1950s, Bayonne was a closely knit, very ethnic, heavily Roman Catholic, and virtually all-white working-class town. The city was about 80 percent Roman Catholic, with so few Protestants that Aaron Lazare, a Bayonne native who became a psychiatrist or, in his words, "a Jewish doctor who can't stand blood," claimed, "I didn't meet a Protestant until I went to college at Oberlin." Most of Bayonne's almost eighty thousand residents were middle class. There were very few pockets of real poverty or of wealth. The latter consisted of a small group of doctors and lawyers who had their practices in Bayonne and lived in a four-block area of predominantly one-family houses near the spacious Hudson County Park. "People were not terribly rich or you wouldn't still live in Bayonne," Barney explained.

The Franks lived in a multi-ethnic neighborhood where Catholics and Jews, Italians, Poles, Irish, and other ethnic groups lived together in relative harmony. The Irish were considered the aristocrats because they had lived there the longest. An Irish family lived on one side of the Franks' house and a Syrian family on the other. The Italian family that lived on the corner included the future mayor of Bayonne, Thomas Domenico.

Despite its reputation as an industrial town with the inevitable noxious byproducts of industry, including unclean air and pollution in the bay, Bayonne, as Barney's brother, David, remembers it, was "not a smelly, oily place." It was a pleasant place where the residents were meticulous in caring for their property and could often be seen sweeping their stoops or hosing the sidewalk in front of their houses. Elsie Frank called it "an ideal place to raise a family," and Barney's sister Ann described it as a city "where you could walk anywhere you wanted to go." Goldie Rosenhan, a former resident of Bayonne, remembers, "We had everything you could have wanted as kids growing up—movie theaters, a diner, three five-and-ten-cents stores, the best hot dogs around, and beautiful parks and tennis courts."

The actress Sandra Dee, who died in 2005, was Bayonne's most famous native. Born Alexandra Zuck in 1942, she appeared in almost two dozen movies in the late 1950s and early 1960s and had the title role in the original *Gidget* film. Her wholesome, good-girl image was immortalized, and satirized, in the song "Look at Me, I'm Sandra Dee," from the hit Broadway musical and film *Grease*.

The Frank children walked to public school. At Washington Elementary School, Barney was elected president of the student council. "That was my first elected office," he said. Many parents had attended the same public schools as their children. "We had many of the same teachers that had educated our parents," Beth Weisberg recalled. There were two Catholic high schools and one public high school in Bayonne. Among Bayonne High School's most notable graduates are the economist Arthur Burns, Sister Miriam Teresa Demjanovich, from the class of 1917, whose nomination for sainthood was sent to the Vatican in 2004, and Chuck Wepner, one of Barney's classmates, who went on to become a journeyman heavyweight boxer nicknamed the "Bayonne Bleeder." Chuck Wepner went fifteen rounds against Muhammad Ali in a 1975 fight, knocking down the champ in the ninth round, and became the inspiration for the film *Rocky*.

Barney's childhood friend Steven V. Roberts described Bayonne as "that rarest of entities—a genuine community." "Everybody in Bayonne was connected in different ways. There was this endless web of connections," he said. "For example, there were all these connections between the Frank and Roberts families. My parents knew Barney's parents. They went to the same synagogue. I knew Doris from a Jewish youth group and we dated for a time. When I worked at the *Bayonne Times*, one of the people who were nice to me was Barney's uncle Rosie, the sports editor, who would give me tickets to Yankees games. Our neighbors were relatives of the Franks."

The Jewish people made up about 8 to 10 percent of the city's population. They were a cohesive minority, and they looked after one another. Their lives revolved around the Jewish Community Center for social activities and the ten synagogues for religious observances and practices. Barney remembers socializing "mostly with other Jewish kids." "The Jewish kids played football and other sports among ourselves," he recalled, revealing some regret. In the fall of 2007, when Barney attended the fiftieth-year reunion of the Bayonne High School class of 1957, he observed that "the Jews still hung out together."

"Bayonne is so close to New York, my twin brother and I could see the Statue of Liberty from the window of the bedroom we once shared," Roberts recalled. Barney remembers that it took him less than an hour to get into Manhattan and from there, "you would take the subway, the A train to 59th Street, and then the D train, and you would be at Yankee Stadium in the Bronx." He was an avid Yankees fan, as was his younger sister, Doris. The New York metropolitan area had three major league baseball teams then, and the Bayonne neighborhood was split among Yankees, Brooklyn Dodgers, and New York Giants fans. Even when Walter O'Malley, to make a statement to Brooklyn leaders, had the Dodgers play more than half a dozen "home" games in 1956 and 1957 at Roosevelt Stadium in nearby Jersey City, a short bus ride away, the loyal Yankees fans in Bayonne could not bring themselves to attend the games.

Bayonne's less than six square miles was mostly filled with narrow two-family houses. There were few apartment buildings. The Frank family lived at 1020 Hudson Boulevard (since renamed J. F. Kennedy Boulevard), three houses from the intersection at West 42nd Street. The house was squeezed on a narrow lot with thin alleys, barely wider than a car, separating their house from their neighbor's. There was a small, eight-by-twelve-foot dirt garden in the front of the house. Although from the front sidewalk, the triple-decker frame house, which was only about twenty feet wide, appeared rather ordinary and narrow, it extended back more than sixty feet. It was a two-family house with lots of rooms. At first the Franks lived on the first floor. After David was born, the second floor and the attic were made into a duplex. The Frank family lived in the duplex and rented out the first floor.

The basement of the Franks' house was very large, with high ceilings. It was not your typical finished basement where one might hold Scout meetings. "We had mirror tiles, leather couches, and an actual bar in the basement," Doris recalled. It was a big party room with gold tiles on the support poles. After a bar in the area went out of business, she explained, "my father bought the contents—lock, stock and barrel." When the teen lounge at the Jewish Center closed at ten o'clock on Saturday evenings, the party would often move to the Franks' basement, less than two blocks away. "Barney would always bring a bunch of friends back to our house," his mother said.

When the Jewish mayor of Dublin, Ireland, came to Bayonne for a fundraiser for the United Jewish Appeal, the cocktail party before the dinner was held in the Franks' basement. In 1958 when Eleanor Roosevelt was the speaker at the Israel Bonds dinner, the cocktail party with her before the dinner also took place in the Franks' basement.

Another visitor to the Franks' basement was a Jewish youngster from Brooklyn named Alan Dershowitz. At the time he was dating a girl from Barney's high school class named Sue Barlach. "I think it was at her Sweet Sixteen party that I first met Barney," the now-famous Harvard Law School professor recalled. "Afterwards, a number of us went to Barney's house and hung out in his basement." The trip from Boro Park in Brooklyn to Bayonne without a car was a major schlep for Dershowitz. "I had to take the subway to 42nd Street in Manhattan, then the Port Authority train to Jersey City, and then a bus to Bayonne," he said. It was apparently worth the effort, since he later married Sue Barlach.

Hudson Boulevard was a grand thoroughfare with three lanes in each direction. The Franks' house was across the street from Hudson County Park (now called Bayonne Park), which extends for twelve blocks from 36th to 48th Street and is proportionately bigger for Bayonne than Central Park is for Manhattan. Barney remembers acres of greenery and trails, playgrounds, softball fields, expansive baseball diamonds, even a track, and a football field in the middle. It was a short walk through the park to reach Newark Bay, on which it borders.

An extension of the park on West 42nd Street held several tennis courts. "My kids grew up on those tennis courts," Elsie said. Because the courts were clay rather than all weather, when it rained the man in charge took down the nets till the courts were dry and could be used. The tennis courts were visible from the back bedroom window of the Franks' house. After it rained, Elsie inevitably received telephone calls that began, "Hello, Mrs. Frank, this is so-and-so. Barney said it was okay to call you to see if the net on the tennis court is up." She would ask the caller to hold, walk to the back bedroom and look out the window, then return to tell the caller the status of the net.

Barney described his childhood as "your conventional middle-class upbringing." "My father worked hard and my mother was the center of family life." Doris said, "My father always thought you were truly American when you had the most current stuff out there on the market." The Franks had one of the first television sets in their neighborhood.

Sam Frank was a worrier and when he had children he wanted to have the biggest possible car to keep his family safe in the event of an accident. He would buy second-hand Cadillac limousines. "My father had various connections," Barney remembers. "I think one of the cars had a bullet hole in it." When Elsie finally rebelled, Sam bought a Lincoln. Those large cars didn't get much mileage, but gas was much cheaper then, and besides, Sam Frank owned a gas station.

Sam Frank's parents came from a small town in northern Poland near the Russian border. Sam's early life in Bayonne revolved around newspapers—reading, selling, and delivering them. When he was sixteen, he dropped out of high school to help support his financially struggling family. His first job was working for the *Bayonne Times* organizing newspaper deliveries; later he served for several years as circulation editor. From an early age, Sam Frank was a hard worker and an entrepreneur. By the time he was twenty-one, he owned three trucks for delivering newspapers. He hired newsboys who would hawk the evening editions of the *New York Daily News*, the *New York Mirror*, and the *Daily Graphic* on the street corners of Bayonne.

The *Bayonne Times* was owned by Judge Herman Lazarus, an elderly Jewish attorney with some political clout whose law office was located above the newspaper. Lazarus, who had been given the newspaper by a client as barter for legal services, had little interest in the money-losing newspaper. When Sam Frank started working for the paper it was being run by a bright young manager named Solomon Isadore Newhouse, known to his friends and family as "Sam." The oldest of eight children of Jewish immigrants, Newhouse had left school after the eighth grade to help provide for his family. He had started as an office boy in Lazarus's law office, landing the job after proposing to Lazarus, "Don't pay me until after I prove my worth." Newhouse was hard working and ambitious and quickly moved up the ladder from office boy to bookkeeper to Lazarus's assistant at the law firm, and from messenger to copy boy to general manager at the newspaper.

Sam Frank enjoyed working with Newhouse, who was several years older, and the two men became friends. In 1922, at age twenty-seven, Newhouse decided it was time to go out on his own. Using his savings and a financial investment from Lazarus, he purchased a bankrupt newspaper in Staten Island called the *Staten Island Advance*, which he soon turned around financially. Beginning with that small newspaper, Newhouse went on to build one of the nation's largest newspaper chains, S.I. Newhouse, and magazine empires, Advance Publications, and eventually became one of the richest men in the country.

In 1981, shortly after his election to Congress, Barney received a phone call from a senior executive in the Newhouse media empire to lobby him to support a particular bill in Congress. Someone in the Newhouse family had apparently kept track of Sam Frank's family and was aware that his older son was a congressman. The executive began the conversation by referring to the longtime friendship between the Newhouse and Frank families, saying how pleased the Newhouse family was that Sam Frank's son had become so successful.

Barney's mother, Elsie Golush, was born in Bayonne, the second youngest of six children. Her parents, who came from a small town near Minsk in Belarus, died within a few months of each other when she was twelve years old. The two oldest children, Fanny, twenty-three at the time, and Jenny, nineteen, were both married. Fanny and Jenny and their spouses purchased a two-family house in Bayonne and each couple took in and raised two of the younger siblings. Elsie moved in with Jenny and her husband, Morris "Rosie" Rosenberg, who was sports editor of the *Bayonne Times*.

Rosie was part of a regular poker group that included Sam Frank and several other men from the newspaper. One evening when the group met for poker at Rosie's house, Elsie, who was thirteen at the time, served them water. Sam took notice. He found Elsie, with her warm brown eyes, charming, beautiful, and smart. Several years later, Sam suggested to Elsie's brother Abe that he bring Elsie to the club they both belonged to and Abe obliged him. Elsie was attracted to this young man, whom she remembered as a bit of a stud, a swashbuckler who had become financially successful, and she and Sam started dating.

Although she graduated from Bayonne High School near the top of her class of 1929, Elsie never went to college. To help out her family during the Depression, she went to work as a legal secretary for a law firm in Bayonne. When she and Sam were married in 1936, Sam was twenty-nine and Elsie was just shy of her twenty-fourth birthday. "I was making twenty-three dollars a week, the highest-paid legal secretary in Bayonne," Elsie recalled. "In those days it was the custom that married women didn't work. We could have used my income but Sam wouldn't hear of it," she said. So Elsie stopped working.

Sam Frank and a partner, Nathan Segel, owned a truck stop, Tooley's Truck Terminal, in Jersey City, less than two miles from the mouth of the Holland

Tunnel. When the two men opened their business in the 1940s, anti-Semitism was still pervasive, so they called it Tooley's, because the name sounded Irish. Tooley was Segel's nickname, acquired in his childhood when his friends would hear his mother from her front porch summon him for dinner by shouting his Jewish name, "Naf-t-o-o-l-e-y! Supper!"

Tooley's Truck Stop was a large, full-service facility for over-the-road truck drivers. It had a diner, a gas station, a scale for weighing the trucks, a clothing store, a convenience store that sold solid and dry ice and other items, and a bunk house with semi-private rooms upstairs where the drivers could sleep overnight. Sam Frank had one of the first integrated facilities in the area and it was the only place locally where black drivers could rent rooms to sleep overnight. He also employed many black workers at the truck stop.

The land behind Tooley's Truck Stop was sometimes used as a dumping ground. "My father would occasionally get a call from a cop in New York asking for permission to search there for bodies," Barney recalled. "It was actually clean fill," he added. "Remember, this was before the Verrazano Bridge was built. So if you killed someone in Brooklyn or lower Manhattan, the quickest way out of New York City was either the Lincoln or Holland Tunnel. If you went through the Holland Tunnel it was the first open spot when you came out of the tunnel."

Bribery and kickbacks were time-honored traditions and mob influence and corruption were part of the fabric of life in Bayonne. Sam Frank was caught in the middle of a bribery investigation by the Hudson County prosecutor involving Bayonne city officials and went to jail in 1946 for refusing to answer questions before a grand jury about his older brother Harry. Harry Frank and a partner owned an auto dealership and got the contract to sell cars to the city. Not surprisingly, they were giving a kickback for the contract to two Bayonne Democratic city commissioners, James A. Mullanaphy and Joseph J. Topoleski. The two commissioners were part of the Hague group, a political machine run by Frank "Boss" Hague, the Democratic mayor of Jersey City from 1917 to 1947, whose motto was "I am the law." The Hague group purportedly had ties to organized crime, the Teamsters Union, and the Longshoremen's Union and was involved in extortion and labor racketeering.

In 1944 the Republicans in New Jersey had taken control of the governorship. Unlike other states, where county prosecutors are elected locally, in New Jersey the governor appointed the county prosecutors. The prosecutor for Hudson County, appointed by the Republican governor Walter Evans Edge, was out to crack the case and believed that Sam Frank either knew something or was involved as a middleman or a courier and put pressure on him to testify. By most accounts, Sam was innocent of any wrongdoing but did not want to testify against his brother. He was also fearful that the Hague group might kill him or harm his family if he testified.

Sam Frank disappeared for a time and hid from the police. The Hudson County police, who were controlled by the Republicans, were looking for him while the Bayonne city police, controlled by the Democrats, were protecting him. According to Elsie, there was once a physical fight outside the Franks' home between a city policeman and a county cop who were both staking out the house. On one occasion, Elsie took the children to visit their father in New York City where he was hiding out. Barney remembers seeing the movie *Robin Hood* with Errol Flynn during that visit. A few days later, a Hudson County police detective came to Washington Elementary School to question Barney about whether the Frank family had visited their father in New York. The six-year-old first grader was summoned to the principal's office to meet with the detective. Fortunately, someone had alerted Barney's Aunt Minnie, a teacher at the elementary school, and she stormed into the principal's office and broke up the interview.

Sam was subsequently arrested as a material witness. When he refused to testify before a grand jury in the bribery investigation, he was found in criminal contempt and spent about a year in jail. "When my father went to jail, we just assumed my father must be right," Ann recalled. "I didn't talk about it, not because I was embarrassed, but because my mother told me not to talk about it." She added, "We never worried what other people thought. My parents raised us to do what was right regardless of what other people may think." Elsie spent a lot of time visiting Sam in jail and bringing him food. Every so often, she would take Ann and Barney with her.

Barney speaks with admiration of his father for not breaking down and testifying. "He was the Susan McDougal of his day," Barney said, referring to the woman who was jailed for refusing to testify against the Clintons during the Whitewater investigation. His high school friend Mark Rose recalled his own parents' admiration for Sam and Elsie Frank. "At least in the circles that my parents were in, there was real sympathy and respect for Sam Frank. There was not a hint of any condemnation." He remembers that his parents were impressed with Elsie because she "held her head up high."

Elsie described Sam Frank as good natured, a brilliant guy with a great sense of humor. Ann remembers his warmth and his good humor. "He would walk with David on his shoulder and sing to him," she said.

Sam took care of his family. He put an older brother and a younger sister through college. He bought a house for his mother, where she lived on the second floor while his older brother Irving, who was never able to make an adequate living, lived downstairs with his wife and children. Sam was always generous to others. When he was a youngster selling newspapers on the streets of Bayonne, his mother would knit wool gloves and hats for him. Inevitably he would come home without the gloves and hat because he had given them to other kids who were poorer and in his view needed them more.

Doris remembers how hard her father worked, leaving for work at the truck stop at five in the morning, six days a week. She described him as "pretty much a nontraditionalist," adding, "He always drove with his shoes off. He was exactly who he was, with no pretenses." Ann said, "My father had a certain disregard for the conventions of dress, much like Barney. He didn't believe in tying his shoelaces." David recalls that his father was "very kind and sweet" and that he had "great wisdom and a sense of treating people fairly." "In a quiet way," David said, "he was magnetic." "People respected what he said and really listened when he spoke."

Barney grew up as part of a large and closely knit extended family surrounded by several aunts and uncles and eleven cousins who lived within a ten-to-twelve-block radius. Aunt Jenny and Aunt Fanny and their families continued to share the two-family house Elsie had grown up in, and Elsie's brother Abe and his family lived only four blocks away. On warm Sundays, the whole family would go on a picnic.

It was a family with a social conscience. When Ann was eight years old, she insisted that her parents put a bumper sticker on their car that read "Boycott Britain" to protest British obstacles to the creation of the State of Israel. Later, at a time when her friends were out selling Girl Scout cookies, Ann collected money for the State of Israel. When she was about eleven, she read an article in the *New York Post* about workers on strike in the Midwest against Kohler, a company that manufactured faucets and other plumbing supplies. Ann made her uncle, a plumbing contractor, promise not to buy any Kohler products while the employees remained on strike.

Everyone called Barney's uncle Morris Rosenberg "Rosie" because of his popular sports column, "Rosie's Round-Up," in the *Bayonne Times*. Rosie liked being a big fish in a small pond and never left the *Bayonne Times*. He wrote that sports column six days a week for over thirty years, covering local sports and the New York City teams, as well as the national sports scene. He was a top boxing writer and loved writing about the sport at a time when people cared about and paid attention to boxing. "Rosie had a way with words," David Frank said. He used "synonym upon synonym and metaphors to describe common sports terms." In a November, 1947 column about Allie Stolz, Newark's foremost contender for the lightweight championship, Rosie described Stolz's recent string of victories: "He dealt out drubbings to Bobby Ruffin and Jay Fontana in New York, traveled to New Haven to whip 'Snooks' Lacey, went down to Baltimore to decision Billy Banks, then up to Boston to add Abie Denner to his list of vanquished foemen."

Rosie's column on August 1, 1946, was about a rookie outfielder on the Jersey City Giants, a phenom from Scotland named Robert "Bobby" Thomson who was belting home runs at a record pace. "The Giants can command $25,000 for Thomson in the open market but consider him too valuable," Rosie wrote about the ballplayer who five seasons later would hit a three-run home run off Brooklyn Dodgers pitcher Ralph Branca to win the pennant for the New York Giants, a blast that would forever be known as "The Shot Heard 'Round the World."

Morris Rosenberg had a big influence on Barney's interest in sports as a child. One day when Barney was eleven, Rosie brought Jackie Farrell, a scout for the New York Yankees, to the Frank house for dinner. Instead of peppering Farrell with questions about the Yankees' rookie prospects or which pitcher was the most difficult for Joe DiMaggio to hit against, Barney asked Farrell why there weren't any black ballplayers on the Yankees. "Well," the scout responded, "they are trying." It took another four years before Elston Howard broke the color barrier with the Yankees.

Elsie took her children everywhere. "My husband was the worker, I was the driver. I schlepped the kids all over the place," she said. She insisted in those days that her children take elocution lessons and later credited that training with her children's ability to think on their feet in front of a crowd. Barney called the lessons "natural self-improvement" and feels they may have helped his speaking ability.

Some of Barney's fondest childhood memories are of the trips to Newark, where his mother took him and his siblings to the movies. One of the movie theaters in Newark featured a "Laughfest" where for two hours the children enjoyed the antics of Abbott and Costello, the visual comedy of Laurel and Hardy, and especially the eye-poking, face-slapping, pie-throwing slapstick of the Three Stooges. The Three Stooges were considered *mishpokhe* (Yiddish for "extended family" or "kin"), because Shemp Howard, the often forgotten Stooge, was related to the Frank family by marriage. In 1925, Shemp Howard (whose last name was originally Horwitz) married Gertrude "Babe" Frank, a first cousin of Sam's. Many of the Frank family elders frowned on the marriage. "My aunt Minnie told me that the relatives felt terrible, they were embarrassed by the marriage," Barney explained. "'He's an actor—a bum,' they said. Then the Depression came and Shemp wasn't such a bum when he supported the family. He wound up carrying them all."

Shemp, his younger brother Moe Howard, and a friend named Larry Fine were the original Three Stooges. When Shemp left the group in 1932 at the urging of his wife and became a show business journeyman, he was replaced in the act by the youngest brother, Jerome "Curly" Howard. In May 1946, Curly left the comedy act after suffering a debilitating stroke and at Moe's insistence, Shemp, after an almost fifteen-year absence, rejoined the trio and his presence saved the act.

From the time he was thirteen, Barney worked part-time at his father's truck stop in Jersey City, usually on Saturdays and during vacations, pumping diesel gas into the large trucks and occasionally operating the weigh station. He was paid ten dollars for the day and that was his spending money for the week. Doris remembers that she desperately wanted to pump gas "like Barney did." "But," she said, "my father would never let me. He was a chauvinist. He would tell me, 'Princess, pumping gas is not something girls do.'" He called Ann "Cookie" until she went to kindergarten and voiced objection to such a childish nickname.

For many years, the Frank family belonged to Talmud Torah, an orthodox synagogue about nine blocks from their house. "There was no reform temple in the area at the time and the conservative synagogue [Temple Emanuel, where most of the wealthy Jews were members] was a little too ritzy," Barney said. In 1953, Barney had his bar mitzvah ceremony, during which he was called to read from the Torah at the orthodox *shul*. Elsie recalled that his favorite part of the bar mitzvah service was when he finished reading his Haftorah and everyone, according to Jewish custom, threw little bags of candy at him. "He quickly ducked under the *bimah*, a raised platform from which the Torah is read, when the candy was being thrown," Ann recalled.

At the time of Barney's bar mitzvah the social hall of the new Bayonne Jewish Community Center, located on the corner of Hudson Boulevard and West 44th Street, a block and a half from the Franks' house, was not complete. But Sam Frank was so proud of his son and of "his building," which he had helped raise money to construct, that he insisted on having his son's bar mitzvah party there. The party was held in the gym, which at the time had only cinder-block walls. Several hundred people attended. Sam invited everyone he knew—friends, family, second cousins, and people with whom he did business.

The new Jewish Community Center was a modern structure with a gym, auditorium, social hall, and meeting rooms that housed the civic, social, cultural, athletic, and spiritual activities of the Bayonne Jewish community under one roof. Barney and his sisters and brother spent considerable time at the Jewish Center and were active with different groups. They attended Youth Council meetings on Monday nights, fraternity and sorority meetings on Wednesdays, and dances on Saturday evenings. The Jewish Center, Mark Rose recalled, was "the place where you hung out evenings looking for girls."

Sam Frank was not a deeply religious man but he was a committed Jew. He contributed money to all the synagogues in the area. He was active in the Bayonne Lodge of B'nai B'rith, the Bayonne United Jewish Appeal, the Jewish

National Fund, and the State of Israel Bonds drive. When people wanted a reform Jewish synagogue in Bayonne, Sam Frank was there to help raise the funds to build Temple Beth Am around the block from the Franks' house. David had his bar mitzvah ceremony there in 1963.

"If you needed to raise money, you would call my husband. If you needed someone to serve on a board or community organization, you would call me," Elsie said. She described Sam as a businessman with a liberal conscience. His idea of a good time was to buy a ticket to a local Bayonne fund-raiser. "I never knew which one we would be going to," Elsie said. "I had to have such a wardrobe for all those charitable events." The friends they socialized with were local people who owned businesses in Bayonne.

Elsie helped establish the Bayonne chapter of Hadassah, a volunteer women's organization committed to Jewish ideals, and served as its first secretary. She chaired the women's division of Israel Bonds and was active in the National Council of Jewish Women. She was also the editor of the Jewish Community Center newspaper.

Although Sam and Elsie Frank were not well educated, they put a premium on education and especially on reading. "The house was filled with newspapers, magazines, and books," Elsie said. "To this day, my children still read and read." In the Frank household reading newspapers was akin to studying the Talmud. Everyone would read the paper and then take part in a family discussion. Many years later Barney learned, to his surprise and dismay, that it is considered rude to bring a newspaper to the dinner table. New York had several newspapers at the time, the *Times*, the *Post*, the *Mirror*, the *Daily News*, the *Herald Tribune*, the *World*, and the *Telegram*, and New Jersey had the *Newark Star Ledger*, the *Newark Evening News*, the *Hudson Dispatch*, the *Jersey Journal*, the *Jersey Observer*, and, of course, the *Bayonne Times*. "We had most of them in the house," Doris said. "If we were out on a Saturday night we would stop and buy the evening edition of the newspapers, which came out at ten o'clock."

"We learned from our parents at an early age that what was happening in the world was important and that there was a direct connection between politics and the decisions being made and the way we were going to live," Ann explained. Barney's friend Jerry Katz recalled having dinner sometimes at the Franks' house. "The Frank family would sit around the dinner table and talk about world events. At the time I didn't know where Ohio was. I was absorbing it all." The conversation around the dinner table usually involved politics and social issues. As Doris recalled, Barney and Ann talked a lot and often argued at the dinner table. Barney was the fastest talking of the four Frank children.

The Frank children, like most siblings, had disagreements and arguments but they generally got along well. "Our family values are evidenced by my children's mutual concern for each other's well being," Elsie said. Today, they continue to support each other, whether by helping out in a political campaign, dealing with a political sex scandal, or providing comfort at the time of a divorce, a spouse's death, or the tragic murder of a daughter.

Barney was drawn to politics at an early age. He remembers watching the Army–McCarthy hearings in 1954 on the family's little black-and-white television set with his parents, whom he described as "passionate liberals." He also watched the 1956 national conventions on television. "There was an attempt by liberals to strengthen the civil rights plank at the Democratic convention," he said. "I remember they took a voice vote on the civil rights plank, and Speaker Sam Rayburn, who was presiding, said, 'The no's have it.' I was angry. Obviously the fix was in to avoid a roll call vote."

One of Barney's earliest passions as a teenager emerged from the horrific death of Emmett Till, a fourteen-year-old black youth from Chicago. In August 1955, while visiting relatives near the small Mississippi Delta community of Money, Till was kidnapped and then savagely murdered, reportedly for whistling at a white woman in a grocery store. Till's mother insisted that his disfigured face and mutilated body be displayed in an open casket at the funeral so that the world could see what had been done to her son. By focusing national attention on the brutality directed at blacks in the South, the murder of Emmett Till stirred the conscience of the nation and became a defining event in the civil rights movement.

Barney could not stop thinking about Emmett Till. "I remember reading about it in the *New York Post*," he said. It was the heyday of the *Post*, which was a Frank family favorite because of its great sports section and its liberal politics, with the columnists Murray Kempton, William Shannon, Max Lerner, James Wexler, and Jimmy Cannon. "Emmett Till was my age but black. He had been murdered and the *New York Post* made it very clear that everybody in town, including the sheriff, knew who did it, and nobody did anything about it," Barney said.

Eventually, however, Roy Bryant, the owner of the grocery store, and his half-brother, J. W. Milam, were arrested and tried for murder in a segregated Tallahatchie County courthouse in Sumner, Mississippi. The defense attorneys suggested to the jury that the body was not that of Emmett Till. The two men were acquitted by a jury of twelve white men, who deliberated for about an hour. The acquittal fueled outrage across the country. The next year, Bryant and Milam admitted in an interview with *Look* magazine, for which they were paid four thousand dollars, that they had beaten and murdered Till because he had whistled at Bryant's wife. The Emmett Till tragedy instilled in Barney a desire to fight for civil rights and put an end to hatred and bigotry.

Sam and Elsie Frank's politics were rooted in the liberalism of the New Deal. They were devoted Roosevelt Democrats who believed in the power of government to do good for people. In the 1950s they were zealous supporters of Adlai Stevenson, the one-term governor of Illinois and Democratic presidential candidate whose eloquence and intellect elevated the level of political discourse in the country. When Stevenson was defeated by General Dwight Eisenhower in 1952, Ann found a piece of black cloth in the house and wore it as an armband to school in protest. (This gesture came thirteen years before the black armband Mary Beth Tinker wore to school to protest the war in Vietnam resulted in a landmark decision by the Supreme Court on the First Amendment.) "Until that moment," Ann said, "I didn't realize that the good guys could lose an election. I remember watching the election results in 1948 and seeing Truman beat Dewey. Elections were exciting. They were important. I thought they were like a cowboy movie where in the end the good guy always won. That didn't happen this time." In 1956, when he was sixteen years old, Barney rang doorbells in Bayonne on behalf of Stevenson's second presidential campaign.

Ann, who had skipped a grade in school, was the first to leave home to attend college, heading to Radcliffe College in Cambridge, Massachusetts, in September 1954 at the age of sixteen. "I heard someone say that Ann was the smartest girl ever to go through the Bayonne schools," Lynda Weitz, whose father was a teacher in the Bayonne public schools, said. Aaron Lazare, who dated Ann once in high school and later became the chancellor and dean of the University of Massachusetts Medical School, said, "Ann was so smart, I felt totally insecure."

The Frank family went to visit Ann at college that fall. They were having breakfast at the old Commander Hotel just off Harvard Square when they noticed that Adlai Stevenson was sitting with an aide at an adjoining table. "My father approached him," Barney said. "My father's version of 'Mack' was 'Chief.' 'Chief,' he said to Stevenson, 'we really need you.' Stevenson was very gracious."

"We had a copy of the *New York Times*, which had a front-page story that President Eisenhower wanted to appoint Adlai Stevenson to some position overseas," Elsie recalled. "My husband showed Stevenson the newspaper and said, 'Chief, they still want you." Stevenson replied, "Thanks, but I've had enough of those guys." A few minutes later, Stevenson's son, a student at Harvard, joined his father for breakfast. Stevenson leaned over and asked Sam Frank, "Can I see your newspaper? I want to show that article to my son." Sam proudly handed the front section of the newspaper to Stevenson.

After breakfast the family visited Ann. They gave her the *New York Times* to read and she noticed that the front section was missing. "Where is the rest of the newspaper?" she asked. "Adlai Stevenson has it," her father replied. "Daddy, will you stop kidding me. Where is the rest of the paper really? Ann asked. "My father was so pleased that he had that encounter with Adlai Stevenson," Ann recalled.

In a city where there were few Jews, Barney was an intellectual Jewish kid with "Coke-bottle" glasses he started wearing in fourth grade. In those days, the public schools would administer an annual eye examination. One day Barney came home from school with a note that said he needed glasses. When his mother asked, "Why didn't you ever tell me that you couldn't see well?" he replied, "I thought everybody saw things that way." Barney was a little on the chubby side, as he describes himself, but "not fat." He was likeable and energetic. "I played softball, football, and tennis, but basketball was the one sport I just couldn't get the hang of. I was too clumsy and uncoordinated for basketball," Barney said. Referring to the basketball team at the Jewish Center, he added, "These were all my friends, so I was the manager. I was actually the scorekeeper. It was a way to hang with the guys during the basketball season."

In 1955, he was the first underclassman to be elected president of the Youth Council at the Jewish Center, and he was reelected the following year. Max Lourie, who at the time was youth director at the center, as well as Barney's geometry teacher, remembers that everybody enjoyed Barney's company. "He was very popular because he was so sincere. He never said anything just to be heard," Lourie, at age ninety-five, recalled. "Barney had this charisma that people gravitated toward him. People kind of looked up to him naturally and wanted him to lead. He helped you see things in a new way," Lynda Weitz, a fellow officer on the Youth Council, said. Mark Rose said, "I don't know anybody who didn't like Barney, other than perhaps a few teachers who thought he was too smart-alecky. He had this aura characterized by his physical presence, a nervous energy, movement, and a tense alertness."

At Bayonne High School Barney played on the tennis team and was sports editor of the school newspaper, the *Beacon*. He had a humor column in the paper called "Confusing Say" that his friend Jerry Katz describes as "unbelievable—sophisticated and funny." He also wrote for the Student Congress newspaper and served as one of the two parliamentarians appointed to the Student Congress. He was a member of the debating club and the National Honor Society and president of the Key Club, which sent volunteers to service organizations in Bayonne.

"I was chosen as editor of the school newspaper over Barney because he wasn't deferential enough. I don't think he really cared," Mark Rose recalled. Rose, who was voted Most Likely to Succeed in a senior class poll, is an associate vice chancellor and professor of English at the University of California at Santa Barbara. "We were in the same homeroom and always did the *New York Times* crossword puzzle in competition with each other," he said. "Barney always won. He is one of the fastest minds I have ever known in my life."

According to Rose, he and Barney were polar opposites in interests and style, "except we were both interested in writing" and "we were on the same page politically." "Barney was interested in sports both as a player and as a fan. Sports weren't in my universe. I was interested in opera and Barney would give me hell about that. 'Why would you want to listen to that stuff?' he'd ask." Rose described Barney's style back then as "aggressively plebian" compared with his own, which he called "very high culture and pretentious." For many teenagers like Rose, Bayonne was a place to escape from. But, Rose said, "Barney never spoke that way."

Beth Weisberg, now a Jewish educator in Seattle, recalled Barney's irreverence. When they attended the Columbia University School of Journalism conference for high school newspapers together, unlike the students who brought copies of their school papers to distribute, she and Barney, at his instigation, handed out copies of the Communist newspaper the *Daily Worker*.

Barney's twelfth-grade English teacher, Betty Harelick, at age ninety-six described him as "very bright, one of my best former students." "Barney spoke too fast even then," Harelick recalled, paused momentarily, laughed, and then added, "I should have done something about his fast talking, but he was a senior." Asked if she was surprised that Barney has done so well in politics, she replied, "No. He would have been successful in anything he did. He was always a liberal. He had strong ideas, but he listened to reason and didn't let anyone put him down. He hasn't changed much."

In high school Barney developed a passion for politics, which he sees as a natural segue from his love of sports. "It was like sports but with a moral content," he said. As a teenager Barney idolized Hubert Humphrey. Ann shared her brother's fascination with politics and doesn't remember ever wanting to do anything other than politics.

"Barney could stand on his feet and speak," one of his classmates recalled. He won second place in the county American Legion Voice of Democracy oratory contest. Goldie Rosenhan remembered that once during his senior year at Bayonne High School when Barney was being honored at a school assembly, "someone from the Rotary Club stood up and said some nice things about Barney and predicted that he would be the youngest senator from New Jersey. It wasn't the Senate and it wasn't New Jersey but the spirit of what he predicted came true."

Beneath the facade of smart, funny, popular, seemingly regular guy who constantly dated girls, Barney suffered the silent pain, fear, and loneliness of being homosexual during the 1950s. "It's hard to explain to people what it's like to be afraid your parents are going to find out or your siblings," he said. He was determined not to tell anyone and terrified that someone would find out his secret. Tim McFeeley, the former executive director of the Human Rights Campaign, described that experience: "Your whole life you have been taught that everything about this is wrong and so you learn to hide it. Hiding was and still is a very devastating part of being a gay or lesbian person because you hide it from your family, which are the closest people to you growing up. You learn to hide, learn to lie, and learn to not be honest with yourself."

When Barney was thirteen years old, some friends passed around a soft-core girlie magazine. Barney didn't get any sexual charge from the photographs. "My first hypothesis was that I just don't have any sex drive. Then I realized that I did. I was attracted to guys. I knew that I was gay," Barney recalled. A year later, Barney and a group of friends were involved in some horseplay in the locker room. "I forget what triggered it," Barney said, "but one of the kids said to me, 'What are you, queer?' and I replied, 'Yeah, I am.' It was a thunderbolt." The other boy thought Barney was joking around but he wasn't. This discovery about his sexuality, which would remain hidden for almost twenty-five years and would not be revealed publicly until Barney was forty-seven years old, would cast a giant shadow over his lifestyle, his relationships, and his career.

As a teenager Barney was frightened, depressed, and tortured by feelings he could not control. He had no crushes but felt sexual urges toward other boys his age. In the early 1950s, being gay was associated with being effeminate in men and masculine in women. "Barney was not effeminate in any size, shape, or form," Mark Rose declared. "You didn't know there was a full range of types [of gays]," Barney explained. "If you weren't like that you didn't fit in. There was a heterosexual majority, and a small number of effeminate men and masculine women and I'm none of the above. What have I got? I thought. I didn't know about other types." This lack of information made it even more difficult for him to come to terms with his homosexuality. And there were no role models for gay youth at the time.

Barney grew up in a society in which prejudice against homosexuals was deep-seated. The outlook was bleak. In December 1950, the Subcommittee on Investigations of the Senate Committee on Expenditures in the Executive Departments, which was controlled by the Democrats, issued Senate Report 241, titled, "Employment of Homosexuals and Other Sex Perverts in Government." It stated: "The conclusion of the subcommittee that homosexuals and other sex perverts are a security risk is not based upon mere conjecture. . . . [It] is predicated on a careful review of the opinions of those best qualified to consider matters of security in government, namely the intelligence agencies of the government."

In April 1953, President Eisenhower signed Executive Order 10450, establishing that "sexual perversion" was grounds for firing a federal employee and for barring the hiring of a homosexual. In 1954, Eisenhower issued another executive order singling out homosexuals as security risks and providing that they could not get a security clearance. It memorialized the negative stereotype that homosexuals are so susceptible to blackmail that they cannot be trusted. That same year, the *New York Times* headlined a news story, "Sex Perverts Fired from State Department." The *Times* wasn't quoting Joseph McCarthy or anyone else. These were the newspaper's own words to describe homosexuals.

"The notion that you have a choice is so bizarre, especially when you are a teenager. It is the last choice any teenager would make back then," Barney explained. He doesn't know of anyone who wanted to be gay. "I can't imagine that anybody believes that a young teenager in the early 1950s would think, 'Boy, it would be really great to be a part of this minority that everybody hates and to have a really restricted life.'"

Barney needed to fit in as a teenager. In 1956, when the movie *Baby Doll*, starring Carroll Baker, was condemned by Cardinal Francis Spellman, his attack made the racy film a must-see for teenage boys everywhere. All of Barney's friends wanted to see the nightie-clad Baker on the big screen and he didn't want to be left out. So he feigned a desire to see the movie with his friends.

Nobody had a clue about Barney's sexuality in high school. Max Lourie recalls that Barney went out on dates with girls most weekends. Thirty years later, Lynda Weitz, one of the girls he regularly dated in high school, was surprised to read that Barney Frank is gay. "I felt like someone was rewriting the history of my childhood," she said.

According to his mother, from the time Barney was a teenager, he wanted to be in Congress. But to Barney, the notion that he would ever be elected to public office seemed pretty remote, almost alien, more because he was Jewish than because he was gay, since that was still secret. Sam Frank once told one of Barney's friends, "I worry about Barney. He is so ambitious and he forgets that he is Jewish." In those days, there were very few Jews in elected office. Barney was aware of the barriers. "When I was growing up in 1957 you could be a Jewish elected official from Brooklyn or you could be a Jew like from Oregon, where you were the only Jew around so they didn't know enough to be anti-Semitic," he said. "I also knew growing up that Hudson County, where politics was corrupt and machine controlled and there was no independent access, wasn't the norm but it still influenced me." Although Barney dreamed of being a congressman, he was a realist, and so in the 1957 Bayonne High School yearbook, the *Garnet and White*, beneath the photo of Barnett Frank, in short hair and black-rimmed glasses, his stated future occupation is "lawyer." He viewed law as a way to help people and make changes in society.

Even as a youngster, Barney was fascinated with Congress. His graduation present from high school in June 1957 was a family trip to Washington. "We had a new station wagon and Barney had just gotten his license and he drove us all to Washington," Elsie recalled. Every morning Barney would drive the station wagon to Capitol Hill and spend the entire day watching Congress in session and attending committee meetings while his mother and Doris and David toured the monuments, museums, and other sights in the city. Barney had asked someone with political connections to help get him a Senate gallery pass from New Jersey senator Clifford Case's office and was grateful for the favor, unaware that anyone could simply pick up a pass at the senator's office.

Most high school students in Bayonne sought employment after graduation. In the Bayonne High School class of 1957 fewer than 75 of the 455 graduating seniors went on to college, and most of those attended state schools and teachers' colleges, such as Jersey City State Teachers' College. Very few students went to college out of town. Barney applied to six colleges. Harvard University was his first choice. "I was playing tennis on the public courts near our house," he recalled, "when my mother came running over waving a thick envelope from Harvard." He was accepted.

3

A Decade at Harvard with Only a B.A. to Show for It

IN THE FALL OF 1957, an idealistic and anxious seventeen-year-old kid who had never strayed far from his Bayonne roots followed his sister Ann to Cambridge, Massachusetts, to attend Harvard. About eleven hundred freshmen walked with him through the historic gate and entered the hallowed grounds of Harvard Yard for the first time. Barney arrived with several books from home so that he would have something to read. Almost everyone at Harvard, he discovered, was smart. The freshmen who had attended Andover or Exeter and had already completed a year or two of college classes arrived with a veneer of intellectual sophistication that was formidable and intimidating.

Barney's freshman roommate was Charles Halpern from Buffalo, New York, who would go on to attend Yale Law School and become one of the country's finest public interest lawyers. "It was a good match," Halpern said, "two smart, funny eastern Jews with similar senses of the world." And they both wore thick-rimmed glasses. Halpern was immediately impressed by his roommate's knowledge of government and his sense of purpose. He remembers that he showed up at Harvard proud that he knew there were two houses in Congress. But Barney already knew the names of all the U.S. senators and most of the members of the House and their voting records, as well as the names of all the congressional committees and committee chairmen.

Barney soon became close friends with another freshman, Hastings Wyman Jr. The two had nothing in common except an obsession with politics, which fueled their friendship. They differed on almost every political issue of the day and would argue constantly and often fiercely. Wyman, a Presbyterian, was a smart, reactionary southerner, very conservative and very much a segregationist, from Aiken, South Carolina, a small town of about five thousand people. Barney became a member of the Young Democratic Club at Harvard and Wyman joined the Harvard Conservative League.

Wyman would later write his senior thesis on the resurgence of the Republican Party in South Carolina, an idea that at the time was not even a blip on anyone's political radar screen. After graduating from the University of South Carolina Law School in 1964 and practicing law in Aiken for several years, Wyman worked for the Republican National Committee as a southern field representative and then served for five years as Senator Strom Thurmond's legislative assistant. In 1978, he started the *Southern Political Report*, a biweekly newsletter covering the politics and politicians of twelve southern states that he continues to write today.

During the semester break, Barney took Wyman to visit Bayonne. To Wyman, "it was a whole different world and a real eye opener." The blocks of row houses seemed to him "kind of dingy compared to pretty houses on large lots in a small town in South Carolina." The Franks were the first Jews he ever knew, and he found them warm and hospitable. He was impressed that Barney's father made a lot of money and did it with little education. In the southern small-town rural environment Wyman grew up in, he said, "people had education but little money."

A year later, Barney visited Wyman in Aiken. Wyman remembers being alarmed when the first thing Barney did after leaving the plane was to walk over to a water fountain with a sign that said "colored people" and take a drink. "Barney made it clear where he stood," Wyman said. His parents liked Barney a lot, "although," he said, "there was this sort of language barrier. He spoke so fast in a Bayonne accent and my parents had a southern accent."

Barney was totally focused on politics. He knew from the beginning that he wanted to be a government major and took almost every government course that was offered. During his freshman year, he became active in student politics and student council activities. At Harvard, he found what for him was a new phenomenon—people to his left politically. But the whole time he was there he stayed deep in the closet. Though he and his roommate, Charley Halpern, often played tennis together and had many dinners in the graduate student apartment where Barney's sister Ann lived with her husband, Gerald Lewis, a student at the Harvard Law School, Halpern had no idea that his roommate was gay. Many times during their freshman year, he fixed Barney up with dates, often with his cousin Kitty. Dating women was part of the camouflage. "It was something you did," Barney explained. But "it became more and more awkward." Years later Barney realized that a student in his freshman dorm that he had found really attractive had come on to him. But Barney had been too terrified to respond to the advance. He did not want anyone to know or find out that he was gay.

Halpern recalled that when he and Barney were at Harvard, "homophobia was kind of the conversational coin of the realm." "There were often gay jokes,

jokes about queers and about fairies," he said. "Barney was part of the group listening and laughing at those jokes. He has this tough exterior but it had to hurt on the inside." It did hurt, and, according to Barney, the pain was even worse in high school. "After a while you get kind of hardened and just accept it," he explained. "It wasn't a daily painful thing. It was almost like having some kind of physical handicap. Human beings can get used to almost anything."

Like Barney, Hastings Wyman knew from the time he was about thirteen years old that he was gay and was living a closeted life. A year or two into their friendship at college, he confided his secret to Barney. "I had no idea back then that Barney was gay. He was the first and only person I told," Wyman said. Barney was sympathetic about his friend's revelation but never said anything about himself. He felt no attraction to Wyman, and besides, he explained, "I was still too frightened. It was unthinkable then that I would tell people." Hastings Wyman came out of the closet in the mid-1990s after several years of marriage and two children.

Barney, in the first of a series of weight losses and binge weight gains, had lost about twenty-five pounds before starting at Harvard. However, he gained a lot of that weight back. According to Wyman, as an undergraduate, Barney had several pairs of khaki slacks in different sizes and wore the one that best matched his waistline at the time.

As a freshman at Harvard, Barney read the *New York Times* every morning while shaving. When Halpern was asked how Barney could do that, he responded, "not very well" and pointed out that Barney was often seen walking to the Harvard Freshman Union for breakfast with dabs of toilet paper all over his face.

Even then he was not fastidious in his dress. Those were the days when students at Harvard were required to wear a jacket and tie in the dining room. Barney kept the same tie crumpled in his pocket and would put it on every day while waiting in the food line. Barney and Halpern chose to remain roommates for their sophomore and junior years and asked Wyman to join them as a third roommate.

During the summer after his freshman year at Harvard, while back home in Bayonne, Barney started dating Goldie Rosenhan, who had just graduated from Bayonne High School, where she was an editor of the school newspaper and a member of the National Honor Society. "Goldie was more Barney's speed intellectually," his high school pal Jerry Katz said. They had first met in French class. "Barney was far brighter in the classroom but I was a better French student," Goldie contended. They would go to parties, to the movies, or out to dinner and regularly did the *New York Times* crossword puzzle together. "Every moment," Goldie recalled, "he had something funny to say."

Barney and Goldie continued to date for almost two years while Goldie was at Brandeis University in Waltham, Massachusetts, about a thirty-minute drive from Cambridge. They got together on weekends and went to parties and occasional football games. Sometimes they double dated with Barney's sister Ann and her husband.

"I remember going with Barney to a football game at Harvard," Goldie said. "He bought me a Harvard pennant at the game. Midway into the game, he shouted, 'Damn it, I bought you that pennant so you could stand up and cheer and wave it.' Everybody around us in the stands started laughing."

Goldie knew how to deal with him. "I had wanted a Harvard scarf," she said, "so I wore a friend's Princeton scarf to meet with Barney in Cambridge just to rouse his ire. He pulled the scarf off my neck, stomped upon it, and said, 'Don't ever wear it again.' The following weekend, he presented me with a Harvard scarf."

Barney and Goldie stopped dating in the fall of 1961. Looking back at her relationship with Barney more than forty-five years later, Goldie remarked: "I was such a naïve, idealistic person going away for the first time in my life to college, and having him as close as he was, adding support and someone to lean on. I idolized him. I adored him. I just felt that the sun rose and set on this brilliant person with whom I was having a relationship. He was the most fun to be with. There was just a glow on everything we did together because he was there." She continued, "I am not sure whether that is the reality of it or simply the way it was to me at the time. It certainly is the way I remember him. To this day there isn't anything I wouldn't do for him."

Scattered throughout Barney's academic odyssey were forays into politics and social activism. In the fall of 1958, a first-year student from the Harvard Law School Young Democrats came to speak to the Young Democrats at the college. He predicted, accurately, that two Democrats, John F. Kennedy, who was running for reelection to the Senate, and Foster Furcolo, who was running for governor, would win without difficulty. But there was a hot race for Congress in what was then the Tenth Congressional District, where the Democrats, whose candidate was John L. Saltonstall, a liberal and the state chairman of the Americans for Democratic Action, had a good shot at beating the conservative Republican incumbent, Lawrence Curtis. The Tenth District included Brookline and Newton, two old Yankee Republican cities that were beginning to turn Democratic, as well as about a third of Boston. The young law student proposed that the Law School Democrats and the College Young Democrats work together in the Saltonstall race in Brookline. "The law school student who made the pitch, a Brookline native, had a certain interest in that race," Barney explained. "He was just entering Brookline politics. That was the first time I met Michael Dukakis."

Four years later, in 1962, at the age of twenty-nine, Dukakis was elected to the state legislature from Brookline.

That fall, Barney canvassed voters in Brookline for John Saltonstall. He stood outside Kehillath Israel, a large conservative synagogue in Coolidge Corner in Brookline, handing out Saltonstall for Congress campaign literature. Twenty-two years later, he himself would be running for Congress and campaigning at that same synagogue.

During his junior year at Harvard, Barney met Allard Lowenstein, a civil and human rights activist who would become Barney's role model and have a major impact on his life and political career. Lowenstein dressed in rumpled business suits and, like Barney, wore thick black glasses. Barney was impressed by how bright Lowenstein was, and by his dedication to fairness in the world; he was also drawn to Lowenstein's combination of liberalism, commitment, and advocacy. Barney admired his magnetism and his ability to stand up before a crowd and move the group using powerful, logical arguments. Lowenstein inspired thousands of students in the 1960s and 1970s to fight for civil rights and to protest the war in Southeast Asia. He galvanized a national effort to stop the war in Vietnam, and in 1967 he organized the Dump Lyndon Johnson movement.

Barney's initial meeting with Lowenstein came when, as a member of the Harvard student council, he, with another student, was assigned to pick up Lowenstein at Logan Airport in Boston and drive him to campus for a speech. During the drive, he and Lowenstein spoke at length about a wide range of subjects. Lowenstein had recently returned from Southwest Africa (now Namibia). Southwest Africa, a German colony, had been taken over by the League of Nations as a trust territory after World War I and in 1919 had been turned over to South Africa as a mandated territory. Lowenstein, who along with others had been agitating at the United Nations to have Southwest Africa declared a free country, had surreptitiously entered the country to gather material for a book about the widespread brutality and authoritarian abuses by the South African government there. He came to Harvard on a national tour to promote the book *Brutal Mandate*, and focus attention on the deplorable conditions in Southwest Africa.

Shortly after Barney left for Harvard, his father, Sam, had a breakdown that Barney believes was triggered by the pardon he received for his contempt conviction twelve years earlier. The pardon had come through the efforts of the Franks' neighbor Thomas Domenico, who was now mayor of Bayonne. When the pardon arrived in the mail, Sam Frank threw the document to the floor and asked his wife, "What did I ever do to deserve going to jail?" He was fearful that because Ann was at Radcliffe and Barney was at Harvard, the two children would be ashamed of him, a high school dropout who had spent time in prison, and that he would lose their love and respect.

On Saturday, April 23, 1960, Sam Frank had a sudden heart attack and died. He was fifty-three years old. Hastings Wyman recalled coming back to the suite and finding Barney and Goldie Rosenhan sitting on the couch with Ann and her husband. Barney was crying. "His father's death was very emotionally difficult. They were close and he felt a lot of affection for his father," Wyman said.

Sam Frank was buried the following day. Although there was no Sunday newspaper in Bayonne to report his death, the news spread quickly around Bayonne. "The funeral parlor was so packed that people were standing on the sidewalk," Elsie recalled.

Elsie stayed home for seven more years to care for her two younger children, Doris, who was sixteen at the time of her father's death, and David, who was ten. When David was ready for college, Elsie, now fifty-five, went back to work to support her family. She was hired as a legal secretary by the Wall Street law firm Cravath, Swain, and Moore.

Barney finished the spring semester of his junior year at Harvard and then took a year's leave of absence to help his mother sort out the family's finances, deal with his father's business associates, and sell and liquidate his father's business. Barney had planned to attend his first National Student Association (NSA) meeting at the University of Minnesota that August, but as the time approached, he began to vacillate, reluctant to leave because of his family situation. Finally, his mother insisted that he go.

Over five hundred students attended the meeting. To Barney, it was a "revelation." He discovered that he had an aptitude for politics. "It was national, it was political, and I was good at it," he said. "I learned that I had the debating and parliamentary skills, and ability to maneuver politically." He was impressed by the sophistication and commitment of the other student leaders he met at the convention, all of whom shared his zeal for politics. Among them were Ed Garvey, who later became director of the National Football League Players Association, and Mark Furstenberg, an Oberlin College student who went on to work for the Kennedy White House, helping to develop a national service program as part of a broad attack on poverty, and who has remained a close friend for nearly fifty years. Al Lowenstein was also at the meeting and Barney spent considerable time with him there and got to know him better.

Several of Barney's Harvard classmates attended the NSA meeting, including Timothy Wirth, who went on to serve in the House of Representatives, from Colorado, for twelve years and in the Senate for six, and Eugene Zagat Jr., the vice president of the student council at Harvard when Barney was the treasurer. Zagat became the most famous member of the Harvard class of 1961 when he co-founded the best-selling Zagat Restaurant Guide.

The two major current issues that appealed to liberals and progressives at the meeting were disarmament and civil rights. "We were dealing with important issues as though what we did counted. It was fun and we learned a lot," Furstenberg said.

Barney, like most of the other students at the time, was unaware that the NSA was sponsored and financially supported by the CIA. "There was a delegation of students at the meeting from Ghana. We were very naïve and assumed that those students paid their own way," Furstenberg recalled. "In 1967, when *Ramparts* broke the story of the CIA's support of the NSA, we were quite surprised. 'Did you know?' I asked Barney and he said no."

During the fall of 1960, while Barney was at home in Bayonne, he became involved at the grass-roots level in Senator John Kennedy's campaign for president. By late October, however, when it became clear that the family was going to sell the truck-stop business, affording Barney some unexpected free time, he decided to apply for the army's six-month active duty and seven-and-a-half-year active reserve program. Applying for military service meant that he had to lie about his sexuality when he encountered that question on the application.

"I wanted to get my military service out of the way," he said. "If I graduated and chose not to go on to graduate school, I would be drafted. If I could have gotten in the six months of active duty before I had to return to Harvard, it would have been a way to do my military service and not have it interfere with later career plans." He took the required test and almost failed the mechanical aptitude part. The program was popular at the time and Barney was placed on a waiting list. By the time the army accepted him for the program it was late April 1961 and there was not enough time to complete the six months of active service before he needed to return to Harvard. He would have had to take another year off from college, and so he declined admission to the program. That was before the Vietnam War escalated.

That spring, Tony Pirozzi, a friend of Sam Frank's who had served time in prison for robbery and kidnapping, asked Barney what he was going to do after he finished college. Barney said he'd probably go to law school. "Barn', that's great," Pirozzi said. "Me and the boyz, we got lots of wurk for you."

"That's not the type of law I want to practice," Barney told him. Pirozzi explained that they had an arrangement with the Hudson County prosecutor and offered to help get him a job in the prosecutor's office. Barney respectfully declined.

Barney missed Harvard. Being part of the "band of brothers" with his roommates was a very important part of his life. In the spring of 1961, he often visited the campus and stayed with his former roommates. He even went to commencement, since it was his class that was graduating.

In Barney's absence, Charley Halpern and Hastings Wyman had added a new roommate, Bob Komenda, who at the time was dating Temma Kaplan, a freshman at Brandeis. Temma spent considerable time with the group. She was most intrigued by Barney and that spring, she began to hang out with him. The two became close friends. Barney described their relationship as "very simpatico." "Even back then, he was a political poet, a great storyteller, and really funny," Kaplan, now a professor of women's studies at Rutgers University, said.

Most young people complain about their parents, but, Kaplan recalled, Barney never did. "Occasionally he would see some item that reminded him of his father, and out-of-the-blue he would say something like 'my father really liked whitefish,'" she said. "He clearly loved his father enormously."

After Barney returned to Harvard in September 1961 for his senior year, he and Temma spent so much time together that people thought they were a couple. They were together at least two days a week. They went to parties and did almost everything as a twosome. "At first we were comfortable in not having an intimate sexual relationship," Kaplan explained. "For a long time, I was seeing a lot of other people and it was a relief not to be in a sexual relationship and to have a really good friend like Barney." Then it became a problem. "It was very hard, we loved each other but weren't sexually involved," she said. "I kind of hoped he was gay because he certainly wasn't interested in me sexually. I really thought of Barney as being asexual at the time. There were plenty of people like that who were kind of afraid or scared in some way," she explained. "It was painful but we never talked about it." The pressure of outsiders seeing them as a couple finally became too great for Barney. He stopped calling and they stopped seeing each other.

Temma Kaplan was very perceptive but didn't suspect that Barney was gay. "Of all the people I should have been the one to notice because I was spending so much time with him but I didn't," she said. "I knew many gay students who had come out at Brandeis where people were more open. I was conscious that Hastings was probably gay. Barney was so closeted then that even I didn't put things together."

From the time Barney returned to Harvard for his senior year, he was uncertain about what he would do after graduation, go to graduate school for a Ph.D. in government or go to law school. Although friends all assumed he would go to law school because they knew he wanted to be in politics, Barney decided to go to graduate school, in part because he thought that as a college professor he would find it easier to deal with being gay. Academia would provide him with a more sheltered life. Also, he was good in school, he liked school, and he appreciated its supportive atmosphere. But the factor that weighed most heavily in his decision was his eagerness to get involved in politics. He was determined to be an aide to politicians and in his view the best way to go back and forth in that kind of political participation was as an academic. John Kennedy had become president in 1961 and there was a model of Harvard academics, including John Kenneth Galbraith, James Schlesinger, and McGeorge Bundy, going to work for Kennedy. The old joke was, How do you get to Washington? Go to Harvard Square and turn left.

In May, Barney graduated from Harvard Phi Beta Kappa and magna cum laude. He was accepted in the graduate program in government at Harvard. Although Barney would spend ten years as a student at Harvard, four as an undergraduate and six as a graduate student and teaching fellow in government, in the end that B.A., he said, was the only degree he "managed to wrest from [Harvard president] Nathan Pusey's deceptively iron grip."

In the summer of 1962, Barney met Stephen Solarz, a recent Brandeis graduate and a future member of Congress, at the NSA meeting in Madison, Wisconsin. During his sophomore and junior years in college, Solarz had dated Lynda Weitz, a fellow student at Brandeis, who had once remarked to him, "You remind me so much of the guy I used to date in high school in Bayonne, Barney Frank." Solarz was intrigued. When he ran across Barney at the meeting, he introduced himself, saying that he'd wanted to meet Barney and explained about dating Lynda Weitz and the comment she'd made. "In a certain sense it was flattering to have been compared to him because he was charismatic and very much politically engaged. He was part of the inner circle of the NSA leadership and well-connected," Solarz said.

"Barney and Steve were both kind of political animals," Lynda Weitz Newman, now a clinical psychologist living in Dallas, said. "Steve was the one more clearly determined to be in political office. He had been the mayor of Midwood [High School in Brooklyn] and wanted to be the mayor of New York City some day."

That summer Barney was part of the Independent Research Service delegation to the Festival of Youth and Students for Peace and Friendship in Helsinki, Finland. The trip was paid for by the CIA. "At that point," Barney explained, "the CIA was sort of the left of the foreign policy establishment in the Kennedy administration." For many years the Soviet Union had sponsored youth festivals but always inside the iron curtain. In 1959, under Nikita Khrushchev, the Russians held their first youth festival outside the iron curtain, in Vienna. The Americans had insufficient time to organize properly for that festival, but an American delegation of about 350 people was ready and well organized for the festival in 1962. Dennis Shaul, one of the event recruiters, called the delegation "truly American" because it was made up of people from all over the country and included big groups from Stanford, from the Midwest, and from the eastern schools, as well as a smaller number from the deep South. "We tried to recruit the broad picture of America," he said.

Barney described the trip as a "battle for the hearts and minds of the third world students, particularly the Africans." For example, he said, "the CIA paid to set up a big nightclub in Helsinki because they knew that the Africans liked American jazz," but the problem, he explained, "was all the Finns kept coming to this front nightclub." His fellow delegate Gloria Steinem, a recent graduate of Smith College, helped to win over Africans from the Communists by appearing "Mata Hariesque as she came slinking through the beaded curtain doorway at the nightclub."

That fall, Barney and many other young liberals at Harvard worked on the Senate campaign of Edward McCormack Jr., the thirty-eight-year-old Massachusetts attorney general, against the political newcomer Edward Kennedy for the Senate seat vacated by President John Kennedy. Edward McCormack, the nephew of Speaker John McCormack, a product of conservative South Boston, had been a progressive, liberal attorney general, creating the nation's first consumer protection division and appointing the state's first assistant attorney general for civil rights. As attorney general, McCormack had played a key role in the Supreme Court's landmark decision in *Gideon v. Wainright*, guaranteeing indigent criminal defendants the right to legal counsel. McCormack's office had prepared a persuasive *amicus* brief arguing for the right to legal counsel. He lobbied other attorneys general across the country to sign on to the brief and persuaded twenty to do so, including the Minnesota attorney general, Walter Mondale. During that 1962 Senate primary campaign, at a debate at South Boston High School, McCormack famously said, "I ask my opponent, 'What are your qualifications?' You graduated from law school three years ago. You never worked for a living; you have never run or held elective office." McCormack then told his rival, "If your name was Edward Moore, instead of Edward Moore Kennedy, your candidacy would be a joke." Kennedy won the primary election by a considerable margin.

In the fall, several of the Harvard Young Democrats who had supported Edward McCormack for the Senate suggested inviting McCormack's father, Edward McCormack Sr., known as "Knocko," to speak on campus. Knocko, the burly younger brother of House Speaker John McCormack, was a gregarious and popular local politician, a South Boston ward boss and, by legend, a bookie. For many years, Knocko, who weighed almost three hundred pounds, served as grand marshal astride a dray horse in the St. Patrick's Day Parade in South Boston. He took umbrage over a scene in the film version of Edwin O'Connor's classic novel *The Last Hurrah*, in which a fictional character based on four-time Boston mayor James Michael Curley attends a wake for a guy named Knocko Minihan. "That son-of-a-bitch killed me," he said.

Barney made the arrangements for the Boston pol to talk to the students and drove to Knocko's home to pick him up. He suggested that Knocko's wife,

Mae, join them. She declined saying, "My husband's going to tell dirty stories and say things that are shocking. I won't be shocked but I'm going to have to act shocked in front of the students. It's too much trouble and I'm too old to do that."

Knocko spoke to the students about Boston politics, including fixing elections. One of the students, a genteel and proper young man from Indiana said, "Mr. McCormack, I'm going to ask you a very personal question. If it is too personal, you don't have to answer it—" Knocko interrupted, "What do you want to know? Do I still fuck my wife? No, I'm too old."

When Knocko McCormack died, Kevin White and his father-in-law, William Galvin, a political boss from Charlestown, went to the wake for Knocko. For many years, Galvin had been the director and Knocko the deputy director of Quincy Market and its restored successor, Faneuil Hall Markets, positions that were political plums. As they walked by the corpse, Galvin remarked to White, "Geez, Knocko and I used to be pretty close. I haven't seen him in years."

Barney had always believed in working within the political process to bring about change. And because he believed that the Democratic Party was a national vehicle for racial justice, he was a natural antagonist of the more romantic radicals at Harvard, the Students for a Democratic Society (SDS), who had no faith in the electoral process and favored demonstrations and civil disobedience. Thus, he took exception to an article in a November 1962 issue of the student newspaper, the *Harvard Crimson*, titled "Political Activity Gives Students Sense of Significance," by Steven V. Roberts, Barney's Bayonne friend and neighbor whom he had encouraged to apply to Harvard. Roberts suggested that student politics had come of age intellectually and politically when members of SDS and other peace marchers gave up waving signs and singing songs in favor of stuffing envelopes and ringing doorbells for peace candidates. Barney took Roberts to task for his implicit identification of the militants of the peace movement with student politics as a whole. In a letter to the editor of the *Crimson*, Barney wrote, "Long before the peace marchers discovered the inefficacy of effervescence there were many students who realized that their political ideals could best be affected within the political process. . . . Had Mr. Roberts paid some attention to such groups as the Young Democrats and Young Republicans during the period in which his heroic radicals were groping in their self-created void, he might have been less 'astounded' at the 'spectacle' of students doing the necessary if unexciting tasks of political campaigning." He concluded, "To argue, as does Mr. Roberts, that this awakening is something wondrous to behold is to lend support to the view that irresponsibility is the norm of student politics."

As a teaching fellow in government, Barney taught undergraduates at Harvard and served as the assistant senior tutor at Winthrop House while studying for his Ph.D. degree and working on a doctoral thesis, which began as a study of the postwar conservative coalition in the House of Representatives. Isaac Kramnick, the head tutor in government at the time, said that Barney stood out as a graduate student and teaching fellow because he was so different. His whole manner was "so un-Harvard." Barney, Kramnick recalled, "spoke like a streetwise city kid, was loud and often vulgar, and he smoked cigars."

During that period Barney dated Doris Kearns, who was a year behind him in graduate school and was also a teaching fellow in government. Kearns would later become a best-selling author and a prominent historian. "It was an artificial relationship," Barney recalled. The relationship ended before Kearns received a White House fellowship in the Lyndon Johnson administration.

As the resident assistant senior tutor in Winthrop House, Barney made a lasting impression on the Harvard undergraduates. All Harvard undergraduates are assigned to a house after their freshman year. The house is not just a place to live but is part of the educational process at the college. According to Donald Graham, Harvard class of 1966, who lived in Winthrop House, Harvard was a pretty cold, impersonal place at the time. The college made no effort to see to it that a member of the faculty looked after any particular student. If a student was depressed or felt lost, as many eighteen- and nineteen-year-olds sometimes do, there was nobody at Harvard to find him. "In that atmosphere Barney Frank was universally regarded, among the kids I knew, as the friendliest and most approachable," Graham, now chairman and CEO of the Washington Post Company, said. "If an undergraduate at Winthrop House was thinking over whether to major in economics or social studies, should they take this course or that, or whatnot, Barney was the person students could talk to." He added, "There were so few faculty members who were really interested in and sympathetic to undergraduates and Barney headed the list. Harvard should have cloned him." "You could talk to Barney about a lot of stuff," Gregory Craig, the White House counsel for President Barack Obama, said. "He would talk honestly about teachers and about their theory and approach to the subject matter." "Barney," Craig described, "moved comfortably among the faculty who were quite fond of him as well as among the students. I think his identity at that time was still as a student although he was in that transition phase."

The British-born Bruce Chalmers, a professor of metallurgy, was the resident master at Winthrop House, and Standish Meecham, described by a former Winthrop House student as a "super duper preppie," was the senior tutor. The undergraduate students regarded Chalmers as a nice person but so quiet and reserved that they couldn't get to know him, and they found Meecham standoffish. In contrast, in the words of Bob Adkins, Harvard class of 1967, "Barney was totally approachable and he really did care what happened to you."

Barney took all his meals in the dining hall at Winthrop House. Smoking was permitted in the dining room then, and Barney always had a cigar in his hand. "Most of the time it was lit, and he was in a cloud of smoke," Michael Epstein, class of 1967, recalls. "He was a brilliant guy even at that point, with his New Jersey accent, his cigar, extremely sharp mind and quick wit. He was just a wonder to behold, especially for an undergraduate one year out of the Midwest. I had never seen anything quite like him. It was great."

According to an article in the *Harvard Crimson* in March 1966, one of the benefits of living in Winthrop House was the presence there of "assistant senior tutor Barney Frank, who combines the virtues of a political philosopher with those of a Jersey ward boss." Barney's profile in the 1966 *Harvard Yearbook* reads: "In a Bayonne, New Jersey accent, the burly, bespectacled Barney Frank displays immense knowledge of government from the arid heights of political theory on down to the personal eccentricities of Massachusetts state legislators." It calls him "a phenomenon, . . . a living demonstration that education can be vital, vibrant, and fun" and notes that "[his] integrity, irreverence and energy command the respect of Frank's students."

According to Jimmy Segel, Harvard class of 1967, "Barney's interest in politics was not limited to just the academic side of political theory or history and this was particularly attractive to students in the mid-1960s when the country was in turmoil."

In the Winthrop dining room Barney would hold court at a big table surrounded by undergraduates who were enthusiastic about politics. Some students would sit down and eat; others would just hang around. One of those students was Gregory Craig, who lived in Leverett House. "You could count on Barney being there on a Sunday from eleven to two," he said. "I thought I was pretty knowledgeable about politics but Barney left me in the dust and so I would go to lunch at Winthrop House on Sundays and join that big circle of students that would sit around with him and talk reform politics." Like others, Craig would come away from a discussion with Barney, savoring comments he would later repeat, starting with, "You gotta hear what Barney said today." For example, he referred to Illinois senator Everett Dirksen as "the Casey Stengel of the Senate" and described him as "a man who has been on every side of every issue to come before the American public in thirty years."

Barney would stay in the dining room for hours discussing politics with anyone who wanted to talk, even if only one student remained. Bob Adkins recalls that though the discussion usually focused on politics, government, and public affairs, there was also a lot of teasing, joking, and gossiping. "Barney," he said, "was a Mecca, invariably entertaining and funny, a source of news and gossip." He was a "walking resource on any issue that might come up."

Donald Graham's first impression of Barney was, "This is a helluva interesting guy, a great conversationalist and so funny." "He wasn't showing off, unlike
some people at Harvard whose main purpose in talking was to show how smart
they were."

Barney's former students describe him as "a great teacher" and, according to
James Roosevelt, the grandson of Franklin and Eleanor Roosevelt and a member of the Harvard class of 1968, he was highly sought after as a tutor. "He respected undergraduates with whom he was having a dialogue in that he is ready
to agree with you when he thinks you're right, and to tell you how little you
know about the subject when he thinks you're wrong," Roosevelt said.

Thomas Oliphant, who lived in Eliot House as a Harvard undergraduate,
remembers that there were "two hot teaching fellows" in the government department at Harvard—Barney Frank and Marty Peretz. "The highbrow types,"
he said, "such as Al Gore, tended to gravitate to Marty, and people who were
interested in getting their fingernails dirty tended to gravitate to Barney." If a
student planned to be a government major, he usually signed up for a tutorial
in government his sophomore year. A tutorial consisted of a small class of about
five or six students that covered a particular subject in government. Michael Epstein recalled the government tutorial that he had with Barney his sophomore
year in 1964: "Once or twice a week we would gather in Barney's slovenly living
room in Winthrop House and sit around and talk politics. He used the 1964
presidential election as a laboratory. We spent a lot of time discussing the presidential contest as well as the congressional elections." According to Epstein,
Barney was not a disciplinarian, but he was able to coax the students to do the
work because of the interesting issues he put in front of the group.

Barney was always a faithful attendee of Winthrop House activities and always part of the fun. Michael Epstein described him as "the soul" of Winthrop
House. Barney "was even less mature that we were," he said. Every year at the
Christmas party, the junior faculty at Winthrop House would put on a show for
the assembled undergraduates about life in the house. During the skit in 1965,
Barney played the infamous Winthrop foam man, clothed from the waist up in
shaving cream.

Barney played on the tutors' softball team and was active in intramural sports.
The undergraduates remember that he was a fairly good softball player and very
competitive. But he was injured so often, turning an ankle or spraining his knee,
that it seemed as though he was on crutches half the time he was at Harvard.

According to Epstein, Barney enjoyed sitting around and provoking, prodding, and debating politics with the students but that he did not seem to be as
focused on his studies as the other tutors were. Epstein recalled a bet that he
made during his sophomore year with Barney. Although Epstein was a govern-

ment major, he planned to attend medical school after graduation and become a doctor. He bet Barney that he would get a medical degree before Barney got his doctorate. Epstein won. According to Epstein, who is now the chief operating officer of the Harvard-affiliated Beth Israel Deaconess Medical Center, in retaliation Barney frequently tells people in Epstein's presence that his greatest accomplishment as a teacher of government at Harvard was that Epstein went into medicine.

The undergraduates at Winthrop House never thought Barney would ever run for political office. They saw him as "the guy who would be working behind the scenes." "He was great fun, always provocative and interesting, but no one in their wildest dreams thought this cigar-smoking, overweight, foul-mouthed, funny talker from Bayonne, New Jersey, would some day be a congressman," Epstein observed. Nor did anyone have any idea he was gay.

Each of the houses at Harvard has a distinct personality and reputation. At the time Winthrop House was known as the "jock house." It had more athletes, minorities, and children of blue-collar workers than did Adams House up the street, where those undergraduates who fancied themselves as intellectuals, lived, or Eliot House, which was known as the preppy house. Barney reached out to the students from working-class families, to the black students, and to those less affluent and in a sense gave them a stage and promoted them and made them seem important. Someone would say something that did not break any intellectual ground and Barney would rephrase it and credit the student for the observation in a way that made him seem more clever and articulate than he was. "Many people, particularly today, think of Barney as being able to use humor to put people down in ways that are totally aggressive," Temma Kaplan observed, "but he also has that special gift to make people look good."

Barney was a passionate supporter of the civil rights movement and as a graduate student participated in the Mississippi Freedom Summer in 1964. In the fall of 1963, the president of the Mississippi NAACP, Aaron Henry, known as "Doc" Henry because he had a degree in pharmacy from Xavier University in New Orleans and was the owner of a drugstore in Mississippi with a large black patronage, decided to run a general political campaign for governor of Mississippi as if he were actually on the ballot. The purpose of this mock election was to refute the argument voiced by white officials in Mississippi that blacks did not want to participate in the political process. Al Lowenstein, who was teaching at Stanford at the time, was friendly with Henry, and he recruited about fifty college students from Stanford and Yale to travel to Mississippi to help in Henry's mock gubernatorial campaign. The campaign strategy was to put ballot boxes in every conceivable place—in restaurants, in homes, and in churches. Eighty thousand people participated in the mock election. During the campaign some of the white middle-class students from Stanford and Yale were mistreated. One was shot at. Others were abused. All of a sudden, the intimidation of white students in Mississippi became national news.

A year later, Lowenstein and a coalition of civil rights groups organized Mississippi Freedom Summer. Its goal was to send hundreds of college students to Mississippi to focus national attention on the plight of blacks in that state and to force the hand of the Johnson administration. The state of Mississippi had the largest black population and it was the state with the most violently anti-black tradition. In December 1963, Lowenstein recruited Barney to be one of his deputies and to coordinate several projects for Mississippi Freedom Summer. According to Barney, Lowenstein had a knack for getting people to do things that they really were not interested in but later were happy they did. In the documentary film *Citizen: The Political Life of Allard K. Lowenstein*, Barney explains how Lowenstein persuaded him to go to Mississippi: "Al said, 'How would you like to go to Mississippi this summer?' I couldn't think of anything I less wanted to do than go to Mississippi, except to go to Mississippi in the summer. Two hours later, I found myself temporarily designated as one of the chief organizers at Harvard for this project, which was typical of Al."

Lowenstein had a falling out with several of the organizers of Mississippi Freedom Summer, apparently for giving the far left too much authority, and pulled out, leaving Barney in an awkward situation. He had recruited several Harvard students to go to Mississippi but he had signed on in a kind of executive role, something that was no longer available to him with Lowenstein's departure. He decided nonetheless to head down south to Jackson, Mississippi, to participate in the civil rights movement as a foot soldier by helping to register black voters. "On some level, the organizers knew they'd get better national press if young white students were being beaten and mistreated along with black sharecroppers," he said.

Six to seven hundred students, mostly white, from all over the country, went to Mississippi that summer to work as volunteers to organize Mississippi blacks who were being denied the right to vote. If you were black in Mississippi then and tried to vote, you had a good chance of being killed. The plan was to refute the assertion made by white leaders in Mississippi that blacks don't vote because they don't want to. The goal was to create Mississippi Freedom Democratic Party and to elect a delegation to go to the 1964 Democratic National Convention in Atlantic City, New Jersey, in August to challenge the state's all-white delegation. This project was put together by the Council of Federated Organizations, which included the NAACP, the Student Nonviolent Coordinating Committee, the Southern Christian Leadership Conference, and the Congress of Racial Equality.

Three of the young freedom riders, Michael Schwerner and Andrew Good-win, who were Jewish, and James Cheney, a young black Mississippian, were arrested by the police in Jackson. After they were released from jail late at night, their car was followed by a death squad, and they were brutally beaten to death with chains. Their bodies were not found until some time later.

Barney spent about five weeks in Jackson. During that time, he did some field organizing but not much, because rural Mississippi blacks had a hard time understanding him. "I had a combination New Jersey/New York and Massachusetts accent, and truth be told, very poor diction. There were few people in Mississippi of either race who could understand anything I said," he explained. "There was one time I went out into the field and I finally gave up trying to explain that my name was not Benjamin Franklin. I just answered to Benjamin Franklin for the rest of the day." He was soon put to work handling the organizational requirements involved in forming the Mississippi Freedom Democratic Party and working as a liaison between the political people in Jackson and those up north.

The white college students were in Mississippi registering black voters in early July when Congress passed the 1964 Civil Rights Act, outlawing segregation in public accommodations. However, an order came down from the civil rights leadership, which included Dr. Martin Luther King, Jr., James Farmer, and Bayard Rustin, not to be confrontational and not to press for immediate integration of lunch counters, movie theaters, or motels. The civil rights leaders wanted the students to remain focused on voting rights and not to divert attention from that goal.

When Barney left Mississippi in July, he was asked to go to Washington to work with Joseph Rauh, the counsel for the Mississippi Freedom Democratic Party and one of the nation's foremost civil rights attorneys. Rauh was preparing a brief to submit to the Democratic National Party on behalf of the Mississippi Freedom Democratic Party, challenging the seating of the state's all-white delegation at the upcoming Democratic convention. Barney presented Rauh with the facts he had prepared. When Barney, in response to Rauh's questioning, assured him that he was not a lawyer, Rauh, who was concerned that the legal establishment might try to go after this young man, said, "Good. That way they can't try to disbar you." Rauh cited Barney Frank in a footnote in the brief as the source of the information.

Barney needed a place to stay while in Washington and contacted some friends he had first met at the NSA meeting in Minneapolis in August 1960, Barbara and Cokie Boggs, the very liberal daughters of Hale Boggs, a Democratic congressman from Louisiana. The Boggs family had a large house in Bethesda, Maryland, just outside of the District of Columbia, and Barney asked whether he could stay there. "Sure thing," Barbara Boggs told him. He arrived in the late evening and the two sisters took him downstairs to stay overnight in the guest room in the basement.

The next morning when Barney came up from the basement, Hale Boggs was sitting at the kitchen table having his coffee. Earlier that month, Boggs had voted against the 1964 Civil Rights Act. As Hale Boggs later told the story:

> I'm just sittin' there havin' mah coffee and this young fella comes up from the basement. At first, I thought he was there to fix somethin'. Then he goes and pours himself a cup of coffee and sits down at the table with me. This surprised me.
> I said, "Hello, son."
> He introduces himself and tells me he had been in Mississippi and explains what he had been doing there.
> I said to him, "Did yah sleep well down there last night?"
> "Yes sir," he answered.
> "Is yer coffee okay?"
> "Yes sir," he answered.
> "So you would say that we are treating yah pretty good?"
> "Yes sir," he answered.
> "Son, would you do me one favor in return?"
> "What's that?" he asked.
> "Just don't ever tell anybody you were here," I said.

Later that morning, Hale Boggs confronted his daughters, "I know that you're trying to get me to do the right thing. Damned, I have enough problems without you turning this house into the local branch of the Underground Railroad."

Unlike most southern congressman at the time, the next year Hale Boggs, the House majority whip, supported the Voting Rights Act. Boggs was very popular with his Democrat colleagues and the House leadership was worried about his being defeated in his bid for reelection and wanted to help him. When the National Football League needed assistance and came to Congress seeking legislation to approve a merger with the American Football League, the price was a football team for New Orleans. The New Orleans Saints football team was born in 1966 to help Hale Boggs. Boggs won reelection to his House seat and was elected as majority leader in 1971.

In the summer of 1965, Al Lowenstein served as director of the Encampment for Citizenship. During the encampment, student leaders and political and social activists from across the country came together and talked about how to change the country most effectively, how to deal with social injustice, and other issues of concern. The event was held on the somewhat secluded eighteen-acre campus of the Fieldston School, a private secondary school in the Riverdale section of the Bronx in New York. At Al Lowenstein's request Barney spent a week or two there as part of the faculty.

At one of these sessions Barney participated in a debate that included Tom Hayden, a radical from Newark, New Jersey, who had been active in organizing tenants to engage in rent strikes against landlords. It was a period when Barney would often debate members of SDS in public forums, defending the classic liberal position against their radical views. The debate took place in a grassy outdoor amphitheater on the campus. Hayden spoke first, refusing to use a microphone and standing among the audience rather than sitting in a position of prominence up on the stage. When Hayden finished, he sat down among the crowd on the grass. Barney looked at Hayden and remarked, "Tom, you're such a grass root. I don't know whether I'm supposed to debate you or come down there and water you."

Barney generally supported the undergraduate students, especially on First Amendment issues. In October 1965, the *Harvard Crimson* reported that an administration official had said that the student May 2nd Committee might have violated a rule safeguarding academic freedom by distributing pamphlets that disputed the views expressed by a sociology lecturer in a class on Communist Chinese society, because the pamphlets reproduced some of the lecturer's statements in class without his consent. Barney was appalled by the university's reaction. In his view, the principle at issue was that this sort of vigorous debate of controversial questions was something that the university should be encouraging, not punishing. In a letter to the *Harvard Crimson* defending the right of students to criticize their teachers, Barney wrote: "I infer that May 2nd stands accused of a crime lying halfway between un-Harvard activities and *lese majeste*. And in one of the most spectacular displays of semantic perversion since *1984* this accusation is justified as a defense of academic freedom." With respect to "this outburst of intellectual impertinence," he added, "I know of few faculty members who fear that their lectures will be over published." Barney subsequently met with the dean of students, who agreed that the pamphlets posed no threat to the teacher's academic freedom or to the order of his class. According to friends, Barney saw himself then as a facilitator, not as a political leader.

In the early spring of 1966, Barney received a notice from the draft board calling him up for active duty. James Roosevelt, a sophomore in Barney's government tutorial that year, recalled having breakfast with him the morning after the draft notice arrived. "Like many liberals Barney had not yet concluded that the Vietnam War was a mistake," Roosevelt said. "While Barney had no wish to go to Vietnam, he didn't see why he had any right not to go since there were fifty thousand young Americans in Vietnam at the time." Roosevelt was impressed that Barney's attitude about his draft notice was consistent with the views he had taken on the war.

Barney did not attempt to avoid military service. He returned the draft notice, pointing out that he was a graduate student and was teaching several classes, and asked whether they could wait a few months until May so that he could finish the current semester before being called up. "He didn't want to leave his students high and dry," Roosevelt explained. The draft board responded that they had not known he was a student and that if he provided the necessary documentation he would receive a student deferment. Apparently, what happened was that his Selective Service records in Bayonne had mistakenly been filed under Frank Barney. By the time the draft board stopped giving deferments to graduate students, he was too old to be drafted.

That spring, Barney was named special assistant for student programs to Richard E. Neustadt, the director of the newly created Institute of Politics at Harvard's John F. Kennedy School of Government. The institute was founded as "a living memorial to President John F. Kennedy that engages young people in politics and public service" and was designed to bring veteran politicians and academics together to work on the problems of government.

Later that year, the Institute of Politics created an honorary associate program to bring government policy makers and public figures to campus to meet informally with small groups of undergraduate students in off-the-record sessions. Secretary of Defense Robert S. McNamara was selected as the institute's first honorary associate, primarily because of his close ties to President Kennedy. Professor Neustadt and Barney both recognized that McNamara, viewed by many as a symbol of the Vietnam War because of his role as President Johnson's key adviser and the principal manager of the war, would be highly controversial and that his presence would likely generate protest. Anti–Vietnam War sentiment had been growing at the university. Several antiwar teach-ins had been held there that fall involving renowned political theorists such as Stanley Hoffman, a professor of government at the institute, and John Fairbank, who had talked to the students about the region, the nationalist movement in Vietnam, and the biography of Ho Chi Minh.

Neustadt and Barney decided it would be best to have Secretary McNamara visit informally with small groups of students in a controlled and secure environment. Barney was assigned to handle all the details of McNamara's visit to Harvard, including coordinating security with the university police and acting as McNamara's escort.

Sign-up sheets were distributed around campus for all undergraduates interested in meeting McNamara. More than 1,500 Harvard and Radcliffe students signed up to enter a lottery for the 120 available spaces to meet with McNamara for dinner, lunch, or a small discussion group. To demonstrate that the selection process would be fair and honest, Barney invited representatives from SDS, Young Democrats, Young Republicans, the Harvard Policy Committee, and other campus organizations to a public ceremony in the Winthrop House dining room to observe the selection process. The sign-up sheets containing the student names were placed on a table in the dining room. Someone held the sheets in place, occasionally rotating them, as a blindfolded Barney Frank jabbed his finger at the top sheet to select a student. Sometimes he missed the paper entirely. Other times he landed between two names. This awkward process continued until the names of 120 students had been selected.

At the outset, Barney used a third-party intermediary to negotiate an arrangement with SDS to avoid a disruptive demonstration. The SDS leaders initially proposed a debate on the Harvard campus between Secretary McNamara and an antiwar advocate. The leadership of the Kennedy Institute of Politics rejected this proposal, stating unequivocally that McNamara would not publicly debate anyone. The SDS leaders then escalated the controversy by sending a telegram inviting McNamara to participate in a debate on campus with Robert Scheer, managing editor of *Ramparts* magazine and an ardent critic of the Vietnam War. This invitation was supported by a petition signed by some fifty faculty members, almost a hundred teaching fellows, and more than a thousand students. Neustadt rejected the idea of a public debate with Scheer on the grounds that the purpose of McNamara's visit was to meet informally and have discussions off-the-record with small groups of undergraduates and that it would create a bad precedent and discourage others from accepting an invitation from the institute as part of its new program.

Barney then attempted unsuccessfully to negotiate an agreement directly with the SDS leaders. He offered to present their antiwar petition directly to Secretary McNamara. When that was rejected, he proposed a peaceful demonstration. That too was rejected on the grounds that he was not offering them anything they did not already have a constitutional right to do.

Secretary McNamara's visit to Harvard on November 7, 1966, began with what he described as a "lively discussion" with students at Quincy House. About fifty students were in the group. According to Dick Morningstar, one of those attending, McNamara essentially told them not to worry about Vietnam, that the administration would take care of it, and that the war would be over in a year. "He told us to go out and march for civil rights because that is what is important," Morningstar recalled.

From there Secretary McNamara was scheduled to address a graduate seminar class in international relations that Henry Kissinger was teaching several blocks away. About three hundred students, many of them anti–Vietnam War protesters from SDS, stood on the street in front of Quincy House waiting for him to exit. Sheets from the Gordon Linen Company, which supplied fresh sheets and towels to Harvard undergraduates, were hung from the buildings around Quincy House, carrying messages such as "Mac the Knife," "Vietnam is the Edsel of U.S. Foreign Policy" (an unflattering reference to McNamara's previous position as CEO of Ford Motors), and "How many people have you killed?" "There was even one sheet that said, 'Black Day for Gordon Linen,'" Bo Jones, then a junior at Harvard, recalled.

It was Barney's job to ensure that the secretary of defense did not get mobbed by student protesters. Barney had a plan in place, in football parlance a fake handoff up the middle. However, he did not take into account the sophistication of the SDS crowd. One of the students, who had worked in the civil rights movement in Mississippi and had been responsible for rigging up the two-way radios from the cars to the freedom houses there, had stationed himself and others on the roof of the buildings around Quincy House with two-way radios to observe McNamara's movement from the building.

Barney had recruited several football players from Winthrop House to lead the blocking. Suddenly, a small group, including a very visible Barney Frank and what appeared to be Secretary McNamara, exited from Quincy House with the football players clearing a path to the Quincy House garage into a waiting car and driving off. Many of the students in the crowd were fooled by the ruse. They did not see that the secretary had been taken out through the back door on Mill Street and escorted to a car that was to be driven to Kissinger's class by a campus policeman. A large group of demonstrators, however, alerted by the students with the two-way radios, descended on McNamara as he entered the car. The mob of students surged and surrounded the vehicle. Some threw themselves on the ground in front of the car. The car was blocked and could not move.

Michael Barrett, a Harvard freshman, who would later manage Barney's first campaign for state representative in 1972, observed the incident: "Students were pounding on the car. It was wild, woolly and tumultuous, [and] it caught everyone unprepared. It was those innocent days before campus unrest became a staple of things." As Secretary McNamara said in his description of the incident in his 1995 memoir *In Retrospect*, "Then all hell broke loose as students began rocking the car." The resourceful McNamara got out of the car, climbed on an adjacent vehicle, and, shaking his finger at the crowd, shouted, "When I was a student at Berkeley in the late 1930s, I was a lot tougher and a lot more courteous than you are today." These words had the effect of baiting the crowd even more. He then said, "Okay. I'll answer one or two of your questions." The first question shouted at him was, "Why did you not tell the American people that the Vietnam War started in 1957 and 1958 as an internal revolution?" This was followed by, "How many innocent women and children have been killed?" Each time the answer was drowned out by the noise and shouts of the demonstrators. As the danger and chaos increased, McNamara jumped off the car and was rushed through a door at Quincy House by campus police and Barney, who had returned to Quincy House after the failed ruse. Then, as McNamara describes it, "[I] found myself in an underground tunnel extending several blocks and linking a number of Harvard buildings. My escort through the maze was Barney Frank, a Harvard [student] who later became U.S. representative for Massachusetts' Fourth Congressional District. Frank and I ran through the maze, lost the students, and emerged in Harvard Yard. I kept my commitment to meet with Kissinger's class, somewhat unnerved." A student who had watched Barney escorting McNamara through a screaming crowd of students said later that Barney "looked pretty tough." But Barney was publicly embarrassed by the incident, which was probably the lowest moment of his decade at Harvard. He said later, "McNamara was very gracious about the incident but I was pretty upset."

An article in the campus newspaper about the incident focused attention on Barney's role, saying that for three weeks Barney had been at the center of preparations for the defense secretary's visit. But all of his efforts had been in vain. The militant and physical confrontation between the student protesters and Secretary McNamara was as much a humiliation for Barney as it was for McNamara.

The incident also did damage to Barney in the eyes of many left-wing students at Harvard, who were angry that he would engage in a ruse to frustrate their opportunity to have an open policy debate on the war. He was one of the few members of the Harvard faculty who had shown an interest in the students on the far left and treated them with respect, attending SDS meetings to debate and to engage the SDS thinkers. Although his views were much more moderate and he believed that some of the changes these students were attempting to bring about were unrealistic, he did not consider them to be unpatriotic at that time.

That same year, 1966, Edward McCormack ran for governor of Massachusetts. Barney served on his policy advisory committee, doing research on policy issues and writing speeches for the candidate. He even did some radio debates on behalf of McCormack. Barney was now twenty-six years old, and this was his first major, serious role in a political campaign. All the major Democratic liberals in Massachusetts were supporters of McCormack, and Barney got to know them during the campaign. Although McCormack won the Democratic nomination, he lost badly in the general election to Republican John Volpe. On election night in November, Barney, still a graduate student at Harvard, did his first radio commentary on an election on station WHRB in Boston. The host of the program was Chris Wallace.

After McCormack's unsuccessful race for governor, Barney received a telephone call from Michael Dukakis, who was then the state representative from Brookline. Dukakis was organizing the Massachusetts equivalent of the congressional Democratic Study Group, consisting of about ten liberal, reform-minded Democrats in the state legislature, and asked Barney, still a graduate student, whether he was interested in becoming the organization's unofficial "executive director," an impressive title for being the group's entire volunteer staff. Barney jumped at the opportunity.

Beginning in December 1966, the group, which included Dukakis, Michael J. Harrington, Katharine Kane, Jack Buckley, Dave Ahern, Charles Ohanian, and Joel Greenberg, met every other Monday at about five o'clock, after the legislative session, in the living room of Katharine Kane's Beacon Hill home on Chestnut Street, a five-and-a-half-story house built in 1820 during the Federal period and located a short distance from the State House. "There were not many liberals in the state legislature back then," Harrington pointed out.

The group discussed legislative bills, including those involving no-fault automobile insurance and civil service reform and particularly those that related to urban issues such as low-cost housing. As the group's unpaid executive director, Barney did almost everything—taking minutes at the meetings, drafting press releases, and doing any research that was necessary. He learned from that experience what a considerable opportunity serving in the state legislature provided to advance the public interest.

Barney was a prolific writer when he was a graduate student at Harvard. Unfortunately, none of this writing was directed to his doctoral thesis. Instead, he wrote a scholarly piece for the *Harvard Review*, a book review for the *Dunster Political Review*, a letter to the editor that was printed in the *New York Times*, and a large number of letters to the editor of the *Harvard Crimson*.

In the 1964 letter that appeared in the *New York Times*, he took aim at Strom Thurmond, a segregationist senator from South Carolina who had advanced some extreme theories to prove the constitutionality of mistreating blacks. Commenting on Senator Thurmond's decision to switch to the Republican Party, Barney wrote, "It is better to give than to receive."

In the article published in the Fall–Winter 1965 issue of the *Harvard Review*, titled "Busy Haunts and Remote Wilderness," Barney defends the Supreme Court's decisions in a series of reapportionment cases, wherein the Court decreed that every citizen must count the same as every other in the distribution of legislative seats. In the twenty-four-page article, filled with Barney's brand of humor, he quotes Shakespeare, suggesting that before entering a discussion on the politics of reapportionment, "the first thing we do, let's kill all the lawyers." To the footnote citation he adds, "Whether or not this is a dissenting opinion is not revealed in my *Bartlett's Quotations*."

Thomas Mann, in a review of that volume of the *Harvard Review* for the January 21, 1966, *Harvard Crimson*, says of the Barney Frank piece, "This is the first article I've ever read in a *Harvard Review* that is just plain fun reading, even if you aren't interested in the topic."

In the article, Barney dissected and rebutted the legal arguments made by dissenting justices John Harlan and Felix Frankfurter. He described the Court's decision in simple terms, saying that equal means equal, and "that a state law — or constitution—which assigns one representative to 5,000 rural residents and one to 50,000 urbanites fails to accord equal treatment to the latter." He wrote, "Within the court itself, Justice Harlan looks on his colleague's handiwork with all the enthusiasm of a nun who has caught less pious sisters smuggling men into the convent."

In *Baker v. Carr*, in which the Justices ordered a federal district court to hear a reapportionment case, Justice Frankfurter angrily dissented, arguing that legislative redistricting is none of the court's business and that the Supreme Court's image as a neutral arbiter would be tarnished. Justice Frankfurter predicted widespread disobedience to the Court's edict, which never came to pass. Barney lamented Frankfurter's contention that the decision "invite[d] legislatures to play ducks and drakes with the judiciary" and "confessed that I would not recognize an intra-governmental game of ducks and drakes even if I wandered unto the playing field," but "it is indisputable that the pattern of legislative response to the apportionment decisions has predominantly been one of obedience."

Barney described Frankfurter's argument that the decision would cause a torrent of bitter criticism of the Supreme Court as the "chicken" school of Supreme Court analysts, whose almost unvarying advice to the Court is "don't stick your neck out." He was unsparing in denigrating Frankfurter's plea for the Court not to act on malapportionment lest it impair its ability to act elsewhere. "[That] is like counseling the President not to spend his political capital on federal aid to education lest he impair his ability to preserve inviolate the appropriation for the Smithsonian Institution," he wrote.

He took direct aim at Frankfurter's suggestion that the victims of partial disfranchisement appeal to the consciences of their disenfranchisers, advice rooted in Frankfurter's lifelong belief that the eradication of social ills must be left to the political process. Barney argued that it makes very little sense to recommend political action to those whose very claim is that the scales of politics have been unfairly weighted against them. He explained: "Urging the tormented to shame their tormentors into repentance has a noble history in this century, but this sort of judicial Gandhism hardly represents a proper discharge of the Supreme Court's Constitutional function. By abandoning the helpless to reliance on self-help, Frankfurter unwittingly pronounced his own *reductio ad absurdum*."

In 1966, Barney wrote a caustic review of James McGregor Burns's book *Presidential Government* in the *Dunster Political Review*. In a critique of that issue published in the *Harvard Crimson*, Robert Herfort comments on the "eloquence and force" with which Barney examined and refuted Burns's assumptions. He notes that Barney's response to Burns's prescription for the federal government to direct a program of cultural uplift is that "the equality of my life is none of the government's business." In a letter to the editor of the *Harvard Crimson*, Barney points out that the quotation should have read "the quality of my life" and suggests that the mistake casts him as an oblique opponent of the civil rights movement. But, he writes, "I believe fully in the government's right to interfere with my choice of neighbors, it is my personal preference for softball over Shakespeare that I wish to protect against the culture-mongers."

Barney was teaching at Harvard and having a wonderful time challenging the undergraduate students. One thing he had not done, however, was work on his doctoral dissertation. By the fall of 1967, he had saved enough money to take a year off from teaching and start writing his thesis. In early September, before moving into a small apartment in East Cambridge, he flew to Stanford University with his younger brother, David, who was starting college, and helped him move in. He returned to the Boston area with plans to work full time on his thesis, while continuing to work part time for the Democratic Study Group. To take advantage of the access he enjoyed through his ties to the Democratic Study Group, he had changed the subject of the thesis from the U.S. Congress to the Massachusetts state legislature.

4

Moving Seamlessly from Political Theory at Harvard to Hardball Politics at City Hall

IN THE CROWDED ten-candidate field in the September 26, 1967, preliminary election for mayor of Boston, Louise Day Hicks finished first with just over 28 percent of the vote. Hicks, a South Boston resident and member of the Boston School Committee for six years, was a strong opponent of school busing for integration whose campaign slogan was "You know where I stand." Kevin Hagan White, the Massachusetts secretary of state since 1961, finished a distant second with a little over 20 percent, trailing Hicks by about 13,500 votes. State representative John W. Sears, a reform-minded Republican much like John Lindsay in New York City and the first GOP candidate for mayor of Boston since 1933, edged out the Boston urban renewal chief Edward Logue, Mayor John Collins's choice as successor, for third place.

White, despite a campaign described by Herb Gleason, an establishment lawyer, Beacon Hill reformer, and key White supporter as "worrisome and terribly disorganized," and run by his brother Terry, who owned a street-line-painting business, was politically well-positioned to face off against Hicks in the November general election. Most of the liberals at Harvard had supported Sears or Logue.

A few days after the preliminary election for mayor of Boston, almost before Barney could put pencil to paper on his doctoral thesis, the telephone in his East Cambridge apartment rang. Chris Lydon, a young reporter for the *Boston Globe*, was calling. Lydon had covered White as secretary of state and gotten to know him well. He also had reported on the Edward McCormack campaign for governor in 1966 for the *Globe* and gotten to know Barney during that campaign.

"Would you be interested in helping Kevin White in the general election campaign for mayor against Louise Day Hicks? Lydon asked. "Barney," Lydon recalled years later, "was the perfect person for the job."

Kevin White had grown up in politics. His father, Joseph, had represented West Roxbury and the North End. His father-in-law, William Galvin, known as "Mother Gal" because as the manager of a bar in Charleston he would deliver regular customers who got drunk and passed out to the front steps of their homes, had been the political boss of Charleston and served on the Boston City Council. A graduate of Williams College and Boston College Law School, White had been an assistant district attorney. With the support of his father and father-in-law, he had captured the Democratic nomination for secretary of state in 1960 and beaten the Republican candidate, Edward Brooke, in the general election.

"Kevin had these Irish bases of support in parts of the city," Lydon explained, but he needed someone to give the campaign for mayor "intellectual coherence as well as political coherence." Lydon knew Barney Frank to be a bright guy, whose ability to write and to focus on issues White desperately needed in the campaign. Lydon acted on his own in attempting to recruit Barney for the mayoralty campaign of his friend and neighbor Kevin White.

"This is an opening for you. It is an opportunity to get in on the ground floor with a candidate who is very interesting politically," Lydon told Barney. He pointed out to the graduate student that it would simply mean delaying his thesis for about five weeks to help the White campaign. Barney characteristically did not hesitate. He replied that it was a door worth knocking on and agreed to set aside his thesis to work in White's general election campaign. "I did it more out of negative feelings about Louise Day Hicks than pro Kevin White," Barney explained. "People said that White was a good guy, but if he had been running against someone like Ed Logue in the general election I wouldn't have gotten involved."

Lydon tried to recruit two people that day for the White campaign. The second person that he called was Chester Hartman, another smart person and a sort of urban radical from New York. At the time Hartman was running the Commission on Low Income Housing in Boston. But he was not interested. "Chester blew it off and Barney made a career out of it," Lydon recalled.

Kevin White lived on Beacon Hill at 158 Mount Vernon Street. Lydon and his wife, Cindy, whom White had introduced to Lydon, lived two doors away. Cindy Lydon's sister Nancy and her husband, Samuel Huntington, a political scientist and the chairman of the Government Department at Harvard, lived in a building around the corner. And Cindy's father, Harry Arkelian, the best-known Armenian rug merchant in Boston, lived around the other corner. In the middle, between the Whites and the Huntingtons, the Pulitzer Prize–winning author and Harvard history professor Samuel Eliot Morison lived. They were all close friends.

Barney's first meeting with Kevin White was scheduled to take place at White's house at four o'clock one afternoon. He rang the bell and was ushered in. White was running late and Barney waited in the front drawing room. He took a book from the bookshelf, *Ward 8* by Joseph Dinneen, a fictional portrait of Martin Lomasney, a legendary ward boss in Boston. When White arrived almost two hours later he was impressed that this twenty-seven-year-old graduate student did not mind waiting around to see him and appeared to be absorbed in the book. But White had to leave immediately for a political event and said he would have to reschedule the meeting. He suggested that Barney take the book with him and finish it.

Barney explained to Lydon that the meeting with White hadn't taken place as scheduled. "But I've got his book," he said, "and I suppose I have to return it." A day or two later, Barney went back to White's house and met with the candidate. Near the end of the meeting, White said, "I want you to work for me in the campaign. People are going to resent you coming in. Listen, do me a favor. If you find you're not doing anything useful at the end of a week, before you walk away, give me a call." According to Barney, that was a positive sign that White knew political administration. "He knew that signing me on didn't give me a real function."

This was Barney's first involvement in Boston politics. He went to work as a volunteer in the White campaign in early October. An outsider, he started out as a researcher, touted as a smart Harvard faculty member. He labored tirelessly and diligently in the campaign and as people got to know him he moved closer to the inner circle. He quickly became the candidate's scheduler. "I was very important to the campaign because during a campaign a lot of people who are good at things have real jobs. I could go [to the campaign office] in the morning and work all day," he explained.

It soon became clear to everybody but Barney that he was going to be working in the administration. "I remember one guy asked me to go to lunch and said, 'You're going to have a big job in the White administration, and I'm going to support you, and I want you to remember me.'" Barney was surprised. "I'm an academic. I have a thesis to write," he thought.

Kevin White won the mayoralty election over Louise Day Hicks by a decisive margin. With the election over, Barney prepared once again to start writing his thesis. But the day after the election, he was awakened by a call from Edward Sullivan, White's first deputy at the secretary of state's office. "Secretary White would like to meet with you," Sullivan said.

At the time Barney was assisting Al Lowenstein, who was in the midst of his Dump Lyndon Johnson campaign. The National Intercollegiate Young Democrats were holding their annual convention in Boston that week at the old Statler Hilton Hotel. Barney was to be the presiding officer at the convention, at which Senator Eugene McCarthy and others were to speak. There was also a dinner event that he was to emcee with John Kenneth Galbraith. Since both mayor-elect White and Barney had busy schedules that week, it was agreed that they would meet the following Saturday afternoon after Barney finished his duties at the convention.

Barney finished chairing the convention at five o'clock, left the hotel, and walked up Arlington Street to the corner of Beacon, by the public garden, and waited by prearrangement for White's car to come by to pick him up. White was driving his son Mark to a youth hockey practice in Wellesley. Barney and White sat in the empty stands at the skating rink in Wellesley while the youngsters practiced. White, who had an eye for talent was direct. "I would like you to come to work for me in the mayor's office," he said.

Barney was stunned. In the few campaigns he had previously worked on, his candidates had never won. "To me, politics was something you did on the side. Being gay, Jewish, and from Hudson County in New Jersey where there was no independent access to politics, it seemed to me this was another world. The notion that politics could be a career had never occurred to me," he said.

Barney responded to the mayor-elect, "I'd love to work for you but I can't do it now. I really have to write my thesis. Let me write my thesis. It will take about two years and then I can go work for you." White wasn't taking no for an answer. He wanted to have the best people he could in his administration. "You want me to be a good liberal and I want to get all these important things done, race and poverty," White said. "You know the people around me. They are very good people but they don't share the same ideas. If people like you aren't willing to help me, then it will be much more difficult for me to do these things. I need your help now."

"I just can't," Barney responded.

He explained to White that as a graduate student at Harvard you have five years from the time you pass your general exams, which he had taken in the fall of 1964, to write your thesis. "I only have two of the five years left to get my thesis written."

"Whose five-year rule is it?" White asked.

"The Harvard Government Department," Barney replied.

White said that he would get back to Barney.

A few days later, White called Barney and told him he had been talking with his good friend and neighbor Sam Huntington, the chairman of the Government Department at Harvard, and that Huntington had agreed to give Barney an extension. "That extension from the five-year rule did not have an expiration date," Barney recalled. "I could probably still write my thesis today." With that obstacle out of the way, Barney agreed to take the job in the mayor's office and immediately started working on the transition team.

Mayor-elect White appointed a five-member talent-hunting task force headed by Huntington. The task force included Richard Goodwin, a former speech-writer for Presidents John Kennedy and Lyndon Johnson who had written several speeches for White during the general election for mayor and had sub-sequently married Doris Kearns. Barney was appointed as the team's executive director.

White had a meeting with the transition team and others who had been active in the campaign to brainstorm names of those he might choose to fill various city government positions. While White's inner circle suggested a few people they knew from the neighborhoods, Barney kept offering several names for every job, people he knew locally and across the country, academics, com-munity activists, and politicos, far more than anybody else in the room. Barney suggested Hale Champion, then a fellow at the Kennedy Institute of Politics at Harvard, who had served for six years as director of finance for the state of California under the Democratic governor Pat Brown before Ronald Reagan's election as governor in 1966, to head the Boston Redevelopment Authority, a powerful agency that oversees urban renewal. He proposed Samuel Merrick, an experienced U.S. Department of Labor official, who had joined the Kennedy Institute of Politics three months earlier, to handle collective bargaining and labor relations with city employees. As reported by Lydon in the *Boston Globe Magazine*, Merrick had once made a casual remark at Harvard that "it would be fun to work for the City of Boston" and in the same tone that "it would be fun to go slide in the snow," and Barney had gotten wind of it. Finally, Rob-ert Crane, the state treasurer, who would serve in that position for a record twenty-six years, took his close friend Kevin White aside at the transition team meeting and asked, "Who's that fat Jewish kid who keeps coming up with all the answers?"

When mayor-elect White announced the appointment of Hale Champion as director of the Boston Redevelopment Authority, Daniel Patrick Moynihan, who headed the Joint Center for Urban Studies at Harvard, was quoted in the *Harvard Crimson* as commenting that among people who know public policy, "there aren't five men in this country with better reputations."

Kevin White was not a prototypical Irish politician like the legendary Boston mayor James Michael Curley. White was a lawyer and a well-educated, cultured man with a self-deprecating sense of humor. Above all, he was a reformer and had visions for the city. White brought many talented, intelligent people into city government, including Herbert Gleason, who left the law firm of Hill & Barrow to become corporation counsel; Edward Sullivan, director of administrative services; and David Davis, director of the office of public service.

Many of the people he appointed he had not known months earlier. "Whatever Kevin White's faults or greatness, he had an eye for picking talent, talent that ranged from old-fashioned Boston pols to people like Barney Frank, who at first glance you would think what the hell is he doing here?" Alan Lupo, a former reporter for the *Boston Globe*, said. Lawrence DiCara, who served on the Boston City Council from 1972 to 1981, commented that no previous mayor of Boston would have surrounded himself with people of such caliber—smart, idealistic, and well-educated—but that White "was never threatened by having people smarter than him working for him." According to DiCara, White disregarded traditional ethnic and neighborhood politics in choosing his staff and brought talented people like Barney Frank into his administration. "These were not people who could deliver votes on Election Day," he said. "Barney couldn't deliver his mother's vote. She was still living in New Jersey."

The late 1960s was a time of rebirth in cities across the nation. Many bright young people were attracted to work in city government for energetic mayors such as John Lindsay in New York City, Carl Stokes, the first black mayor of Cleveland, and Kevin White in Boston. It was an exciting time to be working in city government and addressing longstanding social problems. White was able to attract an impressive collection of talent. Barney was both his chief talent scout and the leading edge of the talent that White had assembled. The group included William Cowin, who joined White's administration in May 1968 as special counsel to the mayor, having worked previously on staff for Edward Brooke when he was Massachusetts attorney general and later U.S. senator. "Young people like me thought that it was the last great frontier," he said.

With the inauguration of Mayor White, Boston City Hall was transformed into a vibrant and accessible place. Mayor White wanted programs to meet the human needs of the city. He created the "Little City Hall" program in the neighborhoods to bring government closer to the people. This program, the first of its kind in the nation, set up small offices in the neighborhoods, usually operating out of trailers, that were staffed by city government employees to provide services to residents and respond to grievances. Each of the Little City Hall managers appointed by the mayor was also an advocate for the neighborhood. White put more police officers on the street and built a thousand units of low-income housing on vacant city land.

Barney came into the White administration with boundless energy and bursting with ideas. During the early part of White's first term, Barney stood out.

He was referred to in the Boston press as the "whiz kid," the "wunderkind," the "man who got things done," the "Mayor's brain trust," and "Kevin White's alter ego." He occupied the office next to the mayor and was involved in everything. He wielded enormous power in governing the city. Peter Meade, a City Hall veteran, described Barney as "the heart and soul of Kevin White's administration during that first term." "He was the guy who held the place together in so many significant ways."

In an administration filled with workaholics and headed by a mayor who on occasion would spend the night in his City Hall office, Barney outworked everybody. He seemed to have no other life. He would be in the office often seven days a week, frequently working sixteen-hour days, and seemed to thrive on it. "Barney had a sense that you needed to enjoy what you were doing and have a good time doing it," Cowin observed.

"Barney became the man of all work—he could write, he could direct, he was the person at Kevin White's side, he was Kevin's eyes and ears, and was very close to Kevin," Lydon recalled. "I always felt that Kevin White was in good hands and that Barney would take care of him. He was tough, strong, clean, purposeful, and principled. Barney was born to be a first-class public man."

Barney had a knack for political tactics and knew what was going on everywhere. He handled all the detail work, made the deals, and got things done. He was involved in just about every big issue and every major project—racial issues, neighborhood problems, the interstate highway, an expansion of Logan Airport—everything but fund-raising. He did political intelligence, dealt with the School Committee, kept watch on administrative departments, decided where the mayor should go each day, formulated a communications strategy and wrote the mayor's press releases, lobbied the City Council, usually one-on-one in a councilor's office, and helped department heads prepare for testimony before the City Council. And if there was a community beef about a local issue, he would be the person attending the community meeting on behalf of the mayor. According to Cowin, "he performed these many duties effectively and without any loss of humanity."

"Barney made it respectable to be a political guy," William "Bo" Holland, a former aide to Mayor White who himself has been known as a political guy for over forty years, said. "Here was someone who had a reputation for being the smartest guy on the block who relished the political parts of his job, and who never shrank from it. He was someone we looked up to."

The *Boston Globe* reporter Thomas Oliphant described Barney as a chief of staff "who worked around the clock and whose tentacles reached into every aspect of the city government, including dealing with the press." "If you were working on a story that involved the mayor in those first months," Oliphant said, "you were as likely to talk to Barney as to Frank Tiffen, the press secretary. He was one of the first people I met in public life who supplied both context and wit." Oliphant's first impression of Barney at City Hall was "sleeves rolled up, dirty fingernails, making things work, doing deals, and making the case for this or that program."

Cowin recalled that when a reporter asked Barney who does what in City Hall, Barney responded, "Well, the best I can tell, I'm responsible for everything that can be done in twenty-four hours or less and Cowin is responsible for everything else." "While this was an exaggeration of my role," Cowin said, "it certainly wasn't of his." According to Cowin, Barney took responsibility for all the things that had to be done quickly, an environment that increased the odds of acting on impulse and making an error or a bad decision. Yet Barney seemed to avoid such pitfalls.

As White's chief of staff, Barney was plunged into a cauldron of urban, racial, and ethnic politics in the rough world of Boston confrontational politics, long dominated by native Yankee Protestants and Irish and Italian Catholics. Barney was White's link with the Boston neighborhoods and the many groups and organizations that wanted something. He was also the "man to see" at City Hall on policy as well as political issues. As a result, people were often lined up outside his office to see him. "You knew where his office was. You could follow the trail of cigar smoke there," Meade said.

White had a tendency to disappear for a week or so. In the mayor's absence, Barney would run the "cabinet" meetings at which about a dozen particular department heads and senior staff would gather to engage in policymaking, discussing various problems and alternatives. At the meetings Barney spoke fast, thought fast, and stayed focused. He had little tolerance for long-winded statements. "You didn't have to explain things to him," one former department head recalled. "Mention two key words and he knew what the issue was and would cut you off." Another one said, "Barney was sometimes abrasive and ruffled feathers but everyone liked him. He understood the subject matter and he understood the politics." Cowin added, "He never did or said anything to suggest that he was superior or better than anyone else."

By all accounts, Kevin White and Barney Frank, the urbane yet street-smart Irish politician and the disheveled academic, came together and had a close professional relationship. In Cowin's view, "Barney was the most important person to Kevin in his public and political life. Kevin depended on him the most. He had the most confidence in his judgment and his loyalty. Barney was the single most influential person with the mayor." Alan Lupo said that because White "appreciated talent, appreciated humor, and appreciated people who were fast on their feet, there was a great deal of respect and affection between the two of them at that time." White was impatient and wanted things said quickly, and therefore he valued Barney for his ability to think and talk as fast as he did. Barney, according to Herb Gleason, "could produce a cascade of information in a moment." White would get "restless listening to almost anybody else." The Boston City Council president, William Foley Jr., said at the time with some dismay, "In the end White only listens to one guy—Barney."

Barney made many of the mayor's decisions, including many personnel decisions. He was successful, for example, at bringing women and minorities into the administration. And although Barney would be careful not to do anything without first consulting the mayor, White would not always pay attention or think things through because he trusted Barney's judgment so much.

The Boston Housing Authority was a mess when White took office. A move was under way to take it out of the patronage arena and put some knowledgeable people on the housing board. In an effort to give public housing tenants a real voice on the Housing Authority, Barney suggested appointing Doris Bunte, a black tenant in the Orchard Park housing project and a respected figure in the black community, as a member. But Bunte, who attempted to reform the Boston Housing Authority, proved to be a real annoyance to the mayor. After one particular episode involving patronage, White stormed into Barney's office and said, "Who's this person you put on the Housing Authority, this Doris Bunte woman?" Barney replied, "I told you about her and you said 'yah, yah.'" The mayor replied, "You've been around here long enough to know that 'yah, yah' means 'no, no'" and stormed out.

"Barney had been described to me by people as a genius who was smarter than everybody, so I kind of expected that," Colin Diver recalled. A graduate of Amherst and the Harvard Law School, Diver had come to work at City Hall after hearing Mayor White give an inspirational speech at the *Harvard Law Review* banquet. "What I didn't expect was the political savvy and earthiness that was rather obvious as soon as you met him." Rent control was one of the issues that White had focused on during the campaign, using the slogan "When landlords raise rent, Kevin White raises hell." During White's first term, some of the neighborhoods put a lot of pressure on the mayor's office because of rising rents. Barney assigned Diver to work on preparing a rent control proposal and ordinance. "I had the benefit of some pretty good training in economics and I had the benefit of conversations with some economist friends of mine," Diver said. He told Barney that rent control was bad economics and that it was not going to work, and he predicted that it would have a long-term disastrous impact on the housing market. Barney said he knew all that and then, according to Diver, "ran through all the arguments that I was going to make and then some that I hadn't considered." But, Barney said, "we're going to do this because

Kevin is getting the shit kicked out of him in Brighton, Allston, and Jamaica Plains [and other neighborhoods] and we have to respond to this problem." Barney and Diver talked about a rent stabilization policy rather than a strict New York City–style rent control law. Although Barney's "heart wasn't in rent control," Diver explained, he understood what needed to be done and the right way to go about doing it.

To some Boston political observers, at times it looked as though Barney rather than Mayor White was running the show. Barney takes issue with that statement, saying "Kevin was in charge. While he wasn't a mastermind, he was a very smart man and he knew what he wanted to do. He deserves the credit." Barney prefers to downplay his role, saying, "I worked for Kevin White. He picked me. I had no independent stature." Barney contends that he stood out because of his personality and image and because the White staff at the beginning was so unstructured. Alan Lupo agrees that while Barney wielded tremendous power and ran the day-to-day city, "it was Mayor White who ran the big city picture and called the shots."

In his role as Mayor White's deputy, Barney regularly met with liberal groups but was never asked to meet with a gay rights group. The gay community in Boston was fairly closeted at the time. Many liberal groups in the Boston area considered Barney "the liberal heart" of Mayor White's administration during its first three years. He was largely responsible for the mayor's decision that the city join the national grape boycott by directing Boston city agencies to cease purchasing California table grapes, an action that prompted an angry telegram to the mayor from California governor Ronald Reagan. He was also responsible for the city of Boston's voting its General Motors stock proxies with Campaign GM, part of Ralph Nader's Project on Corporate Responsibility. Barney was vocal in his opposition to excessive use of police force in several incidents.

In a contemporary analysis in the *Boston Globe*, Lydon described Barney as "brash, a boat rocker, fiercely loyal to White but as much interested in provoking the mayor as protecting him." Lydon wrote: "In policy debates [Frank] argues the liberal side of every question. He pushed successfully, for example, for the appointment of Julius Bernstein to the Boston Housing Authority over City Council rantings that Bernstein was still the head of the Socialist Party in Boston. He fought for more generous treatment than was actually given to militant black demands after Martin Luther King's assassination. He wanted to fight for a tougher Model Cities program and was ready to sacrifice unanimous Council approval to get it."

Boston was a very Roman Catholic, parochial city at the time. It was an Irish city where Italians were generally tolerated but not accepted. Ethnic politics was a tremendous force then. The Jewish population in Boston, which had hovered at about 10 to 15 percent, had shrunk significantly. Nonetheless, "Barney was really the chief operating officer of the city of Boston during those years," according to Jim Segel, a former student of his at Harvard who went to work for him as an assistant in City Hall. "It was so extraordinary. He was kind of an alien in Boston politics. He had attended Harvard, was Jewish, and was from Bayonne. It was the first time anyone like that had been in such a position of political power. Boston was still an Irish preserve." Barney went into this culture and transformed it, showing that he could be accepted as part of the political fabric of the community.

"One day I was sitting in Barney's office at City Hall and he said, 'I think we ought to have a hundred new police officers,'" Bo Holland remembered. "Barney made a decision. He then went and convinced Mayor White that it was the right policy to make, and next thing you knew there were a hundred new cops in Boston. He had that kind of power."

According to White, Barney, like White himself, is a power collector, someone who collects everything he can get his hands on, someone who reaches out for more power to do more things, in contrast to a power user, someone who wants only the power necessary to do his job.

Several years later, when Barney was serving in the Massachusetts state legislature, Ed Markey, a colleague and friend, asked him whether he ever wanted to be the mayor of Boston. "No," Barney replied, "because the mayor will never have as much power as I wielded." J. Anthony Lukas, in his Pulitzer Prize–winning book *Common Ground*, about race relations and the busing for school integration crisis in Boston in the late 1960s, describes Barney as the "de facto mayor." "In a City Hall still populated principally by amicable Irishmen," he writes, "Barney was an anachronism: a Jew from Bayonne, New Jersey who delivered his stinging wisecracks in a thick 'Joisy' accent, through billows of smoke from a cigar which looked like one of Hoboken's belching smokestacks. With his massive belly draped in perpetually rumpled suits, Barney did not look impressive, but few people could slip so nimbly through the corridors of Massachusetts politics."

On April 4, 1968, only three months into his administration, Mayor White was at a movie theater watching the film *Gone with the Wind* when he was informed that Dr. Martin Luther King Jr. had been shot. The mayor went immediately to City Hall. In the book Lukas describes the events and sporadic disturbances in Boston following the assassination of Dr. King. Gangs of black youths roamed about in Roxbury smashing windows and overturning autos. A bus carrying a dozen white people was trapped by a crowd of chanting and jeering blacks. White's first instinct was to summon the police. Barney was concerned that an armed response might only make matters worse. At Barney's urging, the mayor agreed to let black ministers and community workers try persuasion first, and within an hour they were able to quiet the crowd and rescue the white passengers.

The next day, James Brown, the "Godfather of Soul," whose hit songs included "Papa's Got a Brand New Bag" and "I Got You (I Feel Good)," was scheduled to perform in concert at Boston Garden before a largely young and black audience from all over the city. Under the circumstances, Boston Garden officials wanted to cancel the concert. But doing so would have left thousands of disappointed black youths outside the arena in downtown Boston that evening. After much negotiation, the concert went on as scheduled, a television station agreed to carry it live, young people were urged to stay home and watch the concert on television, and the city of Boston agreed to pay Brown the difference between what he would have made from a full house and what he actually took in that night.

Lukas wrote: "Neither the mayor nor Barney Frank had ever heard of James Brown. Barney thought that he was a football player." Barney disputes that statement. "Kevin asked why a football player is giving a concert at Boston Garden. I said that I don't know and would have to ask someone. I had not heard of James Brown but I knew he wasn't a football player. Kevin thought he was a football player."

As the mayor's chief of staff, Barney served as liaison between the reform-minded mayor and the relatively conservative Boston City Council, who were often at loggerheads. The mayor had great disdain for most of the city councilors. And because, at the time, the City Council consisted of nine members who were all elected at-large for two-year terms, they were always running for reelection and competing against each other. Boston was the classic strong-mayor structure of municipal government and the City Council had been statutorily weak for decades. As such, the council members had little power and not much to do. But a city councilor had to produce for his constituents, usually in the form of city jobs or other benefits. Thus, members could thrive rhetorically on the council by calling the mayor all kinds of things, but in private they needed to get together with the mayor and his people and strike a deal on whatever it was they believed they needed and thought the mayor could deliver. Barney had to work with the council, an institutionally hostile body with an inferiority complex, and try to get the members to be allies or, at worst, not to hurt the mayor. By all accounts he was effective at both.

Wearing a rumpled suit that looked as though he had slept in it, a white shirt, and a nondescript tie, and chewing on a drugstore cigar, Barney would frequently testify on behalf of the mayor at council hearings, which often meant fielding hostile questions, particularly during budget hearings. Barney relied on a combination of political savvy, directness, and humor, a flair for the rejoinder, and a knack for making irreverent comments. He clearly enjoyed himself. His political style was described by one observer as "politicking with a wisecrack and wisecracking with finesse and sometimes deadly accuracy." Many years later, Kevin White told the *Boston Globe*, "I still marvel at how this young Jewish kid from Bayonne was so effective at playing hard-nosed politics with the entrenched veterans of city government."

According to Alan Lupo, Mayor White's Harvard-educated young chief of staff was able to have a good working relationship with the veteran Irish and Italian Boston City Council pols of that era because he didn't talk or look like a Harvard grad. His manner of speech was described by one Boston reporter as "more East Boston bartender than Harvard graduate." Council president William Foley said about the rapid-fire delivery of the mayor's chief of staff: "His ultimate ambition in life is to say all the words in a given sentence." The *Boston Globe* reporter Elliot Friedman wrote that Barney had "occasional moments of neatness," but they were "sporadic." Lupo was more direct: "In those days when everyone was trying to look neat like John F. Kennedy, holding a suit jacket over their right shoulder, Barney was 'a total slob,' disheveled, overweight, with foul mouth but with a great sense of humor. If there is anything that helps in politics or anything else in life it is a sense of humor."

There were some real characters on the Boston City Council then, men such as John E. Corrigan, Jerry O'Leary, Joseph Timilty, and the most colorful of them all, Frederick C. Langone. "Fearless Freddie," as the popular councilor from the North End was affectionately known, would regularly launch into tirades against the White administration. Langone's modus operandi was to savage whoever was testifying on behalf of the mayor. He was famous for saying, "You can't trick me, I was born on Halloween," and "I want to know who was there! W-O-H. Who?" But despite his gruff exterior, sharp rhetoric, and extended rants, which at times made him look like a buffoon, he was a bright, shrewd, and street-smart politician, a master at interrogating people. Langone could talk as fast as Barney, and the two men, both puffing on cigars, would go at each other, jabbering away while engulfed in cigar smoke. "People couldn't understand either of them talking. Maybe they understood each other," Jim Segel said. Barney was very good at handling Langone. "Fred Langone and Barney had this relationship; it wasn't antagonistic but rather one of professional respect. They liked to game with each other," Bo Holland observed. "Barney's wit was such that it would sometimes go over Freddy and he wouldn't realize that he had got jabbed," Joseph Timilty said.

The Langone family was an institution in Massachusetts politics. Fred Langone's grandfather had been the first Italian state legislator, and his father, Joseph

A. Langone Sr., the first Italian state senator. His brother Joseph "Joe-Joe" Langone served as a state representative from the North End for several terms and also spent time in prison for assaulting an FBI agent. Joseph Langone Sr. had started Langone's Funeral Home in the North End and, as the funeral director, had literally buried Nicola Sacco and Bartolomeo Vanzetti, the Italian immigrants executed by the Commonwealth of Massachusetts in 1927 for the murder of two men in Braintree, a celebrated case in which many people in the United States and around the world became convinced that they were not guilty. Freddy and Joe-Joe owned the profitable Langone funeral home in the 1960s.

Barney described Fred Langone as "one of those classic guys who would yell for the camera and then come back and make a deal." He would shout blustery comments at you at a public hearing, Barney recalled, "and later come over to you and say, 'Hey kid, you and me, let's go get a drink.'" Once, Barney said, "I was griping about people that wanted a swimming pool in their neighborhood and then would complain about the noise when we were building the pool." "Freddy, who was in his fifties, said to me, 'Hey kid. Ain't you heard the news? Everybody wants to go to heaven but nobody wants to die.'" Every year at Christmas, Langone would send Barney a small gift—a can of shoe polish—because he always wore scuffed, unpolished shoes.

Barney was a political troubleshooter for the mayor who saw action on the front lines of Boston city government. Whenever there was a demonstration on the City Hall Plaza or on Boston Common, he was there to observe in case something happened. When it was reported that a large group of tough-looking motorcycle riders who had made some threats were coming to Boston, Barney traveled with the police to make sure everything was handled well. He and the police watched a small group of very young bikers come into the city who, Barney said, looked "more like trikers than bikers." When it was reported that a group of hippies from New York dedicated to violence had joined a core of about a hundred local hippies and political radicals on the Boston Common to defy the midnight curfew in support of their common right to sleep in the open air on the Common, Barney was there at 3 a.m. to coordinate the police bust.

In the mid-1990s, Elsie Frank was speaking at an event for seniors in Dorchester when an elderly woman approached her and said, "How is Barney doing?" "Oh, you know Barney. From where?" Elsie asked. The woman explained: "In the late 1960s, my husband died while at home. It was in the middle of the winter. There had been a snowstorm and there were several inches of snow on the ground. We lived on a dead-end street in Boston and the city had not plowed the street. The funeral home could not get a hearse down our snow-covered street to pick up my husband's body. It was a Saturday and I frantically phoned everywhere and everybody I could think of but couldn't get any results. I was beside myself and didn't know what to do. A friend of mine suggested, 'Why don't you phone that fat kid who works for the mayor, the one we always see on television who talks so funny?' We thought of his name, looked him up in the phone book, and I phoned him at his office. Within an hour, the street where I live was cleared of snow and the hearse was able to come for my husband." The woman looked at Elsie and said, "Do I remember Barney? How could I forget him? I have been grateful to him ever since."

Despite a crushing schedule, Barney managed to find time to teach an urban government seminar at Harvard. The topic was Boston city government, and several city department heads came as guest lecturers. He even took the students to City Hall one day to meet and discuss issues with Mayor White.

His idea of a vacation was to take a group of Harvard undergraduates with him in a rental car and go to Long Island to campaign for Al Lowenstein, who was running for Congress in 1968. James Roosevelt remembers what a great experience that trip was: "It was a practical way for us undergraduates to change the political landscape."

Herb Gleason believes that during this period with Kevin White, Barney was a deeply unhappy person. "He plowed his energy into his work, which was great for Kevin. His whole life was his job and while he was wonderful at it, his life was incomplete. He didn't get asked to parties, social events, or out for dinner much. I think he was very lonely." At official functions Barney could usually be found off in a corner schmoozing with some politician.

Even though he was considerably overweight, Barney did manage to play softball on Kevin White's office team, known as "Kevin's Krusaders." He was not a gifted softball player but loved to play the game. He played first base because he didn't have to run as much at that position. Colleagues in the White administration remember seeing Barney play softball one day in his socks because he couldn't find the time to buy a pair of sneakers.

"People used to mistake me for Barney," Bo Holland recalled. "People would stop me on the street thinking I was Barney Frank, being a heavy guy with glasses. They were looking for jobs and asking favors of different kinds." At first Holland would explain that he was not Barney Frank. Then he started to go along with it and tell the people "to come up and see me in my office." These people would later show up outside Barney's office.

When asked about his accomplishments working for Mayor White, Barney pointed to White's early liberal racial policies: "Kevin White took office at a time when race was racking the city of Boston. The black population in the city was not part of the process of governance. We brought about racial integration in Boston, ending that racist and segregationist thing. Blacks got fair treatment. Mayor White confronted entrenched prejudices, attitudes, and myths and began to break them open for the better."

On November 1, 2006, on a sunny and unseasonably mild morning, speaking at a ceremony for the unveiling of a ten-foot-tall bronze statue of former mayor White outside Boston's Faneuil Hall, Barney explained that in the face of every good piece of political advice to the contrary, Kevin White tackled the racial divide and achieved racial equality in an important way his first year. "When he took office, most of the black people in this city thought the white people were being treated better by the government. But by the end of the first year he got equality. Most of the white people thought the black people were being treated better by the government," Barney said. "The black people weren't any happier. But you had equal unhappiness. And that was the prerequisite for starting to turn things around."

Barney notes with pride his role in formulating White's transportation policy and persuading the mayor to strongly oppose the construction of destructive superhighways, such as the Southwest Expressway (I-95), which would have been built through Hyde Park, cutting the South End in half, and the proposed Inner Beltway, which would have been routed through the Fenway and cut right into the heart of the park land and existing open spaces and displaced over three thousand families, the majority of whom were low income. "You are not going to build any more highways in my city," Mayor White declared in 1970. In Barney's view, new highway construction would have torn up a large chunk of Boston and resulted in loss of housing, additional air pollution, and disruption to long-established ethnic neighborhoods. "I'm not an esthetic. If the whole world were like Bayonne, New Jersey, it wouldn't bother me," he explains in Alan Lupo's *Rites of Way*, a 1971 book about the politics of transportation in Boston. "It wasn't the sanctity of Fowl Meadow but the effect on the poor that bothered me about I-95. I'm not a Druid. I don't think trees have an independent value."

Almost as soon as Kevin White became mayor he began running for governor. In 1970, he defeated Morris Donohue, the president of the state senate, in a bitter Democratic primary. But many of Donohue's supporters refused to support White in the general election. White, with Michael Dukakis on the ticket as his running mate for lieutenant governor, was easily beaten in the November election by the incumbent Republican governor, Francis Sargent, who won the city of Boston as well. Sargent, the former lieutenant governor of the commonwealth, had become governor in 1969 when John Volpe resigned to join President Nixon's Cabinet as secretary of transportation.

Sargent was an amiable and personable politician who was at the height of his popularity. He had not been in office long enough to generate many enemies and was still enjoying a honeymoon period as governor. He was also clever, and reached out to liberal Democrats during the campaign. "Kevin White lost because he ran against a pretty decent candidate. Frank Sargent fit the profile of a nice Yankee governor," the veteran Boston politico Bo Holland observed. According to Barney, part of the problem, to White's credit, was that he was the first mayor of Boston to say publicly that the city had a race problem and he was going to try to deal with it. "They were calling him Mayor Black," Barney noted. Some people voted against White for governor because they wanted to keep him as mayor. "Sargent was seen as a good liberal and some liberals reasoned that if we elect Kevin White as governor, who knows who is going to be mayor of Boston," Barney said. "A lot of liberals said we have a liberal governor and a liberal mayor and we don't want to change that." In Barney's view, it was more Sargent's popularity than anything else that decided the election.

During the gubernatorial election Barney performed double duty—he ran the city of Boston, making all the decisions while the mayor was campaigning, and helped with White's campaign. As a result, he gained even more weight. "I saw him two days before the election walking down Tremont Street in Boston and he was so fat he looked like he was going to burst," Philip Johnston, former chairman of the Massachusetts Democratic Party, recalled.

In December, exhausted and somewhat disillusioned, Barney resigned from the mayor's staff. "I am resigning because I am tired both physically and mentally—plain worn out," he declared. However, he acknowledged that if White had been elected governor he probably would have gone to the State House with him.

Mayor White tried hard to persuade Barney to stay on in city government and offered him several good jobs, including head of the City Hospital and head of the Boston Housing Authority. "I offered him any position in the administration 'except mayor,'" White said. White was gracious and told his young chief of staff to get some rest and come back later.

"When Barney left City Hall, he wasn't replaced as such because you couldn't replace him with any one person," Colin Diver explained. Larry Quealy, a politico from West Roxbury, sat in Barney's office and dealt with political matters. Bob Weinberg, a former U.S. Budget Bureau official, took over the policy adviser half of Barney's job.

"Many of us had a sense that Kevin White's administration started to lose some of its glow toward the end of its first term and was becoming more of a traditional city machine at that point," Tom Oliphant observed.

Barney was thirty years old and still thought of himself as an academic, a Ph.D. student on leave. Richard Neustadt at Harvard offered him a fellowship at the Kennedy Institute of Politics and Barney decided to accept the fellowship and return to Harvard. He planned to use the fellowship to finally write his on-again, off-again doctoral thesis, the subject of which had changed yet again, this time to a study of city government, relying heavily on his practical experiences at City Hall.

"I had fantasized about how it would be nice to have all this leisure time to write and contemplate but I was just too antsy and restless," Barney said. As he tried to wrestle a doctoral thesis into submission, he kept getting interrupted and had trouble focusing on it. He wound up instead writing an article titled "The Incredible Shrinking Barney Frank" for the *Boston Globe Magazine* about how he lost a hundred pounds, dropping from 275 to 175 in about eight months through strict dieting. "I literally didn't recognize him when he tapped me on the shoulder one day," Philip Johnston recalled. "He looked at me and said, 'Barney Frank minus a hundred pounds.'"

Barney was a compulsive eater who had once described himself as "someone who could always be counted on at a party to single-handedly reduce at least one mountain of cheese to a molehill." In the article, he explains, only a small part of what he used to eat "was due to biological hunger." He discusses his earlier eating habits: "Food performs for me the same functions that alcohol, cigarettes, and Bruins games perform for other people. I eat for fun. In the good old days, when I stopped eating, it was generally because of 1) a depletion of the immediate food supply, 2) embarrassment, and 3) fatigue in my arms and jaw. It was rarely because I had eaten all that I wanted." He explains how he lost so much weight: "I did not undergo amputation of any significant part of my body. Nor did I contract a serious illness, or turn to some variant of Eastern religion based on an exclusive diet of rice husks and Banyan tree bark." Rather, he rigorously followed Dr. Stillman's all-protein diet and lost the weight by sheer strength of will.

Although Barney was confident that he could get tenure at Harvard, he began to recognize that he was better suited to politics than to academic life. "I decided then that I really liked politics and came to realize that I was not sufficiently disciplined to be an academic and was trying to force myself into the wrong place. I would be much better in a line of work where a short attention span was an asset and not a handicap," he explained. "It became clear to me that even though I was gay, I could find a role and a livelihood as an appointed official." He decided he would try to return to politics as an aide.

5

Coming to Washington

MICHAEL J. HARRINGTON, a thirty-three-year-old Irish Catholic who had worked on a beer truck to pay for his undergraduate and law school education at Harvard, had been elected to Congress from Massachusetts's Sixth District in a special election in September 1969, following the death of Republican William Bates. The Sixth District, which included Lynn, Haverhill, Salem, and the port city of Gloucester, was the home of the Saltonstalls, the Lodges, and other prominent, old-line Massachusetts families. This North Shore district was the birthplace of the term *gerrymander*, named after Massachusetts governor Elbridge Gerry, who in the nineteenth century created a distorted, salamander-shaped district to bring together all the Federalist towns. The district had been in the hands of the Republican Bates family for over forty years and the hawkish William Bates had regularly won reelection with about 65 percent of the vote.

Harrington, a state representative, had run for Congress in 1969 on a peace and priorities platform — opposing the Vietnam War and the antiballistics missile defense system. His opponent in that special election was the Republican state senator William Saltonstall, the son of Leverett Saltonstall, the commonwealth's first three-term governor and a U.S. senator for twenty-two years before retiring in 1966. The election was viewed by many as a referendum on the Vietnam War and President Richard Nixon's foreign policy.

In the closing weeks of the campaign, this special election brought together a whole new generation of politicians from eastern Massachusetts, liberals who were active politically but had never been elected to office. Barney Frank was there, as was Thomas O'Neill III. William Delahunt and Edward Markey helped out in the Harrington campaign. "At least ten of us who worked for Michael Harrington in that campaign later ran for the Massachusetts legislature and won," O'Neill recalled.

Mike Harrington received just over 52 percent of the vote in an upset victory over Saltonstall. His plurality was small, less than seven thousand votes, but in winning the election he became the first Democrat to represent the Sixth District in Congress in almost a hundred years.

William S. Wasserman, the owner and publisher of *North Shore Weeklies*, a chain of local weekly newspapers on the North Shore of Massachusetts, had helped run Harrington's campaign for Congress. He agreed to come to Washington temporarily to put together Harrington's congressional office operation. Wasserman served as administrative assistant and ran the office in a no-nonsense way. A few weeks into the summer of 1970 he had fired one of the volunteer interns, a junior from the University of Michigan, for using the Congressional Research Service, part of the Library of Congress, to find an answer to a *New York Times* crossword puzzle.

In the early spring of 1971, after Wasserman informed Harrington that he was planning to leave and return to Massachusetts, Harrington contacted Barney Frank and offered him the position of administrative assistant, a job title on Capitol Hill that has since been changed to chief of staff. Harrington had first met Barney in 1966 when he was the volunteer staff for the Democratic Study Group in the state legislature. Harrington's philosophy was that when one gets a chance as an elected official to hire staff, you're a fool if you don't hire up. "Wherever it went," Harrington explained, "I knew that I would be the beneficiary of at least some exposure to a guy that I thought was among the more interesting people I had come across."

The offer was a turning point for Barney. "It had always seemed to me that if I was as interested in politics as I was, I should spend some time in Washington, even if just as a temporary thing," he said. Barney agreed to go to Washington to work for Mike Harrington, whom he described as "one of the most attractive persons in Massachusetts politics." He committed to stay for eighteen months, through the next election.

Harrington was excited about having Barney come on board and viewed him as an intellectual partner. "Mike Harrington is smart enough so that he doesn't feel threatened by anyone," Barney said. He had explained to Harrington that there were a few things he needed to do, including take a trip to England to observe the parliamentary system, before coming to Washington. Mayor White was reportedly angry that Barney had taken a job with Harrington less than six months after leaving City Hall.

When Barney arrived in Washington in June 1971, Richard Nixon was two and a half years into his first term as president. The war continued to rage in Southeast Asia. It was the last season that the Washington Senators, managed by Ted Williams, would play baseball at RFK Stadium before being morphed into the Texas Rangers. The city of Washington, once a sleepy southern town and a performing arts wasteland, was beginning to blossom with the opening of new cultural venues in the city and its environs—the curtain of the Filene Center amphitheater at Wolf Trap Farm Park in Vienna, Virginia, the first National Park for the Performing Arts, was set to rise on July 1 and the John F. Kennedy Center for the Performing Arts, on the banks of the Potomac, would open on September 8.

More than two dozen summer interns from colleges across the country and about ten regular staff were gathered in Suite 435 of the Cannon Building, the office of Congressman Harrington, waiting to meet the new administrative assistant who had been Mayor White's chief of staff for three years.

The Washington intern program, according to Harrington, was a small part of an effort "to inspire or motivate or at least provide the opportunity for people to get a proximate view of the process, maybe not a traditionally orthodox view of the process." "Michael Harrington had a habit of throwing the doors wide open for interns, turning the office over to the interns, and then he would leave for the summer. The intern business could be somewhat difficult when some twenty-five overachievers are set loose in a small space with no defined task," Barney said.

Barney had arrived in town the evening before, having hurriedly packed everything he owned into his old car, which had a hole in the floor through which the road was visible, for the eight-hour highway drive from Boston. As he was getting dressed that morning he could not find his shoes. But he did not let that interfere with his getting to work on time.

A few minutes past nine o'clock, Barney made his entrance into the crowded room. He was dressed in a rumpled brown double-breasted suit, with a white shirt and a striped tie. On his feet was a pair of white tennis sneakers with Celtics green laces. He stood before the gathered staff, his dark eyes glancing around at the large group through a pair of black-rimmed glasses, and began to speak rapidly in a lingering Jersey accent. His opening words were: "The first order of business. We have to organize an office softball team." I leaned over to Larry Alexander, an intern from Yale (who would later represent Marblehead in the Massachusetts legislature) and whispered, "This guy has a future. He is going to go far." Ten years later Barney had a House softball team of his own—the Congressional Franks.

Barney's hundred-pound weight loss since November 1970 had forced him to buy a new wardrobe. It was a novel experience for someone who had spent most of his adult life on the heavy side and in the husky department—the opportunity to shop for regular-size suits. But nothing else about his disheveled appearance had changed.

Barney was never much for spectator sports. He preferred to be active and a player rather than a fan. If he had a choice between attending a Red Sox World

Series game and playing softball, he would choose to play. He loved softball and tennis. For someone who, in his words, "had the kind of muscular coordination that makes sharpening a pencil an accomplishment," his weight loss was like the realization of a dream. Now, at 175 pounds, he could run, slide, jump, stretch, and accomplish feats on the baseball diamond and the tennis court that he had not been able to do in many years.

Softball is a rite of summer in the nation's capital. Congressional staff, interns, and often members of Congress play on makeshift fields on the mall. Interns are sent out in mid-afternoon in scouting parties to hunt for and reserve (squatter's rights) a field or at least a parcel of grass. Barney was a serious softball player. Although he did not have a picture-perfect swing, he did have some good power. He generally played third base. In later years, like many aging infielders, he shifted to first base.

The softball games were coed and one of the few rules was that a woman had to pitch. One evening that summer, the Harrington team was playing a squad from the office of Democrat Robert Giaimo of Connecticut. The Harrington group was the better team but the difference was in the pitching. The other team's summer intern pitcher, a rising junior at a small college in Connecticut, was a physical education major and the star pitcher for the college women's softball team. She threw the softball with speed and made the ball jump as it whizzed by home plate. In the congressional summer league she was clearly a franchise player. After team Harrington's losing effort, the players on both squads congregated to extend the traditional "good game" to each other. Barney went over to the opposing pitcher and on the spot offered her an internship in Mike Harrington's office the following summer.

The one exception to the "female must pitch" rule was that a member of Congress could pitch. This was known as the Thomas P. "Tip" O'Neill Jr. waiver. When the Harrington team played Tip O'Neill's office, Tip was the pitcher. The affable giant Tip O'Neill stood on the mound with a softball, a glove, a beer can, and a cigar. If the batted ball hit the beer can it was deemed a ground rule single.

Mike Harrington got a seat on the Armed Services Committee after a nasty fight with Louise Day Hicks, the newly elected representative from Boston, who coveted that committee assignment because the Boston naval shipyard was located in her district. F. Edward Herbert of Louisiana, the chairman of the Armed Services Committee, had been elevated to that position because of the seniority system in Congress, which put undue power and influence into the hands of southern Democrats from safe districts, members who were generally conservative and pro-military. There was a great deal of friction between the liberal, antiwar, and reform-minded Harrington and the hawkish Herbert. This was mild compared to two years later when Pat Schroeder, a peace candidate and women's rights advocate from Denver, and Ronald Dellums, an antiwar militant from Berkeley, were elected to Congress and "became members" of the Armed Services Committee over Hebert's vehement objections. Herbert claimed that there was no room on the committee platform for the two of them, so he made them share one chair during the hearings, sitting cheek to cheek. Years later, Barney commented that it was the only half-assed thing that Schroeder or Dellums ever did in their political lives.

Barney hired the first person he interviewed for his secretary, Josephine Weber. Born in Brooklyn, Weber had moved from New York to Washington with her husband in July 1971 and set about looking for a secretarial job. When she arrived for a scheduled interview in Rep. Ed Koch's office, she was informed that the position was no longer available. But the staff in Koch's office told her about a job opening that had not yet been posted in the House placement office. The job was in Michael Harrington's office, as secretary to the new administrative assistant. Weber's job interview with Barney was rather brief. Glancing at her resume, he began by commenting, "So, you're from New York."

"Yes," Weber said.

"What would qualify you to work in a Massachusetts member's office?" he asked.

"When all my ancestors came to this country from Italy, they settled in Massachusetts," Weber replied.

"Where in Massachusetts?"

"In Lawrence."

"Guess that would qualify you," Barney concluded.

Weber had worked for seven years as a secretary in New York City but had no Hill experience. "We will be in touch with you," Barney said at the end of the brief interview.

Weber responded with a let me prove my worth, you don't have to pay me proposal, reminiscent of the strategy employed sixty years earlier by S. I. Newhouse to land a job with Hyman Lazarus. "Let me have the job for a one-week trial period. You don't have to pay me anything. If after a week you are not satisfied with my performance or if I don't like working here, I will leave," she said. Barney liked her spunk and agreed to the one-week trial period. She was subsequently hired.

"Barney was so smart, always funny, sometimes mischievous, and made the office a pleasant place to work," Weber recalled. "He is a kind and gentle person and behind that rough exterior is a teddy bear. If Barney liked you, he tried not to show it outwardly." For Weber's birthday, Barney handed her a book about Senator Edward Kennedy and simply said, "Don't tell anyone."

Christine Sullivan, a legislative assistant in the office who later served as Massachusetts secretary of consumer affairs in Governor Michael Dukakis's administration, recalls that Barney never sat still. "He would be racing around with all those ideas, his rumpled white shirt sticking out, with two bottles of Diet Coke, one in each hand, believing that it was more efficient to carry two bottles because that way he didn't waste time having to go back to get a second bottle of soda," she said. "He was always moving, shaking, and doing," Weber remarked.

With his combination of imagination, creativity, and intellectual rigor, Barney was a star, a stand-out in the congressional office. Several Harrington staffers believed he belonged in public office, that he should have been a congressman, not an administrative assistant.

Stan Brand, who was working for Tip O'Neill in 1971 when he met Barney, called him "an extremely bright guy," "who seemed more like a backroom politician, even though he was only thirty-one years old." "I considered myself worldly," Brand said, "but Barney seemed to be on a different level in terms of his ability to move in the Congress, even as a staff person." Rep. Charles Rangel of New York once said about congressional staff: "There are two types of people in this place. There are members and there are clerks. Those not members are clerks." Referring to that comment, Brand said, "Barney seemed to defy that view that everyone not elected is a clerk. He appeared to be moving, manipulating, and interconnecting with members in a way that seemed a lot more sophisticated than I thought the average staff person would be, and he did so in a way that was mindful of his place."

This was Barney's first taste of life in Congress and he enjoyed being in Washington. He liked organizing things and going to meetings with members of Congress. At that time he worked closely with Bella Abzug, Patsy Mink, Bob Kastenmeir, Sam Gibbons, and Bob Eckhardt.

Tip O'Neill had a table at Paul Young's restaurant several nights a week, usually Tuesday to Thursday. His wife, Millie, had not yet moved down to Washington. "It was a place to hang out in the middle of the week. Everybody and his brother would come by this table. I don't know which lobbyist or company picked up the tab. It was where I learned my politics and government," Tom Oliphant of the *Boston Globe* said. He had moved to Washington in 1969. Like Oliphant, Barney often sat at that table and got a great political education there. "I went there the first time with Michael Harrington and Tip knew who I was from my days with Kevin White," Barney recalled. "I loved being there at Tip's table as one of the disciples. Besides, I was very closeted and repressed and had no independent social life then."

While working for Harrington, Barney always had a messy desk with papers strewn about and the top of the desk barely visible. One day, Barney left his lit cigar on the desk and then dumped some papers on it. The resulting small blaze set off fire alarms in the building. Barney claims not to remember that incident today but admits, "I've set fire to wastebaskets every so often."

That fall, while attending law school at the University of Pennsylvania, I wrote to Barney to tell him that I wanted to work in Harrington's office again the following summer. About two weeks later, I received a response from Barney saying that Harrington was delighted that I wanted to come back and that I should consider myself hired. He added, "Your salary will depend on whether you hit before or after me in the batting order, since the latter situation will swell your RBI total thru no merit of your own."

In early February, I received another note from Barney. He wrote, "In case you outlive me—dubious considering the top-flight physical shape I am in—I send you this so you will know how I want my obituary to look." The obituary that he attached from the *Washington Post* was headlined, "Morris Bealle, Writer, Softball Player–Coach" and focused on the performance of the deceased on the softball field.

Working for a freshman member of Congress can be a tedious and exasperating experience, even more so when the member, like Harrington, does not comport with the traditional role of a House member. "I viewed the job as essentially an educative function," Harrington explained. "A traditional definition of the role in terms of attention to detail and production of legislation was never one that interested me. I used the minor league visibility to raise issues."

As a freshman congressman, Harrington was an outspoken critic of the Nixon administration policy in Indochina. He raised the Vietnam War issue and the need to immediately withdraw U.S. troops from Southeast Asia repeatedly on the floor of the House, in the hawkish Armed Services Committee, in budget deliberations, in appeals to the president, and even in the courts. He was also a leading voice on the need for congressional reform and had delivered his maiden speech on the House floor attacking the seniority system in Congress. The *Boston Globe* described Harrington as "the liberal, the maverick, the intellectual warrior for peace and ecology, the young man who wants inoperative, antiquated governmental systems dismantled." Harrington maintained the image projected during the special election campaign, "He understands what's right and has the guts to stand up for it."

"At that time," Stan Brand pointed out, "it was not common to be a gadfly. Mike Harrington was one of the first." Cragg Hines, a journalist, who in 1970 served as a congressional fellow in Harrington's office, called Harrington "a total gadfly." "He was the person who sort of carried the torch but not the issue. Politics needs both the nuts and bolts legislator who puts coalitions together and the legislator who burns a little more brightly, more intensely and that was always Michael," Hines said. To Oliphant, Harrington's idealism and his "magnificent politicking made him exciting." "He was a jumble of interesting contradictions."

"The only good job in the office of a young congressman is to be the young congressman," Barney told Steve Roberts at the time. "I don't think I was as good at [the job] as I could have been," he acknowledged later. "You can't be better than the principal at the job." According to Barney, part of the problem was that Mike Harrington had little interest in the day-to-day workings of being a legislator. "Michael was an advocate. He didn't want to legislate. He would have been a better senator than congressman," he said.

"Here was Barney working for a congressman who wasn't interested in legislating. All of a sudden he was doing gadfly work. It was hard not to be deeply impressed by how well he did that. It was the first inkling that I got about Barney's versatility," Oliphant said.

"The only legislation that I ever worked on in terms of trying to get something passed was to make sure we got 'three deckers' for the city of Lynn," Barney recalled "It was a program for one- and two-family houses, a federal loan program. I remember going to a member from Massachusetts on the Banking and Currency Committee, Peggy Heckler, to do it."

When Harrington hired Barney in the spring of 1971, he was already thinking about running for the Senate in 1972. But once he realized that Edward Brooke was not likely to lose his Senate seat, his attention began to swing to running for governor in 1974, and his interest in politics shifted to Massachusetts. When there were no votes in Congress, Barney remembers, Harrington got on a plane back to Massachusetts. "There was jockeying and friction between him and Michael Dukakis over who was going to run for governor. Dukakis was on the ground and being in Washington was a disadvantage for [Harrington]," Barney said.

Barney remembers only one time when he influenced Harrington's vote. In an issue involving Alaska and the oil pipeline, some of the environmentalists were pushing for something that was being opposed by Native Alaskans. Barney recalls, "Patsy Mink was arguing with Michael. I said to him, '[The Native Alaskans] are being screwed over' and he agreed."

Barney said he would have advised Harrington not to abstain on a vote in the House to wish former President Harry Truman a happy ninetieth birthday. According to Harrington, his decision to vote present had nothing to do with Truman but rather with the institutional process in the House. He thought it was ridiculous to have a roll call vote on extending birthday greetings to Truman "just to get an extended lunch break."

Barney did not distinguish himself as an office administrator during his stint as Harrington's administrative assistant. "The combination of Harrington and

Frank as far as effective, traditionally defined administration was a disaster," Harrington admits. "Barney was the kind of guy who was great being what he is now, and what he has been most of his life, an extraordinary resource with great range, and great skills when it came to impression but would never be deemed a worthy lineal successor to Bill Wasserman as an administrator." A lot of administrative stuff needed more attention. "When you are an ideas person, constituent mail is not a priority," a Harrington staffer explained.

Barney was a force to be reckoned with, however, on policy issues. Harrington described him as a talented wordsmith. In a statement Barney drafted for Mike Harrington critical of Armed Services Committee chairman Edward Hebert, he wrote that the Armed Services Committee has turned from "constitutional watchdog to lap-dog of the Pentagon."

For many years, the opponents of the Vietnam War in Congress had tried unsuccessfully to end the war through the appropriations process. On November 16, 1971, Edward Boland of Massachusetts was planning to offer an amendment to the appropriations bill to prohibit the use of funds "to finance any military combat or military support operations by U.S. forces in or over South Vietnam, North Vietnam, Laos or Cambodia, after June 1, 1972," subject to the release of all American prisoners of war. Barney drafted a "Dear Colleague" letter over Harrington's signature, urging every member of the House to vote for the Boland amendment. In an effort to make the law socially relevant, Barney relied on the opinion of the First Circuit Court of Appeals in the case of *Massachusetts v. Laird*. In that case the Commonwealth of Massachusetts had challenged the legitimacy of the war in Vietnam on the grounds that Congress had never voted a declaration of war. The court rejected the claim on the grounds that Congress has constitutionally sanctioned the war by voting appropriations for it. Barney wrote in the letter:

> This decision by the highest court to rule on the war's constitutionality removes any question of the appropriateness of the Boland amendment. No longer can it be argued that the appropriations process can be separated from the legitimacy of the war. A vote for the appropriation—absent Congressman Boland's amendment—is a vote to provide the indispensable legislative approval required by the Constitution for the war to continue. The argument that policy matters ought not to be determined in an appropriations bill can hardly be relied upon when a Federal Circuit Court has cited that very appropriations process as conclusive evidence that the policy in question is approved by the Congress.

Barney also took on a very uncharacteristic role for a congressional staffer. He became more quoted in the press than his political boss. Barney did not set out to raise his own political profile at the expense of Mike Harrington. However, many reporters knew Barney from his days in Boston City Hall and found that if they needed a memorable quotation for a story, he was the place to go. When a reporter from the *Salem News* asked him about President Nixon's new economic policies, he commented, "I can't think of any time a chief executive has so thoroughly repudiated his own policies—except perhaps God and the flood. . . . [Nixon] admitted his economic policy was a total failure [showing] that things are even worse than we thought."

Several Harrington staffers recalled one particular article that appeared in the Boston press that was replete with quotations from Barney about policy issues and only in the last paragraph was it noted that he worked for Mike Harrington. It was the type of article that made congressional staffers gasp.

Mike Harrington, however, was not concerned about the press attention that Barney was receiving in the Boston area. "I knew what I was buying when I hired him. I thought Barney had already achieved his own standing. It didn't bother me at all in terms of the benefit [I was receiving], which was idea generation, the sheer range of that."

"I remember Barney in that era having multiple unfinished agendas, among them being a speaking commitment he had made," Harrington said. The two men happened to be on the same flight to Boston, and Harrington noticed that Barney had on a sport jacket, a tie, a shirt, a pair of pants, and sneakers. "When I looked at him with astonishment," Harrington said, "he shrugged philosophically. He had forgotten to take his shoes out of his car." Harrington found it fascinating watching Barney work. "I always wondered where I fit in this broader agenda as the employer-of-record," he said with a laugh. "I was never quite sure, but it was well worth the experience."

During this period, Barney was approached by several reform-minded members of the Cambridge City Council and asked to consider the position of Cambridge city manager. But he turned down the offer because of the commitment he had made to Harrington.

In March 1972, while serving as Harrington's administrative assistant in Washington, Barney won his first elective office, back in Boston, as the leader of a slate for the Boston Ward 5 Democratic Committee. In wards and towns in Massachusetts the voters elect political party committees. For many years, Ward 5 had been a typically "rotten borough" (an election district that has many fewer inhabitants than other election districts with the same voting power). It was heavily Republican and even though the Democrats could not expect to win any elections there, the Democratic committee members from Ward 5 had an equal vote at the Democratic state convention. In 1960, Kevin White and his group of liberal reformers had taken over the Ward 5 Democratic Party Committee in Boston's Beacon Hill and Back Bay neighborhood and had dominated it since then, winning reelection in 1964 and 1968. According to Barney, Kevin White's group had become "sort of the liberal Democratic establishment" and in 1972 was opposed by several other reform slates.

Charlie McGlue was one of the Democratic committee members thrown out of office by the Kevin White slate and he was still furious. McGlue's area of expertise was election law. "You hired him to get your opponents thrown off the ballot. That was his specialty," Barney explained. Although the Kevin White reform slate won at the polls in 1960, McGlue succeeded in getting two members of White's ticket disqualified because they lacked the proper residency qualification, and McGlue got one of those vacancies. "McGlue was bombastic, a terrible man, and we had him around for four years," Herb Gleason recalled. McGlue was finally knocked off the Boston Ward 5 Democratic Committee by the White slate in 1964 and his seat was taken by Kathy Kane, an ally of White. In 1972, McGlue dusted off an old rule that no city official could run for ward or town committee. This was a problem for the White organization because all of the prominent people then serving on the Ward 5 committee were working for the city. Herb Gleason was serving as corporation counsel, Kathy Kane was director of cultural affairs, and Kevin White was of course the mayor. Thus, all of the people who would win on name recognition were not eligible to run.

The Democratic committee election was scheduled to take place in March 1972, and a big turnout was expected because of the presidential primary. The White organization needed someone with name recognition who was not a city official to head the ticket. Barney was well known in the area. He had kept his residence in Boston and although he had given up his Back Bay apartment when he went to work in Washington, his sister Doris, who had moved to Boston in 1969, lived in the Back Bay three doors down from his old apartment. He would stay in Doris's apartment when he visited Boston on weekends. The White organization came to Barney and asked him to head the ticket for Democratic Party Committee in Ward 5. "You want me?" Barney asked, thinking, "I'm good at what I do but I don't have any broad popular appeal. I'm Jewish, gay, and an out-of-towner." Then he reflected, "Wow! Elected office and me, it has this magical quality." He agreed to run for the Democratic Party Committee in Ward 5.

There was another more socially conservative ticket on the ballot, made up of local people, including Charlie McGlue, remnants of a group that White's team had beaten twelve years earlier. Barney topped all the candidates seeking the Ward 5 Democratic Committee membership and the ticket favorable to Mayor White won easily.

Some friends commented on Barney's strong performance and voter appeal and urged him to run for state representative. The Ward 5 seat in the state legislature was being occupied by Maurice "Mo" Frye, a popular incumbent and a progressive Republican in the mold of Francis Sargent. Frye, a member of the Ways and Means committee, was the last Republican to occupy a House seat from Boston, and Barney declined to run against him. "We differed so little on major issues. It's a waste of time and money to run against an incumbent when you agree with him," he explained. Barney was also skeptical that he could beat an incumbent who was a capable legislator, a decent and reasonable fellow, and someone who had won reelection several times rather easily.

6

Running for the Legislature from Ward 5, Where Everybody Knows Your Name

SEVERAL WEEKS LATER, in April 1972, Steve Cohen, whom Barney had hired several years earlier to work at City Hall, telephoned to inform Barney that he and his wife, Shelley, had gotten wind that Mo Frye was planning to retire as state representative from Ward 5. The Cohens and other friends urged Barney to run. Barney visited Frye at his office on Charles Street, where the fifty-one-year-old Frye confirmed that he planned to retire from the legislature and turn his attention to his real estate business in Beacon Hill. He asked Barney not to tell anyone, since his plans were not yet public.

Barney decided to enter the race. But he had made a commitment to Michael Harrington to stay on as his administrative assistant through the 1972 election and felt badly about leaving him in the lurch. He admired what Harrington stood for and what he had done. Harrington's initial reaction when Barney told him he planned to run for the state legislature from Ward 5 was, "I had not thought about you in that context." Harrington, however, encouraged Barney to run for the open seat. "If you have that itch, you've got to scratch it," he said. "You don't want to go through a lifetime and have to say at the end that I wish I had done something like that." He graciously released Barney from his commitment, and Barney appreciated the gesture, especially, he said, because politicians often are not generous about other people's careers. "If Michael had said he didn't want me to do it," Barney said, "I would not have run."

One person who knew them both said, "It's good that they split up before the marriage went bad." Some Harrington staffers believed that their boss was relieved that Barney was moving on. But Harrington said recently, "I have no memory of any misgivings. [Barney's decision to move on] was not something I

97

viewed with ill-suppressed relief. It was foreseeable and entirely consistent with knowing Barney over a period of years." According to Harrington, his aim was to attract talent, use the talent, and, if possible, benefit from it. He was more uncomfortable with someone who wanted to create a permanent niche on his staff and turn it into something like a civil service position than someone who was ambitious and wanted to move on.

In June, when Barney announced to the Harrington staff that he had decided to run for the open seat from Ward 5 in the Massachusetts state legislature, Jo Weber, his secretary, and Ann Morcones, the cute and bubbly office reception-ist, began to give him grief about the way he dressed. They told him that his pants were horrible. "What's wrong with these pants?" Barney asked. "They're clean and don't have any holes." Then Weber pointed to the scuffed pair of shoes on his feet with the outer layer of leather no longer there and said, "How can you run for office in those shoes? They look like crap." Barney replied that he didn't have time to get shoes. "We'll get the new shoes for you," Weber said. Barney agreed but insisted that the shoes be black. He gave the women forty dollars, and at lunchtime they went to Hahn's Shoes in downtown Washing-ton and bought Barney, in Weber's words, "a decent and presentable pair of shoes."

When Barney told people that he was planning to run for the state legislature, he encountered skepticism from everyone except Bo Holland, who at the time was working in the Personnel Department at Boston City Hall. "I jumped out of my chair and told him, 'That's fantastic! It's a great thing to do. You'll love it. You will be a great legislator,'" Holland recalled. "You are the first person in City Hall who thinks it is a good idea," Barney responded.

Barney found that people clearly undervalued the job of state representative, and he had a hard time explaining to them why he was so eager to do it. One of the main reasons for his enthusiasm was that he had seen Michael Dukakis as a state representative in the 1960s play a major leadership role in issues of concern to Barney. Barney viewed Dukakis as a model in showing that "government can be an essential element in improving the quality of our lives."

"Putting your name on the ballot is a fairly egotistical thing," Barney noted, later remarking that "modesty is one of the first casualties of any political cam-paign." But at the time he had feelings of insecurity about running for office. Although he was at ease and in control teaching classes at Harvard and work-ing behind the scenes in government, always as someone's assistant, he feared the negative effects of his being Jewish, somewhat shy, rumpled in appearance, and gay. When most people decide to run for public office, they are resigned to the fact that their public life is going to intrude substantially on their personal life. For Barney, seeking elected office meant sacrificing a private life. "In 1972 I made a conscious choice for a political career over a personal life," he said.

In early June, Barney took out nomination papers and started circulating them in Ward 5 to obtain the necessary signatures to get his name on the September 19 primary ballot. In late June, as the deadline for filing the nomination papers approached, Barney resigned from Harrington's staff. That evening, he took the 10:30 overnight train from Union Station in Washington to Boston to begin his campaign for the Massachusetts legislature. He asked the porter in the sleeping car to wake him at 7:15 in the morning, an hour and fifteen minutes before the train was due to arrive in Boston. The porter, however, didn't wake him until 9:15, explaining, "We're running late, and this is where we would have been at 7:15 if we were on time."

The Ward 5 district encompassed Beacon Hill, the Back Bay, Kenmore Square and the Boston University campus, and parts of the Fenway and South End. Located in the heart of Yankee country, the district was overwhelmingly Republican and over the years had regularly elected Republicans, with only one or two slip-ups. The Democrats had won some legislative seats in the old Ward 5 in the 1880s during the period of Republican corruption scandals. Once, in 1941, when the area was a separate Boston City Council ward, a Democrat won the City Council seat for one term. That candidate was Jewish and his real name was Abraham Freedman, but he ran for the seat as A. Frank Foster. "The only reason Foster won was that his Republican opponent, the very smart son of a very prominent family in the area, was just about the most arrogant man in the world," Barney explained. "His name was McGeorge Bundy." He added, "The next year the Republicans ran a chair (meaning an empty chair or political nobody) and beat Frank Foster."

Although the district had been Republican for many years, Barney believed that it was changing and moving Democratic. Ward 5 in downtown Boston was a mix of wealthy residents, young professionals, blue-collar families, and many newly enfranchised students attending Boston University. The Bull and Finch Pub, a neighborhood bar on Beacon Street that later inspired the popular television comedy series *Cheers*, "where everyone knows your name," was located in the heart of Ward 5. Barney decided that the seat was winnable, particularly since there was no incumbent to topple.

Barney had little money to use for the campaign. His mother was working as a legal secretary in New York City at the time and sent campaign contributions. His younger siblings, David, who had just finished his first year at Boston College Law School, and Doris, helped him set up a campaign organization. Both had lined up summer jobs but chose instead to help their brother. David served as co-campaign manager, and Doris handled the state campaign finance reports and also did some typing. Ann Lewis, Barney's older sister, was active in the campaign at the start but then got involved in handling the George McGovern for President Campaign in the city of Boston.

Michael Barrett, a native of Reading, Massachusetts, and a recent Harvard graduate, was the other co-campaign manager. Barrett had met Barney several years earlier when he took an urban government seminar that Barney was teaching at the Institute of Politics at Harvard. Barney had helped Barrett get his first job after graduation in 1970 with the Boston Housing Authority. Barrett was later recruited to work in Allard Lowenstein's national voter registration effort and national Youth Caucus. When that commitment ended he went to work in Barney's campaign. Barrett had some familiarity with the Ward 5 district, having sold Fuller Brush products door-to-door in the area to help pay his way through college.

Although the conventional wisdom at the time was that a candidate should not overload the voters with enormous amounts of minutia but instead stick to thematic points, Barney took a contrarian's view and paid great attention to substantive detail. "Voters in this district want and will read serious campaign literature," he asserted. His lifelong faith in the printed word stems from his growing up in a family where the newspaper was king. From that initial 1972 campaign to the present, he has devoted considerable energy and resources to campaign literature in the belief that people read things.

Barrett remembers that Barney would sit down in front of a typewriter and produce "incredibly detailed bulleted single-spaced position papers on all these issues at stream-of-consciousness speed." At some point Barrett expressed his admiration about Barney's astonishing productivity, and Barney explained, "I am the best person on the planet in my first sixty seconds' worth of reaction to an issue but then it never gets any better after that." He didn't write drafts because, he said, "my first effort is my best effort."

"From the start of the campaign Barney was authentic. He did not slow down his speaking and did not change his persona," Barrett recalled. Because of his days working for Mayor White, "he had the advantage of having been publicly recognized as a character and as a person who did not necessarily rest on polish but rather on the speed of his brain and the speed of his mouth. People in the district were ready for that." Barrett recalls Barney's standing before a cluster of people in a living room at a coffee meet-and-greet and doing extremely well. "He was funny and smart and the entertainment quotient was always very high."

About ten days before the September 19 primary, I was in Boston visiting friends and headed over to chat with Barney at his campaign headquarters on Boylston Street, a small office located above an Arthur Murray dance studio. A few blocks from the campaign headquarters, I was approached on the street by a man in his mid-thirties. He greeted me, reaching out to shake my hand, "Hi! I'm Vic Themo and I'm running for state representative." During our brief conversation, Themo mentioned repeatedly that he was born in the district and had grown up there and knew from firsthand experience the problems his neighbors faced. "I'm not from New Jersey," he declared. He handed me some campaign literature that focused on his lifelong residency in the district, pointing out that he was educated at Boston Latin, Huntington Prep, Boston College, Harvard, and Boston University Law School. His campaign slogan was "Vic Themo understands the problems of the elderly yet understands the needs of the young."

I was thinking about Tip O'Neill's maxim that "all politics is local" as I continued walking to Barney's campaign headquarters. Themo seemed to be a credible and formidable opponent. I mentioned my encounter with Themo to Barney. He was facing three candidates in the hotly contested Democratic primary—Themo, Charles Tenney Jr., a legal services attorney with no previous political experience who was making his first run for political office, and Mark Townshend, a native of suburban Chicago who was working for the First National Bank in Boston. In Barney's view, Themo was a nice guy but not a strong candidate and was not someone he thought would hurt him in the primary election. He was most concerned about Townshend, a Princeton graduate, whom he described as smart and someone who knew, better than his other opponents, how politics works.

Barney's message to the voters of Ward 5 was that since all Boston city officials were elected on a citywide basis, representing the interests of individual neighborhoods and solving local problems, everything from trash collection to street lights, had become the responsibility of state legislators. His campaign slogan was "Put Barney Frank to Work for Ward 5."

"From my own experience, I'm convinced," he told the voters, "that the overriding principle of government in Massachusetts, at both the city and state level, is inertia. Government will remain at rest unless it's jolted out of it . . . by individuals, by neighborhood associations, or by elected representatives. At the city level I know the government structures very well and I know the individuals who work there."

During the campaign Barney focused on a better urban environment, calling for cleaner streets and sidewalks and a reduction in the number of automobiles in the city, particularly those driven by commuters. He proposed a pilot program banning automobiles from certain downtown pedestrian areas. He advocated lifting the legislative parking privilege on Beacon Hill streets surrounding the State House. "There's no reason why legislators can't walk or use [public transit] or pay to park as other people do," he said. He proposed giving residents parking preference and shifting revenues from new highway construction to mass transit. He pledged to fight to ease the property tax burden. He advocated strong rent control laws, better public health care, and more affordable housing for seniors. He backed several liberal proposals, such as higher welfare payments, and others that might be considered more radical, such as banning handguns for everyone but police, abolishing the abortion statutes, and legalizing, licensing, and regulating marijuana in the same way as alcohol. He recognized, however, that the chances were remote that the conservative state legislature would enact any of these measures. "I'm not going to be a Don Quixote. I can tell the difference between the Golden Dome and a windmill," he said.

None of these issues distanced him from the mainstream in that district. It had been liberal even when represented by a Republican. Barney never had a problem in that race with being considered too far to the left. Instead, he was perceived as an urban, street-smart politician.

Barney never avoided any issue on the campaign trail. When asked at Boston University about amnesty for draft dodgers, he bluntly commented that he favored unconditional amnesty for draft resisters and deserters. "No distinction between them as far as I'm concerned," he told a crowd of students. He proposed creating a super zoning law that would designate drug treatment centers, halfway houses, low-income housing, and waste treatment facilities in various communities so that each community would have its fair share of unpopular facilities. He suggested, only partly in jest, that there be a commissioner of unpopular facilities to administer the program.

In July, Barney issued a campaign position letter detailing his support for civil rights for homosexuals. This leaflet was directed principally at the gay community in Bay Village. He promised that, if elected, he would "sponsor and work for legislation to outlaw discrimination against individuals on the basis of their sexual orientation in housing, employment, public accommodations, or the sale of insurance." He called for the repeal of laws that regulate the sexual conduct of consenting adults in private and an end to mistreatment, harassment, and entrapment of homosexuals by the police. "I've worked with gay groups who've told me about how the state police set up decoys at highway rest stops. Now that's not right. Those people aren't hurting anybody," he argued.

"As a lesbian in Boston in the early 1970s," Ann Maguire said, she thought Barney's first run for the state legislature with talk about introducing a gay rights bill "was quite wow!" Here was somebody she wanted to support and work with.

In early September, David Frank phoned his mother and told her that he planned to take a leave of absence from law school. "I can't leave Barney in the lurch. He needs me. I will go back to law school in February," he said. In February, he would explain to his mother that he was not going back to law school because he found politics much more exciting than law and no longer wanted to be a lawyer.

Barney's established ties to local Democratic leaders and his knowledge of the ways of Boston politics gave him an advantage. "People in the community, ranging from highly educated professionals to working-class persons, had great affection for Barney and admired him from his days in City Hall," Doris recalled. "I remember a police officer coming into the campaign office and asking what he could do to help Barney." Barney's spirited campaign efforts energized a coalition of more than a hundred volunteers—students, liberals, gays, senior citizens, community activists, and other residents of Back Bay and Beacon Hill—who worked several hours or more weekly doing telephone canvassing, preparing mailings, and distributing campaign literature. On the rainy Tuesday of the primary, Barney stayed out campaigning at polling places almost until they closed. It was hard, he recalls. "The last thing people wanted to do was stand and chat in the rain."

Barney crushed his three challengers in the Democratic primary, receiving almost fifteen hundred votes or roughly 80 percent of the vote, with the other three candidates receiving a combined total of three hundred votes. Mark Townshend, who finished second, garnered less than 9 percent of the vote. Victor Themo, the lifelong resident of Ward 5, received only thirty-six votes. "Poor Victor, he got two votes in a precinct in which he, his mother, and his aunt lived," Barney said. Since only about 20 percent of the voters had been born in the district, there turned out to be no advantage to his being a lifelong resident.

With an overwhelming 80 percent of the vote, Barney was one of the biggest winners across the state in the primary elections. He was particularly proud that he won a higher percentage of the vote than Harrington, who had 74 percent in his primary election. But despite his huge victory, Barney was concerned about the general election in November.

"This has been a Republican district for quite some time and I am the challenger here. It's not at all in the bag. I will try to find more ways to meet people and talk to them, but it's hard to do without intruding on them. Door-to-door campaigning is out because of the fear of crime," Barney told a local newspaper. In a campaign letter that Barney mailed to residents of Ward 5 before the general election, he invited voters to call or write to him with their questions.

Much of Barney's concern stemmed from the district's history of electing moderate Republicans to the state legislature. The GOP nominee, Virgil Aiello, was a moderate in the Mo Frye mold, a former marine, and the vice chair of the Ward 5 Republican Committee, who ran unopposed in the primary. A graduate of Tufts University and Boston University Law School, he had a law office on Charles Street and was studying urban planning at MIT. He had been the director of the Beacon Hill Civic Association and was a longtime resident of Ward 5, where his family owned the well-known DeLuca's Market on Charles Street. He was a year younger than Barney and also a bachelor.

Aiello had been the Ward 5 coordinator for Governor Francis Sargent's 1970 campaign, and he went into the campaign with the support of the popular governor and senator Edward Brooke. Governor Sargent spoke at a function for Aiello at the Harvard Club. Senator Brooke accompanied Aiello to a campaign event with a group of senior citizens. "I'll never forget that event," Aiello said. "We were in a building for seniors and one lady told Senator Brooke that she lived with her mother in the building but that her elderly mother was too infirm to come down to the party room to meet him, though she would have loved to. The senator replied, 'After the meeting is over, let's go up and meet your mother.' When the meeting ended, we took the elevator and went upstairs and met the woman. It was a special moment and very touching."

Aiello's campaign slogan was "For the People of Ward 5: A Voice, Not an Echo." Aiello said that he tried to present himself as an independent voice and someone who had lived and worked in the neighborhood. His main issue in the campaign was the high crime rate in the district and the "fear that keeps residents prisoners in their own apartments."

Ward 5 also had a strong tradition of Independent voting, and the November ballot included two Independent candidates. One was Andrew Moes, a twenty-two-year-old recent graduate of Emerson College who received some press attention when he proposed allowing voters to file civil suits against politicians who break campaign promises. The other was Marcia Krafsur, a fairly radical woman in her mid-twenties whose campaign slogan was "Today's Problems Require Today's Answers." Of the approximately fifteen thousand voters in Ward 5, sixty-seven hundred were registered as Independents, fifty-four hundred as Democrats, and twenty-six hundred as Republicans.

In the campaign, Barney was incredibly detail oriented, micro-segmenting the constituencies and targeting voters almost block by block. For example, he produced a lengthy position paper dealing with the reconstruction of the bridge overpass on Storrow Drive that targeted the residents in the apartment buildings on either side of the crossover on Storrow Drive, the people who would be most affected by the reconstruction and resulting traffic tie-ups. Aiello remembers that when Barney came up with a position paper, it was not simply a one-page handout but three or four pages stapled together. Aiello acknowledged that he looked to see what issue Barney thought was important in what area.

No issue was too minor for Barney's attention, even dog litter. Mayor White had vetoed a dog control ordinance on the grounds that it would be too hard to enforce. But Barney felt the issue was serious and proposed an experimental dog control program for Boston using federal money that was available for hiring the unemployed.

The 1972 election marked the first time eighteen-year-olds would be eligible to vote, and, Barney recalled, "all those students at Boston University were going to be voting for George McGovern for president but they didn't know what the hell the state legislature was." Barney's solution was a campaign poster that featured a photograph of him with George McGovern. The caption read: "Who Is That Guy with Barney Frank?" The poster proved so popular that the Frank campaign had to produce more because they kept disappearing and winding up on the walls in the dorm rooms at Boston University.

Barney's campaign also targeted the new young voters with ads stressing the theme "Make your votes count!" in newspapers with large college readerships, such as the *Real Paper*. The ads pointed out that on November 7 readers would have the chance to vote against Richard Nixon, Spiro Agnew, war, racism, and oppression but that there were other offices at stake that day too, noting that Barney Frank was running for state representative because he believed that fundamental change was needed on the state and local levels as well.

Barney coordinated with the McGovern campaign to make sure that his campaign literature would be distributed with the McGovern campaign materials to all newly registered voters in the district. He also publicized, particularly among new voters and college students, endorsements he had received from César Chávez of the United Farm Workers Union, Ramsey Clark, the former attorney general under President Lyndon Johnson, Elaine Noble and Lena Saunders, the chairs of the Massachusetts Women's Political Caucus, and Allard Lowenstein, who in 1967 had organized the Dump Lyndon Johnson movement.

Barney described the campaign as "probably about as hard fought a representative campaign as you could see." He and Aiello generated so much interest in the district that more people cast ballots in the race between them than in the race for the U.S. Senate. The two candidates engaged in debates throughout the district from Emerson College to Bay Village, including one sponsored by the Singles Club of the Arlington Street Church before about fifty people in the church basement. At a debate sponsored by the Back Bay Association, when Barney was asked about his position on highway construction, he replied, "I am accused of do-nothingness on the highways. It's true. Even more, I'm for blowing up a few existing roads." Aiello recalls having fun debating Barney because he was so spontaneous and knowledgeable. "Below his jocular remarks and levity, was a candidate very focused on his message and careful about everything he said, not about to give anything away on an issue," Aiello said.

Like Barney, Aiello tried to reach everyone. "During that race I actually knocked on almost every door in the district," he said, "and I mean door, not just building." Aiello's campaign staff distributed a twenty-four-question survey in the district and received about ten thousand responses. "I did the survey to let people know that I was interested in what they had to say, as well as to develop positions on those issues," he explained. It was a small district geographically and the two candidates often crossed paths. Aiello remembers walking into a student dining hall at Boston University and finding Barney conducting a meeting with a crowd of students.

Aiello's roots in Ward 5 turned out to be too geographically limited to help him. The various neighborhoods in Ward 5 were distinctive and the district was not homogeneous. Furthermore, many people were moving in and out of the district. Aiello's strength was limited to a few precincts in Beacon Hill. Residents on the far end of Back Bay did not frequent DeLuca's Market.

In what would become a hallmark of Barney Frank's electoral career, he did not take anything or any opponent for granted. Although he had name recognition, resources, and volunteers, he continued to work thirteen- to fourteen-hour days as a candidate.

A few days before the general election, David Frank spoke with his mother, who said she planned to take a couple of vacation days from work and would be there. "I think Barney is going to win and we will need to have an election night party. Please bring some money so that we can have a party," he said. The primary and general election campaign had cost about eight thousand dollars.

Barney won the general election decisively with 60 percent of the vote, becoming the first Democrat to hold that seat in over thirty years and only the second Democrat in the twentieth century. He was aided by the eighteen-year-old vote and a large Democratic voter turnout for George McGovern in the presidential election, especially among Boston University students in the district. "I'm one of the few people in the country who can say he benefited from George McGovern's coattails," Barney observed. Aiello believes that he was really beaten by McGovern, who did better than Barney in almost every precinct in the district. "The eighteen-year-olds were hell-bent on voting that year," he recalled. "There was no stopping them and they were not voting Republican." Although the polls closed at eight o'clock in the evening, by law anyone in line at that time could vote. In the precincts around Boston University, the eighteen-year-olds voted in such large numbers that there were still students in line waiting to vote at ten o'clock.

A few weeks after the election, Barney ran into George McGovern at an event at Harvard and told the former Democratic presidential candidate that he had just been elected to the state legislature on his "coattails." At first McGovern thought that this fast-talking young man was mocking him. He had been traveling across the country and constantly hearing negative comments from Democratic candidates who had been taken down by him, such as one who had been the Democratic county sheriff for twenty-six years but lost with McGovern heading the ticket. When Barney explained the situation, however, McGovern seemed genuinely pleased by the news.

Later that evening, when McGovern returned to his hotel room, he phoned Bob Shrum, a speechwriter and media adviser during his presidential campaign, and recounted that story to him. Shrum knew immediately that he was talking about Barney. The next morning, Shrum called Barney and told him that Mc-Govern had come back thrilled. "Somebody had told him," Shrum reported to Barney, "that he had been elected on his coattails." "Did you talk to McGovern last night?" "Yeah," Barney answered. "I figured it was you," Shrum said.

Many years later, when Barney was a congressman, Virgil Aiello bumped into him at National Airport outside Washington, D.C. "Virge, it could have been worse," Barney said. "You could have won that election." Aiello did not run for political office again for twenty years. In 1994 and 1996, he ran unsuccessfully for the Governor's Council, a part-time position, as a Republican in what had become an overwhelming Democratic district in Boston.

7

The Gentleman from the Back Bay

IN 1973, on the first Wednesday in January, the traditional opening day of the Massachusetts General Court, the formal name of the Bay State's legislature, the 240 newly elected members assembled in the ornate chamber to begin the 168th annual session. The 1972 elections brought a new wave of Democrats to the legislature, a group of liberals who opposed the Vietnam War and were committed to civil rights. This new generation of politicians was there to rearrange the political chairs, to end the graft, and to bring about legislative reform.

The class of 1972 that entered the House together that day included four future members of Congress—Edward Markey, William Delahunt, Brian Donnelly, and Barney Frank. It also included Thomas "Tommy" O'Neill III, elected president of the class of 1972, who went on to become lieutenant governor of the commonwealth; Michael Connolly, who later served as Massachusetts secretary of state; and four new African American representatives—Mel King, a longtime Boston community activist from the South End, Doris Bunte from Roxbury, a fighter for tenants' rights whom Mayor Kevin White had tried unsuccessfully to remove from the Boston Housing Authority, and Bill Owens and Royal Bolling Jr.

Democratic state representative Michael Paul Feeney of Hyde Park in Boston, the new dean of the House of Representatives, who at age sixty-five was beginning his thirty-third year in the legislature, assumed the gavel as Speaker pro tem. Feeney had risen to senior member of the House when Nathan Rosenfeld, a Republican with one term more seniority, decided not to seek reelection.

"Michael Paul, occasionally Paul but never Michael, was a canny, secretive Irish pol, a master of old-line politics, a real character, something out of *The Last Hurrah*," Barney recalled. "He was the epitome of let's keep politics small and don't be expanding the vote." To Feeney, the idea of a voter registration drive was anathema, something, Barney explained, "that God would have visited on Egypt to get the Jews out." "You would be walking down the hall in the State House and if Michael Paul wanted to talk to you, you would literally pass a nook and hear Michael Paul whisper, 'Barney, can I talk to you?' You couldn't see him, only hear him," Barney said.

Feeney gaveled the session to order and the opening-day ritual began. Governor Francis Sargent and his Executive Council were admitted to the chamber. The governor administered the oath of office to the members as a group, spoke briefly about his optimism for the prospect of a short, productive, and nonpartisan session, and then he and the council left the chamber. In the ensuing session, Democrat David Bartley of Holyoke was reelected to a third term as Speaker on a traditional party-line roll call vote. Frank Hatch of Beverly was reelected as Republican leader. The legislature then adopted a resolution congratulating Congressman Thomas P. "Tip" O'Neill Jr., a former Speaker of the Massachusetts legislature who had later won the seat in Congress formerly held by John F. Kennedy, on his election as majority leader in the U.S. House of Representatives and adjourned for several days.

On Monday evening, January 8, Governor Sargent delivered his State of the Commonwealth address to the legislature. The governor proposed a total reorganization of state government, describing it as "a plan without parallel in modern times," urgently needed and long overdue. He outlined examples of the waste and duplication that existed throughout government and proposed eliminating unnecessary agencies and commissions that served no purpose. Acknowledging that he was a Republican but that most of the legislators were Democrats, he urged them to make the reorganization a bipartisan effort.

After the governor finished his speech, almost every member had something to say, apart from the freshmen or "rookies," whose role it was to sit back and be quiet—to listen and not speak—that is, except for Barney. According to his fellow rookie Tommy O'Neill, Barney grabbed center stage and everybody paid attention. "He had these great comments about the state budget and why the governor was missing the boat. He was wonderfully partisan and smart in his approach."

Despite the overwhelming Democratic majority in the Massachusetts House, a split in the Democratic Party between the old-guard traditionalists and the new reformers would result in many intraparty battles. At the time, much of the progressive agenda in the commonwealth was being advanced by the Republican Party, by progressive stalwarts such as Governor Sargent, Edward Brooke, and Elliot Richardson. "A transformation was beginning to take place, an ideological shift, a switching of DNA between the parties that would not be completed until the early 1980s," Edward Markey said. But Barney was interested in advancing a progressive agenda, and where it was necessary he would align himself with the Republicans, with whom he was able to build relationships without compromising his liberal positions.

Barney came to the legislature in 1973 with, in the words of Representative Max Volterra of Attleboro, "the clout and knowledge of a seasoned veteran." He called Barney "a dynamo right from the beginning," someone who knew immediately who the players were, how to work the system, and how to get legislation moving. According to Carlton Viveiros, a state representative from Fall River, Barney commanded respect because as Mayor White's chief of staff he had become well known for his brilliance and political savvy.

Like other freshmen legislators, Barney confronted the problems of having no staff to assist in handling constituent matters and committee work and generally too little time to get things done. Time management was his biggest problem. He shared a small, partitioned office with William Delahunt, Brian Donnelly, and Paul Guzzi. Guzzi remembers that Barney's desk was always a mess but that he seemed to know where everything was. From the office entrance, to the right was another small room with desks for several other representatives, including James Smith of Lynn, who was impressed by Barney's persistent questions to him about the rules of the legislature, which Smith described as arcane and confusing but very useful. Barney quickly mastered the rules and procedures in the state legislature and used this knowledge to his advantage.

"With Barney, there was never a moment wasted, no down time. He was always absorbing information. He would be reading anything and everything he could get his hands on," Smith said, "even in the men's room." "A few of us might take a newspaper to read on the toilet seat. Barney, however, would take the newspaper with him to read at the urinal. I had never seen that before, a guy reading at the urinal."

There were no pre-assigned seats for freshmen legislators. The seats they picked when they first arrived in January became their official seats. Edward Markey sat down in seat number 67, and Barney Frank sat down next to him in seat number 68. "That was the first time I met him and for the next four years we were sitting next to each other," Markey said.

Markey couldn't help noticing the unpolished shoes with holes in the bottom that his colleague wore every day. He soon understood, however, that Barney had more important things on his mind than having his shoes resoled or attending to his wardrobe. "Barney's suits and shirts reflected a philosophical view that ideas and thoughts rather than clothes make the man," he said. As minority leader Frank Hatch put it, "He looked a little like an unmade bed, but who cares about that?" Many of Barney's colleagues had opinions about how he dressed. Speaker David Bartley said, "Barney dressed about as good as Second Hand

Rose." And James Smith remarked, "Barney had a unique look that in a way reminded me of Groucho Marx—cigar, sloppy, overweight, misdressed. It was a look that only he could pull off."

Barney was assigned to two committees, Transportation and Social Welfare, and committee work became his top priority. It was a busy time for him as he balanced his work as a state legislator with several teaching jobs.

After only six weeks in the legislature, Barney was featured in the *Boston Globe* in a column by Mike Barnicle, published February 15, 1973, and titled "Barney Frank—the 'pols' can't understand him." The column describes Barney as "a rare commodity on Beacon Hill."

> He's young. He's bright. He's honest and he knows what he's doing. . . . Barney Frank is a "rep." He's a guy who feels that his main job is "public education and advocacy." To some of his 239 fellow "reps" he's kind of hard to figure. He has no law practice. He has no insurance or real estate business and he's not on the make for some other job. He's a full time State Representative and every day he's there in the State House fighting for the 40,000 people who live in his Back Bay–Beacon Hill district. "The pols" can't understand him because Frank is a guy who speaks out about [issues].

The Democratic and Republican leadership respected Barney's ability to debate and to persuade colleagues to vote for a bill. Frank Hatch remembers Barney's spontaneous sense of humor, something unique in the legislature. "He knew how to phrase issues, how to phrase comments in a way that I don't think anybody else had done or has done since in the legislature. I can't think of anyone like Barney. He always had a quip in debate. He could be just devastating and at the same time funny and that is a rare combination. With his wit he managed to present some very unpopular positions which others couldn't begin to do." The Democratic Speaker, David Bartley, recalled Barney's ability to laugh at himself, "which most of the liberals just never understood." "Many liberals thought they were better than you, and they were not only right but morally right. Barney was bright enough to know that's not the way you do it."

Barney's fervent idealism shaped his liberal record in the state legislature. He took public stands on controversial and sensitive issues, speaking out on the ones he cared most about— busing, housing, abortion, gay rights, and affirmative action. The first bill he introduced, on January 4, 1973, prohibited discrimination in housing, insurance, employment, and public accommodation based on sexual preference. It was the first gay rights bill filed in the history of Massachusetts. Another gay rights bill he sponsored that same day would have repealed the centuries-old prohibition in the law against adultery, fornication, unnatural acts, crimes against nature, and lewd and lascivious cohabitation, which he considered to be state interference with people's sex lives. "The ranks of us out on the street would be considerably thinned if police actually enforced the law," he said.

Generally when a legislator has baggage, he tries to hide it and avoid suspicion by not being identified with that issue. But not Barney. "I was not in a position to come out, but I promised myself I would never back away from the issue in a public policy sense. When I sponsored a gay rights bill, I was scared to death," he told *Newsweek* in 1989. It was a struggle. Some legislators derogatorily referred to it as "the Frank fag bill." "At least the bigots were honest," Barney said. "They were very straightforward in their anti–gay and lesbian feelings, saying, 'We don't want to hire fags. We don't want some dyke working for us. We want to be able to fire them. They are undesirable and no good, and no one ought to have to associate with them in the workplace or anywhere else, and we're against your bill.'"

The first hearing on gay rights legislation was that spring before the Commerce and Labor Committee, because the bill prohibited discrimination against gays in employment and in housing. Barney was a little nervous as he sat waiting to testify in support of his bill. He wondered, "Are they going to ask me if I am gay since I am an unmarried thirty-three-year-old?"

Royal Bolling Jr., a freshman legislator on the committee, supported Barney. His statement, "I know what you're talking about in terms of discrimination because I am black. As a black man I am sensitive to injustice and it is very similar," had a lasting effect on Barney. "There is something about the experience of being discriminated against unfairly. There is something about being denied your rights because of some element . . . that you can't control. It is something about being the victim of that kind of discrimination that makes you sympathetic with other victims of discrimination," Barney said.

Barney began his testimony by noting that when he ran for office from Ward 5, he met with homosexuals in the Back Bay district and became familiar with their problems. "You have to talk to pols on their terms," he explained. "On this bill, I told them that this is a constituent service and the homosexuals deserve the same kind of service from me that they give their people. They accept those terms. They don't accept moral superiority. I don't want to be a Bella Abzug. I want to get things done." He attempted to minimize the moral issue of homosexuality by telling the committee members that the bill was not a statement of support for homosexual rights but simply a request from one group of citizens to work on the same terms as everybody else.

When Barney's bill to repeal the prohibition against certain sexual acts came to the floor for a vote on June 6, 1973, he spoke eloquently in support of the measure, arguing that the laws that make it criminal for homosexuals to engage in sexual activities by mutual consent "serve no reasonable public purpose" and are "a terrible prejudice against a minority." "Stigmatizing these individuals exemplifies some of the oppression of minorities we ought to get away from." Private conduct between two people ought to be their business, he said and expressed his hope that that would be the predominant view some day.

Democrat J. Louis LeBlanc from New Bedford, who strongly opposed "deleting crimes against nature and other unnatural acts," urged his colleagues to vote against the bill because in his view if the bill passed, homosexuals in Barney Frank's district "would be free to go elsewhere in the commonwealth" and other legislators would then have trouble. "We'd be wise to leave well enough alone," he cautioned. The bill was soundly defeated.

Barney was not surprised by the result and vowed to introduce gay rights legislation again during the next session. He believed that the bill would have received more votes if it had been by secret ballot. Jim Segel recalls that Barney was not discouraged by the two dozen or so votes for his bill and that he had said to Segel, "If we start now, maybe in twenty years it will change like civil rights."

Every year Barney persuaded more members to support the bill outlawing discrimination against gays in the workplace and in housing. One such member was Joseph DeNucci of Newton, a former professional boxer, who stood up and said that he supported the bill because it is just about ending discrimination and he knew what discrimination is like. Ann Maguire, the gay and lesbian rights activist, said that she will always be grateful to Barney for his support for a gay rights bill and what it meant in those days. "It took a tremendous amount of bravery."

Barney favored a bill to legalize at the state level some forms of gambling, including low-stakes betting on sports teams. Frank Hatch, the minority leader, John Ames, the minority whip, and several other old-time Yankees did not think it was proper for people to bet even a dollar on a baseball or football game and tried to shape the debate as a morality issue. In a speech before the legislature, Barney said, "For many people, their entertainment is to go to their house on Cape Cod or to their place on the beach in Maine. They look forward to getting away to their cottage in the mountains in New Hampshire. But for many other people, there is no place to go. Their only enjoyment many weekends is to just sit at home and watch on television those games that they bet on." He drew on H. L. Mencken's definition of Puritanism to remind his colleagues that there are some people who "have the haunting fear that someone somewhere might be having a good time." "In a two-minute speech, Barney was able to puncture their balloon and deflate the morals of the side that has all the entertainment and shift the whole debate," Ed Markey recalled.

Barney was a strong advocate of using redistricting to give underrepresented minority groups a legislative voice in the Senate, and during his first year in the legislature he spearheaded the effort to create a district in Boston that would insure the election of a black senator. At the time there had never been an African American member of the Massachusetts Senate. The four new African American representatives who entered the House in January 1973 had won in the November 1972 elections in part because they came from single-member districts. Mel King, Bill Owens, Doris Bunte, and Royal Bolling Jr. joined Royal Bolling Sr., a veteran old-school politician from Roxbury elected to the legislature in 1968. The addition of these four representatives meant that for the first time there were enough black legislators to form a black caucus.

Redistricting was necessary in 1973 to reflect population changes in the state and would involve every House and Senate seat. Each Senate district had between 140,000 and 200,000 people. Boston at that time had a population of about 640,000 people, of whom roughly 525,000 or 82 percent were white and 105,000 or 16 percent were black. Historically, the black neighborhoods in Boston had been split and divided among several senatorial districts. Some House districts had a majority of black constituents but there had never been a senatorial district with a majority of black constituents. The population of Roxbury, located in the center of Boston, had grown, but Roxbury had been divided into four pieces, each of which was part of a larger white Senate district.

The largest block of some 45,000 black voters in Roxbury was distributed among several wards in the heavily Irish South Boston Senate district represented by Senate majority whip William "Billy" Bulger. Bulger's district had three times as many white voters as black voters. Bulger liked that arrangement because there were not enough black voters in the district for a black candidate to win. But by 1973 there were enough black voters that if two white ethnic candidates and a black candidate ran in the Democratic primary, the two white candidates would split the votes in South Boston and the black candidate could win the primary. Bulger discouraged others from running against him in a primary, maintaining that "if you run against me you will give the seat to them." Bulger did not want to see his district changed.

The members of the Black Caucus complained that Massachusetts had never had a black state senator because the Roxbury district had been pulled apart. Barney believes now that the Black Caucus could have made out a winning case under the Voting Rights Act. At the time he decided that it would be wrong not to meet this historical challenge and determined to change it. He led a block of energetic liberal Democrats in the House, including Jim Segel, Paul Guzzi, Michael Connolly, James Smith, and others, who joined forces with the Black Caucus in an effort to create, through redistricting, a district in Boston that would guarantee election of a black senator.

"We were under a great deal of pressure to back off," Guzzi recalled. "The real pressure was coming from the Senate because it impacted a Senate seat. The tradition had been that neither branch would interfere or intervene in the other body's redistricting."

"The black Senate seat fight for us started out as a lark," Kay Gibbs, who managed Doris Bunte's campaign for state representative and subsequently became the staff director of the Black Caucus, said. "Never did I think, in my wildest dreams, that we could accomplish this. Barney, however, thought if we worked hard enough we could win."

The effort gained momentum as the press started to focus public attention on the issue. The coalition of liberal Democrats and Black Caucus members treated the effort like a political campaign, trying to gain additional votes every day by lobbying individual representatives. "Barney was the ringleader of that effort," Gibbs said. "The fight to create a black Senate district brought out the best in him. He is a natural leader. There is no question in my mind that we would not have won if it had not been for Barney's persistent ability to figure out how to put together coalitions and his powers of persuasion."

Barney and the Republican leader in the House, Frank Hatch, who were closely aligned on many issues in those early years, became the public face of the effort to create a black senatorial district in Boston, speaking regularly to the press. "This is not giving blacks special privilege. It is only giving a community proper representation," Barney argued.

During the debate in the House on the redistricting bill, George Keverian of Everett, the chairman of the House Redistricting Committee, argued that the Senate redistricting plan would not preclude a black from being elected senator. Keverian opposed the measure proposed by the Black Caucus because it would divide three wards in Boston. He claimed that the redistricting map was drawn "with an eye to maintaining neighborhood cohesion." Barney disagreed. "Boston's ward lines have as much logical coherence as the Austro-Hungarian Empire."

A legislative bill was the only way to get redistricting without going to court, something the Democratic leadership wanted to avoid. At the time, the Massachusetts House and Senate drafted and approved separate redistricting bills, which were sent to the governor. The House coalition consisting of liberal Democrats, the five members of the Black Caucus, and moderate Republicans urged the governor to veto any Senate redistricting bill that did not create a black senatorial district in Boston. On May 30, Governor Sargent vetoed the Senate redistricting bill because, he said, "I will not approve a plan that, in effect, disenfranchises a large number of the commonwealth's citizens." The next day the Senate moved swiftly to override the governor's veto by a vote of 28 to 7.

"Usually you leave the other body's redistricting bill alone unless you want yours fooled around with. The Senate passed the House redistricting bill before the House had passed the Senate redistricting bill. Usually, it's done simultaneously. The Senate made a colossal error. In chess you'd call that 'check,'" Joseph Timilty, a former state senator, said.

When the Senate leadership learned on May 31 that Governor Sargent planned to sign the House redistricting bill, the Senate voted, shortly before 2:00 p.m., to recall the bill. Under the rules of the legislature, the Senate could recall a bill provided it was recalled before the governor signed it. The Senate planned to use the House redistricting bill as leverage to influence House members to vote to override the governor's veto of the Senate redistricting bill. The Senate dispatched a messenger to the governor's office to retrieve the House redistricting bill. When the messenger arrived at the governor's office, he was informed that Governor Sargent had signed the House redistricting bill at 1:45 p.m. "There are people who are convinced that they played around with the time stamp. I have no way of knowing but I wouldn't be surprised," Barney said.

Eighty votes, or one-third plus one of the legislators voting, were needed to sustain the veto. Although most of the Republicans in the House supported the governor's veto, the coalition led by Barney needed about forty Democratic votes to sustain the Republican governor's veto of a Democratic-crafted Senate redistricting plan.

Barney worked feverishly that day to persuade undecided Democrats to support the governor's veto. At the same time the Senate leadership set up a base for their intense lobbying operations in the Senate Ways and Means Committee office across from the House chamber. Some House members referred to this as the "wrestling room."

Barney spearheaded the effort to uphold the veto during a dramatic debate in the House that began that afternoon at about four o'clock. Royal Bolling Sr. assured his colleagues that there was no way under the redistricting plan proposed by the Black Caucus that Senator William Bulger could lose his Senate seat. Frank Hatch argued that it is "a question of simple justice." He spoke of the pressure being put on House members not necessarily by the House leadership but by their own senators. "I have never seen as many senators on this side of the third floor coming to have fireside chats. Very few legislators will have arms left in their sockets if they vote the wrong way."

Ed Markey was lobbied heavily by the Senate and House leadership (except for Speaker Bartley, who did not participate in the lobbying effort) to vote to override the veto. It was a difficult vote for Markey because his constituents were not in favor of creating a black senatorial district. Earlier that day, Markey had asked Barney for advice and Barney had replied, "Do the right thing." Markey was one of the last members to cast a vote. "As I put my hand on the toggle switch to vote, Barney asked, 'What are you going to do?' I told him that I'm going to do the right thing and I moved the switch to the left to sustain the veto," he said. The vote was 139 to 85, 11 votes short of the two-thirds majority needed to override the governor's veto.

With the House voting to uphold the veto, the Senate leadership was finally willing to create a predominantly black Senate district in Boston. "They took the position that if the liberals wanted to give the blacks a Senate seat, we will take one of the liberals' seats," Barney explained. The Senate Democratic leadership took two very liberal Senate districts, one based in Brookline that included Brighton and other parts of Boston and the other in Newton, and combined them into one Senate district.

A lot of personal animosity developed over the issue of a black Senate seat, and it remained after the vote. Barney was out front on the issue and some of his comments were more inflammatory than those of other representatives. Billy Bulger reportedly carried around a newspaper article in which Barney had recommended that the South Boston and Roxbury districts be combined. Six years later, Bulger would become Senate president. "Bulger was furious because we took the black voters out of his district," Barney said. To punish Barney, his Ward 5 Back Bay/Beacon Hill House district, which had been part of Jack Backman's liberal Senate district, was moved into the South Boston Senate district represented by Bulger, a state Senate district he could never hope to win.

Before the vote, Barney had introduced a bill to establish a commission to study converting the parking lot at the State House into a park with an underground garage. The bill, which his Beacon Hill constituents strongly supported, had passed the House and was close to passage in the Senate. However, when Barney told Senate president Kevin Harrington that he would fight against the Senate redistricting bill, Harrington threatened to retaliate by killing the parking garage study bill. In late August 1973 the bill was killed in the Senate, apparently at the behest of Harrington. Michael Connolly and Edward McColgan, who had fought for the black Senate district, also had bills of theirs killed by Harrington. Barney was typically outspoken, charging that Harrington was using the Senate "as an instrument of personal revenge to punish representatives who had voted for a black Senate district in Boston." "I have no intention of sitting quietly by and being mugged by some political hoodlum, even if he is the Senate president," Barney told the *Boston Globe*.

Near the end of his first year in the state legislature, Barney recognized that what he did best was legislate. "My short attention span, jumping around, some of my weaknesses in other contexts became advantages as a legislator. I am much better at doing a lot of things quickly than doing a couple of things over a long period of time. When you are dealing with seven or eight issues a day at the State House, that becomes an advantage," he said.

Alexander "Al" Cella had been a state representative from Medford and Hubert Humphrey's campaign manager in Massachusetts during the 1968 presidential campaign. According to David Bartley, "Cella was the liberal intellectual in the legislature and was very able and well respected." Barney described him as "a bright guy and a good liberal." "He was short and fat and spoke in a raspy, kind of Mafia caricature voice," he said. Cella had bridged two worlds. A street-wise guy from the largely Italian and Irish city of Medford, he had graduated from Harvard and worked there as a teaching fellow in government before being elected to the legislature. While serving in the legislature, he attended Suffolk Law School. But when seeking a third term in the legislature, Cella took his opponent in the Democratic primary for granted and he was beaten by a bus driver, George "Chick" McDermott. "McDermott was the kind of person who would stray from his bus route and drop passengers in front of their houses in bad weather," Barney said. The more socially conservative Bartley, Speaker at the time, who was a practitioner of old school politics and a supporter of the patronage system, had hired the liberal Cella as a resident intellectual on his staff. While working for the Speaker, Cella had joined the faculty at Suffolk Law School, where he taught administrative law and legislation. "I kind of looked up to him as a model in some way," Barney said.

In December 1973, Al Cella said to Barney, "You ought to go to law school." Barney thought for a moment and replied, "Yeah, you're right." In part because having a law degree would make him better at his job in the state legislature, Barney decided to follow Cella's advice. "Most of the laws are state laws," he said. He also thought that since he didn't want to spend his entire life in the state legislature and would probably never be elected to a higher office, he needed some way to make a living after serving in the legislature. And, he said, "I decided to become a lawyer in self-defense. I went to law school because I was tired of everyone on Beacon Hill telling me that I couldn't do something because it wasn't legal."

Barney applied for admission to Harvard Law School in the fall, after rejecting the idea of going to law school at night because of high expectations among his Back Bay and Beacon Hill constituents that he would attend civic association and neighborhood meetings two or three nights a week Also, in the state legislature there are no votes before one o'clock in the afternoon so that members of the legislature could appear in court, and the judges whose budgets they were voting on accommodated them.

After reviewing Barney's application, Harvard Law School professor Charles Fried, the head of the admissions committee, who later served as solicitor general in the Reagan administration, called to inform Barney that he had been accepted. Barney expressed his delight and assured Fried that attending the school would not conflict with his job in the legislature. Fried replied that the admissions committee assumed he would leave the legislature to attend Harvard Law School. When Barney explained that his job was related and would help in law school, Fried told Barney that he would find that the law as he had experienced it in politics was very different from the law taught at Harvard Law School. "That's not good," Barney thought, "because what I am experiencing is reality."

Fried told Barney that he would have to quit the legislature in order to become a full-time student at Harvard Law School. When Barney later told Ed Markey about his conversation with Fried, Markey pointed out that when Harvard Law School had turned down F. Lee Bailey many years before on the same premise—that he would have to give up his private investigator business to attend Harvard—Bailey had gone instead to Boston University Law School and received the highest grades ever. Contending that Harvard's premise was faulty, Markey urged Barney to fight to get the school to change its policy.

Barney took up the challenge and succeeded in breaking the outside employment barrier at Harvard Law School. He called Herbert Gleason, corporation counsel for Mayor White, who was active in Harvard Law School alumni affairs and knew almost all the senior law school faculty. According to Gleason, "the other Harvard Law School faculty were more sensible than Charles Fried, who was a master of theory and ideology but with little sense of reality." Gleason spoke with professor Abraham Chayes, who had been counselor to the State Department during President John Kennedy's administration, on Barney's behalf. At the urging of the faculty, the Harvard Law School administration admitted Barney with the express understanding that he would be able to continue to serve in the legislature.

When Barney worked at City Hall, he had supplemented his income by teaching at the University of Massachusetts at Boston. But as a member of the state legislature he couldn't continue to teach there because the legislature voted on the university's budget and that created a conflict of interest. Instead, he did some teaching first at Boston University, a private college, and later at the Center for Adult Education. In the mid-1970s, to help pay for law school, he started doing a radio talk show on WBZ in Boston on Saturday evenings from eight o'clock to midnight. "I was gay and closeted, and had no social life anyway," he said.

Barney's favorite job outside the legislature was moonlighting on a television show on the UHF public television station in Boston called *Club 44*. The program was filmed in a large studio set up to resemble a night club. "It was a very funny show," Barney recalled. It had Lanie Zera, "who made people laugh," as well as "several acts, and some hosts." He described his role on the show, for which he was paid fifty dollars a week: "I would be sitting at a bar, almost like a Norm Peterson [the overweight accountant who anchored the bar in *Cheers*] and I would do a three-minute monologue."

During his tenure in the Massachusetts legislature, Barney was unfettered.

On April 10, 1974, the House debated a bill he had sponsored to implement the recommendations of the President's National Commission on Marijuana and Drug Abuse. Barney argued that the bill would "allow the police to concentrate on fighting serious drug problems." "Selling marijuana," he said, "should be illegal but not smoking it."

Edward Coury, a Democratic representative from New Bedford, spoke out against the bill, stating that he had read the commission's report and that he saw it as nothing more than "a cute way to injure the youth of the commonwealth." "The commission the president appointed is just as sick as he is," Coury contended. Later Coury took aim at Barney. "If it's not prostitution, if it's not fornication, if it's not support of rights for homosexuals . . . it's this bill [legalizing marijuana]. Mr. Speaker, I want to know when the gentleman from the Back Bay is going to stop," Coury asked indignantly. Barney replied, "Mr. Speaker, it is true that I have introduced bills relating to pornography, gambling, prostitution, adultery, marijuana, and homosexuality. But I am going to make a commitment to my colleague from New Bedford. I will keep on trying until I find something he likes to do."

Two weeks later, the Massachusetts Supreme Judicial Court, in a 4-to-3 ruling, struck down all of the state's obscenity laws as unconstitutionally vague. "People are entitled to know what they may or may not do under the threat of imprisonment or fines. Our general obscenity statutes do not furnish any guidance," the court declared. The commonwealth's obscenity laws did not define with the necessary specificity what types of sexual material or sexual conduct was prohibited, relying instead on general terms, such as *indecent* and *obscene*. This landmark decision, which grew out of the showing of the film *The Devil in Miss Jones*, erased obscenity laws that had been on the books since 1711. The decision alarmed the Democratic representative J. Louis LeBlanc, who described it as a "cancer on society" and called for emergency legislation. To fill the moral void, the state legislature's joint Judiciary Committee drafted a new state obscenity bill containing explicit definitions of *nudity*, *sexual conduct*, *sexual excitement*, and *hard-core pornography*. When Barney started to read the bill's definition of *sexual excitement*, one of his colleagues asked him to stop reading the bill's graphic passages. "There's a typical censor's mentality. The representative wants to keep all the fun for himself," Barney retorted.

Barney challenged the bill's definition of *sexual conduct*, which makes obscene "any touching of the buttocks of the human male or female." "I can imagine what would happen during football games," he said. "The center bends over, and the quarterback places his hands between the center's rectum and scrotum to get the snap. The quarterback does this publicly and repeatedly with tens of thousands of people watching him."

Barney offered an amendment to retain the provisions of the bill dealing with "harmful to minors" and "dissemination to minors" and to strike out all sections that related to adults. He described the bill as "mischievous and harmful" and objected to the bill's "perverted sense of priorities and purpose" in telling every adult in the commonwealth what he or she can read or what movies to attend. "I don't think we should tell a thirty-five-year-old adult what he can see if he does it discreetly. We should not divert the police force to the preposterous task of prosecuting this." He continued, "Dirty old men have rights too. No one goes to the Combat Zone involuntarily. What right does any member of the legislature have to say how others should enjoy themselves?"

One representative said that he and his wife had walked out of a movie that made him "feel dirty," but that he was "no prude." "Are we going to continue to be so permissive?" he asked. "The time has come when people have got to realize there is a certain sense of values."

"I want to know why we should tell law enforcement officials to march forward on people who are reading the wrong books," Barney replied. "If it is permissiveness to say men and women of forty-five can read the books they want, then I hope the age of permissiveness comes." Republican Albert Elwell opposed the Frank amendment on the grounds that "no one has the right to destroy society for all people." LeBlanc spoke out against the amendment, asking his colleagues, "Is this legislature going to condone filth in this commonwealth?" The Frank amendment was defeated 48 to 171.

Barney's personality, his clever quips, his insights on a wide range of subjects, and his willingness to speak on the record about issues other politicians would not touch made him a favorite of reporters covering the state legislature. Unlike many other Boston politicians, Barney made himself accessible to the media and always returned reporters' telephone messages promptly. At that time the Boston newspapers had far more reporters covering the state legislature, and it was the center of political activity in Massachusetts.

Barney was the colorful personality everybody wanted to quote because he always had something amusing or incisive, usually both, to say. When, for example, the press asked him to comment on the House creating an ethics committee in the wake of the conviction of two state senators for extortion, he responded, "Peer policing doesn't even work at West Point. The committee should be banned with saccharine as an artificial sweetener." When a motion was offered in the Massachusetts House to elect an ethics committee, Barney offered an amendment that said the legislators who got the fewest votes should be the members of the ethics committee because only people with no friends in the first place would be effective. He declared that you would not get him to serve on the ethics committee without a subpoena. Some say Barney had the most favorable press coverage of any politician in the state. He was also considered to be a very effective legislator.

Andrew Natsios, Barney's Republican House colleague from Holliston, who later served under President George W. Bush as the administrator for the U.S. Agency for International Development and a top U.S. envoy to Sudan, said that there are two kinds of legislators, "glamour boys and workhorses." He described Barney as a workhorse and said that the basic characteristic of a workhorse is "being effective and being able to get things done." "Barney could do that," Natsios said. "But he was glib enough, articulate enough, and humorous enough to always have a comment that the media would report."

Barney's media popularity and political savvy helped get his legislative colleague Paul Guzzi elected secretary of state in 1974. Largely as a result of Barney's efforts, a Democratic Party caucus selected Guzzi over Boston city councilor Lawrence DiCara and Brookline state representative John Businger to run in the primary against the incumbent, John Davoren. Guzzi was considered a long-shot candidate in challenging Davoren. One day Barney dropped by Guzzi's small campaign headquarters in Newton. The candidate was out campaigning but his wife and newborn child were in the office. Aware that television cameras were down the street outside the courthouse, Barney quickly led Guzzi's wife, Joanne, and the baby down to the courthouse. The television crew immediately recognized Barney, and before the television correspondent could ask Barney a question, he introduced Joanne Guzzi. As a result, a thirty-second story ran that evening on the local television news about the candidate's wife, who was back on the campaign trail with her baby in tow. Guzzi upset the heavily favored Davoren in the September 1974 Democratic primary, and easily beat the GOP candidate, John Quinlan, in the general election.

In 1974 a huge transportation bill was coming up for a vote in the House. Many legislators believed the bill was unaffordable. Barney, the liberal leader on transportation issues and the acknowledged transportation expert because of his work for Mayor White in that area, remained uncharacteristically silent during the contentious debate over the bill on the House floor. The debate ended and the electronic voting call started. The board began to light up with red (no) and green (yes) votes. With about two minutes remaining to vote, Ed Markey asked Barney how he should vote. Barney muttered, "Vote no." Then, when the Speaker was about to bring down the gavel to end the voting, Barney voted yes. "All of a sudden," Markey recalled, "there is a click-click-click and five votes on the board changed from red to green." Almost immediately there were five liberal legislators standing in front of Barney, asking, "Why did we vote yes?" "On balance, I feel the bill perhaps could add to a more diversified transportation portfolio," Barney responded in a most un-Barney-like fashion. "It was a very tough call," he added. The five members walked away scratching their heads.

When Markey asked Barney why he voted yes, Barney replied, "I got them to agree to put Victorian lanterns the entire length of Commonwealth Avenue." Commonwealth Avenue had no street lights at the time and it was dangerous to walk there after dark. Many residents didn't want garish, bright lights, and gas lights would not have given off enough light. "The Victorian lanterns weren't gas lights but looked like them. We had to develop a new light that was both aesthetically pleasing and bright," Barney later explained. Those lights became the signature for transforming Commonwealth Avenue back to the look of the 1890s and are still there today. "That incident shows his pragmatic side as well as his leadership skills," Markey said.

In January 1975, at the beginning of Barney's second term, Speaker David Bartley appointed him to the Ways and Means Committee, which controls appropriations and has jurisdiction over how money is spent. Appointment to such a powerful committee was unusual for a second-term member. But, Bartley recalled, "Barney's appointment was based on sheer ability. I wanted people who were able to think, who were bright, and could evaluate the problems as they existed in Massachusetts." He added, "There were 240 members of the House and there is no question in my mind that Barney was smarter than 239 of them almost put together." Later that year, when Bartley retired, the new Speaker, Thomas McGee, kept Barney on the committee." "It was a mark of approval and respect. It showed that I had arrived," Barney said.

Andrew Natsios was impressed that Barney always knew enough about state law that he could speak right up during a debate and, without doing research, make subtle arguments that were always "fresh and unusual." Natsios recalled introducing an amendment to deal with the inequity in the state tax code between public sector pensions, which were exempt from state income tax, and private pensions, which were not. "My grandfather was a mill worker in Lowell for fifty years and had a $15-a-month pension that was taxed, while Tip O'Neill, when he retired from Congress, would have a $125,000-a-year pension that he would not have to pay state income tax on," he explained. He proposed that the state tax public-sector pensions the same way it taxed private pensions, but with a tax exemption for the first $15,000 of pension income to benefit lower-income people. Member after member rose in the chamber to speak out against the Natsios amendment. Barney did not join them. Instead, he told his Democratic colleagues during the debate that he was embarrassed that a conservative Republican was proposing to correct an inequity in the tax code that hurt poor people and provided a loophole for more prosperous people who were making plenty of money out of state and federal pensions. "Democrats should all be voting for this. Shame on everybody in this chamber for beating up on the gentleman from Holliston for proposing something that is truly a Democratic amendment," Barney said. He was one of only half a dozen legislators to vote in favor of the Natsios amendment, which was overwhelmingly defeated. "For Barney," Natsios recalled, "it was a matter of equity and justice."

"There is no question that the Massachusetts House in those days was a complete dictatorship," Bartley said, adding, "I say benevolent dictatorship, which is the best form of government." Soon after arriving in the legislature, Barney figured out what the leadership was all about and would often clash with the entrenched Democratic leadership. "Barney is not going to follow a path just because it is there. Just because someone says this is how you are going to march, he is not going to do it. That is part of his value, part of his attraction," Frank Hatch said. Barney seemed to know how far he could go in opposing the Democratic leadership, but, as Natsios recalled, Barney always did so if he felt they took the wrong position on issues involving social equity and social services for the poor. "I don't consider him Machiavellian. He does understand the chess board. He knew which moves would get him closest to conquering the king. He could stay several moves ahead of other people. He never did anything to jeopardize his ability to be effective," said Andrew Card, a state representative from Holbrook at the time and later chief of staff to President George W. Bush. According to Card, Barney was never a gadfly. "He probably was a horsefly. He could buzz around and provide a pretty deep bite but he never caused the horse not to reach its final destination." Card remembers Barney as a leader of the reform movement, sometimes championing issues that were not in his own political interest. "That impressed me because he had the courage to stand up against some of the Democratic leaders."

Barney's popularity with his constituents soared as he became an institution in the Ward 5 district. He was totally committed to politics and government, often working seven days a week. The part of the job of being a state representative that involved the greatest expenditure of time, especially in Boston, was dealing with local problems and performing constituent services. If there was a problem that needed fixing, Barney was there carrying the ball. His biggest effort was in trying to preserve the residential quality and character of the neighborhood in the heart of Boston. When Beacon Street residents complained about the noise created by heavy truck traffic at night, he alerted the City's Department of Traffic to the problem and successfully lobbied the department to ban truck traffic on Beacon Street between 11:00 p.m. and 7:00 a.m.

Barney spent many evenings attending community meetings. These included meetings held by the two main civic organizations, the Neighborhood Association of the Back Bay and the Beacon Hill Civic Association, as well as meetings of the Fenway Civic Association, the Bay Village Association, the Kenmore Square Residential Association, the Beacon Hill Business Association, the Back Bay–Beacon Hill Tenants' Union, Friends of the Public Garden, and the Back

Bay Committee against Nuclear Energy. Tom Oliphant, who had moved to the *Boston Globe*'s Washington bureau, would occasionally return to Boston. "When I had some time to kill, there was nothing more fun than to go to one of Barney's community meetings on Beacon Hill," he said. "Barney knew the people who showed up at the meetings by name. Everybody there had an opinion on everything and something they wanted him to do for them. He had a disarming charm and gentleness about him. He could talk to a woman who clearly needed [a sedative] as if she was an aunt or something. I did that four or five times and had a ball."

Boston's Combat Zone, an area of raucous nightclubs, topless bars, adult bookstores, pornographic movie houses, and rampant prostitution in downtown Boston, bordered some residential neighborhoods in Barney's district. Many of his constituents were concerned that prostitution, pornography, and other forms of vice and public nuisances were spreading out beyond the existing Combat Zone. Women complained that while walking in their own neighborhoods they were sometimes harassed by men who assumed they were prostitutes.

In 1975, at the suggestion of the Boston Police commissioner, Robert DiGrazia, Barney introduced a bill in the state legislature to designate the Combat Zone as an adult entertainment district, in an effort to isolate and segregate the area. In Barney's view, this legislation served a dual purpose: it would remove prostitution and other forms of vice from residential areas and confine them to one small area where they had existed for many years, and, by legalizing prostitution, it would provide a way to regulate the trade and pimps would be mostly eliminated. "Prostitution conducted at midnight in a residential block of Newbury Street is a nuisance that ought to be prohibited but when it occurs in the Combat Zone, it is of no concern to anyone except those voluntarily involved in the transaction," Barney contended. The bill was not passed by the state legislature.

Barney believes that private sexual behavior of adults is "none of the state's business" but it is the state's business to protect citizens "from nuisance and disturbances" near their homes and businesses. Tim McFeeley, a lawyer who lived in Bay Village in Ward 5 and was active in the neighborhood association, recalled how helpful Barney was in dealing with local nuisance problems. When McFeeley and the association tried to get the Varas brothers, owners of two gay bars, Jacques and The Other Side, that were sites for vice and drugs and had been the source of an extraordinary amount of violence, including murder, to roll back their hours and make other changes, the owners would not cooperate. According to McFeeley, they tried to hide behind the banner of gay rights. Barney and Elaine Noble, who represented the adjoining ward, sent a joint letter to people in the gay community urging them not to be manipulated by the Varas brothers, whose only interest was to protect their profits. McFeeley, who later served as executive director of the Human Rights Campaign in the early 1990s, says he shocks friends by telling them that the first project he and Barney Frank ever worked on together was to close a gay bar in Boston.

Politics was Barney's whole existence during his years in the state legislature. His idea of a vacation was a trip to Washington to watch Congress in action. He had almost no personal or social life, the price he paid for being gay and totally closeted. Some of his colleagues in the legislature noticed that Barney sometimes seemed depressed. "I remember him putting on more weight or being lost in thought or isolated in his office. You could kind of track Barney's mood by how much he shared time with other people. I remember feeling sorry for Barney when he was struggling for a greater definition of his life," Card said.

"I came to really dislike much of popular culture because it celebrated love and romance and I froze myself out of that," Barney said. One notable exception was a romance that began in 1974 with Kathleen Sullivan, the daughter of William H. "Billy" Sullivan Jr., the founder and president of the New England Patriots Football Club. Barney met Kathleen after Billy Sullivan wrote a letter to him asking whether he might give some advice about how to win an election to Kathleen, a twenty-nine-year-old school teacher who was eager to run for the Boston School Committee.

Kathleen Sullivan grew up in a large Irish Catholic family with two sisters and three brothers. She attended Ursuline Academy, a Catholic girls' high school. After graduating from the Manhattanville College of the Sacred Heart, she taught school for a year in Bedford–Stuyvesant in Brooklyn and then for three years in Harlem in New York City. At the time she met Barney, she was teaching children with special needs at a school in the Dorchester section of Boston.

Philip Johnston, who dated Kathleen briefly in high school, described her as "very warm, fun loving, smiling, laughing, and very political." She ran for the Boston School Committee in 1973 on the slogan "Kathleen Sullivan: She's the one who cares about the kids." She ran an energetic and very visible campaign, spending considerable time out in the streets meeting with voters, and that together with high name-recognition as the daughter of Patriots owner Billy Sullivan enabled her to finish in second place among twenty-two candidates to win a seat on the Boston School Committee. At the time she served on the school committee she attended the Harvard Graduate School of Education as a doctoral candidate.

Things changed dramatically in 1974 when Judge Arthur Garrity Jr. issued a ruling on school integration and busing that polarized the city of Boston. Sullivan credits Barney's knowledge of history and pragmatic counsel for helping her to understand and navigate what she referred to as the Scylla and Charybdis of Boston politics during the ensuing desegregation crisis that prompted thirty thousand families to pull their children out of the public schools. At an antibusing meeting at Hyde Park, Sullivan stood up to the jeering crowd, telling them that their children were going to receive an integrated education, no matter what. Sullivan, currently the dean of development for the City College of San Francisco, said Barney's strategic insights helped her win first place in the School Committee race in 1975, when, only months before, people had refused to sign her nomination papers and she had been booed at public hearings across Boston.

Barney and Kathleen Sullivan started going out together in 1974 and dated for almost two years. They both loved politicking, and during that period every year one or the other of them ran for office. "Barney was very much taken with her. He really liked her," Barney's friend Mark Furstenberg said.

Barney attended several of Kathleen's family get-togethers at the Sullivans' house in Wellesley. Billy Sullivan liked to talk to Barney about business, because, as Barney recalled, "he claimed that I was antibusiness." At a party on Christmas Eve in 1975, Sullivan approached Barney and told him there was a way that he could help business in Massachusetts. Sullivan explained that the law required that a merger be approved by a two-thirds vote and it would really help business if the law could be changed to approval by a simple majority. He gave Barney several memos about the law and Barney said that he would look into it.

To avoid a conflict of interest because of his dating Kathleen, Barney passed the material along to a colleague, David Swartz of Haverhill. Swartz told Barney that about twenty states required only a simple majority. The bill sounded reasonable to Barney and he made clear that it didn't relate to just the Patriots. Swartz filed the bill June 8, 1976, and it was quickly approved in both houses. "After [the bill] was filed, I didn't have much to do with it. We didn't sneak it through. There wasn't much opposition that I remember," Barney explained in a deposition in a law suit subsequently filed against Billy Sullivan by several minority stockholders in the Patriots. Sullivan had used the new law to buy out the minority shareholders and take over control of the team.

Barney and Kathleen spent a great deal of time together. "It was a real romance," a colleague in the state legislature recalled. "Those two just looked great together. It was a very good fit and they always seemed to be quite happy together," Tom Oliphant said. In the view of Tom Winship, the editor of the *Boston Globe*, Barney Frank and Kathleen Sullivan were the hot young power couple in Boston. According to Oliphant, "Tom Winship really thought that [Kathleen] was the one [for Barney]," and Chris Lydon said, "Winship saw Barney as a kind of studly young squire as well as a politician." "They were both smart and fun

and there appeared to be genuine warmth and affection between them," former
Harvard Law School professor Lance Liebman recalled.

During the latter part of the period when Barney dated Kathleen Sullivan, a
few of his friends sensed that something was troubling him about the relationship. One friend thought that Barney's dilemma related to whether a rich Irish
girl and a nice Jewish boy could find happiness together, the so-called *Bridget
Loves Bernie* problem popularized by the 1972–73 CBS television situation comedy, since almost all the women he had previously dated were Jewish.

On one occasion, Barney remarked to a fellow representative, "What is it
about these Irish girls?" Assuming that Barney's problem related to sex—in the
words of a later Billy Joel song, that "Catholic girls start much too late"—the
lawmaker responded, "She comes from a very traditional family. You can't appreciate the influence of a thousand years of Catholicism, particularly Irish Catholicism." None of Barney's friends had any inkling of the real problem.

If Barney had had a choice about his homosexuality, he would have picked
Kathleen. "That is when I decided that I had to deal honestly with being gay. It
was unfair to Kathleen. I really liked her a lot. She was wonderful, smart, and we
had a lot in common. I realized that it was crazy. That was the last effort to avoid
being gay," Barney explained. When they broke up he did not tell her that he was
gay. "I don't think she was shocked at the time," he said. After his breakup with
Kathleen Sullivan, Barney never had another relationship with a woman.

On April 10, 1976, Kathleen Sullivan flew to San Francisco to speak about desegregation at the National School Board Convention. "I remember Kathleen
telling me that she was going to San Francisco and her father recommended
that she have lunch with Joe Alioto, the former flamboyant mayor of San Francisco, because the two men knew each other from football, and that started the
romance," Barney said. Kathleen Sullivan and Joseph Alioto were married in
1978.

In late 1976, at a charity dinner and political roast of Barney, Governor Michael Dukakis poked fun at Barney because he had lost Kathleen Sullivan to Joe
Alioto. The crowd burst into laughter. Barney forced a smile. The remark hurt
him more than Dukakis ever imagined. Barney didn't lose Kathleen. It was a
forfeit beyond his control.

Being back in Boston, near some of his favorite Italian restaurants, such as
Joe Tecce's, proved too much of a temptation for Barney. Soon after joining the
legislature, he gained back most of the weight he had lost. "I like food. I like
fattening food and I like to eat a lot of it," he said. "I can't blame anyone else. I
can't blame God or my genes." His signature dish was meat with a side of pea-
nut butter with Béarnaise sauce.

Barney decided to turn his appearance into a reelection asset. "I kind of made
a virtue out of necessity," he said. "There was no way I was going to win as a

glamorous candidate. You don't run as a five-foot ten-inch, 270-pound pretty boy. [So] I said to people, I may be fat and not too neat but that just shows how much I concentrate on my job."

Barney's campaign slogan for reelection to the state legislature in 1974 was "Neatness Isn't Everything." Under that tagline the campaign poster features a photograph of a characteristically disheveled Barney, overweight and dumpy, with a pug nose, a tiny mouth surrounded by a doughnut of sagging flesh leading to a double chin, his uncombed long hair shaggy and sprouting over his ears and collar, in need of both haircut and shave, peering out from behind his trademark thick black-rimmed eyeglasses. In this black-and-white poster Barney is seated by a desk holding his hands together with his fingers clasped, his nails a manicurist's nightmare. He is wearing a dark, rumpled sports jacket, which appears to merge into the black border of the poster, making it difficult to see where one ends and the other begins. Below the photo in large bold print are two lines: "Re-elect Barney" followed by "Barney Frank for State Representative."

Barney's sister Doris thought the poster was a riot. "Barney is who he is," she remarked. His mother, Elsie, was horrified when she saw the poster for the first time while walking on Beacon Street on her way home from work. Shortly after Barney's election to the state legislature and at a time when many of her friends were moving to Florida, Elsie Frank had relocated to Boston to be near her children. "I liked my job and was making good money then. It was difficult to move away from my sisters and cousins, leave all my friends, sell my house in Bayonne, and start a new life in Boston," she said. She went to work as a legal secretary for Morgan, Brown, a large Boston law firm that specialized in representing the management side of labor disputes. "That's where the money is," she explained. She lied on her job application, claiming that she was fifty-five years old when in fact she was sixty.

Tim McFeeley, an attorney living in the Back Bay, prided himself on being the first person in line to vote when his neighborhood polling place opened. He would arrive in the early morning, bringing a newspaper to read. On Election Day in 1974, when he arrived at his usual time, he was surprised to see that someone had beaten him to the polls. The first spot in line was taken by Elsie Frank. She could not wait to pull the lever to vote for her son for state representative. She greeted McFeeley warmly and said, "I hope that you will vote for my son, Barney Frank."

Two months earlier, Barney had entered Harvard Law School. "Barney Frank was a legend in law school," his classmate Charles Tiefer said. "First-year law students at Harvard were uptight and needed some laughter and Barney provided that relief." Another classmate, Amy Totenberg, said that Barney was uninhibited and independent, and his identity didn't depend on law school. "His eyes were on activities and concerns outside of law school. He did not try to ingratiate himself with the professors," she said. Because of the stories she had heard about Barney from her mother, Melanie Totenberg, who had worked closely with him on liberal causes with the Americans for Democratic Action, she expected him to be aggressive and rambunctious. Instead, she said, "Barney had this understated, bemused persona. His responses in class were sometimes cynical, often funny. He was quick as a whip in his responses, and did so almost effortlessly." She found Barney aloof but not obnoxious or arrogant.

Many of Barney's fellow first-year students were in awe of him not simply because he was a state representative but because he was a quick thinker, funny and articulate and unintimidated by any of the law school faculty. Douglas Ginsburg, a professor at the law school from 1975 to 1983 and later a judge on the D.C. Circuit Court of Appeals, said Barney was the brightest law student he ever had, noting especially his analytical abilities and how quickly he could think on his feet.

Lance Liebman had joined the Harvard Law School faculty in 1970. A summa cum laude graduate of Yale University, with a master's degree in history from Cambridge University, Liebman had graduated magna cum laude from Harvard Law School in 1967, where he had served as president of the Harvard Law Review. Following a Supreme Court clerkship with Justice Byron White, he had worked as a deputy to New York City Mayor John Lindsay, handling transportation and community issues.

In the spring of 1975, Barney took a course in property law with Lance Liebman, who, like most of the other junior faculty members, was concerned about whether he would be given tenure as a professor at the law school. Liebman had been assigned to teach first-year students the basic course in property law. It was a subject in which he had little expertise, and so he tried to learn as he was teaching. When he entered the lecture hall for the first property class, he noticed Barney among the students, sitting in the last row. Barney was a contemporary, a graduate student in government and highly visible on campus in the mid-1960s, whom Liebman had met while attending law school at Harvard. "Oh no!" Liebman recalled thinking. "That's all I need, to have Barney whose I.Q. was a million, embarrass me in class. I'll never get tenure." After the first class, Liebman approached Barney and said, partly in earnest and partly in jest, "Barney, can you please do me a favor and not correct me or embarrass me in class." "Sure thing, no problem," Barney replied.

Barney kept his word. "He was soft on me" Liebman said. "He didn't ask any questions, attempt to correct me, or make my life difficult, which he certainly could have." But there was one occasion when Barney could not resist speaking up. Liebman was discussing an advisory opinion by the Massachusetts Supreme Judicial Court on the issue of beach access by non-property-owners. Citizens who wanted access to the public oceanside land of wealthy property owners had put pressure on the Massachusetts legislature to act. The legislature asked the court for an advisory opinion on the proposed statute, which would have granted on-foot right of access for very limited purposes between 10:00 a.m. and 4:00 p.m. The court said that such a statute was unconstitutional. Barney, who had been in the legislature when the opinion was requested, could not control himself and from his perch in the last row, without raising his hand, launched into a rapid explanation of why the legislature had asked for the court's opinion. He explained how useful it is for a legislative body to shift such matters over to the courts so that they can then say, "The court told us it was illegal and so we couldn't do it, when the legislature didn't want to do it in the first place." "It was a great performance," Liebman said. He was named a full professor at Harvard Law School in 1976 and later became the dean of Columbia Law School, where he still teaches today.

Exam week in May 1975 coincided with a busy period in the legislature. The appropriations bills were coming to the House floor and as the leading liberal on the Ways and Means Committee, Barney was busy making the case to his colleagues on behalf of social programs. When Ed Markey, in the adjoining seat, asked Barney why he had a stack of law books sitting on his small wooden desk on the floor of the legislature, Barney explained that he had a final exam the next day. Markey wondered how his colleague was going to study with the legislature in session.

The House concluded its business that day by early evening. Markey went home to Malden and put on the radio as he sometimes did in the evening to listen to Jerry Williams, an aggressive, opinionated, and popular Boston radio talk show host, whose program was on from ten o'clock to midnight. At the start of the program Markey heard the announcement, "Tonight, substituting for Jerry Williams, the special guest host is Barney Frank." "I listened to the program more out of curiosity to see how he could do this when he had a Harvard Law School final exam the next morning," Markey said. "Listeners were calling in with questions but they weren't asking about contracts or torts."

At midnight, a new talk show host, Larry Glick, came on the air. He had the time slot from midnight to 6:00 a.m. Glick would ordinarily converse for a minute or two with the host who was about to go off the air. This time he said, "Barney, that was a very interesting subject you were just talking about. Is there any way you can come on with me after the midnight news?" "Okay," Barney replied, "but I can't stay long because I am going to be a little busy tomorrow." "Barney comes on after the midnight news and swaps a few stories with Larry Glick, then says good night because he has to get up early the next morning to do a few things," Markey said.

The next day, when Barney sat down in his seat in the House chamber, Markey asked him why he stayed over for the Larry Glick show. "It was the first time

Larry Glick ever asked me to stay on and I didn't think I should say no to him," Barney replied.

Despite how time-consuming his responsibilities as a legislator were, Barney did exceptionally well in law school. When his first-year grades came in, he was invited to join the Harvard Law Review but turned down the honor because he had neither the interest nor the time to do it. Barney told the law review editors that he had read *Tom Sawyer* and was not about to paint their fence. "I had no interest in [spending my time] doing sub-cite checking."

It was sometimes difficult for Barney to juggle being a full-time law school student and a state legislator. Although the House was not in session in the fall, during the spring semester Barney often worked sixty hours a week in the legislature. To keep up with his schoolwork, he often studied at his desk on the House floor while the legislature was in session. Occasionally, he dozed off. "When I would wake up and open my eyes, if I was surrounded by people with liver spots I knew that I was in the legislature, if they had zits I knew that I was in law school," he said.

Lance Liebman recalled that one morning in May of Barney's second or third year of law school, as he was exiting the State House subway stop at Park Street at about nine o'clock, he saw Barney entering the subway station. He asked Barney what he was doing. Barney explained that the legislature had been in session all night debating the budget and he had to take his securities law exam at ten o'clock. "I was just amazed," Liebman recalled. "He had been up all night fighting over the budget and was going to take a three-hour exam." On one or two occasions, when the House was in session, the school allowed Barney to take a proctored exam at the State House.

In fall 1974, Barney campaigned heavily for his friend Michael Dukakis in the gubernatorial election. Dukakis won the Democratic nomination and then easily defeated the incumbent Republican governor, Francis Sargent, in the general election with 56 percent of the vote.

About a week after the election, governor-elect Dukakis asked Barney to join his cabinet as secretary of transportation, a position described by one veteran Massachusetts pol as "one of the most powerful jobs in state government." Dukakis had first offered the job to state senator Jim McIntyre from Quincy, who turned it down. "Barney and I had been deeply involved in the anti-highway pro-public-transit fight," Dukakis explained. "Barney had a lot to do with Mayor White's fundamental decision to oppose the master highway plan. I wanted someone who was very capable and shared my commitment."

Barney agonized over the job offer. "I was playing on a touch football team in law school and I was thinking about whether or not to accept the cabinet position. I wasn't able to focus on the game, kept missing my blocks, and was having a lousy first half," Barney said. "I kept going back and forth and finally at half time made the decision not to join Dukakis's cabinet because I enjoyed being a legislator." According to Barney, with that decision no longer on his mind, he then played a great second half of touch football. After the game, he phoned Dukakis from a pay phone at the law school to inform him of his decision. "That was the right choice," Barney said, looking back. "I would have been torn if I had gone to work for Dukakis and might have felt compelled to resign in protest over his actions in going after social programs and poor people."

When Barney turned down the position, Dukakis named Frederick Salvucci as transportation secretary. Salvucci, a community activist and a leader in the fight against unnecessary highways, had a degree in engineering and city planning from MIT and was a bright and dedicated transportation planner, whom Dukakis later described as "an absolutely superb and outstanding transportation secretary." "It was one of the best personnel moves Dukakis ever made," Barney said.

Dukakis inherited what he described as a fiscal "mess." On November 18, less than two weeks after the election, Dukakis reported that the state faced a three-hundred-million-dollar deficit. Human services programs accounted for about half of the state's spending. A reporter asked the governor-elect whether it might be necessary to use a scalpel to cut human services in order to avoid a tax hike. He responded that he would use a meat cleaver.

In mid-December, Barney and representative James Smith proposed a tax package that would raise fifty million dollars in new taxes. "We knew in advance that the state was going to run out of money before the end of the fiscal year and that you would eventually have to raise taxes and that it is easier to act quickly," Smith explained. Dukakis, who had made "a lead-pipe promise" to the voters during the gubernatorial campaign that he would not raise taxes and had pledged to reduce the state budget deficit through superior management, opposed that effort.

As the leading liberal on the Ways and Means Committee, Barney became the point person in the effort to get Governor Dukakis to reexamine his pledge. Barney recognized how badly social programs would be hurt by the governor's budget. Because of his experience working for Mayor White, he understood what each program did and the impact it would have on the poor and the elderly. In Barney's view, you have to first determine what you need to do to take care of people's suffering and then determine how to pay for it, and that you cannot start with a self-contained budget box as the governor did. According to one prominent state legislator, Michael Dukakis had an autocratic attitude when he first got elected and believed that the decision making was his and his alone as governor.

At the beginning of his administration, Governor Dukakis invited about half a dozen liberal legislators who had supported him in the election to the governor's office for lunch. As the group was being seated at a long conference table, Barney poked Phil Johnston and whispered, "Where the hell is the food? I don't see any food?" Soon after the governor began speaking about his plans, Barney muttered to Johnston, "I am hungry. Where is he hiding the food?" About five minutes later, an aide walked in carrying one small brown paper bag and handed it to the governor. The governor opened the bag and withdrew the sandwich he had brought from home. The legislators learned that lunch with the governor meant bring your own.

The Democratic legislators hoped that the new, Democratic governor would give them the long overdue salary increase that the Democratic-controlled legislature had failed to push for during Francis Sargent's term as governor. Barney, considered by many of his colleagues to be a leader though he was only a sophomore legislator in 1975, was confident that he could deliver this legislative pay raise for the Democratic leadership. But Governor Dukakis refused to go along with a pay hike because the deficit was so huge. Some legislators believe that Dukakis's refusal created bad feelings between Barney and the governor that only worsened from there.

Barney's relationship with the forty-two-year-old Dukakis quickly deteriorated when the governor began, in Barney's words, "waging war against the poor." He cut back in nearly all the nonfederal human service programs that benefit the poor and the elderly and impounded funds for medical services for welfare recipients. Barney became one of the most outspoken and strident critics of Dukakis, a friend he had supported for election and who had offered him a cabinet post. Barney's constituents in Beacon Hill and Back Bay, few of whom were welfare recipients, were unaffected by the cuts. But to Barney it was a matter of policy and principle not politics. "Barney really cared about groups of people who were disadvantaged. It was genuine. It wasn't political empathy," Frank Hatch said. Barney acknowledges that some human services cuts were inevitable in the situation Dukakis inherited in 1974, but, he said, "by his own conscious, deliberate choices, he exacerbated the situation and inflicted social damage far beyond what had to occur."

In early 1975, Barney blasted the governor for his decision to deny a legally mandated minimal cost-of-living increase to recipients of public assistance. He charged that, in an effort to uphold campaign pledges to introduce no new taxes, the governor was scapegoating the poor. "Politically, this may make sense. Morally it is despicable," Barney said. "We have heard a good deal of talk about 'administrative toughness' and 'biting bullets.' But all we have seen to date is a blanket decision to punish the large majority of deserving, eligible welfare recipients by denying them the money they need to buy the basic necessities of life." Dukakis cut general-relief recipients, people who were getting less than a hundred dollars a week in assistance. Barney called the governor "a Robin Hood in reverse—he steals from the poor and gives to the rich," remarking that "only he could live like a king on ninety-eight dollars a week."

Dukakis continued to maintain an austere and frugal life style after becoming governor and shunned the trappings of office. He commuted to work every day on the trolley from his home in Brookline. "It is terrific that Michael Dukakis rides the subway to work," Barney said. "The problem is that he gets off at the State House."

The fiscal mess Dukakis had to deal with included the largest state deficit proportionately, as a percentage of the total budget, of any state in the country. Because of that deficit, *Time* magazine called Massachusetts "the new Appalachia." Barney, Dukakis pointed out, certainly did not create the problems, but he had been in the legislature and "participated to some extent and had to share some responsibility for it." "As it turned out we had to raise taxes big time; we had to cut big time," he said. "The bond rating services were killing us. We had to pay 9 percent in tax free bonds to cover the gap. It was a terrible year."

Dukakis admits now that he "personally handled it rather badly" and that ten years later he would have done things much differently. "I would have called in the Barney Franks, the advocates, the constituents, and the others and said, 'Okay, guys, here are the numbers. Now what do you want us to do?'"

In the spring of 1975, as the state fiscal crisis mounted, Governor Dukakis was finding ways to take liberties with and redefine the budget calendar. He asked the legislature, in a deficiency budget request, to use the funds normally allocated for June to pay the state's expenses in April and May. Barney came to the microphone on the floor in the House chamber and proposed to his colleagues a novel solution for solving the state's budgetary crisis, that Massachusetts temporarily eliminate the month of June. "In a spirit of cooperation with our governor, I am willing to take the next logical step and do away with the whole inconvenient month," he said. "I know it will be difficult for some people to get used to the idea that Memorial Day and the Fourth of July will only be one weekend apart this year, but any governor who can persuade people to ignore a three-hundred-million-dollar deficit ought to be able to get them to overlook thirty humid days." He made it clear that this would be a one-time-only thing: "I will give the voters of Massachusetts a lead-pipe guarantee that there will be a June next year." He went on at great length, developing his idea with growing sarcasm. "The governor knew in January that we would have to get rid of one month this year, and if he had been willing to bite the bullet earlier we could have abolished February instead of June, which would also have allowed us all to save on our heating bills." Governor Dukakis let Barney know that he did not appreciate being mocked.

One of Barney's most enduring and prophetic quips from that period involves Boston's "Big Dig." Thirty-five years later, it is still quoted in Boston. The Central Artery, an elevated highway carrying traffic through downtown Boston, was constructed in the 1950s. By 1975 the rusty highway structure was an eyesore. It had no merge or breakdown lanes and was in a state of almost constant traffic gridlock. When Frederick Salvucci, Dukakis's transportation secretary, first proposed moving the Artery underground, Barney asked, "Wouldn't it be cheaper to raise the city than to depress the Artery?" That project of sinking the Artery expressway to a network of tunnels below the city, formally called the Central Artery/Third Harbor Tunnel project, came to be known as Boston's Big Dig. Excavation for the project began in 1991 at a projected cost of six billion dollars and the almost two-decade construction of the Big Dig became the most expensive public works project in the nation ever at a cost of nearly fifteen billion dollars.

Barney attended a party held at Joe Tecce's restaurant to celebrate the appointment of the former state representative from East Boston and Charlestown, Dennis Kearney, as sheriff of Suffolk County. The position had become available when the former sheriff was indicted. James Smith was at the party and recalled: "Dennis comes over to Barney and me clearly distressed, 'I just shook hands with a guy and he gave me five hundred dollars in my palm. What should I do?' he asked us. I didn't know what to advise him. Barney instinctively said, 'Give me the money.' He went over to the man and said, 'He's not that type of guy' and gave him the five hundred dollars back. Barney had the street smarts to know exactly what to do. It was all over in sixty seconds. In the process the word went out that Dennis Kearney is not that type of sheriff and that the sheriff's office is under new management."

In 1975, the *Boston Globe* referred to Barney as "the leading liberal spokesman in the legislature" with a "flexibility that the old-line politicians admire." "A lot of other people didn't want to be the leading liberal. There was a wave of post-Vietnam conservatism. I got the job probably by default. It wasn't the most coveted position," Barney explained.

Barney was very liberal on social issues, but there was another side to him that confused people. "He was a little Republican on good government, ethics in government, cracking down on welfare fraud, and in dealing with public employee unions," Natsios said. The *Boston Herald* columnist Warren Brookes called Barney "one of those refreshing liberals who understand that the success of socially compassionate government depends on tough and effective management." As a state legislator, he was the chief sponsor of a bill to use computers to catch welfare cheats by cross-checking employment records of people who are working against records of those who are receiving welfare, unemployment benefits, Aid to Families with Dependent Children payments, and other such benefits. It also would check bank accounts to ensure that recipients of various benefit programs were not holding assets in excess of the amount allowed by law. This legislation would enable the state to run more efficient public assistance programs. Barney tried to get other liberals to understand that the best way to help the poor is to make the programs work efficiently. "Liberals ought to be tougher vigilantes on the trail of welfare fraud. You can't help the genuinely poor if you let other people cheat," he said. "Barney expected people to play by the rules and was offended by welfare fraud. Most people expect that liberals would not take on that issue but he did. It wasn't the stereotypical knee-jerk approach to the issue. That gained him a lot of respect with his colleagues," William Delahunt said.

Barney detested wasteful spending and government inefficiency. "It's the liberals' responsibility to try to save money because if we don't save money in the right places, it's going to be cut in the wrong places," he said. As a liberal he is an enthusiastic supporter of trade unionism. But he took the lead in efforts to reduce the powers of public employee unions in Massachusetts. He sponsored legislation to limit the power of the Massachusetts Bay Transit Authority (MBTA) unions because he thought they were out of control and their demands for salary and benefits were excessive and contrary to the public interest, and he wanted to curb what he viewed as the excesses of civil service and the intolerable inefficiency at the MBTA. Barney did not own a car at the time and commuted most places by riding the MBTA. He described the company in these words: "Never has one organization paid so much to so many people to do so little." He was outraged that MBTA workers were getting substantial pay raises without regard to productivity or betterment of services. He complained that MBTA work rules "required three people to change a fuse—two to carry the ladder and one to supervise." "You can't hire them, you can't fire them, you can only yell at them," he said with frustration. He wanted to make it easier for managers to discharge MBTA employees for poor performance. "I'm not looking to make it easy to fire a hundred MBTA employees. I just want to make it a reasonable task to fire one employee," he said.

"The balance has tipped much too far in the direction of the public employee," he argued, pointing out that civil service makes for inefficient, uncivil civil servants. In 1974, the Massachusetts legislature granted state employees full collective bargaining rights in addition to civil service job protection. "This means that public employees are doubly insulated from management efforts to increase productivity—once by civil service and again by their unions and the agreements they sign," he argued in a WBZ television and radio editorial. "It is virtually impossible to fire or discipline a public employee for poor work performance."

Barney championed a series of controversial bills to make public sector employees more manageable and the personnel system more efficient. He proposed allowing communities to opt out of the civil service system and run their own personnel systems. He wanted legislative changes to give public managers some capacity to differentiate between the majority of conscientious public employees and the minority of abusers and to make productivity achievable. "As long as we continue to operate a system which insulates public employees from effective management techniques, government in our state will continue to be inefficient, expensive, and frustrating," he contended.

He was the only Boston legislator to vote against forcing cities to submit to binding arbitration for police and fire wages, objecting to a law that gives control over tens of millions of dollars in city wage costs to a nonelected official. "An arbitrator neither raises nor pays those taxes," he told his colleagues. "I believe we have an obligation to pay well the men and women who risk their lives for us. But that doesn't supersede the democratic process on the local level, and that's what this bill would do," he explained. He believed that giving arbitrators the final say would mean that, in effect, they would be running the police and fire departments. Furthermore, an arbitrator, he said, "is not equipped to deal with the decisions of allocations of resources."

In 1976, he proposed repealing the law requiring that MBTA collective bargaining disputes be submitted to binding arbitration because he felt that MBTA employees should be treated the same way other state employees were. The previous year the legislature had raised taxes and denied a cost-of-living increase to other state employees but MBTA employees got an adjustment through arbitration. His measure was defeated by a vote of 84 to 138.

Barney, however, did not give up. In 1978 he bucked several labor unions to win approval of legislation to bring about reform of MBTA operations and collective bargaining, to cut substantial waste, and to bring greater efficiency to the MBTA. This bill strengthened the management right to control labor costs, for example, by hiring part-time workers for peak hours rather than hiring them all day, and by contracting out such jobs as cleaning and security. The legislation amended the MBTA enabling statute by establishing criteria that must be considered by an arbitrator in deciding wage issues. It required an arbitrator to compare the salaries of MBTA employees with those of other in-state public employees rather than of transit workers in other cities, such as New York, Chicago, and San Francisco. The Carmen's Union called this legislation the most antilabor bill to come from the legislature. In 1981, the First Circuit Court of Appeals, in a decision written by then Judge Stephen G. Breyer, upheld the validity of this legislation, overturning a district court ruling that parts of the law were unconstitutional.

Tip O'Neill faced a tough opponent in the Democratic primary in 1976, the year he was to become Speaker of the House, largely because of the school busing issue in Boston. O'Neill's congressional district included East Boston, an Italian community separated from the rest of the city by the harbor, and Charlestown, a tightly knit Irish urban village on the slopes of Bunker Hill that had been included in Phase II of Judge Garrity's school-integration busing plan. There was tremendous opposition in these areas to the busing plan. O'Neill was being challenged in the primary by state representative Edward Galotti, a conservative, antibusing, antiabortion candidate who waged a hard-hitting campaign against him. Galotti ran a series of campaign commercials that poked fun at O'Neill's propensity for foreign travel as a member of Congress, referring to him as "Trip O'Neill." In one memorable television ad, the announcer says, "Well, Johnny, it is time to meet your congressman," and then little Johnny is seen at Logan Airport waving to Tip O'Neill as an airplane flies overhead.

Barney's Ward 5 in Beacon Hill/Back Bay was part of O'Neill's congressional district and Barney offered to help. He coordinated a campaign rally for Tip O'Neill in a large barn owned by Kennedy Studios of Beacon Hill, just outside the Ward 5 boundary. "Tip came from an era when Ward 5 was 90 percent Republican and he didn't realize that there were many Democrats there now," Barney said. There were over three hundred people at the rally and O'Neill was impressed. "Barn," he said, "I didn't think there were this many Democrats in the whole ward."

O'Neill stood on top of a large printing press and gave a powerful speech against the war in Vietnam. "It was hard to get him to stop," Barney recalled. "People were yelling 'Hooray Tip O'Neill.' He was overwhelmed. To go campaigning on Beacon Hill and be cheered while forty years earlier he had been the arch enemy of the people of Beacon Hill."

O'Neill was old school and before the rally Barney had said, "Now Tip, don't call the women girls." But when Barney introduced O'Neill to Elsie Frank, he exclaimed, "How ahr ya, dahlin'. Oh, what a good lookin' girl—" Catching himself, O'Neill turned to Barney and asked, "Can I say that?" Barney said it was okay in that one instance.

Galotti's "Trip O'Neill" television commercials got under O'Neill's skin but had no impact on the electorate. O'Neill trounced Galotti in the Democratic primary with almost 80 percent of the vote.

Barney supported Morris Udall, a liberal congressman from Arizona, for the Democratic presidential nomination in 1976. "Here was Barney Frank, a state representative from Ward 5 in Boston, and the Udall camp had him cut radio ads before the Massachusetts primary endorsing Udall. His endorsement of Udall carried weight and had a big impact with liberals in the commonwealth," Philip Johnston said. Johnston was co-chair, with Tommy O'Neill, of Indiana senator Birch Bayh's presidential campaign in the state. Barney's sister Ann Lewis was the deputy national campaign director for Bayh for President.

Washington Senator Henry "Scoop" Jackson won the Democratic presidential primary in Massachusetts, though Udall finished ahead of Bayh. Udall came in second to Georgia governor Jimmy Carter in several primaries. Barney admired Udall enormously. "Morris Udall was such an appealing person, had such good judgment, and would have been a much better president than Jimmy Carter," Barney said decades later. "America would have been a different place if he had been elected. I think he would have been reelected to a second term."

In early 1977, Kay Gibbs, staff director of the Black Caucus in the Massachusetts House, responded to a request for a favor from a reporter, who was a friend of hers, to tell him something negative about Barney. He had been unable to find anyone to do so, either on or off the record. Gibbs said that Barney had one fatal flaw—he was loyal to a fault—and she criticized him for continuing to back Mayor White despite all the investigations and problems White was having. When the article appeared, Barney was furious. He telephoned Gibbs and angrily accused her of ruining his reputation. He considered her comment to be an act of betrayal. "It is my reputation and it is very important to me," he said. In 1979, Barney broke with Kevin White and supported Mel King in the primary.

In April 1977, when Barney read a column in the *Boston Globe* by Bob Healy that said Barney Frank was a leading candidate to run against Senator Edward Brooke next year, he promptly dispatched a letter to the editor at the *Globe* to put to rest the story that he was planning to run for the U.S. Senate. "Bob Healy's assertion that I am a leading candidate to run against Senator Brooke makes me feel like the ninety-year-old man hit with a paternity suit: while there isn't any truth to the notion, it is so flattering that I hate to deny it," Barney wrote. Nonetheless, in response to Healy's column, Barney received a campaign contribution for a Senate race. "It is hard enough these days for politicians to cope with the laws regarding contributions for office for which we are running," Barney said. "Only God and John Gardner [president of Common Cause] know how to handle checks proffered for nonexistent campaigns."

Barney graduated cum laude from Harvard Law School in June 1977 but put off taking the bar exam until February so he could concentrate on his work in the legislature. At the time he described his future plans: "I do not plan to practice commercially now, but will teach part time at the Kennedy School starting next January, run for reelection, and do some volunteer lawyering for the American Civil Liberties Union—only First Amendment, race, sex and penumbra stuff." He went on to say that he is not "a big search-and-seizure liberal" and that he has never been against "a little judicious immunity." In Barney's view, "evidence obtained by police officers who commit procedural errors while making searches in good faith and for reasonable cause ought to be a welcome addition to the trial process if it proves that someone has robbed, murdered, raped or burglarized."

In July 1977 Barney attended a four-day conference in Denver of the National Conference of Alternative State and Local Policies that was organized by some of the prominent political activists of the peace and civil rights movements of the 1960s, including Sam Brown and Tom Hayden. The conference attracted about 450 participants—state and local officials, rising politicians with liberal backgrounds, labor representatives, lobbyists and public interest advocates, and community organizers from across the nation. Martin Smith, the political editor of the *Sacramento Bee*, wrote that Barney Frank's "flamboyance" made him the star of the gathering. "Better than any other speaker, Frank expressed the conferees' scorn of what he called the 'New Liberalism,' the prevailing reluctance of state and national Democratic administrations to spend more money on social programs," Smith said.

Barney contended that the new breed of liberals, including Massachusetts governor Michael Dukakis, President Jimmy Carter, California governor Jerry Brown, New York governor Hugh Carey, and New York City mayor Ed Koch, offered impeccable liberal credentials on issues such as the environment, consumer affairs, and women's rights but ignored the unpopular issues of racism and poverty. "Politicians today understand that advocating on behalf of the poor is a very bad thing to do. They find if they're good on the environment, consumer, and women's issues, they can still get 95 percent of the middle-class liberal vote," he said.

At the conference Barney argued that it was time for activists on the left to adjust their strategies, to become more skillful in the art of politicking, and to develop new coalitions to push for a more liberal response from the Carter administration on many issues. "I was for Carter as a choice between Dr. Jekyll–Mr. Hyde and Mr. Hyde. I am almost completely dissatisfied. Life under the Democrats is going to be a whole lot like life under the Republicans," he said. He criticized the new Democratic administration for backing away from welfare reform and any effort to achieve full employment and for allocating more resources for defense, adding, "the fundamental flaw with Carter is his total lack of commitment to do anything for poor people." He suggested that the only way for the conferees to work effectively against the Carter administration's policy of deliberate neglect was to begin organizing opposition to Carter's policies that might culminate with a primary challenge to President Carter in 1980.

In 1974, the voters in Massachusetts had overwhelmingly passed a ballot measure promoted by the League of Women Voters to reduce the state House of Representatives from 240 to 160 seats in the name of efficiency. In January 1977, it was announced that under the proposed new House district lines for the 1978 election Barney Frank's and Elaine Noble's districts would be merged.

Barney had close ties to Elaine Noble and the idea of competing against her troubled him deeply, particularly because she had come out while he was still closeted. In 1970, when the National Women's Political Caucus was created, Noble chaired the Massachusetts Women's Political Caucus with Lena Saunders and Ann Lewis, who was working for Mayor White and living in Boston at the time. When Barney returned to Boston in 1972 to run for the state legislature from Ward 5, his sister introduced him to Elaine Noble and they quickly became friends. Noble endorsed Barney in that first campaign and helped him gain the support of the many gay and lesbian voters in Ward 5.

During redistricting in 1974, Barney volunteered part of his district, Ward 5, one of the largest districts, with over forty thousand people, and it became the heart of the adjacent Ward 6. Four of the ten precincts in Ward 5 went into the new Ward 6, which included some of the Back Bay, Suffolk, Kenmore Square, and the Fenway. Ann Lewis had shown Elaine Noble the map when the new Ward 6 was drawn and urged her to run because she could win it.

Barney stayed neutral in the Democratic primary in Ward 6 in 1974 because Noble's opponent was a woman from the Back Bay who had strongly supported him in 1972. Noble won the Ward 6 primary and Barney endorsed her in the November general election. The two candidates placed a joint campaign ad in the local newspaper.

Elaine Noble had grown up in the poor central Pennsylvania mining town of Natrona and moved to Boston to attend Boston University. She later earned a master's degree in education from Harvard. Noble had a long record of work in the community. The night she won the seat in the state legislature from Ward 6 with 59 percent of the vote, national television networks and national newspapers were there to cover her victory. Barney told the *New York Times*, "It sounds condescending and I don't mean it to be, but you could not have a better individual to be the first openly gay person in office. She's going to walk around this place breaking stereotypes just by her own style and intelligence. To meet her face-to-face dispels stereotypes."

The thirty-eight-year-old Noble quickly gained acceptance in the clubby male-dominated legislature. "Everyone looked at her kinda funny at first because they'd all read she was a lesbian. The funny thing is she's very popular with the members now. When we have a late night session, she'll be in my office with all the guys having beer and pretzels," the House majority leader William MacLean, a conservative Democrat, said at the time. "Elaine made a strategic decision to be closer to the leadership. Part of it related to the good feeling of being an outsider who was accepted," Barney explained. "I think she got a little too cozy with the leadership. In a couple of cases she voted with the leadership on some non–gay/lesbian issues and some of my liberal, reform-minded friends got angry at her."

Elaine Noble was not a one-issue state representative. She took on many neighborhood problems and became a champion of those related to the elderly. Barney and Noble worked together in meeting the needs of their overlapping constituencies, and in 1975, they held a joint press conference to endorse Mayor White for reelection.

Noble was adamant about seeking reelection in 1978. She told the *Boston Phoenix*: "I've worked hard to become a multi-dimensional politician. I am really wrapped up in being a state rep. I enjoy getting people new streetlights, helping them with snow removal problems. I enjoy walking into a pizza shop and talking with people. . . . My personal identity is caught up with being a state rep. It fills my needs. I'm not getting out."

Faced with the prospect of running against her, Barney told the *Boston Phoenix* that he would not feel comfortable being the vehicle for Noble's losing power and influence. "I have been trying to think of some principle with which I can justify saying that affirmative action applies to every other white male but me, but I can't find one. Elaine is part of two sorely underrepresented groups. If there is no alternative for her, I'll give up the seat," he said.

Both lawmakers were extremely popular with their constituents. However, about 70 percent of the newly redrawn district came from Barney's Ward 5, and of the remaining 30 percent that had been part of Noble's Ward 6, about three-quarters of the area had been part of Barney's district in 1972. He was considered the odds-on favorite in a race against Noble in the new district and was confident that he would win. Nonetheless, he was prepared not to seek reelection. He felt that such a campaign would be an expensive waste of liberal money and efforts. "What would we have to debate?" he asked. He was also concerned that he might suffer politically in the future by beating Noble.

Barney did not think that he could be elected to any other office of consequence. He quickly dismissed the suggestion that he run instead for a seat on the relatively powerless Boston City Council, referring to it as "an unattractive zoo." "There are two reasons why I will not run for the City Council," he said. "First, I might lose. Second, I might win." He also remembered what Joe Moakley, who had elected to the Boston City Council in 1971, in between congressional races, had told him: "World War II was better than being on the City Council." Barney considered temporarily leaving politics to practice law or teach.

When rumors surfaced in the spring of 1978 that Barney planned to drop out of the race because he believed it was important to have an openly lesbian person continue to be visible in the legislature, a group of leaders of the lesbian community asked for a meeting with Barney to encourage him to seek reelection. The group included Ann Maguire, who had been Noble's campaign manager in 1974, Sherry Bardon and Lois Johnson, an older couple who had been pioneers in lesbian politics since the early 1950s, Byrd Swift from the Swift Meats family, Pat Hanratty, an activist who was in a Ph.D. program at MIT, and several other local women. The group of eight women was accompanied by Joe Martin, a gay rights lobbyist and activist who, with Hanratty, had co-founded the Massachusetts Gay and Lesbian Political Caucus. Many of those in attendance had formed the core of Noble's first campaign organization in 1974. The meeting took place in the evening at Byrd Swift's large house on Commonwealth Avenue, a block from where Barney lived.

The group urged Barney to run for reelection and assured him of their support, telling him that though they helped to elect Elaine Noble, they believed he was more talented as a legislator. "Barney was far better than Elaine in knowing how to get things done in the legislature," Ann Maguire said. "We told Barney that it was really important for us that he stay in the legislature because he better represented our interests." "There was no comparison in their talent. We felt that Barney was far more valuable to the gay and lesbian community staying in the legislature than Elaine would have been. Also, Elaine had a cozy relationship with the Speaker and the majority leader that troubled us. Barney didn't know how disenchanted we were with Elaine's legislative performance," Martin explained.

Part of the disenchantment grew out of a feeling among some in the group that Noble had gone Hollywood, becoming a celebrity and forgetting about the people who had done the grassroots work that helped get her elected. "There is no such thing as an old friend of Elaine's because she is too interested in making new friends," one member of the group said.

"We knew that we would piss off some members of the gay and lesbian community who thought that Elaine was so invaluable because she was out," Martin said. "Besides, half of the people at the meeting thought that Barney was probably gay but closeted." "Even if he wasn't gay, he was the most sympathetic person that we had come across in the legislature and he genuinely cared about the gay community and what was going to happen," Maguire explained.

Barney knew they were right. "Legislating is a very strange business and I am good at it. I am not good at many other things," he thought. He had introduced gay rights legislation in 1973 before Noble had been elected to the legislature. But as the nation's only openly gay or lesbian state legislator, Noble had became a national symbol for gays and lesbians, and she received around 250 letters a week from all over the country. "She was the representative for the whole world. No human being could have done what she was asked to do," Barney explained. He had observed that Noble was overwhelmed by the letters, and because she felt a need to respond to every one, with little or no staff to assist in dealing with this national constituency, she did not have the time to do the job of legislating well.

Finally, Barney agreed to run for reelection to the state legislature. "It was this group of lesbians at the meeting who gave me moral permission in my mind to run for reelection," he said. In 1978 Noble told the *Advocate* that the expectation of the gay community was difficult for her to satisfy. "Because I was considered the gay politician, I had not only more work, but got more flack, more criticism, more heartache from the gay community than from the people who elected me. . . . I really tried the best I could and it wasn't good enough for the gay community," she said.

With Barney determined to run for reelection, Noble decided to drop out of the race for state representative and to run instead in the Democratic primary for the U.S. Senate. Barney felt obligated to endorse her in the Democratic primary. "People understood that I supported her because she had gotten out of the state representative race for me," he said. He also knew that Noble would not be a factor in the crowded field of candidates vying for the Democratic nomination. Barney would have preferred to remain neutral in that race because the field of candidates included his friends Kathleen Sullivan Alioto and Paul Guzzi and the liberal, progressive congressman Paul Tsongas.

Tsongas won the Democrat primary and the opportunity to try to unseat the incumbent, Republican senator Edward Brooke, in November, with 36 percent of the vote. Guzzi finished second with 31 percent. Kathleen Sullivan Alioto, who had campaigned with her husband, the former mayor of San Francisco, at her side and was the beneficiary of a fund-raising event at Anthony's Pier 4 Restaurant featuring Frank Sinatra, a close friend of her husband's, finished third with 19 percent of the vote. Howard Phillips had 15 percent running as a Democrat, and Elaine Noble finished last with only 6 percent.

In the general election, Barney snubbed the Democratic candidate, Tsongas, and endorsed Brooke, a moderate Republican and the first African American to be popularly elected to the Senate in 1966. Barney acted as co-chair of the Democrats for Brooke Committee because, he said, "We have to do the right thing." "I went with Ed Brooke because I believed then and now that race is the greatest single problem in America and there was only one African American in the Senate and that was Brooke. The African American community widely admired Ed Brooke, having him in the Senate meant a great deal to them, and they were heartbroken when he lost. I would have done the same thing if the Democratic nominee had been Paul Guzzi, Elaine Noble, or Kathleen Sullivan," he explained. According to Kay Gibbs, there were bitter feelings in the black community about Tsongas's running against Brooke. "Brooke was a good senator, a good man, and a black man," she said.

In April 1977, Barney described his relationship with Governor Michael Dukakis as civil and added that it might improve "if he doesn't get reelected." In
January 1978, about a dozen people gathered at the home of Bob Wood, the
president of the University of Massachusetts, whom Dukakis had alienated by
cutting the school's budget. The group, which included serious political players, such as state representatives Philip Johnston, Mel King, and Doris Bunte,
tried hard to persuade Barney to run for governor against Dukakis. Johnston
told him, "You're the one who can take him on. You, better than anyone, can
articulate the reasons why Dukakis has been a disaster." "You've got to run,"
Wood said. The group pushed Barney hard to run. But Barney said, "I just can't
do it," explaining his fear that David Liederman, Dukakis's chief of staff and a
former legislator would go after him "on personal stuff" and that would detract
from the real issue of Dukakis's performance as governor. Nobody in the group
pressed Barney on the nature of that personal stuff.

A few months later, with Dukakis 42 percentage points ahead in the Democratic primary in the early polls, Barney made a serious blunder. Later he said, "I
made two mistakes, opposing Dukakis in 1978 and supporting him in 1974." In
an effort to teach Dukakis a lesson for his meat-cleaver attack on state programs
for the poor, Barney actively supported a protest candidate, the liberal social activist Barbara Ackerman, a fifty-three-year-old former mayor of Cambridge, for
the Democratic nomination. Barney was probably the best-known politician to
break with Governor Dukakis and back Ackerman, who had no realistic chance
of winning. "The real point of Ackerman's campaign," Barney explained, "was to
show Dukakis that there was a price to be paid for hurting poor people."

Dukakis says now that he was surprised by Barney's endorsement of Ackerman. "Whatever my sins those first years, we had gotten the state moving
again. By 1978 we not only had the place pretty well stabilized but were starting to move in the right direction and to do really good things, things that
seemed to me people like Barney ought to feel good about. I was upset since I
doubted very much that he thought Barbara Ackerman would be an outstanding governor."

Barney had underestimated the voter strength of Dukakis's conservative challenger, Edward J. King, who ran the Massachusetts Port Authority and headed
a business group. King, a political rookie, had once played professional football
with the Buffalo Bills and the Baltimore Colts. Campaigning on emotional issues—in support of the right to life and capital punishment and against busing—stressing his managerial skills, and promising to cut taxes by five hundred
million dollars, King upset Dukakis in the Democratic primary, with Ackerman
getting 7 percent of the vote.

Many people in the liberal community blamed Barney for Dukakis's loss.
The day after the primary, Kay Gibbs phoned Barney. "Hello, Barney," she said.

"This is Kay. It is not your fault." "That is the first nice thing anyone has said to me all day," Barney replied. "I think that Barney learned an important lesson from that experience—some sense of moderation," Gibbs said later, and Barney acknowledged that he made a mistake and learned a lesson. "One of Barney's refreshing and endearing qualities is that he admits when he has made a mistake," Bo Jones, who has known him since the mid-1960s at Harvard, said.

"The Massachusetts Democratic Party is in about the same shape as the Holy Roman Empire—it's in shambles," Barney commented following the primary. Speaker Tip O'Neill, whose son Tommy had served as lieutenant governor under Dukakis and was on the Democratic ticket as Edward King's running mate, endorsed King after the primary and tried to bring about party unity.

Barney led an exodus of liberal Democratic state legislators away from the Democratic gubernatorial nominee, Edward King, and supported the GOP candidate, Frank Hatch, the moderate minority leader in the state legislature. Hatch's running mate for lieutenant governor was William Cowin, whom Barney also liked and had worked closely with in City Hall in 1968–69. "Barney helped my campaign enormously," Hatch recalled. "He held a reception for me and actively campaigned for me in Boston. With his assistance, I carried the city of Boston, which was quite unusual in those days." King went on to defeat Hatch in the general election with 53 percent of the vote. "It's always dangerous for a Democrat with ambitions for higher office to support a Republican," Andrew Natsios commented. Yet Barney did so not once but twice in 1978.

Edward King proved to be a disaster as governor. His administration was almost immediately flush with scandal and riddled with incompetence. Less than six weeks into his administration, King lost four of his appointees to scandal. Asked for his assessment of Governor King's administration, Barney told the *Washington Post* in March 1979, "The good news is that Ed King is Superman. The bad news is that Massachusetts seems to be made of kryptonite." King planned to cut taxes at the expense of welfare recipients and to ask private charities to play a greater role in assisting the poor. Barney remarked, "He thinks he's Jiminy Cricket: Wish and it will be so." When someone suggested that King be impeached, Barney responded that Massachusetts has no recall election provision and "incompetence is not an impeachable offense." "Barney and Governor King were like oil and water," Paul Guzzi said. Guzzi served as the governor's chief of staff and yet managed to maintain his friendship with Barney.

In January 1979, the orientation for newly elected members of the U.S. Congress was held at Harvard. The session relating to urban problems took place at Boston City Hall with Mayor White and Barney Frank among the speakers. "It was obvious quickly that [Barney] knew more about urban issues than anybody else in the room," William Ratchford, then a freshman Democratic congressman from Connecticut, said. "He wasn't showing off or being boastful. That was not his personality. You just said to yourself 'Wow!' and he did it with such a great sense of humor." The praise for Barney's performance at the orientation session was bipartisan and came from such Republican members as Carrol Campbell of South Carolina and Jerry Lewis of California.

In 1979, Barney taught part-time at the Kennedy School of Government at Harvard. One morning he met Joe Martin for breakfast at the school. They went through the cafeteria line and carried their trays into the faculty dining room. It was early and there was only one other person in the dining room—Michael Dukakis, who was also teaching at the Kennedy School. "Barney, why don't you come over here and bring your friend and let's sit together," Dukakis suggested. Barney said no and just kept on walking to another table. Martin was uncomfortable. "I kept looking at Dukakis and he made eye contact, and neither of us could really understand why we weren't all sitting together," Martin said. Barney could not bring himself to accept the olive branch Dukakis extended, partly because he was still angry at the governor for going after social programs but mainly because he was embarrassed about his own actions in the primary and felt responsible for King's being elected governor.

When Ted Kennedy announced in the spring of 1979 that he was running for president, Barney offered his support. Like other liberal Democrats, Barney was greatly disappointed with Carter. "With Carter now deciding he needs the neutron bomb more than he needs welfare reform, the long-term prognosis for Boston is negative," he said. The Kennedy campaign staff asked Barney to go to New York to run Kennedy's campaign in the Empire State. The Massachusetts legislature had adjourned and he was free for a few months. But he encountered tremendous resistance not to him personally but to any outsider coming to New York. "I got to New York, and three days later I was dismissed and sent back home," he said.

At the time of the 1975 mayoralty election campaign, many liberals were troubled by the way Mayor White was running City Hall. In the closing days of that campaign, Barney came to White's rescue by rallying liberal support behind the mayor. This last-minute assistance helped White narrowly defeat his challenger, state senator Joseph Timilty. Four years later, however, Barney supported state representative Mel King, the only black candidate, in the preliminary election, and then endorsed Timilty in the general election against White, who was seeking a fourth term as mayor. The latter endorsement was the most surprising because in the late 1960s when Barney was Mayor White's chief of staff, Timilty, a city councilor, was White's adversary and someone Barney often clashed with at council hearings. "It was absolutely unimaginable in the late 1960s that ten years later Barney would be supporting Joe Timilty for mayor over Kevin White," Alan Lupo, a former *Boston Globe* reporter, said. Yet, there was Barney, in the final week of the 1979 mayoralty campaign, splitting with his former boss and endorsing Timilty. "Barney had been such a key player in 1975 and we welcomed his support, though we would have preferred to have had it earlier," Timilty said.

Joseph Timilty had undergone a political metamorphosis and his views of the issues had changed dramatically over the years. When Barney was elected to the state legislature and Timilty to the state senate in 1972, they had developed a good working relationship. The two men had cooperated on antidiscrimination legislation based on sexual orientation and a host of issues in the legislature, including housing and the creation of a "black" Senate seat. According to Barney, while Timilty had started out as a fairly provincial Boston politician in the 1960s, he had grown, broadened his outlook, and moved to the left.

Barney explained that he broke from Mayor White in 1979 because White's administration had become antidemocratic and had politicized services. In 1972, White had been George McGovern's first choice for vice president until, according to the *Washington Post* columnist David Broder, Senator Edward Kennedy vetoed White, and McGovern turned instead to Missouri senator Thomas Eagleton.

"Kevin White went from being a potential vice president in 1972 and a national interplanetary leader, which people used to joke Kevin thought of himself as, to having to fight hard for reelection in 1975 to a job he had had for eight years," Barney said. "Kevin was furious. He felt it was demeaning to him. After he narrowly won reelection as mayor in 1975, he decided he was going to build the kind of power base that would make him immune from challenge, and I think that he lost his bearing for a while."

Barney felt Mayor White was "undermining democracy" and "creating a political machine of the worst kind." One example was the mayor's wholesale firing of a city department after some of the employees had failed to buckle when pressured to join White's reelection campaign. Barney also pointed to a state representative race in the Brookline–West Roxbury district. Elinore Meyerson, a former Brookline selectwoman and in Barney's estimation a solid and good person, was running for reelection to the seat against a political ally of the mayor's from West Roxbury. According to Barney, some of White's people played games with the election machinery and appeared to have engaged in election fraud in that contest. Although Mayor White was not involved personally in the fraud, he looked the other way.

Barney didn't feel that he was being disloyal when he supported other candidates against his former boss. "I worked for Kevin White, then the mayor of Boston, and was very high on him—thought he did a great job. But then I came to disagree with things he did and opposed him when he ran for his last term.

People said I was being disloyal. But the idea is not to work for a person but for your ideals. You are working for the public interest," he explained in a 1999 *Playboy* interview.

Barney applies that same standard to himself and candidly points out that sometimes he doesn't agree with himself or his own voting record. "The only person I agreed with 100 percent was me the first time I ran for office," he remarked. "By the time I ran for reelection, I had a couple of problems with my record. But I decided I was the best candidate in the race, so I worked as hard as I could for me anyway."

The *Boston Globe* political columnist Robert Turner would write that Barney already had a national reputation "that is probably greater than of any other state legislator in the country since Julian Bond." He was often quoted in the *New York Times* and was once featured in the newspaper's Quotation of the Day. "Massachusetts State Representative Barney Frank discussing the success of the elderly in lobbying for increased social services: 'If socialism ever comes to America, it will come in a wheelchair.'" He was one of the young leaders profiled in David Broder's 1980 book *Changing of the Guard: Power and Leadership in America*.

In early December 1979, Barney wrote in his regular column for the local newspaper in Ward 5: "This is the time of year when legislators present judiciously selected accounts of their efforts on behalf of truth, justice and the American Way in the guise of reports to their constituents. Indeed one of the minor advantages of legislative office is this license to write our own report cards," he began. He said he had been in the House for seven years and, though his voting record had diverged from the Speaker's too often for him to be appointed to any paying leadership position, he had been on the Ways and Means Committee for five years. "Now as I approach my 40th birthday," he concluded, "I am a lot more respectful of tradition than I used to be."

8

Mr. Frank Goes to Washington
with Help from Pope John Paul II
and John Kerry

IN 1980, the year he turned forty, Barney felt "bummed out." He was going through a mid-life crisis. He described himself to a colleague in the state legislature as "clinically depressed." He was frustrated with his job in the legislature and frustrated with his personal life, and he began to take inventory. When he first ran for the state legislature, in 1972, he thought he could have a career as an elected official and give up his personal life. But he soon learned, he said, "When you try to make your public career a substitute for your private life, the electorate becomes your lover, and that's not healthy. I was really feeling the pressure of being closeted, not having a social life or an emotional life. It started to get to me. I had sacrificed an awful lot but was not going anywhere politically." He felt he had reached a dead end in the state legislature.

With the exception of Senator Edward Kennedy, Barney was on the outs with almost all of the major Democrats in the state. "By 1980, the mayor of Boston, the current and previous Democratic governors, and one Democratic senator had reason not to be exactly thrilled with me," he said.

In the late 1970s, Barney had told a few gay people about his sexual orientation. One was Joe Martin, who had met Barney during the summer of 1973, right out of college. Martin was house-sitting on Beacon Hill, and because he had time on his hands, he often went to the State House to listen to hearings. He was immediately impressed by Barney and soon became a big fan. Barney was impressed that Martin had come out while in college and lived an openly gay life. Martin recalled his surprise when Barney told him he was gay and recounted their conversation, which began one evening when the two men were in Barney's studio apartment in Boston. Barney was sitting in a recliner, smoking a cigar and flipping ashes in the direction of an ashtray that stood on a stand next to the recliner. There was a two-to-three-foot stack of newspapers on a nearby chair. Barney suggested that Martin go to the refrigerator and help himself if he was hungry. Martin opened the refrigerator door and saw only several cans of diet soda, a jar of pickles, and some mustard.

Barney suddenly asked, "How would you feel if Ralph Nader was gay?" At the time Martin's two biggest heroes in politics were Ralph Nader and Golda Meir. Martin replied that it wouldn't make any difference to him at all. Barney persisted, "But how would you feel if Ralph Nader was out of the closet? Don't you think the corporations would go after him in a more ruthless way than they already are? Would you want him to be out of the closet?"

When Martin said he'd have to think about it, that he wasn't sure, Barney said, "I want to tell you something. I am gay."

"I was floored," Martin recalled. "My radar hadn't detected anything." He had read several articles about Barney's romantic relationship with Kathleen Sullivan and asked Barney about it. He also expressed surprise that Barney was so good on the issue of gay rights while he was closeted. Martin assumed a politician who was closeted would run in the opposite direction.

Barney explained that he felt close to Kathleen Sullivan, whom he described as "a wonderful woman," but, he said, "This is who I really am." He also explained his support of gay rights. "I made a commitment when I was running for the legislature. It is a basic civil rights issue and I would feel strongly about it whether or not I am gay."

In early 1980, Barney started coming out to a small circle of straight friends, usually privately during one-on-one conversations. "I never thought of it before," Barney remarked during an interview for this book, "but I think that my decision to start coming out reflected that I had just eliminated one of the few openly gay or lesbian politicians in America, Elaine Noble, and felt that there was a need to fill the vacuum."

He came out to his longtime friend Jim Segel, a former state representative, during breakfast one day at the Ritz-Carlton in Boston. "It was a singular moment for me," Segel recalled. "No one had ever said that to me before." When Barney asked, "Doesn't everybody think I'm gay?" Segel replied, "I don't believe most people think about it one way or the other." Barney wanted to come out publicly, but Segel discouraged him from doing so, arguing that coming out would be devastating if he had any further political ambitions.

Barney had dinner with Joe Martin and asked for his views on how he should come out. Martin was surprised that Barney had come to him for such advice. "I was approaching thirty years of age. Barney was my hero. What did I have to offer him? I might have been a role model in some sense in that I had come out while in college," Martin said. Aware that Barney was depressed and felt he had nowhere to go politically, Martin thought it was probably a good time to get the issue out of the way, and so he advised Barney not to make a big deal about it, not to hold a press conference and make an announcement that he is gay, but instead just to let the information get out naturally.

A few days later, on March 14, Allard Lowenstein, Barney's close friend and political mentor, his inspiration for wanting to make a difference in society, was murdered. He was fifty-one. Dennis Sweeney, a mentally troubled young man with whom Lowenstein had crossed paths during his varied career, walked into Lowenstein's law office in New York and shot him seven times, killing him.

Barney was devastated by Lowenstein's death. He said about Lowenstein, "Outside of my family, no single person has had more of an impact on my life." Barney was drawn to Lowenstein's passionate combination of idealism and pragmatism on behalf of social justice and fairness. "Al Lowenstein was a very important political figure. He was everything I thought you should be in life," Barney said. "He was the first guy I met who was absolutely passionate on liberal issues but also willing to blow the whistle on the far left, the communists. He did not shy away from debating critics to the left who advocated tactics which he believed to be ineffective and self-defeating." Barney learned from Lowenstein that if you want to be an idealist you have to be pragmatic about it, "Nobody ever got me to do more things that I swore I wouldn't do and was glad that I did than Al," Barney said. "He was among the greatest moral teachers of all time."

Jenny Littlefield, Lowenstein's widow, believes that the friendship between Lowenstein and Barney stayed so strong because "they were both independent thinkers, their politics were the same, and neither became terribly radicalized. There was never a left–further-left split. They were both advocates of using the political system to bring about change." Lowenstein greatly respected Barney and often consulted him about the best way to approach a problem.

"Barney was an important friend of Al's because they saw the world the same way, caring enormously about how to make the world better. They thought strategically and pragmatically," Greg Craig said. "Whenever Al had an idea about a strategy or a way of approaching a problem that he cared a great deal about, he talked to Barney about the problem because he respected Barney's brainpower so much."

Barney was unaware that Al Lowenstein was anything but heterosexual. "I have never claimed to be exceptionally perceptive in personal matters of this sort and was certainly not before I came out myself. However, I think back to one or two potential incidents," he said recently. It is ironic that Barney saw Lowenstein as an important role model without realizing how much the two had in common and that Lowenstein was probably struggling with some gay feelings himself.

On March 31, Barney turned forty, adding to his sense of melancholy. Jim Segel, Dick Morningstar, and a group of Barney's friends from his Harvard graduate student days took him out to dinner at the Harvest restaurant in Cambridge to celebrate his birthday and to try to cheer him up. "He was turning forty, he didn't see the legislature as a permanent career, and he didn't really know what he was going to do," Morningstar said. There was several other fortieth birthday parties that friends had thrown for him but the therapy did not help. At one of those parties, Mark Shields, a political pundit who was then writing political editorials for the *Washington Post*, warned his friend, "You can win the Pulitzer Prize or write a symphony and they will never again refer to you as 'the young Barney Frank.'"

In early April, Barney told his three siblings separately, within a twenty-four-hour period, that he is gay. "It was a very, very difficult thing to do but they were very supportive," Barney said. "I could not think of any reason why this would make any difference," his sister Doris said. She was surprised by the revelation. She knew Barney had dated women and that he was very popular and did not seem to be a loner. But when Barney asked Doris whether he should tell their mother, she said no. "I don't know why I said no. That is something I always regretted and wish I could take back because she would have been the most supportive person," Doris said. David and Ann were also surprised by the disclosure. Ann said, "I should have known."

In mid-April, Barney was the featured speaker at Gay and Lesbian Awareness Day at Harvard, a series of seminars and workshops on topics ranging from coming out at Harvard to homosexuality and the Third World community. The final event was an evening plenary session at which Barney was the keynote speaker. As he waited to address the group, he looked at the faces of the near-capacity crowd at the Science Center and contemplated coming out to the group. He reflected on how meaningful such a revelation would be to them. "Why not come out then?" he thought. He saw little political downside. His political future did not appear promising and he was resigned to running for a last term in the state legislature.

"The purpose of an event like this is to make events like this irrelevant," he began. "It is always hard for me to speak on the affirmative about gay rights, about the rights of other people to be themselves and enjoy themselves without affecting a third party. Before I entered the state legislature, the case appeared to be self-evident. I couldn't imagine how you could debate it." But after several years of encountering resistance to gay rights in the legislature, he explained, "I don't understand the arguments. It's hard to take the arguments seriously."

He urged the group to continue the efforts "to get government not just off people's backs but out of their beds," describing the issue of gay rights as "painfully simple." "Individuals ought to be free to live their own lives as they see fit, as long as they don't impose their choices on others," he said. "People who in the name of I-don't-know-what, take it on themselves to interfere [with that right] ought to be regarded as about the most fundamental violators of liberties there are."

He emphasized to the crowd that while people should be free to express their sexual orientation, they have a responsibility to conduct their intimate relations in private. "I'm not saying that I want open, public sex. . . . We have a right to ask each other to be discreet about it, but to go beyond that—it just baffles me."

When Barney finished speaking, he received a loud ovation from the crowd. But he was disappointed in himself that he had not come out. When the opportunity appeared, he just could not do it.

For many years, Barney had made it clear that he had aspirations for higher office and was eager to run for Congress. "In a state legislature there are a narrower set of issues than in Congress. You can become bored," he said. He wanted to move on from issues such as rent control to talk about foreign policy and civil liberties. He likened his ambition to run for Congress to that of a pretty good shortstop playing Class A baseball—he wanted to move up to the major leagues.

The road to Washington was blocked, however, by Speaker Tip O'Neill. The Beacon Hill and Back Bay ward that Barney represented in the state legislature was part of O'Neill's congressional district. Barney often thought about running for Congress when O'Neill retired. He told John Marttila, a friend and professional campaign strategist, "If you ever hear on the news that Tip is retiring, check your telephone answering machine immediately because there will be a message from me wanting to hire you to manage my campaign for Tip's open seat."

Barney fantasized about running for Tip O'Neill's open seat against Tommy O'Neill, Joe Kennedy, and James Roosevelt. In his mind, he had already planned a television commercial using his mother: "Hello, my name is Elsie Frank. I am here to ask you to vote for my son Barney who is running for Congress. He is very talented and cares about working people. I want to make one thing very clear—Barney is not running for Congress on my coattails." (When O'Neill retired in 1988, Joe Kennedy and James Roosevelt and several other candidates did run for the open House seat, which Kennedy won.)

Barney also thought that if Father Robert Drinan ever left Congress he would run for that seat in the adjoining congressional district. His friend Paul Guzzi, the Massachusetts secretary of state, assured Barney that if Drinan ever got out he would support Barney. Barney was concerned about competition from John Kerry. "We will have to deal with that if it comes up," Guzzi told him.

Many of Barney's liberal colleagues and friends in the Massachusetts legislature had moved on. Guzzi had been elected secretary of state in 1974, Edward Markey was elected to Congress in 1976, James Smith left the legislature in 1978 and ran unsuccessfully for Michael Harrington's vacant seat in Congress, Bill Delahunt became a district attorney, and Tommy O'Neill became lieutenant governor. Another close friend, Jim Segel, was redistricted in 1978 and left the legislature after three terms.

In the state legislature Barney was chafing under the autocratic rule of Speaker Thomas McGee, who was supported by the Senate president, William Bulger. As one of the few remaining liberals in the legislature, Barney was left to do battle with the conservative governor, Edward King, and the conservative Democrats in the legislature. When asked if he was "the last liberal left," Barney replied, "No, but there aren't a lot of us." "I feel a little like John Kennedy when he was asked how he became a war hero and said, 'The Japanese sank my boat.'"

Barney resigned himself to running for a fifth and final term in the state legislature, with no plan for what would follow. "In my mind, I was acknowledging the end of my political career and trying to figure out what life would be like as an openly gay man, how it would be helpful that I had been in office and had that credential, and where I would go from there," he said. He was considering practicing law or perhaps beginning a new career as a writer or a gay rights activist or undertaking some combination of the three.

Then Barney received a belated birthday gift when the Pope, of all people, opened up a congressional seat for him. As if by divine intervention, Pope John Paul II suddenly and unexpectedly instructed Father Robert Drinan, a five-term Democratic congressman, to leave elective office. Relying on an obscure edict from early in the twentieth century by Pope Benedict XV prohibiting priests from holding secular political office, which had never been enforced, Pope John Paul issued a decree forbidding clergy from holding public office. According to Drinan, the Vatican changed canon law by removing the discretion in the law that had been given to cardinals to permit priests and nuns around the world to hold public office. Drinan had received permission to run for Congress from Cardinal Richard Cushing, who, Drinan said, was "very enthusiastic about it."

This change in papal law was aimed at forcing Father Drinan to step down. Pope John Paul did not want Jesuit priests in Congress. When journalists traveling on the papal jet asked the Pope a question about Drinan, he responded, "Politics is the responsibility of laymen and a priest should be a priest."

Most observers assumed that the Vatican directive was in response to Drinan's active and vocal support for liberalized abortion laws, which, according to one story, the Pope learned about on October 1, 1979, the first evening of his six-city pastoral visit to the United States. After celebrating Mass before more than four hundred thousand people on the Boston Common, the Pope spent the night at the residence of Cardinal Humberto Medeiros in Brighton, on the Boston side of the Newton border. He was to leave early the next morning for New York City to address the United Nations. During the evening someone told the Pope about a priest in the diocese who votes for abortion rights as a member of the U.S. House of Representatives. "That cannot continue," the Pope reportedly responded.

Drinan never felt comfortable discussing the edict that forced him out of Congress—even twenty-five years later. In April 2005, following the death of Pope John Paul, Drinan, appearing on *CNN Late Edition*, was asked by Wolf Blitzer to comment on the Pope's action in 1980 that forced him out of Congress. "For better or worse, history will judge," he said. When Blitzer followed up, asking, "Just as they changed canon law in your case, should they do it again to allow priests to get involved in politics and political life?" Drinan replied, "History will have to judge that. I don't know."

Drinan did speak publicly about the matter once, in 1996, when he delivered the Joseph Rauh Lecture at the University of the District of Columbia School of Law. Discussing his ten years in Congress, he mentioned that moment when the Vatican informed him that the Pope thought it was inappropriate for a Catholic priest to be a member of Congress, and so he did not seek reelection. Then he paused momentarily and said, "I have often contemplated what the Pontiff would have done if he had known that Barney Frank was going to take my place in Congress."

After the death of Pope John Paul II in April 2005, Barney ran into Father Robert Drinan one evening at an event on Capitol Hill. At the time, the eighty-five-year-old Drinan had been teaching at Georgetown Law Center for twenty-five years and had become a prolific author. When Barney said to him, "I have a kind of divine-constitutional-theological question for you." Drinan asked with some apprehension what it was. Referring to the new pope, Barney said, "If the new guy changes his mind, do I have to give you the seat back?" Drinan laughed out loud.

In 1980, the Fourth Congressional District of Massachusetts was an amalgam of five cities and fifteen towns that snaked from the heavily Jewish Boston suburbs of Brookline and Newton through Waltham, the home of Brandeis University and Bentley College and a Catholic working-class city once known for its watch factories, to Wayland and Framingham in the center of the district. It twisted through the moderate Republican towns of Lincoln, Sudbury, Harvard, and Bolton and then northwest through the small, conservative, blue-collar Catholic towns of Lancaster, Leominster, Westminster, and Fitchburg and ended in Gardner. It is about an hour's drive from the tip of the district in Brookline on the Boston border to the other end of the district in Gardner.

In the late 1960s, the Massachusetts congressional delegation for the most part was made up of men like Tip O'Neill, Torbert McDonald (John F. Kennedy's roommate at Harvard College), Edward Boland, Speaker John W. McCormack, James Burke, Harold Donohue, and Philip Philbin, whom Barney described as "mainstream meat and potato, good union liberal Democrats, who thought abortion was 'Oh my God,' and didn't think much about environmental issues."

In 1968, a few candidates from the left ran in the Democratic primaries on the issue of the Vietnam War. Philip Philbin, an old-time politician who supported the Vietnam War, had three opponents in the primary and finished with only 49 percent of the vote. He went on to win the 1968 general election, where he was held to 48 percent of the vote in a three-candidate race. Chandler Stevens, an Independent antiwar candidate, finished second, winning six of the towns and cities in the district that included Newton but not Brookline, which was added to the district in 1972.

Politics in Massachusetts started to change with the election of Michael J. Harrington to Congress in 1969. In 1970, Philbin, who had represented the district since 1942, was the primary target of the new left. Although he had a liberal voting record on domestic issues, he was a hawk on the Vietnam War from his perch as the second most senior Democrat on the Armed Services Committee. The liberals in the district decided to hold a citizens' caucus to select one antiwar candidate to oppose Philbin in the Democratic primary. The plan was an outgrowth of what had occurred two years earlier when they had attempted unsuccessfully to get one of the two liberal candidates running against Philbin in the Democratic primary to withdraw.

Jerome Grossman, a wealthy businessman and longtime liberal activist who came to symbolize the peace movement in Massachusetts, had planned to be the liberal Democratic candidate to oppose Philbin in the primary. But he subsequently dropped out of the contest after persuading the reluctant Drinan to run. Grossman first met Drinan, the dean of Boston College Law School and a strong critic of the Vietnam War, at a dinner at Boston College in October 1969, a day or two before the Vietnam Moratorium.

The citizens' caucus met to endorse a candidate on February 22, 1970, in Concord. When the caucus started at 9:00 a.m. in the auditorium of the Concord–Carlisle High School, most of the nearly two thousand attendees assumed that Drinan, the overwhelming favorite among several candidates, would easily win the caucus.

John Kerry, who was barely known in February 1970, appeared at the caucus as a candidate. "I think that John Kerry knew that the caucus was a train that had already left the station. My supporters had the necessary votes even before that day began," Drinan recalled. But, as Grossman writes in his 1996 memoir *Relentless Liberal*, Kerry, a "totally unknown Vietnam veteran," was "the surprise of the caucus." He "stunned the delegates with the power of his message and delivery" and almost stole the nomination away from Drinan. Unlike Drinan, Kerry was "tall, handsome, young, and smooth," and he began to pick up support from other candidates as they were eliminated ballot by ballot.

Around six o'clock that evening, believing that the vote for Drinan was secure unless his supporters went home, Grossman, in what he describes as his "best Richard Daly style," records that he "locked the doors to the high school and prevented anyone from leaving." Drinan was nominated, and immediately Kerry stood up and said he would not contest the decision in the primary and would work for Drinan. "I walked over to John Kerry afterwards," Grossman writes, "and told him we will never forget his action. I have been supporting him ever since based on what he did then."

Recalling the event over thirty-five years later, Kerry said, "It was a close vote and Drinan won by only a small percentage. I had only been [in the race] for a few weeks. There was nothing that compelled me to concede at the caucus. I could have said I'm going to the people and taken my candidacy to the ballot box." But he chose not to, he said, because he saw "a larger purpose." He recognized that everyone at the caucus had the same cause as he—they wanted to beat a major pro-war candidate and end the war—and so he made it unanimous and "gave energy to the effort to propel" Drinan. According to Kerry, it was a spontaneous decision and it was a right decision. "I'm glad I did it," he said.

Drinan, running as a vocal opponent of the Vietnam War, challenged Philbin in the Democratic primary. Relying on a grass-roots campaign featuring energetic and resourceful students and other enthusiastic volunteers who canvassed the district most weekends, and guided by the political campaign consultant John Marttila, Drinan defeated the fourteen-term Democratic incumbent by a 46 to 36 percent margin.

Philbin did not bow out of the race gracefully. He ran in the general election as an Independent and garnered over 45,000 votes, around 27 percent. Drinan received about 37 percent of the vote and won a narrow 3,367-vote victory over the moderate Republican state representative John McGlennon of Concord to become the first Roman Catholic priest elected to Congress. In Barney's opinion, the liberals overestimated the extent to which Catholics would automatically vote for a priest. Some Catholics opposed the idea of a priest in Congress.

The takeover of the Massachusetts delegation by the new liberals, one seat at a time, which began with Harrington in 1969 and Drinan in 1970, continued with the election of Gerry Studds in 1972, succeeding the seven-term Republican Hastings Keith, who did not seek reelection, and Ed Markey in 1976, replacing Torbert McDonald.

A conscientious and extremely competent and hard-working representative, Drinan was a vocal opponent of the war in Vietnam, a strong supporter of Israel, and a champion of human rights. Through determination and the force of his personality he focused attention in Congress on the plight of Soviet Jews. According to Tip O'Neill, Drinan, who was "always devoted to the poor and the humble," "really thought he was doing God's work" by being in Congress. Drinan was a member of the Judiciary Committee and in July 1974 he offered one of the articles of impeachment against President Richard Nixon.

In late April 1980, Dorothy "Dottie" Reichard, the director of Drinan's district office, spoke with Drinan on the telephone and sensed that something was troubling him. She phoned Clark Ziegler, Drinan's administrative assistant in Washington, and asked what was wrong with the boss. "I don't know for sure," Ziegler said, "but something is wrong between him and the church and he gets very quiet."

Drinan had been informed privately about the papal decision that priests were not to run for public office, and the news caught him by surprise. He appealed the decision, but on May 3, a few days before the May 6 filing deadline for the September primary election for Congress, he learned that his appeal had been turned down by the Vatican. Stunned and shattered, Drinan broke the news to some of his closest friends and staff. When he phoned Reichard and announced, "The Pope said that I cannot run again for Congress," she suggested that they meet in the Waltham office later that afternoon.

"It was a dramatic meeting," Tom Kiley, Drinan's pollster for ten years, said. When asked whether he planned to leave the church, Drinan adamantly replied no. "I would never leave the church," he said. Drinan was first and foremost a Jesuit priest. "There was never a single word of discussion about him not obeying the order from the Pope," Grossman recalled. Drinan had hoped to reverse the papal decision but he had been unsuccessful. Drinan put his vows above his desire to stay in Congress. He accepted the decision with regret and pain.

With only about seventy-two hours left for a candidate to obtain the necessary signatures to get on the ballot, the group turned to the issue of finding a good liberal candidate, an appropriate successor to Drinan in Congress, someone whom they could all unite behind. The first person Grossman phoned was former governor Michael Dukakis. "Dukakis was the most logical and we knew he would be responsive to the peace constituencies," Grossman said. "Dukakis could have had that House seat for the asking."

Dukakis declined. "When I got beat in 1978, I thought it was over. A guy who I didn't have a hell of a lot of respect for had beaten me," Dukakis said. He had young children at the time and no interest in going to Washington to serve in Congress. If he ran for anything, he said, it would be for governor again (in 1982).

The second person Grossman phoned was former state representative Lois Pines of Newton. "I knew her to be a very ambitious person, always ready to take on a challenge," Grossman said. Pines declined to run because she felt she could not move to Washington and uproot her children. According to Grossman, Pines called him back a few days later to say that she had changed her mind and asked whether the position was still open. Grossman told her it wasn't.

Grossman then approached state senator Jack Backman of Brookline, whom many Democrats considered to be Drinan's logical successor, to see whether he was interested in running for the open seat in Congress. Backman declined because his wife had cancer and he needed to be with her.

Grossman next phoned John Kerry and urged him to enter the race for Congress. Kerry indicated that he was inclined to run but needed some time to think about it. Grossman was surprised by Kerry's tepid response: "I had expected John Kerry to jump through the phone after getting a call like that," he said.

Nobody in the Drinan camp even thought about Barney Frank. It wasn't anything against him. "He didn't come to mind because he didn't live in the district," Reichard recalled.

May 4 began as a normal Sunday for Barney. In the morning he played squash with a friend at the Harvard Club. On the way home, he stopped off to visit his mother, who lived a few blocks away, and returned to his small apartment on Commonwealth Avenue at about one o'clock to drop off his squash racket and change before going out again. He left the apartment, and as he was walking down the stairs he heard his telephone ringing. He ran back up the steps, opened his apartment door, and picked up the telephone on about the fifth ring. He curtly demanded to know who was on the phone, and when Marge Segel, the wife of his friend Jim Segel, identified herself, he bellowed, "What do you want? I'm in a hurry. I am going to the movies and ran back to the apartment when I heard the phone ringing."

When Marge asked, "Did you hear that Father Drinan isn't running again?" Barney was suddenly more interested in the phone conversation than the movie. She told him about the papal edict and said she had just received a phone call from David Mofenson, a state representative from Newton. When Mofenson had asked her whether Jim knew that Drinan wasn't running for reelection, she had answered no. Then Mofenson had said, "If Jimmy doesn't know, that must mean Barney doesn't know."

"There was something about what David said that made me feel uncomfortable," Marge Segel recalled. "I had the feeling something funny was going on." It seemed to her that someone didn't want Barney to know that Drinan was not running for reelection, and so she told Barney, "If David thought it was interesting that you didn't know, I thought you should know. I decided to call you because Jim is not home." "Where is he?" Barney asked. When she replied, "He's visiting his grandfather in Cambridge and is due home any minute," Barney said, "Have him call me."

About fifteen minutes later, Jim Segel arrived home and phoned Barney. Segel had been a student of Barney's at Harvard and had later worked briefly for him at City Hall. The two men had served together in the state legislature. Segel had represented Brookline for six years before getting redistricted. Barney asked him whether he was going to run. Segel said no because he had two small children but that if Barney was interested, he would support him.

Segel knew that Mofenson wanted the position, but he promised to support Barney. "Let's talk about it," Barney suggested. Barney had not owned a car since returning to Boston in 1972 because, as he once explained to a reporter, "I'd never remember to get it inspected." "I'll take the subway and pick me up at Reservoir," Barney told Segel.

On the drive from the subway stop, Segel pressed Barney about whether he would run, and when Barney said, "Well, I'm thinking about running—" Segel interrupted. "If you want to run I'll help you. If you haven't decided by now, I'm going home to take my kids to the movies."

"Thank you. I thought about it and I'm running," Barney said. He realized this was the moment he had been waiting for and jumped into the race for Congress from the Fourth District, in which he had never lived.

Barney was the first person to announce his candidacy for the seat in Congress Drinan was vacating. He told the *Boston Globe* later that day, "You feel almost embarrassed trying to put something together in a short space of time. You have to feel anguish for [Drinan]. It's a tough thing personally [for him]."

"It was fortuitous in that the week before I had been in Maryland helping out the Ted Kennedy campaign against Jimmy Carter," Barney said. "If the campaign trip to Maryland had been a week later, I would not have been in Boston and it might not have been possible for me to react quickly and enter the race."

"It was a difficult decision for me to support Barney over David Mofenson, whom I had also been close friends with," Jim Segel said. "I always thought Barney would make a great congressman because he was bright and committed. He was living a rather lonely life and I thought it would be more important to his life than to others. Although he had his siblings and his mother, he didn't have a family of his own to fall back on."

David Frank was in Washington, driving over the Duke Ellington Bridge on his way to the National Zoo, when he heard the news on the radio that the Vatican had told Drinan that he could not run again. He then heard Dottie Reichard say on National Public Radio that Congressman Robert Drinan would not seek reelection to a sixth term. David knew Reichard well. He had been Drinan's press secretary from January 1977 until early March 1979, before moving on to work for Stephen Solarz on the House Foreign Affairs Subcommittee on Africa. He parked the car, went to a phone booth, and called his mother. "Is Barney running?" he asked. "Yes, he is running," she said.

Barney knew he could never be elected to Congress if he were honest about his sexuality. That afternoon, he called his sister Doris. Her husband, Jim Breay, had worked in the Office of Public Service at City Hall when Barney was the mayor's chief of staff, and Barney had introduced him to Doris. Barney had come out to Doris and Jim several weeks earlier. When Jim answered the telephone, Barney said, "The noise that you just heard is my closet door slamming shut." Jim was puzzled until Barney added, "Father Drinan is not seeking reelection by order of the Pope. I am running for Congress."

On Sunday, May 4, with fifty hours to go before the 5:00 p.m. filing deadline, Barney asked his sister Doris for help getting signatures. She picked him up and they went to an Israel Independence Day rally at the Jewish Community Center in Newton to collect signatures from registered voters on the nomination papers. Soon Barney had an army of volunteers all over the district collecting the necessary signatures. He needed two thousand certifiable signatures from registered voters in the district and had to file the nomination papers before the five o'clock deadline on Tuesday to secure a spot on the ballot for the September primary.

At a press conference that day at the Newton Marriot, an emotional Father Drinan revealed what had happened and announced that he would accede to a papal order to abandon public office. Tom Vallely, a former marine who, after returning from Vietnam, had volunteered to work in Drinan's first campaign for Congress in 1970 as the candidate's driver, recalled that press conference: "After Drinan finished his remarks, a woman in the front row stood up and said, 'Father Drinan, why didn't you just refuse to do what the Vatican said?' Drinan paused. He didn't seem comfortable. He was emotional and finally replied, 'I am a priest.' Being a priest was very important to Drinan."

The next day at a press conference in Washington, Drinan said, "I am proud and honored to be a priest and a Jesuit. As a person of faith, I must believe there is work for me to do which somehow will be more important than the work I am required to leave. I undertake this new pilgrimage with pain and prayer."

That Sunday evening, Barney phoned several people, seeking their support in the race for Congress. One was Thaleia Schlesinger, Senator Paul Tsongas's twin sister, who lived in Brookline. Schlesinger agreed to support Barney but only on one condition. Barney asked, with some apprehension, what it was. "You have to buy three new suits and three new pairs of shoes. You can't run for Congress dressed like a schlep," she told him. "Fine," Barney said, somewhat relieved.

The next morning, they met for breakfast at the Ritz Carlton Hotel on Arlington Street in Boston, near Barney's Back Bay apartment. Barney regularly ate breakfast at the hotel restaurant. It was one of his few financial splurges. At breakfast, Schlesinger agreed to serve as campaign press secretary and spokesperson. She had been doing press advance for Ted Kennedy's presidential campaign and was familiar with the reporters who covered politics. She had also dealt with most of the Massachusetts press in her brother's Senate campaign two years earlier, where she often acted as a surrogate for the candidate.

After breakfast, the pair walked up the street to Brooks Brothers and Schlesinger helped Barney pick out three new suits. "It didn't take much time. He's not into spending a long time shopping for clothing," she explained. Schlesinger had once described Barney's shoes as looking "like a dog ate them." However, she wasn't going to get involved in buying new shoes for him. "A size ten triple E is not my specialty," she said.

Barney felt it was very gracious of Schlesinger to support him, since he had backed Senator Edward Brooke rather than her brother two years earlier. (In 2007, Barney repaid the favor by the Tsongas family when he became the first major politician in Massachusetts to endorse Niki Tsongas, the widow of Senator Paul Tsongas, in the race to fill the Fifth District seat in Congress vacated by Martin Meehan.)

"Bob Drinan had been such a wonderful representative for the Fourth Congressional District. He was someone I had enormous respect for and affection," Schlesinger said. "In terms of holding a grudge against Barney because he had not supported Paul, I don't think you can do that when you are looking at this kind of race, someone to replace Bob Drinan. In my mind Barney was clearly someone whose values on issues I agreed with. I thought that Barney was clearly the most qualified candidate and was the kind of person who would best represent the people of the Fourth District," she explained. "Besides," she added, "it isn't as if Barney worked to undermine Paul. I understood the reason why he supported Senator Brooke. He did it based on a principle I could respect, the need to have an African American in the Senate."

On Monday, May 5, Barney's sister Doris prepared the papers to establish a campaign committee and went to the Mutual Bank and Savings in Newton Center and opened up a bank account for the Committee to Elect Barney Frank to Congress. She wrote out a personal check for $25 to open the account. Ultimately, the campaign committee would spend about $450,000 in the primary and general election. "Doris was the key in setting the campaign in motion," David Frank, who was the campaign manager in the primary election, said. "We needed someone smart, calm, disciplined, and well-organized to make things happen. We couldn't afford to let the other Democratic candidates get a head start."

Later that day, Barney phoned Dick Morningstar, one of the students he had tutored at Winthrop House, who was then an attorney with the Boston law firm of Peabody, Brown, and asked whether he would be the campaign treasurer and help raise money. As the treasurer, Morningstar had to file the necessary campaign finance reports, including one that listed the candidate's assets. "Barney literally had nothing," Morningstar recalled. "He had a tiny bit of money in the bank, maybe a desk in his apartment, his clothes, a baseball glove, and a tennis racket. Those were his total assets. I couldn't believe it."

While Barney raced to get his papers in order and put a campaign committee together, a crowded field began to take shape. It was a frantic couple of days as eleven potential Democratic candidates and an army of campaign workers jockeyed for position at shopping centers and busy pedestrian-traveled streets in communities across the Fourth District in an effort to collect the necessary signatures in only two days, a process that usually takes four to six weeks. "It was like the gold rush. I remember standing there at Coolidge Corner with a bunch of other candidates trying to get nomination signatures. There seemed to be more candidates than commuters. The people getting off the train didn't want to be bothered and I didn't particularly want to bother them. People couldn't get off the Green line without someone hitting on them," Barney recalled.

On Tuesday, May 6, a cartoon of the newly declared candidate appeared on the editorial page of the *Boston Globe*. It shows a beefy Barney Frank, hair disheveled, wearing thick-rimmed glasses, with a cigar in his mouth and a cigar in each hand. He holds a Barney Frank for Congress campaign button. Affixed to his jacket are campaign buttons for candidates he supported in the past, all of whom lost—Ted Kennedy for President, McGovern for President, Udall for President, Hatch for Governor, Ackerman for Governor, McCormack for U.S. Senate, Mel King for Mayor, Timilty for Mayor. The caption repeats a comment Barney made when he announced his candidacy for Congress, "If I endorse anybody this time . . . it'll be my opponent."

The horde of Democratic hopefuls gathering signatures was congested with liberals, including state senator Edward Burke of Framingham, state representative John Businger of Brookline, and former state representative Jon Rotenberg of Brookline, as well as John Kerry and David Mofenson. Moderate and conservative Democrats seeking to get on the ballot included Waltham mayor Arthur Clark, Fitchburg mayor David Gilmartin, Brookline town clerk John

Kendrick, Newton executive councilor Herbert Connolly, and assistant secretary of environmental affairs Edward J. Reilly of Newton. A twelfth Democrat, twenty-six-year-old Robert Shaffer, a conservative Fitchburg businessman who ran a speed-reading school, had planned to challenge Drinan and had filed the needed signatures a week earlier. Barney submitted six thousand signatures and Clark tendered nine thousand.

Kerry and Barney were the two liberal frontrunners for the Democratic nomination. They had first met ten years earlier while participating in a campaign rally for the Kevin White/Michael Dukakis ticket for governor. A day or two after the filing deadline, Barney and Kerry had a meeting to discuss the race for Congress. Tom Vallely, a political consultant and a close friend of Kerry's who had been his political director in a 1972 campaign for Congress, attended the meeting as well.

Both men were politically ambitious. For Barney, this was the break he needed. It was his first and possibly only chance to run for Congress, since there was a political biological clock that was ticking away within him. He sensed that he could not afford to wait for O'Neill's seat in the Eight District to become vacant. He knew it was likely that he would come out as gay before O'Neill's seat had opened up, and he recognized that his running for Congress as a gay man would divert attention from important economic and social issues and significantly reduce his chances of capturing the seat.

Furthermore, Barney might have a better chance to win in the Fourth District. "Massachusetts was a very ethnic place then and this was the district for Barney to run in because Newton and Brookline were heavily Jewish," Jim Segal said. "Tip's district didn't have a Jewish population, and it would have been much harder for him to win there." That view was echoed by the Republican politico John Sears, a resident of Beacon Hill, who said, "Tip's district would have been tough for Barney to win because of its ethnicity."

For Kerry, the open seat provided an opportunity to end eight years in political exile. For many years, he had dreamed of being a congressman and had tried unsuccessfully in 1970 and 1972. Ironically, Kerry, who had been accused of blatant district-hopping eight years earlier, was living in the Fourth District.

Several days earlier, Kerry had told Grossman that he was prepared to be a candidate and his supporters had collected the necessary nominating signatures from registered voters. But he had not firmly made up his mind. "I don't want to make a precipitous decision but a sound one," he told friends. Kerry had lengthy conversations with his brother Cameron, his brother-in-law David Thorne, and Tom Vallely. In the end he withdrew. Looking back on the decision, Kerry said, "I took the time to look at it. I sort of started the process because that's how you have to feel it. It comes to you and you either feel right or you don't. It just

didn't feel right at the time and I made the decision based on my gut." His decision to bow out of the contest, he said, was not related to Barney's being in the
race. "I had great respect for Barney. I knew he was a formidable figure. But I
certainly thought that if I had run I would have won. I had a lot of credentials
and a record."

John Kerry, three years younger than Barney, appeared in many ways to be
the stronger candidate. He lived in the Fourth District in Newton. He had been
married for ten years and had two young daughters. He was stylish, charismatic,
and impeccably dressed. And although he was a liberal, he was also a crime-
fighting former prosecutor, an attribute that would appeal to many voters in the
small, conservative towns in the western part of the district. Kerry was knowledgeable on the issues, and he had national contacts and the ability to raise large
sums of money for a campaign. But he also carried some political baggage.

Eight years earlier, at age twenty-eight, he had run unsuccessfully for Congress. Having made headlines as the face and voice of the Vietnam Veterans
Against the War with his dramatic testimony before the Senate Foreign Relations Committee (where he had said, "How do you ask a man to be the last man
to die in Vietnam? How do you ask a man to be the last man to die for a mistake?"), Kerry was then politically ambitious and impatient, and he had searched
for a congressional district in Massachusetts from which to run. In February
1972, Kerry and his wife, Julia, purchased a house in Worcester, a working-class
city, so that he might run in the Democratic primary against Harold Donohue,
an aging congressman who appeared vulnerable. But when President Richard
Nixon nominated F. Bradford Morse, a generally liberal Republican congressman, to replace the late Ralph Bunche as undersecretary of the United Nations,
creating an open seat in the Fifth District, Kerry and his wife rented an apartment in Lowell, an old textile mill town and small blue-collar city northwest of
Boston, and he ran for Congress there instead. Kerry was hurt by his district
hopping and was out of place in the Fifth District. Paul Cronin, a lackluster,
former two-term Republican state representative from Andover who had served
as chief of staff to Congressman Morse, easily won the general election with 53
percent of the vote.

Barney offered many political strengths and impressive credentials as a candidate. He had an encyclopedic knowledge and understanding of local, state,
and national policy issues and was well known throughout the Boston area and
suburbs. But his image as an acerbic, wise-cracking, eccentric, often profane,
cigar-chomping, Jewish Boston politician who spoke with a New Jersey accent
and his strong identification as a champion of liberal causes in the legislature,
such as gay rights, abortion rights, and women's rights, while advantageous in
Newton and Brookline, liberal energy centers with heavy Jewish populations,

would hurt him in the small conservative towns in the northern and western parts of the district. Barney lived outside the Fourth District in the Back Bay on Commonwealth Avenue, less than a mile from the district line at the eastern end of Brookline, and he had no roots in the district.

There was also the appearance problem. The *Boston Globe* columnist Alan Richman described him as "a 40-year-old from Bayonne who dresses like his hometown looks," adding, "Goodwill donates clothes to Barney Frank." John Marttila, a respected and experienced political strategist, had advised him to "just try not to look disgusting." But, "when you are five feet ten inches and you have a forty-six-inch waist and your thighs rub together, your clothes have a way of not looking good," Barney explained.

In addition, Barney had a reputation as a party renegade for having supported Republicans Frank Hatch, for governor, and Edward Brooke, for senator, in 1978. Another significant concern was his deteriorating relationship with former governor Michael Dukakis, Brookline's favorite son and still a major player among liberals in the Fourth District. Only two years earlier, Barney had led the "Dump the Duke" drive.

John Kerry agonized over the decision to withdraw. "John's family situation was bad. He had two young daughters and the marriage was in trouble. It was not a good time for him to run. He had personal things to take care of," Tom Vallely said. "I knew that Barney would run and I knew Barney would be a tough candidate." Vallely told Kerry privately, "What are you agonizing over? It's simple, let's call Barney and get this over with."

Tom Vallely wanted to run for Barney's Ward 5 seat in the state legislature. The thirty-year-old Vallely, a former marine who had been only eighteen years old when he went to fight in the war in Vietnam, had earned a Silver Star in combat. He and Kerry, now close friends, had first met during Drinan's initial campaign for Congress in 1970. Kerry supported Vallely's decision to run for Barney's seat. He planned to pursue statewide office in the future and, in the state legislature, Vallely would be better positioned to assist Kerry in a statewide race.

Kerry also knew that it would be a mess if both he and Barney ran in the Democratic primary and that they would likely split the liberal vote in Newton and Brookline, allowing Arthur Clark, the fifty-nine-year-old conservative mayor of Waltham with voter support in the large city of Waltham and in the conservative towns in the western part of the district, where Philip Philbin had done so well, to win the primary. Kerry feared being viewed as the divider because of the negative impact that might have on a future run for statewide office. "If John and I had both been in, it would have been impossible," Barney said.

The meeting between Kerry and Barney, attended also by Vallely, lasted about thirty minutes. Barney was direct. He was determined to run for the seat regardless of whether Kerry ran. Kerry informed Barney that for family reasons he had decided not to run and that he would endorse Barney for Congress. Barney expressed his gratitude to Kerry for his support and pledged that he would be helpful when Kerry decided to run for statewide office, perhaps attorney general or lieutenant governor. Thus, it was agreed that Barney would run for Drinan's vacant seat in Congress with Kerry's endorsement. Kerry would wait for the next political opening, probably a race for statewide office, and run with Barney's support and assistance. And Barney would endorse Tom Vallely for the open seat from Ward 5 in the state legislature.

It is likely that Barney would have endorsed Vallely, who lived in the Back Bay, for his open seat anyway. Vallely had worked for John Marttila's political campaign consulting group and Barney had known him since Kevin White's first campaign for mayor in 1967. Also, Vallely had strong ties with Barney's siblings.

On Friday afternoon, May 9, Barney and Kerry held a joint press conference at the Howard Johnson's Motel at Newton Corner. The two friends met in the parking garage and walked in together, a study in contrasts. At six feet, four inches, Kerry, the slim Massachusetts Brahmin, towered over the chubby Barney Frank, who was six inches shorter. In his new, not-yet-rumpled Brooks Brothers suit, Barney was dressed almost as well as Kerry, who wore a well-tailored blue pin-striped suit. "I felt like it was something out of a movie," Barney recalled.

Although Barney was the candidate for Congress, the press conference belonged to Kerry. Kerry spoke first, describing his genuine affection for Robert Drinan, reminiscing about Drinan's courageous underdog campaign for Congress in 1970 and talking about how Drinan had served the people of the Fourth District with honor and distinction. Kerry then discussed his own difficult decision not to run and gracefully withdrew, expressing concern that he and Barney might split the liberal vote. "Politics doesn't always need contentiousness," he said. Kerry concluded with a strong endorsement of the candidacy of Barney Frank who "can carry on the Drinan legacy." Barney was sitting on Kerry's left and appeared to be deeply moved by Kerry's comments.

When Barney spoke, he was uncharacteristically subdued. "The most disabling form of naiveté is excessive cynicism. That is what we are suffering now. Liberals and conservatives are designated as incapable of achieving anything," he said. He described himself as a "progressive" who stands for "peace and social justice." He remarked that Kerry had pulled out of the race because he thought it was better for the party and thanked Kerry for his "extraordinarily noble initiative." Barney added, "It makes me all the more determined. Not only Bob Drinan's legacy, but John's endorsement will push me on to work even harder."

"It worked out for the better," Kerry said, reflecting on that decision more than twenty-five years later. "I'm glad that I supported Barney. I did the right thing and he has been an absolutely superb congressman ever since." Kerry's decision to defer to Barney and to forgo the race for Congress turned out to have a significant and beneficial impact on the political careers of both men. Barney got a clear shot to run for Congress, won the election, and went on to become a star legislator and an icon for the gay and lesbian community. Had he waited for Tip O'Neill to retire and run in the Eight District, it is doubtful that he would have won, especially if he had "come out" before the election, in a crowded primary field that included formidable candidates such as Joe Kennedy.

"John Kerry made the right decision personally and ultimately politically. I don't think he knew that at the time. If John had run for Congress in 1980 he wouldn't be running for president today," Vallely said in May 2004, by which time Kerry had wrapped up the Democratic nomination for president. He added, "John Kerry's decision not to run for Congress was incredibly important to him because it cemented a friendship and created an alliance with Barney Frank, who was an extremely significant figure in Democratic politics in Massachusetts. Kerry benefited greatly from Barney's energy, intellect, and vision."

By withdrawing from the congressional race, Kerry was finally able to shake the image many had of him as a self-centered political opportunist and make amends for his district-hopping run for Congress eight years earlier. As Barney sees it, "If John was purely motivated by ambition, he would have run. It did him a lot of good with liberals because it showed that he was committed to the cause. John had other options and I didn't. I was not then a plausible statewide candidate or anything else and John was. It was a very generous, self-sacrificing act. I felt enormously grateful." "Politics," Barney said, "is a business where egos often get in the way of cooperation, yet John Kerry stepped aside from a race he had a good chance to win to help me. We all benefited from his selflessness, a selflessness that is rare in Massachusetts."

Two years later, Kerry decided to run for lieutenant governor. According to Vallely, "John Kerry would not have been able to become lieutenant governor without Barney Frank's assistance." Kerry was not well known in Boston political circles, and at the state Democratic convention in Springfield in May 1982, he was not the party choice for lieutenant governor. But Barney helped him obtain the 15 percent of the delegate votes needed to qualify for the primary ballot in September. In the Democratic primary, Kerry prevailed over the candidate chosen by the Democrats at the convention, Evelyn Murphy, who had served as environmental secretary during Michael Dukakis's first term as governor. In November, John Kerry was elected lieutenant governor on the ticket with Michael Dukakis.

In 1984, Kerry narrowly won the Democratic nomination for the Senate seat that had unexpectedly opened up when Paul Tsongas retired because of illness. Kerry edged Rep. James Shannon, a former Michael Harrington intern and a protégé of Speaker Tip O'Neill, who had the support of the Democratic establishment and organized labor, by fewer than twenty-five thousand votes in a four-candidate primary election that included secretary of state Michael Connolly and former Speaker David Bartley. "It would have been very difficult for John Kerry to move on to the Senate without Barney's loyal political support, both at the convention and during the primary," Vallely said. "It was my impression at the May 1980 meeting that Barney only agreed to help John Kerry once, but Barney chose to help him a second time, in the Senate race."

In early May 1984, Edward Markey dropped out of the Senate race, deciding instead to run for reelection to the House. That left Barney free to work for Kerry. "Most of the congressional delegation was for Jim Shannon and my supporting John Kerry was a big thing. I had no ties to Shannon, who had sort of passively helped me get redistricted in a bad way in 1982. Besides, I really thought that John Kerry was the better candidate and would make a good senator," Barney said.

In the Republican Senate primary, Ray Shamie, a conservative businessman, upset Elliot Richardson, a self-proclaimed public service junkie who had one of the most impressive résumés in the United States. In the general election, Kerry easily defeated Shamie with 56 percent of the vote.

Many residents in Ward 5 were disappointed that Barney was leaving the Back Bay/Beacon Hill area to run for Congress elsewhere. Several weeks after his meeting with Kerry, Barney endorsed Tom Vallely to be state representative from Ward 5. His endorsement was tantamount to election because of his popularity in the district. "The only issue in the race for state representative in Ward 5 was who Barney wanted," Vallely recalled. At a meeting with gay and lesbian leaders in the district, Barney told them that he wanted Tom Vallely to replace him in the legislature. When one of the leaders objected, saying, "But Vallely is very arrogant," Barney responded, "It's a prerequisite for the job." He urged the group to support Vallely because, he said, "we want to pass the gay rights bill and you need a marine fighting at your side." Vallely's campaign poster featured a photo of him with Barney titled "Barney's Choice . . . Tom Vallely." Beneath the photo was the slogan, "Keep the Progressive Tradition." "Barney was nice to me," Vallely said. "He is not nice to everyone." Vallely easily won the election against five other candidates, including the perennial candidate Victor Naum Themo.

Barney's 1980 campaign for Congress was a family affair. During the early weeks of the campaign, while his brother, David, searched for office space to rent, the living room of his sister Doris's home in Newton Center served as campaign headquarters, Six months earlier, Doris and her husband had moved from Charlestown to Newton Center. They had initially searched for a house in Arlington or Belmont, in Tip O'Neill's district, because they assumed Barney would be running for Congress in that district when O'Neill retired. However, they could not find the right house in that area. It was fortuitous that they had purchased a house in Newton Center because of its schools and were living in the heart of the Fourth District from which Barney was running for Congress. When David found an office in Brookline, the whole operation, including Doris's two children, ages four and two, moved to the new quarters.

Doris helped to organize the financial side of the campaign. Every day she picked up and sorted the mail, recorded the campaign contributions on index cards, and, with her children in tow, went to the bank to deposit the checks. Her husband, Jim, prepared the reports that had to be filed with the Federal Election Commission. Ann Lewis, who came from Washington to the district for about a month to work on the campaign, was a "behind the scenes" strategist and adviser. Her daughters, Patti, Susan, and Beth, assisted in the campaign as well. Elsie Frank came to the Brookline office every evening after work and stayed until nine or ten o'clock typing letters. "I typed and I typed and I typed—thank you notes or whatever else needed to be typed—and I ran errands," she said.

Barney does not enjoy campaigning. "Candidates who tell you that campaigning is fun are either (a) crazy or (b) lying, and either way unfit for office," he declared. On a rainy day in May, the *Boston Phoenix* reporter Richard Gaines accompanied Barney as he campaigned at the Chestnut Hill transit station, his first stop of the day. Gaines, who watched as a subdued candidate deferentially and enthusiastically began to introduce himself to random passers-by, describes the scene:

> It is now 7:30. Commuters are beginning to arrive more frequently. . . . A short fellow with an umbrella crosses the tracks that separate the parking lot and the station. As Frank approaches, the man says, "I don't vote in the district, Mr. Frank." The candidate retreats. "I appreciate your anticipation, sir."
>
> And then, yet another presumed Republican. Frank approaches dutifully, if somewhat hopelessly. "No, no," says the man. "Not even a maybe?" The candidate smiles playfully. "No." "I think that was a general 'Leave me alone,'" he notes.
>
> The rain intensifies. Barney Frank takes a yellow umbrella from an aide. Holding the umbrella over two gray-haired women who apparently feel they know him personally from television, he discusses the nuances of campaigning. The women are enjoying themselves. A harried commuter rushes past, intent on not missing a car that is about to leave for Boston. The candidate does not move in for the interception. "Never keep a commuter off a train or bus," he observes. The women nod in agreement.

By the end of the campaign, Barney had learned, he said that "commuters aren't very talkative in the morning but it's better to see them then than after work. They'll run right over you on their way home."

Doris recalled an incident early in the campaign that had infuriated her. "Barney had been sent out to a busy street corner in Brookline to leaflet and shake hands. He hates that sort of thing and usually would return quickly. He was gone quite a while, which was surprising. I went out looking for him and found him sitting on a stool at a nearby Brigham's finishing an ice cream cone and reading a book."

The Drinan Advisory Group was an informal organization of about forty Drinan supporters, primarily Drinan campaign coordinators from cities and towns across the district, which had functioned as an advice-giving council or brain trust to Robert Drinan. The group, led by Jerome Grossman, had formed in 1970 around the Vietnam War issue and then selected Robert Drinan as their candidate. "Drinan referred to this group as 'his minions,' more of a religious term. Others called it 'Drinan's mafia,'" Grossman said.

In May 1980, in an effort to find a worthy successor to Drinan and avoid liberal fratricide, the Drinan group took it upon themselves to attempt to narrow the unwieldy Democratic field to one consensus liberal candidate. "At the beginning, I didn't see the Drinan organization as being so instrumental in the Democratic nomination process, but they were," Jim Segel, Barney's campaign manager in Brookline, said. The candidate who received the endorsement of the Drinan group inherited Drinan's city and town campaign coordinators and became the beneficiary of Jerry Grossman's talents as a fund-raiser as well.

The Drinan group agreed to interview all of the Democratic candidates and select for their support the one who was closest to Robert Drinan ideologically and who was most electable. Drinan had no involvement in this effort.

Two candidates, Robert Shaffer and Jon Rotenberg, chose not to participate in the interviews, which took place on Sunday, May 18, at the home of Dottie Reichard in Chestnut Hill, near Boston College. Each of the candidates was assigned an interview time. The first candidate, Herbert Connolly, showed a weak grasp of the issues when he revealed that he had no knowledge of the Hyde Amendment, which would prohibit Medicaid-funded abortions. Arthur Clark, a conservative who had never been a Drinan supporter, showed up and argued the case for his candidacy before the liberal audience. "Arthur Clark was a typical small-town mayor who reflected the mores of his conservative city, and had a limited view of things based on his experience," Grossman said. "There was a lot of feeling for liberal state representative David Mofenson, who had represented Newton ably for many years," Mary Beth Cahill, a member of the Drinan group from Framingham, said. Mofenson, one of the pre-meeting favorites to pick up the group's endorsement, did not perform as well as expected. He seemed to consider himself the heir apparent to Drinan and put the group off with his "you-owe-me" message.

Barney was scheduled to appear last. The Drinan group waited and waited but there was no sign of him. While Reichard paced up and down the sidewalk in front of her house, an increasingly impatient Grossman, thinking it was Reichard who had leaked the information to Barney two weeks earlier about Drinan's not running for reelection, said to her sternly, "Your candidate hasn't arrived yet." Finally, Barney appeared at the house, about half an hour late. His driver had gotten lost. The driver, Bill Mulrow, a graduate of Yale University, had been a student of Barney's that spring at the Kennedy School at Harvard. When Reichard asked Mulrow, "Don't you know Newton? Are you from Brookline?" he replied, "No, I'm from the Bronx."

Barney entered the house. He knew most of the people there and greeted each one. "He was very charming," Reichard said. "Barney did everything right. He was bright and witty and had the right answer to all the questions, ranging from SALT to the MX missile system, and like Drinan, he took the issues from the parochial to the national and international level." "Barney, who followed national affairs religiously, was on a different level than the other candidates," Cahill described. He also was sensitive to the plight of Robert Drinan. At the end of the interview, Barney was told, "We will let you know" and he left. The conclave of cardinals of the Drinan group then caucused and the white smoke from the burned ballots signaled that a successor to Father Robert Drinan had been chosen. The group selected Barney Frank overwhelmingly on the first ballot.

"Barney was the best of the bunch from our perspective," Grossman said, though he had personal reservations about Barney because he had supported Edmund Muskie in 1972 and had gone out of his way to try to destroy the McGovern movement, which he thought was "impractical." Grossman was also concerned that Barney had the odor of a Boston politician, and he considered the fact that Barney lived outside the district to be a serious political weakness. Barbara Ackerman, the former mayor of Cambridge, who had challenged Governor Michael Dukakis in 1978, had contacted Grossman and highly recommended Barney. That recommendation was important to Grossman.

At a press conference the Drinan group held the next day, Grossman explained that several of the candidates the group had interviewed were "eminently acceptable on ideological and philosophical grounds" but that unquestionably Barney Frank was the most electable candidate and the one best able to raise money and build an organization to win the difficult contest. Privately, Grossman was not at all sure that Barney would beat Arthur Clark. "If I had to handicap the race, I would have given the edge to Clark," he said.

Sidney Blumenthal, a reporter for the *Real Paper*, an alternative Boston week-ly, wrote that Barney was "a worthy successor to Drinan." "He is idiosyncratic, obsessive, a workaholic, a different kind of priest for the parish. Better yet, Bar-ney Frank can't be removed from office by the Pope. He has a reputation in the state legislature for being well informed, innovative." Like Drinan, "he didn't ask the leadership before he took a stand."

Barney moved into an apartment on Floral Street in Newton Highlands. He boasted to a friend that the apartment was within walking distance of the MBTA trolley line and that everything he needed was nearby—a sub shop, a dry cleaner, and a drug store—and there was lots of neon in the area.

In late May, Barney went to Drinan's district office and asked Dottie Reich-ard, a former teacher and member of the Newton School Committee, to work on his campaign. According to the *Newton Tab*, "No one knows the Fourth District better than Dottie Reichard." She took a leave of absence as Drinan's district director and went to work at Barney's campaign headquarters.

"We had our first poll," Reichard recalled. "In those days, you didn't hire a group of people to make phone calls. We sat around the campaign headquar-ters and made the phone calls ourselves." Tom Kiley presented Barney with the results, a large blue binder marked, "For Candidate's Use Only." Barney took the binder with him for an interview with the *Newton Tab*, planning to refer to select parts. Sometime later, the campaign headquarters received a call from the newspaper informing the staff that Mr. Frank had left behind a large blue binder marked "For Candidate's Use Only."

One day early in the campaign, Bill Black, who often drove Barney to cam-paign events, went to the headquarters in Brookline to pick him up. It was clear to him that Barney was preoccupied with something, but he insisted, "We've got to go. We're running late for the first stop." When Barney finally got in the car, he was unusually subdued, almost weeping. He handed Black a telegram he had just received from Dorothy DiCintio, Allard Lowenstein's sister, wishing him good luck in the campaign and asking him "to carry the torch." Barney was deeply moved by the telegram and it rekindled all his memories of Lowenstein, who had been murdered a few months earlier. "I considered Barney as some-body I wanted to see take Al's place in the Congress. I don't want to say that he was Al's successor because Barney is such a brilliant person in his own right. I kind of felt he was my representative in the House," DiCintio explained. She added, "I think that Al respected and admired Barney as much as Barney did Al. Al just lead the way, getting into Congress earlier."

During the campaign, at a time when a tide of conservatism was sweeping across the country and many candidates tried to avoid being labeled as a "lib-eral," Barney did not flinch in his unabashed liberalism or mask who he was. He told the *Boston Globe*, "I'm proud of being a liberal. I'm proud of what it means. But I heard somebody call me an ultra liberal. I'm not ultra anything, not even ultra handsome."

Being a liberal, however, hurt Barney in the conservative blue-collar Roman Catholic communities in the western part of the district, the factory towns of Fitchburg, Leominster, and Gardner. As David Gilmartin, the popular mayor of Fitchburg, who decided to drop out of the race, explained: "A small town working man with two bologna sandwiches in his lunch pail thinks a liberal politician is someone who wants to give one of them away." An ultra-liberal would no doubt be seen as someone who wanted to give both bologna sandwiches away.

The conservative western part of the Fourth Congressional District provided as much as 40 percent of the potential vote in the Democratic primary. The voters in many of these small towns never recovered from the loss of Philip Philbin in 1970 and never really accepted Robert Drinan. In the 1978 Democratic primary Drinan eked out a mere seventeen-vote victory in Leominster over a virtually unknown challenger.

By the time of the first candidate debate on June 5, the Democratic field had been narrowed to Arthur Clark, David Mofenson, Robert Shaffer, and Barney. Jerome Grossman, whom *Boston Globe* columnist Robert Healy once referred to as "the Mayor Daly of the left," in supporting Barney, had successfully pushed all of the other liberal candidates, except for David Mofenson, out of the Democratic primary. Mofenson, a mild mannered, hard-working and solidly liberal legislator, chose to give up certain reelection to the state legislature to stay in the race for Congress. Mofenson, who felt he should have had the endorsement of the Drinan group, called Barney's decision to enter the race "rank opportunism."

The debate was held at the Newton Marriott Hotel before a crowd of about 150. The other candidates almost immediately went on the attack against Barney, leaving him feeling as though he were in a tag-team wrestling match. "Different people kept coming into the ring to fight," he said. Arthur Clark, who was deep-voiced and spoke rather slowly, commented in his prepared opening statement, "Baaarrr-ney has represented interests foreign to my district."

David Mofenson was a conspicuous and imposing figure at nearly six feet, seven inches tall. A graduate of Tufts University and Boston University Law School, the thirty-seven-year-old Mofenson was completing his tenth year representing Newton in the state legislature, where he served as chairman of the Committee on Human Services and Elderly Affairs and had a reputation for constituent service. Mofenson contrasted his role as a quiet, methodical, workmanlike legislator with that of Barney and asserted, "The United States Congress does not need a self-proclaimed guerrilla fighter." Barney responded, "I try to be noisy and my district has benefited from it. I'll do the same in Washington." Barney explained that his style would be similar to that of Robert Drinan. "Drinan was a noisy congressman. He always took a firm stand and put up a fight. That's the kind of congressman I'd be—pugnacious. I'm good at thinking on my feet. I'm not always as polite as I should be but I'm a good man to have around in a legislative brawl."

Mofenson, who had lived and worked in the district for twenty years and believed that it was his turf, bitterly resented the encroachment of his one-time liberal ally into "his district" and accused Barney of being a "carpetbagger." Barney, who had been living in Boston three-quarters of a mile from Brookline, replied, "The notion that three-quarters of a mile from the line one way or another matters really baffles me. The problems and issues that would face my constituents and me, nuclear power, housing, and inflation, are not made any different by an accident of three-quarters of a mile."

Clark read almost all of his answers from prepared cards. When Clark was questioned about tax policy, Barney sarcastically remarked that he didn't have a card on taxes, so he couldn't answer. At one point in the debate, Clark pounded the table and promised not to accept a penny in campaign contributions from the large oil companies. Barney added, "I will not accept any of the oil company money that none of us have been offered."

Drinan had remained neutral in the Democratic primary. In late June, however, he decided it was important for him to support Barney in order to hold the seat for a liberal. According to Drinan, the decision to endorse Barney in the primary "was simply natural and almost inevitable." He called Barney and said, "Do you want me to endorse you in the primary? I don't want you to feel beholden to me." Barney instantly responded that he would gladly take the endorsement and thanked Drinan for his backing. Barney considered Drinan's endorsement to be valuable in pushing those on the fence, torn between Mofenson and himself, into his camp.

At a press conference at the Barney Frank campaign headquarters in Brookline on Saturday morning, June 21, Drinan enthusiastically endorsed Barney as his successor. "In terms of electability, in terms of effectiveness for the people he seeks to represent, in terms of an imaginative and unwavering commitment to economic justice, to civil rights and civil liberties, Barney Frank is the right man at the right time for the citizens of the Fourth Congressional District," he said. Drinan praised Barney as an "individual of uncommon character and achievement" and said he was "someone who will not sound retreat, someone whose commitment to the public interest is so deep-seated that he will retain the courage of his convictions and resist repeated efforts to run for political cover." Drinan concluded his remarks by saying that Barney "has the courage and the ability to become an outstanding congressman."

When Drinan had finished his prepared remarks, a reporter asked whether he needed permission from the Roman Catholic Church to make the endorsement. Drinan, with an edge in his voice, replied, "I am the congressman until January 1. I'm committing political acts every day."

As a courtesy, Reichard had phoned David Mofenson to inform him in advance that Drinan planned to endorse Barney that Saturday. Mofenson had been a strong supporter of Drinan over the years and had been actively seeking Drinan's endorsement. "It was a bit painful because I had nothing really against the two or three other prominent people in the Democratic primary," Drinan said. He remembered being confronted by one of the candidates (Mofenson) after his statement that morning about why he had not chosen him. "I simply said that the statement speaks for itself," Drinan recalled. Mofenson was angry and bitter. He felt betrayed by Drinan's endorsement of Barney and charged that Drinan had broken a promise to remain neutral. Mofenson told the press, "Today's statement by Robert Drinan is clear evidence that Barney Frank cannot win this race on his own record. Frank's candidacy has become stagnant."

Drinan's endorsement of Barney was a blow to Mofenson's struggling campaign, but Mofenson remained in the race. Under repeated pressure from fellow liberals to drop out in favor of Barney, Mofenson declared, "I will not be pulled out of this race. I will be the next congressman from the Fourth Congressional District." Despite his low polling numbers and inability to raise the campaign funds needed to seriously compete in the congressional race, Mofenson was adamant and even zealous about remaining in the race. Later he admitted that when he entered the race he had underestimated the influence of money. "There will be no second mortgage on my house. When the money is gone, that's it. It's a long shot but we'll make it a good shot," he said.

Once Drinan endorsed Barney for Congress, he campaigned with him throughout the Fourth Congressional District, against the wishes of many in the church hierarchy. Their first joint campaign appearance was in Framingham, at an event coordinated by Mary Beth Cahill, a twenty-six-year-old political hand who later became director of EMILY's List, the organization that helps pro-choice female candidates win elective office, and who in 2004 took over as manager of John Kerry's floundering presidential campaign, turned the campaign around in the Iowa and New Hampshire primaries, and helped Kerry win the Democratic presidential nomination. As a member of the Framingham Democratic Committee, Cahill had run Drinan's Framingham district office and had managed his campaign in that area in 1978 and therefore knew everyone who had supported Drinan. "Barney didn't have many relationships in Framingham, a key battleground in the primary, and it was important for him to get as much support in Framingham as possible," she said.

Drinan was devoted to getting Barney elected and did almost anything he could to get attention from voters. He would chase women who were pushing their shopping carts to their cars in the supermarket parking lot, pointing to Barney and calling out, "You have to meet this man. He's going to be your new congressman." Bill Black remembers seeing Drinan stand up on a bench to draw a crowd of people to introduce them to Barney. "When you saw this cadaverous-looking priest who had such an abrupt manner out campaigning it was a sight to behold, because he loved politics, was very interested in people, and drew enormous energy from crowds," Cahill said.

Barney saw that Drinan's decision to accede to the papal order to abandon public office caused him great anguish. "It denied him the chance to do something that he thought was terribly important to his well being." Campaigning with Barney reopened some of the pain for the priest. "It was a hard thing for him to do but he did so graciously," Barney said.

Bill Mulrow, who had finished his second year at the Kennedy School, had planned to work for the Democratic National Committee that summer preparing for the presidential convention being held in New York City. But when Barney decided to run for Congress, Mulrow joined the campaign, ultimately becoming a deputy campaign manager. During the first few months of the campaign, Mulrow did some driving and served as the "body guy," spending almost all his time traveling with the candidate around the district. "Having an Irish Catholic kid next to Barney was a good fit politically, particularly in the western part of the district," Mulrow said. He described Barney as "the hardest-working candidate I have ever seen." "If he needed to get up at four a.m. to be at a factory gate in Leominster, he wouldn't complain. He demanded a lot of himself and accordingly demanded a lot of those that worked for him."

Mark Horan, a volunteer driver who would later run Jim Segal's unsuccessful campaign for state treasurer and is now a senior aide to the mayor of Somerville, Massachusetts, said he has never seen a candidate more dedicated than Barney. "On Sunday mornings, I would drive Barney from one Jewish deli to another in Newton and Brookline because Jewish people would be going out to pick up their dozen bagels and other items," Horan said. "Don't forget to wrap the onion bagels separately" soon became part of his vocabulary. "Barney didn't care for that duty but he did it. I've seen candidates you had to drag out of bed to do it."

"Barney was focused on winning the primary and campaigned at a relentless pace," Mary Beth Cahill recalled. "We did three coffees a night and whatever else we could do during the day." "Sometimes I would pick him up on a Sunday morning," she said. "He would buy a newspaper and go to the trash can and throw three-quarters of the paper away immediately—the lifestyle pages, all the real estate ads, all the car stuff, et cetera—and enter the car with a greatly reduced newspaper. He would just open up the newspaper and start reading it. You knew when to talk and when not to talk."

As the primary campaign progressed, Barney, who had started out believing that his election was a long shot, began to realize that the job he had always dreamed of was now within his grasp and he wanted it desperately. "The more Barney could see that it was doable and winnable, the more intense he got and the more difficult to get along with," Jim Segel said. "I knew him as a warm, caring person but he wasn't during that campaign. People would go out of their way for him and he would be rude. He would go to a house party, stay in the kitchen, and then come out for a few minutes." Segel remembers that at one such event, Barney put his cigar ashes on the floor of the host's living room. At another neighborhood coffee, when asked about rumors that a prison will be built in the area, he shouted back, "What is this? Not in my backyard?" all the time shoving jumbo chocolate chip cookies into his mouth. "I'd rather have a prison next door to me than a school. If the prisoners get out, they leave as fast as they can. If the kids get out, they just want to hang around and get into trouble," he said.

The candidate was often preoccupied with food. According to several drivers, any time they were near Jack and Marian's Deli in Brookline Village, Barney would stop for a sandwich. "Where are we going tonight?" he would ask the driver. "Wayland" one driver said. "WASPs," Barney replied. "There isn't going to be any food." They would stop and get a sandwich before going to the event.

Reichard recalls that Barney sometimes spent twenty hours a day campaigning, and "he was pretty heavy then," she said. "The more anxious he was, the more he ate, the more he became unhappy and abrasive. It made for some tense moments."

When Tom Kiley met with most of his other campaign clients after conducting a major poll, he would first make a presentation to the candidate, sometimes using a slide show. It was different with Barney. "Barney would say, 'Let me take a look,' and grab the report out of my hand," Kiley said. "He would thumb through the report in a matter of minutes, digesting most of the polling information, while saying, 'Not doing as well as I thought there,' 'That issue is not cutting,' '65—we should be getting 70 percent there.'" Barney would have some questions and then he and Kiley would discuss the report. "Yes, Barney spoke a mile-a-minute. Yes, he thought faster than anyone else in the room. However, he created a sense of team. He assembled everyone in a room and discussed matters and got our input. You felt a part of the venture," Kiley said.

The Democratic primary became largely a two-horse race between Barney and Arthur Clark, a solid but not flashy, suburban Roman Catholic conservative, with no intellectual pretense. Clark had entered the race at the urging of friends who told him there would be several liberals in the primary and suggested that the district was more moderate than people thought. Also, Clark was not risking anything, since he did not have to give up the mayoral office to run. There was no single issue that dominated the campaign. It centered on differences in ideology, a liberal-conservative tug of war, and style. To many, Clark symbolized the old guard, while Barney looked like the next generation of leader.

Clark had a reputation as a shrewd politician, and he was a formidable opponent. He was born in Waltham, where he grew up and graduated from high school. He served as a U.S. Navy intelligence officer during World War II and later was a manager at Quirk Tire Company in Watertown. In his first race for public office, the 1969 mayoralty election in Waltham, Clark trailed after the initial vote tally but eventually won by fifty-six votes in a citywide recount. He became a popular mayor of a thriving city with a budget surplus. He was regarded as a solid money manager and credited with bringing several high technology companies into Waltham. Clark had been active in the Massachusetts Mayors Association, including as president and chairman of the board of directors. He had also been chairman of the New England delegation to the U.S. Conference of Mayors during the fight for reenactment of revenue sharing. Clark had been reelected more times (six terms) than any other mayor in the city's history and had never lost an election. He had a real base of support and a strong hold on this conservative, Catholic, heavily Italian, working-class city of about sixty thousand people.

"Clark was regarded as being a tough behind-the-scenes player. He had the kind of polish that being a mayor for a long time can teach you. He knew how to talk to strangers and work a room," Dan Payne, the media adviser for the Barney Frank campaign, said. Cahill described him as "a back-slapping full time pol" who drove around campaigning in a big bus. Clark was also a good fundraiser and had the endorsement of Democratic senator Henry "Scoop" Jackson of Washington State, who had won the 1976 Democratic presidential primary in Massachusetts.

Clark made few mistakes during the campaign. He campaigned with confidence, smiling frequently and moving well through a crowd. He was a working-class businessman, a former tire salesman with five children and two grandchildren. At six feet tall and 180 pounds, he had a grandfatherly look about him that many people found comforting. Clark was not a very enlightened or creative mayor but he had few negatives. His administration was relatively scandal free. In essence, he did not turn voters on or off.

Clark reminded voters that Barney was not from the Fourth District and did not represent the same type of constituency he did. "I think the Fourth District is entitled to its own congressman. I don't think Back Bay and Beacon

Hill need two congressmen," he contended. Clark's tire company in Waltham was unionized, and he had cordial relations with municipal unions as mayor of Waltham and considerable labor support in the campaign. The Massachusetts AFL–CIO, with its four hundred thousand members, including forty thousand in the Fourth District, endorsed Clark in the race. In addition, the Amalgamated Transit Union, which represented most of the employees at the Massachusetts Bay Transit Authority, strongly supported Clark as a means of exacting revenge against Barney for his efforts as a state legislator to pass an MBTA management rights bill that limited the union's powers and did away with several previously untouchable practices.

The International Ladies Garment Workers Union and several other manufacturing labor unions supported Barney, in part because he had introduced legislation calling for a boycott of products made by J. P. Stevens, a strongly anti-union company.

Clark considered himself a "moderate-conservative" and favored Governor Edward King's "businessman's approach" to government rather than Drinan's liberal activism. Clark supported a balanced budget for the federal government and said he wanted to bring "fiscal sanity" to Washington. On the abortion issue, Clark was strongly "pro-life." He also endorsed a bigger defense budget as a means for strengthening the position of the United States abroad and creating more jobs in the district. He was an ardent supporter of the MX missile system and so comfortable talking about defense that, inevitably, when he was asked a question about health care or education, he would work into his answer that he believed in a strong national defense.

The city of Waltham, with just under thirty thousand voters, accounted for about one-sixth of the voters in the Fourth District. With a hotly contested race between two Waltham city councilors, Joseph Maguire and Peter Trombley, for the Democratic nomination for an open state representative seat, the primary turnout in Waltham was likely to be high, a distinct advantage for Clark. Barney was irked that many leading liberals in the administration at Brandeis University, in Waltham, were supporting Mayor Clark.

While Barney and Clark were locked in a tight Democratic primary race to succeed Drinan, Mofenson touted the support of Massachusetts House Speaker Thomas McGee (whom Barney had irritated in the legislature time and time again), who called Mofenson "the most credible liberal in the House." In mid-August, Mofenson intensified his campaign attacks on Barney, often failing to even mention Clark. He was bitter and territorial about Barney's running in his district, feeling that Barney was invading the territory of an ally. "What is he, NATO?" Barney asked. "I could never abandon my constituents overnight like that and move into a new community to run for office," Mofenson told the

Boston Globe. "What will Barney Frank do after the election, continue to forum shop? I will continue to live in Newton after this election is over and after the Fourth Congressional District is redistricted." The *Boston Globe* political columnist Robert L. Turner pointed out that Mofenson's legislative district in Newton comprised less than 7 percent of the Fourth Congressional District and noted that there were twenty-two cities and towns in the Fourth District. "Mofenson doesn't live in 21 of them. Frank doesn't live in the 22nd. So what's the difference?" Turner asked. Although Mofenson later dropped out of the contest and supported Barney, he remains bitter today, almost three decades later, about Barney's entry into the race.

Barney became the target of constant attack from Clark, Mofenson, and to a lesser degree, Shaffer. Barney's record and personality became the central focus of the campaign. At an August 13 candidate debate, Arthur Clark dubbed Barney "an ultra liberal," out of touch with the district. David Mofenson continued his attack on him as a carpetbagger, hopping from one district to the other. Richard Jones, who had entered the race before Drinan announced his decision not to seek reelection and was running unopposed in the Republican primary, complained that Barney has always been on government payrolls. Barney was quick to reply, pointing out the irony of having Jones, an army dentist for twenty years who had retired at age forty-three as a full colonel with an army pension, attack him for being on the government payroll. He suggested it was like having the six-foot-seven-inch Mofenson accuse him of being too tall.

At a press conference on the morning of August 27, Robert Shaffer, a businessman from Fitchburg who was the most conservative Democrat in the race and in last place in the polls, dropped out of the contest and threw his support to Clark. At a candidate debate two weeks earlier, Shaffer had said, "I wish we could take the whole Democratic Party and put it in a time machine and take it back to 1952 and bring back Harry Truman." At the press conference he said, "Arthur Clark means jobs, security for our country and a businesslike approach to government." Shaffer had kind words for Mofenson but went on the offensive against Barney, calling him a "political opportunist" and charging that he had already changed his stripes several times. At the time, Tom Kiley's poll showed Barney with 33 percent, Arthur Clark with 25 percent, David Mofenson with 11 percent, and Robert Shaffer with about 7 percent of the vote. Thus, Shaffer's departure put the race in a dead heat between Barney and Clark. "I became very pessimistic when this happened because the race was so close," Barney said.

Following Shaffer's withdrawal, the Barney Frank campaign agreed that unless they redoubled their efforts to persuade Mofenson to withdraw from the election, Barney might lose. The strategy for getting Mofenson out of the race focused on identifying twenty key Mofenson supporters, presenting them with the poll showing that Mofenson had no chance of winning, and pressuring them to urge him to withdraw. "Mofenson's support in Newton and Brookline cut sharply into Barney's liberal base. Any vote Mofenson got would be a vote taken away from Barney," Tom Kiley said.

In late August, John Kerry organized a breakfast meeting at a hotel in Newton Corner with Kiley and David Frank, who was managing his brother's primary election campaign. Kerry volunteered that he was well aware that Mofenson was siphoning votes away from Barney, especially in Newton, and that he wanted to speak to Mofenson about dropping out. "We just sat there and agreed with Kerry," David said. "We thought—wow, this is terrific, with the race so close, how great it would be if Mofenson, who like Barney was liberal and Jewish, dropped out."

"It was important that Barney win and that we try to do everything we could to unite our side, the same thing we did with Bob Drinan in 1970," Kerry recalled. He subsequently met with Mofenson and urged him to drop out of the contest.

In an August 27 editorial, the *Boston Globe* endorsed Barney in the Democratic primary. The newspaper explained its choice: "The Democratic primary includes two progressive and effective state legislators. In normal circumstances Representative David Mofenson would be a clear choice for the job. But there is a difference this year. It is Representative Barney Frank. He is an exceptional politician and he deserves the votes of 4th District Democrats." A few days later Robert L. Turner wrote that "Barney Frank was born to be a congressman." "When it comes to a grasp of issues that affect both a district and a nation—and the ability to make a difference in a body of 435 members—Frank stands alone." Turner observed that Mofenson, a liberal, could draw just enough votes from Frank to throw the election to Clark, a pro-life conservative, and noted that Mofenson's continued presence in the race could well betray the cause he represented. Clark, however, continued to describe the primary as a three-candidate contest and attempted to make Mofenson appear as a viable candidate so that liberal voters in Newton and Brookline would not be dissuaded from casting their primary ballots for him.

In early September, rumors circulated that Mofenson might drop out of the race. On Wednesday evening, September 3, Mofenson failed to appear at a candidate forum at Temple Israel in Brookline, the first debate in the campaign that he had missed. Later that evening, Barney met with Mofenson. Dick Morningstar, Barney's campaign treasurer, had learned from his next-door neighbor, Sidney Boorstein, a close friend of Mofenson's and his chief fund-raiser, that Mofenson was dropping out of the race.

The next morning, September 4, at a joint press conference at the State House, Mofenson announced that he was dropping out of the contest and was backing his fellow liberal, Barney Frank. Trailing by a wide margin in the polls and faced with a thirty-thousand-dollar campaign debt, Mofenson had no realistic chance to win. He had made the decision to withdraw the previous evening, he said, after weighing his prospects in the light of the increasing and fierce pressure from the Barney Frank camp to withdraw and from the Arthur Clark camp to continue. He cited an empty campaign treasury as his prime reason for leaving the race.

"The district must have a clear choice between progressive and conservative candidacies," Mofenson asserted. "I want to see a progressive voice and vote in Congress in the Fourth Congressional District. Barney Frank will be the voice of progressive Democratic policies." Mofenson referred to Barney as "a good friend" and added that although the two men had some differences, they agreed on "an overwhelming majority of the issues." Mofenson did not want to be the spoiler and throw the Democratic primary race to Clark.

"That was important," Barney said. "If Mofenson had gotten five thousand votes, I could have lost the election." At a fund-raiser in October to help Mofenson retire the thirty-thousand-dollar campaign deficit, an event attended by former governor Michael Dukakis, Lieutenant Governor Thomas O'Neill III, Speaker Thomas McGee, and others, Barney expressed his "admiration for the graciousness and generosity David showed during the campaign."

As the primary campaign entered its final week, Clark introduced a radio commercial that painted his opponent as a big-city candidate lacking an understanding of suburban problems. As the ad begins, the announcer says, "Barney Frank wants to legalize prostitution. In Arthur Clark's opinion, nobody in the Fourth District wants to move the Combat Zone here. Barney Frank may know all about the Back Bay and Boston. But just because he moved into the Fourth District doesn't mean he's changed what he stands for. And what does Barney Frank stand for?" In the background, a women's voice is heard softly repeating the words "racial pressure," "busing," "crime," "prostitution," "Combat Zone."

Barney immediately confronted Clark about the ad. "To exploit racial tension in a metropolitan area where people are actually being killed is irresponsible," he declared. "There are no racial issues in the Fourth Congressional District." He accused Clark of using the New Right tactics of innuendo, smear, and distortion.

At a September 8 candidate forum at Waltham High School that was broadcast on the radio, Barney took aim at the Republican candidate Richard Jones's "cruel position" of opposing federal rent subsidies for housing for the elderly and price controls on energy. Clark talked about "cutting the waste and fat out of government" and pledged that his businesslike management of Waltham would be continued in Washington. In response, Barney argued that voters deserve specifics. "How many 'pro-waste, pro-unemployment and pro-inflation' candidates have run for office recently?" he asked. "Unless a candidate is willing to be specific," he said, "no waste will be cut back."

On Wednesday evening, September 10, Governor Edward King attended a fund-raiser for Arthur Clark, where he said, "Given the choice of the two candidates, I would choose Arthur Clark for the Fourth District." The Frank campaign pounced on this statement and began airing radio ads linking Clark with King. In the spot the announcer says that the same political strategists who brought Massachusetts Ed King now want to put Arthur Clark in Congress. At the end of the ad, Barney says, "You can fool some of the people some of the time, but you can't fool the same people twice in two years."

Barney stopped his personal campaigning for Congress at sundown on Wednesday, September 10, in observance of the Jewish holiday of Rosh Hashanah and announced that he would resume campaigning after the holiday.

The lift in the Barney Frank campaign organization created by David Mofenson's withdrawal from the race was short-lived. The next morning, five days before the Democratic primary election, Cardinal Humberto Medeiros, the Roman Catholic archbishop of Boston, issued an open pastoral letter denouncing abortion as a "horrendous crime and deadly sin" and urging Catholics to "save our children, born and unborn" by voting in the primary against candidates who did not favor right-to-life legislation. Although the letter did not mention any candidates by name, it was clearly aimed at defeating Barney and the first-term Democratic Congressman James Shannon, a twenty-eight-year-old Irish Catholic seeking reelection in the adjoining Fifth District, who was being challenged in the primary by Robert Hatem, a conservative Raytheon executive from Lowell. The letter was an effort to turn the Democratic races in the large Catholic-populated Fourth and Fifth Districts into a referendum on abortion and a barometer of church influence. It read: "Those who make abortion possible by law—such as legislators and those who promote, defend and elect these same lawmakers—cannot separate themselves from that guilt which accompanies this horrendous crime and deadly sin. It is imperative that Catholics realize the law of God extends into the polling booth. . . . Your answer to this call to vote must not be taken lightly since it could be a matter of life or death for millions yet to come. May our values be a living witness of the faith and hope and love we show."

The Barney Frank campaign staff had no advance notice of Cardinal Medeiros's intentions. But the letter gave the race a high profile, and, as Barney's press secretary, Thaleia Schlesinger, recalled, "Everybody showed up. Television cameras showed up. Radio people showed up. The local and national press showed up. Jack Germond, a political columnist for the *Baltimore Sun* and a regular on the *Today Show* and the *McLaughlin Group*, showed up." Schlesinger did not try to contact Barney. She issued a brief statement to the press that it was very unfortunate that the attack came on a day when Barney Frank was in synagogue observing one of the important Jewish religious holidays and would not be available to respond and that the campaign would have no further comment. Later Schlesinger said that the letter threw everything out of kilter and created a sense of uncertainty. "Who knew what the response would be at the polls? We did not have a clue. There was no sense in polling. It was too late to change anything and in any event what would you do?"

That morning, when Shannon was informed by his staff that Cardinal Medeiros had issued a letter urging Roman Catholics to vote against candidates who were pro-choice on abortion and denouncing him and Barney Frank, and that the press wanted to know his response, he was taken aback and asked, "What was Barney's response?" Told that Barney could not respond because he was in temple praying on Rosh Hashanah, Shannon said, "Tell the press that I am in temple too. I'm going to temple right now."

Barney was also taken aback by the cardinal's statement. Having served in the state legislature for four terms, he knew the important role the Catholic Church played in Massachusetts politics. He was also disappointed because he had worked with the church on social justice issues while in the legislature and thought that he had a better relationship with the Catholic Church than was manifest in the cardinal's letter.

After the Jewish holiday, Barney chose not to respond publicly to the cardinal's statement. "That was the time to turn the other cheek," he said. But Senator Edward Kennedy, who was supporting both Barney and Shannon, publicly disagreed with Cardinal Medeiros's admonition that Catholics should not vote for candidates who are pro-choice on abortion. Kennedy avoided criticizing the cardinal but urged voters "to make up their minds on the whole range of issues before us today." "That has been the tradition in our state," he said. Speaking at a previously scheduled fund-raiser for Barney at the Sidney Hill Country Club in Chestnut Hill on Friday evening, September 12, Kennedy exhorted the crowd to "reject the forces of negativism, the voices of despair, the voices of distortion and misrepresentation, and the New Right."

The letter from Cardinal Medeiros was printed on the front page of the *Pilot*, the official newspaper of the archdiocese, and copies were distributed to over four hundred Catholic churches in the district. Priests were directed to read the cardinal's letter from the pulpit to their congregants at services that Sunday before the Tuesday primary.

Cardinal Medeiros, who succeeded the charismatic, energetic, and witty Cardinal Richard Cushing, had avoided controversy and made few public comments. Many church observers were surprised by his action. The *Boston Globe* reported that Cardinal Medeiros was moved to write the letter by his outrage over the support the outspoken and highly visible Father Drinan had given Barney in the race, campaigning with him throughout the district and taping several radio ads for him.

Barney was the object of a double-barreled attack by the Roman Catholic Church. That same day, September 11, a public letter was released that was signed by Rev. Leo Battista, the coordinator of pro-life activities and director of Catholic Charities in the Worcester Diocese, and thirteen other clergy members, asking Father Drinan to withdraw his endorsement of Barney Frank. Battista attacked Barney for being an advocate of prostitution, pornography, and X-rated films on television, activities that he called a "direct threat to the Judeo-Christian family." The Battista letter was circulated in Catholic churches in the Fourth District.

In response, a coalition of fifty-five clerics, including Boston-area ministers, priests, rabbis, and nuns, signed a letter and held a press conference denouncing the Battista letter as an attack on the character of Barney Frank. Barney called the letter "a deliberate and systematic distortion of my record" that came on Rosh Hashanah when he could not respond. "You can debate whether or not there should be a Combat Zone in Boston. But to say I want a Combat Zone in every city or town is a blatant lie," he said.

The Medeiros letter inflamed both sides. Some Catholics considered the Church's action to be overreaching. As soon as the letter went out, the Barney Frank campaign headquarters started receiving phone calls from people identifying themselves as Catholics, who said, as Reichard recalls, "I am Catholic and I don't believe in abortion. But, I am going to vote for Barney Frank because I don't need the church telling me what to do." Or, "The church should stay out of politics. Isn't that what they told Drinan to do?" In Newton and Brookline, residents were doubly outraged that the cardinal's sneak attack occurred during Rosh Hashanah. Over the next few days, cars would pull up to the Barney Frank campaign headquarters and people would jump out and deliver campaign checks along with a request to use the contribution against what the cardinal was doing.

Roger Sohn, a young man from Newton, who had just started a residency in orthopedics at Tufts University Hospital and had never before actively participated in a political campaign, was so angered by the cardinal's statement that he felt a need to act. That Sunday, he drove to the Barney Frank for Congress headquarters in Newton and asked for a large campaign sign. He took the sign and drove to the busy intersection at Route 9 and Hammond Street in Newton, across from the Longwood Cricket Club, a highly visible spot. There he stood on the corner, holding up the large Barney Frank for Congress placard for passing motorists during most of that day. In mid-afternoon, a passenger in a car waved at him and yelled to thank him for his support. It was the candidate, Barney Frank.

Robert Drinan did not waiver in his support of Barney. He rejected the request by Battista and other clergy members to reconsider his endorsement, declaring, "We stand at another crossroads this year. I can think of no one I would rather take my place than Barney Frank. We can choose the right path; we can send Barney Frank to Congress." Drinan kept campaigning for Barney as if nothing had happened. He campaigned with him in the heavily Catholic town of Fitchburg on Saturday, September 13. "I'm Congressman Drinan, meet your new congressman," he would say as he introduced Barney to people along Main Street. When the two men entered the Barney Rosen Company on Main Street, Drinan said, "I always buy my socks here." "I think I'll get a pair too," Barney said. "All my socks are black. I don't like to sort socks."

Later that day, Barney campaigned at the busy Weston town dump, a sanitary landfill facility. "Are you going to help me unload?" a man searching through the back seat of his car for plastic bags filled with trash asked. "In my business, we just deliver," Barney replied. John Kerry joined Barney in campaigning at the Weston dump site that day.

The cardinal's comments galvanized the Barney Frank campaign staff, and some began to view the race for Congress from the Fourth District in Massachusetts as a referendum on the influence of the Catholic Church. At the final televised debate on Sunday, September 14, Clark, who backed a constitutional amendment banning abortion and opposed Medicaid funding of abortions for poor women, supported the cardinal's action. "The Church has a right to step in," he said. "The cardinal got involved because there is an erosion of moral fiber in this country."

The cardinal's action stimulated a near-record turnout in the primaries, bringing around thirty thousand more voters to the polls than expected. Alan Licarie, the executive secretary of the Newton Election Commission, whose past voter turnout predictions had always been accurate within 3 percent, had predicted that thirteen thousand Democrats in Newton would vote. More than twenty thousand Democrats voted in Newton. Over eighty thousand people, or almost 20 percent of the district, turned out to vote in the Democratic primary. The *Boston Globe* columnist Ellen Goodman, a resident of Newton, wrote: "People in my town went to the polls angry. . . . I haven't seen anything like it in years." The near-record voter turnout in Newton and Brookline, with over 50 percent of the eligible voters going to the polls, accounted for almost 40 percent of the Democratic primary vote in the district and they voted overwhelmingly for Barney Frank.

Jim Segel had served as the Barney Frank campaign coordinator in Brookline, and Conan O'Brien, later of NBC's *Late Night* and *The Tonight Show* but then a Brookline High School senior, had been a precinct organizer. Barney carried the town of Brookline with 10,284 votes, the largest primary vote in Brookline history, and overwhelmed Clark with 78 percent of the vote. To put that vote total in Brookline in perspective, the 10,284 votes cast for Barney was more than the combined total of votes received there by Ted Kennedy, Jimmy Carter, and Jerry Brown in the Democratic presidentail primary six months earlier and more than the combined total of votes received by Michael Dukakis, Edward King, and Barbara Ackerman in the 1978 Democratic primary for governor.

Barney won Newton by a 7-to-3 margin, or roughly eight thousand votes. His margin of victory in Brookline and Newton was large enough to overcome Clark's lopsided win in Waltham, where he captured 90 percent of the vote, and Clark's victories in the cities and towns in the conservative western part of the district. Clark carried four of the five cities and seven of the fifteen towns in the Fourth District. Barney won the Democratic primary by fewer than five thousand votes, 52 to 47 percent. Jim Segel and Robert White, Clark's campaign manager, agreed that if Mofenson had stayed in the race, Clark would have been the Democratic candidate for Congress.

Barney claimed victory that night at a gathering of more than eight hundred supporters jammed into the ballroom of the Sheraton Tara Hotel in Framingham. He told the cheering supporters that they had "reaffirmed the fundamental principle that government is meant to serve us" and paid tribute to Robert Drinan. "It was ten years ago that Father Drinan won his first congressional primary," he said. "I feel humble and proud to acknowledge part of the reason I won was because Drinan earned the respect of people around the district. This enhances my winning enormously."

The Democratic nominee for Congress wasted no time in focusing attention on his GOP opponent in the general election. Charging that Richard Jones held the view that the government cannot do anything at all to address society's ills, Barney said, "I don't think that government is omniscient. I do think we can work to make government serve us."

He concluded his remarks with a good-natured ribbing of his press secretary, Thaleia Schlesinger. "I have gone now since early May without saying anything outrageous. If Thaleia bites her lips any more she is going to look like Herbert Hoover." "I wouldn't say he went from May without saying anything outrageous, but he tried," Schlesinger recalled.

James Shannon was also victorious in the primary. Cokie Roberts sent Barney a telegram that read, "Black hats 2, Red hats nothing." The headline in the *Boston Herald* the next day was "Teddy 2, Cardinal 0."

Barney was very successful in raising campaign funds because of all the connections he had developed over the years. He received a tremendous amount of financial support from people in Ward 5 in Boston, from residents in Newton and Brookline, and from all over the country. Barney spent over $315,000 in the primary election, compared with Arthur Clark's $190,575. He set a record for spending in a congressional election in Massachusetts, eclipsing the previous high set by Nick Mavroules, who spent $290,000 in 1978 for both the primary and general election.

After Barney won the primary, most people assumed that the general election was a mere formality. A week before the Democratic primary, Renee Loth had written in the *Boston Phoenix*: "The winner next Tuesday is all but guaranteed a seat in Congress since not even the most imaginative or insecure could write a reasonable scenario that allowed for victory in November by Richard Jones, the ultra-conservative Republican libertarian."

Mayor Clark and the people in his camp never made peace with Barney. Clark waited almost twenty-four hours after the election results were in before conceding defeat publicly. He was furious over losing the primary and refused to endorse Barney in the general election, saying he and Barney were "miles apart philosophically." Clark considered running in the general election as an Independent, as Philip Philbin had done ten years earlier after losing to Robert Drinan in the Democratic primary, but decided not to.

While Clark did not publicly endorse the Republican candidate, Richard Jones, he supported him in any way he could, privately urging his supporters to back Jones and putting a lot of pressure on people in Waltham not to support Barney in the general election. Many of those in Clark's inner circle supported and worked hard for the conservative Republican nominee in the general election. The Massachusetts State Labor Council, which had strongly backed Clark in the primary, stayed out of the general election at the urging of the MBTA unions.

Tip O'Neill had remained neutral during the Democratic primary. Most of the staff in his office, however, had supported Clark in the primary because they knew him and he was their contemporary. After Barney won the primary, O'Neill campaigned with him in the general election. While they were campaigning together in Waltham, O'Neill asked Barney what committee he wanted to be on in Congress, and Barney answered, "the Banking Committee, because it has the jurisdiction over urban affairs and housing." "Well, you're on it!" O'Neill responded.

Michael Dukakis had remained neutral in the primary in deference to David Mofenson, whom he described as "a good guy" with whom he was "close." But he was not a vindictive person and he endorsed Barney two days after the primary, despite all the grief Barney had caused him when he was governor, which Dukakis admitted made him "very unhappy." But, Dukakis said, "don't talk to Kitty about those years. She still has great difficulty getting over what went on there with Barney. But you're talking about who is going to represent you in Congress. I had no doubt that Barney would do that well." Back in August, at a political gathering in Nantucket, when Kitty had been asked to try to persuade David Mofenson to get out of the race because the Barney Frank primary was important, she had looked out over the sea and said, "Some things are unforgivable."

In his endorsement of Barney, Dukakis said of him, "He has demonstrated a rare ability to combine sensitivity for the needs of his fellow citizens with leadership in the attempt to root out waste and fraud in the state welfare system." Dukakis even recorded a sixty-second radio ad for him in which he said, "I've known Barney for many, many years, and I can tell you he is one of those rare public officials who calls them as he sees them, who isn't afraid to speak out for what he believes is right, and who is as forthright and honest as anyone I have ever known in public life."

One day, Barney wanted to have his picture taken with President Jimmy Carter when the president arrived at Boston's Logan Airport, so he persuaded Mark Horan, who worked for the president of the University of Massachusetts during the day and drove Barney around some evenings and weekends, to call in sick so he could drive. "We kept going through checkpoints. You could never do that today obviously, to see the president of the United States. I don't remember what we were using as a cover story, probably just that Barney was a state representative," Horan said. "I remember driving down a runway practically to get to Air Force One. Barney told me, 'Whatever you do, make sure to zig and zag when they start shooting at the car.'" Most of the Democratic candidates were at the airport to have their photos taken with the president. Perhaps it was Barney's accent. When the White House sent him a signed photo, the inscription read: "To Bonnie Frank, Good luck on your campaign."

On October 8, Barney debated Richard Jones at a candidate forum held in the auditorium of Weston High School. On the question of the Equal Rights Amendment, Jones described his position as "mixed," explaining that while he supported the basic thrust of the amendment, equality for women and equal pay for equal work, he opposed many of the likely effects of the amendment. He warned that passage of the amendment would result in women being drafted into combat duty and mother-daughter and father-son banquets being prohibited. "You can't vote 'mixed' in Congress," Barney responded. "You get a yes card and a no card." He pointed out to Jones that the state equal rights law passed four years earlier by the Massachusetts legislature had no effect on mother-daughter or father-son social functions. "I know of no police officer who has intervened to stop them," he asserted.

According to friends and staffers, Barney, who had not been pleasant to deal with during the primary, became unbearable during the two-month general election campaign. He was impatient, temperamental, and abrupt in his contacts with campaign staff and others, especially those who drove him to campaign events. He had decided ideas about the best route to take to the destination and would direct the driver where to turn and comment on the person's driving skills, often reducing the driver to tears. "We had to get a different driver for him almost all the time," Jim Segal, who managed Barney's general election campaign, said. He usually had three drivers a day, the morning driver to pick him up at home at six o'clock, the afternoon driver, and the evening driver, who would drop him off at home late at night. He was especially intolerant of female drivers because he considered them to be too timid behind the wheel. After driving Barney one day, Rita Kelliher was left sobbing. She described him as being "all seven dwarfs wrapped into one. He's sleepy, grumpy . . ." When LeAnn Shields got lost driving him to an event in the Fitchburg and Gardner area in the western part of the district, she was relieved to see that he had fallen asleep in the back seat and considered conking him on the head to make sure that he was unconscious when she committed the cardinal sin of pulling into a gas station to ask for directions. The campaign staff composed a song for election night titled "Where Have All the Drivers Gone?"—with a stanza for each of the drivers.

"Part of our job was to keep Barney away from people. He was alienating everyone he came in contact with," Segal said. "During these two months, Barney was better in the abstract than in person. When he was with people he was so uptight because he wanted this so badly, felt that he could win it, and didn't want to blow it." People on the campaign staff did not feel good about the candidate. But nobody quit. "If he wasn't such a good friend, I would have walked out. You have to love Barney Frank to like him," Segal said. "During that general election he was not at all likeable." "At the end of the campaign, I was ready to kill him. He did try one's patience. You have to have a certain amount of affection for him not to bop him," Thaleia Schlesinger recalled. He was consistent, though. "Barney didn't pick on anyone in particular, he didn't discriminate, whoever was there got it," Dottie Reichard said.

Barney explained why he was so frustrated and irritated: "Everyone thought I was a shoo-in, but I was worried. I knew it was a real race and could not afford to take my Republican opponent lightly. In my mind, I realized that it was going to be a good year for the Republicans. The power of New Right candidates cannot be underestimated. I had this opponent, Richard Jones, who was a member of the John Birch Society and nobody knew about it. He was an extremist. But he had no record, so he was free to take any position he wanted. The guy was a John Bircher but looked plausible as a candidate."

The Republican nominee, retired army dentist Richard Jones, was a little-known, arch-conservative forty-six-year-old who had recently moved to the town of Harvard in the western part of the district and was making his first run for public office. Jones had no prior political experience. The media consultant Dan Payne described him as "an odd ball, a political nobody who really didn't know why he was running" and who "at best was a Reagan clone" and "at worst he was a nut who didn't belong in the race." In 1977, Jones was chairman of the Central Massachusetts chapter of TRIM (Tax Relief Immediately), which described itself as part of the nationwide network of committees launched by the John Birch Society.

Jones had little campaign money and his supporters never imagined that the Reagan Revolution was coming and would almost sweep him into office. After the primary, Jones ran little ads in small newspapers across the district with questions for his opponent. Payne remembers that the ads were kind of clever, though very small, like an ad for a painter or a tradesman, and they were scattered around the newspaper. In the last few weeks of the campaign, however, Jones ran a flurry of radio ads viciously attacking Barney's liberal positions in the state legislature, accusing him of being an advocate of hard-core pornography, prostitution, and homosexuality. In one sixty-second ad, the announcer says: "Barney Frank says he's a champion of women's rights. Yet he has sponsored bills to legalize prostitution in every city and town in Massachusetts. He voted to allow hard-core pornography, which degrades women, on television. Frank says he's a champion of the elderly. Yet he has sponsored a tax on public pensions and other taxes that hit the elderly the hardest. Frank says he wants to do in Washington what he did on Beacon Hill. On Beacon Hill he sponsored new taxes and a homosexual rights amendment to the constitution. Yet Barney Frank calls his opponent far out. Richard Jones says he wants to go to Congress to cut inflation, cut taxes, and get the bureaucracy under control. To Mr. Frank, that is far out."

In another ad Jones accuses Barney of trying to "sneak through" a pay raise for state legislators. Barney explained his vote in favor of the legislation to increase the legislative salary to $20,800 a year effective January 1, 1980, saying simply, "I think the salary was too low and I voted to raise it." Of Jones he said, "He thinks anybody getting a public salary is stealing it, except him."

Barney was out in the field campaigning every day, talking to people, paying heed to questions voters were asking about claims Jones was making, and seeing the doubt on their faces. He understood what was happening—people were listening to what Jones was saying about him and the race was tightening. He knew that what he was hearing on the street belied the two-week-old polling numbers showing him with a twenty-point lead over Jones. Jones made Barney look alien, particularly in the parts of the district outside the metropolitan area. "What he said was, 'Here's this guy from New Jersey, he's Jewish, never been married, he supports gay rights, he doesn't think you should make babies or say prayers. He wouldn't make it a crime not to pledge to the flag, he's for smut and pornography on cable TV, and he's from Boston? It was rough. People believe that stuff if it is not rebutted," Barney said.

Barney believes that the public has a short attention span and there is a limited amount of time they can give to politics. If negative ads are not promptly rebutted, people tend to believe them. "It is unrealistic to expect the public automatically to know you're a good person without defending yourself. You can't say I have so much confidence that the public will ignore it," he observed. This was especially true in 1980 when Barney was unknown to much of the electorate in the Fourth District. According to David Frank, Cardinal Medeiros's letter had split the district, leaving people in the western part with strong feelings against Barney, giving Jones's negative campaign more fertile ground in which to take root.

John Marttila and Tom Kiley, Barney's campaign strategists, who had also guided Drinan through all his congressional elections, were dismissive and initially resisted Barney's pleas to respond to Jones's ads and attack him as a John Bircher. They advised Barney to rise above it and to keep the campaign positive. "You're practically the congressman-elect at this point," they told him.

Barney's instinct about the Ronald Reagan phenomenon and the damage that Jones was inflicting, however, were both correct. "This was the one time that I was right and my campaign people were wrong," he said. Kiley admits that Barney was right, that it was a serious race and that his campaign strategists thought he was worrying too much. "It was such an energetic campaign and there was so much enthusiasm. You fool yourself. You think it is the whole universe. We underestimated Jones and should have taken him more seriously. We just couldn't believe that Jones, with his limited credentials, could be a serious candidate," he said.

The Barney Frank campaign began airing commercials portraying Richard Jones as a tool of the New Right and hammering away at the fact that Jones had briefly been a member of the extreme right-wing, ultra-conservative John Birch Society. In the radio ads, the announcer says: "Can you imagine people from Massachusetts sending a former member of the John Birch Society to the United States Congress? Yep, this Republican was an active local leader in the Birch Society just three years ago. So if you run into this Republican, remind him that this is Massachusetts, not Texas, and tell him, around here we're supporting the Democrat for Congress, Barney Frank."

Jones later complained to the *Boston Globe* that the ads portrayed him as "someone to the right of Attila the Hun." He maintained that he had been a member of the John Birch Society for only eight months, had never gone to any membership meetings, and had attended only one dinner, just to hear the speaker, Congressman Larry McDonald of Georgia, a John Birch Society member.

In print ads the Barney Frank campaign began highlighting some of Jones's positions on the issues: "Can you imagine anyone running for Congress in Massachusetts in 1980 who is against putting limits back on home heating oil prices? Well, the Republican running against Barney Frank is against limits on energy prices. And can you imagine anybody wanting to cut off federal housing subsidies for older people. The Republican's against that too."

The Frank campaign literature highlighted Jones's response to a question about possible restitution for fisherman in the George's Bank who might be harmed by oil spills: "I'm a dentist. I'm not an expert on fish and I'm not an expert on oil or on energy in any of its forms. I do know I like to use both and hope to be able to continue." The Frank campaign ads hammered away at the theme that sending Jones to Congress would be a tragedy for the country and an embarrassment for the Fourth District.

Election night 1980 was an agonizing one for Democrats, especially liberal Democrats. Ronald Reagan was elected to the White House in a landslide victory, winning even Massachusetts, the only state that had voted for George McGovern in 1972. A conservative Republican tidal wave swept across the country. In the Senate, the Democrats' 18-seat majority turned into a 6-seat minority. The liberal Democratic titans George McGovern of South Dakota, Birch Bayh of Indiana, and Frank Church of Idaho, as well as the veteran senator Warren Magnuson of Washington State, a leader on consumer rights, were all voted out of office. The Democrats' 114-seat margin in the House of Representatives shrank to 51.

Proposition 2½, a conservative proposal requiring that total property taxes not exceed 2½ percent of fair market value, was on the ballot in Massachusetts and it brought many voters to the polls on Election Day. Proposition 2½, the most sweeping ballot initiative in the state's history, which would cut property taxes by an average of 40 percent statewide and reduce automobile excise taxes by 62 percent, won in Massachusetts, and people who voted for Proposition 2½, which Jones supported, were generally not Barney Frank voters.

"That night was longer and more painful than we expected," Bill Mulrow recalled. "There was a lot of tension that evening. You could see it on people's faces," Tom Kiley said. Barney was fighting the conservative tide. For hours on the night of the election the vote was slow coming in and the outcome of the race in the Fourth Congressional District was too close to call. Barney and several hundred supporters spent several long and uncomfortable hours awaiting the results at the Newton Marriott Hotel. Marge Segel volunteered to keep Barney company in the hotel suite as they awaited the election returns. "I didn't realize when I said I would stay with him why everyone looked at me with great relief," she said.

In a nearby room, campaign staff tallied the results as city and precinct workers called in to report the results. They took turns running into Barney's room to give him the numbers. Barney had a significant lead in the early returns, winning Brookline and Newton by a large twenty-four-thousand-vote margin. Jones, however, won decisively in Waltham by four thousand votes and as the vote tallies began coming in from the western part of the district, Barney's lead began to shrink, leaving the candidate tense and fidgety. He started breaking pencils in half and throwing them across the room.

"I tried to be comforting, being a school teacher and guidance counselor, and I gently put my arm on his shoulder," Marge Segel said. But Barney yelled, "Don't touch me. Just leave me alone." "I thought he was going to jump on me," Segel said. "It was a horrible night, one that I will never forget."

Barney had resisted the pleas of his senior campaign advisers to leave his suite at the Marriott and address the crowd of well-wishers. Finally, at about 12:45, he relented and briefly addressed his supporters, beginning, "They say one of the keys to a successful political career is timing, knowing the right year to run. Obviously I haven't mastered that yet." Even though he was in the lead, it was premature to claim victory. "I apologize that it has been a longer night than I anticipated. But I think it will be a good night. At least, I'd rather be us than him right now. It's looking good, but it's too early to be sure," he said. "We're running against the national tide and if we win, I think we will win, I guess I'll go down there [to Washington] and spawn," he said wryly.

Barney refused to claim victory until most of the votes had been counted in Framingham, which Clark had carried in the primary by about three hundred votes. Those results were the last to come in, because Framingham used paper ballots. The vote count in Framingham showed Barney winning the town by a little more than a thousand votes. He held on to his lead and managed to eke out a narrow eight-thousand-vote victory with 52 percent of the vote. Barney won only five of the twenty-three cities and towns in the district. "When we won, there was a feeling not of elation but of relief," Jim Segel said. "It was the most painful victory I have ever been through," Thaleia Schlesinger remembered.

Barney entered the hotel ballroom shortly after two in the morning to declare victory. The crowd of five hundred well-wishers had shrunk to about a hundred die-hard supporters, who greeted the victorious candidate with a loud ovation that lasted well over a minute. "We won," Barney declared. He appeared tired and worn out as he joked to supporters in a hoarse voice, "I have to call the Department of the Interior tomorrow. I have to apply for status as an endangered species."

Barney was deeply saddened by the defeat of so many liberal Democrats across the country. "We won but we didn't win by enough to take anything for granted. It is not a happy night for us because so many decent people across the country became martyrs; I think that is a good word for it. We cannot allow the wholly negative and nasty strain of politics that is emerging to succeed. There are people in this country who, in a cynical and calculated way, have capitalized on the very understandable frustration the voters felt," he said. He thanked Robert Drinan for his support in a time of "personal anguish." Focusing on the job ahead, he asserted, "The first priority has to be to show that fiscal responsibility and social responsibility are compatible."

Years later, in explaining his narrow margin of victory over a relatively unknown Republican in the 1980 general election, Barney said, "I had only had one serious race before that, in 1972. In that contest I had to persuade a lot of upper-middle-class, highly educated professionals to vote for me. It was easy geographically. It was not a problem how you translated what you thought into more straightforward language." "In the 1980 race I didn't realize that I was coming across as unlikeable, particularly in the general election. That right-wing John Birch extremist was coming across to voters as more likeable." He said he ran in 1980 as though he were arguing a case before an appellate court, "trying to get every last point in, rather than speaking to a jury." He described some of the problems that he encountered in that election, including feeling the sting of anti-Semitic comments while campaigning in the working class towns of Fitchburg and Leominster. "I was Jewish, liberal, and an outsider. I had moved to the district from Boston. I was a double outsider. Nobody in Massachusetts ever referred to me as a Bostonian until I moved out of Boston to run for Congress. When I lived in Boston, they used to say that I was from New Jersey."

The election campaign had a remarkable influence on the family of Barney's sister Doris and her husband, Jim. Their home in Newton had started out as the base for the campaign. After the election, Barney, Doris, Jim, and their two children, Jeffrey, four and a half years old, and Julie, two and a half, all went to Berkshire County for some rest and relaxation. One day Julie was bothering Jeffrey and kept asking him questions. Finally, Jeffrey turned to her and said, "Ju-wee, stop interviewing me." "That is part of who they were," Doris explained. "The campaign was a tremendous family experience."

In early December, Barney went to Washington, where a lame-duck session of Congress was being held. He went up to the doorman stationed outside the entrance to the floor of the House and said, "I'm Barney Frank. Could you tell Representative Jimmy Shannon that I want to talk to him?" The door man replied, "Oh, Mr. Frank. You're a member-elect. You are permitted to go on the floor."

Barney walked up the two steps to the House floor and bumped into Morris Udall. Four years earlier, during Udall's campaign for president, Barney had been a driver for Udall and had gotten to know him well. "Hi, Barney!" Udall said. "Hi, Mo!" Barney replied. It was a brief conversation but it had a deep emotional impact on the member-elect. Now, all of a sudden, he was Mo Udall's colleague. Twenty years later, Barney told that story to Mo Udall's son, Rep. Mark Udall of Colorado. "That's the way I felt when I first bumped into you on the House floor," Mark said. "I won't be having a kid that is going to bump into you. I think it ends here," Barney replied.

After the election, Barney gave his interpretation of the Reagan Republican landslide to David Broder of the *Washington Post*. "The voters were saying they are unhappy with the state of the world, and they think the Democrats and the liberals are to blame for it. We've been running the show for so long. I think we got ourselves painted as the defenders of the status quo," he said. "Liberals have got to change perceptions, to show people that it is possible to be socially conscious and economically prudent at the same time."

Unlike many other Democrats, Barney had a strategy for dealing with the new president and the Reagan program initiatives. He described this strategy to Broder: "We Democrats don't obstruct Ronald Reagan. He is the president and he and his supporters are entitled to their shot. It would be a great mistake for the Democrats in the House of Representatives to let Ronald Reagan say he was blocked from doing what he and the Republican Senate wanted to do by a group of willful Democrats in the House. We can't let him run around the country in the 1982 campaign saying we kept him from changing the status quo."

Speaker Tip O'Neill kept the promise he had made during the campaign and helped Barney become a member of the Banking, Finance, and Urban Affairs Committee, his first choice of committee assignments because of its housing jurisdiction. He was also appointed to the Government Operations Committee.

In December, O'Neill sent his assistant, Ari Weiss, a bright, young intellectual, to tell Barney that he wanted him on the Judiciary Committee. When Barney protested that he was already publicly committed to serving on the Banking Committee and that he had promised his constituents housing, Weiss explained that O'Neill wanted him on Judiciary as well because the Democratic leadership was having trouble getting liberals to go on that committee because of abortion, school prayer, busing, and other divisive issues before the panel. "We need Democrats who will vote against anti-abortion and pro-school-prayer legislation in committee to keep those bills from reaching the House floor. Some Democrats are fearful that conservative groups will use those votes against them at election time," Weiss told him.

When Barney protested that he was no more eager than his colleagues to put himself in the line of fire of those right-wing conservative groups, Weiss replied, "But all the members of those groups generally hate you anyway so you have little to lose."

Barney joined the Judiciary Committee in part as a favor to Speaker O'Neill, who wanted liberals on the panel, and in part because Robert Drinan had served on that committee and asked him to go on it. Drinan had suggested to Theodore Hesburgh, who had just finished serving as chairman of the Select Commission on Immigration and Refugee Policy, created in 1978 to conduct a study and evaluation of immigration and refugee laws, policies, and procedures, and to Peter Rodino, chairman of the Judiciary Committee, that Barney Frank would be a good member for Judiciary. Rodino and Hesburgh lobbied Barney in the members' dining room to become a member of the Judiciary Committee and help with immigration legislation. The Democratic leadership put several liberals—Pat Schroeder, Mike Synar, and later Chuck Schumer and Dan Glickman—on Judiciary as an extra major committee assignment.

In commenting about Democratic congressman Bill Hughes of New Jersey, who chaired the House Judiciary subcommittee on crime, Barney explained, "In Congress, if you are from Kansas, you go on the Agriculture committee. If you're from Cape Cod, you go on the Merchant Marine committee. If you're from New Jersey, you go on the crime subcommittee to protect your major industry."

When the size of the Select Committee on Aging was expanded, Barney was given a seat on that committee as well. As a freshman, he served on four committees, the only Massachusetts representative on each of those committees, and seven subcommittees.

9

Rookie of the Year

BARNEY FRANK'S swearing-in ceremony and party in January 1981 was one of the few celebrations for liberals that year. Morris Udall called Barney's election "one of the best things to happen to the House of Representatives in years." Robert Drinan, who had joined the faculty at Georgetown University Law Center, attended the swearing-in of his successor.

Within days of arriving in Congress, Barney remarked that he could stay in the House for the next thirty years and feel his life fulfilled. "I've been like a kid with my nose pressed against the candy-store window for a long time," he said. He made no effort to win over his colleagues with charm, leaving some to wonder, "Who the heck does this guy think he is?" Rep. Tom Downey was put off when he called Barney to look at someone's résumé and interview that person for a job on his staff and Barney had responded with a curt, "Send me the résumé" and hung up the phone. "Doesn't he know that I am three terms senior to him?" Downey recalled thinking. "You're supposed to be cheerful. 'Yes sir, I'd be happy to do it.' He did not pay attention to this natural pecking order that I thought existed," he said.

Within a few months, however, Barney and Tom Downey became good friends. "Underneath the gruff exterior was not only a man of enormous intelligence and wit but a tremendous guy," Downey said.

"Most new members couldn't care less about the rules of the House, [but] from day one, Barney Frank was interested in the process and always had that propensity to understand the House rules and act on that understanding," the retired House parliamentarian Charles Johnson recalled. "At odd times he would come up to us on the House floor to pursue questions about the rules. Those discussions about the rules have continued over his entire House career." Barney is fond of saying, "I always follow the rules of the House when there is a Parliamentarian present."

Arthur Clark never forgave Barney for beating him in the Democratic primary. Five months later, on Sunday, February 1, 1981, when the city of Waltham held a parade and homecoming celebration in honor of William Keough Jr., a Waltham native and one of the fifty-two returning hostages who had spent over fourteen months in captivity in Iran, Clark did not invite Barney Frank, the congressman from his district, to march in the parade, to sit with other dignitaries on the extended parade reviewing stand that had been erected in front of City Hall, or to present a plaque or other memento to Keough at the ceremony following the parade. John Kendrick, however, the town clerk of Brookline, was on stage to present a plaque to Keough. Although Clark's action was an intentional snub, Barney was philosophical, observing that as a state legislator, he had never liked walking in parades because he never knew what to do with his hands.

Barney went to the parade anyway with his mother. Initially he stood around in the cold winter weather, mixed with and greeted constituents, and then joined the crowd on Main Street to watch the parade. "I didn't do it to embarrass Clark but it sort of boomeranged on him," Barney said. The press and many constituents reacted negatively to Clark's pettiness. A crowd of about four hundred thousand, the biggest parade in Waltham history, lined the two-mile parade route to cheer Keough, who rode with Mayor Clark at his side in an open limo bedecked with yellow ribbons.

Clark never smoothed things out with Barney. He could not bring himself to approach his congressman to seek assistance in getting federal funds for Waltham. That November, Clark was reelected as mayor of Waltham and prevailed again in 1983 for an eighth term. In 1985, however, after sixteen years as mayor, Clark was beaten in his bid for reelection. He died in May 1990.

Barney quickly made his mark in Congress. In February 1981, the Consumer Affairs and Coinage Subcommittee of the Banking Committee, chaired by Frank Annunzio from Chicago, approved the Cash Discount Act, a bill that Annunzio, its chief proponent, touted as being pro-consumer. While Barney supported the provision providing incentives for merchants to grant discounts to cash-paying customers, he strongly opposed the prohibition against surcharges by merchants on customers who elect to use credit cards. In Barney's view, when you impose a rule that merchants may not charge more for the credit card user than for the cash customer, it means that the cash payers, the poorer people, are subsidizing the wealthier credit card users. Several consumer organizations, such as the Consumer Federation of America and Consumers Union, also opposed the credit card surcharge ban.

Barney offered an amendment in committee to delete from the bill the prohibition on merchants charging more for credit card purchases. He saw no reason why merchants should not be able to pass along these costs to the credit card customer and considered it a terrible mistake for Congress to interfere with the free market by dictating to the retail industry what they should or should not do with regard to a very basic marketing decision. "To deregulate oil but to regulate the small merchant seems to me to be a silly way to work with the economy," Barney said.

His amendment was overwhelmingly defeated, but he said he would offer it again when the bill came to the House floor for a vote. Soon after, Annunzio's longtime Banking Committee staffer Curt Prins, described by friends as a character and by others as disagreeable, warned Richard Goldstein, Barney's legislative assistant, "Tell your boss something from my boss—if he offers that amendment, he'll never get a fucking thing through this committee," he said. Goldstein passed along the message to Barney.

The next day, Barney, who had been in Congress less than two months, confronted Annunzio, a veteran legislator first elected to Congress in 1964 and considered by some to be a cross between an old-time machine politician from Chicago and the mob's representative in Congress. "Frank, your guy told my guy that if I offer the amendment you will see to it that I never get anything through the committee," Barney said. He added, "Is this how things work around here? If it is, I understand. Tell me, Frank, is this how the game is played here?" Annunzio, caught off guard by the freshman lawmaker's directness, assured Barney that there had been a misunderstanding and that though he would oppose the amendment, Barney had a right to offer it. "You learn early on in the legislative body that you cannot back down," Barney said. Barney earned Annunzio's respect by standing up to him. According to Goldstein, "After that time, there couldn't have been two closer members of Congress."

The Cash Discount Act was brought up on the House floor on February 24 under suspension of the rules, a procedure under which amendments are prohibited and a two-thirds majority vote is required for passage. The bill passed overwhelmingly by a margin of 372 to 4. Barney was one of those who voted no.

In an exchange with Jack Valenti, a former special assistant to President Lyndon Johnson who had left the White House in 1966 to head the Motion Picture Association of America, Barney further established himself as someone not to be taken lightly. Valenti had persuaded Barney, a member of the Judiciary Subcommittee on Courts, Civil Liberties, and the Administration of Justice, to carry an amendment for him on a bill before the committee. Barney was the chief proponent of Valenti's position. The bill related to an issue on which the movie studios and broadcasters were at odds. At the time, Valenti had been the president of the Motion Picture Association for almost fifteen years and was considered to be one of the premier lobbyists in Washington. When Valenti decided to cut a deal without talking first to Barney about it, Goldstein brought the deal to Barney's attention. Barney, hearing about it for the first time, was livid.

He set up a meeting with Valenti and told Goldstein, who ordinarily sat in on meetings with lobbyists if they related to an issue in which he had been involved, not to attend this particular meeting. "I'm going to talk to Valenti alone, just the two of us, so don't come," he said.

Goldstein watched as Valenti walked confidently into Barney's office and closed the door. From outside, Goldstein heard Barney shouting at Valenti, though between the closed door and Barney's rapid-fire delivery, he could not understand what Barney was saying. When Valenti left Barney's office, Goldstein recalls, he staggered out looking shocked, and when staffers in the reception area greeted him, Valenti walked hurriedly by them without a word.

"You really have to establish this right off. You can't let people play games or you get marginalized," Barney said. "This is a business where reputation is so important." After the incident, according to Goldstein, Valenti did only good things for Barney and raised a lot of campaign funds for him over the years.

In April 2006, when Jack Valenti, who retired in August 2004 after thirty-eight years as president of the Motion Picture Association of America, was asked about that incident, the eighty-five-year-old lobbyist did not recall it. "That was not my style to do anything behind the back of a member of Congress," he said. "I learned from Lyndon Johnson to never break your word because if you do, you lose your credibility."

Barney took the lead with other members of Congress in attempting unsuccessfully to stop the sale of AWACS (Airborne Warning and Control System) planes to Saudi Arabia in 1981. He felt that by taking this initiative the Reagan administration would be rewarding the Saudis for their intransigence, and he viewed the sale as counter to America's interest that there be a strong and independent Israel. But the AWACS sale went through, according to Barney, because of the votes of eight right-wing senators backed by the Moral Majority, including the most anti-Israel member of Congress, Senator Jesse Helms of North Carolina. "In 1981, there was no significant effort by the Moral Majority on behalf of Israel," Barney said. "Jerry Falwell never said, 'Jesse, it's a *shande* [shame] the way you talk about Israel.'"

Barney was surprised that some critics questioned the right of Jewish members of Congress to oppose that sale, calling into question their patriotism. He compared the relationship between Saudi Arabia and the United States to that of Lucy van Pelt and Charlie Brown and the annual October cartoon in which Lucy repeatedly assures Charlie Brown that she will hold the football for him to kick despite his skepticism but always pulls it away at the last moment and down he goes. "That's us and the Saudi Arabians," Barney said. "Every time they want something, they persuade us. We give in to them and they pull the football away. It has been an enduring problem."

When Barney was elected to Congress in 1980, the unedited televising of House sessions by C-SPAN was in its infancy. In an early episode of the long-running television series *The Simpsons,* as Homer Simpson scanned the cable television channels for the first time, he gleefully exclaimed, "Wow! Pro wrestling from Mexico. You know down there it is a real sport." Another channel, to his delight, was broadcasting the World Series of Cockfighting live from New Orleans. He paused momentarily on C-SPAN as a congressman said on the House floor, "Mr. Speaker, if I could call your attention to the retroactive subsidy appropriations override bill. I refer you to page four thousand five hundred and—" "They think people will watch anything," Homer remarked.

Eventually, however, C-SPAN turned the legislative process into a spectator sport. As the C-SPAN cable television audience grew from thousands of political and federal government junkies to millions of households that tune to C-SPAN and find entertainment in watching their government in action, Barney's multitude of fans expanded exponentially.

On occasion, though, Barney, like Homer Simpson, pokes fun at C-SPAN. At a Judiciary Committee hearing in 1993 about the FBI assault on the Branch Davidian compound near Waco, Texas, in which some eighty members of the religious cult, including many women and children, were killed in a blaze, Attorney General Janet Reno was painfully explaining how in retrospect she wished she had pumped sleeping gas into the Branch Davidian compound. Barney relieved some of the tension when he asked, "Couldn't you pipe in C-SPAN?"

Barney was most flattered when, because he was a single, unmarried member of Congress, his name appeared on a list of the two hundred most eligible bachelors in the world, and he boasted to friends of this accomplishment. At the time, Prince Charles headed the list. In late February 1981, he was delighted to note that Prince Charles had just become engaged. "We all move up one spot on the list," he said.

That spring, Barney phoned Don Graham at the *Washington Post* not to discuss politics or public policy but to challenge the *Washington Post* in softball. Graham took his advertising department to play Barney's team, the Congressional Franks. Barney rarely missed a softball game. He played first base and always batted first in the line-up, which gave him more at bats but reduced his RBI total. He brought his impatience from the office to the softball field. "C'mon, let's go, it's getting dark," he would shout to keep the game moving so as to get in a full seven innings. At a game on June 21, one of his staff responded, "Barney, it's not getting dark. This is the longest day of the year."

One night he wanted to play in a softball game but had a black-tie event to attend. He asked his secretary, Patty Hamel, to drive him to the event after the game. They were about halfway to the hotel where the event was being held when Hamel stopped the car at a red light. Barney, sitting in the front passenger seat, suddenly opened the door and darted into the back seat of Hamel's Toyota Celica hatchback and started changing into his tuxedo. This was no easy task even for a contortionist. But Barney had practice changing clothes in small areas. During the 1980 campaign for Congress he had on occasion changed his clothes in the back seat of a Ford Pinto. The small Toyota Celica was shaking from the movement in the back seat and Hamel asked what was happening. "Oh, I forgot that you went to Catholic school," Barney said. "That's okay. Do what you have to do," she replied. Minutes later, Hamel pulled up to the hotel and proceeded to the line with all the limos. "Barney exited from the back seat, zipped up his pants, said thank you, and walked into the hotel," she said.

Barney spoke often on the House floor. "From day one, he stood out personality-wise and intelligence-wise," Charles Johnson, who at the time was deputy parliamentarian in the House, said. He impressed Johnson with his insight and ability to engage in debate on a wide range of issues. He also impressed Democrat Tom Foley of Washington State, who said of Barney, "His kind of humor is in short commodity. It enlightens, but does not obscure; . . . it amuses, but doesn't offend." During a House debate on a bill to assist the textile and apparel industry, Barney used humor to ridicule the exaggerated arguments from opponents of the bill. "To hear a grosser set of exaggerations, you would have to hang around a college fraternity house on a Monday morning and hear them describe how well they did on the weekend," he said. "We have been told that this is going to lead to sixty thousand retail jobs being lost. Are we to believe that people are going to fly to Hong Kong to buy their T-shirts?"

Barney recognized that in the state legislature he had been too sarcastic and confrontational toward his colleagues during debates. In Congress, he softened his tone and tried to be more open-minded. His remarks on the floor were clever but not mean-spirited or personal. He knew how to deal with arguments advanced by other members that were not cogent. "If the gentleman wants to beat strawmen," he told one of his colleagues during a House debate, "he should find a field somewhere." Nonetheless, he could still be impatient, rude, and caustic toward witnesses at hearings. At a July 24, 1981, hearing by the Aging subcommittee on retirement income, Howard Phillips, who had been a rival of Barney's in college and later became the founder and director of the Conservative Caucus, made the mistake of answering one of Barney's questions with a nod. The following exchange occurred:

BARNEY: It is very hard to get nods into the record, Mr. Phillips.

PHILLIPS: As James Michael Curley said, never talk when you can smile; never smile when you can wrinkle your brow; never wrinkle your brow when you can nod, and at this stage I am nodding.

BARNEY: I believe James Michael Curley also made it a practice never to volunteer and testified only when subpoenaed. If you find testifying on these issues a burden, I am sure the chairman would be glad to excuse you. I don't mean to intrude on your privacy, but it seems to me there is a certain obligation of witnesses to respond to questions.

On another occasion when Phillips was testifying at a Judiciary subcommittee hearing on abortion rights, the two men went at it and, by all accounts, Barney made Phillips look foolish. Near the end of his testimony, Phillips remarked, "Mr. Frank, you are not giving anything I say any respect." "That is the first thing you said that I agree with," Barney responded.

"You could always count on Barney to bring a little humor to the most serious things," veteran Hill staffer Gerry McMurray said. He often used wit to take the raw edges off otherwise acrimonious debates. On July 29, 1981, during a debate on the House floor on President Reagan's tax cut plan and the bill's special tax breaks for the oil industry, Jack Fields, a conservative GOP freshman from Houston, warned that "the eyes of Texas are upon us today." "I do not object to the eyes of Texas being upon me; I object to the hands of Texas being in my pockets," Barney said, referring to the bill's special provisions for the oil industry "that only about fifteen Members of this body are prepared to defend on the merits."

During a debate on September 10 about restricting the number of flights at National Airport, which Barney considered to be anticompetitive and a form of reregulation, the conservative Democrat Buddy Roemer of Louisiana referred to him as a born-again supporter of airline deregulation. "I do not believe that I have been born again, but I think in this case I was simply feeling immaculate from the beginning," Barney replied. "The fact is that deregulation and an increase in competition has always been a goal of mine." He had taken that same position two years earlier on the PBS television program *The Advocates* on the subject of federal deregulation of trucking, arguing that deregulation will inevitably lead to lower prices and increased efficiency in the trucking industry because of increased competition.

Barney recognized early on the importance of good personal relationships in the legislative process that often cross party, sectional, and ideological lines. According to Charlie Wilson, a Democrat from Texas, one would not have expected Barney, because "he's liberal, he's from Massachusetts, he talks with a Northeastern accent, and he smokes a big cigar," to have much influence with conservatives, but his warmth and wit and keen mind won him respect in Congress. "He stands up for his principles, and gets things done, too," Wilson said. Barney understands that being a legislator is a very collegial occupation. "We work with each other, we lobby each other, we do each other favors, and we try to persuade each other. The nature of the legislative process demands collegiality or it does not work," he said. "In some ways being effective in a legislative body is a lot like being popular back in high school, the personal relationships become very important. It's more serious, but in many ways it's the same." He sees a fine line between being effective and serious and putting people off.

Barney's signature legislative event during his first term was the successful battle to save the Legal Services Corporation, created in 1974 to provide access to the courts for the poorest people in the country, when President Reagan tried to dismantle it. Reagan had been a foe of Legal Services since the time he was governor of California and lost a lawsuit brought by Legal Services in the state. Barney was in the forefront in building a bipartisan coalition in the Judiciary Committee to support a bill to save the Legal Services Corporation. The bill, which restricted the corporation's mandate to providing basic legal assistance to people with family disputes, landlord–tenant disputes, and other kinds of disputes of the most mundane sort, was unanimously approved in subcommittee and passed overwhelmingly by the Judiciary Committee, with a majority of both Democrats and Republicans on the committee voting for it.

When the bill reached the House floor in June 1981, Barney was forceful and persuasive in defending the legislation during three days of often acrimonious debate and fending off dozens of harmful amendments offered by opponents. "If you abolish the Legal Services Corporation, you do not punish the lawyers, you punish the poor people," he told his colleagues.

James Sensenbrenner, a conservative Republican from Wisconsin, warned that unless his amendment was adopted, to give the Legal Services Corporation the flexibility to deal with the reduction in funding contained in the bill, the Legal Services Corporation would be in a procedural straitjacket. Barney candidly responded, "The gentleman is a dedicated legitimate opponent of the bill. It really does not seem to me to be credible that he would be worried about putting them in a straitjacket when what he really wants to do is put them in a guillotine." Barney added, "He has every right to try and wipe them out. But let us not pretend that this is an effort to help them when we know the gentleman wants to blow them up."

Barney resisted an amendment by Charlie Wilson to prohibit the Legal Services Corporation from bringing class-action lawsuits. "We are being asked to adopt an amendment which says we have two rules of law: one for everybody and a separate one for the poor," he explained. "If you are representing poor people, we are going to tie one hand behind your back. . . . It is the most blatant form of discrimination on the grounds of economics that I have ever heard of."

Even though the committee bill contained language that Legal Services funds could not be used for general advocacy in changing the legal status of homosexuality, Democrat Larry McDonald of Georgia went further and offered an amendment to bar the Legal Services Corporation by regulation from promoting, defending, or protecting homosexuality. "If anyone thinks he or she has to vote to prevent the Reagan board, which will probably [consist of] Howard Phillips and ten of his clones, from adopting these regulations, he or she has spent the last year in a time capsule, which may, in fact, be the most attractive place to have spent it," Barney argued.

Legal Services was reauthorized for two more years, and even though it emerged with only 75 percent of its previous funding, it was a significant victory for the liberal Democrats in Congress and one of the few defeats President Reagan suffered in 1981. As Barney left the House chamber after the vote, a group of Legal Services supporters standing in the hallway broke into spontaneous applause.

Barney was applauded again for his debating prowess when he showed that he knew what he was talking about and held his own against a dozen members of Congress from dairy-farming districts. The dairy lobby spent a considerable amount of money fighting attempts by Congress to cut dairy price subsidies. As a result, the Reagan administration had trouble finding a member of Congress to offer such an amendment on behalf of the president. On October 7, 1981, when the farm bill came before the House, there was liberal Massachusetts Democrat Barney Frank acting as the unlikely field general for the Office of Management and Budget director David Stockman in the battle to cut the costly dairy price support program. "No one else wanted to offer the Reagan administration's proposal so I did it. I offered the amendment to cut dairy subsidies because I thought Ronald Reagan was right about that. I just wish he recognized that that extends as well to tobacco, peanuts, and sugar," Barney explained. "It's a political and economic necessity for liberals to find ways to cut the budget."

To Barney, this federal program that supported dairy prices by offering to buy milk at a fixed floor-price based on a formula was the federal equivalent of the MBTA. In his view, largely because of the excesses of this price support, U.S. dairy farmers have produced far more cheese, butter, and milk than the market can accommodate and the government has been forced to purchase the surplus. He contended that the price support inflated prices and stimulated overproduction.

Barney stood alone at the podium on the floor of the House for half an hour to introduce and defend his amendment on behalf of the Reagan administration. As he began speaking, farm state members from both parties started queuing up to challenge him.

"The dairy price support program is a classic case of a problem which brought forth a solution which has in turn eclipsed the problem and become the problem in itself," he stated. "We are talking about an unmanageable surplus. Indeed, when people worry these days in the *Reader's Digest* that the debt is a trillion dollars, and calculate their share of the national debt, I guess the one assuring thing is that they also each own a pound of butter they did not know they had because, thanks to the dairy program, we have got a couple of million pounds of butter in surplus with no sensible thing to do with it. . . . [It is] a surplus which threatens to leave us awash in butter—to mix a metaphor."

Several minutes into his remarks, members from farm belt states began peppering him with questions. Among them, Democrat Tom Harkin of Iowa questioned the figures Barney was relying on. "They are a range of figures, and . . . frankly, my confidence in the ability of our economists to predict what the cows are going to do is a little bit weak," Barney replied.

"The gentleman's figure of five hundred million dollars does not mean anything, then?" Harkin asked.

"If I did not think I was going to be spending less for dairy farmers and all those interests I would not see all these dairy farmers standing up here getting ready to oppose the amendment . . . and stop me from getting my point across," Barney responded.

Harkin proceeded to test the freshman lawmaker's expertise by accusing him of mixing apples and oranges in his assumptions, comparing his proposal to the Bedell amendment, which aimed to reduce the support price somewhat. Barney explained: "The critical differences are these: First, the figure of 72.5 percent [of parity in the Bedell proposal] is for one year and we are at 70. But even more importantly, there are two triggers. Our trigger says that if we have miscalculated and the program has produced too much government expenditure, we can go below $13.70 to $13.10 [per hundredweight]. [Mr. Bedell] says that if we exceed beyond our expectations and get below $3.5 billion, then we can go higher. The gentleman has a trigger that goes up and I have a trigger that goes down."

Texas Democrat Charlie Stenholm stepped up and asked, "Does the gentleman have a concern about the price of milk in the grocery store?"

"I do have that concern as well," Barney replied. "My primary concern is how much it is costing the government. If the gentleman wants to make a point about the prices in the grocery store, he can do that; I am not entirely going to play straight man."

"I was noticing as I was eating a bowl of cereal last night that the price of a gallon of milk in Arlington, Virginia, is $1.97, which is 9 cents less than it was three years ago when I came to the Congress," Stenholm pointed out.

"At that rate the gentleman could put it in his car," Barney replied.

"My question . . . is this," Stenholm continued: "In April of this year we lowered the dairyman's income, his net take-home pay, by $7,000. The effect of [this] amendment would be to lower it at least another $7,000."

"I am going to make a heretical statement to the head of the Conservative Democratic forum. I do not want to set any particular level; I want the market to do that. . . . My answer, in all seriousness is, 'no,' it is none of my business to set the price of milk. I am not a good milk price setter, and I do not think anyone else is because the people who are the experts set a price for us that resulted in a lot of surplus and a $2 billion expenditure. I honestly believe the price of milk can best be set by the market," Barney answered.

Republican Tom Hagedorn of Minnesota prefaced his question by commenting that he was "impressed and intrigued" by Barney's "new-found interest in our dairy support program."

"There have been a couple of references to my new-found interest in the dairy price support program," Barney said. "Before I came here I was in the Massachusetts legislature, [which] does not have a dairy price support program. I was first a member of that body and later a Member of this body. I apologize for not being prompt and expressing my interest before, but this is the first time a legislative body in which I served as a Member considered a dairy price support program. So I think I have been reasonably prompt in my interest."

Hagedorn then argued that it was important that Congress not go overboard the other way in reducing the percent of parity, and Barney replied: "I do not think it is going overboard in penury to continue a program at a level which will be continuously above . . . half a billion dollars a year. We have heard a lot about the market, and I have read Milton Friedman and all the others. I have not found the footnote that says, 'except dairy farmers,' or the footnote that says, 'a free market absent agriculture.'"

"Does that also hold true for the deregulation of natural gas? Let the market apply?" Stenholm asked.

"Yes. If the gentleman wants to take the percentage drops in the natural gas regulation and apply them to those agricultural programs, then there will be a Frank/Stenholm or—seniority will win—Stenholm/Frank amendment tomorrow to change that. I will [gladly] do that because if we were to deregulate dairy at the pace to which we are committed [to] deregulating natural gas [which I support], the dairy farmers would be a lot madder at the gentleman from Texas than they are at me," Barney answered.

Democrat Floyd Fithian of Indiana argued that the Frank amendment would be disastrous to the dairy industry and would put thousands of small dairy farmers out of business. Barney replied: "We are told that we have to do that because there should be small farmers. I am for small farmers and for small everything. I am not for institutionalizing as a policy of the American Government that we are going to guarantee financially your right to be a small farmer or small grocer or small baseball player or small timer. With fiscal constraints, we simply cannot agree to institutionalize a policy of a federally subsidized right to remain in business as an X, Y, or Z."

The city slicker from Bayonne, the Harvard-educated politician from Boston debated and got the better of about a dozen members of Congress from dairy-farm, agrarian districts. The House rejected the Frank amendment to lower the support price to 70 percent of parity by a vote of 153 to 243 and adopted the Bedell amendment, which reduced the dairy support price only slightly. Barney, however, was given a standing ovation on the House floor. Conservative Republicans Ron Paul of Texas, John Hiler of Indiana, and others came over to congratulate him on his performance. Barney later explained to a reporter why he couldn't offer an amendment to cut price supports for both dairy and cattle, "Being Jewish, with the high holidays [approaching], I can't have milk and meat in the same amendment."

Barney Frank soon became a congressman whom agency officials feared at hearings. The columnist Mary McGrory referred to him as someone skilled at "drawing blood from bloodless bureaucrats." "The art of interrogating witnesses is something that most members of Congress have lost, partly because we do so little oversight. Barney is par excellence at that function," former representative Dan Glickman observed.

On November 17, 1981, the Judiciary Subcommittee on Immigration, Refugees, and International Law held a hearing on a bill introduced by Republican Stewart McKinney of Connecticut to provide preferential entry into the United States for Amerasian children, those half-Asian, half-American children fathered by American servicemen in Southeast Asia. The legislation was designed to remedy the plight of the abandoned Amerasian children, who were being mistreated in the countries of their birth because of their mixed parentage, by allowing these children to come to the United States, where they would have an opportunity to live more fulfilling lives.

The two State Department officials who testified on behalf of the Reagan administration, Diego Asencio, the assistant secretary for Consular Affairs, and Cornelius Scully, the director of the Office of Legislation, raised reservations about the bill. They expressed concern about abuse and fraud. "You mean that you are afraid some half-European or half-Australian kid might slip in?" Barney teased.

After getting the State Department officials to concede that these children were suffering severe discrimination because they had American fathers, Barney asked the bureaucrats whether they had an alternative. The State Department officials shifted gears to a delaying tactic, pointing to the marvels of a new scientific breakthrough blood test that could pinpoint the home state of the father. To Barney's persistent challenges, they conceded that the blood test was still in the laboratory stage at the Communicable Disease Center. When Barney asked about the cost of this miraculous blood test, they had no idea what it would cost. He asked whether or not the blood test could establish if the father was a serviceman: "Do you pick up antigens of occupation?" "No, sir," admitted the government officials. "So your problem would not be solved by [this] blood test," Barney concluded.

When the French left Vietnam in 1954, they took twenty-five thousand children with them. The French government paid for the schooling of those who stayed behind. When those children turned twenty-one, they had the option of French citizenship. Barney summed up the issue before the subcommittee: "France wasn't worried at all that some half-French, half-English child might slip in. We were in Asia for our own purposes. Therefore, it is our obligation to bring our kids home."

Barney began receiving accolades for his legislative skills and pragmatism from his colleagues and from the media that covered Congress. In a poll of members of Congress conducted by *U.S. News and World Report*, Barney Frank was chosen the most promising and effective freshman among the seventy-two new members of the House. He was also named the outstanding freshman in the House by the public television program *The Lawmakers* and by *Washingtonian* magazine.

In 1981, Barney received a zero rating from a Christian group, Christian Voice, for his voting record in Congress on religious issues. As Barney tells the story, he complained to a former member of Congress, "Bob, I know that I am Jewish, but still they said I was a total zero on Christian values." "I understand that you're upset but to tell you the truth I am not very sympathetic," the former member replied. "They used to give me a zero too and I think I have even more right to complain," said Robert Drinan, the Catholic priest whose vacated House seat Barney had won.

Barney explained the zero rating. "It is not just Christianity they rate, but a very specific form of Christianity. They find the Equal Rights Amendment unbiblical and say you're a bad Christian if you voted to ratify the Panama Canal treaty, if you are for the nuclear freeze . . ." He added, "People have every right to decide that in their version of the Bible, men are superior to women. I do not subscribe to that idea, but that's their right in their private relationships. But it should not be carried into public policy."

Barney also played an active role in constituent matters, often getting involved personally. When Roger Sohn, the surgeon-in-training who had campaigned for him in the 1980 election, was planning to do a residency in orthopedics at a hospital in Ireland, he learned after all the travel arrangements had been made for him and his wife, Fran, that he had been denied an Irish medical license because of a technicality. He wrote Barney a letter, with little faith that anything would happen as a result. But a week later, as he was coming out of the operating room, he received a phone call from Barney, who instructed him to wait by the same phone for five minutes. The second call was from the Irish ambassador to the United States, who told him that the Irish medical license would be granted and apologized for the inconvenience. Barney had phoned the State Department himself and then had spoken to the Irish ambassador. "Because of Tip," he later explained, "if you were in the Massachusetts delegation you got to know the Irish [ambassador] very well."

Baby Barnett, 1940.
Melville Photo Studio,
Bayonne, N.J.

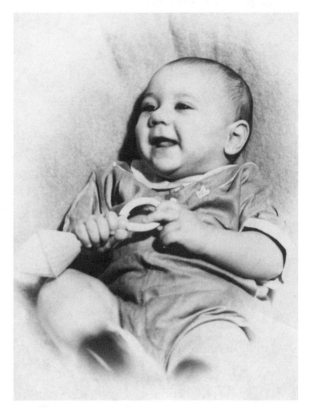

Barney with his sister Ann, 1945.

Ann, Barney, Doris, and Elsie, 1947 (David wasn't born yet). This was one of Elsie's favorite photos.

Classic Bar Mitzvah photo with his parents, Elsie and Sam, 1953. Note that the cake reads Barnett Frank.

Sporting a bowtie, c. 1954.

Barney at the plate, 1956. David is in the background (right) watching his older brother bat.

The Frank family (Doris, Sam, Barney, Ann, Elsie, and David) at Brown's Hotel in the Catskills, 1957.

Elsie and Barney with Eleanor Roosevelt (center) when she visited Bayonne to speak at an Israel Bonds dinner, 1958.

Barney (second from right near stairs) and other students at the Freedom Summer training program in Oxford, Ohio, before going to Mississippi to register black voters, June 1964. *Photo by Mark Levy. Courtesy of the Queens College/CUNY Civil Rights Archive.*

Barney (standing to left of portrait of President Kennedy) at first board meeting of Institute of Politics, Kennedy School of Government, Harvard, 1966. Sitting at the table (left to right) are *Los Angeles Times* publisher Otis Chandler, former treasury secretary C. Douglas Dillon, former World Bank president Eugene Black Sr., senior national security aide Michael Forrestal, Jacqueline Kennedy, former New York governor Averill Harriman, Institute of Politics director Richard Neustadt, *Washington Post* publisher Katharine Graham, Washington senator Henry "Scoop" Jackson, and Columbia College dean David Truman. *Courtesy of the Institute of Politics.*

"Neatness Isn't Everything" campaign poster, 1974.

Barney slides head first into home plate in 1982 campaign ad. *Courtesy of Dan Payne.*

Front and back of campaign baseball trading card, 1984.

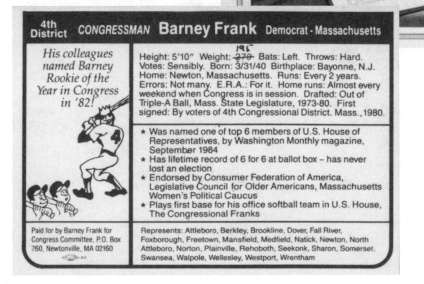

BARNEY FRANK

CONGRESSMAN

4th District

DEM. - MASS.

4th District	CONGRESSMAN **Barney Frank** Democrat - Massachusetts	

His colleagues named Barney Rookie of the Year in Congress in '82!

Height: 5'10" Weight: ~~270~~ 195 Bats: Left. Throws: Hard. Votes: Sensibly. Born: 3/31/40 Birthplace: Bayonne, N.J. Home: Newton, Massachusetts. Runs: Every 2 years. Errors: Not many. E.R.A.: For it. Home runs: Almost every weekend when Congress is in session. Drafted: Out of Triple-A Ball, Mass. State Legislature, 1973-80. First signed: By voters of 4th Congressional District. Mass., 1980.

★ Was named one of top 6 members of U.S. House of Representatives, by Washington Monthly magazine, September 1984
★ Has lifetime record of 6 for 6 at ballot box – has never lost an election
★ Endorsed by Consumer Federation of America, Legislative Council for Older Americans, Massachusetts Women's Political Caucus
★ Plays first base for his office softball team in U.S. House, The Congressional Franks

Paid for by Barney Frank for Congress Committee, P.O. Box 260, Newtonville, MA 02160

Represents: Attleboro, Berkley, Brookline, Dover, Fall River, Foxborough, Freetown, Mansfield, Medfield, Natick, Newton, North Attleboro, Norton, Plainville, Rehoboth, Seekonk, Sharon, Somerset, Swansea, Walpole, Wellesley, Westport, Wrentham

Reading to his niece and nephew, Julie and Jeffrey, with Elsie looking on, 1982.
Photo © Richard Sobol.

Barney and Rep. Tom Carper with Rabbi Menachem Schneerson during trip to Israel, 1984.

Foreign trips weren't always exciting. Italy, 1984.

With Yelena Bonner outside her apartment in Moscow, 1986. *Photo © Richard Sobol*

Elsie's 84th birthday party, 1996.

Reps. Barney Frank and Tammy Baldwin testify before a Congressional hearing on workplace discrimination against transgender Americans, June 2008. *Courtesy of the Human Rights Campaign.*

On parade in his district, 2008. *Photo by Jim Ready.*

Speaking to reporters on Capitol Hill, September 22, 2008. *AP photo by Charles Dharapak.*

Jim Ready, Barney, and President Barack Obama on Inauguration Day, January 20, 2009. *Photo by Stephen Ayres, courtesy of Jim Ready.*

10

Running against
Heckler-Reaganomics

BARNEY LOVED LIFE IN CONGRESS, working on legislation to advance the values he believed in, making political deals, lobbying members to support his bills and amendments, and schmoozing with colleagues in the cloakroom near the House chamber between votes. He also enjoyed relaxing in the Speaker's lobby off the House floor, puffing a cigar and chatting and joking with reporters. He had the job he had always dreamed of and he turned out to be pretty good at it.

Because of his narrow margin of victory in the 1980 general election, Barney was always nervous about being reelected and was in effect running for reelection from the first day he entered Congress. He therefore chose not to establish roots in Washington and moved into an apartment near Capitol Hill with some rented furniture. He was aware, however, of the considerable advantage of incumbency in races for Congress, and that gave him some comfort.

Then it happened, an incumbent's worst fear—redistricting. For all House members redistricting is politically life-threatening. It occurs every ten years when state congressional districts are redrawn to conform to population changes as recorded in the census. Even Claude Pepper, Democrat from Florida, the dynamic chairman of the House Select Committee on Aging who championed the rights of the elderly and who served for fifteen years in the Senate and then twenty-eight years in the House, was reportedly worried in 1988, at age eighty-eight, about redistricting in 1992.

The 1980 census figures showed a population growth in the Bay State of less than 1 percent during the 1970s, and this meant that Massachusetts had to reduce its number of congressional districts from twelve to eleven. The redistricting process was in the hands of the Democratic-controlled state legislature, which had the task of redrawing the political map.

In the months leading up to the redistricting decision in Massachusetts, Republican Congresswoman Margaret Heckler had kept her political options open, hinting that she might run for statewide office, either for senator against Edward Kennedy or for governor, to keep the Democrats from carving up her congressional district. Democratic governor Edward King was chummy with Heckler and threatened to veto any redistricting plan that put her at a disadvantage. King, who had not forgotten that Barney had backed Republican Frank Hatch for governor in 1978, openly supported sacrificing Barney's House seat.

On the streets of Boston, the word seemed to be that Barney was in trouble. One day in early December 1981, when Thaleia Schlesinger was walking near the State House in Boston, she overheard a conversation between two young men in conservative business suits walking a few steps behind her. One of them said, "Margaret is going to destroy Barney Frank and then she is going to run for the Senate in two years against Paul Tsongas and beat him also." At the intersection, she stopped, turned around, and said to the men, "Let me introduce myself. I am Thaleia Tsongas Schlesinger. I am Paul Tsongas's sister and I was Barney Frank's campaign press secretary." As the light changed, she walked away.

Barney's abrasiveness and his knack for antagonizing Democratic leaders during his four terms as a state legislator had put off many of the conservative old-guard Democrats, and he was well aware of the feelings against him. At our regular Monday night tennis game a few days later, as we were waiting to enter the tennis bubble, Barney, clearly preoccupied, said to me "Some of my former colleagues in the state legislature are trying to get even with me. They are using redistricting as their weapon. They plan to carve up my district and put me together with Margaret Heckler."

Barney's first serve was powerful and sizzled off the racket but straight into the net. His second serve was a lob. But it too failed to clear the net. A double fault. Not a good start for Barney. I won the first set easily. Instead of his usual hand-to-hand combat style of tennis, Barney appeared to be going through the motions. As we were changing sides of the court for the second set, he said, "I'm sorry. I just can't focus on playing tennis tonight." He seemed defeated, and not just on the tennis court.

Barney knew early on that when Massachusetts lost one of its twelve congressional seats, his district might be in play. He recognized that a Democrat had to be matched up against Heckler, an eight-term incumbent and one of only two Republican members in the Massachusetts delegation, and he realized that as the most junior member of the state's congressional delegation, that Democrat would most likely be he. Silvio Conte, the other Massachusetts Republican, whom Barney affectionately referred to as "the poet laureate of

Berkshire County," represented the First Congressional District in the western part of the state, a rural area that was more isolated and harder geographically to cut up. Heckler's Tenth Congressional District bordered several Democratic districts and was easier to divide up. But what Barney didn't expect was that the Democratic-controlled state legislature was prepared to draw the lines of the new district in a way that overwhelmingly favored Heckler. Redistricting is in essence a pure political act by elected officials.

State senator William "Billy" Bulger, who had been majority whip during the redistricting battle in 1973, had become the Senate president. Bulger and House majority leader George Keverian co-chaired the Special Commission on Congressional Redistricting, a seventeen-member committee consisting of thirteen Democrats and four Republicans. Four years earlier, when the Massachusetts House Redistricting Committee plan was subsequently changed to eliminate Jim Segel's legislative seat in Brookline for what Barney considered personal, partisan reasons, Barney had spoken out against that action, taking aim at Keverian and the House Speaker, Thomas McGee.

Bulger, described by a former state legislator as "a payback kind of person" and someone whose guiding philosophy is "Don't get mad, get even," was determined to hurt Barney for leading the coalition effort in 1973 to create a district that would elect a black senator. Bulger considered that effort, which affected his white, working-class, Irish-Catholic, South Boston district, an attempt to unseat him. He originally attributed it to bigotry by liberals who were anti-Catholic and anti-Irish and were out to punish South Boston. Bulger got his revenge in 1982 by merging the congressional districts of Barney Frank and Margaret Heckler and malevolently drawing the new district in a way that tremendously favored Heckler. Bulger punished Barney by creating a district in which he could not win. "Billy Bulger wasn't afraid to show that he controlled the process and congressmen didn't," Andrew Card, then a state representative from Holbrook who ran for governor in 1982, said.

Fourteen years later, however, in his 1996 memoir, *While the Music Lasts: My Life in Politics*, Bulger was almost apologetic when he wrote of Barney: "However much I have disagreed with him at times, I have always believed his positions were sincere and not based on personal or ethnic antagonism. We have remained friendly throughout the years, and I have supported him in campaigns."

When the congressional redistricting commission formally revealed its redistricting plan on Wednesday, December 9, Barney began a feverish lobbying campaign to keep much of his old Fourth District in the new district by amending the plan. He wanted Framingham, a town of about 65,000 residents, which had been put in James Shannon's Fifth District, in the new district to give him a fighting chance against Heckler. Although Barney had lost Framingham by several hundred votes in the 1980 Democratic primary and had carried the town by only a thousand votes in the general election, he had made major inroads there since taking office, working hard at constituent services and becoming well known and popular.

John DelPrete, the chairman of the Framingham Board of Selectmen, citing a hearing Barney had arranged for the board with the U.S. Department of Transportation about the transportation of hazardous waste and vinyl chloride through the community on trains, said of him, "He has gone overboard to help Framingham. I have never seen this type of support from a congressman." That sentiment was echoed by the local newspaper, the *Middlesex News*, in a December 11 editorial: "Frank had begun to give Framingham the kind of one-on-one service that it had long wanted from representatives at the state and federal level but never got." A cartoon by Dave Granlund in the *Middlesex News* shows a bespectacled Barney Frank in the form of a snowman melting in the sun of congressional redistricting.

In the effort to keep Framingham in the Fourth District, Barney brokered a deal that meant Democratic members from safe districts would cede heavily Democratic areas to the new Fourth District and acquire areas that Margaret Heckler had represented. This complicated transaction was akin to a four-team trade in baseball. Joe Early would acquire Attleboro and North Attleboro, Heckler strongholds near the Rhode Island border. In exchange, Early would give up some towns north and east of his Worcester hub to Jim Shannon. Shannon would also pick up Concord and some other liberal Boston suburbs from Edward Markey. In return, Shannon would give Framingham back to Barney and Billerica, Tewksbury, and presumably another town to be named later to Markey. "Any way you want to move me is fine," Markey had told Barney. In a separate transaction that Barney engineered, Joe Moakley agreed to take the town of Berkley in southeastern Massachusetts, which had been part of Heckler's district and was to be included in the new Fourth District. Moakley admitted to the *Boston Globe* that he was happy to help Barney out, though, he said, "I don't know where Berkley is, but I'll love it, I'm sure."

Barney's efforts to orchestrate a deal to keep Framingham in the Fourth District proved futile. When Democratic Party activists from Washington phoned Bulger to urge amendment of the redistricting plan, he responded that Barney Frank had caused him grief in the state legislature for eight years. Despite a request by House Speaker Tip O'Neill, Bulger refused to go along with the plan to put Framingham back in the Fourth District. Because it was December, Barney was inspired to compose a new Christmas carol, titled "O Little Town of Framingham."

On Friday evening, December 11, Barney confronted Bulger at a Democratic Party fund-raiser in Boston. "I have something to talk to you about," Barney said. "No politics tonight," Bulger replied dismissively. "How about geography and arithmetic," Barney suggested.

On December 14, the Massachusetts legislature debated the congressional redistricting plan. Keverian, the majority leader, explained the process. He began by acknowledging that everyone knew the merger would be a freshman Democrat and a Republican woman who live closer together than any other members of Congress and that the only debate was about the configuration of that merged district. Keverian explained that because of a population explosion in southeastern Massachusetts, it was necessary to take away more of the Fourth District, since more members of Congress needed that population in their district. He called the plan "fair and equitable" and observed that it was the first unanimous redistricting report in his memory.

Rep. David Cohen from Newton responded that while he accepted the fact that Barney Frank's district had to be merged with that of Congresswoman Heckler, the cards have been unfairly stacked in Heckler's favor. "We are not asking that Congressman Frank be handed a district on a silver platter. We expected that it would be a shootout at the O.K. Corral. But this is the Alamo," he said. "The reality is that it essentially cuts the throat of one of the most effective congressmen in Washington today," he said. Rep. John Businger of Brookline added, "I cannot believe that a Democratic representative would have written a plan in which a Republican is given preference over a Democrat. It is not a fair fight."

Rep. John Flood of Canton was more direct: "Fairness my foot. This is a political issue. This is a Democratic House and a Democratic state. If anyone is to be protected in redistricting it should be Democrats. When members of the Democratic leadership cannot tolerate the philosophy of Democrats that is different from their own, they cannot be called Democratic leaders. Barney Frank is a Democrat, an intelligent Democrat, and a Democrat who represents the people."

Rep. Michael Barrett from Reading, who had been Barney's campaign co-manager in his first race for state representative in 1972, referred to the redistricting plan "as a devil's pact, an unholy alliance between Edward King, Margaret Heckler, and William Bulger." Barrett, in an attempt to dramatize Barney's victim status, told his colleagues: "This is not a debate. It is a funeral oration. There is no way Frank can survive in this particular district. His career is being called to an end with the cooperation of both parties." Barrett suggested that when the bill is sent to the governor for signature, there should be several moments of mourning. "We are losing one of our brightest stars. Three or four years from now, all of us will look around for the likes of Barney Frank."

Keverian responded to Barney's supporters that he tried hard to keep Framingham in the new district but there was no consensus. After several hours of heated debate, the Massachusetts House, following the directive of its Democratic leaders, voted to reject the pro-Frank amendment to include the town of Framingham in the new district, with 39 in favor of the amendment and 117 against.

At a press conference at the State House after the vote, a tired and dejected Barney spoke out, because, he said, "it is unhealthy to the political system to take a mugging quietly." "I don't mean to be egomaniacal but if you asked legislators to draw a map in which Barney Frank would never be a congressman again, this would be it," he said. He asserted that the redistricting had been done the way it had in retribution for his having been so outspoken on a multitude of issues while serving in the state legislature. "I am in a high-risk business," he told the reporters. "It is inevitable that you lose your job because people [vote] you out. It is a little hard to take when you get legislated out." Andrew Natsios, a victim himself of redistricting in the state legislature, said, "That's the way the political game works. If you go after too many people, they go after you."

The next day, Senator Edward Burke of Framingham offered an amendment to include Framingham in the Fourth District, contending that Framingham is similar socially and economically to Newton and Wellesley but has little in common with Lowell and Lawrence in the Fifth District. The "Barney Frank–Framingham" amendment was defeated in the Senate by a vote of 15 in favor to 23 opposed.

The end result was that Barney's old Fourth District was carved up into six pieces and redistributed. He had been stripped of almost his entire district, retaining only Newton and Brookline, and the numerical name of the Fourth District. Bulger reportedly had wanted to slice up Newton and Brookline as well but no one else wanted those towns. Certainly not Tip O'Neill. Brookline had once been part of O'Neill's district and he was happy to lose the town in 1972. "Brookline—10 percent of the district, 50 percent of the mail," he said. "They make phone calls, come to my office. I don't want to have to deal with this any more."

Seventy percent of the population of the redrawn Fourth District came from Heckler's old district. Thus, the newly drawn district had 360,000 people whom she had represented in Congress for sixteen years, compared with 140,000 whom Barney had represented for one term. At the time, Heckler represented nineteen of the twenty-three cities and towns in the new Fourth District. Two towns, Walpole and Dover, came from Joseph Moakley's district, but even those towns were once represented by Heckler.

The Democratic leadership in the state legislature "certainly tried their best to get rid of Barney," Frank Hatch, the Republican leader from 1971 to 1978, who had left the legislature in 1978 to run for governor and was living in Vermont at the time, said. "Even Tom DeLay couldn't have done a better redistricting," he said. Others agree. "They were absolutely trying to redistrict Barney out of a congressional seat," former state representative Philip Johnston said. And former state representative Max Volterra from Attleboro described Barney as "an overwhelming underdog against Margaret Heckler."

There were a few politicians, however, who thought that Barney could beat Heckler and viewed the redistricting as a way to get rid of Heckler rather than Barney. "The only Democrat who thought that Barney Frank was going to lose to Margaret Heckler was Barney. I never had a question in my mind about Barney winning," Tommy O'Neill, lieutenant governor at the time, said. Joseph Timilty, a state senator, believed that Barney would win because Heckler, despite her sixteen-year incumbency, was out of touch with her district and out of touch with the issues.

The redistricting decision by the Massachusetts legislature was a major embarrassment to Speaker Tip O'Neill. He had been traveling across the country, warning about the thin Democratic majority in the House and urging Democratic state legislatures to protect their own in the redistricting process. But he had been unable to persuade the Democratic legislative leaders in his home state to alter the political map on Democrat Barney Frank's behalf. O'Neill was mortified that Massachusetts could well lose a Democratic seat in Congress because of redistricting.

Barney was devastated by the redistricting and began to feel sorry for himself, complaining about the unfairness of it all to anyone who would listen—staff, constituents, or reporters. He would walk around the office like a despondent Prince Hamlet moaning about how unfair it was that he could no longer be a congressman. Mary Beth Cahill, a legislative assistant on his Washington staff, was good at handling those conversations. "Get off of it. That's not going to play," she said. She urged him to get busy campaigning. "Pick yourself up and let's get going," she said. He seriously considered not running for reelection because he had no hope of winning.

His opponent, Margaret Heckler, then fifty years old, was born in Flushing, New York, the daughter of an Irish New York City hotel doorman. The five-foot-two-inch blond-haired legislator was energetic, outgoing, and always impeccably dressed. She was known as sweet and genteel on the outside but wily and shrewd on the inside. A popular incumbent, a savvy campaigner, and a formidable opponent, she had many friendships in the state legislature and in Congress that crossed party lines. Heckler, a graduate of Albertus Magnus College, had received a law degree from Boston College Law School in 1956, where she was an editor of the *Law Review* and the only woman in her class. In 1962, as an attorney and a member of the Wellesley town meeting, Heckler became the first woman elected to the eight-member governor's council, a largely ceremonial body dating from the eighteenth century. The position gave her visibility though little power.

In 1966, Heckler challenged Joseph Martin of North Attleboro, the seemingly unbeatable eighty-one-year-old former Speaker of the House (1947–49, 1953–55) who had been in office since 1924, in the Republican primary. Martin was in ill health and had said that he wanted "just one more term." State senator John F. Parker from Fall River, part of the Senate leadership, who was in line to succeed Martin, like other Republicans, was prepared to wait, but not Heckler. She ran a strong, active campaign, traveling around the district, knocking on doors, and meeting voters. She promised the voters vigorous representation. Her campaign slogan was "We Need a Heckler in Congress." She quoted from Martin's 1924 campaign, in which he had ousted an eighty-three-year-old incumbent who had been in Congress too long. Heckler won against Martin and narrowly defeated Democrat Patrick Harrington of Fall River in the general election.

Heckler was a moderate on most issues and prided herself on exemplary constituent service. As a member of Congress, she was respected and generally liked, although in her sixteen years there she had never served in a leadership position. She was the most senior woman in the House, but had diluted her seniority by committee hopping, spending two years on Government Operations, then six years on Banking and six years on Agriculture before moving to Science and Technology. In 1981 she was a member of the Science and Technology Committee and the Veterans' Affairs Committee. Margaret Mary O'Shaughnessy Heckler was important to the Republican Party, in the state and on the federal level, and as a successful female Irish American politician could easily raise the campaign money needed.

Since her first victory in 1966, Heckler had had little difficulty over the years getting reelected. She received less than 60 percent of the vote only once, in 1970, when the Democratic candidate, Bertram Yaffe, held her to 57 percent.

The syndicated columnist Jack Anderson once referred to her as Margaret "I'd-walk-a-mile-for-a-camera" Heckler. In 1976, when President Gerald Ford came to Boston during the Bicentennial, he appeared at a political event at the Museum of Science. Margaret Heckler was there, standing on the platform, close to the president, and inserting herself, according to one observer, in fifty-nine of the first sixty photographs of the president. She was standing so close to the president that when Carlton Fisk, the Boston Red Sox catcher and 1972 Rookie of the Year, showed up, and President Ford, a former Michigan football star and enthusiastic sports fan, pivoted abruptly and darted over to greet Fisk, he knocked Heckler off the platform.

Joe Moakley described Heckler to the *Boston Globe*: "She's always on the move. If gasohol comes into the district there's Peggy Heckler with a hard hat filling up someone's car. If there's a flood there's Peggy Heckler going down the river in a canoe. She's a good campaigner and a hard worker. Margaret Heckler is a formidable opponent."

This new salamander-shaped Fourth District extended south from its core in Newton and Brookline through the wealthy, WASP Republican towns of Wellesley and Dover, past Natick, Medfield, and Sharon to Attleboro. From there it continued south past the blue-collar, heavily Portuguese, struggling old textile-mill city of Fall River, which was heavily Democratic but generally conservative, to Westport on the Rhode Island border. It was an expensive district to campaign in, since it included two separate television markets. The only plus for Barney in the redistricting map was that the Democratic but conservative city of Waltham, where he had not faired well with the voters in the 1980 election, was no longer part of the district. It had been moved into Tip O'Neill's district.

In January 1982, John Marttila and Tom Kiley, Barney's campaign strategists, told him that he probably couldn't win but that he could get his percentage of the vote up to the high forties and make a respectable showing. Barney decided privately to throw in the towel and not seek reelection because he did not think he could win. "I am not going to be a participant in my own mugging," he said. He hated having to impose on relatives, friends, and others for campaign contributions, and he was awkward socially and detested campaigning. He did not want to put himself through exhausting eighteen-hour campaign days only to lose. "Campaigning is bad enough, but if you cannot win it is far worse," he said. "I had a chance to be a congressman for another year and wanted to be the best legislator I could be."

Barney visited his old friend Mark Furstenberg, who lived in Newton at the time. The two men spent the morning talking about what Barney could do for a living when his term in Congress ended. Recalling their meeting, Furstenberg said, "He really didn't think he could beat Heckler and clearly had made up his mind not to run for reelection."

Barney then told his brother, David, about his decision not to run. And though David mentally worked out the percentage of the vote Barney would need in each city and figured he had no more than a one-in-three chance of winning, and thought he would probably lose, he urged his older brother to reconsider and run for reelection rather than quit. "I understand how you feel. Nobody can force you to run," David said. "But suppose [and he named a number of likely candidates] runs and he gets 47–48 percent of the vote against Heckler, how are you going to feel?" Jim Segel was more forceful when Barney asked him how people would react to his quitting. "Everybody is going to think that you are a fucking asshole," Segel said. "A lot of people wanted that seat. David [Mofenson] wanted it and others. People busted their ass to help you get that seat. Now it is tough and you are walking away. That is what they are going to think."

Ed Markey encouraged Barney to run for reelection, but for a different reason. "You should run because people in the know understand that it is a hard seat to win. If you do a good job you can move back and run for Tip's seat when he retires," he said.

Amy Isaacs, a friend whom Barney had known since 1969 when she was an intern at the Americans for Democratic Action and he served on the board, advised him that it could be worse. "It's not like your opponent is Jesus Christ," she said.

The message from Barney's top staff—Dottie Reichard, Mary Beth Cahill, Doug Cahn, and Jim Dolan, his administrative assistant in Washington who had worked as Heckler's press secretary several years earlier, was that if you don't stand up and fight for reelection, there won't be another chance. You have to try. If you lose, there will still be doors open to you.

Finally, at the urging of family and friends, Barney reconsidered his private decision not to run. They convinced him that he owed it to his supporters to take a shot at Heckler. "He walked into the campaign against Heckler assuming that he was going to lose. When you are not expected to win, you can be looser, and that helped him," his sister Ann Lewis said.

A February 1982 poll of five hundred likely voters conducted by Tom Kiley showed Heckler leading by a substantial margin, 52 to 34 percent. Barney was well liked in Newton and Brookline and carried that area easily in the poll, while Heckler led in her much larger part of the district. Kiley did some message testing in the poll, trying out certain potential attack lines, and found that when the voters surveyed were read a description of the candidates and their positions there was a dramatic swing toward Barney in Heckler's part of the district, particularly in Fall River, where large numbers of conservative, ethnic Democrats had been voting for Heckler for Congress for years. Kiley believed that this disclosure showed potential.

One of Barney's first acts after deciding to run against Heckler was to visit Carlton Viveiros, the Democratic mayor of Fall River, at his home and seek his support. Barney and Viveiros had served together in the state legislature for three terms. Viveiros, who had been elected mayor of Fall River in 1978, had not supported the liberal Democratic state senator Robert McCarthy two years earlier in the race against Heckler. Viveiros was a conservative legislator from a blue-collar district. Yet there was a certain quiet chemistry between the two men. "I had a solid personal relationship with Barney which meant a lot. He is extremely capable and of high moral standard," Viveiros said. "Barney can have a relationship with people, I think, without being a back slapper or a stroker, and without necessarily going out and having a beer with you." Barney was much more liberal than Viveiros would have liked in a candidate for Congress, but he agreed to support Barney and worked hard to elect him. Barney feels that Viveiros's endorsement was very important in that election. "The hallmark of Barney's political career is that he connects with a lot of people on a personal level and they become his friends regardless of his position on the issues," Tom Kiley said.

The blue-collar city of Fall River was a key battleground in the campaign. Close to half of its ninety-two thousand residents were of Portuguese descent. The voters in Fall River were traditional Democrats but they liked and respected Heckler. She had carried the city in every run for Congress, except for the first one, when her opponent in the general election was from Fall River.

After the two congressional districts were merged, one of the people that Barney made it his business to meet with was Mark A. Sullivan, a native of Fall River and the director of the city's community action and local antipoverty program. Sullivan administered an array of community programs, including fuel assistance, weatherization, senior aid, and Head Start. His influence and power in the community had come from block grants that his organization received.

The first time Barney met with the mustachioed thirty-nine-year-old Sullivan, Sullivan told him that he had no interest in supporting his candidacy. "You don't have a prayer," he said. Barney came back a second time a few weeks later and again Sullivan was not interested. But Barney persisted. The next time he went to see Sullivan, he brought Lieutenant Governor Tommy O'Neill with him. Sullivan's father had been the president of the Eastern Massachusetts Bus Drivers Union and a friend of Tip O'Neill's from the time O'Neill was Speaker in the Massachusetts legislature. "I started to be intrigued by this sitting congressman," Sullivan recalled. "He grew on me. I was captivated by his intellect and impressed by his ability and his terrific sense of humor, often self-effacing." Sullivan did some research and examined Barney's voting record. He was drawn to Barney for his philosophical and moral commitment to fairness and equality, recognizing that Barney would relate well to the people in Fall River, who were concerned about jobs and paying the rent.

Sullivan had heard rumors that Barney was gay and was not bashful about asking him a direct question. At their next meeting, he said, "Listen, I don't care personally. But if you are gay it will probably become an election issue and I just want to know what kind of campaign to expect." Barney denied that he was gay. "I was lying to a couple of people at that time about being gay," Barney recalled with some understatement.

Sullivan had a close personal relationship with Heckler, who had been an ally of his in his community work during the past eight or nine years. Ronald Reagan, however, changed the equation. Barney made a persuasive case to Sullivan that the amount of block grants was dwindling under the Reagan economic program and that the administration policies Heckler was supporting were hurting the people of Fall River. If Heckler had voted against the Gramm–Latta bill, which substantially cut programs for the poor, the elderly, working people, and students, Barney acknowledges now, he would never have had Sullivan's support.

"In my whole life that was the toughest thing I ever did politically and the smartest," Sullivan said. "I put my life and my family on the line."

The people in the district had been voting for Heckler for sixteen years and she was popular. Barney's campaign strategy was to tell voters that, because of Ronald Reagan, Heckler was not the same person they had voted for. She had been a moderate, but the Reagan people were cracking down on moderate Republicans.

In April 1981, less than three weeks after being shot and wounded by John Hinckley outside the Washington Hilton Hotel, President Reagan began spending several hours a day phoning members of Congress to drum up support for his economic program, particularly the Gramm–Latta bill, which would dramatically cut nondefense programs. The president used a phone list of moderate Republicans and conservative Democrats that had been prepared by the White House Office of Congressional Affairs and contained a short biography and political summary of each member. The call card for Margaret Heckler, as quoted in Richard Reeves's 2005 biography *President Reagan: The Triumph of Imagination*, read: "North suburbs of Boston and Fall River. . . . Peggy wants to support the president but feels vulnerable because her district is likely to be reapportioned and she will be pitted against Barney Frank, a liberal Democrat." According to Reeves, President Reagan wrote the following note after he spoke with Heckler: "Has a very real problem. . . . There is no doubt of her personal support & desire to be of help. We need to give her good rational explanations re: the cuts such as student loans, etc."

Barney made Heckler's support of Reagan's economic policies the overriding issue in the campaign, coining the term *Heckler-Reaganomics*. He emphasized the unfairness of the Reagan pro-business economic policies, saying they caused "one of the most serious economic crises since the Great Depression" and inflicted enormous harm on vulnerable people. Heckler, he pointed out, had voted for President Reagan's budget in 1981 and that budget reduced funding for Medicare, housing programs, public transportation, and elderly lunch programs and cut student loans for middle-income students while significantly increasing military funding, including spending for the MX missile program. With Margaret Heckler's help, he pointed out, the Reagan administration also cut fuel assistance. "Many people in Fall River won't be able to heat their homes this winter because Ronald Reagan said the oil companies need a tax cut and we can't afford fuel assistance," he said. Also, the budget Heckler had voted for "recommissioned forty-year-old battleships from the mothball fleet while decommissioning eighty-year-old women from their Social Security minimum benefits" and funded, at billions of dollars, "a shelter for the homeless MX missile while severely defunding programs to weatherize our human shelters." "I have a rule," Barney told reporters, "that I never vote for any weapon that is older than I am."

Barney explained to voters that the conservative, Reagan position was that government takes care of the basics, such a cleaning the streets and providing police, but that beyond that it is up to private charity to help people. The Reagan administration's policy, he said, reflected the credo of David Stockman, director of the Office of Management and Budget: "Nobody is entitled to anything."

Mark Sullivan was more qualified than almost anyone else to talk to voters about the impact Ronald Reagan's economic policies was having on working people and the elderly in Fall River. When he had gone to Washington to plead Fall River's case and asked Congresswoman Heckler not to vote for Gramm–Latta and several other bills that cut or abolished all the programs that were being used for the revitalization of Fall River, she had told him that the pressure on her to vote with the administration was enormous. At a press conference to endorse Barney, Sullivan warned the Fall River community that Heckler had been voting the party line and that as bad as the current year budget cuts were, they would be five times worse the next year. "To return Margaret Heckler back to Congress to continue Reaganomics," he said, "is to cut your nose off to spite your face."

"The more I met Congressman Frank the more I understood that all I had to do was get him with people and he could sell himself," Sullivan said. "We just had to get him in the door. He was a natural. He did not know how good a campaigner he was by Fall River standards." Barney went to practically every community event in southeastern Massachusetts, including the Firemen's Ball in Fall River, where he participated in the grand march with the fire chief.

Barney had ended the 1980 general election with a ninety-five-thousand-dollar campaign deficit resulting from the unexpected need in the last two weeks of the campaign to respond to Richard Jones's negative advertising. He had spent most of 1981 retiring that campaign debt. As an incumbent congressman who was widely known, it was much easier for him to raise money for the 1982 campaign. Senator Edward Kennedy and Speaker Tip O'Neill hosted a forty-second-birthday fund-raiser for Barney on April 4, 1982. O'Neill told the crowd, "In just one year in Congress, Barney Frank has done more than many people do in fifteen or twenty years." Three weeks later, Harvard Law School professor Alan Dershowitz hosted a fund-raiser for Barney at his home, and Professor Lawrence Tribe had one in the fall.

"The Heckler campaign underestimated our ability to raise money," Thaleia Schlesinger, who had been elevated from press secretary in 1980 to campaign chair in 1982, said. The race became a national cause célèbre and money started flowing into the campaign. "I have a great fund-raiser," Barney said, "a fellow by the name of Reagan." "I have raised an awful lot of money in small contributions from people who care about the environment, desperately frightened by what James Watt is doing to protect our resources. I get money from women who think that there should be equality in this society and they are appalled to see Phyllis Schafly appointing the people who are running the women's movement."

Barney's campaign against Margaret Heckler was one of the most closely watched and bitterly fought House races and the most expensive congressional race in the nation in 1982. This meant a lot more trips to the bank for his sister Doris, with her young children in tow, to deposit mounds of campaign checks. Barney spent just over $1.5 million on the campaign, while Heckler spent a little under $1 million.

The Frank–Heckler election became a referendum on Reagan's economic policies, and the Reagan White House considered Heckler's race against Barney Frank their second highest priority among the 435 House races, topped only by the reelection of Eugene Atkinson of Pennsylvania, who had switched parties to the GOP a year earlier. The White House was active in ensuring that Heckler received campaign funds from various Republican Party committees. Ronald Reagan's Political Action Committee, which generally did not provide financial support to incumbents, contributed to Heckler's campaign because "she had supported the president on several votes that were tough for her district." Vice President George Bush, treasury secretary Donald Regan, transportation secretary Drew Lewis, and White House aides James Baker, Edward Meese, Lyn Nofzinger, Ed Rollins, and Ken Duberstein appeared at fund-raising and campaign events for Heckler.

In contrast to Heckler, who had not faced a tough election campaign in many years, Barney had an experienced campaign organization in place from the 1980 election. His campaign staff included enthusiastic young people who believed in him and were willing to work tirelessly on his behalf. "The affection and respect for Barney from the [1980 campaign] really manifested itself in the number of people from our first race who volunteered to help him hold on to his seat in Congress in the new district," Mary Beth Cahill said.

One memorable early television commercial that was a big hit, and Barney's favorite, was designed to introduce the rookie congressman to the residents in Fall River and the southern part of the new congressional district by showing him in tune with Americana by playing softball. According to Dan Payne, who created and directed the commercial, the idea was that Barney would hit an-inside-the-park home run and the announcer would explain that he was rookie of the year, voted best freshman congressman—without, as some consultants say, "looking like a complete brown-nose."

The ad opens with Barney in the batter's box, looking like the Bambino, or at least like William Bendix playing Babe Ruth in the 1948 film *The Babe Ruth Story*. The announcer says, "In 1981 Barney Frank's colleagues named him rookie of the year in Congress." Swinging the bat from the left side of the plate, Barney, unassisted by performance-enhancing drugs, blasts a towering drive that sails over the outfielder's head. As Barney runs around the bases the announcer recites his legislative accomplishments during his first House term: "They were impressed with how Barney chopped millions of dollars in wasteful farm subsidies, how he helped stop the Republicans from cutting Social Security, how he opposed the Reagan tax program because it favored the rich over average people, and how he even stood up to a Democratic tax plan that favored big oil." The ad ends with Barney sliding head first into home, touching the plate ahead of the relay throw to the catcher, and accepting congratulations from his jubilant teammates. The announcer concludes, "Barney Frank, the best new Congressman in Washington. A congressman you can trust."

The softball commercial was filmed at what was then called the Beaver Country Day School in Newton. A few weeks earlier, a Jewish group that was planning a softball marathon in which they would play an inning or two against a series of teams invited Barney to participate and he fielded a team made up of campaign volunteers. The group warmed up by playing softball for about forty-five minutes before shooting the commercial.

"Barney had hurt his knee and was not running well," Dan Payne recalled. "He was crabby about the whole idea that this was going to be a set-up and we would control everything." Before the camera started to roll, Barney told Payne, "You can fake everything else but I want to do a head-first slide because you can't fake that."

"I knew Barney was a pretty good hitter but I was surprised at how hard and far he hit the ball," Payne said. Barney whacked the ball deep over the outfielder's head and started running around the bases. The outfielder retrieved the ball and threw it to the shortstop as Barney, waved home by third-base coach Mark Horan, rounded third base. The shortstop caught the ball on the outfield grass, turned, and fired the ball to home plate. "Barney is running down the third base line and we have a camera waiting for him," Payne said. "The throw comes in and Barney having slid too early is out by about two feet."

"We go back, put him on third base with a big lead and do it again," Payne explained. "The shortstop has the ball, turns and throws it home and Barney is out again, sliding head-first right into the catcher's tag." On the third try Barney made it home safely, sliding head-first under the tag of the catcher, Peter Kovar, a campaign volunteer from Newton who has been Barney's chief of staff in the Washington office since early 1991.

Payne liked the baseball commercial because he thought it was the best metaphor for Barney. Although many of Barney's campaign staff worried that in the ad Barney, who was overweight and clearly a weekend athlete, might not look congressional enough, Payne said he was able to pull it off. "Barney Frank was more coordinated than I expected," Kevin Casey, the first baseman, who was on assignment from Lieutenant Governor Tommy O'Neill's staff, said. "He reminded me a little of Jackie Gleason, who, despite his appearance, was exceptionally well coordinated."

After the commercial aired, people, particularly from Fall River, started phoning the campaign office to challenge Barney's team in softball. "I knew we had something going. We had bridged the cultural gap between the Newton liberal and the Fall River conservative voters," Payne said. "It sort of set the tone for the campaign, the whole idea of Barney Frank coming at politics differently." "The softball commercial really humanized him and was a big hit in Fall River," Bill Black, who worked on the campaign staff in Fall River, said. "At first, the people in Fall River looked upon Barney as a liberal from Boston, but when they got to meet him they found him to be an average guy they could relate to."

At the start of the 1982 campaign, David Frank told his mother that it was time for her to retire from her job as a legal secretary because Barney needed her in the campaign. Elsie protested at first but in the end she took a leave of absence from the law firm where she worked. "If Barney needs me, I can't say no," she said.

Elsie added immeasurably to Barney's campaign by appearing in a television ad that focused on protecting the elderly from cuts in Social Security. In the sixty-second spot, the camera zooms in on a white-haired woman sitting in an overstuffed chair. The woman says: "I just retired and I'm looking forward to my Social Security. In fact, I'm depending on it. So all this talk about cutting Social Security is really making me nervous. That's why I'm glad Barney Frank is in Congress. Barney helped stop the Republicans from cutting cost-of-living and Medicare benefits, and he'll keep fighting to protect our Social Security. How can I be so sure Barney will do the right thing by us older people? Because he's my son."

David Frank had suggested using his mother in a campaign commercial. The brilliance of the commercial was in its reality. It used the candidate's mother, who was then sixty-nine years old, about to retire, talking about retirement and Social Security and tied that to Barney's strong stand on Social Security. "Elsie gave the Social Security argument life and meaning," Payne said. "Barney wouldn't have been able to develop the Social Security argument the way he did without that ad."

The commercial was filmed in the living room of Elsie's apartment in the Back Bay in Boston. It was hot in the room under the lights of the camera. The air conditioner in the bedroom didn't have much impact in the living room, and the windows were closed to keep out the traffic noise from Beacon Street three floors below. The camera crew put black cloth on the windows to keep out the natural sunlight. Elsie was preoccupied that morning because one of her grandchildren, Ann's daughter Beth, was in the hospital being operated on for an infected tooth. Elsie had promised Beth she'd be there when she woke up.

The filming seemed interminable to Elsie. Payne kept paring down the script, till finally he said to her, "You do it with the words you feel comfortable with," and Elsie did it perfectly. Then there was a problem with the camera. Finally, everything came together and, after telling the crew just to leave the cloth on the windows, Elsie dashed out of the apartment and hailed a taxi to New England Baptist Hospital. She went to her granddaughter's room and found her asleep. As Elsie sat down on a chair next to the bed, Beth opened her eyes and said, "Grandma, I'll be all right. You can go home."

The Frank campaign began running the commercial with a limited distribution to reach seniors concerned with retirement. They purchased time on the *Lawrence Welk Show*. But soon they had to run the ad in prime time in response to all the phone calls that came into the campaign headquarters from people who said they had heard about the Elsie Frank commercial and wanted to know when they could watch it on television. "It became a general consumption commercial," Payne said. And Elsie became something of a celebrity. She appeared on the cover of the April 1983 issue of *Harper's*, illustrating an article on the best television commercials of the 1982 political campaign titled "Barney Frank's Mother and 500 Postmen." The article, by Nicholas Lemann, calls Elsie "irresistible." The television political ad "Mrs. Frank" was awarded first prize by the New England Broadcasting Association. In the next election cycle, candidates across the country imitated the Elsie Frank commercial with help from their mothers.

In the spring of 1982, Barney and Heckler appeared together for the first time at a candidate forum at the Newton Marriott. It was not a debate and the two candidates made separate twenty-minute presentations. "Heckler didn't want to deal with him at all. She hated being in the same building with him," Payne said.

Heckler went first and spoke about her many years of service to the district and all that she had done for her constituents. When it was his turn, Barney pointed out that constituent service is part of the job and that every member of Congress provides it. Furthermore, "we have staff to do that," he said. "So far as I am concerned we begin this race even. I am going to do exactly what she does. Now that we've got that out of the way, let's focus on the differences between us." "That was the single most devastating thing that Barney did to Heckler during the campaign. He took away her constituent service advantage," Payne said.

Heckler underestimated Barney and made the mistake of assuming that she would not have that hard a fight against Barney because he had won in 1980 by only a slim margin over an unknown dentist. She acted as though Barney were little more than a nuisance, allowing him to benefit from her inaction and spend ten months establishing himself as a credible, interesting politician. "The difference was that Heckler was not accustomed to the kind of opposition she was coming under or to the type of work she had to do to hold the seat," Mary Beth Cahill said.

By not campaigning, Heckler allowed Barney to set the tone of the campaign. He traveled all over the district introducing himself to voters and portraying Heckler as an ardent supporter of President Reagan's economic policies. Particularly devastating was the comment he frequently made to audiences, "I wasn't the one the president kissed." He was referring to President Reagan's televised State of the Union speech in January 1982. Heckler arrived early at the event and secured a seat on the aisle. When the president entered the chamber and started walking to the Speaker's rostrum, she shook his hand. When he had delivered his speech and started walking back up the aisle, Heckler, easily visible in a bright red dress, greeted him warmly and got national television exposure when she then kissed the president. "That was the kiss of death for Margaret Heckler," Dottie Reichard said.

Barney was much more confident about himself and his position on the issues in 1982 than he had been during the 1980 campaign. He tried to spend every minute he was not in Congress in the district campaigning. If he couldn't be at an event in person, his campaign staff organized a telephone hookup. In Sharon, which has a substantial Jewish population, Barney campaigned at every synagogue more than once. He burrowed in underneath an entrenched incumbent and did so the old-fashioned way. "It's important to be seen and to make your face known. This may not be much of a face, but it's going to be seen," he declared.

Despite his improved self-confidence, however, Barney continued to lack certain social graces. When state representative Max Volterra and his wife hosted a campaign party for Barney at their home in Attleboro, Barney came in the house, schmoozed with the guests, and left. "My wife complained that he didn't even say goodbye or thank me," Volterra recalled. "I phoned Barney and told him that my wife wasn't too happy and that one of the things you have to do is thank people." Barney immediately called Max's wife, apologized, and thanked her for her effort.

In contrast to Barney's energetic campaign, Heckler's was lackluster. The candidate was rusty, and she didn't realize that politics had changed since her last competitive race. She had grown accustomed to simply working the crowds at Portuguese, Italian, Irish, and other ethnic festivals, and she counted on her popularity, her sixteen years of exemplary constituent service, and her moderate record to pull her through. Barney had opened four campaign offices—in Brookline, Newton, Fall River, and Natick—before Heckler had opened one. He also benefited from some infighting on Heckler's campaign staff. They could not agree, for example, on what shade of pink to use on her bumper stickers, and so there were no Heckler bumper stickers for the first six weeks of the campaign. Heckler's husband, John, and her campaign manager reportedly came to physical blows, and Heckler herself remained inaccessible to the press for interviews during the campaign. A press release about the official opening of her Newton–Brookline campaign office wasn't received by many newspapers until several weeks after the event.

Barney was successful in getting the working-class Democratic voters in Fall River, where Reagan's economic policies had taken a toll, to pay attention to the issue differences between the candidates. Speaking at senior citizen centers, outside factory gates, and at church bingo games, Barney repeatedly reminded his audience that he and Heckler had voted differently on a wide variety of issues affecting women, the poor, the elderly, the unemployed, and the environment. He remarked that even Pennsylvania GOP Senator John Heinz, of the Heinz ketchup family, found it unpalatable when the recent menu for school lunches proposed substituting ketchup for a real vegetable and tofu for real meat.

The message began to sink in. As one local labor official said about Heckler, "She's not the same person. We didn't walk out on her. She walked out on us. We came to her for things but she wouldn't listen. She became part of the Reagan Republican Revolution." The Massachusetts state AFL–CIO, which had supported Heckler the previous ten years, switched over and endorsed Barney, largely because he was there with labor during the fight against the unfairness of the administration's economic policies.

The residents of Fall River started to gravitate toward Barney Frank because they saw him as someone who was going to help them. "The people in Fall River responded to Barney because he is genuine and sincere. He is not concerned about his appearance and wasn't full of himself," Mayor Viveiros said. The columnist Colman McCarthy had described Barney's suits as "hanging over his bulgy frame like overfilled Hefty bags." Barney maintained that there was nothing wrong with the suits he wore and pointed out that the suits came from the Darwood factory outlet store in Fall River, a union shop. People would come up to him and say, "That's a very ill-fitting suit," and he would respond, "No, it's a very well fitting suit. I just don't happen to be the person it fits."

Barney brought Democrat Tony Coelho of California, the only Portuguese American member of Congress, to Fall River to campaign with him in the city's Portuguese neighborhoods. Coelho praised Barney as a champion of the interests of Portuguese Americans. In other areas of Fall River, Barney brought in state representative Joseph DeNucci, a one-time middleweight contender ranked in the top ten who had ended his professional boxing career with a respectable 65–12–4 record. The two men had worked out their differences since the Democratic primary for Congress two years earlier when DeNucci, as a supporter of David Mofenson, had backed Arthur Clark after Mofenson dropped out of the race. DeNucci now enthusiastically endorsed Barney. "Barney came up like me: the hard way. And with a good family behind him," DeNucci said.

Both candidates had entertainment stars to help bolster their campaigns. Wayne Newton performed at a fund-raiser for Margaret Heckler, though she hardly knew who he was. When a reporter interviewed Heckler at the event and asked her to name her favorite Wayne Newton song, knowing none, she answered, "Oh, I love them all." The actress Liv Ullmann and Mike Farrell from the popular TV series *M*A*S*H* came to support Barney. Farrell was a long-time political activist who had been involved in dozens of political campaigns. "I am not sure who introduced us but Barney was a pal of Al Lowenstein who was a dear friend of mine. I was sick at the loss of Al and I was happy to help someone who Al believed in and who believed in Al," Farrell recalled.

As Barney and Farrell drove around Fall River, Barney pointed out the closed mills and factories that had moved south where labor costs were cheaper. The unemployment rate in Fall River had climbed to almost 15 percent, and people were lined up waiting for unemployment checks. Barney, sitting in the back seat with a campaign aide, explained to Farrell, in the front passenger seat, how the president's economic policies had hurt the residents of Fall River. "I was just knocked out by him, his wit, and his incredible grasp of the issues from a perspective that many people don't see. He had a real appreciation of the common people, their rights and their dignity. It was something that really caught me," Farrell said.

"It was a big deal when a television star like Mike Farrell . . . came to Fall River to campaign for Barney Frank," Mark Sullivan said. People loved the character he played on *M*A*S*H*, Captain B. J. Hunnicut, and his willingness to come to Fall River to campaign for Barney gave the candidate added stature.

Claude Pepper, the oldest sitting member of Congress and the strongest defender of the Social Security and Medicare programs in the country, also went to Fall River to urge people to vote for Barney Frank, referring particularly to the work he had done for the elderly. "I'm asking you, as chairman of the House Select Committee on Aging, don't let them take away the best man we've got," he declared.

Barney used the Reagan administration's assault on women's rights against Heckler. "It was the early days of the women's movement and it was gratifying to see women moving away from Heckler and into Barney's camp," Ann Lewis said. Most feminist groups in the district supported Barney because of Heckler's record opposing publicly funded abortions for women who were poor. The Massachusetts Women's Political Caucus, which Heckler had founded, also supported Barney.

Barney contrasted his strong and consistent position on women's issues with that of Heckler, a record characterized by contradictions. He pointed out, for example, that in April 1981 Heckler had placed in the *Congressional Record* a detailed and devastating analysis of the ways in which the Reagan budget proposal would disproportionately harm women in housing, legal services, education, job training, Social Security, and many other areas. In page after page, her analysis shows the negative impact the president's budget will have on women. Yet one month later, on May 7, 1981, Heckler voted for the Reagan budget, thereby endorsing the same cuts she had described as so destructive to women. "If [Heckler] wants to say she's been able to influence President Reagan's policies towards women, then God help us," Barney asserted.

Heckler fought back, telling women that she was a champion in Congress for equal pay for women. She pointed out that she was the one who took the lead in ensuring that female hairdressers were paid the same wages as male barbers in the House barber and beauty shops.

Many of the congressional leaders in the battle for women's rights, including Pat Schroeder, Barbara Mikulski, and Geraldine Ferraro, went to the Fourth District to campaign for Barney. They praised his efforts on behalf of women's rights and contended that he had been more supportive on issues important to women, family, and children than his opponent. "With respect to Margaret Heckler, what really surprised me was her complete voting reversal," Mikulski said. "She really went for [Reagan's] program. She gave it a hug. She embraced it. She advocated it. She worked for it. And now after redistricting occurred, we noticed a shift back."

By late spring, Barney had gained in the polls. As a result, in June, Heckler abandoned President Reagan and voted against the budget introduced by the conservative Republican Delbert Latte. "The election had a good influence on her and she kind of switched. I am afraid that if I am not around, she's going to relapse," Barney told voters. When Heckler changed her position and voted against the MX missile, Barney pointed out that he had consistently opposed the MX missile, whereas Heckler "has had more positions on the MX missile than they have suggested basing systems for the missile." Heckler had shadowed his voting record in 1982 to such an extent that some of his House colleagues suggested that he was in control of two votes. Rep. William Ratchford from Connecticut pointed out that during close votes in the House in 1982, Heckler would always wait to see how Barney voted before casting her vote at the last minute. "I haven't had such a good influence on someone since my kid brother got too old to listen," Barney said.

By the summer, Barney had pulled almost even with Heckler in the polls. A July 1982 poll conducted by Boston's WBZ-TV showed Heckler with 27 percent and Frank with 24 percent. He had been successful, particularly in the blue-collar areas, in tying Heckler to Reagan's economic policies.

Later that month Barney arranged for the House Select Committee on Aging, of which he was a member, to hold a field hearing the following month in Fall River to examine the effects of what had come to be known as the Notch Act. This measure, enacted by Congress as part of the 1977 Social Security Act Amendments, reduced Social Security benefits for persons born between 1917 and 1921—the notch—by as much as $110 a month. Thus, workers born days apart at the end of 1916 and the beginning of 1917, who paid the same Social Security taxes for many years, would receive benefits that differed by more than $1,300 a year. Claude Pepper delegated authority to Barney to chair the August 13 field hearing.

Two days before the hearing, Congresswoman Heckler sent Barney a letter demanding that she be permitted to testify at the field hearing. Barney responded that despite her tardy request he would fit her into the hearing schedule. He added that this was the first request he had received from a member of Congress to testify at a field hearing, noting that the main purpose of field hearings was to get the views of affected constituents.

The night before the hearing, Heckler persuaded Robert Dornan, a victim of congressional redistricting in California who had been defeated in the Senate primary election, to resign from the Aging Committee. She then arranged for the Republican leadership to appoint her to the vacant committee seat in an attempt to upstage Barney at the field hearing. Barney did not learn about the new appointment to the committee until about an hour before the hearing.

When Barney gaveled the field hearing to order on Friday morning, August 13, at Bristol Community College in Fall River, Margaret Heckler was in attendance as a member of the Committee on Aging sitting in the chair to Barney's right. Howie Carr, a columnist for the *Boston Herald American*, described Heckler's entrance: "Margaret Heckler's wig arrived here at 10:57 Friday morning. The rest of the congresswoman from Wellesley showed up at 10:59." "Both would have been better off staying home," Democratic committee member William Ratchford recalled.

Before a battery of television cameras on hand to film the expected fireworks, the two candidates sat shoulder-to-shoulder exchanging comments during the almost three hours of testimony by more than a dozen witnesses.

In his opening remarks, Barney told the audience of advocates for the elderly and about two hundred senior citizens, many of whom were turning sixty-five that year and would receive reduced benefits, "the Notch Act is an inequity that must not be allowed to continue." "It isn't fair for people who have worked hard all their lives to be penalized just because they were born in the wrong month," he asserted. "No one has ever documented that people born after January 1, 1917, pay less at the store, pay lower utility bills, or have lower medical bills."

Barney said with a straight face in introducing Heckler, "I'm also glad to welcome our newest member of the Committee on Aging, my colleague, Mrs. Heckler, who was appointed to the committee last night, so we have the junior member of the Aging Committee." Heckler read a long opening statement that consumed more than ten minutes. She began by emphasizing that she has been an advocate for the elderly on many committees since entering Congress in 1967. She defended her December 1977 vote in favor of the Social Security Act Amendments, a bill intended to shore up the solvency of the Social Security system, and argued that Claude Pepper had supported the measure and that Speaker Tip O'Neill and most members of the Massachusetts congressional delegation had voted for the bill. "It was the end of a session and we were going home for Christmas and it was a time when the Social Security system was bleeding," she explained.

Barney told the audience that Gerry Studds of New Bedford had voted against the bill because of the Notch provision. "He paid some attention to the game," he said, to cheers and applause.

Heckler contended that there was no separate vote on the Notch provision and that it was an up-or-down vote on the entire bill to save the Social Security system. But Barney got the better of her by reminding her that when an important bill is defeated it comes back on the floor twenty minutes later with the objectionable part removed. He advised Heckler, "Next time they stick you with a stinker on a take-it-or-leave-it basis, let's leave it and come back and do it right the next day." He countered Heckler's argument that "the technicians made a very big mistake in this case" by pointing out that it was not the technicians but the members of Congress who had not paid attention when Robert Myers, the director of the Social Security Administration, had warned Congress in public testimony in 1977 that the change in the formula for calculating benefits would cause problems for people born after 1916 and would create an inequity. "When you get elected to public office you are responsible for decisions you make and the votes you make," Barney said.

Heckler declared that she supported legislation to eliminate the inequity resulting from the Notch Act. Barney remarked that it was not until he entered the race that she attempted to change this inequity.

Heckler suggested that she was going to send all of the testimony from the hearing on the Notch Act problem to the National Commission on Social Security Reform, scheduled to report to the Congress in the next few months, and ask them for solutions to the Notch problem. Barney responded that it would be a mistake to wait and put too much weight on the Presidential Commission on Social Security. "Expertise is sometimes more overrated than the dollar. That is how we got into this problem in 1977, the 'experts' said it. I am not waiting for any commission." Rep. Bill Ratchford, who had served as Connecticut commissioner of elderly affairs before being elected to Congress in 1978, did a fine job playing Ed McMahon to Barney's Johnny Carson by adding: "The last thing we need is one more study of Social Security. You could fill the Library of Congress with all the studies of Social Security. Anyone telling you that we need to wait for the report of the Commission simply hasn't looked at the problem. Another study? Hell, we need action."

"It was like watching Barney hit softballs out of the park—boom, boom, boom," Ratchford said. Heckler was consistently on the defensive and her responses did not play well with the crowd.

One of the witnesses from Fall River, Sebastian Russo, testified that when he retired and went to fill out the necessary paperwork, the employee at the Social Security office told him that in 1977 Congress had passed the Notch Act, which cut his Social Security benefits. He said he had written three or four letters to Rep. Heckler, who had represented the Fall River area for many years, about the problem of the Notch provision but never got a response, and then he contacted Rep. Frank's office about the inequity. "My slogan is remember in November when you vote," he said to loud applause from the audience.

After the hearing, Heckler complained that she had walked into a "stacked deck." In an article in a local newspaper headlined, "Heckler in the Lion's Den," Kevin Convey wrote: "The lamb (Margaret Heckler) lay down with the lion

(Barney Frank) here yesterday with the predictable result: The lamb was eaten alive."

Republican Senator Rudy Boschwitz, who is Jewish, spoke at a fund-raiser for Heckler in Newton in an appeal to Jewish voters. "Peggy can be more effective on Israel because she has more credibility with the administration," the freshman senator from Minnesota contended. Barney responded in the press, "Senator Boschwitz said that the reason to vote for Congresswoman Heckler over me is that she has more influence with the Reagan administration and that they really like her and they don't like me. I just wish he would say that more often."

Heckler made an appeal for the Jewish vote by attacking her opponent for voting against foreign aid to Israel. When asked by a reporter for his reaction, Barney exclaimed in Yiddish, "Vey iz mir!" (an expressive term that means "Woe is me!"). "That type of blatant ethnic pandering is not a terrific idea," he said. In his view, many ethnic groups have legitimate concerns that ought to be addressed, but he objected to Heckler's using Israel as bait. He had voted against the $11.3 billion foreign aid bill because he thought it squandered billions of dollars and included military aid to El Salvador, removed the ban on military aid to Argentina, and contained too much assistance in general for dictatorships of various sorts. "If you give aid to Israel, does that mean you also have to give aid to anti-Semitic Argentina?" he asked.

During the campaign Barney pointed to bills that he had introduced in the state legislature with the conservative Republican Andrew Natsios—civil service reform, restraining the MBTA unions, and using a computer cross-matching system to catch welfare cheats, legislation that had saved the commonwealth fifteen million dollars in welfare fraud. Natsios, a close friend of Heckler's, was the Republican state party chairman in 1982. Heckler complained to Natsios that Barney was "killing" her with Republicans by going all over the district saying he and Natsios had filed the bills together. "I want you to get up and say he's lying," she said. But Natsios assured her, and other Republicans who asked him, that it was true. "It was an unusual coalition and that's why those bills passed. Barney was a good government Democrat and they were really good government bills," he said.

On Friday, September 17, at a press conference in Fall River, Barney announced plans to introduce legislation in Congress, similar to the bill he had pushed through the Massachusetts legislature in 1978, to require every state to use computerized cross-matching to prevent welfare abuse. Almost immediately after the announcement, Heckler's Washington staff asked the Legislative Counsel's office to draft a bill along the lines that Barney had outlined. On the following Tuesday, Heckler introduced H.R. 7148, a bill to provide that states administering needs-related federally assisted programs must verify the income, assets, and eligibility of applicants for and recipients of benefits under such programs by cross-matching them against relevant public records. She claimed that her bill would save as much as sixteen billion dollars in welfare abuses.

The Barney Frank campaign cried foul and responded with a sixty-second radio ad titled "Echo," reviewing for voters Heckler's last-minute move to get on the Aging Committee and her taking credit for Barney's idea about stopping welfare fraud. The ad ends, "So if you like Barney Frank's ideas for protecting Social Security and cutting welfare fraud, why accept an echo? Vote for Barney Frank, a congressman you can trust."

The Frank campaign also did a series of poster ads that ran on the Green Line of the MBTA subway from Newton and Brookline to Boston. Copies of the poster hung above seats on the trolley and read: "Ronald Reagan wants this seat for Margaret Heckler. Don't give Reagan this seat. Vote for Democrat Barney Frank." The problem with the posters was that they proved to be too popular. People kept stealing the posters from the MBTA and taking them home as collectibles.

For most of the campaign, Heckler had avoided direct debates with her opponent. However, when the polls indicated that she was in some trouble she agreed to a series of four debates—in Newton in September and in Wellesley, Fall River, and Attleboro in early October. Many observers believe that the debates were pivotal, particularly in an election matching two incumbent members of Congress.

The first debate took place on Friday evening, September 10, at the Newton City Hall War Memorial Auditorium before a crowd of over three hundred people. Doug Cahn, who was with Barney backstage before the debate, described Barney as "a mess." "He was physically exhausted. He was uncomfortable having to keep to a tight campaign schedule and to raise money, and doing things he didn't enjoy. He was biting his nails before the debate."

For ninety minutes the candidates engaged in largely testy, personal exchanges that foreshadowed the tone of the subsequent debates. Barney accused Heckler of voting in lockstep for Reagan budget cuts and tax cuts for the oil companies and tax loopholes for the wealthy. Heckler defended herself by arguing that she had voted for the Reagan budget cuts in 1981 in response to the 1980 presidential election and "America's mandate to get government off our backs . . . and cut waste and fraud." Barney pointed out that Heckler sat on the food stamp subcommittee for six years while food stamp funds tripled and she never introduced an amendment to cut waste or fraud.

At one point, a flustered Heckler paid her opponent a backhanded compliment, calling him "a rhetorical Houdini able to transfer any issue to any context he chooses." She took umbrage at her opponent's attempt to portray her as a captive of the Reagan White House. "No one controls Heckler," she declared. "I'm unbossed and unbought."

People most remember the second debate, held October 4 at Babson College in Wellesley. This one-hour debate, sponsored by the local League of Women Voters, was the only debate televised live statewide. Supporters carrying placards for the candidates circulated in the parking lot, while Babson's twelve-hundred-seat Knight Auditorium filled to overflowing.

The debate format allowed each candidate to respond to the other's answer and rebuttal. The moderator, Bernard Redmont, the dean of the Boston University School of Public Communications, a former CBS News foreign correspondent with forty years of experience in print, radio, and television journalism, needed all that skill to maintain order as the candidates traded verbal punches in what became a no-holds-barred fight. Although the audience had been instructed not to applaud during the debate, that rule was broken continually, almost from the beginning of the debate.

Wearing a red tailored suit with a violet scarf, a feisty and combative Heckler came out swinging at the opening bell and squarely landed the first verbal blow. Heckler began by expressing how shocked she was to read about her opponent's attitude toward constituent services and bringing federal programs and funds home to the district. He had said in a *Boston Globe* interview: "A political fact of my life is that I can get political credit for the slop that I bring into my district. Incumbents can survive forever just by slopping the hogs." In a sharp voice, Heckler declared, "I don't believe the people are the hogs or the programs and projects and needs that I answer are the slop."

Barney defended his comments about legislators who "try to buy people's votes," charging that their votes "for the pork" for their districts are the reason "we have water projects for billions of dollars that waste money." Referring to Heckler, he said, "I am critical of her and other politicians who try to base a political campaign on the simple fact of providing constituent services. She and I and every other member of Congress get half a million dollars a year to provide constituent services. . . . I object when people are told that they ought to have to pay with their votes for services they have already paid for with their taxes."

Throughout the debate, Barney focused attention on President Reagan's failed economic programs and tied Heckler to the shortcomings of Reaganomics. He accused the president, who, he said, inherited a weak economy, of making the country's economic problems worse, adding to the deficit, and keeping up interest rates with his huge military-spending program and a tax bill that had excessive tax loopholes for the very wealthy and the oil companies.

"It is the height of demagoguery to talk about big oil," Heckler responded. She charged that Democratic legislators had started a bidding war to provide tax breaks and that Republicans upped the bidding. She said that she opposed it.

"You see another difference between us," Barney said. "My rhetoric and my voting record coincide. Mrs. Heckler talks about the oil tax cuts, but she tells you everything about the oil tax cuts except one fact, that she voted for it." He continued, "Yes, the Democratic leadership and the Republican leadership both wanted oil tax cuts. The difference between us is that I said no to both leaderships and she said yes."

One of the panel members, John Desmond, the editor of the *Wellesley Townsman*, asked Heckler a question relating to her claim that she had no chance to vote against certain program cuts, such as student financial aid programs, on the 1981 budget: "Can you explain why you had no chance when the *Congressional Record* records you in favor of procedures that prevented any chance?"

"Mr. Desmond, you'll have to talk to the Democratic leadership because they devise the rule under which legislation is considered by the House of Representatives," she replied. Heckler defended her action by suggesting that "it was a package approach," that President Reagan's budget came before Congress as an entire package on which members had to vote yes or no, with no chance to amend it. "There was no opportunity to vote for a line item," she contended. She stated that had there been an opportunity she would have voted against cuts in student loans and Social Security.

Barney was ready. That morning he had asked his campaign press secretary, David Abbott, to obtain a copy of the *Congressional Record* for June 26, 1981, the date of the budget vote, so that he could flaunt the document during the debate and read from it. But there was not enough time to have a copy of that volume of the *Congressional Record* sent to Massachusetts by Barney's Washington office, so Abbott, who had just graduated from Harvard Law School, sent a campaign aide over to the Harvard Law School Library to get the volume. Knowing that copies of the *Congressional Record* were "for reference only" and could not be checked out of the law library, he instructed the aide to put the book in his coat and just walk out with it, assuring the aide that they would return the book the next day. It was the only way he could think of to get a copy of the *Congressional Record* on such short notice. When Barney brandished the *Congressional Record* during the televised debate, he was unaware that it had been temporarily purloined from the Harvard Law School Library.

Barney was not about to let his opponent on stage get away with doing what he calls a "reverse Houdini," tying herself in knots and then telling her constituents, "Gee, I wish I could help you, I'd like to vote for that bill, but I can't because I'm all tied up in knots." He was referring to a favorite practice of legislators, who vote for rules that limit debate or prevent amendments before voting on a controversial bill and then explain to unhappy constituents that they had been forced to vote yes or no on the whole package because they weren't allowed to offer any amendments.

"The question was did Mrs. Heckler vote to prevent amendments to the budget? The answer is irrefutable," Barney asserted, holding up the *Congressional Record*. No amendments were allowed, he pointed out, because Heckler and other pro-Reagan members of the House voted in favor of rules to prevent any amendments from being offered, amendments that could have saved some social programs. "There was a key vote on the floor. Should we or should we not allow amendments to the budget? Congressman Jones says, 'If he is allowed to amend the budget he will put in more money for student loans, he will restore Social Security cuts, he will restore nutrition programs,'" Barney said, reading from the *Congressional Record* and adding, "Mrs. Heckler, in obedience to her party's leadership, voted to prevent that amending process."

On June 26, 1981, on Roll Call No. 112, 215 members voted to move the previous question on the key motion and prohibit amendments, and 212 members voted against it. "Congresswoman Heckler is one of the 215 and that simply is a fact right here in the *Congressional Record*," he declared.

Heckler attacked him for leading the fight in 1979 for the "secret Halloween heist" pay raise for state legislators, voted late at night with an unrecorded vote and later repealed by the Bay State voters. In response, Barney questioned why, if Heckler found such offense with a six-dollar-a-day pay raise for state legislators being paid nineteen thousand dollars a year, she had voted for a seventy-five-dollar-a-day tax break for House members making sixty thousand dollars a year. "And she does it on an amendment sneaked into a black lung bill, and calls that democratic," he said. He pointed out that he voted against the tax break for House members.

Heckler spent much of the debate attempting to shift the focus to Barney's record in the state legislature. Referring to Barney as "a very taxing gentleman," she criticized him for sponsoring a tax on all public pensions, for voting against exempting the elderly from the regressive meals tax, for voting against property tax rebates for the elderly, and for voting to impose an excise tax on hospital beds and students attending colleges.

Heckler's new tack led Barney to comment that state representative Royall Switzler of Wellesley should be nervous. "Mrs. Heckler appears to be interested in running for the state house of representatives." He in turn accused her of distorting his record and indicated that the excise-tax measure, which did not pass, was an idea to raise revenue from the large number of tax-exempt institutions in Boston as a means to provide property tax relief.

During the debate one of the panel members asked a question about the possibility of raising the retirement age. Initially, Heckler was in favor of that but then later in the debate appeared to retract that position. Barney jumped on the fact that his opponent had taken two stands during the debate on the issue of raising the retirement age—initially to extend the present age limit and then later to maintain it. "She has apparently changed her mind in fifteen minutes, which is a record even for her," he contended.

Each candidate was given three minutes for a closing statement. The order was decided by a coin toss before the debate. Heckler won the toss and chose to go last. Barney would have no opportunity to reply, and so she would have the last word. "I'm flattered that Congresswoman Heckler finds nothing in my congressional voting record that she can disagree with," Barney said in his closing statement, declaring that he wanted to cut waste but also wanted to retain a sense of social responsibility.

When Barney finished, Heckler introduced a new issue, launching what has been dubbed her October offensive. She had a large collection of related attack ads ready to run on television and anti-Frank campaign literature ready for distribution.

With her voice rising, Heckler turned to her opponent and attacked him for supporting pornography and legalized prostitution while he was in the state legislature. You could almost hear the audience gasp. As Heckler continued, her supporters cheered and Barney's supporters booed. She said emotionally: "Mr. Frank has voted consistently for the exhibition of pornographic literature and for pornographic television. . . . The television coverage he has supported in his votes in the State House exploited and degraded the position of women in this society and contributes to the climate of violence against them. The Combat Zone proposal which he proposed five times in five years was unwarranted and unwished by any constituency in this district. And indeed it did not solve the problem but provided a sanctuary for those who profit from the vices." The television cameras showed what appeared to be a stunned Barney Frank.

The *New York Times* quoted a woman at the debate who said, "That wasn't proper. Margaret Heckler must be getting desperate." Dottie Reichard observed, "Walking out, I heard these lovely, proper Republican women from Wellesley saying, 'I've never seen her act like that.'"

Perhaps it was because Heckler hadn't taken her opponent seriously for so long, that when she did, she overdid it. Perhaps it was the frustration of trailing in the polls. Perhaps it was desperation. At the second debate the electorate saw another side of Heckler, an unpleasant side. She came across as an angry, strident, and aggressive street fighter who did not mask her considerable dislike of her opponent. This image was totally at odds with her established image as a proper lady. In contrast, Barney's campaign strategists John Marttila and Tom Kiley had urged him not to pick on Heckler, "She's a woman. Don't make her a sacrificial lamb." Those comments were echoed by Barney's family, friends, and campaign staff, who advised him just to make his point at the debate, not to yell at Heckler, and not to appear strident and allow people to feel sorry for her.

A poll of four hundred registered voters in the Fourth District conducted after the televised debate found that 63 percent had not seen the debate, 16 percent felt that Barney had won, and 6 percent believed that Heckler was the winner. A poll conducted during the first week of October, right after the debate, showed Barney ahead, 42 to 37 percent, within the poll's 5 percent margin of error, and with 21 percent undecided. "We were tracking the race through the spring, summer, and fall and knew we were really moving," Dan Payne said. "Democrats were accepting Barney and rejecting Heckler. Her unfavorables were increasing as Barney's favorables were going up." People who had supported Heckler in the past, upon learning about her recent voting record, were moving their support to Barney.

"Heckler was grasping and went to the lowest common denominator that resonated in the 1980 campaign, figuring that if she did what Jones did it would have the same effect," Thaleia Schlesinger said. "Her attack à la Jones backfired because people knew Barney then and he had a record in Congress." In tough campaigns, Payne said, "you have to roll the dice and trust your instincts. Once the campaign momentum started moving away, she didn't seem to know how to get back into the game."

Heckler distributed fifty thousand campaign leaflets titled "You Have a Right to Know" with a list of seventeen bills Barney had backed during his eight years as a state legislator. The text highlights his support for adult entertainment zones, prostitution, and pornography and emphasizes that he voted in favor of higher taxes, a pay raise for state legislators, and bills to block stiffer penalties for certain crimes. On the back of the leaflet, under a photograph of the Heckler family, the message reads: "Margaret Heckler, the senior ranking woman in Congress, a wife and mother of three, opposes Barney Frank's stand on each of the issues inside. During her 16 years as your elected representative she has sponsored and voted for legislation that reflects her feelings and those of the people she represents."

One of the most negative television ads Heckler launched takes aim at the Barney Frank campaign tagline "A Democrat you can trust." The announcer begins by listing the bills Barney supported: "As a state legislator he sponsored a bill to permit legalized prostitution and allow Combat Zones in every city and town in Massachusetts and voted against increased penalties for criminals who distribute pornography to minors, and last year he voted to reduce the sentence for violent rape." The words "Prostitution" and "Pornography" are superimposed across a black-and-white still photo of his face. Then the ad shifts to a color film clip of Margaret Heckler walking down the street, smiling in the sunshine, while an American flag waves in the background and the announcer repeats the tagline, "Keep Margaret Heckler. She has a record we can be proud of."

Barney knew that he had to respond swiftly to Heckler's accusations. The day after the debate, he sent a statement to over a thousand campaign workers to set the record straight. He later held a press conference to respond to Heckler's attack and systematic distortion of his legislative record and to denounce her deliberate decision to stop talking about national issues. "I think by bringing these tactics to light you make them less effective," he said at the press conference.

"Margaret Heckler and I have an obligation to tell people what we will do about unemployment, about protecting the right of retirees to full Social Security benefits. . . . I think the voters are entitled to know about how to reduce unemployment . . . how to stop James Watt and Ann Gorsuch from destroying our environment," he argued. "For her, on the advice of her paid consultants, to refuse to discuss these any more, to announce that instead she is going to talk about issues that have been dead for five or six years, and in a distorted fashion, really disserves the democratic process," he asserted. "There isn't a thing in her latest round of ads or leaflet that is relevant to the issues that face the American people today."

One of Heckler's campaign advisers had boasted to the press that she was going to stop talking about Reagan and national issues and "change the subject of the discourse." "What are we supposed to talk about?" Barney asked. "Chickens? English literature?" "No matter how many more hired guns Margaret Heckler brings in . . . and they can all give her advice about . . . how to change the subject, and they can dig up any issue they want. I expect that pretty soon we will be debating the nuances of the Emancipation Proclamation at the rate she is going historically. I intend to continue to discuss the issues of this campaign," he declared. "I think it's perfectly legitimate to change the subject if you're having a conversation but changing the subject of an election from the issues that are before the voters to those that aren't seems to me to be a bit of a problem."

Heckler had accused Barney of voting in 1981 "to reduce the sentence for violent rape," suggesting that he wanted to go easy on rapists. This was the only federal issue she spoke of in her barrage and it referred to one vote out of over seven hundred he had cast in two years in Congress. Heckler's inability to find anything else in his congressional voting record to criticize was, Barney said, a "backhanded compliment" and "the single most blatant distortion in politics" he had ever seen.

He explained that the rape bill in question was one that the District of Columbia government had passed at the passionate request of women's groups and D.C. law enforcement officials to facilitate rape prosecution. This new law expanded the definition of rape, adding new grounds on which rape charges could be brought, such as covertly administering drugs to get someone to engage in sex and same-sex rape, and it abolished spousal immunity in rape cases. The new law took the focus off the conduct of the victim with regard to consent. It also reduced the maximum penalty for rape from life in prison, which was thought to make jurors reluctant to convict, to twenty years.

Barney pointed out that the District of Columbia Rape Law was supported by the Rape Crisis Center, the National Coalition Against Sexual Assault, the Washington, D.C., Commission for Women, the Chief of Police of Washington, D.C., "those radicals in the American Bar Association," the Greater Washington Central Labor Council, AFL–CIO, and "that notorious pro-rape group, the Women's Legal Defense Fund."

Conservatives in Congress introduced a resolution to disapprove the criminal code revision by the District of Columbia. "I voted to support the right of the District of Columbia to have its own rape statute. I think that American citizens who live in the District of Columbia ought to be able to set their own criminal code. I wasn't sent to Congress by the voters of the Fourth District to be the extra member of the District of Columbia City Council," Barney said. On the merits he was supportive of the new law, which was viewed as an advance in prosecuting rape.

According to Barney, the Moral Majority made the District of Columbia rape law its number one issue in 1981, whipped up its troops, and decided to make it a test of their strength. "Margaret Heckler, at the behest of the Moral Majority, voted to veto the District of Columbia rape law. It is another example of her giving in to immediate political pressure," he said.

Barney also explained that the intent of the bill he filed in 1975 was to clean up and protect residential neighborhoods in Boston from Combat Zone sprawl. He noted that his initiative was never enacted into law and that he stopped filing this bill to establish a legal adult entertainment district in the Combat Zone when the city of Boston abandoned this approach and decided to use other tactics to remove crime and vice from residential neighborhoods.

Barney brought out a letter that Robert DiGrazia had written two years earlier when Arthur Clark and Richard Jones had attempted to distort these same actions by him as a state representative, in which the former Boston police commissioner corroborated that it was at his request that Barney had sponsored this legislation. "It was not softness or approval of vice which led to your sponsorship of the bill; it was a practical hard-headed effort to get vice out of the neighborhoods where people live," DiGrazia said.

Barney also released a statement from Janet Koltun, a former Back Bay constituent, then residing in Brookline, to counter the charge that he was soft on prostitution. "When I lived in the Back Bay, there was a serious prostitution problem on the corner near our house," she wrote. "Barney Frank took the lead in ending this problem. . . . He worked hard and successfully for increased police activity and a change of traffic patterns to drive the prostitutes out of our area . . . and to preserve the residential character of our neighborhood."

Asked about the similarities between Heckler's attacks on his record in the state legislature and the messages that Jones had used with some success in the final weeks of the 1980 campaign, Barney responded, "Margaret Heckler is apparently very lucky that Richard Jones, the very right-wing Republican, the John Birch member that I ran against last time didn't copyright his literature because what she has done is reissue it." "It's not surprising because she hired his campaign workers," he said, referring to Gerald Lange, one of Heckler's senior campaign advisors, who had been Jones's campaign manager two years earlier.

"Heckler was hoping not to use that material," Barney said in retrospect. "When the race began, Heckler was confidently telling people she was going to win easily. When polls suggested that I was ahead and showed that Heckler's pro-Reagan voting record was not popular with voters in the district, she decided she had to throw the bomb."

The Frank campaign responded to Heckler's accusations with a television ad in which the announcer says, "Barney Frank has been in politics long enough to know that your image suffers a little at election time," while a hand pencils a mustache and goatee on a still photograph of him. "But this time things have gone too far. Margaret Heckler is so worried about her own record, she's painting a distorted picture of Barney's," the announcer continues while a clearly female hand scribbles and messes up his face with a red magic marker. Then to the message, "There is a word for this kind of tactic," the screen is filled with the single word SMEAR. As the smear of red marker disappears from Barney's face, the ad concludes, "The truth is Barney Frank has always fought against crime and vice and to protect families, from students to senior citizens. Wipe away the smear and you see why Barney Frank is still a congressman you can trust."

The *Boston Globe* blasted Heckler's line of attack in an October 8 editorial titled "Political Pornography," saying, "It is unfortunate—and maybe even instructive—that in the closing weeks of the campaign she has chosen not to run [on her record in Congress] or even to run against the congressional record of her opponent, Rep. Barney Frank. Instead she has sought to make an issue of one small aspect of Frank's record in the state legislature and in the process has distorted it in a fashion so outlandish that ultimately it may backfire on her campaign."

The *Boston Herald American*, which rarely agreed with the *Globe* on anything, charged Heckler with "deliberately and callously" distorting Barney's action. The *New Bedford Standard Times* denounced her "unsavory campaign tactics that do a disservice both to voters and to the office she seeks to retain." Anthony Lewis in the *New York Times* accused Heckler of resorting to "right wing gutter politics" and using such techniques that "the ghost of Joe McCarthy must be grinning." Lewis wrote: "The voters sometimes see through McCarthyism, but not always. It may work. But what would it profit Mrs. Heckler to win the seat and lose her political soul?"

The final Frank–Heckler debate took place on Monday, October 11, in the auditorium at Attleboro High School and was broadcast live on radio stations in Fall River and Attleboro. The debate attracted over a thousand people, including, along with supporters of the two candidates, many others who were there to watch a confrontation that promised, according to a description of the earlier debates in the *Boston Globe*, to be akin to going to a Bruins ice hockey game. The sportswriter Dan Shaughnessy, who lived in Newton, began an article in the *Globe* about a heated, hard-played basketball game between the Boston Celtics and the Milwaukee Bucks with the words, "It was fought with the intensity of your average Barney Frank–Margaret Heckler debate."

There was loud applause and cheering as the candidates separately entered the auditorium, much like a championship fight, and then began to duke it out on stage. The debate moderator, Doug Reed, managing editor of the *Attleboro Sun Chronicle*, should have begun with the words "Let's get ready to rumble." Throughout the debate, the audience at times cheered, heckled, jeered, snickered, and on several occasions interrupted the candidates. Every time Heckler threw a verbal punch at her opponent, a man in the back of the auditorium wearing a Peg Heckler baseball cap shouted, "Go get 'em Peg!" And whenever a candidate went over the allotted two minutes to answer a question or the one minute given for rebuttal, the crowd began to chant, "Time, time." In terms of audience participation the debate was a cross between old-fashioned melodrama and a midnight showing of *The Rocky Horror Picture Show*. The *Attleboro Sun Chronicle*, which sponsored the debate, commented that the two students who led the pledge of allegiance were the only speakers that night who were not booed. The newspaper concluded that "the confrontation delivered all it promised and more."

"I am delighted to be in Attleboro, a community that Mr. Frank fought to keep out of this district, which he sought to make at that time a suburb of Worcester," Heckler began. She then went on the attack, pointing out that the excise tax Barney had proposed on every college student in the commonwealth was not fifteen dollars per student as he had suggested at an earlier debate but seventy-five dollars per student, that the property tax relief he promised did not show up in any of his tax bills, and that while he said that he introduced legislation to establish a combat zone in Boston, under his bill every city and town can establish such zones. "You are right Mr. Frank," she concluded. "Someone is distorting the record. But it is not me."

Barney replied, "We have 10.1 percent unemployment. We have elderly people whose Medicare has been cut, students who can't afford to go to college, working men and women who can't find jobs. We have a candidate running for Congress who sees fit voluntarily not to mention one of those." Then he said that the *Boston Globe* and the *Boston Herald* had both editorially condemned Heckler's distortions of his voting record and went on to point out that yes, he did file legislation that he hoped would give the cities and towns an alternative to property tax and that, in contrast to his opponent, he did not think that the students at Wellesley, Boston College, Brandeis, and Harvard should get free police and fire service from property taxpayers.

"She has voted for more taxes than I have ever thought of voting for," Barney said. He noted that in 1969 when Richard Nixon needed a tax increase of six billion dollars to fight the Vietnam War, she voted for it, and in 1977 she voted for what President Reagan later referred to as the largest payroll tax increase in history, simultaneously objecting to the use of general revenues to ease the strain on Social Security.

Barney asserted during the debate that the central issue was the economy and reminded the audience of Heckler's unwavering support of President Reagan's economic and budget policies in 1981. "If Margaret Heckler and other Ronald Reagan supporters get reelected on November 2, Ronald Reagan will continue his course," he warned. "The only way we will get the change we need to put people back to work is if the voters send a message to Washington that they are unhappy with current economic policy."

Turning to the audience, Heckler declared, "The votes I cast in 1981 were designed to remove the excesses of programs and indeed, even in that year, I cast many other votes that were not sponsored or favored by the administration, although Mr. Frank would like to picture me as a Reagan clone. I am not a clone. I have served under five presidents and I voted my conscience, independently, unbossed and unbought." Her words were greeted by loud cheers of "Way to go, Peg."

Asked whether he was going to be worried in Congress about protecting the Back Bay and Beacon Hill against prostitution and vice, Barney swung and connected on that softball question. "No, it's not part of the congressional job. I'll spend more time on unemployment and protecting American workers against unfair imports." He reminded the audience that as a member of the state legislature he had fought hard to protect his neighborhood against crime and vice and that with the cooperation of the police he had driven prostitutes from the neighborhood. "Yes, I will continue to work as hard for my constituents in this district as I did when I represented them in downtown Boston," he said. "Problems will differ but they will get the same kind of attention from me." He concluded with a jab at his opponent. "I have already begun to help the people of Attleboro by inducing Mrs. Heckler to open her first constituent service office in Attleboro in her sixteen years [in Congress]," he said.

During the debate, Barney was asked whether his fiscal feelings were in tune with the Attleboros and whether they could expect further relief from federal taxes. "I hope so," he responded, and charged that it was Congresswoman Heckler who had voted for several tax increases at the federal level. When his response was drowned out by loud boos and shouts from Heckler supporters in the audience, he showed that he knew how to handle all types of hecklers. "Truth is often unpleasant. You'll get used to it," he said.

Heckler again won the coin toss and chose to go last in delivering a closing statement. Looking at her opponent, whom she had always addressed as "Mr. Frank" during the debate, she said, "Barney, you and I know that for eight months you've been distorting my record and you have conducted a very negative campaign against me. You feel that only one year of my vote is relevant and not the sixteen years which I have been an effective and really responsible, committed member of Congress." She expressed pride in her record in Congress as a strong voice for business, for women, for the elderly, for veterans, and for this district. "If my record is at issue, so is yours, Mr. Frank!"

Swinging for the fences in her last at bat, she attacked Barney's record, knowing that once again he would have no opportunity to respond. "Will you tell us, Mr. Frank, why you voted against increased penalties for convicts who start riots?" "Why on earth did you introduce a bill to give serious criminals the right to vote by absentee ballot?" "How do you justify voting against the property tax rebates for the elderly and against exempting the elderly and the handicapped from the meals tax?" she asked. "Why, Mr. Frank, if you are such a supporter of women, did you vote against requiring sellers of pornography to keep the material out of public view?" She continued until the bell rang, marking the expiration of her time and the conclusion of the debate.

At a nuclear freeze forum on October 16, Barney referred to T. K. Jones's having said that the way to survive a nuclear attack is to have dirt thrown on you. "One more debate and I'll be invulnerable to any kind of radiation," he joked. He criticized the Reagan administration for having no serious commitment to arms reduction and for its view that "we can arm ourselves into world security." "The administration wants to undo the test ban treaty, and their latest proposal for the MX missile, that weapons system out of Pirandello [author of *Six Characters in Search of an Author*], all those kilotons in search of a basing mode, requires an ABM missile in violation of agreements we are abiding by," he charged.

Although Barney continued to maintain an official silence about his sexuality, there was a whispering campaign and rumors were spreading. After an event in Fall River, a man who had been in the audience came up to Barney and asked whether he was part of the Mafia. Barney was surprised at the question. "What makes you think that?" he asked. "That woman you are running against said that you are one of those boys from Providence." Barney laughed. He was not about to explain to the man that what Heckler probably said was that he was one of the boys from Provincetown, a large gay community on Cape Cod.

Heckler, in an attempt to win back working-class voters in Fall River, referred to Barney as an unmarried forty-two-year-old who had supported gay rights and tried to paint him as a person who did not believe in "family values." When a reporter asked Barney about the rumors coming from Heckler's camp relating to his being unmarried, he replied, "Margaret draws inferences from my being unmarried but she also complained that I did political favors for Billy Sullivan when I was taking out his daughter. And I said, 'Look—one way or the other.'"

Cable television, still in its infancy, played an important role in the campaign in the key battleground of Fall River, a city with an excellent cable television system and a large Portuguese population. The local Frank campaign organization rented a theater marquee, the only one remaining in Fall River, and used it to advertise Barney's next talk on cable television.

At the time cable television was significantly cheaper than network television and allowed the candidate to target a particular audience. The campaign purchased time on the "Portuguese channel" and produced three half-hour panel discussions and a dozen thirty-second ads. "At any given time the audience for cable television was low, but it was so cheap you could afford to saturate the market," Barney said. Almost without his opponent's being aware of it, according to Richard Armstrong, an expert on the use of new communication technologies in American politics, Barney used cable television "like a Trojan Horse to sneak into the very heart of Margaret Heckler's district."

On October 19, Senate Majority Leader Howard Baker came to the district to campaign for Heckler. Barney welcomed Baker's appearance because it gave him an opportunity to reiterate the link between Heckler and the Reagan administration, which he said "needed Heckler's votes for the cuts in programs for the elderly, the ill, and students." "He should campaign for her," Barney said. "They agree on Reagan's policies."

The following day, Speaker of the House Tip O'Neill campaigned with Barney. At a rally in Fall River, he described Barney as "a man with a heart." "I find him so able, so talented, so dedicated. . . . He has been a strong right arm to me," he said. Heckler, who had developed a warm and cordial relationship with O'Neill during her tenure in Congress, berated O'Neill for campaigning against her. But O'Neill stood his ground. This was politics and Heckler was a Republican. O'Neill reportedly told Heckler that even if his own brother were running as a Republican he would campaign against him.

O'Neill and Barney did a joint radio call-in show in Fall River. One of the first callers, addressing O'Neill, said, "I want to talk to you about the Notch Act and the unfairness it is creating for many senior citizens." There was a short pause and Barney jumped in. "It is a terrible thing. It cuts Social Security. Margaret Heckler voted for it."

O'Neill didn't utter a word in response to the question. When the program was over, O'Neill, Barney, several members of his campaign staff in Fall River, and Bob Healy from the *Boston Globe* went to dinner at the Venus de Milo restaurant in Fall River. As the group was taking their seats around the table, O'Neill turned to Barney and asked, "What the fuck is the Notch Act?" Barney replied, "It cuts Social Security and you voted for it. But don't worry, I am not running against you."

With her new-found recognition and celebrity status from the television commercial, Elsie Frank began to make public appearances representing her son, particularly at events for seniors. Shy, with no public speaking experience, and initially terrified about addressing crowds on the campaign stump, Elsie became more confident with each speaking engagement. Thaleia Schlesinger described her as "fabulous." "She stepped up to the plate big time. She became a very effective advocate. She became a star," Schlesinger said. "It soon became clear that she was just as assured a public performer as her son was," Mary Beth Cahill observed. "We knew that our mother was smart, but we didn't know that she would be such a forceful and dynamic speaker," David said.

Elsie had been unaware of the myriad problems faced by the elderly. But traveling around to campaign events, nursing homes, and housing projects, she said, "It was an eye-opener for me. I discovered that for many seniors, the seventy-five-cent lunch was their big meal of the day. I realized I had been living in a cloistered world. I began to think, 'Maybe I can do something for other elderly people.'" And so at the age of seventy, Elsie Frank became an activist, a lobbyist, and a champion for senior citizens, speaking out on issues impacting the elderly and lobbying for bills in the Massachusetts legislature. She co-founded, with Ruth Cowin, the mother of William Cowin, who worked with Barney in Mayor Kevin White's office, the Committee to End Elder Homelessness. In 1986, following the death of Frank Manning, the Claude Pepper of elder advocacy in Massachusetts, Elsie became president of the Massachusetts Association of Older Americans, an eighteen-thousand-member organization that spoke and lobbied on behalf the elderly. Soon thereafter, Elsie Frank was being referred to as "the Bay State's leading advocate for the elderly."

To celebrate Elsie's seventieth birthday, the campaign hosted a party on October 21 at the Venus de Milo restaurant. Busloads of seniors, about a thousand people, were invited to the event. Besides a good party, it was an opportunity to demonstrate that Barney was a family person. Barney and Elsie went from table to table introducing themselves and shaking hands. "Feeling the warmth in that room, I had a very positive feeling that Barney would win," Elsie recalled.

Speaker Tip O'Neill appeared at the party and urged the crowd of seniors to send Ronald Reagan a message by returning Barney Frank to Congress.

On Monday October 25, a week before the election, Democrat Henry Waxman of California came to the Fourth District to appear with Barney at a forum designed to focus public attention on the Reagan administration's record on the environment. "This administration has made protection of the environment a partisan issue for the first time," Barney said, describing its position on the environment as "Let's back off." "I believe in cost-benefit analysis only a little more than I believe in unicorns."

The next day, former congressman John Anderson, who had run as an Independent in the 1980 presidential campaign, came to the Fourth District to campaign for Barney. There were more than a hundred thousand registered Independent voters in the Fourth District, and in some of the towns in the district as much as 20 percent of the voters had voted for Anderson in 1980. Anderson began the press conference by remarking that although Barney Frank will never make *GQ* (*Gentleman's Quarterly*), a fashion magazine, he had been selected by *CQ* (*Congressional Quarterly*) as one of the three most outstanding new members of Congress. Anderson praised him for his "rugged independence on the issues" and for standing up to President Reagan's assault on working-class people.

Barney remarked that Anderson's appearance in the district underscored the importance of this congressional race nationally. "Margaret Heckler and I differ on how we should spend the resources of this country. This is a race that people will look at nationally to see how Ronald Reagan is doing. Margaret Heckler denies that this is a race with national implications," he said "Last week she denied that to the *Washington Post*, the *Minneapolis Tribune*, and Japanese television."

Michael Dukakis ran for governor in 1982 against Republican John Sears, and he had an overwhelming lead. He was concerned, however, about voter apathy, and so his radio ads during the final two weeks of the campaign focused on that issue. "Are you going to vote in the governor's race on Tuesday, November 2, or do you think your vote doesn't matter much because Mike Dukakis is going to win anyway?" the voiceover says. It goes on to warn that if enough Democrats and Independents who support Dukakis stay home on Election Day, the next governor could well be the Republican John Winthrop Sears. (Dukakis defeated Sears by a margin of almost 23 points.)

Dukakis told his campaign coordinators that Barney Frank's race against Margaret Heckler was critical and instructed them to work with the Frank campaign and help them get out the vote. He campaigned with Barney in Brookline and wrote a letter of support that was mailed to every residence in Brookline. With

Dukakis and Edward Kennedy, who was running for reelection to the Senate, heading the ticket, liberals were more likely to go to the polls.

In late October, the *Boston Herald* endorsed Barney, referring to Heckler as "a sixteen-year incumbent who has lost touch with the people of her district," and praising Barney for being "most of all, an innovator—a bright, articulate voice for the people of his district" and noting that "in his two short years in Congress he has done more than enough to earn our endorsement." Yet Heckler had the endorsement of the *Attleboro Sun*, the *Fall River Herald*, and for the first time in her career, the *Providence Journal*.

On October 27, a few days before the election, Kennedy spoke at a Barney Frank campaign rally in Fall River before a packed house, which included Democratic state legislators, party officials, and labor leaders. The senior senator emphasized to the crowd "who have been so effective in so many campaigns in the past, who have been good and valued friends and strong supporters of mine as they had been my brother before me" the importance of the upcoming election. "The eyes of the country are on this congressional district," he said. "Make no mistake about it. There is a very clear choice between whether the people of this district want to follow the course of the past two years with an individual who has supported that economic program or someone who believes that we can do better and has spelled out during the course of this campaign how that can be done."

The weekend before the election, Tom Kiley reported the results of a final poll that showed Barney leading by 15 percentage points, 53 to 38 percent. One of the campaign advisers asked, "Barney, what are you going to do next, walk on water?" Barney replied, "You've got the wrong group. We don't walk on water, we part the water."

On election night the practice in Fall River was to count the first fifty or one hundred votes in each precinct and release that tally, and then go back to a full count. That preliminary count, though unscientific, was 60 percent in favor of Barney Frank and was considered a good omen. When all the votes in the Fourth District were counted, Barney convincingly trounced Margaret Heckler by a vote of 121,802 to 82,804 and won reelection with 62 percent of the vote.

That evening at the Hilton Inn in Natick, Barney addressed a crowd of ecstatic supporters wearing buttons that read, "Frankly, I Knew That Barney Could Do It." The jubilant candidate proclaimed, "Back in January, a lot of people were saying I couldn't win. I was one of them. Fortunately, my family and staff didn't listen to me. A funny thing happened to me on the way to defeat—I got reelected."

He told the crowd that he didn't consider the victory "a personal triumph but as a statement by the people in the Fourth District that what has been going on in Washington the past two years has not been fair." He referred to Margaret

Heckler kindly and called her "a tough campaigner." Then amidst cheers and chants of *Elsie! Elsie!* he introduced his mother. "I've always been glad that she's my mother," he told the crowd. "I learned this year that I'm glad she's not my opponent."

At the end of his speech, Barney said to the television cameras, "To the people in Fall River, I'm coming there now. 'Call *vavu*.'" That reference to *vavu*, which in Portuguese means "grandfather," had become a victory cheer, a phrase used whenever something good happened in the Portuguese community in Fall River. It had started with a small group of men in Fall River who regularly played basketball together. Whenever this one particular player did something good on the court, he would say to the others, "I have to call my grandfather" or "call *vavu*" and that developed into a victory cheer.

Barney was concerned about avoiding any appearance of snubbing or neglecting his new constituents in the southern part of the district. He wanted to go to Fall River to address his supporters so the people there would feel they were as much a part of the new district as Newton or Brookline. He had chosen the Hilton Inn in Natick as the site for his victory celebration primarily because it provided easy access for driving to Fall River. He made a quick exit from the victory celebration in Natick and was driven to Fall River to speak at a similar event.

Barney was elated on election night. During the drive to Fall River, he and Mary Beth Cahill sang songs from the Broadway show *Guys and Dolls*, and from Barney's favorite show, *Fiorello!* It includes "The Bum Won," which begins, "Even without our help look at the way he won. Everyone sold him short." A supporter of the upset winner later sings, "Someone pinch me, maybe this is just a beautiful dream . . . I'd like to know just how the hell it happened, what we did right."

The ballroom at the Holiday Inn in Fall River was overflowing with supporters as Barney entered. "It was like a movie moment. The crowd loved him and went wild," Bill Black, from the campaign staff there, said. "Barney was so moved that he could hardly speak. I watched him working his jaw. It took a while for Barney to compose himself. It was an emotional moment."

That evening President Reagan watched the election returns in the living quarters of the White House with his wife, Nancy, and several White House aides and their spouses. According to Richard Reeves in his biography *President Reagan—The Triumph of Imagination*, when Reagan heard the announcement that Massachusetts congresswoman Margaret Heckler had lost her seat, he said, "Gee, I'm sorry to lose Heckler. She was a good little girl."

The front-page headline in the *Boston Herald* the next day read: "Winners— Duke, Teddy, Barney." Barney surprised the experts by winning with a large margin a race he was supposed to lose. He carried Newton and Brookline with 77 percent of the vote, held Heckler to 57 percent of the vote in her hometown of upper-income Wellesley, which she had carried by more than 2-to-1 in 1980, and held her to only a 5-point win in Attleboro, a town she had won by 34 points two years earlier. Most important, he won 58 percent of the vote in Fall River. The only mistake he made in this campaign, he told the *Herald* after the election, was to feel sorry for himself at the beginning.

Looking back at the race against Margaret Heckler over twenty-five years later, Barney said he believes he won the election because the bad economy hurt Heckler in the blue-collar areas and, when she got desperate, she started attacking him for what he had done in the state legislature. Jones had run similar ads in 1980 attacking Barney's liberal positions in the state legislature, particularly his support for gay rights and for designating the Combat Zone as an adult entertainment district. Jones's ads had been successful, whereas Heckler's ads two years later had backfired. Barney sees several reasons why: "First, I had no congressional record and people didn't know me as well two years earlier when Jones ran those ads. Second, Jones did it in a narrow window period and it took me a while to fight back. Third, Jones did it more coolly. Finally, to be honest, there was some sexism back then. A woman got treated differently then if she was tough. It was harder for a woman than for a man to be perceived as tough twenty-five years ago. Also, Heckler had cultivated the image of being a very sweet, kind, feminine person, and she didn't do the attacks in the right way. She was too angry and bitter. She thought that she could use social issues to take the blue-collar areas away from me, but the economy was so bad that they stayed with me."

After the election, Barney went to Florida for a ten-day vacation to recuperate. What began in May 1980 as a six-month campaign to get elected to the U.S. House of Representatives had turned into a nonstop thirty-month campaign to win a House seat and then a post-redistricting battle to keep the seat.

Barney began to arrange for staff and offices for the new 70 percent of the district. The majority of his congressional staff would work in Massachusetts to provide constituent services. Soon after the election, he gathered his Washington staff together for lunch in the Members' dining room in the Capitol and told them, "My priority is poor people. I'm going to do a lot of housing committee work. Tell the environmentalists that I am still going to vote their way but I am not going to be carrying their amendments any more."

Barney had spent over $1.5 million during the campaign, about $100,000 more than he had raised. He wasted little time in beginning a successful effort to retire his campaign debt, starting by drafting the official Barney Frank Campaign Debt Retirement Jingle, to be sung to the tune of "I'm in Love Again," a

musical classic by a man who, according to Barney, had been, in one unfortunate respect, one of his role models growing up, Antoine "Fats" Domino.

> Yes, it's me, and I'm in debt again,
> Had no money since you know when.
> I spent a million, that is true,
> But that's 'cause I had a district that was new.
> Need some money and I need it bad,
> So in '84 we'll all be glad.
> Hoo-ee baby, hoo-ee,
> Baby, won't you give some dough to me.
> Ee-ny mee-ny—min-ey mo,
> Out of debt is where I want to go.
> Hoo-ee baby, hoo-ee,
> You get a tax credit if you give to me.

What happened to Margaret Heckler? At the beginning of 1983, the Reagan
administration was concerned about the women's vote and had a genuine need
for conspicuous women as it prepared for the 1984 campaign. Thus, partly as
a reward for her loyalty to the president and largely to increase the visibility of
women in the administration, on January 12, 1983, President Reagan appointed
Margaret Heckler secretary of the Department of Health and Human Services.
Heckler had no particular expertise in the programs she was to administer. By
December 1985, Heckler was no longer "needed" and the White House chief of
staff, Don Regan, critical of her job performance, eased her out of the cabinet.
Soon after she was named ambassador to Ireland, one of the best jobs in the
Foreign Service because of the fringe benefits, which include a large mansion in
Phoenix Park in the middle of Dublin. Heckler served as ambassador to Ireland
until 1989.

11

Barney, We Hardly Recognize Ye

"I GAIN WEIGHT when I am nervous, which I usually am during campaigns," Barney explained. "I was particularly nervous [during the race against Heckler] because I was afraid I couldn't win." Barney coped with the tension of the 1982 campaign by eating. "When you're under stress, you *fress*," he said. He ate everything in sight and then came back for dessert. He often ate half a pecan pie and five hamburgers as a snack between meals. In his eating habits, he followed the advice of Miss Piggy, who once said, "Never eat more than you can lift."

"We would take him places in Fall River to meet people and all he would look at was the food. 'You'll eat afterwards,' I would tell him," Mark Sullivan said. Sullivan recalled attending a campaign event with Barney in a private home. Just as the host came up to be introduced to Barney and reached out his hand, Barney grabbed a sandwich and took a bite, causing sauce to spurt out all over his tie. "I'm not full but my tie is," Barney said as the introduction began. At a 1982 fund-raiser for state representative Philip Johnston hosted by Johnston's sister at her home in Boston, Barney was a featured speaker. Johnston recalls that his sister had already set out most of the food when Barney arrived. "He was like a vacuum cleaner and ate all the hors d'oeuvres before the other people got there," Johnston said.

Campaigns in the United States, according to Barney, have always been very food-centered. He would spend fifteen to sixteen hours a day campaigning throughout the district and go to ten or twelve events, all of them centered on food—be it bagels or lasagna. "You are meeting with the elderly, better give them coffee and a donut because that is hospitable. You are going to a Portuguese festival or a Jewish event, you have to sample the food," he said. At these campaign events he would eat, in the words of Pooh Bear, "a little something" at each of them. "I have a very fast mouth. I talk fast and I eat fast." By the end of the campaign, he had gained more than 55 pounds and his weight had ballooned back up to 270 pounds.

During the congressional recess in the spring of 1983 when Barney was traveling around the district, he ran into Kevin Poirier, a friend with whom he had served in the state legislature. Poirier was the Republican representative from North Attleboro. When Poirier asked Barney, "How does it feel to have a safe seat?" Barney said he was sort of shocked and realized for the first time that maybe he was in pretty good shape politically and that maybe he could keep his job if he worked at it.

After that conversation with Poirier, feeling that the pressure was off, Barney began to act more relaxed. Staffers who had worked for him during his first term in Congress found that he was less moody, less prone to temper tantrums, and easier to get along with. Also, he began to share the reins with senior staff and to delegate more. "That first term, I couldn't send a letter to a constituent on a stupid issue without running the letter by Barney," Richard Goldstein, who had been one of Barney's legislative assistants, said. "Now it turns out that Ronald Reagan has been kind of a role model for me. I've learned to delegate a lot better. As far as management style goes, Ronald Reagan was right and Jimmy Carter was wrong," Barney said at the time. "For years, I really let the job run me and in the last couple of months I've finally learned how to control my time."

With the confidence of knowing that if he did a good job he could hold onto the House seat for a while, at least until redistricting in ten years, Barney established himself more permanently in Washington. Barney was then able to work on the other parts of his life. The first project was to lose weight, which was no easy task for him. "Food was a very important part of my life. I like to eat. Food made me feel good," Barney said. The challenge for Barney was to find other ways to feel good.

Barney was so successful in his effort to lose weight that the *Newton Tribune* spoke of his metamorphoses from rotund representative to svelte lawmaker. Barney reasoned that cutting down on food and increasing exercise was the only way he could lose weight, since a congressman's hectic schedule does not allow for the regular meal planning that most formal weight-loss programs or prescribed diets require. Along with a strict diet, he started exercising regularly, lifting weights four or five times a week and playing tennis twice a week.

"I didn't eat anything I liked and not much that I didn't like," Barney said. He explained the two maxims of his avoid-food diet with Phyllis Richman, food critic for the *Washington Post*: (1) A carrot has less calories than a pizza; and (2) Nothing has less calories than anything. When Richman asked whether he nibbled carrots and such, he responded, "I don't think any human being likes raw vegetables, but I eat them."

Barney pointed out that Raymond, the man who runs the snack bar in the cloak room of the House of Representatives, had to apply for a Small Business Administration disaster loan when Barney went on a diet.

To help him avoid food, Barney instructed his office staff not to schedule any business-related meal appointments for him. "Let's do breakfast," "Let's discuss it at lunch," and "Let's get together for dinner" were no longer part of his vocabulary. Barney often wonders why it is that in Washington two civilized people cannot communicate with each other without food in their mouths. "I think we are probably capable of having a conversation where neither of us puts anything in his or her mouth. That is a strain on people." His new philosophy was, "Except to my constituents, I would rather be rude than fat."

He talked freely about his weight loss so that people would understand what he was up against and that would make it easier for him to say no to food without fear of offending anyone. He would still attend political dinners in Washington or go to people's homes for social dinners but not to eat. He would tell the host in advance, "I would like to come, but I will not be eating. Don't think whether I eat has anything to do with how I feel about you." He would try to eat a salad or an appetizer before the dinner and just go and sit at the table with an empty plate. "For me it's not such a big change. I used to eat so fast that I'd spend most of the evening with an empty plate," he said.

Barney stayed away from fried foods, butter, and desserts, as well as sugar and salt. During a House debate on sugar subsidies, Barney remarked, "We have had people here speaking from the consumer perspective and the producer perspective. I am here speaking from the former consumer perspective of sugar." The contents of his refrigerator were just enough to warrant keeping it plugged in. It usually contained a little light cottage cheese, maybe a few slices of bread, and some Lean Cuisine meals in the freezer. In general, he liked to keep his house stocked, he said, "only with foods that are not easy to eat."

He rarely used the stove in his Capitol Hill apartment to cook meals. On one occasion when he was hosting a dinner party for a few friends, John and Amy Isaacs volunteered to cook a Thai dinner at his apartment. They planned to bring all the pots and pans for cooking. Just as they were getting ready to leave their apartment, Barney called and asked them to bring pliers because the stove didn't have any knobs.

Barney substituted sleep for his once habitual midnight snacks. He told *Boston Magazine*, "I live alone and I don't keep any food in the house. I wake up hungry at three o'clock in the morning, but I'm also naked and tired. Two out of three wins, so I go back to sleep."

When Barney was not hungry he no longer tended to eat, even a little, and he would skip meals whenever possible. Barney planned his meals around his work, so that the distractions of hunger didn't take him away from important work. "I make sure I'm only hungry when I can be distracted. For example, paperwork at my desk can only be tackled with a full stomach. On the other hand, I can be hungry and be on the floor. I can be in a committee meeting and be hungry. I can socialize and be hungry," he said.

Barney started his weight-loss program in April 1983. Over the next twelve months he lost over fifty pounds. In January 1984, when Barney returned to Washington following the lengthy congressional recess, the press wanted to know what his constituents were saying. "You are not as fat as you look on TV" and "You know you don't really look that bad," Barney replied. He recognized that keeping trim required permanent self-denial, saying, "The day I die, I will either be fat or hungry."

During a television interview about his diet with Charlie Rose on *CBS News Nightwatch* on March 22, 1984, Barney explained, "When you lose a lot of weight people notice. There is a certain advantage for politicians. If you get people talking about your weight you are going to lose fewer votes. Politicians like to avoid contentious issues. I don't think there is an anti-diet vote there, although there may be in some Italian restaurants in my district which I have offended." Rose asked whether his self-esteem was better because of the weight loss. "Most definitely," Barney responded. "My self-esteem is sufficiently better that I can talk about my self-esteem."

Middle-age vanity, at age forty-four, helped drive Barney's total physical makeover. He began exercising and working out regularly in the members-only House gym in the subbasement level of the Rayburn Office Building and at the Dupont Athletic Club in downtown Washington, lifting weights and doing some calisthenics. When he was in Massachusetts, he continued his regular workouts at the Jewish Community Center near his home in Newton, at the Metropolitan Health Club in Boston, at the Attleboro YMCA, or at the gym at the Boys Club near his district office in Fall River.

Barney began to enjoy the physiological effects of his rigorous weight-lifting workouts. The exercise made him feel less tired, more energetic, and more alert. During an interview on the television program *Bodywatch*, which filmed Barney pumping iron in the gym, he commented on his new physique. "I still have a kind of fat self-image. Every so often I will catch a glimpse of myself. I was coming out of the shower and saw somebody approaching in the mirror and I said 'Gee, that guy looks like he is in pretty good shape,' and I was pleasantly surprised to find out it was me."

Barney believed that exercise helped insure weight loss in the right places. "When you start to approach middle age you can lose a lot of weight and I would not like it to just go wherever it wants. I would like to have something to say about it," he said. "If you lose weight and don't exercise you look like a Kewpie doll that was left next to the radiator." The weight loss increased his stamina and he began playing tennis three times a week. He also started running, usually about a mile from his Capitol Hill apartment to the House office building.

Barney also shed his signature black-rimmed eyeglasses in favor of contact lenses, revealing his warm brown eyes and making him look less scholarly and more debonair. His thick, dark hair, once shaggy, was now fluffy and wavy. It was not only combed but neatly styled and blow-dried. Barney explained to the *Jewish Advocate*, "I have good Jewish hair, but all I do is have it cut differently." His hallmark rumpled suits were given away to Goodwill, and he began to wear fashionable new clothes that hung better on his five-foot-ten-inch frame.

Barney was like the middle-aged woman in the old joke who has a heart attack and is rushed to the hospital. While on the operating table she has a near-death experience, during which she sees her guardian angel and asks if this is her time. The angel says no and explains that she has another forty years to live. Upon her recovery, the woman decides to stay in the hospital for a few more days to have a facelift, liposuction, and a tummy tuck. She even has someone come in to change her hair color. She feels that since she has another forty years to live it is worth it. As she is leaving the hospital she is killed by an ambulance speeding up to the hospital. When she arrives in heaven, she sees her guardian angel again and says, "I thought you said that I had another forty years!" The apologetic angel says, "I'm sorry. I didn't recognize you."

People did not recognize the new Barney Frank. "He came up to me one evening at the Hyatt Regency and said, 'Hi Jack.' I didn't recognize him. It sounded like Barney but didn't look like him. He had lost a lot of weight, was not wearing glasses, had on new clothes, and even his hair was different," Jack Valenti said.

Barney had transformed himself from an unkempt, overweight, self-proclaimed slob to a trim, debonair, well-dressed congressman. His weight had plummeted and his waistline had shrunk from a forty-six to the mid-thirties. When a reporter reminded him of his earlier "Neatness isn't everything" marketing strategy, Barney responded "Neatness is gaining."

One evening in early 1984, Barney entered the Cannon House Office Building. He had been playing tennis and was wearing a pair of dark-blue gym shorts and a gray tank-top shirt. He had left his wallet and identification in the car. The Capitol police officer on duty stopped him and asked where he was going. When Barney said he was Massachusetts congressman Barney Frank, the rookie officer opened the desk drawer and took out the *Congressional Pictorial Directory for the 98th Congress*, a publication popularly referred to as the mug book. The book includes black-and-white headshots, a little over two square inches in size, of each member of Congress by state. This book, however, had been printed in December 1982. The officer leafed through the small book until he came to Massachusetts and found the headshot photo of Barney Frank, a heavyweight with layers of fat under his chin and wearing thick eyeglasses. The officer looked up at the physically fit, muscular man in front of him, glanced down at the photo once again, stared at the man and said, "You are not Barney Frank. You don't look anything like him."

It was the same in his district. When Barney marched in the Fourth of July parade in Fall River, some people complained that he didn't even show up. When he appeared as the speaker at a Golden Age Club meeting for Jewish seniors at a Newton synagogue, the seniors did a double take. "Where's Barney?" they asked, mistaking him for one of his aides.

In the fall of 1984, Barney attended a political event in Brookline for Democratic presidential candidate Walter Mondale. The event took place in the large backyard at the home of Bob Farmer in Chestnut Hill. The next day a photo of Mondale and Barney appeared on the front page of the *Providence Journal* over the caption, "Walter Mondale and an unidentified supporter." The *Providence Journal* offered to run a correction but Barney said no. "I didn't want the newspaper to say, 'We have just learned that the person in the photo with Walter Mondale is your congressman.'"

Behind the contact lenses and the new slim body, however, lurked the old Barney. Below the well-groomed appearance and well-tailored suit, he still wore his old, comfortable, scuffed and battered shoes. Nor had his table manners changed. The *Providence Journal* reported that during a campaign stop in Medfield, at a lunch with city leaders, Barney "practically inhaled the bread sticks" and "after coffee in a cozy rustic restaurant full of business suits, Barney used the butter knife for dental floss." When he spoke before groups and rattled off a few nonstop sentences, or jingled the change in his pockets, or stood idly on one foot, the people knew it was the same old Barney.

There were a few complaints about his new appearance. Some constituents preferred the old, chubbier, teddy-bear-like, rumpled version. In endorsing him for reelection, the *Fall River Herald News* said: "The only fault that one can legitimately find with Barney is with his image, which when he was first elected, was, well, roly-poly. Everyone became accustomed to Barney as he was when, lo and behold, he turned up svelte and almost unrecognizable." The newspaper editorial noted that the people of his district are getting to know him all over again and urged Barney not to drastically change his image in the next two years, stating, "One such alteration is enough."

Dave Granlund, the political cartoonist for the *Middlesex News*, griped: "The one thing we cartoonists count on is a static appearance. No way can I do anything with Barney's face now. My only hope is that he loses his contact lenses and goes on an eating binge." And one constituent remarked, "If I didn't know it was Barney Frank, the guy with the sense of humor and all that, I'd think he was connected or something, you know, a mobster."

Amidst the confusion stemming from Barney's makeover, Elsie Frank remarked, "It's not a new look to me. This is how he looked when he became a bar mitzvah. What you're seeing is the 'old' Barney." That was true except for the glasses. By December 1984, he had lost nearly 75 pounds and weighed about 195.

After the transformation, female staffers on Capitol Hill started noticing the new Barney Frank. A woman on Henry Hyde's staff mentioned to Bill Black, a legislative assistant, that whenever Barney spoke on the floor all the women in Hyde's office crowded around the television set to watch him because he looked so handsome now. When Black reported to Barney that the women in Hyde's office thought he was "hot," Barney did not seem pleased. "That was meant to be a compliment," Black said. "Women have lower standards for men than men do," Barney replied.

In early 1985, Barney became overzealous in his weight-lifting efforts and suffered a hernia. As he described it, "I have the stamina of a teenager, the body of a twenty-two-year-old, and the hernia of a middle-aged Jewish man who should have known better." In August 1985, after suffering a leg injury playing tennis that required the help of crutches, Barney remarked to a group of senior citizens in Foxboro, Massachusetts, in an aphorism that would make Yogi Berra proud, "I used to be a lot healthier until I decided to be physically fit." There was a photo spread on Barney Frank in the January 1986 issue of *People* magazine. He joked to his Washington office staff, "They got my biceps, triceps, and deltoids in the last picture, but they didn't get my pecs. Maybe they should do a coming-out-of-the-shower shot."

During his first term in Congress, knowing that he faced a tough reelection race in 1982, Barney did not travel outside the United States. When the banking industry invited him to a meeting in Bermuda, he couldn't be bothered and sent his domestic legislative assistant in his place. As a prominent Jewish member of Congress he received repeated requests from Jewish organizations to travel to Israel, but he turned them all down. In part, he didn't want to be associated with the perks and trappings of office. "I didn't travel my first term since I was a little nervous about reelection. After getting reelected I figured it was safe to leave the country and that there would still be a district when I got back. The first term I thought there would be a district but they moved it," he said.

Finally, in mid-September 1983, he took his first overseas trip. "I went to a part of the world where a large number of my constituents feel a great kinship, where they are very proud of its democracy, very proud of its pro-Americanism, and where they feel great heritage ties. I went to Portugal and the Azores," he said. About seventy-five thousand of the five hundred thousand constituents in the newly drawn Fourth District, mostly in Fall River and the adjoining towns, considered themselves to be of Portuguese descent. Barney spent eight days in

Lisbon, the Azores, St. Michaels, Pico, and the other islands, and visited the United States' Lajes Air Base in the Azores. It was a combination vacation and business trip during which he met with Portuguese government officials and discussed trade, immigration, and relations between the two countries.

Barney wanted to maintain the delicate balance between the northern and southern parts of the newly redrawn Fourth District and avoid being perceived as favoring one constituency over the other. Therefore, he also agreed to go on a trip to Israel in late 1983 sponsored by the B'nai B'rith Anti-Defamation League. Three other members of Congress, all freshmen, went with him, Thomas Carper of Delaware and Edward Feighan of Ohio, both Democrats, and Tom Lewis of Florida, a Republican. Congressional staff and employees from several Jewish organizations were also part of the group. The delegation flew nonstop from Kennedy Airport in New York to Egypt, where they would spend a few days in Cairo meeting with senior Egyptian officials, including President Hosni Mubarak, before heading to Israel and a side trip to Lebanon.

Thomas Carper had served as Delaware state treasurer for six years before being elected to Congress in 1982. He had defeated veteran GOP congressman Thomas Evans, whose reelection campaign struggled because of his acknowledged extramarital affair with the lobbyist and one-time *Playboy* model Paula Parkinson. Carper, a few weeks shy of his thirty-seventh birthday, was single at the time, handsome, and, according to some women on the trip, very much on the make. As soon as the pilot turned off the Fasten-seat-belts sign, Carper began to walk about the cabin, chatting with people and searching for female companionship. In short order, he found his prey. At this point memories diverge. According to Carper, he came upon two attractive, single, smart, and lovely American women who were traveling to Cairo for vacation. However, according to others on the trip, he romanced one of the flight stewardesses, a woman described by one passenger as "a real babe."

Because the flight would be arriving in Cairo on December 31, the trip organizers had arranged for the group to attend a New Year's Eve gala banquet, with music and dancing, at the Cairo Hilton Hotel overlooking the Nile, where they would be staying. When Carper invited the stewardess to the party at the Cairo Hilton, she said that she would love to go but couldn't abandon her friend, another stewardess on the flight. Since Lewis and Feighan were traveling with their wives, Carper then approached Barney, the only other single member of Congress on the trip. Carper and Barney knew each other from serving together on the Banking committee.

Barney was sitting in his seat voraciously reading newspapers, as he tended to do on trips. "I just met these two lovely women on the plane. We should invite them to the New Year's Eve banquet at our hotel. They look like fun dates. Tom and Ed have their spouses," Carper said, "I'm not interested," Barney replied, hardly glancing up from the newspaper he was reading. But Carper would not take no for an answer. He kept badgering Barney, who simply wanted to be left alone to read his newspapers in peace. Barney declined each invitation, claiming he was tired, busy, not interested, whatever. Finally, to get Carper off his back, Barney agreed to the double date. When Carper said to the women, "Congressman Barney Frank of Massachusetts and I would be honored if you join us at the New Year's Eve party at the Cairo Hilton," they readily accepted the invitation.

At the party, Carper introduced Caroline, who happened to be from Massachusetts, to Barney. The group sat at a long table for dinner. "I am sitting with my date, we're talking, and getting to know each other," Carper recalled. "I look and Barney is talking and engaging with other people but there is not a lot of interaction between him and his date."

Barney was "cold as ice" and had little conversation with Caroline at dinner. He was uncomfortable at the table and tired. Faith Morningstar, who was on the trip with her husband, Dick, Barney's campaign treasurer, told him that he was being rude to Caroline. "I was nice to do this at all for Tom," Barney replied. When Caroline left the table briefly, Barney muttered to Faith and Dick Morningstar, "I have to get out of here. I am gay." "I don't care what you are. You're staying until midnight," Faith Morningstar told him.

After dinner the music and dancing began, and Carper noticed that Barney was not dancing with his date. Instead, he was at the table talking with almost everyone near him except her. At the stroke of midnight, Carper and his date hugged and kissed on the dance floor. A few minutes after midnight, when Carper glanced over at the table he saw that Barney was gone and Caroline was sitting alone. This put a crimp in Carper's plans, since his date wouldn't leave her friend alone. The next morning, Carper ran into Barney in the hallway outside their hotel rooms and asked, "What was the problem last night? Didn't you like Caroline?

"Well, to be honest with you," Barney replied, "I would have liked her brother better."

"Do you know her brother?" Carper said, thinking that maybe Barney knew her brother since Caroline was from Massachusetts.

"Boy, you really are dumb. I don't even know if she has a brother," Barney answered. He then told Carper that he was gay. At the time, he had come out to only a few friends and family.

"I reacted kind of nonchalant. I did not have a big overt reaction," Carper recalled.

When the group arrived in Israel a few days later, they stayed in Jerusalem at the King David Hotel, Carper and Barney had often worked out at the same time at the House gym. Carper knocked on the door of Barney's hotel room and said, "C'mon, let's go work out at the Jerusalem Y across the street." "That meant a lot to me," Barney said. "He was making the point that the fact I was gay was not going to keep him from working out with me."

Carper, who went on to serve two terms as governor of Delaware and was elected to the Senate in 2000, was one of the first House members that Barney came out to but not the first. Barney and Gerry Studds of Massachusetts had come out to each other. The first House member Barney came out to was Mike Synar, a Democratic representative from Oklahoma. Synar had been elected to Congress in 1978 and almost immediately angered the oil industry by voting to protect areas of the Alaskan wilderness from development. Synar sat next to Barney one morning at a Judiciary subcommittee hearing. He turned to Barney and for no apparent reason asked whether he had a girlfriend. Barney said no. When Synar asked if he was gay, Barney answered yes. "I just decided that I would answer," he explained. Ironically, in Synar's last House race in 1994, when he was defeated in the Democratic primary, Synar, who had dated several women but never married, was the subject of an underground whispering campaign that, since he was forty-four years old and had never married, he was gay.

The trip to the Middle East included free time for sightseeing in Cairo. Everybody in the group went to see the pyramids except Barney. He turned down an invitation from Dick and Faith Morningstar to join them, saying, "If I want to see buildings that my ancestors built, I'd just go see some houses in Bayonne." Then, when Doug Cahn, his administrative assistant, and his wife, Barbara, also invited Barney to join them to see the pyramids, Barney was arrogant when he turned down the invitation, calling the trip a waste of time. "Why would I want to go to the pyramids when I can see photos of them? I have more important things to do." Barney stayed in the hotel room reading back issues of the *New York Times*, some over two months old, that he had brought with him on the trip.

Most people pack clothing in their suitcases, Barney packs newspapers. Allard Lowenstein had a similar habit of carrying around old newspapers to read on trips. Dick Morningstar recalled traveling with Barney to Los Angeles during his first term in Congress when he was invited to address the Motion Picture Association of America. "He brought this big carry-on briefcase, ninety-five percent of which was filled with newspapers and the other five percent with clothing. He did not bring a suitcase on the trip. Soon after takeoff, the area where we were sitting became a den littered with newspapers." Several former staffers recall Barney often coming into the office with a weeks-old newspaper article and asking them to look into the substance of a story.

After the race against Heckler, Barney started to get involved in other ventures, appearing more frequently on television and doing some writing. In June

1983, he participated in several panel discussions for the PBS television series *The Constitution: That Delicate Balance*, produced by Fred Friendly. The shows were taped in Independence Hall in Philadelphia.

The first program, which aired in 1984, was moderated by the Harvard Law School professor Charles Nesson and focused on crime and insanity. The panel included Gerry Spence, an attorney, U.S. Appeals Court judge Irving Kaufman, and Rudolph Giuliani, then the U.S. attorney for New York. William Gaylin, a psychiatrist with the Hastings Center for Bioethics, argued that our society has compassion and has recognized for over fifteen hundred years that some people, a small number, are not responsible for their actions. Barney, however, shared the public's skepticism at the idea that a person can be crazy enough to kill someone but can then be sane again within a short time. "The notion that society will extract no penalty from you and will not protect itself from you because [you were insane] when you pulled the trigger doesn't have a lot of appeal to me," Barney asserted. "People who kill people ought to be kept away from the rest of us, particularly those they may kill. Society has a right to be protected from that individual."

In July 1982, Barney had introduced legislation to abolish the insanity defense at the federal level. He had begun to focus on this issue in early 1980 when his close friend Al Lowenstein was murdered and the murderer was judged not guilty by reason of insanity and treated in a way that Barney felt allowed him to walk the streets at any time and be a danger to others. Barney thought that the time was right for this legislation because just weeks earlier, on June 21, 1982, after an eight-week trial, John Hinckley Jr. had been acquitted by reason of insanity of shooting President Ronald Reagan, his press secretary, James Brady, a police officer, and a Secret Service officer. To many Americans who were stunned and outraged by the verdict, the trial had shown that the insanity defense makes a mockery of the judicial system.

Barney introduced the bill with these words: "We don't these days divide the world into a small group that is totally out of control or insane and the rest that are totally sane. Most of us talk of mental illness as a spectrum. It is only in the law that we are locked in an unfortunate way into sane and insane. [The murderer] has clearly done it and because he or she may do it again society has a right to say we want you locked up. I don't want people walking around who are prone to take pot shots at others. . . . Maybe it is not their fault in a moral sense but that is not the purpose of the criminal justice system, simply to have trials to say you're a good person or a bad person."

Barney went on to explain that he does not believe, as an intellectual matter, that we can know when someone had recovered from mental illness. "It is not the same as a broken arm. They can tell when your arm heals. They can tell when the pneumonia has left your lungs. We cannot say with any degree of certainty when someone who is mentally ill is no longer mentally ill," he said. Later, at a press conference, referring to the psychiatrists who had testified at Hinckley's trial that he was sane all along, he said, "I don't think we ought to continue in our law a system where a man who is guilty of that kind of violent act might be free in a year or two because they happen to choose for the psychiatric panel the psychiatrists who were on the prosecution side." "Jodie Foster has a right to be very nervous about that," he added.

In the legislation he proposed a two-step process. First, there would be a trial to determine whether the individual charged is guilty of the crime. Should the jury find that the individual charged is guilty of committing that crime, that person would be given an appropriate sentence of confinement befitting the crime. "It may be that the person ought to get treatment during that period of confinement. What kind of treatment that person gets is a different issue," Barney said. "The fellow should be locked up. The function of the criminal justice system is to put something between them and us for our protection."

The second step would be a separate proceeding before the judge to allow evidence of mental illness and arguments that the convicted person should be given a particular type of treatment, or that some part of the sentence could be served in a mental institution with proper security. This second hearing, however, would not go to a not-guilty finding or to shortening the sentence or to releasing the person. The Democrats in Congress considered Barney's bill too harsh and it didn't move.

The second program in the PBS series was titled "The Sovereign Self: Right to Live, Right to Die" and was moderated by the Harvard Law School professor Arthur Miller. That panel included Gloria Steinem, Phil Donahue, Court of Appeals judge Abner Mikva, Meg Greenfield, the editorial page editor of the *Washington Post*, some prominent physicians, and several members of the Senate and the House.

The first hypothetical situation posed by Miller was one involving an adult patient in terrible pain, a medical certification that the patient is terminal and will live less than sixty days, and a request from the patient to the doctor to end his life right away. Miller asked whether Barney would support legislation allowing the doctor to do so. Barney answered that he would support legislation along those lines with certain safeguards relating to medical certification and to protect against coercion. In his view, when the patient decides that his life will be unbearable, the patient's individual autonomy ought to prevail.

Henry Hyde and Robert Drinan, who had joined the Georgetown Law Center faculty after leaving Congress in 1981, were on the program panel as well, and both disagreed with Barney. Drinan asserted that such power has never been given to the state and "It is God's right alone." Hyde noted initially, "I agree with Father Drinan for the first time in my life." He stated that he would not give the medical profession immunity against murder. He spoke about the sanctity of life and contended that the right to life is paramount." Barney challenged him, "Henry, you say there is a right to life. What is the right to life? A right belongs to someone. If I am a desperately ill person in terminal pain, whose right is it—the right to life? If it isn't my right, who else has a right to my life, my insurance company?"

Barney has always enjoyed writing, and he wrote a long essay on the use of metaphors in politics and government. The article, titled "Is This a Dagger Which I See Before Me? No, Congressman, It's Korea," appeared in the *Washington Post* on July 27, 1983. This essay was Barney at his best, witty, irreverent, and refreshing. It was a topic that he had planned to write about for several years.

In the article he calls on people to stop obfuscating political arguments with metaphors about pointed daggers and soft underbellies or mixed metaphors, such as the one by William Goodling of Pennsylvania, who, in a budget debate on the House floor in May 1982, insisted that the Democrats "stop milking a dead horse." Barney has argued that if there is any change in the First Amendment, it should be to ban the use of metaphors in the discussion of public policy, particularly foreign policy. Absent such a change in the First Amendment, he is resigned to continuing to live his life among camels putting their noses into tents and lawyers sliding down slippery slopes.

In Barney's view, although people claim to use metaphors to advance understanding by explaining complex phenomena in terms of simple and familiar ones, the fact is that people become so enamored of a simplistic figure of speech that they substitute it for reality and consequently their comments become distorted and mechanistic. He notes in the article that physical shapes of countries lead otherwise sensible people to discuss international events in the terms tenyear-olds use when assembling geographic jigsaw puzzles. Metaphor-mongers understand the value of making them graphic. Underbellies must always be soft, and threats always aimed at one's rear, except of course, when they are aimed at one's heart. Barney pokes fun at another physical metaphor popular in foreign policy discussions: the country-as-a-weapon: "I have grown up being told that Korea is essential to our security because it is pointed like a dagger at the back of Japan. First of all, I doubt very much that countries have fronts or backs. And if Japan does have a back, it seems unduly ethnocentric for us to decide that it is the part nearest Asia. . . . It is relevant that Korea is near Japan. It is wholly irrelevant that it is roughly dagger shaped. Unless levitation is far more advanced in the East than I realize, the danger of Korea's being stuck into Japan seems negligible."

He also casts aspersions on the domino theory: "It is undeniable that events in one country can have a profound effect on its neighbors. It is demonstrably untrue that the 'fall' of any one nation automatically or even probably means the 'fall' of all of its neighbors. (Apparently, countries, unlike dominoes, can fall in several directions at once.) . . . Incidentally, the domino theory is at its most impressive when it describes the impact of an island nation on its neighbors across the water. Presumably this variant is the domino wave effect."

12

Subcommittee Chairman Frank

In January 1983, Barney, beginning his second term in Congress, ascended, on the basis of seniority, to the chairmanship of the Government Operations Subcommittee on Manpower and Housing. It is rare for a sophomore member to have enough seniority to land a subcommittee chairmanship, even with the proliferation of House subcommittees in the early 1980s. Barney explained how he came to make the transition from individual member to subcommittee chairman in only his second term: "It took three retirements, one death, two incumbents being beaten in the election, and a party switch."

The Government Operations subcommittee was an oversight panel rather than a legislative committee and was responsible for overseeing the programs and operations of several departments and agencies, including the Department of Housing and Urban Development (HUD), the Department of Labor, the National Labor Relations Board (NLRB), the Equal Employment Opportunity Commission (EEOC), and the Office of Personnel Management (OPM).

Barney revived and energized an obscure subcommittee that had been moribund for several years under the leadership of Cardiss Collins of Illinois. He was aggressive, going after the Office of Management and Budget for interfering in the legislative process and taking on the navy for exposing its workers to asbestos at the Kittery–Portsmouth Naval Shipyard. Administration officials began to feel the heat of Barney's caustic, prosecutorial style.

At a subcommittee hearing about the importance of preserving the existing housing stock for low-income people, HUD assistant secretary Maurice Barksdale testified that some parts of the country had more subsidized housing for the poor than needed. Barney expressed his incredulity and asked for proof. In response, HUD provided the subcommittee with a list of underutilized subsidized housing projects they considered surplus. The subcommittee staff researched the list and found that forty-three of the forty-seven projects it named were fully occupied and some had waiting lists of up to two years. "In some projects there were no waiting lists because there was so little turnover and waiting time so long that they stopped keeping a list," Richard Goldstein, the housing counsel, said. Barney told the press, "HUD has found an innovative way to deal with the housing shortage, which is to define it out of existence. It's a triumph of ideology over reality. When people have to distort reality to justify their policy, that's a pretty good indication there's something wrong with the policy." HUD then submitted a revised list of fourteen surplus projects.

At a follow-up hearing on October 5, 1983, HUD undersecretary Philip Abrams apologized for submitting inaccurate data to the subcommittee. He admitted that the revised list of fourteen projects was also incorrect and that the actual number of surplus projects was just four. Abrams took this new list of surplus projects and tore it in half. "I'm sorry," he said. "I appreciate your admitting that," Barney replied. "If [HUD officials] wanted to screw this up intentionally, you could not have done it better."

On a Monday evening in November 1983, Barney and I had finished playing tennis under the bubble at Haines Point and gathered our belongings. As we were leaving the court, Barney, seemingly out of the blue, asked, "What is you career goal?" "I am waiting for a Democratic administration so that you can get me the NLRB general counsel position," I replied candidly.

"Are you interested in becoming my subcommittee staff director and chief counsel?" he asked. "Most of the jurisdiction is in the labor area and I could use someone with a strong labor background. Besides, it would be a good stepping stone for NLRB general counsel." He added as a sweetener, "And you get a free parking space in the Rayburn garage."

"A free indoor parking spot in the Rayburn Building," I thought, "that's an offer I can't refuse." One question, however, came to mind. "As chief counsel where would I be sitting at the hearings?" I asked. He looked a little puzzled and I promptly clarified the question. "Would I be sitting at the table next to the chairman like Roy Cohn or in back of the chairman like Robert Kennedy?" He instantly recalled the 1954 photo of Senator Joseph McCarthy chairing the hearings by the Senate Permanent Subcommittee on Investigations on communism in the army that I was referring to and replied, "You would be sitting on the dais next to me like Roy Cohn, but hopefully there will be a better result." I was flattered by the unexpected job offer and told him that I needed some time to think about it and to discuss the matter with my wife. He said that would be fine and asked me to tell him my decision at tennis the next week.

The following Monday night, while we were waiting for the bell to ring, signaling the start of our one hour of court time, I accepted the job offer. After the match, Barney drove me to the Metro stop next to the Cannon Office Building. As we were approaching the Metro stop, he said, "There is something you should know before you take the job." Then he added, "I am gay."

I was caught by surprise and as I exited the car I muttered awkwardly, "Fine. I'll see you next week at tennis." During the thirty-minute Metro ride home, I could not think of anything else. I recalled his publicized romance in the mid-seventies with Kathleen Sullivan, whose father owned the New England Patriots, and my vision of tickets on the fifty-yard line when the Patriots played the New York Jets.

When I arrived home, I immediately told my wife what Barney had said. I asked her whether I should reconsider my decision to take the staff director position not because I was homophobic but because Barney could get "outed" and my job would be dependent on his continued reelection to Congress. "Absolutely not," she said. "He thought enough about you to share his secret with you. That had to be a difficult thing for him to do."

As subcommittee chairman, Barney was interested in uncovering waste and abuse in government programs. In his view, it made sense programmatically and politically to be tougher on waste and fraud in the programs that you care about, like HUD, than those you don't, because money badly spent hurts housing programs. He was not interested, however, in going after officials and bureaucrats for minor lapses, such as cronyism and using the government chauffeur for personal business. "If people want me to be a cop, they have to give me a gun and a holster and a badge," he said.

I was nervous as I prepared for my first subcommittee hearing on the subject of wage discrimination against women and the issue of equivalent pay for equivalent work. On February 28, 1984, the evening before the hearing, at about seven o'clock, a woman from the staff of EEOC chairman Clarence Thomas phoned the subcommittee office and informed us that Thomas had decided not to testify at the hearing. There was no reason given for this last-minute cancellation.

I panicked. Should I postpone or cancel the hearing? Without Thomas, it would be a one-sided hearing, consisting of several women's rights groups and other sympathetic witnesses charging that the EEOC had been "sitting" on some 250 complaints of sex-based wage discrimination and had failed to take action on that issue.

I tried unsuccessfully to track down Barney. Finally, at about ten o'clock, I reached him at home and explained what had happened. "That's Gr-r-reat," said Barney in a voice that sounded like Tony the Tiger hawking Frosted Flakes. "Don't worry," he added. "We will subpoena him."

At the beginning of the hearing, Barney recounted the events of the previous evening relating to Thomas's last-minute withdrawal and announced his intention to subpoena the EEOC chairman to discuss the agency's handling of sex-based wage discrimination.

Barney avoided any discussion of the controversial concept of "comparable worth" and focused on sex-based wage discrimination. "Strong federal involvement is needed if the wage gap between traditionally male and female jobs is to be closed. Yet despite its status as the country's chief civil rights enforcement agency, the EEOC has failed to take a lead role in wage bias actions," he said. He expressed concern over the delay by EEOC in carrying out *County of Washington v. Gunther*, the 1981 case in which the Supreme Court held that female employees who claimed that their jobs were undervalued because of intentional sex discrimination could sue under Title VII of the 1964 Civil Rights Act, even though their work was not identical to that of male coworkers receiving higher pay. "The EEOC's failure to develop a policy on that issue for nearly three years is inexcusable. It's EEOC's responsibility to give guidance. It isn't doing that," Barney said.

Rather than appearing in person, Thomas submitted a written statement in which he acknowledged the need for further commission policy on wage discrimination following *Gunther*. To address that concern, Thomas stated that he had established a working group at the EEOC made up of attorneys, a statistician, and a research psychologist to study the pay equity issue and to prepare a series of option papers for commission consideration. Barney labeled this action "too little, too late."

Later that morning, when Barney returned to his congressional office, he found a stack of yellow phone messages on his desk. One showed that Thomas had called shortly after ten, asking him to return the phone call and noting that it was "important." When Barney returned the call and Thomas came on the line, Barney, with his usual abruptness, interrupted the pleasantries and demanded, "What do you want?" Thomas explained that his nonappearance had been based on a "misunderstanding and a miscommunication." He readily agreed to appear before the subcommittee the following week without the need for a subpoena. But the damage to EEOC and its chairman had been done. A hearing by a relatively obscure subcommittee that probably would have received minimal press attention became news because of Thomas's failure to appear. The next morning, an article on page A3 of the *Washington Post* was headlined, "EEOC Head Threatened with Hill Subpoena for Failing to Testify."

The subsequent hearing on March 14 took place before a room overflowing with spectators, several television cameras, and a press table filled to capacity to witness Thomas's delayed appearance before the subcommittee. This first face-to-face encounter between Barney Frank and Clarence Thomas quickly turned into a sparring match that lasted over an hour.

At one point, Barney asked whether the EEOC would consider opposing the Justice Department if it sought reversal of a recent federal district court judge's decision that Washington State had violated Title VII by failing to pay employees in predominantly female job classifications at the same rate as men holding jobs of equivalent difficulty and responsibility. When Thomas refused to take a position, Barney said, "If you can't answer that, you might as well stay home and we'll mail you your check." Thomas then stated his belief that the EEOC does not have authority to file briefs in public sector cases and could not block a Justice Department brief arguing for reversal.

Thomas assured the panel that the EEOC would vote in the next two months on a policy to address *Gunther*-type cases, with the hope of investigating and litigating them. He testified that a newly created internal task force was already addressing the broader question of pay equity. Thomas disagreed with the allegations that EEOC had been "sitting" on 250 cases of sex-based wage discrimination. He stated that a recent "staff analysis" of those charges determined that they are "all comparable worth cases—not *Gunther*-type." Barney expressed concern over the agency's delay in moving on wage discrimination cases since the Supreme Court's 1981 decision in the *Gunther* case. "It looks like the commission didn't do a thing until the subcommittee took action," he said. "What we've got now is a hasty review of cases and a task force. I just don't think it's acceptable to work at this pace."

John "Jock" McKernan of Maine was the ranking Republican on the subcommittee. The personable and photogenic thirty-six-year-old McKernan, the offspring of a well-to-do New England family, educated at Exeter and Dartmouth, where he was captain of the tennis team, was an attorney and former state legislator. He was a moderate-to-liberal Republican with higher political ambitions. At the time he was dating and subsequently married Olympia Snowe, the other House member from Maine, who was later elected to the Senate. After four years in the House, McKernan was elected governor of Maine in 1986 and served for two terms. Senior Republicans had opted for more desirable subcommittee assignments on the Government Operations Committee, and so, as a freshman congressman, McKernan unexpectedly found himself as the senior Republican on the subcommittee.

McKernan played an active part in changing the name of the subcommittee from the anachronistic Manpower and Housing to the gender-neutral Employment and Housing. At a July 26, 1984, subcommittee hearing to examine the Women's Bureau, part of the Department of Labor, McKernan overheard a child in the audience ask her mother, "If this is a hearing about women, why is this committee called 'manpower'?" McKernan wrote letters to the Government Operations Committee chairman, Jack Brooks, and the ranking Republican member, Frank Horton, strongly endorsing Barney's proposal to change the name of the subcommittee. Brooks responded that he would do so—but next year at the commencement of the 99th Congress. Brooks had no problem with the name change, but he had just ordered a new supply of stationery for all the subcommittees.

The subcommittee consisted primarily of first-term members. At a hearing in early 1984, Joe Kolter, a Democrat from Pennsylvania (who achieved some notoriety in the mid-1990s when he pleaded guilty to embezzlement charges in connection with the House post office scandal), asked the witness a rather naïve, somewhat stupid question. Barney leaned over to me and commented, "Believe it or not the guy he beat in the election was even dumber." At the next hearing, Kolter wandered into the room about forty minutes late. When it was his turn to question the witness, Kolter posed a totally irrelevant question. Barney leaned over to me and asked, "Who invited him to this hearing? We have got to stop sending him notice of our hearings."

In Barney's view, the dumbest member of Congress ever was Senator William Scott of Virginia. In the mid-1970s, Scott was named the dumbest member of Congress in an article in a rather obscure publication (*New Times* magazine). In response, Scott held a statewide press conference to deny the charge and, as a reporter observed, thereby confirmed the accuracy of what he was denying.

Another freshman Democrat on the subcommittee was Major Owens from Brooklyn, New York, who represented the Bedford–Stuyvesant and Brownesville sections of the borough. That seat had previously been held by Shirley Chisholm. When Chisholm, an African American woman, was first elected to Congress from this urban district, she was assigned to the Forestry Subcommittee on the House Agriculture Committee, which she believed was irrelevant to her urban constituency. Her classic comment was, "Apparently, the only thing these people know about Brooklyn is that a tree grows there." Major Owens was the only librarian serving in the Congress.

On May 24, 1984, the Subcommittee on Manpower and Housing held a joint hearing with the Banking Subcommittee on Housing and Community Development, chaired by Henry Barbosa Gonzalez of Texas, to examine a fifty-page, $138,000 report on the homeless issued by HUD earlier that month.

The first Mexican American ever elected to Congress, Gonzalez had experienced bigotry growing up in Texas. When Barney arrived in Congress in 1981, one of his first acts was to vote for Gonzalez to be the chairman of the Subcommittee on Housing and Community Development in a contested election. Barney shared Gonzalez's genuine passion for helping working people and poorer people and the two men had a close working relationship over the years. "It was close because Barney was respectful of him and tolerated his idiosyncratic way of thinking and doing things," Gerry McMurray, the housing subcommittee staff director, said. "Barney often covered for Henry B. and made him look good," another housing subcommittee staffer said. Barney believes that Gonzalez was a crusader and vastly underrated as a legislator and that many of his accomplishments, such as pressing the Federal Reserve Board to open the minutes of its meetings to the public and helping to clean up the mess of the Savings and Loan scandals, have been overlooked.

As the senior subcommittee chairman, Gonzalez presided at the joint hearing to consider HUD's report that sought to minimize the problem by contending that the number of homeless in the United States was much smaller than had been previously estimated. The HUD study estimated the nationwide homeless population at 250,000 to 350,000 persons. Previous estimates had put the country's homeless population at over two million.

In his opening remarks, Barney suggested that "the people now employed in counting the homeless use the same statistical approach to computing the national debt." He called HUD's effort "intellectually shoddy, methodologically lacking, and morally incredibly callous."

At the beginning of the Reagan administration, when the issue of the homeless had first come up, some Democrats in Congress were critical of HUD secretary Samuel Pierce for not doing anything. Pierce said that the homeless were not his problem. "I guess he is a very literal-minded man," Barney commented at the time. "What makes one homeless is the absence of housing. So apparently the secretary of the Department of Housing thinks that if people do not have any housing, they are not his responsibility."

Shelter administrators, church leaders, social workers, and advocates for the homeless from across the country charged that the research for the report was inaccurate and deceptive, and they testified to a pattern of undercounting. Witnesses claimed that the information they provided HUD researchers was ignored, distorted, or wrongly quoted. One witness testified that in estimating the number of homeless people in New York City, the HUD report said the figure of 12,000 was within the "reliable" range even though the number of homeless people actually sheltered and counted authoritatively was more than 16,000. Louisa Stark, co-chair of the Phoenix Consortium for the Homeless, said that she gave HUD researchers figures indicating that the homeless population in Phoenix was 1,500 to 3,000 people. The HUD report stated, however, that "the most reliable estimate of homeless people in Phoenix was between 750 and 1,400."

The joint hearing began at 9:30 in the morning and did not end until almost eight o'clock in the evening. As was Gonzalez's custom, the hearing proceeded without any breaks. It was rumored that Gonzalez could go an entire day without having to go to the restroom. As the ranking Republican on the Government Operations subcommittee, John McKernan felt an obligation and responsibility to be present for the entire joint hearing. It was a long and agonizing day for McKernan. Subsequently, if Barney ever needed McKernan's support to approve a subcommittee report, he would threaten to hold another joint hearing with Gonzalez's subcommittee. McKernan would plead, "Please, no, anything but that. I will do whatever you want."

In early 1983, McKernan had asked Barney to hold a field hearing dealing with health and safety conditions at the Kittery–Portsmouth Naval Shipyard, located on the Maine–New Hampshire border, partly in McKernan's congressional district. Barney agreed, and on April 18, 1983, the subcommittee held a field hearing in Kittery, Maine, focusing on whether the U.S. Navy was complying with Occupational Safety and Health Administration (OSHA) rules for medical surveillance of employees exposed to asbestos and reasonable access to medical exposure records. As a result of the subcommittee intervention, the White House directed the navy to comply with the applicable OSHA rules.

In 1984, a different health problem developed at the Kittery–Portsmouth Naval Shipyard. The Federal Employees Metal Trade Council, the union representing the federal workers at the site, again asked McKernan for help and, at his request, Barney agreed to do another hearing but this time in Washington. At the hearing on August 9, 1984, George Ackley, a shipyard employee, testified about health conditions in the sawmill building. The main problems were an outdated, almost nonfunctional ventilation system, which did not remove wood dust and other harmful substances from the air that workers breathed, and a lack of heat in the building. During the winter, Ackely said, the temperature in the work area was often below ten degrees.

The subcommittee then heard testimony from Paul Clark, the production engineering superintendent of the shipyard. "Does it seem reasonable that people ought to be working day in and day out in a building which has no heat in Maine and we are not talking about Gulfport here?" Barney asked. Clark pointed out that the shipyard is in the Northeast and during the winter there is some work that has to be done outside and sometimes it is twenty degrees below zero. Without missing a beat, Barney retorted, "If that is your attitude, why not just tear down the sawmill building and then at least you won't have the ventilation problems."

In May 1985, at the request of Bob Wise, a Democrat from West Virginia (who went on to serve as governor of that state until an extramarital affair ended his political career), Barney agreed to hold a subcommittee field hearing in his district on delays by the Labor Department in processing black-lung claims. Barney was eager to help. He was sympathetic to the plight of coal miners; in his view the delays were a legitimate problem and the subcommittee should intervene. Earlier that year, after the Wilberg Mine disaster in which twenty-seven miners were killed in Orangeville, Utah, in the district of Howard Nielson, who had succeeded McKernan as the ranking Republican on the subcommittee, Barney had agreed to travel to Utah to hold a field hearing. However, when Mine Safety and Health Administration officials offered to take him on a tour of a mine, he drew the line and curtly responded, "I don't do mines." The hearing in Charleston, West Virginia, was scheduled for June 24, 1985.

As a courtesy, both West Virginia senators, Robert Byrd and Jay Rockefeller, were invited to appear at the hearing. Ten days before the hearing, Byrd, the Senate Democratic leader, informed the subcommittee by letter that he would be unable to attend the field hearing because of a conflict but that he would submit a written statement. A few days later, Senator Rockefeller accepted the invitation. When Senator Byrd learned that Rockefeller would be attending the black-lung hearing in Charleston, his schedule was abruptly changed so that he too could attend the hearing, though he would be arriving a little late. Byrd, who had played his fiddle at various campaign stops when he ran for the state legislature in 1946, was not about to play second fiddle to Jay Rockefeller.

Barney had several constituent events in his district the weekend of June 22, and the plan was for him to fly to West Virginia on Sunday evening. He was ticketed on the five o'clock flight from Boston to Washington National Airport, where he would change planes and take the six-fifty flight to Charleston.

Barney, however, has a propensity for cutting it close with airline flights. A few months earlier, Bill Black, his legislative assistant, and his wife, Rita, were booked on the same flight as Barney out of National Airport and they offered to drive him to the airport. As they drove by the Capitol on the way to the airport, Barney abruptly declared that he needed to stop in the office to pack some newspapers to read. After what seemed like an eternity to the Blacks, Barney returned to the car and they proceeded to the airport. When they encountered heavy traffic on the 14th Street Bridge leading to National Airport, Black got anxious and said to Barney, "I have never missed a flight in my life." "If you've never missed a flight, you're wasting too much time in airports," Barney replied. That was part of the time-management philosophy that Barney follows.

On this particular Sunday afternoon, Barney did not leave himself enough time to catch his five o'clock flight from Boston to Washington. When he arrived at the terminal he found passengers in line to board the six o'clock flight to Washington. Barney spotted an acquaintance in line, told him he was in a hurry, traded tickets, and managed to board the flight. When he arrived at Washington National Airport, the last flight to Charleston had already left. The earliest flight the next day would not get him to Charleston until late morning, and the hearing was scheduled to begin at 9:00 a.m.

Barney called Doug Cahn, his administrative assistant, at his home in Takoma Park, Maryland, and without any introduction or greeting, bellowed, "I missed the flight to Charleston." Cahn quickly grasped the problem and told Barney that he would check out the options and call him back shortly. Cahn made a few phone calls to check airline and bus schedules, but found there was no way to get Barney to Charleston in time except to put him on a Greyhound bus for a long overnight trip (with a bus change and a two-hour layover in Roanoke at 2:00 a.m.)—or drive Barney himself. Barney opted to have Cahn drive him but insisted that he have a second driver with him.

Cahn phoned Bill Zavarello, the subcommittee assistant clerk, then drove his Jetta into Washington and picked up Zavarello. Since Zavarello could not drive a stick shift, they had to take his small Toyota Corona. At the airport, Barney climbed in and took over the back seat. He was longer than the car was wide. He got a pillow and lay on the back seat with his bare feet dangling outside the open car window in the night air. He fell asleep almost instantly and started snoring. He barely moved through the whole night's drive.

The trip took about ten hours, and the trio arrived at the hotel in Charleston about an hour before the hearing was to start. Cahn and Zavarello dropped Barney off at the hotel for fifteen minutes to shower. After driving Barney to the hearing, Cahn and Zavarello, who were facing a ten-hour drive home, returned to the hotel, where they went to Barney's room to sleep for a few hours. "It doesn't happen every day," Cahn said, "but on this particular day, Barney wrote one of the most appreciative thank you notes to us. It was on the table in the hotel room when we arrived. It was a nice end to a long night."

At nine o'clock sharp, a well-rested Barney Frank banged the gavel in the ballroom of the University of Charleston to begin the hearing. The room was packed with coal miners and their families. In his opening statement, Barney noted that the hearing was called at the suggestion of Representative Wise. He summed up the problem:

> This hearing deals . . . with the outrageous situation in which the Federal government promises to compensate miners who have been victimized by black lung disease and then fails to live up to that promise for many years.
>
> Nothing could be more of an embarrassment to this Government . . . than the spectacle of men who have worked for years in the mines to produce the energy that this country has needed and has been built upon, having these men become ill, apply to their Government for compensation to which they are legally entitled, and die while waiting for adjudication of their claims.
>
> It literally adds insult to injury to say to men who have become ill with black lung that they should have to go through the bureaucratic process with years of delay, frustration, and anguish, because they cannot get what is rightfully theirs. We intend to put a stop to that.

After opening statements by the other members in attendance, Barney called the first witness, Senator Rockefeller, who was soon joined at the witness table by the arriving Senator Byrd. The subcommittee members and staff were seated on a podium overlooking the witness table. The air was full of smoke from Barney's cigar. Barney leaned over and whispered to me, "If my father could see me now, sitting up here as a House subcommittee chairman with a Rockefeller and a Byrd testifying before me." It was the first time that I had ever heard him talk about his father.

Robert Byrd, the son of a coal miner, had risen from the working class and had represented West Virginia in Congress since 1952, when he was first elected to the House. He was elected to the Senate in 1958 and in 1976 he became the Senate Democratic majority leader. Byrd began his testimony that morning by discussing his efforts in the early 1970s to get President Richard Nixon's support for the black-lung benefits program. At the time Nixon was seeking Byrd's support for the Vietnam War. Barney picked up a pencil and scribbled a note on the yellow legal pad in front of him. He tore off the page and handed it to me. It read: "GREAT—He'll probably support war in Nicaragua for 10 new ALJs [administrative law judges]."

The Labor Department sent two witnesses to the hearing, Nahum Litt, its chief administrative law judge, and Robert Ramsey, the chairman and chief administrative appeals judge of the Benefits Review Board. Litt testified first and read a brief statement. He told the subcommittee that he had met with Labor secretary William Brock three days earlier to discuss the backlog of black-lung cases and stated that the secretary had asked him to convey to the hearing his "personal commitment to resolving this unacceptable situation." Litt reported that Secretary Brock has directed his executive staff to develop a formal analysis of the situation and to present a plan, within three weeks, to address the resources and timetable necessary to eliminate the present backlog of cases as soon as possible.

When Barney asked Judge Litt whether the Labor Department had a policy in place to try to resolve conflicts between the circuit courts in black-lung cases, Litt stonewalled. Barney then went on the offensive, chastising the witness for appearing as Secretary Brock's spokesman and reading a statement from him and then turning around and acting as though he had nothing to do with the secretary or the department policies. "We asked the Department of Labor to send us a representative and you were their designated hitter. I guess that I should have suggested that I wanted someone who could play the field as well. So I guess I will have to ask the Department of Labor in the future to send me a representative who does not turn his representative function on and off depending on the issue that is before us," he said. Later, when Judge Ramsey attempted to provide information that was not asked for, Barney cut him off, saying, "You had your opening statement, Judge Ramsey. I do not think that is a relevant question. While I have enjoyed being in West Virginia, it is not my intention to take up permanent residence in Mr. Wise's district. I think he represents it well enough. And I have got a plane to catch."

Barney has little patience with witnesses who waste his time with irrelevant details. Former representative Dan Glickman recalled what happened at an Administrative Law Subcommittee hearing that Barney chaired in the late 1980s when the witness started talking about the Nobel Prize he had won. Barney interrupted him in mid-sentence, saying "Look, I can read. I don't care what you've done. I don't care how many schools you went to and how many degrees you have. I don't care how many diseases you've cured. I stipulate that you are the most brilliant person to ever testify before this committee. Let's get the message going." The witness, according to Glickman, "was just stunned."

At subcommittee hearings Barney had to keep busy doing something. When a witness read from a prepared statement, some committee members followed along line by line, others formulated their questions, some stared into space, and one or two might take a nap. Barney, often looking bored, always puffing on a cigar, spent this time reading constituent mail, signing letters, or reading the newspaper or a magazine on his lap. Just when you thought he was oblivious to the witness's ongoing testimony, he would interrupt and interject a perceptive comment.

Barney's impatience caused him to be explosive at times, snapping at or scolding a staff member for making a mistake. Joy Simonson, who in 1992 would be inducted into the Women's Hall of Fame in the District of Columbia for her pioneering efforts to achieve equality for women, was in her mid-sixties when Barney enticed her out of retirement to join the subcommittee staff to handle women's issues. On one occasion, after Barney had asked a particular question and the witness responded, Simonson attempted to hand him a document that contradicted the answer given by the witness. She wanted Barney to rely on the document as a basis for a follow-up question. Barney snapped, "Joy, Joy, you cannot, you just cannot do that. I cannot look at that now. You have to give me all the material before the hearing. You cannot expect me to look at it now." Simonson was dumbfounded by the scolding Barney gave her. In time, however, she began to laugh about the incident and to mimic Barney's eruption, which had stemmed from impatience and was not malicious.

Joe Martin, who worked as a legislative aide in Barney's Washington office from 1985 to 1991, recalls that Barney had a way of being critical that was "painfully harsh." "I don't think he realized how much he upset the staff regularly. It was hard for me to take personally because I was torn between having tremendous admiration for him and not having much patience for that type of behavior," he said. Accordingly to Martin, Barney brought every woman who worked in the office to tears at one point, except for Kay Gibbs and Patty Hamel. Martin wondered to what extent some of this behavior toward staff was rooted in anger against himself for being closeted.

Patty Hamel had worked for Joe Early before coming to work for Barney. But the pace in Early's office had been too slow and she was not using many of her secretarial skills. Once when she asked Early to give her more work to do, he suggested that she simply type slower. Hamel found the first year and a half working for Barney "really intense." "I was nervous and on edge," she recalled, until the day Barney came into the office and raised his voice in anger at her in front of everyone in the office for something she had nothing to do with. She went into Barney's private office and confronted him. "First off, I'm not responsible for what you are angry about. Second, even if I was, if you have something to say to me, call me in here and say it, don't do it in front of other people," she said. Barney apologized. "After that there was a different dynamic," Hamel, who worked for him for eight years, said. "He has more respect for people who speak their mind and tell it to him like it is."

Unlike some members who often blur the distinction between personal and official duties, he paid Hamel extra money from his own pocket to manage his financial accounts, pay his personal bills, and maintain his checkbook.

A current staff member described Barney as "intense, a little high strung on occasion" and given to "volcanic eruptions on rare occasions." "Interns and people who don't really know him sometimes take his eruptions personally," this staff member said, adding, "Barney's bite is not really as bad as his growl. You have to be around to appreciate him."

Barney has never tried to shift the blame for an error to the staff publicly. "One of the least attractive characteristics of people in my profession is blaming their staff for mistakes," he has often said.

At a July 1985 subcommittee hearing on HUD's proposal to allow the sale of some public housing units, Barney quoted from a memorandum that raised questions about this policy and cited the former HUD undersecretary Abrams as the author of the memo. A week after the hearing, Barney learned that the memo had been written by HUD staff and not by Abrams. The memo had inadvertently been attached to a copy of a memo written by Abrams that a subcommittee staff member had given to Barney. Barney telephoned Abrams and apologized for mistakenly attributing the memo's authorship to him, never suggesting it was a staff error. He also issued a press advisory publicly apologizing for mistakenly referring to Abrams as the author of the memo and insisted that this press statement be sent not just to the reporters who had attended the hearing but to the entire housing press release list.

That same year, in December, Barney offered an amendment on the House floor to the Superfund bill to create a federal cause of action for persons injured by hazardous substances. Other members had proffered the amendment in prior years without success. The amendment that had been put forth the previous year keyed liability to "the discharge, deposit, injection, dumping, spilling, leaking, storing, treating, or placing of hazardous substances into or on land or water." When Barney's legislative assistant Bill Black met with the lobbyist for an environmental group, the woman suggested adding the word *air* to the amendment, since the amendment already covered toxic waste and pollution on land and in the water. Black saw no reason not to and made the change in the amendment. He then tried without success to explain the additional word to Barney before he offered the amendment.

As soon as Barney proposed the amendment on the floor of the House, John Dingell of Michigan, who sided with the auto industry and opposed the Clean Air Act, asked whether it was the same amendment offered the previous year. Barney, sensing that there was a problem from the tone of Dingell's inquiry, responded that it was substantially the same. Dingell persisted, asking, "Exactly the same?" Barney wasn't prepared and uncharacteristically stopped yielding the floor to Dingell for questions.

After the debate, while Barney was sitting in the House chamber with Black at his side trying to explain the problem, Dingell came over and sat down next to him. "Sorry, John, I didn't have enough time," Barney said, apologizing for not yielding, upon request, to the powerful chairman of the Energy and Commerce Committee. He did not attempt to shift the fault to his young legislative assistant.

13

A Frank That Relishes
the Perfect Job

ON THURSDAY MORNING, January 12, 1984, Senator Paul Tsongas stunned the Massachusetts and Washington political establishment by announcing that he was retiring from the Senate after just one term, for medical reasons. There are five major sports in Massachusetts—Red Sox baseball, Celtics basketball, Patriots football, Bruins hockey, and running for political office, though not necessarily in that order. In many ways, politics in Massachusetts, like rooting for the Red Sox, transcends sports and is followed with almost religious zeal. The newspapers, newscasts, and radio talk shows were immediately inundated with speculation about possible candidates for the open Senate seat. Potential candidates included just about every present and former political officeholder—Lieutenant Governor John Kerry, several members of the Massachusetts congressional delegation, including Barney Frank, former Speaker David Bartley, secretary of state Michael Connolly, and even former representative Michael Harrington.

The night before the public announcement, Thaleia Schlesinger phoned Barney with the news that her brother would be announcing his retirement the next morning. "I felt close enough to Barney to give him a heads up about Paul's retirement," Schlesinger said. She suggested that members of the Tsongas family would likely be supportive if he decided to run for Paul's Senate seat. Barney was sympathetic and said he appreciated the call, but he had no interest in running for the Senate. He had just been through two very grueling House races. "I never gave it another thought," he said.

On the morning of January 12, while driving Barney to an event in Washington, Richard Goldstein, his legislative assistant, asked what he was going to do about the Tsongas Senate seat. "There is only so far a fast-talking, left-handed, Jewish, gay guy from Jersey can push the voters in Massachusetts," Barney responded. "That was the first time Barney told me he was gay," Goldstein said.

That afternoon, Barney called Doris and greeted her with the message, "It's me and I'm not running for the Senate." He could hear her breathe a sigh of relief over the phone. Doris had put two and a half years of her life into Barney's campaigns for Congress and was exhausted. But still she was committed to her brother and was prepared to support whatever decision he made and work tirelessly on his behalf.

Barney considers being in the House of Representatives "a wonderful job." "It's exciting, stimulating, as fulfilling as a job can be," he said. He dislikes hearing colleagues complain about the terrible burdens under which they labor, pointing out that "voting is not heavy lifting." The legendary Henry Clay of Kentucky, who served in both the House and the Senate in the 1800s, said that he preferred the House because it is more vital, more active, and more dynamic. Barney agrees. When asked by a reporter for the *Newton Tribune* about running for Tsongas's Senate seat, Barney replied, "I'm happy where I am. The House is more congenial and open than the Senate and better suited to my temperament, and depending on the issue, I think I can have more impact here. I like this place and I think I'm good at it."

During his first term in the House, Barney had been voted most promising new member. In his second term, however, he came of age, gaining the respect and admiration of his colleagues for the crucial role he played in the debate over revising the nation's immigration laws, a persistently unpopular subject. As a member of the Judiciary Subcommittee on Immigration, Refugees, and International Law, he was intimately involved with immigration reform and became a key member of the coalition that was to rewrite immigration law over the next decade. In a *Wall Street Journal* article published in October 1984, David Rogers describes Barney Frank's new status in the House: "Respect, a precious commodity in a legislative chamber, has little to do with a member's party or philosophy. In subtle, often personal ways, the institution looks beyond first impressions and judges the substance of a member. Reps. [Dan] Lungren [of California] and Frank experienced that rite of passage this year."

Lungren, who had pledged during his 1978 election campaign to get involved in immigration issues in Congress, volunteered for the immigration subcommittee, which, he said, "usually you have to shanghai members to serve on" and which "had not had a stellar record in the past." As he traveled around his district in southern California, Lundgren found that in every group he met with, rich and poor alike, the issue of illegal immigration always came up.

In 1984, many House liberals adopted the hard-line strategy of Hispanic, civil libertarian, and other groups opposed to the immigration reform measure. Barney believes that illegal immigration is a pressing national problem and that some change in the immigration laws is necessary and proper. In his view, when you have a large number of people who are here and cannot legally support themselves, you are inviting desperate behavior. "If it were possible through our law enforcement capacity to remove all of those who are here illegally, then I would be in favor of doing so," he stated.

Barney decided early on to support the basic scheme of giving amnesty to millions of immigrants who entered the country illegally before a certain date in exchange for imposing sanctions and fines against employers who hire undocumented workers in the future. "Employer sanctions and amnesty are indissolubly linked, if not logically then politically. If we do not have the enactment of both in this bill, we have neither," he said. On the immigration subcommittee he was a key player in the drafting of a compromise bill designed to balance the needs of different groups. Hispanic groups supported the amnesty provision but opposed employer sanctions. Conservatives backed employer sanctions but opposed the amnesty provision.

Barney made his mark during the 1984 debate on the immigration bill. He stood up to Judiciary Committee liberals and other traditional allies who raised fears that the legislation would require a national identification card. He called such fears "a non-issue." "We are not talking about anything that has to be carried on your person or in your car or alongside you. We are talking about a method of verifying at the time that you apply for a job that you are legally in this country," he said. "Some people on the left have been wrong in saying this would produce a 'police state.' It's a much more liberal bill than people think. The alternative is to allow continued exploitation of the people who are hired and unfairness for labor."

Barney defused arguments by opponents of the bill about sanctions. "Members have said two things about the sanctions: number 1, that they will not work at all; and number 2, that they will work so well that they will keep not only illegal aliens from being hired, but will keep legal people from being hired. I can understand both arguments being made, but not by the same people," he said.

During the floor debate, Barney introduced an amendment to combat the potential discrimination by employers against noncitizens and workers of Hispanic origin. Under the amendment, a special counsel would be created to handle complaints about discrimination and to see to it that victims have recourse. One of the bill's opponents, Democrat Robert Garcia of New York, the chairman of the Hispanic Caucus, rose to support the Frank amendment on the grounds that the amendment was an admission that the legislation had discriminatory aspects. "If the bill becomes a reality, we will go into plants and factories across America, to make sure that there is no discrimination. If we have to take test case after test case, we will do just that," Garcia told his colleagues.

Barney recycled a line he had used a decade earlier in the state legislature, "When my good friend from New York got up again to help me, I felt like I was on the *Lusitania* and I just got word that the *Titanic* had set sail to rescue me.

I appreciate his support. But enough already before you sink my amendment."
He argued that support for the amendment was not a concession of discrimination. The Frank amendment was adopted by a vote of 404 to 9.

Barney was angered when the House adopted an amendment by Democrat
Leon Panetta of California that gave agriculture a virtually total exemption from
the immigration laws and gave agricultural growers the right at will to bring
large numbers of "guest workers" into the country for up to eleven months.
"There are a lot of these temporary agricultural workers who will spend more
time in America than the average member of Congress," he said. "I have no objection to these people being here. I want to again state I have no Apache blood
whatsoever. I am not here to tell anybody else they cannot come to America.
What I object to is a class of people being brought here, . . . not as citizens, not
as fellow human beings with full rights, but just as that group of domestics that
come and go. Maybe they will not do windows, but they will do everything
else."

Barney considers the term *guest worker* to be one of the great oxymorons of all
time. "Do you have someone say welcome to my house, will you go clean the
bathroom?" he joked. Henry B. Gonzalez of Texas referred to the guest-worker
program as "rent-a-slave." Barney agreed to vote for final passage of the immigration bill only after Republican senator Alan Simpson of Wyoming, the bill's
chief sponsor in the Senate, assured him that the guest-worker provision would
be dropped in the House–Senate conference committee.

Liberals voted overwhelmingly against the immigration bill when it came up
for a vote on the House floor in June 1984. But Barney's support helped win
House passage of the bill by a narrow 5-vote margin, 216 to 211.

During eight days of House–Senate conference committee meetings, Barney
insisted that the final measure include his controversial provision to combat job
discrimination against legal aliens, workers of Hispanic origin, and foreign-look-
ing job applicants and those with foreign accents. Barney told the conference
committee, "Sanctions carry with them at least the potential for discrimination."
The amendment created a mechanism for combating blanket refusals to hire
such people by establishing a special unit in the Justice Department to investigate and prosecute employers for job discrimination against workers because of
their national origin or because they are aliens. It would protect only citizens,
legal aliens, and those to whom the bill would grant such status. It would not
apply to illegal aliens, who are not entitled to work in the United States. The
Frank amendment was not acceptable to the Senate conferees, however, who
believed that the provision went far beyond existing federal antidiscrimination
law and created a new cumbersome bureaucratic unit.

A reporter from *USA Today* asked Barney to predict the immigration bill's
chances without the Frank amendment. Because Barney considered an immi-

gration bill without his antidiscrimination amendment to be dead and buried, he responded to the reporter's question by chanting in Hebrew, "*Yisgadal v'yiskadash sh'me rabbo*," the opening line of the Kaddish, the Jewish prayer for the dead.

Barney called the immigration bill the Rasputin of the 98th Congress—clubbed, shot, and poisoned, the bill refused to die. The House and Senate versions differed markedly, however, and a conference committee was unable to bridge the gap. Finally there was no time remaining to compromise as the legislative clock ran out and the immigration bill died when Congress adjourned for the November election.

From the time he joined the immigration subcommittee in 1981, Barney's heart and mind were focused on finding a strategy to repeal the archaic and offensive provision of the Immigration and Nationality Act that barred gay and lesbian foreigners from entering the United States. The final report of the Select Commission on Immigration and Refugee Policy, issued in March 1981, had recommended a reexamination of all grounds of exclusion.

The 1952 immigration law banned "psychopaths" from entry into the United States. At the time homosexuality was commonly viewed as a form of mental illness. The U.S. Public Health Service represented to Congress that the term *psychopathic personality* would encompass homosexuals and sexual perverts. However, in April 1962, the U.S. Court of Appeals for the Ninth Circuit held this provision to be unconstitutionally vague because homosexuality was not sufficiently encompassed within the term *psychopathic personality*.

The John Kennedy administration then proposed and the Lyndon Johnson administration subsequently endorsed an amendment to the 1952 immigration law that banned those who practiced "sexual deviation" from legal entry into the United States. Surprisingly, no effort was made by any of the liberals in Congress in 1965 to delete that homophobic provision. The amendment simply deleted the word "epilepsy" as grounds for exclusion, on the basis that medical advances have brought the condition under control with medication, and substituted the words "or sexual deviation," and it was enacted without controversy.

Barney was acutely aware of the impact of barring people from entering the United States solely because of their sexual orientation. His friend William Capron, a colleague from his days as a teacher at Harvard University, and his wife, Peg, had a son, Bear, who was gay. Bear had become a Dutch citizen and was barred by this provision from coming to the United States to visit his parents. Barney believed that no valid public cause was served by a law that prevented Bear Capron from visiting his parents.

In 1983, Barney was one of thirty-five cosponsors of a bill introduced by Democrat Julian Dixon of California to repeal the provision in the immigration law that excludes admission to the United States based solely on sexual deviation. In 1984, Barney had recognized that the timing was not right for repealing the ban because Congress and the American public were not ready to do so. In 1985, he took the lead on the immigration subcommittee in rewriting the exclusionary provision of the immigration law in general, and the anti-gay exclusion in particular. His strategy was to take the legitimate bases for excluding people from the United States and embody them in a new section that would replace the existing offensive section. "I would deal with the anti-gay exclusion simply by leaving it out of the redraft. Thus, no separate vote would be taken on whether to repeal this provision, because its abolition would be accomplished by omission," he said.

The congressional leadership and the Ronald Reagan administration and later the George H. W. Bush administration needed all the support they could muster to get the comprehensive immigration bill passed. Barney had the leverage to insist that repeal of the anti-gay exclusion be included as part of the immigration reform package. "I remained sufficiently in tune with majority sentiment in the immigration subcommittee and ultimately in Congress as a whole. I could promise to be a supporter of the final package, so long as I was satisfied by the redraft of the exclusion provision," he explained. "Had I disagreed with the basic outline of the legislation, my leverage would have been negligible. A threat to withhold your support from a bill you are going to oppose in any case does not buy you much." Similarly he would not have gained much leverage by threatening to withhold his support from a bill that was certain to pass.

As Barney wrote in "American Immigration Law: A Case Study in the Effective Use of the Political Process," a chapter in the 2000 book *Creating Change: Sexuality, Public Policy, and Civil Rights*, edited by John D'Emilio, William B. Turner, and Urvashi Vaid:

> If all participants feel equally intensely about all parts of the legislation, bargaining is difficult. In this case I was in an ideal situation because while I was in favor of the overall bill, I cared most of all about the exclusions, and I was prepared to try to defeat the bill if I was not successful in reforming what I considered to be the most outrageous aspect of American immigration law, the anti-gay, anti-free speech, McCarthyite hangover. On this issue, the main priority of the Democratic and Republican leadership was passing the overall bill. My priority was reform of the exclusionary provisions. In the end they accommodated me on the exclusion issue because I was prepared to be a loyal soldier in their battle for the comprehensive legislation.

The Judiciary Committee decided to deal with immigration reform in two separate bills, beginning with the Simpson–Rodino bill, which was passed by Congress in 1986 to address the perceived crisis in illegal immigration. The Democratic leadership on the committee designated Barney as the lead negotiator on exclusions because of his effort to prevent the full set of exclusions from applying to those being given amnesty. He negotiated with the Republicans on the committee led by Hamilton Fish and Dan Lungren. They, however, were not ready to repeal the exclusions. The object was to find a way to prevent the exclusions from interfering in the amnesty provision. The compromise was that a few exclusions were continued, notably those dealing with legitimate public health and safety issues that would, for example, prohibit people with contagious diseases from entering the country. Some of the exclusions were waived in the amnesty, and a third set of exclusions, including the gay exclusion, were made waivable by the commissioner of the Immigration and Naturalization Service.

On June 22, 1988, the Democratic leadership of the Judiciary Committee presented Barney's redraft of the grounds-for-exclusion section in the form of a separate bill. The object was to get a test vote to determine whether the provision would be supported by a majority of the Judiciary Committee. If the vote showed that the provision would have majority support, it would be inserted into the comprehensive immigration reform bill without further controversy. William Dannemeyer of California, the leading gay basher in the House, offered an amendment in the committee to reinsert the homosexuality exclusion, using the "psychopath and sexual deviant" label. The Dannemeyer amendment was defeated by a vote of 10 in favor to 23 opposed. Fish, the senior Republican on the full committee, and Lungren, the senior Republican on the immigration subcommittee, broke with their GOP colleagues and opposed the amendment.

Barney believes that the cooperation that had developed between him and Lungren on behalf of the overall bill had an influence on his vote on the gay and lesbian exclusion. Lungren said he opposed the Dannemeyer amendment mostly because he believed that the exclusion of gays was unnecessary and was the wrong thing to do. But, he added, he probably did it in part because some could construe the amendment and the psychopath and sexual deviant label as "a direct slap at Barney Frank, who I found to be an honorable legislator."

A year or two earlier, the House was considering a hate-crime-reporting bill. Lungren did not support the measure because of concerns about the definition of a hate crime and about the reliability of the underlying data. But when a Republican from Georgia proposed an amendment not to count crimes against people because they are gay as a hate crime, Lungren urged his colleagues to defeat the amendment. He argued that while he did not support the underlying bill, he firmly believed that crimes against people who are gay and lesbian solely because they are gay and lesbian must be included. Lungren managed to get enough votes to defeat that amendment. Afterward, Barney sent him a handwritten note in pencil that said: "I know this didn't seem like a big deal but it was important. Thank you."

Lungren did not run for reelection in 1988 and left Congress. He was appointed by California governor George Deukmejian to be state treasurer in California and serve out the remainder of the term of the late Jesse Unruh. Lungren went through a very nasty confirmation process in California. "Some liberal groups said they were going to 'Bork me,'" he said. Many gay and lesbian organizations in California strongly opposed Lungren's appointment because of his anti-gay voting record in Congress. Barney, however, spoke out on Lungren's behalf, saying that while he didn't agree with him on a lot of things, Lungren is someone who can be trusted, and that they had worked closely together on several issues. Barney took some heat from several liberal groups and the gay and lesbian community in California for undercutting their efforts to stop the Lungren nomination.

The comprehensive immigration reform bill passed by Congress in 1990 and signed into law by President George H. W. Bush was the culmination of Barney's successful effort to repeal the anti-gay provision of immigration law. The House Report on the bill explains that the "sexual deviation" exclusion ground is "not only out of step with current notions of privacy and personal dignity, it is also inconsistent with contemporary psychiatric theories." The report concludes, "In order to make it clear that the United States does not view personal decisions about sexual orientation as a danger to other people in our society, the bill repeals the 'sexual deviation' exclusion ground." Barney's effort resulted in the mirror image of what had occurred twenty-five years earlier when the anti-gay exclusion was tightened by Congress. It was accomplished without controversy and no effort was made to reinsert any of the exclusions

Barney upset many liberals by helping to secure House passage of some bills that were part of President Reagan's legislative agenda. He explained to the *National Journal* in August 1984: "Liberalism is not perfect. There is a tendency for people—both liberals and conservatives—to be inconsistent and rigid. . . . I'm not trying to change liberal principles, but we sometimes differ in our application of them. . . . I reserve the right to determine how my liberal principles are best served, rather than to take inflexible positions."

One such bill was the 1984 Equal Access Act, on which Barney broke ranks with liberals, some civil libertarians, and Jewish groups, such as B'nai B'rith, by supporting the right of student religious groups to have equal access to school facilities after classroom hours. He had opposed the earlier version of the bill that the Reagan administration had proposed, which singled out religious clubs for special protection. It would have permitted religious clubs to meet during the school day and did not prevent outsiders from coming in for the meetings That version was defeated by the House.

The final version of the federal Equal Access Act allows students to use public school facilities during nonschool hours for all extracurricular activities, wheth-

er for a religious meeting or a meeting of the chess club. When a compromise
bill approved by the Senate reached the House floor on July 25, 1984, Barney
was the first lawmaker to speak on its behalf. He considered the equal access
legislation to be significantly different from prayer in the schools. He takes issue
with proponents of school prayer who argue that praying in school is somehow
voluntary or who contend that no one will be offended. "Yeah," he said, "every
nine-year-old kid who wants to pray can get up and pray and all the weird kids
can go in the corner."

Barney believes that the coercive aspect of school prayers led by teachers is
wrong, that it undercuts fundamental freedoms and ought not to be allowed.
But wholly voluntary activities, where outsiders can be prevented from coming
in, as under the 1984 bill, that meet after school and are initiated by the students themselves, whether for religious, political, or philosophical purposes, he
considers legitimate. "If any group is allowed to meet, then all groups, as long
as they don't break the law or the furniture, should be allowed to meet in the
school buildings," he argued.

Barney sees the legislation as a "teenager rights bill." "We ought not to infan-
tilize teenagers," he said. "I do not see any damage that comes to the fabric of
this society because some teenagers might decide to have a meeting of a radical
political group while others might decide to have a meeting of a particular religious society. I think those of us who think teenagers ought to be treated with
some respect for their individuality ought to welcome this bill."

He also differed with fellow liberals by supporting a bill to raise the national speed limit to sixty-five miles per hour. "The first thing I told liberals who
criticized me was that I'll only listen to people on this issue who actually drive
fifty-five miles per hour. That eliminated almost everybody," he said. In 1987,
the House passed the Transportation bill, after Barney, in an effort to build the
largest possible coalition to combat a presidential veto, persuaded a group of
urban eastern Democrats to support the sixty-five-mile-per-hour speed limit for
their western colleagues. President Reagan vetoed the bill as expected, and the
Democratic members of Congress from the West were crucial in the subsequent
vote to override the veto.

In May 1986, Barney broke ranks with many environmental groups and
sharply criticized a decision by the federal Environmental Protection Agency
(EPA) that killed a planned forty-million-dollar shopping mall project in Attleboro in his district because it would have required the filling of thirty-two acres
of wetlands known as Sweedens Swamp. The EPA stated in its decision that
the filling would result in a significant loss of wildlife habitat. Barney took issue with that assessment, saying that there was nothing unique about the land,
"there are no condors" on what he called "a piece of junky land." "There's more
wildlife in my basement," he said. The project's developer had offered to create

new wetlands to offset the loss at Sweedens Swamp and the Army Corps of Engineers had approved a filling permit. Barney stated that it was a mistake for environmentalists to interpret the wetlands-filling law "too strictly" because it "only builds up a counter pressure" that could undo legitimate wetlands protection in the future. When a reporter expressed surprise that a liberal like Barney Frank would side with a developer in a battle with environmental groups, he replied, "If there was the expectation that I was going to be taking orders from any particular group, they're wrong."

In June 1984 Barney was elected national president of Americans for Democratic Action (ADA), the nation's oldest and largest liberal lobbying and advocacy organization. He had been an active member since the mid-1960s. The group was founded in 1947 by such eminent liberals as Eleanor Roosevelt, Hubert Humphrey, John Kenneth Galbraith, Arthur Schlesinger Jr., and Walter Reuther. In the days of Hubert Humphrey, ADA was a major player in national politics.

In April 1971, Allard Lowenstein ran for president of ADA in a hotly contested election against Dolores Mitchell, the chair of the ADA chapter in Massachusetts. Barney ran Lowenstein's successful campaign for the presidency. At the same time, Barney was elected national secretary, becoming the first male national secretary in the group's history. "The women members creditably refused to continue filling this heretofore sexually segregated job," he said. He worked with Lowenstein on youth voter registration and antiwar organizing at ADA.

In the early 1970s, Barney and Lowenstein served together on the board of the ADA. The women's movement was under way and people were becoming sensitive to political correctness. At an ADA board meeting, when the chairwoman sneezed, Barney reacted and instantly blurted out, "God bless you madam co-chair person." "Al used to tell everyone that story because he thought it was the funniest thing he ever heard," his widow, Jenny, recalled.

By the early 1980s, the ADA's membership base had dwindled to a mailing list of about eighty-five thousand and a paid membership of about half that. In early 1984, some ADA officials tried to persuade Barney to become ADA president. Barney asked his friend Amy Isaacs, whom he had known since 1969 when she was an intern at ADA, whether the organization was ready for a gay president. "I wouldn't want to be affiliated with ADA if it wasn't," she replied.

Barney's other concern was that Leon Shull, the ADA's longtime national executive director, had retired and Barney's sister Ann Lewis had applied for the position. She really wanted the job. Barney made it clear that if his becoming president would stand in the way of his sister's becoming executive director, he would back off. At the same time he didn't want to interfere with the selection process for executive director.

When Barney won the election and took on the presidency of ADA he was already sitting on four committees and seven subcommittees and chairing a Government Operations subcommittee. He succeeded Robert Drinan, who had headed the organization since June 1981. Having replaced Drinan in Congress from the Fourth District of Massachusetts, Barney pointed out that he had now followed Father Drinan in two occupations, "but that's it."

Ann Lewis was selected as the group's new national executive director. Barney was quick to point out that he stayed out of the selection process and that his sister got the job strictly on merit.

While a student at Radcliffe College, Ann had married Gerald Lewis, an attorney who shared her attraction to politics. The couple moved to Coral Gables, Florida, and Gerald Lewis ran for the Florida legislature in 1965. Barney went to Florida to be with his sister and brother-in-law on election night to hear the returns come in. At the election night party, Barney met Janet Reno, one of Lewis's law partners. Reno remarked that she found Barney "bright as could be, funny, but abrasive." Lewis won the election and was reelected in 1967. Ann worked on her husband's campaigns and spent the rest of the time at home caring for their three daughters.

After the couple divorced in early 1968, Ann moved back to Massachusetts with her children. She arrived in Boston just after Martin Luther King was murdered. "We were in the midst of the aftermath of the King murder, and Ann helped organize things," Barney said. Mayor White was impressed with Ann and directed Barney to hire her. She worked with Barney as an assistant at City Hall for about a year. Mayor White then promoted her to be his political chief, and she worked in White's campaigns for governor and mayor.

Ann Lewis worked actively in the 1972 presidential campaign, first for Senator Edmund Muskie and then for Senator George McGovern. She left Boston City Hall in the spring of 1975 to work on a commission established by the Massachusetts legislature to investigate what changes would be necessary to bring the state's laws into compliance with the federal Equal Rights Amendment. When Indiana senator Birch Bayh, whose White House bid she was supporting, asked her to serve as his deputy national campaign manager, she accepted the offer and moved to Washington to operate out of Bayh's national campaign headquarters. When Bayh dropped out of the presidential race, Ann stayed in Washington and went to work as administrative assistant to Rep. Stan Lundine of New York and later for Rep. Barbara Mikulski of Maryland. She served for three years as political director of the Democratic National Committee before being selected for the director position at ADA.

At ADA meetings, when Barney didn't know the answer to a question, he would tell people to talk to his sister. Some ADA insiders observed that it was a difficult situation for Barney because he didn't want to interfere with his sister.

In their view, Barney backed away from taking a leadership role in order to give Ann free rein.

Barney and Ann attempted to revive the moribund organization, to increase its clout, and to do a better job of spreading liberal ideology. They wanted to put liberalism back on the political landscape and realized that because ADA for most of its life has been a major player in the Washington political game and not as much in the grass roots, they would have to work throughout the country building membership and holding events in liberal communities. Barney's goals as ADA president were to focus more attention by white liberals on domestic poverty and to repair damage to relations between blacks and Jews caused by the Jesse Jackson presidential campaign and radicals on both sides.

By that time Barney was a popular figure in Congress and in his district. He was a fixture in the Boston television and radio market, and it was hard to pick up a newspaper in Boston without seeing him quoted or referred to.

One morning Barney was in the terminal at Logan Airport in Boston waiting to board a flight to Washington. He was talking to Red Auerbach, the legendary Hall of Fame basketball coach of the Boston Celtics, when they were approached by a boy about fifteen years old. He held out a blank sheet of paper and said, "Can I have your autograph?"

"Sure, son, I'd be happy to sign it for you," Auerbach said.

As Auerbach was reaching into his pocket for a pen, the youngster said, "Who are you, mister? I want Barney Frank's autograph."

Barney leaned over to Auerbach and said, "Red, can I borrow your pen?"

The annual congressional baseball game between Democrats and Republicans is a Washington tradition that dates to the early 1960s. At the 1982 and 1983 congressional baseball games, Barney was part of the broadcast team on C-SPAN, sitting in the booth providing color commentary on the games. In the spring of 1984, he decided he would join his Democratic colleagues and play in the baseball game that summer. His weight was down, his stamina was up, and he was coming off a career season in softball.

The Democrats practiced at seven o'clock most weekday mornings at a field near the Capitol, and Barney regularly attended the practice sessions. He was surprised to find that the skill level on the field was much higher than it appeared from the broadcast booth.

The 1984 congressional classic was played on Wednesday evening, June 20, at Four Mile Run Park in Alexandria, Virginia, the home field of the minor league Alexandria Dukes. The pregame warm-up had the look of a major league all-star game. Most members of Congress wore the uniforms of professional baseball teams from their city or state. Mel Levine of California, the Democrats' starting pitcher, warmed up on the sidelines wearing a Dodgers blue uniform. Silvio

Conte, the manager of the Republican team, wore the uniform of his beloved Boston Red Sox. Ron Dellums of Berkeley was dressed in the green and gold of the Oakland Athletics. Henry Gonzalez, who had played in the game in his younger days and served as first-base coach for the Democrats, wore a Washington Senators uniform. On the sidelines, outfielder Tom Downey of New York, wearing Yankees pin stripes, played catch with shortstop David Bonior of Michigan, who wore the uniform of the Detroit Tigers. Barney wore a Newton High School baseball jersey.

The eight-member Government Operations subcommittee that Barney chaired was well represented in the congressional baseball game. John McKernan had two hits in the game, two walks, two RBIs, and several fielding gems in center field and was named Most Valuable Player. Dan Schaeffer of Colorado, a subcommittee member who had been elected to Congress in a special election in March 1983, following the death of former Apollo astronaut Jack Swigert, was the starting pitcher for the Republicans.

Speaker Tip O'Neill threw out the ceremonial first pitch. The Democrats scored runs in four of the first five innings to lead four to one. The Republicans bounced back with five runs in the bottom of the fifth inning and took the lead.

Barney was not in the starting lineup and as the game progressed it appeared that he might not get to play. But in the bottom half of the sixth inning, Democratic manager Bill Chappell sent him into the game to play right field. Playing right field, as the song "Right Field," written by Willy Welch and popularized by Peter, Paul, and Mary, says, is "easy you know, you can be awkward, you can be slow." Ron Paul of Texas walked to begin the bottom of the sixth inning. The next batter, Phil Crane of Illinois, doubled down the third base line. McKernan then came to bat and hit a line drive past the second baseman into right center field. Barney caught the bouncing ball cleanly on the outfield grass and threw it back to the infield, holding McKernan to a single. That was Barney's only fielding opportunity as the Republicans exploded for seven runs that inning.

In the top of the seventh and final inning, Mike Synar flied out to McKernan in centerfield. After Ron Dellums got a base on balls, pinch-hitter Harry Reid hit a slow roller to first baseman Carl Pursell for the second out. Jim Bates of California walked. That brought Barney up to bat. The Republicans were leading thirteen to four. There were two outs and two runners on base. Dan Schaeffer had pitched the entire game for the Republicans, allowing only four scattered hits. Barney took a few practice swings as he stepped to the plate. He was wearing his glasses as he stood in the batter's box. The left-handed batter looked at Schaeffer on the mound as he started his wind up. The first pitch was a fast ball that appeared to be a bit high but Barney swung at the pitch anyway and missed. It was clear that he was at the plate to be a hitter. He had not put in all that practice time to try to get a base on balls. Schaeffer's second pitch was another fast ball, this time down the middle of the plate. Barney swung and connected. He hit the ball solidly, a hard one-hopper that the pitcher fielded cleanly and threw to first baseman Pursell, several steps ahead of the sprinting Barney Frank. That was the final out of the game. Barney was pleased that he was not a strike-out victim, had managed to hit the ball solidly, and had not embarrassed himself in the game. It was his first, and only, appearance in the annual congressional baseball game.

In September 1984, the *Washington Monthly* did a cover story titled "The Best and Worst of the House of Representatives." Barney was selected one of the six best members of the House, along with John Dingell, Al Gore, Henry Hyde, Henry Waxman, and David Obey. The article noted with respect to Barney Frank and Henry Hyde that "the political arena is filled with men of strong ideas, but there are few who can promote those ideas with an open-mindedness and humor that can take the raw edges off otherwise acrimonious debate." The article also said about Barney: "Frank's old-time liberalism is leavened by a healthy dose of common sense. He was one of three Democrats on the banking committee to support restrictions on aid to victims of mortgage foreclosures so that only those who really need it would get it. If liberals don't 'deal with waste and fraud in a sensible way,' he has argued, 'conservatives will use it as an excuse to destroy the whole program.'" It also noted that Barney has shown himself to have the makings of a tough investigator.

On October 2, 1984, the Human Rights Campaign Fund, a small, embryonic organization and national political action committee established to support gay rights, held its first dinner in Washington. About three hundred people attended the hundred-dollar-a-plate fund-raiser at the Capital Hilton to honor Reps. Barney Frank and Silvio Conte from Massachusetts. Vic Basile, the organization's executive director, said that they chose Barney because he was a champion of gay rights and they wanted to recognize his leadership. They chose Conte, a senior Republican on the Appropriations Committee, because they wanted a Republican and he had been an early supporter of funds for AIDS research. In the early 1980s, when the District of Columbia City Council had repealed its sodomy law and Congress had overruled the District government, Conte had voted against overruling the District government. Conte, however, sent an aide in his place to accept the award, because, according to Basile, "it was too big a leap for Conte to make at the time."

Morris Udall, to whom Barney Frank has often been compared in terms of bigness of spirit and someone he greatly admired, was there to present him with an award for his active role on behalf of federal gay rights legislation. Udall said of Barney's contribution to human rights: "I measure politicians by what they stand for [and] . . . this good man cares about people, the oppressed, and the less fortunate in our society. Someone said not too long ago that America didn't create human rights—human rights created America. That's what Barney Frank is all about."

In the fall of 1984, Barney faced an easy reelection campaign. After his overwhelming victory over Margaret Heckler in 1982, none of the established Republican office holders in the Fourth District was eager to run against him. The GOP nominee, Jim Forte, a 1980 graduate of Boston University, was a political novice, a twenty-six-year-old conservative businessman from Newtonville who was not well known in the district. Forte ran unopposed in the Republican primary.

"It's a long shot, but Barney Frank is not unassailable," Forte said, in announcing his candidacy. The GOP candidate declared that he offered a different approach to the heavy spending and taxation policies that Barney Frank represented. Forte's campaign slogan was "A Frank Alternative." Forte stated that he would also be running against Barney Frank's personality. "Some people tell me [this] is an issue on which I may be vulnerable," Barney remarked.

From time to time, Barney had been lobbied on legislation by former members of Congress who had been voted out of office because they had underestimated their opponents and decided that they had no need to campaign. He was not eager to join their ranks. "You cannot take anything for granted," he maintained. "The one time I'm not concerned about an election will be the last time I'm elected and I love the job." When a local reporter asked whether he was disappointed that he had a Republican challenger in 1984, Barney replied, "If I was really determined to have a political career with no opposition, I'd move to Chile and run for office there."

Barney was highly visible and campaigned actively across the district. A fundamental campaign strategy for incumbent members of Congress is that if you are running against a little-known opponent, avoid your opponent and certainly don't agree to debate him or her. Not Barney. He enjoys debates. It's a sport to him. He has never refused to debate any opponent in any campaign. "I debated Robert Shaffer from Fitchburg in 1980 when I wasn't sure who he was," Barney said. He debated Forte at night on a radio talk show and once at a student assembly at Norton High School, with social studies students determining the debate format and asking the questions.

Barney had retired his campaign debt from the 1982 race against Heckler and was delighted at the prospect of not having to face a serious and well-financed opponent for reelection. He switched from rock 'n' roll to a Broadway musical for his 1984 campaign contribution jingle, set to the tune of "Get Me to the Church on Time" from *My Fair Lady*. The words he wrote reflect his upbeat mood: "I'm going to be reelected, for '84 the path is clear. We'll win all over, except maybe Dover, 'cause you got me out of debt this year. . . . The right wing can't bear me, but they no longer scare me. . . . I won't be nervous or grouchy anymore, 'cause I know that I'll be reelected."

In a poll Barney's campaign conducted among Fourth District voters a month before the 1984 general election, Barney received a 78 percent favorable rating. The *Fall River Herald News*, which had endorsed Margaret Heckler two years earlier, endorsed Barney in an editorial that reads: "Not only is Barney Frank an able and industrious representative of his constituents in the Fourth Congressional District. He is fun to have around. . . . He deserves the victory he seems certain to achieve. Barney is in there fighting for this area's best interests all the time. He is a fighter and a doer, and we are all pleased to have him representing us." The paper also comments that though few people knew Barney when he started campaigning two years earlier, "since then the relatively few people hereabouts who weren't acquainted with Barney Frank have come to know and like him. . . . Barney has appeared at so many functions and dinners in this area in the past two years that it is almost surprising to find how active he has been in Washington where his fellow Congressmen have given him accolades for his effectiveness."

Barney won the general election by a landslide over Forte, receiving 74 percent of the vote, and in the process was able simultaneously to keep his nerves and his appetite in check. Reflecting on the campaign, Barney told the *Providence Journal* on November 7 that the difference between this race and the race against Heckler two years ago was "the difference between the Korean War and a walk on the beach."

After the election, Barney wrote to Walter Mondale, who was beaten decisively by President Reagan, stating how proud he was of their association over the years and complimenting Mondale for running a strong and unwavering campaign that focused on the important issues facing the nation. The former vice president responded with a note expressing his gratitude for Barney's support: "I am hopeful about our party's future because I know it rests in such capable caring hands as yours. When I look back on our campaign, I believe we can all be proud of what we did. We leveled with the American people about our country's future. Our cause was a just one, and I hope you will continue the fight for peace and social justice, which can make this great country even greater." At the bottom of the typewritten letter, Mondale had added a hand-written message: "You stuck with me and I appreciate it. Stay Liberal—we don't have enough of your kind."

Even though he was not a member of the Armed Services or the Appropriations Committee, Barney led the fight in the House against the MX, a weapon that could deliver ten warheads on an intercontinental mission with accuracy.

He considered the MX to be "an ill-conceived and unnecessary weapon, a great waste of money, about $20 billion at best, and more like $30 billion, and a weapon which will be useless if we are lucky, and dangerous if we are not."

On May 16, 1984, during the debate on funding for the MX weapon, Barney dissected the Aspin amendment, offered by Les Aspin of Wisconsin, calling it "the latest figleaf" advanced by supporters of the MX, who were arguing then that the MX was needed because the United States was not having talks with the Russians. Barney mockingly called the amendment a "brilliant scheme for punishing the Russians [by] bringing them to the table" but not necessarily to make them negotiate. Thus, he said, "the table in question may be the breakfast table or the multiplication table or the table of contents, or perhaps the table of elements." He elaborated: "They said if we voted for [the MX] last year, Ronald Reagan would be for arms control. They got some people to believe that. Now they have got a new argument. If we vote for it, the Russians will come to the table."

Barney was on a roll:

Talk about the separation of powers. You know who gets to decide if we build the MX under this? The Russians. . . . If they do not want us to build the MX then they will look very reasonable. April 1 (the most appropriate date in an amendment I have ever seen) will come, and the President will say, we do not build the MX. Then they will wait a month, and then they will get bad again. And then we will have to build it again, and then they will be good. It is like, remember when Harpo Marx of the Marx Brothers was looking in the mirror and trying to anticipate the other guy? They will go like this, and we will go like that. . . . They will turn that pipeline on and off and on and off until, of course, the summer of 1985 because then [Aspin] will have a new rationale for the MX. Then it will be to get the Chinese to behave.

Barney concluded, "If you believe . . . that you need [the MX] because the Russians are by race not negotiators . . . then you vote for it. If you believe, as many of us do, that it is a first-strike weapon if it is useful at all, and that it costs too much money, you vote against it. But please, fig leaf me no fig leaves. Do not try to hide behind this piece of transparency because you are going to get bagged for lewd and lascivious."

When the new session of Congress began in January 1985, the House Democrats voted 121 to 118 by secret ballot at their caucus to oust the frail, eighty-year-old conservative Melvin Price of Illinois as chairman of the Armed Services Committee. Price had been elevated to chairman in 1975 after a group of moderate Democrats had successfully staged a coup and removed the authoritarian and hawkish F. Edward Herbert of Louisiana as chairman. The loss of Price's chairmanship was a sharp blow to the seniority system, according to which the chairman of a committee is the most senior member.

Speaker Tip O'Neill had pleaded unsuccessfully with his Democratic colleagues to give Price one more term as chairman so that he can "leave the House with the same thing he brought here—dignity." Price had promised to give up the chairmanship after two years. The Speaker defended the seniority system, arguing that it protects everyone equally.

Barney, who believed that Price was incompetent and incapable of chairing the committee, responded, "The rewards for diligent service and old age should be respect and maybe a good pension but not a committee chairmanship."

After rejecting Price, the Democratic Caucus passed over the next most senior Democrat, the seventy-four-year-old Charles Bennett of Florida, and reached down the ranks to elect the forty-six-year-old Aspin, who was seventh in committee seniority as chairman of the Armed Services Committee. A former systems analyst in the Pentagon under defense secretary Robert McNamara and an articulate critic of the military, Aspin was well respected by his colleagues for his expertise on defense issues and grasp of technical detail.

Barney and other liberal Democrats provided the votes that put Aspin over the top in his bid for the chairmanship. The liberals had been critical of Aspin for defying the Democratic majority and backing the MX missile system. It was a difficult vote for Barney, one he "had to wrestle with." Barney, however, was misled by Aspin. "I was in New York visiting friends when Aspin phoned and left a message on my answering machine that he would vote against the MX if he became chairman," Barney said. "I'm not very good at operating machines and I somehow erased that message."

Aspin defied the will of the Democratic Caucus and went his own way on the MX and budget cuts at the Pentagon. On March 27, 1985, on the floor of the House, Barney admitted his mistake in voting for Aspin for chairman of the Armed Services Committee in January. That same day, he predicted: "We were told last year we needed [the MX] because we were not having any talks with the Russians and we need it this year because we are having talks with the Russians and if the talks break down, we will be told next year that we need the MX missile because we used to be having talks with the Russians."

With little advance notice, Barney launched an attack on the MX missile program on October 30, 1985, by offering a "very straightforward amendment" to the Defense Department Appropriations bill to cut $1.7 billion out of the budget for building twelve additional MX missiles (ten plus two spares) "that no one thinks we need." "There is no strategic argument whatever for the twelve additional missiles," he said. The House budget had capped the MX missiles at forty, the number that Congress had already committed to. Then the measure went to the Senate, and there the number was raised to fifty. "In conference we did one of our usual compromises," Barney explained. "The House said forty, the other body said fifty, we added forty to fifty, divided by two, and came up with fifty."

Barney sensed that the new atmosphere and concern in Congress about the budget deficit that had given rise to the drastic deficit-reduction legislation initiated by Republican senators Phil Gramm of Texas and Warren Rudman of New Hampshire, mandating across-the-board budget-cutting when Congress cannot do it, could be used to reduce outrageous military spending. He appealed to members who said they wanted to cut the deficit and described his amendment as "a free Gramm–Rudman deficit reduction scorecard vote" because you can save $1.7 billion and "no one is going to tell you that you have damaged our national security." "No one, with the possible exception of Caspar Weinberger, and it would take him some time, thinks it makes any strategic sense to have fifty versus forty," Barney told his colleagues.

The Frank amendment caught supporters of the MX missile program by surprise and it passed by three votes, 211 to 208, with thirty-seven Republicans voting for the measure. "Barney caught us distracted. He caught us being lax," Trent Lott, the Republican whip, said.

That victory was short lived. Two hours and five minutes later, after feverish lobbying by House Republican leaders and a full-court press by the Reagan administration with the message that killing these twelve MX missiles would undercut the president in dealing with Soviet leader Mikhail Gorbachev at the upcoming summit in Geneva, the supporters of the MX were able to force a second vote. Barney stood at the door as members arrived on the floor for the final roll-call vote and handed out flyers that began: "Attention, Deficit-Reducers, Get a head start on meeting your own personal Gramm–Rudman target without injuring national defense." The House reversed itself and restored the funding for the twelve MX missiles by a narrow vote of 214 to 210. "Several people who were with me switched and some of them disappeared," Barney said. He told the *New York Times* that the reversal exposed the "hypocrisy" of many lawmakers who support a balanced budget but refuse to cut arms spending. "There are a couple of hundred fakers when it comes to deficit reduction," he charged.

The next day, on the House floor, Barney spoke out against, and listed the names of, forty-one cosponsors of the Gramm–Rudman deficit reduction measure, "people who tell us how urgent it is to reduce the deficit, who at the same time voted against the president's request to scale down the very expensive Dairy Program subsidy and voted to spend the $1.7 billion for those dubiously necessary MXs."

Barney vigorously opposed the Gramm–Rudman legislation. "We had in the past what was known as Gramm–Latta in 1981. This is the sequel. This is the Gramm–Lateral. It is an effort to get rid of the ball. It is an effort to have Congress avoid making the tough choices," he said. "The Gramm–Rudman proposal probably ought to be called the 'Emasculation Proclamation,' because it is a decision by the [Senate] to divest itself from responsibility for the budget deficits." Speaking on the House floor, he called the Gramm–Rudman bill an "instead of" measure—"something you do that looks easy instead of something that you should do and do not want to do because it is too painful," he explained. "We are going to do this instead of really tackling the defense budget and the agricultural budget and bringing spending under control. We are going to do this instead of putting priorities into the budget. We are going to do this instead of thinking. . . . It is . . . a substitute for political courage, a substitute for thought."

He ridiculed the concept of across-the-board cuts or freezes, calling it "mindless" and "intellectual laziness." He objected to freezes that applied to starved and bloated programs alike and opposed the Gramm–Rudman legislation because it would cut equally medical care desperately needed for elderly ill people, funding for educational assistance to poor children who are not learning well, and honey-bee subsidies.

Perhaps no issue in the 1980s was more revealing of Barney Frank as a person of independent mind and conviction than the contentious battle in the House over whom to seat in the extremely close 1984 election between incumbent Democrat Frank McCloskey and Republican challenger Richard McIntyre in what came to be known as Indiana's "Bloody Eighth" District. McCloskey had led by seventy-two votes after the first count. After corrections were made for some double counting in a Democratic county, McIntyre was ahead by thirty-four votes. State Republican officials quickly certified McIntyre as the winner. However, a recanvass in another county put McCloskey ahead again by seventy-two votes. The House declined to seat either candidate.

For several weeks, Barney was the Democrats' point person in the debate on the House floor about the disputed Indiana election. On March 19, 1985, several GOP members challenged Barney to explain the difference between the election in Indiana and a similarly close election in Idaho, where the House seated the apparent winning candidate. There is genuine doubt about who is the winner in Indiana, he pointed out, whereas no such doubt exists with regard to Idaho. Rep. John Myers from Indiana's Seventh Congressional District argued, however, that the certificate issued by the state of Idaho was clouded because someone in the secretary of state's or the attorney general's office sent a letter to the clerk of the House, after the certificate was issued, stating there was a possibility that twenty-three hundred fraudulent votes might have been cast. "So there was a fraud," Myers said.

"The gentleman does not mean to say there was a fraud. He means that somebody, he is not sure whom, sent the letter suggesting there might be one. That is a little different than saying there was a fraud," Barney responded.

"Well, that is a cloud, a cloud that is not on Indiana," Myers said.

"There is a difference between a fraud and a cloud. Frauds do not have silver linings," Barney remarked.

Barney recognized that there were some genuinely difficult issues about the election in Indiana. The results had been reported by the state of Indiana three different times, and each time they gave a different total. "I do not think you simply decide by two out of three wins it. This is not a basketball playoff. This is an election which we are trying to decide what the intention of the voters was," he said.

Barney argued that the fair thing to do, as the three-member task force established to investigate the election in Indiana and decide whom Congress would seat had proposed, was to allow the neutral and respected General Accounting Office (GAO) to count all the ballots. "We are in a complicated situation where the exercise of judgment is necessary and inevitable and therefore the focus ought to be on the right people to judge that," he said.

Robert Walker was Barney's favorite foil. When Walker contended that the task force ought to throw out all the punch-card ballots that had been placed in unsealed envelopes to ensure that no fraudulent ballots were cast, Barney countered, "I do not think the penalty for not having licked an envelope with sufficient moistness ought to be that an individual loses his or her vote."

During the debate on April 2, Dan Lungren raised the issue of the burden of proof in a recount. "I do not know how you do a recount with the burden of proof," Barney replied. "If you have a recount and people have been told to recount the votes, is the burden of proof like a point spread? I mean, does the burden of proof mean you have to win by 15 or more?"

When House Republicans threatened on April 22 to become confrontational about the contested election in Indiana, Barney countered, "If [confrontational] continues to mean subjecting the American people to the reading of the Federalist Papers at 12:30 at night, . . . that might come under the heading of cruel and unusual punishment if they have to listen." He then commended the Republicans for keeping the House open all night, night after night. "It is probably the first genuine step on behalf of the homeless the Republican Party has taken. Those who don't have air-conditioning probably can get a little bit of relief from the heat here tonight."

After the GAO conducted the recount and judged the Democratic candidate McCloskey the winner by four votes, the task force voted to seat McCloskey. In the end, Barney did not support either the Democratic proposal to seat Mc-Closkey or the Republican measure to seat McIntyre. He voted with the GOP to declare the House seat vacant and hold a new special election. Barney praised the integrity of the task force chairman, Leon Panetta, and did not question the fairness of the recount process, but he believed the vote was too close to call and that the final decision should be made by the voters in a special election. He felt a greater loyalty to democracy at large than to his party. "You couldn't tell who won. Democracy is very important to me. Democracy is as core a value as I have. It seemed to me we were wrong. We were violating democracy," he explained.

A reporter asked Barney how Speaker O'Neill reacted to his vote on the contested election in Indiana. "Tip was mad at me until I explained myself, and then he got furious. Sometimes don't explain," he said.

"Special order" speeches on any subject or issue are delivered by members on the floor of the House at the end of the legislative day, after the House has finished its regular legislative agenda. The speeches are usually delivered to an empty House chamber but are televised to a national audience on C-SPAN.

In the early 1980s, Bob Walker, Newt Gingrich, and other Republican members of a group called the Conservative Opportunity Society were the first to recognize the potential of special orders to tap a growing television audience. The Republicans harvested the rewards of these staged after-hours discussions of issues of their choosing in the House chamber. Many television viewers were unaware that this so-called debate was one-sided and was taking place in a virtually empty House chamber. In 1984, Speaker O'Neill ordered the C-SPAN cameras to show the empty seats.

These televised special orders made Bob Walker a matinee idol to many viewers. As the story goes, in the early 1980s, Republican Jack Kemp of New York, a former professional football quarterback, was walking on a beach in Puerto Rico when a star-struck tourist ran up to him and asked, "You're Jack Kemp, aren't you?" Kemp, flattered at being recognized, said, "Why yes, I am." The tourist then asked, "Do you know Bob Walker personally?"

Following the success of a special order that he had organized with Democrats Byron Dorgan, Pat Schroeder, and Bruce Morrison to focus attention on Attorney General Edwin Meese's legal fees, Barney wrote a memo to Democratic deputy whip Bill Alexander of Arkansas about the need to make special orders a major priority for the Democrats. Although Barney had spoken previously with Alexander and his staff about the need for special orders by the Democrats, he believed it useful to try to write some of it down. "I've always been a believer in the wisdom of a remark James Reston made during a newspaper strike, 'How can I know what I think, if I can't read what I write,'" Barney said.

Barney began the memo, "We are doing well this year, in my judgment, countering the right-wing special-order witch's brew (eye of Newt, tongue of Vin, god-only-knows-what part of Bob Walker)." But, he wrote, "I think we've been a little thin in taking offensives at special order time. Since I joined in objecting to the rule that would have limited special orders, I've felt an obligation to spend more time carrying some share of the load. And I've found that it's not only politically useful, but fun."

He recommended several areas where the Democrats could take the initiative during special orders, such as trade, the Reagan budget, right-wing extremism in the Republican Party, and the Reagan attack on health. He reasoned that if the Democrats succeeded in getting right-wing Republicans to debate them, the Democrats would have the advantage because the topics would be of their choosing and several of them would be present. Barney suggested that Alexander call a meeting of "a few of our people who are good on their feet," including Henry Waxman, who "could do the NIH-health one off the top of his head" and get commitments from them to take on responsibility for regularly doing special orders on topics of our choosing.

On April 2, 1985, the House voted 412 to 1 for a bill to repeal the Internal Revenue Service's contemporaneous record-keeping requirements. A year earlier, in an effort to make the tax code fairer and increase compliance and tax revenue, Congress, as part of the Tax Reform Act of 1984, had enacted a measure requiring that records substantiating use of vehicles for business purposes be contemporaneous with usage. In response, the IRS had issued rules requiring taxpayers to keep detailed contemporaneous daily records showing the date, mileage, and purpose of each trip taken in vehicles for which business-use deductions were claimed. Congressional offices were swamped with phone calls and letters from business interests and angry constituents demanding immediate repeal of this controversial rule.

The bill to retroactively repeal the contemporaneous record-keeping requirement moved swiftly through the House. It was approved by the House Ways and Means Committee that morning and brought to the House floor for a vote that afternoon. During the brief discussion on the House floor before the vote, several members demagogued the contemporaneous record-keeping requirement, with one member stating that "people were being asked to drive with one hand and keep records with the other."

Barney was the sole member of the House to vote against the bill. He explained his vote: "I thought with all the talk about tax reform and tax equity, one person in one chamber ought to vote for it once." He added, "I do think it's a harbinger that with all the passion about tax reform in general there may be few votes for it in particular." Barney's action in voting against the measure prompted Tom Bacon, a columnist for the *Conroe Courier* in Texas, to write: "I'd like to meet this guy and shake his hand, get his autograph, maybe. Whether he was right or wrong on the call doesn't interest me. It's just that I have a visceral admiration for anyone who is willing to buck such a powerful tide, who refuses to collapse under terrific lobbying pressure, who says, in effect, 'Here I am and here I stand, folks, like it or not.'"

Barney is always ready to jump into the fray. One day in May 1985, when he was sitting at his desk eating a salad for lunch, his administrative assistant, Doug Cahn, burst into the room exclaiming, "Barney, you've got to see what is being debated on the House floor. It is unbelievable." Cahn turned on the television set in Barney's inner office and they watched Republican Trent Lott, the minority whip, calling for an immediate investigation of what he referred to as "the case of the missing bullets."

Since 1978, the House had been operating under a rule that all remarks, insertions, and extensions not delivered during debate on the House floor had to be preceded and followed by a bullet symbol in the *Congressional Record* so they would be clearly distinguishable from words that were actually spoken. Lott charged that two weeks earlier, during the debate on the House floor concerning the election of the representative from the Eighth District of Indiana, there were two instances in which the remarks of Democratic members appeared in the *Congressional Record* as if they were delivered during debate, without the required bullet symbols, when in fact not one word of either statement was actually spoken. Moreover, similarly nonspoken remarks by a Republican member that appeared in the *Congressional Record* between those of the two Democrats had the requisite bullets.

Barney watched the television screen as Lott stated, "I do not know whether the case of the missing bullets is a crime of commission or omission. It is curious, though, that the Republican in the middle got a bullet to the head and tail-end of his remarks, while the two flanking Democrats weren't even grazed." "This is going to be fun," Barney said as he dashed off to the House chamber to join in the debate, leaving the half-eaten salad on his desk.

When Barney arrived winded on the House floor, Lott was talking about an incident in 1982 (which came to be known as "Altergate") when a staffer had edited and doctored up a Government Operations committee hearing record in order to portray the exact opposite intent of what Rep. Robert Walker had said, causing embarrassment to Walker.

Barney strode to the microphone to speak on "the great dot inquiry." He said he had just overheard that the subject of dots had become a matter of congressional debate. "I could not resist joining in, because I have not had a chance to debate dots for some time. We used to connect them, and now we are disconnecting them," he said.

Then he took a jab at Walker: "[Trent Lott] did refer to an unfortunate situation where there were some apparent, deliberate altering of the remarks of the gentleman from Pennsylvania, and those of us who have been privileged to hear the remarks of [Walker] certainly do not want to have them altered; we prefer to have them preserved in pristine form."

There were a few House members whom Barney disliked, and Bob Walker was near the top of the list. Walker had been named by *Washingtonian* magazine in its annual "best and worst" issue as the "Biggest Windbag" and "Dreariest" in the House. Barney considered him to be "a pompous ass."

A year earlier, when Speaker O'Neill was asked by reporters about new GOP television ads attacking him, he replied, "I understand the young fellows, the regressives, the John Bircher types, absolutely insisted they run the ads on me." The Speaker named Newt Gingrich, Bob Walker, and Vin Weber and said, "They want to turn back the clock to the days when there were only the rich and the poor in America." The next day, Walker interrupted the legislative business of the House and requested, as a point of personal privilege, an hour to respond to being called a "John Bircher type" by Speaker O'Neill. Walker demanded an apology from the Speaker. Walker's interruption of the business of the House to complain that his feelings were hurt prompted Barney to make a parliamentary inquiry. "Mr. Speaker, is the term 'crybaby' an appropriate phrase to be used in a debate in the House?"

Continuing to address the great dot inquiry, Barney stated that he hoped that no one was suggesting that "there was hanky panky with the dots" or that "there was someone deep in the bowels of the House who is dotting unfairly." "I think the American public has the right to be reassured that no one is playing fast and loose with the dots deliberately, and it was just an administrative error," he asserted.

Lott interrupted and stated that "these are generally referred to as bullets as opposed to dots." Barney responded, "I also believe, I must say, in accuracy in reporting, and I think that while the technical jargon term is 'bullet,' we ought to be clear what we are talking about; it is a little black spot in the *Record*."

Barney remarked that there are two separate issues. The first is did someone fail to follow the rules. "It is not that someone put a dot where they shouldn't have, but someone didn't put a dot where they should've," he explained. The second issue is whether the *Record* should become a verbatim account of what is actually said on the House floor with no opportunity for members to revise their remarks.

Barney challenged Lott, saying that he would vote to do away with the revise-and-extend provision if Lott wanted to make such a proposal. In support of that proposal, Barney argued, "The poor people on our staff will not have to do any more of that work late at night, checking over what was said, cleaning it up for us." Lott did not take Barney up on his offer.

On June 27, 1985, during a debate on whether to inject U.S. combat forces in Nicaragua, a Republican member accused the Democrats of "micromanage-ment." Barney expressed his opposition to the proposed invasion by taking issue with the word "micromanagement." "If a proposal comes forward that you do not like, you do not debate it on the merits, you do not point out what the matter is with it, and you denounce it as micromanagement. It is a substitute for a reasoned argument," he said. "I can understand people talking about micromanagement when we are [examining specific contracts] at the Pentagon. We are talking about war here. We are talking about whether or not we should invade a country and under what circumstances. That would seem to me at least to be mainframe management." Then he asked, "If it is micromanagement when we are talking about the possibility of invading a country and people being killed because it has got three million people, at what population level does a country move out of the micromanagement category?"

He also told the *Brookline Citizen*: "I think we should use military force only when our own security is at risk, and I disagree with those who claim that we are, in fact, at risk because of what happens in Nicaragua. The United States fearing Nicaragua is a little bit like being afraid of Connecticut."

During a House debate on funding for the Nicaraguan Contras, Barney pointed out that the Republicans had lamented, about a month earlier, during a set of passionate special orders, the unfairness of closed rules on controversial issues. Yet the House voted to suspend the one-day waiting period for bringing a bill to the floor so that the resolution dealing with the Contras could be taken up under a closed rule and bypass the committee. "Every single Republican voted for it. When they find it useful, committees can be bypassed, the rules can be closed, the waiting period can be suspended," he said.

Walker interrupted, saying, "We had a [plant closing] bill on the floor yesterday . . . that did all these same things, and you voted for it." Barney took up the challenge and they sparred for a while.

> BARNEY: I never said that I was upset about a closed rule. I am not saying closed rules are bad. I am saying that pretending that you think closed rules are bad is bad. When we had a closed rule yesterday, I voted for it. We have got a closed rule today, I voted for it, but I am not one of those on the other side who says, "Oh, a closed rule, what would James Madison have said? Oh, my God, we bypassed the committee. Thomas Jefferson is turning around in his grave." The fact is the gentleman has found a nonexistent inconsistency. I did not object to closed rules. I did not object to bypassing the committee.

> WALKER: I want to point out that this side did not request a closed rule. We are for open rules. We believe in open rules.

> BARNEY: You said we requested an open rule. You just voted for a closed one. Now, did you make a mistake? Did somebody change the machine? Was it rewired, like the time your dots disappeared. You say you wanted an open rule. . . . When you guys want an open rule, you vote for an open rule, and when you want a closed rule, you vote for a closed rule. It is perfectly reasonable to

proceed in this way, in my judgment, but it also shows that your special order of a month ago meant as much as Tomas Borge (a Sandinista leader notorious for his brutality) saying that the First Amendment is his favorite document.

Barney continued to debate the issue with Rep. Gerald Solomon of New York. "[Mr. Solomon] says that this is a gag rule because he cannot offer an amendment that he would like to. It all depends on whose ox is being gagged." "How much protest did we hear from him when he [put the hammer on other members by saying that you cannot amend our Contra bill]?" Barney asked.

"When the majority and minority are in agreement [as with the aid to the Contra bill] we will then agree to closed rules, but that was not an agreement here today," answered Solomon.

"Apparently, the theory of democracy that the [Republicans] are talking about has a footnote. . . . People should be allowed to speak and the representatives should be allowed their voice, and nobody should be gagged unless both leaderships say it is OK. So [Mr. Solomon] is not opposed to the idea of a gag rule, what he really opposes is a gag rule where he does not have half of the gag in his hands. So we are not talking about whether or not to gag, but who gags, but it is enough to make you gag," Barney responded. He concluded by saying, "The fact is that when it was convenient to the Republican Party they were for a closed rule. . . . Now that it is not convenient, they are against it. Democracy is not a matter of bipartisan convenience. . . . Members cannot simply turn on and off a belief in open rules, in democracy, like a faucet."

In early September 1985, in response to a question posed by a news reporter in his district, Barney frankly and publicly expressed his opinion that Senator Edward Kennedy should not run for president in 1988. Although Barney greatly admired Ted Kennedy and thought he was an outstanding senator and would be a great president, he believed it would be a mistake for him to run because he was too liberal to be elected president. "I would hate to trade a first-rate senator for a defeated presidential candidate," he said. He predicted that if Kennedy ran in 1988 he would likely get the Democratic nomination but would lose to the Republican nominee. He believed that right-wing attacks had taken too heavy a toll on Kennedy for him to have any realistic chance of being elected president, adding, "It's a little unfair, because the perception of him is that he's the embodiment of liberalism and all that the right wing says is wrong with the Democratic Party." Many prominent Democrats and Kennedy loyalists privately shared Barney's fears about a Kennedy candidacy, but none of them had the temerity to go public with those concerns and risk Kennedy's ire.

Barney's public comments that a Ted Kennedy candidacy in 1988 could be a disaster for Democrats were newsworthy because he was a respected liberal member of the Massachusetts congressional delegation, national president of

ADA, and a longtime supporter of Kennedy, for whom he had worked during his short-lived campaign against Jimmy Carter in 1980. Even though he was beholden to Kennedy for his strong support in the past, especially for coming to his defense in the midst of a tough Democratic primary for Congress in 1980, Barney thought that it was important for people to speak up because that way perhaps Kennedy could be deterred from running again.

Kennedy reportedly felt betrayed by Barney and angered by his comments. Barney sent Kennedy a note expressing his regret about how he had handled the matter. In hindsight, Barney recognized that he should have spoken to Kennedy directly as a friend before making his thoughts public. Barney's "Kennedy-can't-win" comments proved to be effective, because later that year Kennedy announced that he would not be a candidate for the Democratic presidential nomination.

On September 26, 1985, the House voted to reject efforts by the Reagan administration, supported by consumer groups, to scale down the farm bill's dairy- and sugar-price supports. Farm Belt legislators asserted during the House debate that the farm economy, which had not been in worse shape since the Great Depression, could not withstand the reductions sought by the administration. A year earlier, Barney had spent several days touring Iowa farms on a trip arranged by Democrat Berkley Bedell to educate urban congressmen. It was an opportunity for him to observe how farm families live and work and to put the "barn" in Barney. (In 1974, the celebrated author John Updike, while teaching at Boston University, lived in Beacon Hill in Ward 5 when Barney was the state representative. Updike, also a talented artist, had once drawn a sketch for Barney that consisted of a big, old-fashioned red barn, a plus sign, a shiny E, and a hot dog on a bun with mustard and other condiments.) Barney renewed his attack on agricultural subsidies. "Now I know our friends would like us all to worry about poor Ma and Pa Kettle, six chickens, a couple cows, [and] a row of lettuce. That is not who gets this [subsidy]." He pointed out that the bill did not target the smaller, vulnerable farmers. "In fact," he said, "it goes the other way. It is anti–means tested. The more you produce, the more you get." He maintained that he was "in favor of helping small needy farmers but not in an inefficient upside-down manner."

"Since we now have enough butter to slather Wyoming into complete slipperiness," he asserted, "let us stop paying the people all this money to produce this butter for which there is no earthly purpose—and no one has suggested a celestial one, although as part of Star Wars we are going to slip and slide off those missiles by greasing something up there." "What we are doing is paying people more money than we have to produce more butter than we need," he told his colleagues.

On October 1, Barney offered an amendment, in keeping with the Reagan administration's position, to phase out the farm subsidy by 5 percent a year. "When you find Barney Frank and Ronald Reagan in agreement," Democrat Dan Glickman of Kansas said, "either they are both crazy or they are both right, and I prefer in this case to believe the former is true." Barney insisted to his colleagues that he was serious about trying to save $5.5 billion and not perpetuating a situation in which larger farmers are paid more money even though the Agriculture Committee set a nonserious tone for the debate "by telling us that we should continue, for instance, to build a fort out of butter in Kansas with federal subsidies." The Frank amendment was soundly defeated by farm state legislators in a vote of 93 to 334.

Barney continued to debate the issue that evening on PBS's *MacNeil/Lehrer Report* with Republican representative Wes Watkins of Oklahoma, who opposed cutting supports during a crisis in farming. Barney dismissed Watkins's argument that the domestic agriculture industry is important to U.S. national security because, he said, we should not be dependent on other countries for our food supply. "The spectacle of our country being starved to death by the Russians is a little bizarre," he said. "We heard last week that the sugar industry is very important to our national security. Presumably, when the Russians invade we are going to put it in their gas tanks as part of our guerrilla warfare." Barney called the national security argument "the last refuge of obscurantism on Capitol Hill." When Watkins snapped back, "You don't understand the technicalities of the farm program," Barney said, "That is the second refuge of obscurantism on Capitol Hill."

On the evening of December 16, 1985, Barney led a revolt on the House floor against a Defense Department conference report that gave the Pentagon more money than it could reasonably spend to the detriment of virtually every other element in society. The revolt ended in House rejection of the conference report.

The columnist Mary McGrory described Barney's successful parliamentary attack on outrageous military spending, noting that "when that same catch-all appropriations bill returned to the House, an extra $1.3 billion had been trimmed from military programs and a military procurement reform measure had been added."

On September 11, 1986, two months before the congressional elections, the House, seeking to capitalize on a politically popular issue, passed by an overwhelming 392-to-16 vote a six-billion-dollar omnibus drug bill to combat narcotics trafficking and discourage the use of illegal drugs. The bill was put together in six weeks and rushed through the House in two days. It provided for stepped-up enforcement, education, and international eradication efforts. It also authorized the death penalty for drug-related murders and bestowed on the military the authority and responsibility to seal U.S. borders against drug trafficking and to pursue and arrest drug smugglers in U.S. territory.

Members outdid each other in attacking drug traffickers and showing how tough they were on the issue. Every amendment to stiffen penalties for drug crimes or to add monies to drug-abuse education and treatment programs was passed. Colorado Democrat Pat Schroeder referred to it as "political piling on before the election." Barney called it "a bidding war" to demonstrate opposition to drugs and said the amendments were the "legislative equivalent of a tantrum." He was one of only sixteen House members who, in the words of the *Washington Post*, "had the guts to vote against the final bill." In voting no, Barney commented, "I'm afraid this bill is the legislative equivalent of crack. It yields a short-term high, but does long-term damage to the system and it's expensive to boot."

Two years earlier, Barney had voted against having the U.S. Navy do drug enforcement. "I want to be there the first time a Trident is fired across the bow of a cabin cruiser as a warning shot. I am not sure that is the best use of the navy," he said.

In 1986, in lieu of his biannual appeal for campaign contributions, Barney began his letter to contributors: "I don't say as many things that you're not supposed to say as I used to, but I still think it is a good idea for politicians to talk like normal human beings part of the time, so here goes: it is unlikely that I will be defeated for reelection this year or in the foreseeable future. . . . This time, I am writing not to ask for anything, but simply to report on my congressional activities, which your efforts have helped make possible."

Barney was challenged in the September 1986 Democratic primary by William Rosa, a candidate affiliated with Lyndon LaRouche, the ultra-conservative perennial presidential candidate. He debated Rosa several times before the primary. In late August, during a two-hour radio debate in which the candidates responded to listeners' questions, Barney tried to focus on issues such as reducing the federal deficit and maintaining social services in the light of President Reagan's budget cuts. Rosa, however, attacked U.S. attorney William Weld and argued that Weld should be executed for drug trafficking, and he accused the Bank of Boston of laundering drug money. "You're not listening to the *Twilight Zone*," Barney assured the radio audience. He received 90 percent of the vote in the Democratic primary against Rosa.

In the general election that year, Barney was opposed by Thomas DeVisscher, who had gone to court to legally change his name to Jesus Christ. Barney's pal Joe Moakley kidded him, "You're running against Jesus Christ. Bet there will be sharp issues in that campaign." Barney won the election with 89 percent of the vote against the token GOP opponent, and for the first time ever carried the town of Dover with 56 percent of the vote. Asked by a reporter how his GOP opponent, who had spent just over a thousand dollars in the campaign, managed to get 11 percent of the vote, Barney explained, "Some people voted for him because they thought he was Jesus Christ and others voted for him because I wasn't."

Barney is not an easy person for reporters to interview. He has a short attention span, little patience, and can be abrasive and intimidating. Sally Quinn, who interviewed Barney for the Style section of the *Washington Post*, wrote: "He loves sparring with reporters and takes great satisfaction in insulting them in interviews, almost daring them not to like him." If a reporter repeats a question, Barney is likely to say, "You already asked me that. If you want to ask it again, ask somebody else."

Barney's maxim is "I would rather be rude than bored." In April 1989, a representative from the Columbia University Oral History Project interviewed Barney about the life of Allard Lowenstein. The interviewer began by noting that he was only halfway through reading the Lowenstein papers and was up to 1965, when Barney interrupted him. "You're going to think I'm rude and I don't care. Don't tell me what I don't need to know—it takes up a lot of my time. Ask me questions and I'll answer them."

When Hanna Rosin, a reporter for the *Washington Post*, interviewed Barney in March 2004 for an article about the wave of same-sex marriages in San Francisco and asked whether he had any personal, as opposed to strategic, reaction to the weddings, Barney responded, "What the hell is wrong with you?"

Lesley Stahl interviewed him in December 2008 for a profile on *60 Minutes*. Referring to a committee hearing on the automobile industry rescue bill in which the heads of the three big automobile makers testified, she said, "There is a theory out there that you, the congressman, had this public spanking of these guys in order to cover yourselves—" Barney interrupted, "That is the kind of argument that people who do not have any idea what they are talking about like to make." "Are you telling me I do not know what I am talking about?" Stahl asked. "By making that argument, yes," Barney replied. "Ouch!" Stahl said.

Although Barney is demanding and can be intimidating and often testy, generally staff enjoy working for him. A good gauge of a lawmaker's personality is staff turnover. Barbara Mikulski and Arlen Specter, who have reputations for being difficult to work for, tend to have a brisk turnover of staff. It was reported in the *Philadelphia Inquirer* in 1984 that a secretary for Senator Specter left him a resignation note that said, "Life is too precious to spend another minute of it with you." Stories abound of senators and representative berating staff over petty matters. There is the tale of Tom Lukens, a Democrat from Ohio, who in the early 1980s scolded a staffer for not being able to sing the proposed official song for the merchant marines that was coming up for a vote on the House floor. There is the tale of Carroll Hubbard, a Democrat from Kentucky, who berated his receptionist for answering the phone with "Good morning" at about one minute past noon.

Barney, in contrast, has had relatively low staff turnover. He has had only three administrative assistants or chiefs of staff in his Washington office in twenty-eight years in the House (and one of them, Doug Cahn, left Barney's employ in 1991 only because his wife had been offered her "dream job" in the Boston area) and only two personal secretaries or executive assistants during that time. Dottie Reichard has been the director of his Newton district office since he was first elected to Congress in 1980. He is good to his staff. "His model for that was Tip O'Neill who had a longtime loyal staff," a former House member said.

"I know some people who work for House members and Senators who don't have a life of their own. They are on constant call," Reichard said. "Barney respects our personal life. If he is going to a weekend meeting, he doesn't expect the staff to be there." Many House members feel naked going to an event without a staff entourage, but not Barney. "He doesn't have this attitude that staff need to be with him all the time," Peter Kovar, who heads his Washington office, said. "If the House is going to be in session into the late evening, and it is not to debate a bill of Barney's, we don't have to stay late just because he's there." Nor does his staff have to spend time preparing floor speeches, drafting opening statements, or writing questions for him at committee hearings. In many other offices the legislative staff often prepares voluminous briefing materials in three-inch-thick binders for the member. Barney doesn't need that. In Barney's office there is not a lot of wasted effort.

According to Reichard, the key is learning Barney's style, anticipating what he wants, and trying to be one step ahead of him. "Barney sets the stage. He is demanding. The staff sees how honest, how hardworking Barney is. Sure, he can be difficult at times, but anyone who comes to work for Barney needs to believe in his ideas and philosophies," she said. Despite all Barney demands from his staff, he insists that everyone call him Barney rather than Congressman Frank. "He never presents himself as better than others," Kovar said.

One of Barney's pet peeves in Congress is the 150-year-old House rule that forbids members from making direct reference to the Senate of the United States during a debate in the House. This archaic rule, written in 1797 by Thomas Jefferson, who had served as vice president of the United States and presiding officer in the Senate from 1797 to 1801, as part of Jefferson's Manual, was adopted by the House in 1837. Under the rule it was a "breach of order" for any member of the House to take any notice during debate of what is said or what is debated in "the other body." The rule states: "The opinion of each House should be left to its own independence, not to be influenced by the proceedings of the other." Jefferson's rule was premised on the belief that references to actions taken by the other body infringed on the necessary degree of independence between the two Houses to separately consider and vote on matters.

Barney believes that senators and representatives should be able to talk about each other and stop the pretense that "each is off on some other planet some- where uninfluenced by and uninfluenceable by the other." He believes that Jef- ferson's premise is spurious, especially in the modern age of television when the proceedings in the House and Senate are televised on C-SPAN. "Barney was always testing the limits on references to the Senate, knowing that he was going to be gaveled down," Charles Johnson, former House parliamentarian, said.

In 1986, during a debate on the House floor, Barney tried to explain to his colleagues that a housing bill that had been passed by the House had been pigeonholed by a Senate committee. "Yes, we passed it, but something has to happen, someplace else," he said. When that effort drew only blank stares from his colleagues, he started singing, "Somewhere over the Rotunda . . ." Barney explained to David Broder of the *Washington Post*: "It was ridiculous. We were the only people in the world who were not allowed to tell the truth about the United States Senate, that it had scuttled the housing bill."

On January 6, 1987, the opening day of the 100th Congress, the House voted to amend its rules to permit members to refer to the Senate of the United States. Barney was the catalyst behind the rules change. He had persuaded the Demo- cratic majority to change the rules to allow impersonal references to the Sen- ate, such as votes in the Senate or quotations from Senate proceedings, to help elucidate legislative history. "He was kind of skirting around the edge, taking the least offensive references to the Senate and making them in order. He knew that the House speaker then was not going to buy into a more expansive rules change on this subject," Johnson, the parliamentarian, said.

14

Accompanying Yelena Bonner Back to the USSR

ON SEPTEMBER 5, 1985, Barney led a group of half a dozen members of Congress to the Soviet Embassy in Washington to deliver a letter to Soviet officials concerning the plight of Andrei Sakharov and his wife, Yelena Bonner. Sakharov, a distinguished physicist who had helped develop the Soviet hydrogen bomb, a 1975 Nobel Peace Prize laureate, and an outspoken dissident and victim of Soviet persecution, had worked courageously, together with his wife, for basic human rights in the Soviet Union. In 1980, after he criticized the Soviet invasion of Afghanistan, Sakharov was banished without the benefit of a trial to internal exile in the remote city of Gorky, about 250 miles from Moscow. Bonner was exiled to Gorky in 1984 following her conviction on charges of slander against the state for distributing anti-Soviet propaganda. On several occasions, Sakharov had gone on hunger strikes to focus attention on the urgent need for his wife to receive medical care in the West.

Officials at the Soviet Embassy refused to accept the letter and to answer questions about whether Sakharov and Bonner were alive or dead. Barney later told reporters that before leaving, the members of the congressional delegation "made a very strong appeal" that the issue of human rights be addressed and improved and that failure in that regard would create "a very bad environment" for the upcoming summit talks.

After the passage of resolutions by the House and the Senate and demonstrations of solidarity with the Sakharov family in Washington and elsewhere, President Ronald Reagan felt compelled to put the plight of Sakharov and Bonner on the agenda for the November summit talks with the Soviet Union. Shortly before the summit, however, in the face of pressure from the West, the Soviets, in a historic act, gave permission for Yelena Bonner to go to the United States to receive medical treatment. As a condition for leaving the Soviet Union, Bonner had to agree not to talk to the press.

That November, the sixty-two-year-old Bonner came to the United States for eye treatment and heart surgery. In January, she underwent quadruple heart-bypass surgery at Massachusetts General Hospital in Boston and then stayed in the Boston area with her family, including her married son, Alexei, her married stepdaughter, Tatiana, her grandchildren, and her mother. Bonner recuperated at the home of Tatiana and her husband, Efrem Yankelevich, who lived in Newton in Barney's congressional district.

Barney had played an active role in condemning the treatment Sakharov and his wife had received from Soviet authorities and in pressuring the Soviet Union to allow Bonner to visit the United States for medical treatment. He met with Bonner twice during her stay in the United States and spoke with her on the telephone from time to time. Barney arranged for a "Members Only" meeting on March 19 where Bonner could discuss her husband's situation with House and Senate members. He also wrote a letter to the Soviet Union, signed by nearly every member of Congress, expressing support for Sakharov's dissident efforts.

In May, when it was time for Bonner to return to the Soviet Union to rejoin her husband in exile in Gorky, Yankelevich asked Barney, at his mother-in-law's request and on behalf of her family, to accompany her back to Moscow. Barney agreed without hesitation. The world was still in the midst of the cold war and Barney understood that Bonner was afraid to go back alone, fearing that she might disappear after her return. The other purpose in accompanying Bonner was to demonstrate the American people's concern for her welfare and that of her husband.

The family's fear was grounded in the fact that in 1986 Mikhail Gorbachev was still evolving in his role as Soviet leader and there was no indication that under his leadership there would be any thawing in the relationship between the Soviet Union and the West. At the time, Gorbachev was considered the logical successor to Nikita Khrushchev and Leonid Brezhnev. Also, Gorbachev probably assumed Bonner would stay in the United States. "She was an old woman and had children and grandchildren here," Barney said. Neither the family nor the U.S. government had any way to know how the Soviets would respond to her returning, probably unexpectedly, to join her husband.

Barney learned from Speaker Tip O'Neill that travel funds were available through a discretionary fund but that the fund was bipartisan and he'd have to find a Republican to go with him. Barney asked Dan Lungren, with whom he served on the immigration subcommittee and whose company he knew he would enjoy, to join him in accompanying Bonner back to Moscow.

Lungren was flattered by the invitation. "I think Barney knew about the work I had done on Soviet Jewry," Lungren said. "I was one of those active, in concert with the Reagan administration, in efforts to put pressure on the government of the Soviet Union to treat the dissidents in a reasonable fashion." Lungren had

"adopted" a Jewish family in the Soviet Union, spoken out on the family's behalf on the House floor, and written letters to the Soviet embassy urging them
to allow the family to emigrate to Israel. Lungren's participation would help
send a message to the Soviet Union that the support in the U.S. Congress for
Bonner and her husband was bipartisan.

A few days later, Speaker O'Neill phoned Barney and told him the U.S. ambassador to the Soviet Union had called him and expressed a strong view that
it was not a good idea for the congressmen to travel with Bonner to Moscow.
O'Neill asked Barney to talk with the ambassador and he agreed to do so. But
first he spoke again with Bonner's family, and they affirmed unequivocally that
she wanted Barney to travel with her.

The ambassador phoned Barney and repeated what he had said to O'Neill
in an effort to discourage Barney from making the trip to the Soviet Union.
Barney replied, "Mr. Ambassador, I would defer to you ordinarily. I do not
claim to know the situation that well. So I am not going to say that my opinion
outranks yours but hers does. She wants me to go and her children want me to
go. So I am going."

"The Speaker told me that I would not be able to dissuade you from going.
It is fine if you want to go," the ambassador replied.

The two congressmen received visas on short notice to accompany Bonner
as far as Moscow. They did not seek a visa to go with her all the way to Gorky,
a city that is closed to foreigners, because that action might be considered too
provocative.

"Frankly, it's not my idea of a great weekend," Barney told the press before
the trip. "But Yelena Bonner asked me and I can't think of anything I can deny
her." He added, "Members of Congress don't usually provide escort services. It
proves how important we think the whole human rights question is in the Soviet Union." Because of the timing of the trip, Barney would miss his twenty-fifth
class reunion at Harvard, but he was willing to make that sacrifice to provide
reassurance to Bonner.

Bonner traveled ahead to Europe with her son and stepdaughter, visiting
Paris, London, and Rome, and meeting with French president François Mitter-
rand, British prime minister Margaret Thatcher, Italian president Benito Craxi,
and other European officials to seek their help in gaining her husband's freedom. She was scheduled to fly from Milan to Moscow on an early morning Ali-
talia flight on Monday, June 2. The two congressmen met in New York, where
they held a joint press conference, and flew to Italy that weekend to join Bonner
for her return to Moscow.

Recognizing that Barney would have a lot of downtime on the long flights,
I gave him a subcommittee report I had drafted to review on the plane. The

report was titled "The Administration Strikes Back: Retaliation against Loretta Cornelius and William Hunt for Testifying Truthfully before Congress." The report found that the Reagan administration had fired two OPM employees, the former deputy director and former associate director of administration, after they had told the Senate Governmental Affairs Committee, during Donald Devine's reconfirmation hearings as OPM director, that they were unaware that Devine had delegated authority to himself to continue running the agency after his term ended and he stepped down as director to await reconfirmation, and that Devine had tried to cover it up.

When Barney and Lungren met Bonner, at the airport in Milan, they found her hugging her son. Barney was moved by the scene. "This woman had no reason to think she would ever see her children and grandchildren again. This incredibly courageous woman was leaving her family, perhaps forever, to share the fate of her husband," he said.

When they boarded the plane to Moscow Barney and Lungren joked about which of the other passengers might be KGB agents. There was only a handful of passengers—Richard Sobol, who was there to take photographs for *Time*, Robert Arsenault, a friend of the Bonner family and former aide to Paul Tsongas, a few students, and some other men whom Barney described as "Italian, Russian, and American CIA types."

When the flight arrived at Moscow's Sheremetyevo Airport, the passengers were directed to depart the plane but to leave all their belongings on board for inspection. KBG agents spent more than half an hour thoroughly searching Bonner's possessions. They also spent considerable time going through Barney's small bag, examining his papers, including the subcommittee report. One of the agents later told Barney, "That was a good report. You cannot trust the Reagan administration." When Barney returned to Washington, I asked him whether the draft report was okay. "The Soviet KGB agent liked it," he said.

"We decided during the flight that one of us would be in front of Mrs. Bonner and the other behind her," Lungren said. "Our thought was that if the Soviets did something untoward, if they used physical action against her, in a sense they would have to go through us to her, not that we could physically stop them, but we would be witnesses to whatever occurred." "We were not James Bond and we were not going to fight anyone," Barney said.

The State Department had told the escorts nothing about what they should expect, and so they were nervous and anxious when the plane landed. When Bonner got off the plane, Barney went ahead of her and Lungren followed behind, the two men serving in effect as Bonner's bodyguards. They all went through passport control and a customs check at the airport without trouble or incident.

When they entered the airport terminal, they encountered, to their surprise, a large crowd of diplomats, western journalists, and Soviet friends and well-wishers all pushing and shoving in an effort to greet and welcome Bonner. Barney described the scene: "It was very moving. All of the NATO ambassadors were there to greet her." Bonner was allowed to talk to reporters at an impromptu airport press conference. When asked how she felt, Bonner replied, "It's complicated. I was staying with my family there, but my husband was here. If I didn't have a husband here, I wouldn't have come back." She did not respond to a reporter's question about whether her campaign in the West to free her husband from internal exile would help their plight. "Obviously, the Soviet government made a decision that they weren't going to make an international incident out of this," Lungren said.

The U.S. embassy had a black sedan and a driver waiting for them. "The people greeting Yelena Bonner so pressed around us that literally we had trouble getting into the car," Lungren said. "It seemed like people's hands and faces were on the car as we drove off."

As they left from the airport on the big boulevard to the city of Moscow, the two congressmen observed to Bonner that the clothing the people were wearing was not as drab as what they had seen in old photos and that the high-rise buildings that flanked the boulevard looked in better shape than they expected. "Wait until you get close," Bonner said.

The driver took the group to Bonner's Moscow apartment and parked the car by the curb in front of the building. A lone tree stood in front of it surrounded by little stubbles of grass. Lungren started to get out of the car and step on the grass, but Bonner stopped him, saying, "No, no. Don't do that. We've never had grass grow here before."

She had not been in her apartment for several years. The group walked into the apartment building and entered an enclosed, nondescript foyer. Bonner glanced around and with a look of amazement exclaimed that the foyer had been painted. "It has never been painted before," she said.

They went upstairs. Bonner had a key and opened the door to her apartment. "We went into her apartment, which had also been painted. She was very proud of her apartment. She was home. It was a magical moment for her," Barney said. Bonner was pleasantly surprised to find that there were no KGB agents at her apartment and soon learned that friends were allowed to visit her there. "What happened was that Yelena Bonner was allowed to be, for at least a day in the Soviet Union, a normal human being with the rights a normal human being would like to have. We are pleased that that happened." Barney said. "Despite what [Soviet officials] say, they pay attention to what the rest of the world thinks of them." The two congressmen left Bonner in her apartment, where she was going to stay for a few days before taking the train to Gorky to rejoin her husband.

From the apartment, Barney and Lundgren were driven to the U.S. Embassy, where they were ushered into a secure room to speak with embassy officials. Barney half expected to find a Cone of Silence like the one popularized in Mel Brooks's spy-spoof television series *Get Smart*. Instead, the two lawmakers were told to "assume that everything you say outside this room is going to be heard" and that if you have something to say "wait until you are outside in the open."

After the meeting at the U.S. Embassy they walked to a small car, where an embassy driver was waiting to take them to visit a group of Soviet Jews who had been refused the right to emigrate. "The guy started driving like a bat out of hell," Lungren said. The driver said something to the effect that the Americans know the Soviets are watching and following us but we are not going to make it easy for them. After about ten minutes, the driver stopped the car, jumped out, went to a pay telephone, and made a quick, confirming call to the refuseniks. The driver hung up the phone, jumped back into the car, and said, "They might have heard that or they might not, but we're not going to make it easy for them." They drove round and round until they finally arrived at what Lungren described as a tall, ugly building.

The driver parked the car and they entered the building. The dingy entrance hall was lit by a single bulb. They rode up the elevator a few floors and entered another dark, empty hallway lit by a small, dusty bulb. The driver knocked on a door. The door opened to a room full of bright lights and a lively gathering of people who were overjoyed to see the two members of the U.S. Congress. "What I most remember," Lungren said, "was people asking us to intercede with their government to allow them or members of their family to leave the Soviet Union, not for good, but to get adequate medical attention and then return. It was a sad situation, people feeling that two relatively junior congressmen from the United States can intercede with their government to allow them the opportunity to obtain medical care."

The two lawmakers spent the night at a mid-level hotel where foreign tourists were allowed to stay. They had to pass a guard who sat at a desk by the elevator on their floor. "You had that feeling that no matter what you said or did, someone was listening or watching," Lungren said. Perhaps, the two men joked to each other, if they just spoke loud enough that they needed new towels to replace the ones full of holes that had been provided, they might be supplied without having to ask.

Barney and Lungren left early the next morning, after spending less than a day in Moscow, because Barney had to be back in Washington on Wednesday for the debate on a housing bill. On the way to the airport they asked the driver to stop briefly in the huge Red Square. It was too early in the morning for the buildings to be open, but they enjoyed looking at the architecture.

"As the wheels of the plane lifted off the ground of the Moscow airport, you felt like some sort of weight of oppression had been lifted from your shoulders. We really got that feeling," Lungren recalled.

In December 1986, Gorbachev allowed Sakharov and Bonner to leave Gorky and return to Moscow. Sakharov died three years later. Bonner, now eighty-six, remains an outspoken advocate of democracy in the former Soviet Union. She often returns to the United States to visit her two children and her grand-children.

15

Coming Out

At a Holocaust Memorial Dedication in New Bedford, Massachusetts, in May 1998, Barney told the religiously and ethnically diverse audience that as a twenty-year-old he had had an interest in public service but because of the pervasiveness of anti-Semitism in the United States at the time, it seemed to him unlikely that he would ever have the opportunity that he did have. "The fact that I could run for office and be held accountable for my own individual faults but not for some group problem—I have enough individual faults to handle it—I am a beneficiary, in my own life and in my own ability to do what I hoped to do, of the diminution of prejudice," he said.

When Barney was elected to Congress in 1980 he became the second Jewish congressman from Massachusetts. The first, Leopold Morse, a clothing merchant from Boston, served five terms in the House of Representatives, from 1877 to 1885 and from 1887 to 1889. At that time Morse was the only Jewish member in the Congress. To this day, Leopold Morse and Barney Frank are the commonwealth's only two Jewish congressmen ever to serve. George Fingold, state attorney general from 1953 to 1958, is the only Jewish statewide officeholder in Massachusetts history.

Today, being Jewish is no longer a factor in politics. But it can fuel Barney's sense of humor. Watching Democrats Samuel Gejdenson of Connecticut and Norm Sisisky of Virginia, both of whom are Jewish, on the House floor one day debating the best location for a submarine repair facility, with each member touting his own district, Barney commented, "The House is watching a fascinating spectacle—two Jews arguing about pork."

On the evening of March 5, 1984, Republican representatives started an all-night special order of speeches about school prayer on the floor of the House of Representatives. During this school-prayer marathon, Barney found himself in the Speaker's chair serving as the presiding officer. Speaker Tip O'Neill had no desire to stay up all night, and so he gave younger Democratic members "the great honor of presiding over the House at six o'clock in the morning." "It was an honor if you had not read *Tom Sawyer* and you can paint my fence—how'd you like to preside over the House of Representatives?" Barney said. His shift in the Speaker's chair began shortly after dawn.

One of the speakers, Marjorie Holt, a six-term Republican from Anne Arundel County, Maryland, who was a Presbyterian and a strong supporter of prayer in public schools, remarked that during the twenty years since prayer had been outlawed in public school, "there has been a deterioration of the standards that we have set in this country for ourselves." She attributed the loss of standards to "our stressing the secular side of our education and not really emphasizing that this is a Christian nation, in God we trust, and that we are built on that premise."

Barney took exception to her final point and, when a reporter asked him about Holt's reference to the United States as "a Christian nation," he said, "If this is a Christian nation, how come some poor Jew has to get up at five-thirty in the morning to preside over the House of Representatives?"

The next day, Holt expressed regret on the House floor for referring to the United States as "a Christian nation." She said that she was sorry for using "a narrow and exclusionary term which does not represent my true feelings." "I was thinking of the religious heritage of our country and the Judeo-Christian history that is the foundation of our respect for the rights of the individual," she explained. "My Christian faith does not cause me to believe that my religion should be given favored status in public policy."

Holt apologized to Barney personally, adding, "I meant to say Judeo-Christian nation." "Marjorie," Barney responded, "I've never met a Judeo-Christian. What do they look like? What kind of card do you send them in December?"

Barney objected to the Moral Majority and others saying that the United States is a Christian nation. "It is not a Christian nation. It is not in the Constitution. It is not in our laws. The notion that this is a Christian nation makes [Jewish people] second-class citizens. I am not a guest in someone else's country. I am here as a Jewish American citizen in a land of equality," he declared. "I have no objection to Christians being more Christian. I object to them making America more Christian."

While Barney has never hidden that he is Jewish ("I outed myself with a bar mitzvah," he once said), the decision to reveal publicly his sexuality was a long time evolving. In 1979, he came out to a few close friends. In early 1980, before running for Congress, he told his siblings. When he got to Congress in January 1981, he was tempted to come out publicly but decided to keep the matter private for fear of jeopardizing his political career.

After his reelection victory over Margaret Heckler in November 1982, Barney told his senior staff. He spoke first with Dottie Reichard. "We were in the process of juggling staff around and I went into his office to ask him some questions," she recalled. As she was leaving his office, Barney called her back. Relieved that she had not been called back to be handed a pink slip, Reichard responded, "Oh, that's fine. Thank you for telling me. I am sure that was difficult for you to do."

Doug Cahn was equally unconcerned though somewhat taken aback when Barney told him. Barney offered him the job of administrative assistant, which he eagerly accepted. Then Barney said, "Doug, there is something you should know about me. I am gay." Cahn remembers a pause that seemed to him "like an eternity." Finally, he replied, "I'm glad you said it and it doesn't make any difference."

With his seat in Congress relatively safe and secure, Barney started telling friends. In 1984, he told Kevin White, who seemed surprised. After almost every weekend that Barney was home in the district, he would return to Washington and report to Cahn everyone he had come out to. "He wanted people to know so that he could be himself," his assistant Patty Hamel said. Barney flirted with the idea of coming out publicly but changed his mind.

By 1984, Barney was living, in his words, "kind of half-in and half-out of the closet." Many of his colleagues knew or suspected that he was gay. Barney recalled the subtle way his colleague and friend Joe Moakley let him know that he knew. "We were talking about someone who was gay and Joe said, 'Hey, not everybody likes vanilla. That's why Howard Johnson has 28 flavors.' It was his gentle way of saying, 'Hey, don't worry about it,'" Barney recalled. His sexual orientation was well known, however, among gays in Washington. He often went to gay clubs, bars, and gyms in Dupont Circle and elsewhere in town.

"It is not uncommon for gay men who come out later in life to have a delayed adolescence because you are not allowed to have adolescence when everyone else is having one. Society doesn't want to acknowledge that your sexuality is in existence at that age," Joe Martin, the only openly gay person on Barney's staff at the time, said. As one of Barney's friends described that period in his life: "He was discovering and feeling his sexuality and attractiveness for the first time. He had lost a lot of weight and would parade around in muscle shirts. Most people go through that at age eighteen. For Barney, it was delayed mid-life adolescence." Another friend observed: "Barney was trying to figure things out. He was just learning about a part of himself that had been suppressed for over thirty years. This was not a part of his life that was well developed and it showed." The friend added, "Barney was clearly experimenting and making the mistake we all do as adolescents. Sometimes when you are young you do stupid things and hang out with the wrong sort of people." As Barney acknowledged to a staffer, "I am in my mid-forties but socially I'm still an adolescent and I'm catching up."

Barney had a series of relationships that didn't make sense to anybody. Some "dangerous dudes," as one person described the men he went with. Barney acted recklessly while he was out there catching up. He misjudged many of these people. Although he later got hurt emotionally and politically by his involvement with Steve Gobie, some of the other people he was involved with, according to a friend, were much worse and "he was damn lucky that he didn't get hurt physically."

Barney also dated Ken Mayer, a doctor from Brookline, and Tom Stoddard, the executive director of the Lambda Legal Defense Fund, whom Martin thought were "great for him." But, Martin said, most of the other people were not "in his best interest."

Friends and staff were worried about Barney because he seemed to be promiscuous. They felt that despite the brilliance he showed in matters of public policy, he showed tremendous lack of judgment in personal matters. One staffer in the office said, "We hoped that he would get through this period quickly."

In the summer of 1984, Barney finally decided to tell his mother. He had told his siblings four years earlier and thought it was rude not to tell his mother. It was a difficult thing for him to do. He told her one day when he was driving her somewhere in his car. Elsie had no idea that her son was gay. Barney had dated women in the past, though it seemed to her that whenever things got serious he would break up with them. Her reaction was, "So he's gay. So what?"

"When my husband, Sam, died and I was a nervous wreck, and Barney took a year off from college at Harvard to help me get my head straight, did it matter if he was gay or not? You judge people for who they are, their character, not what their sexual orientation is. Please excuse my language, but I knew an awful lot of bastards who are straight," Elsie said. She told her older sister Fanny, who wrote to Barney, "To me you're the same Barney, what difference does it make?"

During this period when Barney was coming to terms with his own sexuality, an unattractive streak of nastiness began showing itself in the form of ugly outbursts, particularly against women. Amy Isaacs once overheard Barney shouting angrily at Edie Wilke, who worked for the Arms Control Foreign Policy Caucus and was the wife of Democrat representative Don Edwards, because he disagreed over a strategy and tactic. Isaacs was appalled by Barney's conduct and wrote him a letter that said, "You don't treat anyone like that, especially the wife of a colleague." Barney thanked Isaacs for making that known to him. After a similar outburst against a female reporter at a social function, his longtime friend Cokie Roberts felt compelled to speak to him about that. "He often does it unconsciously and I don't think in his mind he is insulting people but he is," Sergio Pombo, who was later Barney's partner for seven years, said.

June Koch (pronounced "cook") an assistant secretary at HUD, consistently brought out the worst in Barney. On the evening of December 23, 1985, Barney appeared with June Koch and New York City mayor Ed Koch on the *MacNeil/ Lehrer NewsHour* to discuss the plight of the homeless. June Koch was in the Washington studio with the moderator, Jim Lehrer, Barney was in Boston, and Mayor Koch was in New York.

Lehrer began by asking assistant secretary Koch a soft question about what the Ronald Reagan administration was doing to help the homeless. In her response, Koch attempted to place the blame on prior administrations. Barney went on the attack. "That is not an appropriate response from a federal official, to blame other people, people in the 1960s and the 1970s," he said. "Blaming other people is not going to put a warm bed under the homeless." He acknowledged that there had been problems in the past, but accused the Reagan administration of ignoring the problems of the homeless and spending only "a pittance" to help them. Furthermore, he said, "This administration has consistently cut back on every program to build any houses for low-income people while gold plating the Pentagon."

Koch proceeded to list the various housing programs and the monies the Reagan administration was providing. Barney interrupted. "That is just dishonest, June. That was previously voted money and you asked to rescind those programs that you are taking credit for," he said. Koch contended, however, that according to a HUD study, the number of homeless people is not 2 million as many suggest but only 350,000, and many of these have mental problems.

Lehrer asked Barney for a response and he said, "No intellectually honest person, let me repeat that, no intellectually honest person pretends to know the number of homeless."

June Koch maintained that there was no availability problem for low-cost housing. Mayor Koch replied, "It is nonsense what you say. In New York City we have a ten-year wait for public housing. When you have the nerve to say there is no demand for low-cost housing, I want to throw up."

Barney jumped into the fray, mocking the contention that there was no problem with national availability of housing. "You mean that if you average everything out, you have an excess of housing perhaps in Tucson and a shortage in Pittsburgh, and these people are not so mobile as to get from one place to the other?" he said.

When the HUD assistant secretary contended that what had been cut back was the rate of growth in new housing units, pointing out that a hundred thousand new units had been put on line, Barney interrupted her once again, saying, "No June, you are lying." Then shouting and pointing his finger for emphasis, he declared, "Those units were voted by previous administrations. You don't build a house right away. Units that were previously voted in other administrations are still being built. You are not asking for any new units."

People were appalled by Barney's performance that evening. A viewer from Bethesda, Maryland, sent Barney a letter commenting on "the unbelievably bad manners (or no manners)" he had displayed. The writer suggested, "You are still a young man, and it is not too late for you to make your considerable talents count by learning to curb your urge to interrupt and to call the thoughts and judgments of others 'dishonest' and to say repeatedly that your opponent is lying." The writer, it turned out, was actually a fan of Barney Frank and admired his "quick wit and ability to cut through the wrappings and pretty bows of flawed legislation" during spirited debates on the House floor. However, the writer asked, "Is it only the rules of the House which oblige you to keep a civil tongue in your mouth? Or, was last night the real Barney Frank—a combination of a three-year-old having a temper tantrum, a pier-six brawler, and 'the Terrible Tempered Mr. Bang'?"

When Barney first went to Washington, he anticipated that although he wouldn't be out publicly, he wasn't going to be totally closeted any more either. After the 1982 race against Heckler, when he began to relax more and he lost weight, exercised and worked out, and changed his appearance, his self-esteem increased and he was hopeful that he would now finally start to have a romantic life. But it didn't happen. "I realized part of the problem was the awkwardness of being publicly closeted," he explained. "How are you going to meet people? Where are you going to go? I did date a couple of guys, but we can't go here, we can't go there," he said. "That is not necessarily the case if you are in many lines of work, but if you are very prominent, a public figure, there is no halfway point. I was not meeting people."

Barney endured psychic pain and did some stupid things. In a 1999 *Playboy* interview, he said: "I had a hard time meeting people. I hired men for sex, and then tried to make a friend out of them. I thought there was something the matter with me, some flaw. Being a prominent person in the closet meant it was hard not only meeting people but also developing emotional relationships. Why can't I relate to people better? I finally realized it was because I was keeping this secret. I couldn't be myself and I was afraid. I had to be careful who knew. I couldn't be seen in many places. I had to be careful who I called. Relationships are difficult anyway, but I was multiplying the difficulty."

By early 1985, after a few years in Washington experiencing the awkwardness of being publicly closeted and trying to have a social life with men in the shadows, he realized that it was just not working and was making him crazy. He found Abraham Lincoln's aphorism to be as relevant to an individual as to a country. "I could not live half slave and half free, privately free to be a gay man but publicly a slave to the prejudice that would not allow me to acknowledge it," he said. But still he did not come out.

Barney's Massachusetts colleague Gerry Studds had been outed when he was censured by the House in July 1983 for having a sexual relationship with a male teenage congressional page and had just survived a difficult reelection fight in November 1984. Studds represented New Bedford and Barney represented Fall River. "It was just too odd to have the two of us coming out so close together," Barney said. "I decided to wait another election cycle."

"You could see how much pain it caused him to have to equivocate with reporters and other people during that time when he was sort of out, but not really out," Bill Zavarello, a staff member at the time, said. "When are you going to be able to answer that question yes?" Zavarello asked. Barney looked at him sadly and said, "I don't know Billy. I just don't know."

Sunday, March 31, 1985, was Barney's forty-fifth birthday. As he sat in the living room of his Capitol Hill basement apartment, he could find no cause for celebration in his private life. He was lonely, depressed, and emotionally vulnerable. The apartment was dimly lit, with linoleum floors and little furniture. There were a few pieces of Scandinavian-style furniture in the living room. The only wall décor was a calendar of the U.S. Capitol, the kind that members of Congress provide to their constituents, which hung crooked on the wall in the living room. There were black Hefty trash bags taped on the few windows in the apartment in place of curtains. The refrigerator was empty. Boxes served as furniture in the bedroom. There were no bookshelves, and books were stacked on the floor. A box spring and a mattress sat on the floor in the bedroom. A grease stain showed along the bedroom wall where his head rested when he read the newspaper. A lamp on the floor next to the bed had no shade, just a bare bulb. "It was a total dump. It was like a dungeon," Patty Hamel said. "He was born without the gay decorating gene," Vic Basile, the Human Rights Campaign Fund's first executive director, said.

Several months earlier, Joe Martin, who was in town house hunting, stayed in the apartment while Barney was in Massachusetts. Martin invited some friends over for drinks before going out to dinner on Capitol Hill. One friend declared the apartment a "pigsty" and asked who lived there, "some poor, starving college kid?" Martin replied that a member of Congress lived in the apartment. "I just can't believe a congressman would live like this," the friend replied.

As Barney sat in the living room on his birthday, feeling despondent, he started to leaf through the March 22 issue of the *Washington Blade*, a long-established gay newspaper. He read the front-page story, which reported that Jeff Levi, whom he knew, had been appointed director of government and political affairs for the National Gay Task Force. He read that Senator John Kerry intended to reintroduce the Gay Rights bill submitted in past years by his predecessor, Paul Tsongas. In the news-across-the-nation page, he was dismayed to read that Boston City Council member Dapper O'Neill had complained that he had to "sit next to the faggot," the openly gay council member David Scondras, at council meetings, because he "might catch AIDS." Finally, he came to the classifieds and began to scan the ads. One particular ad under Personals/Situations caught his eye. It was sandwiched between "CLOSE ENCOUNTERS. If it takes something special to satisfy your needs call us. . . . Private, discreet" and "TALL, ATHLETIC, Swede, Eric . . . " and it read: "Exceptionally good-looking, personable, muscular athlete is available. Hot bottom plus large endowment equals a good time. Greg."

In the past he had on occasion hired male prostitutes. He dialed the phone number listed in the ad and asked for Greg. At the other end of the telephone line was Stephen L. Gobie, a smooth-talking twenty-eight-year-old who free-lanced in male prostitution and used the alias Greg Davis in personal ads. They arranged to meet at Barney's apartment the next day.

The young, sandy-haired Gobie appeared at Barney's door in the early evening of April 1 (a prophetically appropriate date). To Barney he looked preppy, wearing slacks and a jacket and carrying a copy of the *Washington Post*. Barney paid him eighty dollars in cash for an hour of sex. Over the course of several meetings at which Barney paid Gobie for sex, the two became friends. Gobie recognized early in their relationship that Barney was vulnerable. "This was the first time Barney Frank felt good in a relationship. Here's a guy who didn't have a social life until he was forty-five," Gobie said.

In 1982, Gobie had been convicted of oral sodomy, possession of cocaine, and producing child pornography. Barney thought that Gobie had potential but for many reasons had messed up his life. He tried to help him, hoping that he could turn the young man away from drugs and prostitution and strengthen his social skills. He offered him odd jobs, running errands, driving Barney to appointments, and performing chores around the apartment, and paid him a few dollars for the work. He allowed Gobie to stay in his apartment when he was out of town.

In May 1985, the slender and cocky Gobie appeared mysteriously at one of Barney's office softball games. When I asked Doug Cahn who that was playing left field for us, that I didn't remember ever seeing him in the personal office, Cahn grimaced and said, "His name is Steve Gobie and he is Barney's driver, personal assistant, and man-Friday." He told me that Barney was using his own money to pay him.

It seemed odd to me that Barney would have hired someone to drive his little blue Chevy Chevette, the most downscale car imaginable, without air-conditioning or power steering and with only a radio. Barney generally enjoys driving and knowing how fast he likes to drive, I could not understand why he would relinquish control of the wheel to someone else, other than perhaps Richard Petty. Then Gobie misjudged the first fly ball hit to left field. It was clear to me that he was not a ringer. As Gobie ran after the ball that had gotten by him in left field, I had the feeling that something was awry.

Joe Martin was the only openly gay person on Barney's congressional or subcommittee staff at the time. They had a friendship going back to Barney's early days in the state legislature. Martin would occasionally see Barney socially after work in the company of other gay men. Soon after Barney met Gobie, he asked Martin for his read on Gobie. "I told Barney that I didn't like him, I didn't know what he was up to, and I didn't trust his motives," Martin said. "I knew from the start that Barney had hired him as an escort and I felt extremely uncomfortable. I asked, 'What if he ever goes to the press?' Barney said that would never happen." Martin raised those same concerns a second time and Barney's response was the same, and so Martin didn't pursue it.

Barney's relationship with Gobie did not stay intimate for long because Gobie was principally heterosexual. He was living with a woman in Dupont Circle at the time. The relationship changed after two months as the two men became more friends than sex partners. Barney confided in Joe Martin that the sex with Gobie had ended. But, he said, "I feel bad for the guy and want to help him straighten out his life." Barney even took Gobie with him to attend a bill-signing ceremony at the White House.

The relationship continued for almost eighteen months. Gobie never moved in with Barney, but in time Barney came to realize that Gobie was using him. During the summer of 1987, Barney was away a lot, spending more time in Massachusetts. In August 1987, Mary Jo Daugherty, his landlady, became concerned. She phoned Barney, who was on vacation, and said, "Something is going on in the apartment. All these women coming and going, it looks like a hooker ring." Barney immediately kicked Gobie out of the apartment and ended his relationship with him.

A few weeks later, someone called Barney's office asking for Steve Gobie. In the past, Gobie's girlfriend would occasionally call the office looking for him. The intern who answered the phone asked whether anybody knew a Steve Gobie. Hearing that question, Barney told several staff members, "That man is history. I'm having nothing to do with him. He's completely out of my life."

Barney felt no compulsion to talk about his personal life. In interviews with the press, he consistently refused to discuss his social life or sexual orientation, citing the right to privacy. He told one reporter, "If I answered that question, where would it stop? Which part of your body is your favorite? I get embarrassed even thinking about it." The only things that are public information, he said, are his phone number, his address, and how much money he makes. "What I like to eat used to be a secret until I went on a diet. Only when the law is broken should a public official's private life be in the spotlight."

When a reporter from the *Washington Post* invited Joe Martin to go out for drinks one evening, he agreed. The reporter had been a classmate and close friend of one of Martin's best friends back in Cambridge. After Martin had consumed two drinks, the reporter matter-of-factly asked whether Barney Frank was gay. Joe Martin had been asked that same question countless times since the 1970s. His standard response over the years had been that it is a possibility, but Barney puts all of his energy into his job and he probably doesn't have a sex life. This time, however, Martin, who was a little woozy from the alcohol, said he thought Barney "may be oozing out of the closet." Martin assumed it was an off-the-record conversation with a friend of a friend. The next day, Barney called Martin into his office and said, "I understand that you went out for drinks with a *Washington Post* reporter last night and told her I was 'oozing out of the closet.'" Martin was mortified and offered to resign. But Barney told him he didn't need to resign. "Consider it a lesson learned," he said. "We are not in Boston. This is hardball. This is the big leagues. There are people in this town who would love to see me destroyed. You have to keep that in mind."

In June 1986, Barney was compelled to tell colleagues that he was gay because of a passage in a book by former Republican congressman, Robert Bauman of Maryland, that focused attention on Barney's sexual preference. The ads for the 1984 film *Angel* used the tagline "High school honor student by day . . . Hollywood hooker by night." Bauman, first elected to Congress in August 1973 in a special election in Maryland's First Congressional District, had also been leading a double life—a religious family man, married with four children, a respected arch-conservative member of Congress who preaches family values and crusades against gay rights by day; prowling the streets and back alleys of Washington looking for young men for anonymous sex by night. Bauman would cruise seedy, local gay pick-up areas around town in his car with the Maryland "U.S. Congress 1" license plate.

Several weeks before the November 1980 general election, Bauman, an adviser to the Republican presidential candidate, Ronald Reagan, who appeared to be coasting to reelection, was arrested and charged with a misdemeanor for soliciting sex from a sixteen-year-old male hustler and exotic dancer. Bauman was defeated in his bid for reelection by Democrat Roy Dyson. He lost everything—his seat in Congress, his political career, and his marriage.

In 1986, Bauman wrote a book about his experience titled *The Gentleman From Maryland: The Conscience of a Gay Conservative*. In this book, Bauman describes his experience battling alcoholism and the compulsion to seek anonymous sex with young male hustlers at night. He was still bitter about being voted out of office and felt that he had been treated unfairly. He was disappointed that Republican political leaders did not stand by him. In chapter 2, he writes that Gerry Studds of Massachusetts was reelected by his constituents despite his having been censured by the House for having a homosexual affair with a teenage male page. In the discussion he alludes to Barney's homosexuality: "His Massachusetts colleague, the witty liberal Barney Frank, appears at Washington's annual Gay Pride Day in a tank top with his usual young companion and their picture appears in the *Blade* without comment. Most gay members of Congress choose to be more closeted but their names are known to many in and out of gay circles, including the media, which has its own gay contingent."

In June 1986, excerpts from Bauman's book, scheduled to be released in August, appeared in *Washingtonian* magazine. Although Barney's name had been deleted by the magazine, reporters got wind of the fact that Barney Frank was the congressman Bauman had named in the book. As soon as the magazine appeared on newsstands, Doug Cahn, Barney's administrative assistant, who doubled as press secretary, started fielding phone calls from reporters. "Barney marches in the St. Patrick's Day parade each year. Does that mean that he is Irish?" he told reporters. "Barney is an outspoken supporter of gay rights. Since his election to Congress he has marched in six or seven Gay Pride Day parades, both in Washington and in Boston, to demonstrate his support and solidarity with gays and lesbians," he said. He pointed out to reporters that the photograph in the *Washington Blade* that Bauman referred to had been shot with Barney's knowledge and consent and "the youthful companion" was a political activist friend of Barney in his late twenties. When asked whether Congressman Frank was gay, Cahn followed Barney's lead and said he would not comment further, citing the right to privacy. Bauman's book was not a big seller and moved fairly quickly to the remainder bin.

Once the excerpts from Bauman's book were published, Barney started to warn his colleagues. The first person he visited was Speaker Tip O'Neill. That morning Barney had phoned Tommy O'Neill and said, "I'm going to be seeing your father this afternoon and I am going to tell him that I am gay." "You are doing it at your own peril," the younger O'Neill replied.

In 1979, as a closeted state representative, Barney had rounded up every gay Irish activist he knew in Tip O'Neill's district to attend the gay rights march on Washington and to accompany him to lobby the Speaker for gay rights legislation. The group met with O'Neill in his private office in the Capitol. O'Neill was sympathetic but was not prepared to take the lead on this issue. "Some people say that homosexuals shouldn't be in office because they can be blackmailed," he said, adding, "Why don't all of you just reveal that you are homosexual and then you don't have to worry about anybody blackmailing you. That will put an end to the problem." "Tip came up with this idea on his own," Barney said.

Although Tip O'Neill was the master of old-school politics, he understood the new school as well and was able to adapt to the concerns and needs of a new generation of Democratic legislators in the 1980s. "Tip legitimately evolved. He wasn't just being political," Barney said. In Barney's eyes, Tip O'Neill was much smarter than people gave him credit for and was intellectually the equal of most college professors. Barney had a close friendship with O'Neill, who had always been gracious and supportive of him in the past. Like O'Neill, Barney always wanted to be a politician. Barney shared O'Neill's maxim that politics is an honorable profession.

"Bob Bauman is coming out with a book in which he mentions that I am gay," Barney told O'Neill.

"Oh, for Christ's sake, pal, don't be payin' any attention to that shit. You should read the garbage that these people have been writin' about me lately," replied O'Neill.

"Tip, there's one problem," said Barney.

"What's that?" O'Neill asked.

"It's true. I am gay," said Barney.

O'Neill, an old-fashioned politician and a devout Catholic, was surprised. He had trouble accepting the news. "No, no, that's not true. I don't believe that. You're one of the back room guys, smoking cigars." Barney reiterated that it was true. Clearly saddened by the revelation, O'Neill put his arm around Barney and said, "I'm sorry to hear that. It's a shame. You are well respected by your colleagues and have so much going for you. I thought you were going to be the first Jewish Speaker some day." O'Neill later told his press secretary, Chris Matthews, "We need to be prepared to deal with press inquiries. I think that Barney Frank is gonna come out of the room."

When Robert Bauman appeared on the television program *Crossfire* to plug his book, Robert Novak expressed surprise that Bauman had named one member of Congress "who has never to my knowledge been identified as a homosexual, Democratic representative Barney Frank of Massachusetts." Bauman replied that he had made a mistake, that he regretted mentioning that Barney was gay, and that if he had it to do over again, he would not mention it. "Frankly," Bauman said, "I thought that was something that was known." He added, however, that Barney had not denied in any subsequent interview that he is gay. Novak followed up by commenting, "People in the gay community, Mr. Bauman, say they knew all about you for years and didn't say anything, and that it is outrageous that for money you're putting the finger on one of your former colleagues." Bauman denied mentioning Barney to make money, explaining that if he had wanted a best seller he could have named a lot of people in public life, from high Reagan administration officials to senators and members of Congress to journalists. "My only defense to what obviously was a mistake was that I thought Mr. Frank, in particular, was already known. I know on occasions journalists had asked him that question and I thought his response was in the affirmative but it was a mistake," Bauman said.

Barney did not know Bauman well and was surprised and troubled by the reference to him in the book. "That's generally not considered the thing to do, especially when you're someone who has enjoyed the cover himself," Barney said. He believes that Bauman was motivated by jealousy over the fact that Barney appeared to have it all. Several months later, Bauman apologized to Barney, telling him that he mistakenly believed that Barney was out of the closet when he wrote about him. "I don't think it was a mistake," Barney said.

Barney was particularly rankled at being mentioned in Bauman's book because, he said, "the book was about Bauman's experiences having sex with young boys, about him being beaten up on several occasions, and that kind of stuff. I didn't want to be associated with that kind of thing."

He took issue with Bauman's description of him appearing at the Gay Pride Day event "with his usual young companion," calling it "just flat-out wrong." "It made it sound like I had this young boy. Well, my young companion wasn't so young—he was twenty-seven—and he was a friend, not a lover."

As Barney was edging toward publicly acknowledging his homosexuality, he candidly discussed the matter with his former boss Mike Harrington at a meeting in the Newton district office. According to Harrington, Barney thought that coming out would not be a problem in his district but that it would foreclose his looking at statewide office in the future.

Barney was increasingly being seen at events in Boston accompanied by a man. A gossip column in the *Boston Herald* mentioned that Barney Frank had been seen at some event engaged in "alternative dancing."

Several weeks before publicly coming out, Barney told a few key people in his district about his plans, including Fall River mayor Carlton Viveiros and Jerry Grossman, who urged him not to come out. Grossman approached the matter not from a moralistic but from a political point of view, weighing larger issues that he was concerned about, including the peace issue. He insisted that though Barney felt that after all it was his life they were talking about, he nonetheless had no right to make the announcement. "We put you in there and if you do this you might lose the seat. You have no right to jeopardize the seat just because you want to do this," he said.

Barney had always believed that what he did outside of the office, his private life, was not subject to the Freedom of Information Act, the Sunshine Act, or any other public right-to-information statute. But as Barney spent more and more time publicly discussing his diet, his bodybuilding efforts, and his new appearance in interviews with reporters, he realized that to some extent he had already crossed the divide between public and private life.

The catalyst for the timing of his decision to voluntarily come out of the closet was the May 7 death of Stewart McKinney, a closeted bisexual Republican member of Congress from Connecticut with whom Barney had served on the Banking Committee. McKinney's obituary said that he died of AIDS. There was a lot of denial at first, about the cause of death, whether it was AIDS related, how he had contracted AIDS, and then whether or not he was homosexual. Finally, at McKinney's funeral, Barney decided, "This is crazy." He later explained to the *Washington Post* reporter Lois Romano, "It touched off something. An unfortunate debate about 'Was he or wasn't he? Didn't he or did he?' I said to myself, I don't want that to happen to me. Now I have no reason to believe I'm not going to live until I'm eighty—except for the fact that given my job I have to fly Eastern Air Lines a lot these days. . . . But I didn't want the speculation. I didn't want my family to cope with that."

In early May, when Barney was asked directly by the *Boston Herald* whether he was gay, he skirted the question. "People don't want to hear about my sex life. I think if you asked, 'Are you gay?' or 'Are you this or that?' the most appropriate answer as far as most people are concerned would be 'Yeah, so what?' You shouldn't put your lover on the payroll, whether it's a male or female. You shouldn't be engaged in some sexual activity that distracts you from your job. But other than that, people don't care."

Barney was not ashamed of his gay lifestyle, but he was not eager to advertise it either. He realized, however, that if he continued to sidestep questions about his sexuality, the inference would be that he was embarrassed by it, and he was not.

In late May, Barney reluctantly chose to go public with his homosexuality. It was a risky decision and was viewed by many as an act of political courage. The climate for coming out was much different in 1987 than it is today. "I was pretty sure that if I came out I would not lose my job, having at that point been elected to Congress four times," he explained. "But I assumed it would have some negative impact on my influence in Congress."

When several liberal members of Congress asked Barney to confirm the rumor that he was going to come out, he said, "Yeah, I gotta do it." They urged him not to. "The prevailing view back then in the mid-1980s," Barney said, "was that once I came out, my ability to be effective in any area but gay and lesbian rights would be diminished, and that I would be a one-issue guy not by choice but by reaction." He did not disagree with his colleagues, though he hoped they were wrong. He told them, "You may be right but I just can't continue to live this way. My sanity requires me to come out." Looking back, Barney explained, "I didn't come out for any great political purpose, I just did it to keep from going nuts. My primary motive was that I could no longer live like that."

Barney points out that when gays and lesbians are honest about their sexuality and discuss it with others, it's called "coming out." Yet when heterosexuals want to discuss their sexuality with others it's called "talking."

Barney had an understanding with Bob Healy, the chief political correspondent at the *Boston Globe*, that when he decided he was ready to come out publicly it would be to the *Globe*. Earlier that year, Healy had spoken to Barney and explained that it would be a big embarrassment to the *Globe* if he came out to another newspaper. It was essentially agreed that the *Globe* would not run anything then and when Barney was ready to come out, the *Globe* would get the story.

In late May, after months of dithering, Barney phoned Healy and said that he was ready. But he did not want it to seem like an announcement or some sort of press conference. His attitude was, "I have nothing to hide, nothing to advertise." He wanted to be able to say that being gay is not relevant to how he does his job. "How do you call a press conference and say, 'I want to acknowledge the following irrelevant fact'?" The *Globe* wanted the story to look as though it was at Barney's request, but Barney wanted it to appear that it was at the newspaper's initiative.

John Robinson, the *Globe*'s chief congressional correspondent in Washington, happened to be on vacation at the time. In Robinson's absence, the *Globe* sent Kay Longcope, an openly lesbian reporter who had once been Elaine Noble's lover, to interview Barney on Capitol Hill. Barney told her, "If you ask the direct question: 'Are you gay?' the answer is: 'Yes. So what?'" He also said, "I don't think my sex life is relevant to my job. But on the other hand I don't want to leave the impression that I'm embarrassed about my life." Barney discussed one of the fundamental problems with coming out, "If you don't acknowledge the fact that you're gay, people wonder what you're hiding. If you do, they wonder why you're making a big deal of it." In Barney's view, "The average voter says get the bridges built, stop nuclear testing, find shelter for the homeless, and don't write 'Dear Ann Landers' letters." Barney's coming out was a voluntary, straightforward, this-is-who-I-am declaration.

It was difficult for Barney to say those words to Longcope. He would have preferred for people just to know. "It was hard for Barney to come out in such a public way," Ann Maguire, a gay and lesbian rights activist, said. Barney had waited until he was forty-seven years old to come out of the closet publicly.

Longcope's story was supposed to appear in the *Boston Globe* the following Sunday. Robinson heard from friends at the newspaper that Longcope had interviewed Barney and had the scoop. He reacted angrily, telling the editors at the *Globe* that it was his beat, not hers, and that he had been waiting to do this story for years. The editors at the *Globe*, in an effort to resolve a turf battle, decided to print the story under Robinson's byline and to run a second article the next day, a feature story by Longcope, based on the contents of her hour-long interview with Barney, analyzing why a gay politician comes out.

In the Saturday, May 30, 1987 edition of the *Boston Globe*, Barney Frank became the first member of Congress in history to voluntarily come out publicly as a gay man. Four years earlier, his fellow Bay State Democrat Gerry Studds had become the first member of Congress to publicly acknowledge his homosexuality, following revelations of his sexual affair with a congressional page, for which he was censured by the House. Robert Bauman, Fred Richmond of New York, and Jon Hinson of Mississippi all claimed initially they were too drunk to remember what had happened or gave some other excuse.

"The story appeared in the *Globe* the day before we were expecting it," Mary Beth Cahill said. Barney assumed that it would be a small story buried somewhere inside the newspaper. It was a front-page above-the-fold story headlined "Frank Discusses Being Gay," with the subhead "Says It's Not 'Relevant to My Job.'" The first sentence of the article read, "U.S. Representative Barney Frank, after years of ambivalence about disclosing the nature of his private life, has decided to acknowledge publicly that he is gay." Barney Frank's sexuality was the second lead story on the television evening news in Boston, following a story about the Celtics 117–114 win over the Detroit Pistons in the seventh game of the NBA Eastern conference championship.

Barney was relieved. "I don't know any human being who doesn't have a combination of physical and emotional needs that allows them, without cost, to exist without a personal life," he said. "When I first ran for office, I made a decision that I would sacrifice a private life for politics. After a while, I became increasingly jealous of the people who were 'out.' I thought, 'Why am I leading this unhealthy life where I have to be dishonest?' People said to me, 'Well, you don't have to be dishonest. Just don't mention it.' . . . You cannot go forty-eight hours in this society and be honest and not tell people your sexuality. . . . I defy any human being to . . . honestly answer every question put to you and not give away your sexuality. 'What'd you do last night?' 'Are you married?' 'Are you seeing anybody?' Unless you're a total hermit, you're going to give away your sexual orientation."

That Saturday morning, Barney was scheduled to march in a Memorial Day parade in Attleboro, the most conservative part of his district. Attleboro always celebrated Memorial Day on May 30, regardless of the date of the official holiday. "This is not the place you would choose to make your first appearance after you come out as a gay elected official," Cahill said. Joanne Moore, who ran Barney's district office in Attleboro, was anxious because she was unsure what kind of reception Barney would receive from the tough crowd in Attleboro. Moore's husband, a navy veteran, wore his military uniform and marched with Barney in the parade. Cahill also marched with Barney. Barney's staff felt he was generally well received and that if his being gay was accepted in conservative Attleboro, it would be accepted elsewhere.

That Saturday evening, at a benefit performance of the Big Apple Circus for the Boston Children's Museum attended by, as the guest of honor, Christopher Reeve, the actor who played Superman, and other dignitaries, including state senate president William Bulger, Ken Brecker, the museum director, concluded the introduction of dignitaries by saying, "And we are much honored to have Congressman Barney Frank here with us tonight." Barney received the biggest and loudest ovation of any of the dignitaries. "It was extraordinary," Barney said. "Chris Reeve didn't understand then why I got such a big hand." Tim McFeeley, who was there with his partner, got all choked up and thought how really wonderful this was for the gay community.

The next day, when Barney was introduced at a "From All Walks of Life" AIDS fund-raising event that attracted over five thousand walkers despite the ninety-degree heat, he received sustained, thunderous applause, a hero's welcome, from the members of the gay community and AIDS activists in the crowd. The show of support moved him to tears.

Afterward he told reporters, "This is my private life and it has nothing to do with the job I do in office. I hope voters will look at my record, not my private life." "I think the amount of interest in the social life of a middle-aged politician is not enormous," he joked. "People know the difference between their congressmen and Dr. Ruth. They look to me for constituency services and for advocacy. I don't think I was elected as a sexual role model." When *New York Times* reporter Linda Greenhouse later asked whether he would be a role model for gay men, Barney replied jocularly, "Will I become a role model for thousands of young gay men who smoke cigars and talk too fast? I don't think so."

Barney's constituents in the Fourth District did not appear to be troubled by the disclosure. According to an informal poll of fifty voters interviewed by the *Boston Globe* that weekend outside supermarkets in Newton, Fall River, Somerset, and Wellesley, only about one in twelve expressed concern about Barney Frank's sexual orientation or said they would not vote for him because of it. Even older voters seemed to be taking it in stride; Mark Sullivan in Fall River recalled getting a phone call from his mother, a contemporary of Tip O'Neill's, who said, "Did you hear the news? Barney is out of the cupboard."

Barney believed that any aspirations for higher office "went out the window" when he revealed his homosexuality. "Had I not been gay I might have been thinking about maybe running for a House leadership position or thinking of a

Cabinet job," he said. Barney thought that the admission that he was gay would diminish his influence in Congress, but it did not. He had a well established reputation in the House. The general reaction among his colleagues was enormously supportive. The difference, according to Barney, is that if the first thing people find out is that you're gay, "then the universal stereotypes come into play."

Senator Alan Simpson, a conservative Republican from Wyoming, was one of the first lawmakers to phone Barney to tell him how much he admired his courage and to wish him well. "It takes a lot of guts to do what Barney did," he said.

Barney's revelation was a cause for pride and celebration in the gay community. "Having one of the brightest and most politically savvy members of Congress come out was a big deal. It was huge because he was so well known, a rising star, a go-to-person for the media," Vic Basile said. "There is nothing as powerful about changing people's hearts and minds as someone coming out. It really changes people forever. Those who know and love someone who they now discover is gay, they are different people. We grew exponentially as people became more aware of the issues."

Several days later, when Barney started to thank members of the Gay Political Task Force for their help, it was an emotional moment. In a quavering voice he began, "I just want to thank a lot of people in this room for . . ." He lost his composure and broke into sobs as he tried to finish the sentence: ". . . making this possible." He continued, "What I thought was going to be a very tough time turned out to be a surprisingly easy one."

Barney's coming out gave courage to many gay men and lesbians. On the Monday after the story appeared in the *Globe*, Barney's sister Doris was mowing the front lawn of her home in Newton when the letter carrier came up and gave her a big hug. "It was odd," she recalled. "I knew the letter carrier and we were friends but I was taken aback." The letter carrier said, "I just want to make sure that you thank your brother for me. I am gay and now I feel so good."

After he had come out publicly, a few of Barney's friends questioned why he had to do so. Two years later, when the Gobie scandal broke, Barney would tell these same friends, "Now you know why I had to come out. It was not being fully out that drove me to do stupid things like getting involved with Gobie." After he came out, there was no need for prostitutes. He was finally able to have a social life openly.

Looking back at his decision to come out, Barney said, "One of the stupidest things I ever did was to wait so long. I didn't realize this at the time." He added, "Virtually everybody I have met and talked to, thousands of people, have had a better experience with coming out than they expected. . . . I think when you can help other people at a relatively low price to yourself you ought to do that.

I do think for me not to have acknowledged being gay would have been to deny a lot of vulnerable people help they could have gotten."

The expected reaction of shock and disapproval by his constituents did not take place. Following his disclosure, Barney had a poll taken in his district. The poll showed that overall his constituents were not disappointed or upset to learn that he was gay. However, twice the number of people thought he would lose votes as a result of being gay than the actual number that said they would change their vote because of it.

After coming out, Barney still believed that his being gay was irrelevant to his job in Congress, but he started talking about it. "Being Jewish is also irrelevant, and I don't refuse to talk about being Jewish," he rationalized. Just as he often poked fun at being Jewish, he started to joke about being gay. "What I am really doing is making fun of the prejudice," he said. "Another reason why I joke about being gay is that I don't want to discourage people from coming out. I want to say, 'Hey, this is fun. Come on in. The water's fine.'"

Barney believed that having openly gay and lesbian people in Congress helped dispel prejudice. However, he refused to publicly discuss the inner pressures and feelings of being a gay man. He told Lois Romano of the *Washington Post* on July 2, 1987, "I don't want to kvetch in public. It's a Yiddish word for complain, whine and bitch. How I feel about the inner pressures is nobody's business." When the reporter persisted, Barney responded, "Who wants to know that? Do they want to be eating breakfast worrying about the inner emotional turmoil of a middle-aged politician? Let them tape *Dynasty!*"

In some ways Barney had to work harder in Congress to dispel any perception that all he cared about were gay issues. After serving in the House for three terms, Barney no longer had a need to actively publicize in his district his numerous and varied activities in Congress. But now he felt that he would have to, to ensure that his constituents did not think that gay issues were his only concern. Barney pointed to his record on women's issues and civil rights and declared, "It would be a lousy world if the only people who were concerned about mistreatment or discrimination were the victim."

In the mid-1970s, Barney had watched Elaine Noble, then the only openly gay or lesbian state legislator in the nation, deal with the gay and lesbian national constituency. She felt the need to respond to every letter and was being drowned in the process. When Barney came out, he put an assistant in charge of the gay and lesbian national constituency and set up a process for referring letters to the appropriate organization. By 1987 there existed a network of gay and lesbian organizations that made such referrals possible.

After Barney came out publicly and had to deal with being openly gay as part of an effective political career, two people served as his role models, though one, the Reverend Adam Clayton Powell Jr., was not only straight but militantly so.

Barney sees Powell as the first African American member of Congress prepared to stand up for equality and confront the racism of the Congress itself. "When Powell arrived in Congress, he was told he couldn't use the swimming pool, he couldn't eat in the dining room, and he couldn't go to the barber shop. In each case he basically told them to stuff it and just did it," Barney said.

He read Charles Hamilton's political biography of Adam Clayton Powell because it describes Powell's struggle with prejudice and discrimination in Congress. In confronting the institutionalized homophobia in Congress, Barney tried to model himself on Powell's dignified but defiant and militant refusal to be discriminated against when he was elected to Congress from Harlem in 1944. Following Powell's example, Barney insisted on being treated like anyone else and insisted on the right to bring the man in his life to all events to which other members of Congress might bring a spouse or companion and to fight for equal treatment in every relevant respect, whether as an individual or as a member of a couple. "There is a symbolism here," he said. "If I as a member of Congress allow people to discriminate against me, then I make it easier for people to discriminate against gays and lesbians all over the world."

His other role model was Steve Endean, who had died of AIDS. Endean was the first openly gay person to become a member of the board of Americans for Democratic Action and led the way in insisting that as an openly gay man he be accepted and treated like any other ally of liberal politicians. "Today the kinds of things Steve fought for are taken for granted, but they were hardly gimmes at the time. He was a very important role model for me in how to integrate effective political liberalism with openness about one's sexuality," Barney said.

After Barney came out, he was demonstrably happier and more relaxed. Colleagues found him better adjusted and much easier to work with. "Coming out made me better at my job, because my job is based on a lot of interpersonal reaction. When you're self-hating and frustrated and repressed and frightened, you're not as effective in this kind of job," he said.

Now Barney could be himself in the office. He could joke about being gay and put people at ease. "I was sitting on the couch in the reception area talking with a lobbyist," Joe Martin recalled. "Barney had just returned from San Francisco and someone had given him a pink satin baseball cap. He stuck his head out of his office wearing the hat and asked, 'So what do you think?'"

"It didn't happen overnight," Doug Cahn said. "It was wonderful. I could see it in his eyes, the way he carried himself. He was a nicer person." Cahn no longer received phone calls from people complaining, "Barney yelled at me." Instead he would get calls from people saying, "Oh, I saw Barney and he was so nice to me." Barney's sister Doris summed it up best, "After coming out, he is calmer now, happier now, and at peace with himself. Barney can now just be himself."

Out of the closet, liberated, and with Stephen Gobie out of his apartment, Barney was able to let his social life begin to blossom. After some steady relationships, he met Herb Moses, a thirty-year-old economist and gay activist, who had sent him a fan letter. Herb Moses was seventeen years younger than Barney and about three inches taller. Barney described him as "a thoroughly thoughtful and sensible guy." "He's younger than I am, but he's more mature as a gay person. He came out while he was in college and had more experience than me living out."

During the first two years of Barney and Herb's relationship, Herb attended business school in New Hampshire. In 1989, he moved to Washington. Barney, a senior member of the House Banking Committee, which oversees the Federal National Mortgage Association (Fannie Mae), wrote a letter to the CEO of Fannie Mae, asking for his help in getting a job for Herb at Fannie Mae. Herb Moses was hired by Fannie Mac as a financial analyst.

Barney soon fell in love with Herb and they lived together in a monogamous relationship. Under Herb's watchful eye, Barney began to pay more attention to his appearance and dress. Herb often bought clothes for him. Several days after the Gobie sex scandal broke, Barney told the *Boston Globe* that he wished he had met Herb Moses five years earlier. "Herb provided emotional and intellectual support that make a big difference—the absence of which contributed to the extent to which I was stupid personally earlier," he said.

"Herb very much liked to be the congressional spouse. He liked all the perks that went with it," Patty Hamel said. "He wanted to be in places where hc could be seen and in the spotlight. Barney is not a spotlight seeker." Hamel compared Herb Moses to Margaret Heckler in his desire always to be in the picture.

Barney and Herb shared a split-level townhouse near Dupont Circle that Herb had found. "Herb brought some aesthetics to Barney and really decorated the unit nicely," Vic Basile, who was their neighbor, said. On the living room wall there were photos of Barney and Herb with President George H. W. Bush, President Bill Clinton, Israel prime minister Yitzhak Shamir, Jerry Rawlings, the president of Ghana, and other world leaders. "It was like on the *Donna Reed Show*," one friend said. "Barney would come home from work and kiss Herb as he entered the apartment."

Barney told Claudia Dreifus of the *New York Times*, "It was unimaginable that I could live as a gay man with someone like Herb and have an emotionally satisfying private life that was not an interference with public life. In my own life things have moved forward."

Barney and Herb soon became the most prominent and high-profile gay couple in Washington. Barney began to refer to Herb as his "spouse." They did everything together. They went to the White House Christmas party and other social events that members of Congress usually attend with their spouses. "Our rule was very simple," Barney said. "We almost never did anything to make a point. But we never did anything to make somebody else's point. We just decided we're going to live the way we want to live and if that bothered people that was their problem." But conservative Republicans and homophobes objected. Wesley Pruden wrote in the *Washington Times*: "[Barney Frank] takes male dates to congressional conferences at the Greenbrier, there to dance cheek-to-cheek with his studly boyfriend, to the consternation of colleagues who were there with small children."

During the Clinton administration, Bill and Hillary Clinton and Al and Tipper Gore invited them to small gatherings at the White House of about ten congressional couples. "That meant a great deal to us. It seemed one more step toward prejudices being over," Barney said.

The House had a practice of issuing "spouse cards" and "spouse pins" to the wives and husbands of members to give them special access to the Capitol for parking and other amenities. Herb proudly wore his pin to events in Congress and at the White House until several right-wing members demanded that Congress rescind the perk for him. He returned the spouse card but kept the pin and was issued a "domestic partner" card instead.

In the Harvard College Class of 1961 Thirty-fifth Anniversary Report, Barney wrote: "I feel very lucky in my personal life and my job. If I didn't have to choose constantly between obesity and hunger, I'd be perfectly content." He listed himself as "Married: Herb Moses, August 7, 1987." That was the day of his first date with Herb.

Barney was a strong supporter of Governor Michael Dukakis in his run for the White House in 1988. In September of that year, at a meeting at the Georgetown University Law Center, he urged a group of gay rights activists to put aside their differences with Dukakis over his policy of not allowing gays to serve as foster parents in Massachusetts when they went to the polls in November. He advised the audience to consider which of the two candidates could better meet their goals. "I don't think it's a bad idea to think about an election as a one-night stand. Just pushing a button for someone doesn't mean you're going to call him in the morning," he said. "To further the analogy a little bit, on Election Day, it's ten minutes to 2 in the morning and the bar's about to close, and you don't have the choice that you had at 11 o'clock." Barney predicted that a lot of gay men who had voted Republican in the past were going to switch because they had been repelled by the way Vice President George H. W. Bush courted the far right. "There are a large number of gay men who are well-to-do who have voted their pocketbooks. But when your friends die and you're afraid of dying, you begin to feel differently," he said.

On September 28, at a lively forum between surrogates at the University of

Massachusetts Boston Harbor campus, Barney represented Michael Dukakis and Andrew Card, a former state representative from Holbrook, who had served in the Reagan administration as Deputy Assistant to the President and Director of Intergovernmental Affairs and was a consultant to the Bush campaign, spoke on behalf of Vice President George H. W. Bush. "The vice president has made it very clear that his priorities will be different from Ronald Reagan and one of those priorities is education," said Card. Barney, with a comic's timing, promptly interjected, "I think that's bizarre. The faithful George Bush will not even tell us whether he whispered in Ronald Reagan's ear that selling arms to the Ayatollah was wrong, all along in his secret heart of hearts disagreeing with Ronald Reagan on education and wanting to be the Education President. If you believe that we have a bridge to sell."

The moderator, Bob Kuttner, asked Card how Bush's flexible freeze would help eliminate the federal deficit. Card responded that "Bush would cut spending somewhere." "Somewhere?" exclaimed Barney. "Well, that certainly is a firm statement of priorities. He is going to cut where, somewhere, somewhere over the rainbow." "That's the problem of debating Barney Frank. That's Barney," Card recalled in October 2005 while serving as President George W. Bush's chief of staff.

Barney had built a reputation in the House for integrity and was genuinely concerned about the need to reform campaign finance laws. The problem of money in politics is pervasive—honoraria, contributions to political action committees, and the whole system for financing congressional campaigns. In an April 1984 speech at Boston University's School of Public Communications, he suggested that the system be changed so the public does not pay his salary and he is not forced to raise his campaign funds from the private sector. "Give me public campaign financing and let me raise my salary privately, with a limitation of eighty thousand dollars," he said, reasoning that by having to raise less money, he would be less beholden to fewer people.

"Elected officials are the only human beings in the world who are supposed to take large sums of money on a regular basis from absolute strangers without its having any effect on their behavior," he said. "If a player sliding into home plate reached into his pocket and handed the umpire a thousand dollars before he made the call, what would we call that? A bribe. And if a lawyer handed a judge a thousand dollars before he issued a ruling, what do we call that? A bribe. But when a lobbyist or CEO sidles up to a member of Congress at a fund-raiser or in a skybox and hands him a check for a thousand dollars, what do we call that? A campaign contribution," he said. "If we can give to our community chest each year, then surely we can give two dollars each year to create a system which frees public servants to serve the public."

Although Barney wanted to change the system for financing political campaigns, he was good at political fund-raising. He played by the rules and did not hesitate to exploit the current fund-raising system. "If the guy on the other end of the tennis court is wielding a racket the size of a bass banjo, one would be a fool not to use one too," he said.

Barney's Republican challenger in the 1988 general election was Debra Tucker, a thirty-three-year-old realtor and mother of two from Plainville. Tucker, who was little known outside of Plainville, where she had been elected to the Plainville Finance Committee, had served as the director of media relations and issues for the televangelist Pat Robertson's campaign in Massachusetts. When she announced her candidacy to unseat Barney Frank in Congress, Tucker declared, "What won't be an issue is Frank's acknowledged homosexuality." "There are enough good clean issues to talk about," she maintained. Tucker seemed undaunted by Barney's landslide reelections to Congress in the past. "The bigger they are, the harder they fall; the tougher the battle, the sweeter the victory," she said.

As the fall campaign heated up, however, Tucker increasingly touted her support for traditional family values. She asked the audience at a Republican Candidates' Night event in Attleboro, "How many [parents] would feel safe letting Barney Frank take our kids away for the weekend?" Many of the forty-five people in attendance laughed or snickered at the question. When asked about Tucker's comment, Barney called it "outrageous" and "despicable." "Unfortunately, that's what you get from the far right when they're desperate."

Barney won reelection overwhelmingly with 70 percent of the vote and captured twenty-two of the twenty-three cities and towns in the Fourth District, including Tucker's hometown of Plainville. He lost only the town of Dover, by a margin of 82 votes. Although he slipped a few percentage points from 1986, there was no drop in the Jewish areas in Newton and Brookline. He ran far ahead of the Democratic presidential candidate, Michael Dukakis, who received only 57 percent of the vote in the district. He saw the results as proof that his private life "is of very little interest to most people."

For several years, Barney had listened to the homophobic tirades of California Republicans William Dannemeyer and Bob Dornan when they spoke out on the floor of the House against AIDS legislation advocated by public health officials. They repeatedly accused health officials and House members of being out of touch with the will of the people and bemoaned Congress' unwillingness to listen to the American people with respect to AIDS. On February 1, 1989, Barney drafted a "Dear Colleague" letter. Although "Dear Colleague" letters are traditionally used by members to solicit support for specific bills or amendments, this letter was about AIDS, the voters, and William Dannemeyer. Barney wrote:

In 1986 Mr. Dannemeyer backed an initiative [in California] put together by the prominent felon and medical authority Lyndon LaRouche, and when that effort to deal with AIDS was overwhelmingly repudiated by the voters, its supporters attributed its defeat in substantial part to the unpopularity of Mr. LaRouche. So in 1988, Mr. Dannemeyer put his own initiative on the ballot, one in which he was free to frame the proposal as he wished. The proposal he put forward bore, not surprisingly, a strong resemblance to some of the proposals he has offered unsuccessfully on the floor of the House.

Dannemeyer's proposal would have, among its provisions, required physicians to disclose the name of individuals known or suspected of being infected with the AIDS virus.

Barney included in the letter the election returns in California, where Dannemeyer's AIDS proposals, Proposition 102, were soundly defeated. Barney noted that in Dannemeyer's own congressional district, "doubtless as a tribute to the respect his own constituents have for him," his initiative did better than it did on the statewide ballot by 6 percentage points—losing by a margin of 60 percent to 40 percent. Barney ended the "Dear Colleague" letter by stating that he was eagerly awaiting this year's debate on AIDS issues, in which they might be told that "the trouble with this country is that the people are out of touch with themselves." He told the *Boston Globe*, "There are limits to when you restrain yourself from calling a fool a fool."

In early June 1989, following the resignation of Speaker Jim Wright of Texas, some Republicans began a smear campaign against the new Speaker of the House, sixty-year-old Tom Foley of Washington State, by questioning Foley's sexual orientation. Mark Goodin, the communications director of the Republican National Committee (RNC) and an aide to its chairman, Lee Atwater, prepared a memo titled "Tom Foley: Out of the Liberal Closet." In this memo, addressed to "Republican leaders" and circulated to the media, Goodin broadly hinted that the new Speaker of the House was gay. The memo highlighted Foley's liberal voting record, comparing it to that of Massachusetts representative Barney Frank and stating that Foley voted the way Barney Frank did 81 percent of the time. "I thought that showed a certain deficiency in Mr. Foley. He could do better, but it's a good base," Barney later said during an interview on the *Dick Cavett Show* on CNBC.

Barney faced a dilemma over how to deal with the memo. According to Barney, if people are hurting you by insinuation or by saying bad things, the traditional political view is to ignore them and rise above them. But, he told Cavett, "I was angry because Mr. Atwater has a certain record of this kind of activity. I decided the time had come to say, 'Hey, this goes too far.'"

Barney said he was unhappy about the underlying premise of the closet memo. The Republicans referred to Foley's being gay as if there were something bad about it. "Obviously I'm gay and I don't think there is anything the matter with being gay," Barney said. "But in society, there's still a lot of prejudice. What happens when someone is trying to use something that you don't find offensive as if it were offensive?"

The historical model Barney relies on is the effort by some enemies of President Franklin Roosevelt in the 1940s to spread the rumor that he was Jewish. Roosevelt aides eventually determined that it was appropriate to say he was not Jewish. "I'm also Jewish and I don't think there is anything wrong with being Jewish," Barney said. "When people are using something that is perfectly legitimate in a negative way you do have an obligation. The problem is not whether you are gay or Jewish or anything else but [they're] using it as a club against people and that has to stop."

The memo was largely ignored by the media until Barney took the offense, claiming it was a crude attempt to smear the new Speaker. "They put my name on it. It was despicable. They could have picked other liberals and put someone else in the headlines," Barney told the Associated Press.

Initially, the RNC denied that any sexual innuendo was intended and maintained that Barney Frank was chosen for comparison not because of his sexual preference but because he was a well-known liberal who used to be president of Americans for Democratic Action. Barney told the *New Republic*, "Let's put it this way. I don't think I was selected as a result of a regression analysis."

Barney publicly threatened that if the Republicans "didn't cut the crap," he was going to expose five gay people on the Republican side. His threat was not to expose gay Republicans in general, because he believes there is a right to privacy, but to expose those gay Republicans who attack other people for being gay. In Barney's view, there is a right to privacy but not to hypocrisy. John Locke, the great seventeenth-century British philosopher and theorist of liberalism, he pointed out, had espoused the principle that in a democratic society one great guarantee that laws will be fair is that the people who make the laws be bound by these laws. "A person who votes for one set of rules for sexual behavior and then regularly violates them is a legitimate issue," he said. "It is hypocritical to live a life style and then penalize others for it," he told Ted Koppel on *Nightline*. "Hypocrisy is something the public has a right to know."

In 2007, when Republican senator Larry Craig from Idaho was arrested by an undercover police officer and charged with lewd conduct in a men's bathroom at the Minneapolis airport and pleaded guilty to a lesser charge of disorderly conduct, Barney denounced Craig's hypocrisy in voting to deny equality to gays and lesbians but then engaging in gay behavior. Craig had supported a constitutional ban on gay marriage, resisted efforts to add gays to hate crime laws, and opposed legislation to outlaw employment discrimination against gays. At the same time, however, he defended Craig's refusal to resign on the grounds that the senator's action was not an abuse of office in the sense that he was taking money for corrupt votes. "It's one thing to say that someone can't be trusted to vote without being corrupt, it's another to say that he can't be trusted to go to the bathroom by himself," Barney told the Associated Press.

Looking back at that threat in 1989 to publicly out gay Republicans, Barney told the *Boston Globe*, "I honestly don't know if I'd have done it." He pointed to a scene from Gore Vidal's 1960 political play *The Best Man* in which a presidential candidate threatened to smear his chief opponent for the nomination by calling him a homosexual, in an effort to bring about a moratorium on mud throwing.

The Republicans backed off and the rumors and unfounded insinuations about Tom Foley were never heard again. Barney was successful in squelching the anti-Foley smear campaign, and the campaign generated a backlash. The memo was condemned by members of both parties. President George H. W. Bush called the memo "disgusting." Senate Republican leader Bob Dole commented, "I would say this is not politics. This is garbage." As a result, the RNC chairman was forced to backpedal. Atwater personally apologized to Tom Foley. Mark Goodwin, the memo's author, resigned, under pressure, from his job with the RNC.

Wesley Pruden, in a column in the *Washington Times* on June 9, described what Barney Frank had done: "The humiliation of the Republicans was total—done in by a Democrat in lavender drawers." Hendrik Hertzberg wrote in the *New Republic*: "Frank has done wonders for the image of gay people by facing down the bigots. . . . Right now Barney Frank is the baddest dude in town, and more power to him."

16

In Surviving a Washington Sex Scandal, the Importance of Being Frank

IN JANUARY 1987, Barney Frank had left the Employment and Housing subcommittee to chair the Judiciary Subcommittee on Administrative Law. Two years later, he rejoined the housing subcommittee. Since he was not chairing the hearings, he was more relaxed and more approachable. But because he was no longer the chairman, he was more partisan, combative, and unrestrained in his questioning of witnesses.

On April 26, 1989, Paul Adams, the HUD inspector general, issued a report criticizing apparent favoritism by the department in awarding Section 8 Moderate Rehabilitation Program funds between 1984 and 1988. The program had been established by Congress in 1978 to encourage developers to upgrade substandard rental housing and make units available to low-income families with the help of rental subsidies. The audit report revealed that developers had hired influential, politically well-connected individuals to push and lubricate their applications for these increasingly scarce moderate rehabilitation funds and paid many of these consultants exorbitant fees for these fleeting services. Former interior secretary James Watt had received three hundred thousand dollars in 1986 from a developer for three telephone calls and a meeting with HUD secretary Samuel Pierce to obtain subsidized funds for a housing project in Maryland.

Subcommittee chairman Tom Lantos jumped on the report, and his initiative turned into a series of twenty-seven hearings over fourteen months in what came to be known as the HUD scandal. These hearings on abuses, fraud, favoritism, influence peddling, and mismanagement at HUD during the eight-year tenure of Secretary Pierce resulted in Congress's enacting the HUD Reform Act of 1989, as well as the appointment of an independent counsel to investigate possible criminal wrongdoing by Pierce and others.

On the morning of May 25, room 2247 in the Rayburn Building was over-flowing with press and spectators. More than a dozen television cameras lined the back wall in the hearing room, ready to be clicked on. Former HUD secretary Pierce, who had not commented publicly about the scandal, was scheduled to testify. The opening witness was Judith Siegel, the Maryland developer who had hired James Watt to help obtain moderate rehabilitation units for a project in Essex, Maryland.

In response to a question from Chairman Lantos, Siegel responded that Watt was a business partner and that there was no quid pro quo. When Barney questioned the witness, she confirmed that there was no quid pro quo, that Watt's fee was contingent on the success of his efforts on behalf of the developers. "Well, that sounds like a quid pro quo," said Barney. "If he did this and it succeeded, he got that. I mean, that's what a quid pro quo is, the quid were the Section 8's, and the quo was the three hundred grand, and if he did not get the Section 8's, he did not get the three hundred grand. If that is not a quid pro quo, I do not know what is." Siegel insisted that Watt "was a member of our team." "He was a business partner on a contingency fee? I missed that in law school," Barney said.

Barney subsequently focused on why Siegel had not gone instead to her senator or congressman for assistance in funding the project. That would have cost her nothing. "Sometimes people call me and I'm grumpy. I mean I can't imagine that someone would say, well, I could call my congressman or I could pay three hundred grand and boy, he might be in one of his moods and I'd rather pay the three hundred grand." He said to her: "So I have to believe that being a rational person with a responsibility to your investors and others, that you did this as cheaply as possible, and the fact that you decided based on your experience that the cheapest way to get this project approved was to pay three hundred thousand dollars for a man who contributed nothing in terms of expertise, nothing in terms of substantive advice, but simply political influence, is very unfortunate."

Samuel Pierce was the next witness, and he began by reading a prepared statement. Barney had no respect for the secretary. He once remarked, "Jack Kemp is an enormous improvement over Sam Pierce, although a vacancy would have been an enormous improvement over Sam Pierce."

When the former HUD secretary had finished reading his prepared statement, Tom Lantos questioned him about his meeting with James Watt. Pierce began his response by saying, "Over the eight years, I saw thousands of people in my office." Barney leaned over and whispered to me, "Yeah, through his window."

A single sentence in Pierce's statement caught Barney's eye. At the bottom of page 4 was a comment that the report by the inspector general (IG) talks only

about Republicans, adding, "They do not cover the extent to which those affiliated with the Democratic Party benefited through the Moderate Rehabilitation
Program." Barney asked, "Are you suggesting that the IG deliberately refused
to do that?"

"No, I'm not saying that. . . . I just said that—that's not covered by the report," Pierce replied.

"Do you think that he forgot to do it or deliberately didn't or maybe it wasn't
there?" Barney inquired.

"I don't know," said Pierce.

Barney continued to probe. "But you are accusing the IG of giving an incomplete report and one that gives an unfairly partisan complexion to that?"

"No," Pierce said.

Barney tried again, "You are saying here that the Inspector General neglected
to talk about Democrats who were also there. I want to know, doesn't that
mean that the IG's report was incomplete and gave an unfairly partisan view?"

"I am saying exactly what I said there. There is nothing in there about Democrats. . . . I want to know whether he did or did not," responded Pierce.

"There is nothing in here about Frenchmen either," Barney quipped.

Barney accused Pierce of making an irresponsible statement that he couldn't
support. "Why do you think he didn't [investigate if Democrats were also in-
volved]?" Barney asked.

"I don't know," answered Pirece.

"Do you think he failed to do that—"

"I don't think anything. I'm just—" said Pierce.

"Well, that has become clearer and clearer as this proceeds," Barney shot
back.

Several minutes later, Pierce finally said, "I believe, yes, there are Democrats."
Asked whether he has a list of them, Pierce said no.

"What makes you think there are Democrats who were involved?" Barney
followed up.

"I believe it," said Pierce.

"With any basis?" Barney inquired.

"Just say I believe it," replied Pierce.

"Have you talked to the IG about this?" Barney asked.

"But I think I will now," said Pierce.

"Oh, first you make your public statement and then you'll talk to the Inspector General," said Barney.

There was another issue Barney wanted Pierce to address—access. "You said
you saw Mr. Watt like you would see other people. Would Ms. Siegel have been
able to see you as easily as Mr. Watt?" he asked.

"No. I don't think so. No," Pierce replied.

On Friday, June 9, James Watt testified before the subcommittee. Barney had had little respect for Watt during his tenure as interior secretary. During his 1982 reelection campaign against Heckler, Barney had criticized the Reagan administration for, among other things, "unleashing James Watt on the poor, unsuspecting, dumb animals and on the wilderness."

Watt asked the panel for permission to make a twenty-minute presentation without interruption. Chairman Lantos was reluctant to make such a commitment. But Barney said, "I will make the most supreme effort of self-control of my life and promise not to interrupt Mr. Watt. I can't promise not to squirm, grimace, and wiggle, but I will try not to interrupt." "If Barney can do it we all can," another member announced.

Watt declared that the lobbying for which he was paid more than $420,000 was "legal, moral, ethical and effective." He testified that $131,000 of the money that he received for the Essex, Maryland, project went to his partner.

Barney challenged him. "Did your partner do anything in this? Your partner gave you a ride? Did he look up the phone number?" he asked.

"The partner gave me backup and support. . . . I had to have understanding so that when I made this visit, I spoke with confidence and I would not have my reputation tarnished. . . . Sam Pierce had a right to know Jim Watt wouldn't be— "

Barney interrupted, "I must say in preparing yourself with a lot of detail for meeting with Secretary Pierce, you showed a great excess of caution. I think you were in less danger of being questioned on a specific process than any other time in your life."

Barney was the panel's most effective advocate and questioner during the HUD scandal hearings. Frederick Bush, a former deputy chief of staff to Vice President George H. W. Bush and the president's nominee to be ambassador to Luxembourg, attempted to explain that he had a meeting with Deborah Dean, Secretary Pierce's chief of staff, simply to get information about how a HUD program worked and that he always goes to the top to get information. Barney asked him, "If you need to mail a letter, do you go see the Postmaster General?"

Barney's next target was Marilyn Harrell. She was one of the hundreds of private closing agents hired by HUD to handle real estate transactions in response to efforts by the Reagan administration to privatize operations. As the number of foreclosures rose, HUD took over these properties and then sold them, using private contract agents.

Harrell used the opportunity for personal gain. She was later dubbed "Robin HUD" in the press because she gave part of the monies that she had embezzled from HUD to charity. At the time, Marilyn Harrell had stolen more money from the federal government than any other single individual in the history of the nation. As a closing agent, she would attend closings for the sale of fore-closed properties on behalf of HUD. The checks for the property sales would be written out to her. She would deduct her commission and send the balance of the sale proceeds to HUD. That was how the system was supposed to work and did work for several months.

When Harrell found herself in a personal financial crunch, she delayed send-ing a check to HUD. Nothing happened. Shortly thereafter, Harrell stopped sending any sales checks to HUD and pocketed the money herself. She contin-ued the practice for several years without incident. It was only when she decided to leave the job that somebody at HUD, while processing her exit paperwork, noticed that she had not forwarded any sales proceeds to the agency for several years.

Harrell was near the end of reading her prepared statement and apologized for diverting funds without the authority to do so, explaining that she justified her actions by reminding herself that because she gave some of the money to charity, she had "followed a higher law in an attempt to ease suffering." As she began to read a biblical quote from John 15:12–14, Barney leaned over and whis-pered to me, "Who do you think is going to play her in the made-for-television movie?" As I began casting the role in my mind, he blurted out, "Rue McClana-han from *The Golden Girls*." It was a good choice since Rue McClanahan bore a striking physical resemblance to Harrell.

Barney began asking her a series of questions about the sequence of events. "In September 1988, HUD was expecting some money, and it wasn't forthcom-ing. They then did what?"

"Extended my contract for two months," she replied.

Looking somewhat incredulous, Barney proceeded. "Oh, I see, because you hadn't given them the money they expected, they extended your contract. Your Eighth Amendment rights against cruel and unusual punishment may be in jeopardy here more than your Fifth Amendment rights. [This] was a contract you asked to terminate?"

"That is correct," she answered.

Barney summarized, "You said, 'I want my contract terminated.' HUD said, 'No, there's something fishy going on here, you better keep doing it for two more months.'"

He then focused on the letter she had written to HUD. "You wrote a letter to HUD in July saying, I don't want to do this anymore, I want to talk to you."

Harrell replied that she had written such a letter but that HUD did not answer it.

"Actually, I guess we're now into the 13th Amendment, involuntary servitude, you are a walking compendium of constitutional grievances," Barney remarked.

During August, the HUD hearings went on summer hiatus while Congress was in recess. As always, it was a slow news period. Then suddenly a political bombshell hit, one that rocked the nation's capital. The *Washington Times* published a story about Massachusetts congressman Barney Frank's relationship with a male prostitute. More than two years after Barney had come out publicly, almost two years after he had parted company with Steve Gobie, and at a time when he was living a healthy and happy life with a loving partner, Herb Moses, Barney's political world exploded. He suddenly found himself enmeshed in a major Washington sex scandal that stoked a media tidal wave as his private, past conduct became front-page national news.

In late 1987, Stephen Gobie was at home one evening watching television with some of the women who worked for him. They were watching *The Mayflower Madam*, a made-for-television movie based on the life of Sydney Biddle Barrows and starring Candice Bergen. Barrows, a onetime debutante and Mayflower descendant, had run a high-class escort service in New York City. Watching the movie, Gobie realized, he later said, that he was in the middle of a developing story that could be worth something someday. He made up his mind to become rich and famous by parlaying his tale about Barney Frank into a male version of *The Mayflower Madam* book and television movie deal. Gobie told the women he was with, "One day, don't be surprised if you see me on TV."

In the summer of 1989, Gobie tried to shop his story around Washington. He couldn't out Barney because Barney had been out of the closet for over two years. Gobie needed more. He found an eager audience for his story at the *Washington Times*, a conservative newspaper founded in 1982 and controlled by the ultra-conservative Unification Church, headed by the Reverend Sun Myung Moon, which broke the story.

During the second week in August, Doug Cahn had received a phone call from a press officer in the Virginia attorney general's office who told him as a courtesy that the attorney general's office had received a Freedom of Information Act request from the *Washington Times* concerning the records of a Mr. Stephen L. Gobie. The press officer stated that in the disclosure they were required by law to provide was a reference to Barney Frank. "The caller offered no opinion. He was just telling me this fact," Cahn said. He went into Barney's office to tell him.

On Wednesday morning, August 23, as Barney was leaving his Capitol Hill apartment, two *Washington Times* reporters confronted him about his relationship with Gobie. He invited the reporters into his apartment and answered their questions, acknowledging what was true and denying what was false. Barney described it as "a sexual relationship that turned into a friendship."

"I realized that I shouldn't be hanging out with prostitutes. But I was being careful," Barney recalled. "In the letter to the probation officials, I never said that he was working for me in government. I thought that I had avoided all the things [former New Jersey governor James] McGreevey later fell into, such as putting his lover on the public payroll and giving him perks. What shocked me was that [the *Washington Times* reporters] told untruths as if they were true."

That evening, Barney phoned Cahn at home and alerted him that there could be a news story in the *Washington Times* about Gobie's running a prostitution ring out of his apartment. He told Cahn that he had not known anything about it and that when he learned about it from his landlady he had kicked Gobie out of the apartment. Neither Barney nor Cahn knew in advance that the story would be coming out on Friday morning, August 25. They were not sure that there would even be a story.

On August 25, shortly after 5:00 a.m., Cahn was awakened at home by a phone call from a reporter for WEEI, an all-news radio station in Boston. The reporter asked him to comment on the story about Barney in the *Washington Times*. Cahn replied that he hadn't seen the newspaper story and would get back to the reporter after he read the story.

Cahn immediately contacted Barney, who was in Washington and was scheduled to fly to Massachusetts that morning. Barney said he would take care of returning the reporter's call. Barney's immediate reaction was to respond openly and honestly to the *Washington Times* story.

Cahn's second phone call was to Dottie Reichard, the district office director. He told her what he knew without yet having seen the *Washington Times* story. A few minutes later, Barney called to say he was on his way to Massachusetts and wanted to hold a press conference. Reichard called the district office staff to tell them that they needed to be in the office for a meeting at seven o'clock. She gave no explanation until they gathered at the office and she told the shocked staffers what had happened. She then sent someone to pick up Barney at the airport and made arrangements for the press conference.

An anxious two hours passed for Cahn until Reichard phoned to tell him that Barney would hold a press conference at the Newton Community Service Center. Cahn went to National Airport and boarded the first available flight to Boston. At the airport he purchased a copy of the *Washington Times* and read the story on the plane.

The front-page headline proclaimed, "Sex Sold from Congressman's Apartment," with the subhead, "Frank's Lover Was 'Call Boy.'" The article ran on the top right side of the page, next to a color photo of the Capitol Hill basement apartment where Barney lived. It began: "A male prostitute provided homosexual and bisexual prostitution services from the apartment of U.S. Rep. Barney Frank on Capitol Hill on a periodic basis from late 1985 through mid-1987, the *Washington Times* has learned." The article charged that in the spring of 1985 Barney had solicited a male prostitute, identified only by the pseudonym Greg Davis, who was a convicted felon, had written supportive letters to probation officials on his behalf, and had knowingly permitted him to run a brothel providing sexual services from Barney's Capitol Hill apartment. The article provided a detailed account of their relationship, and the *Washington Times* even printed a copy of the lurid sex-for-hire personal ad in the *Washington Blade* that Barney had responded to.

On the top left side of the front page was a color photo of Chevy Chase Elementary School, located in the affluent suburb of Chevy Chase in Montgomery County, Maryland, near the District of Columbia line. The article beside the photo revealed that Gabriel A. Massaro, the forty-eight-year-old school principal, had purchased sex from this same male prostitute and had permitted him to use the elementary school for his prostitution operation in October and November 1987, providing him with access to a guidance counselor's office and a telephone. Massaro admitted that he had had a four-year relationship with the prostitute but vehemently denied that he was aware of any prostitution operations going on in the school.

In a sidebar story headlined "Tenacity, Gumshoe Probing Confirmed Prostitute's Story," the *Washington Times* tried to cover itself by revealing that the prostitute had failed every aspect of a polygraph test he took. The story noted, however, that Barney Frank and Gabriel Massaro, when confronted by the newspaper, had confirmed most of the charges.

Hundreds of reporters, including Paul Rodriguez and George Archibald of the *Washington Times*, who had broken the story about the congressman's relationship with Gobie and had flown to Boston for the press conference, and television cameras, even a film crew from the BBC in England, filled the large room at the Newton Community Service Center.

As Barney entered the room, he knew that his political career as an elected official was in jeopardy. He approached the press conference with great anxiety and absolute seriousness. He began by telling the assembled reporters to take their seats, for he intended to stay there as long as it took to answer all of their questions.

Later Barney explained his approach: "Gobie decided not just to talk about me having paid him for sex, which was true, but to talk about a lot of other things that weren't true. And the only way I could convincingly deny the things that were false was to admit the things that were true. Admitting your wrongs becomes the basis to refute the things you didn't do." He added, "Everyone is in favor of telling the truth in the abstract but often not in the particulars. I look at it the opposite way. If you deny the plausible then people will believe the implausible, that I knowingly allowed Gobie to run a prostitution ring out of my apartment."

Barney had learned the value of being open with people when he was in the state legislature. Jerry Stevens, the secretary of Health and Human Services during Michael Dukakis's first term as governor, came before the legislators and Barney asked him a question, the answer to which was embarrassing to Stevens. Rather than attempting to be evasive or trying to defend the policy, Stevens just admitted it. "I agree with you. Yes, regrettably that would be the case. It is an unfortunate policy. We had no choice." Startled, Barney asked, "So, you admit that?" "Yes," Stevens responded unequivocally. "If he had tried to evade answering the question, I could have kept that going for at least half an hour," Barney recalled. "He just got it over with."

For well over an hour, Barney methodically took questions and answered them with extraordinary candor. He admitted what was true and denied what was false. He was contrite and humble. He acknowledged a grave error in judgment and expressed deep regret for what had happened. He was penitent but also strong in his own defense. He never deviated from the facts. It was painful for him to discuss in humiliating detail what he had done.

Barney acknowledged that in the spring of 1985 he had answered that ad in the *Washington Blade* and paid for sex several times with a male prostitute whom he identified as Stephen Gobie. Then, he said, the sexual link ended and their relationship became platonic and one based on friendship. He subsequently hired Gobie as a chauffeur and personal aide. He insisted that he paid Gobie with personal funds and that no government or campaign funds were involved. He explained that he had not withheld federal income taxes or Social Security taxes from Gobie's wages or filed tax information because he considered him to be an independent contractor.

Barney explained that he befriended Gobie and hired him as a personal aide because he hoped he could help him get his life in order and turn him away from prostitution and drugs. He stumbled when explaining that his actions were motivated in part by criticism that "liberals are interested in helping humanity at large, maybe with a vote or a check, but don't get involved in particular situations or particular individuals who might need help." Barney likened himself to George Bernard Shaw's Henry Higgins. "Thinking I was going to be Henry Higgins and trying to turn him into Pygmalion was the biggest mistake I've made." This statement prompted a few quiet chuckles from some members of the press corps, who considered Gobie a questionable Eliza Doolittle. One reporter whispered, "Henry Higgins never paid Eliza Doolittle for sex."

Barney admitted that he had written letters on congressional stationery to Gobie's probation officer in Virginia stating that he had hired Gobie as a personal aide. However, he denied at the press conference that he had used any political influence to reduce the length of Gobie's probation. "He asked me and I refused to use political influence," Barney asserted. "What I did was hire him a lawyer." He pointed out to the press that Gobie's probation was not reduced.

Barney stated that he allowed Gobie to use his car and his apartment when he was out of town and affirmed that he had fixed some parking tickets that Gobie had incurred. But he strongly and unequivocally denied having any knowledge of Gobie's operating a prostitution service out of his apartment. "The notion that I knew what was going on is false," he declared. "As soon as there was any evidence I kicked him out." He went on to explain that he had fired Gobie in August 1987 after receiving complaints from his landlady when he was out of town about activities taking place in his apartment that may have involved prostitution. "And the suggestion that he was procuring other sex partners for me is an absolute lie," he asserted.

Barney was embarrassed. Many of the positive aspects to his coming out were being undone by his naïveté and stupidity. He described himself as a victim in his relationship with Gobie. "It turns out that I was being suckered. [Gobie] was, among other things, a very good con man," he said.

For the first time, Barney publicly revealed his angst about what it is like to be gay and lonely, how he tried to make do with only a public life, and how he could not handle the strain. He attributed his poor judgment to trying to work out being gay. He acknowledged that he was stupid for trying to resolve his own emotional gaps and the frustrations of being closeted by using a prostitute and getting too close to him. "I guess I was still coming to terms with being gay. It was a difficult period," he told the audience of reporters.

Barney acknowledged that he had broken the law by patronizing a prostitute. "I should not have done that," he said but added, "In Washington, D.C., that is not a law that the police pay any attention to." He conceded that he was guilty of poor judgment and gross stupidity but maintained that he had not violated any ethics laws or congressional rules. "The last time I checked, acting stupid wasn't a violation of the House rules," he asserted.

Barney insisted that there was no need for a House ethics committee investigation because his actions bore no relation to his work in Congress. He maintained that a politician's private life becomes a relevant topic for public debate only if the official's activities involve abuse of public trust or position, if they point to some character flaw, or if they are hypocritical.

Asked by a reporter at the press conference whether he was going to resign, Barney responded, "I misjudged an individual out of an effort to help someone change his life. I was victimized in part by my own gullibility. But there were never any public funds. I don't happen to think that is the kind of thing over which you resign."

When asked about the impact this incident would likely have on his prospects for reelection, Barney acknowledged that it would likely be used against him in a campaign and added, "If I was planning strategy, this is not one of the events I would propose."

There were a few questions he did not feel a need to answer, such as whether he had paid other male prostitutes for sex. "I will acknowledge that I made a mistake, but I am not going to turn this into a general seminar on my sex life," he said.

After the press conference, Barney, Doug Cahn, who had arrived to witness the last fifteen minutes of the press conference, Mary Beth Cahill, and Dottie Reichard walked the one block from the Newton Community Service Center to the district office, where they found all the telephones ringing. Barney went into his personal office, closed the door, and made a few phone calls. Former Speaker Tip O'Neill was one of the first people to call Barney and offer words of consolation and encouragement.

Dottie Reichard wore a purple dress that day. She never felt right wearing that dress again and threw the garment away. About a year later, when she mentioned it to Barney, he replied, "I understand. I have never again worn the tie I had on at that press conference."

Ann Lewis and her husband had been at Logan Airport waiting to board a flight back to Washington when she heard the news about her brother. They canceled the flight and headed to Barney's office, where Ann immediately began working as Barney's political arm. The small group of senior staff and family that gathered in Barney's office after the press conference, minus Barney, tried to manage the fallout. It was agreed that Doug Cahn would phone the administrative assistants of the other members of the Massachusetts delegation, let them know about the story, and inform them that Barney did not knowingly allow Gobie to operate a prostitution service out of his apartment and that as soon as Barney learned about it, he took decisive action. The group anticipated that there would be a congressional probe and decided that it would be better for Barney to request an ethics committee investigation than to have one thrust on him.

They canceled the fund-raiser that had been scheduled for that evening. When Barney, referring to a parade that Sunday that he had committed to march in as part of the annual summer Fall River Celebrates America Festival, said, "I'm not marching in the parade," his mother said sternly, "Yes, you are. And we are marching with you." According to close friends, Elsie and Ann were the only two people who could consistently win arguments with Barney.

The next day, Barney met with about a dozen people—family, campaign advisers, senior staff, and close friends—at the Newton home of his longtime campaign treasurer, Dick Morningstar, and told them the details of the story. According to Tom Kiley, Barney felt terrible that he had let them all down. "Barney usually drives things—'first, we do this, then we do that, third we do this.' He was so despondent, so unlike Barney. We closed ranks behind him and were giving him emotional support," he said.

After first confirming with the organizer of the Fall River parade that he was still welcome, Barney marched on Sunday along a parade route that was lined with over a hundred thousand people. Carlton Viveiros, the city's mayor, walked at his side. Viveiros had no reservations about doing so. "Barney is a friend and I respected him. He was always there for me as the mayor of Fall River. I was there for him," he said. Barney wore a sport jacket and tie and carried a small American flag. He appeared subdued and unsmiling as he walked along the two-mile parade route. His entire family, except for his sister Doris who was on a family vacation in Ohio, marched with him in the parade.

"The people in Fall River cheered him and stood behind him because he was such a good congressman. They adored him in good times and bad," Mark Sullivan said. The front-page story in the *Fall River Herald News* the next day was headlined "Cheers Greet Frank; Says Political Future in Doubt." The newspaper article reported that Barney "received a shower of support as he walked the parade route, many constituents calling out to him, 'Way to go, Barney' or simply applauding when he appeared." Although there were a few scattered boos, most of the people watching the parade applauded and many gave Barney thumbs-up signs and called out words of encouragement. The article quoted Mark Montigny, the president of the Fall River Area Chamber of Commerce, who said of Barney, "He's one of the best congressmen in the country. I hope he stays in Washington doing what he's doing."

Barney was heartened by the display of support at his first public appearance since the press conference two days earlier. After the parade, he told reporters, "It's a good feeling. I can only infer it's because I am doing a good job. In general, they're probably more enthusiastic than I would have expected." With respect to his actions, he added, "I don't think acting stupid is a rules violation. I don't think being conned is a major violation of the House rules." But he retreated from his assertion at the Friday press conference that there was no need for an ethics committee investigation, saying, "But an inquiry can be a good thing." Asked whether he planned to run for reelection, Barney replied: "It would be arrogant for me to go forward as though nothing has happened. I don't own this job. I've got to earn it. . . . If it seems to me that I am not the best possible candidate to push for the issues I care about, it would be time for me to do something else."

When the sex scandal became front-page news, Barney was living with Herb Moses and had been for about a year. After discussing the matter with Herb and getting his consent, Barney made their relationship public for the first time. He told the *Boston Globe* on August 29, "[Herb] has made such an important difference in my life that this has been a tolerable experience."

A few days later, when Doris returned to Massachusetts, she sat down with her older brother and had an emotional one-on-one conversation with him. Doris, perhaps even more than the other siblings, had been totally devoted to Barney's political career and had spent many weeks away from her family and her career as a teacher working on his campaigns. "I was angry and almost shouting at him," she recalled. "You wanted more than anything in the world to be a congressman," she told him. "How could you jeopardize all that we worked so hard for?" she asked. "I just don't know," Barney responded. He was feeling remorseful and was near tears.

After the story broke in the *Washington Times*, friends, colleagues, and constituents shook their heads in disbelief, unable to imagine how such an intelligent, savvy person could do such a dumb thing and put his career in the hands of a sexual predator like Steve Gobie. But leaders in the gay community understood that Barney's action in using the services of a prostitute and then befriending him grew out of the frustration of living in the closet. "When you are closeted, you are sometimes driven to do desperate things. You don't behave rationally," Vic Basile, the first executive director of the Human Rights Campaign Fund, said. "You can use the analogy of men doing stupid things with call girls but it is not quite the same. It is a deeper emotional situation. I think that he became attached to and dependent on Gobie," Tim McFeeley, who followed Basile as executive director of the Human Rights Campaign, said.

A gay friend of Barney's related his own experience resulting from the effects of being in the closet. For the first year after starting a new job in a new city, he was celibate. Then one day he picked someone up and drove him to his apartment, hoping to have sex with him. When he suddenly recalled that a week earlier a close friend had picked someone up who resembled this man and had had his wallet stolen while he was in the shower, he came to his senses, concocted a story, and asked the man to leave. The man refused, saying that he wanted to be paid first for his lost time. Barney's friend was so fearful that he paid.

"Sometimes when you're not willing to live a life that is honest or you can't, you make stupid, ill-advised decisions and pay for that," Barney's friend said. "That has happened to me and many of my friends. Barney's situation was not that different from others. Some of my friends feel lonely and there are people who take advantage of that. To get some kind of relief or friendship they get involved with the wrong person. That happened to Barney in a more public setting."

The revelations were met with sadness, sympathy, disappointment, and some anger by constituents in the Fourth District. Barney was extremely popular in the district. Many constituents referred to him simply as Barney. For the most part, his constituents stood by him and seemed willing to overlook this apparently isolated lapse of judgment based on his many years of distinguished service to the district and his record of accomplishment in Congress. Barney's office received hundreds of telephone calls from constituents, and they ran 8 to 1 in support of him.

A *Boston Globe*/WBZ-TV telephone poll of four hundred registered voters in the Fourth District conducted the Friday evening that the story broke showed that 65 percent did not think Barney should resign, and 22 percent thought he should; 60 percent thought he should run for reelection, and 59 percent said the revelations would have no impact on their voting. To the question "Who do you believe is telling the truth?" 40 percent responded that they thought the congressman was telling the truth, and 16 percent said they thought Gobie was.

On Saturday, August 26, the *Boston Globe* columnist Tom Oliphant, appearing on the television program *Inside Washington*, voiced strong support for Barney. "I've known Barney Frank since I was in college. He's a man of surpassing integrity that I've never known to be questioned. I think he's a master politician, which people forget. He's also a magnificent congressman, and above all, there is nothing in this episode that counters any of those other images, and I would expect him to survive this smear in good standing," he said. He later wrote those same thoughts in the *Globe*.

Recalling that time, Oliphant said: "It was one of the early political scandals of the modern kind. You see the excesses of the press, which became more dramatic in the Clinton era, and you see the attack machines on the other side. What I did was in reaction to seeing this new attack machine start to form. It was a time when newspapers and mainstream political culture was having trouble coming to grips with gay people and their problems."

Barney needed a complete investigation so that all the facts could come out and clear his name. A year earlier, he had said on national television in connection with the ethics allegations against Speaker Jim Wright: "If there are accusations against those of us in public office, in the interest of public confidence, they ought to be investigated."

Doug Cahn prepared a letter to the ethics committee over the weekend. By noon on Monday, August 28, the three-paragraph letter addressed to Chairman Julian Dixon was hand-delivered to the ethics committee, formally called the Committee on Standards of Official Conduct. It begins: "Questions have been raised about my employment of a personal assistant during [the] period 1985–1987. I have publicly responded to these questions, and I have expressed regret for the mistaken judgment involved." He requested an investigation by the committee in an expedited manner "to ensure that the public record is clear."

When the House returned from its summer recess on September 5, William Dannemeyer rejoiced in reading the *Washington Times* articles aloud on the House floor with all the sordid and titillating details. Robert Dornan remarked, with seeming delight, "Barney's radioactive. Nobody will come near him."

When Barney returned to Washington and found a bank of television cameras set up outside his office to film his comings and goings, he angrily told the camera crews, in a effort to shelter his staff: "If you want to talk to me, we can set up a time for an interview. If you want background footage of me leaving the building, outside the building, crossing the street, that's fine. But I don't want cameras in the hallway photographing my staff every time they walk out of the office."

In early September, Barney addressed his staff at a meeting in the Washington office and offered to help them all find other jobs, saying, "You didn't bargain for any of this." The staff all committed to staying on and offered him words of encouragement.

Many messages of support arrived in the office, including one on videotape from the comedian and actress Whoopi Goldberg. After filming an interview with ABC's *Good Morning America* on the set of the movie she was making at the time, she had asked the television crew to videotape a message to send to Barney Frank. Goldberg looked straight at the camera and spoke without notes. She said: "You don't know me . . . but I just want to tell you I am a staunch supporter of yours and I would be really devastated if you resigned because I think you are one of the few clear bells we have in Washington. . . . So if it is any solace to you, I think if you left, we would be a sadder, much sadder, and a more devastated nation than we already are. . . . So please, please, please don't let that man win by having you resign. . . . It would really be . . . a terrible blow to everyone around us who is trying to make the world better. So please hang in there. Anything I can do, you let me know through the people at *GMA*. Goodbye." Goldberg added a handwritten note to the label of the tape that read:

Dear Mr. Frank

Hang in there. There are a lot of us out here who think that you are the cats PJ and know that if your voice were gone from Washington, we'd be a sadder nation for it.

Be well and in touch.
Yours,
Whoopi Goldberg

The scandal did not subside and the rash of negative publicity continued. For several weeks, follow-up articles appeared regularly in the *Washington Times*.

According to the *Washington Post* media reporter Howard Kurtz in his book *Media Circus*, from August 25 to September 22, the *Washington Times* ran forty-five stories on the Barney Frank case, twenty-two of them on the front page. The paper also ran an editorial calling on Barney to resign. On Monday, August 28, the *Washington Times* reported that John Banzhaf, a law professor at George Washington University, had filed a detailed legal complaint with U.S. attorney Jay Stephens seeking prosecution of Rep. Frank on charges of sodomy, which carries a penalty of up to ten years in prison in the District of Columbia.

On Friday, September 1, with the front-page headline "The Gobie Story: Frank's 'Call Boy' Tells All," the *Washington Times* trumpeted its exclusive interview with Stephen Gobie. The text of the question-and-answer interview with Gobie and the accompanying article filled an entire page of the newspaper. Gobie claimed that his nickname for Barney Frank was "Sweet 'n' Low," because he wanted a sugar daddy, but Barney turned out to be "a sweet guy, low on cash." The interview, however, was about Gobie and provided little new information about his relationship with the congressman. According to Gobie, his area of expertise was in escorting female clients. When he was asked about the first time he had sex with a man, Gobie replied, "I have no comment whatsoever at this point about my own personal sexuality." He later added, "The strength of my relationship with men was strictly on my character, personality and humor."

In 1975, at the age of seventeen, Gobie was convicted for the felony sale and possession of cocaine in Fairfax County, Virginia. Later that year, he was placed on four years' probation in the District of Columbia for sale and possession of narcotics. In June 1982, he was convicted in Alexandria, Virginia, on felony charges of cocaine possession, oral sodomy with a fifteen-year-old girl, and production of obscene material involving a juvenile (taking photos of the fifteen-year-old girl performing various sexual acts). He was sentenced to three years in prison, with all but ninety-three days suspended. He was placed on probation for three years, during which he was ordered to undergo psychosexual therapy. His probation was extended until April 1987 for failing several drug tests, missing meetings with his probation officer, and failing to take part in drug and psychosexual therapy sessions.

In the September *Washington Times* interview, Gobie stated, "I coached Barney's softball team in the congressional league. They had a real funny name, Frank's Hot Dogs or Frank's Franks or the Franking something. I've got a Barney Frank t-shirt." In fact, Gobie was not the coach of Barney's office softball team, the Congressional Franks. Maybe at times he operated as a first or third base coach to guide inexperienced players along the base paths, in a role that several players alternated doing during a game. Gobie was certainly not "the coach" or manager in baseball parlance. In an earlier article in the *Washington*

Post, on August 27, Gobie stated that he helped coach and played left field for Barney's team in the congressional softball league and boasted "I was the star player." He was a utility player at best.

There were other lies, big and small. Gobie claimed that Patty Hamel also knew that he was using the congressman's apartment to run a brothel. Hamel was the person who regularly dealt with Gobie, telling him when to pick Barney up at the airport or directing him to take clothing to the dry cleaner or run other errands. "The guy turned out to be a total liar," Hamel said. "I was shocked when it came out about him using Barney's apartment as a house of prostitution. I could see why Barney was fooled by this guy because I was too."

Another newspaper article stated that Gobie had been running a prostitution ring out of the congressman's "posh" Capitol Hill apartment. How could a dimly lit, barely furnished, basement apartment with Hefty bags for curtains and boxes for furniture be considered posh?

Yet the press continued to print stories full of inaccuracies. Most of the articles in the *Washington Times* and in several other newspapers in effect accepted all or most of the unproven allegations made by Gobie, a con artist and convicted felon. Two days after the initial *Washington Times* story, an article in the *Washington Post* cast doubt on the veracity of some of Gobie's allegations.

Newspapers across the country published editorials about Barney. Some were pretty harsh. The (Phoenix) *Arizona Republic* in an August 30 editorial referred to Barney as a "degenerate" and contended that "to seek male companions through the 'personal' columns of the homosexual press suggests an appetite for debauchery, not the social conscience of Mr. Frank's flowery defense." An editorial that same day in the *Omaha World-Herald* pointed out that the rules of the House require that a member act at all times in a manner that shall reflect credibly on the House and declared, "If the Massachusetts congressman's activities reflect credibly on the House, words have lost their meaning." An editorial in the *Atlanta Journal* on September 9 declared: "His effectiveness is at an end. He should do what he can to spare himself and his constituents further embarrassing details."

The *Register-Guard* in Eugene, Oregon, however, expressed a more universal feeling when it said in a September 6 editorial: "The saddest part in all of this is that Frank is not some sleazy degenerate. He is a caring, intelligent, persuasive, effective and articulate representative whose influence has spread well beyond his district. The country has benefited from his service. It will now benefit more if he voluntarily ends that service."

In a September 1 column in the *Washington Post* titled "No Double Standard For or Against Barney Frank," Carl Rowan argued that Barney should be treated the same as a heterosexual congressman who hired a woman prostitute, bedded her down in his domicile, and let her operate a prostitution ring from his residence. "We would be asking for the resignation or ejection from Congress, of the heterosexual lawmaker on grounds that his behavior was egregiously offensive and his judgment so bad as to render him unfit to make the laws of the land," Rowan wrote. "It is no assault upon gay rights or anything else to say that what Frank did was lacking in taste and discretion, and beyond that simply dumb, dumb, dumb." Rowan concluded, "Frank has sullied the House of Representatives and all who serve there in some ineradicable ways. He let lust lay on him stupidities that are almost beyond belief. He ought to admit this and resign immediately, without forcing the House Ethics Committee to go through long, X-rated hearings, about Frank's culpability in this wicked extravaganza."

The garrulous Gobie, enjoying his celebrity, began to add new details and to level additional unsavory allegations in newspaper interviews and television talk-show appearances in an effort to squeeze more juice out of the scandal story. In press interviews, Gobie insisted that Barney knew what was going on in his apartment: "He knew exactly what I was doing. It was pretty obvious. If he had to come home early [from work], he would call home to be sure the coast was clear. . . . He was being vicarious though me. He said it was kind of a thrill and if he had been 20 years younger he might be doing the same thing."

According to Barney, Gobie was inspired in part by some advisers at the *Washington Times* who told him that the story wasn't going far enough and it didn't "have the legs to destroy this guy." So he began to "amplify it in ways that were crazier and crazier." Gobie added some lurid embellishments. He claimed that he and Barney masturbated in the House members' gym, ejaculating into the open locker of then Vice President George Bush, that he also serviced congressional wives, and that he used Barney's car for trysts.

Gobie expressed no regret or remorse for the damage he had done to the careers of Barney Frank and Gabriel Massaro. In his mind these revelations were only the beginning. He planned to write a book about his experiences. "I think I'll just slap a book together. Sydney Biddle Barrows made in excess of a million. 'Capitol Offenses' would be a nice title," Gobie told the *Washington Post*.

Barney Frank became an object of ridicule, the butt of jokes on the late-night talk shows. During his opening monologue on the *Tonight Show*, Johnny Carson said, "Representative Barney Frank claims he didn't know what [Gobie] was doing. Here's a clue, Barney. When your aide shows up on Capitol Hill with a Chippendale's bow tie and Jim Palmer shorts, that's a clue."

Everyone got into the act. Robert Bauman, who nine years earlier had been in the news headlines after being arrested for soliciting sex from a sixteen-year-old boy, began to offer expert commentary on the Barney Frank affair. In an op-ed piece in the *Washington Post* on September 3, Bauman defended Barney:

I do know something of the depth of despair that society's prejudice against
gays inflicts in a thousand ways, few of them subtle. . . .

Nor is it so improbable that a middle-aged gay man could have a genuine
altruistic interest in a younger man he cared about, a desire to see that person
better himself and pull away from a life of squalor, and make something of
himself. It happens frequently in gay and straight society as well, all the snickers
about Henry Higgins notwithstanding.

Poor self-image afflicts many people, but it is epidemic among gays—
often concealed behind a façade of hyperachievement in other compartments in
life. . . .

And who among us can deny that when emotion takes over our lives,
judgment is not only affected but often distorted beyond any reasonable self-
interest.

Bauman pointed out that Barney's case was one involving consenting adults. He
believed that Barney should not resign. Citing an editorial in the *Baltimore Sun*
almost a decade earlier, in a similar situation involving him, Bauman said the
question should be left for the voters to decide.

The conservative *Boston Herald*, which had earlier described the revelations
about Barney's two-year relationship with a male prostitute as "one of the most
tawdry episodes in modern Massachusetts politics" and had run a story by the
columnist Howie Carr calling Frank "a sicko who happens to be a pol," urged
him to resign his House seat. The Massachusetts Republican Party, as well as
Republican leaders in Washington, called for his resignation, charging that his
conduct had violated the public trust.

On Sunday September 17, the *Boston Globe*, traditionally one of Barney's
biggest supporters, called upon him in an editorial to resign, arguing that his
transgressions were serious enough to warrant his departure from Congress.
The editorial, prepared by Martin Nolan, stated that what was at issue was
"not homosexuality but prostitution, which is illegal." The newspaper asked,
"What would be served by an exhaustive examination of it? Does he want to
answer how many times he sought the services of a prostitute? Does it do anyone any good to learn about it?" The editorial pointed to Barney's diminished
effectiveness and asked, "If former Housing Secretary Samuel Pierce testifies
before the subcommittee on which Frank sits, can Frank chastise Pierce for doing favors for friends at HUD?" Citing the "chasm between the high ideals of
his public life and the squalor of his private life," the newspaper declared that
"for his sake, for the Congress and the causes he has served well, Barney Frank
must go."

Barney and his staff were shocked by the *Boston Globe* editorial. "To para-
phrase John F. Kennedy, the *Boston Globe* urging Barney Frank to resign from
Congress is like *L'Osservatore Romano*, the official publication of the Vatican,

calling on the Pope to step down," Doug Cahn said. A classic line by Murray Kempton composed during the glory days of the *New York Post* that Barney often quotes in speeches reverberated in his mind after the *Globe* editorial: "The function of editorial writers is to come down from the hills after the battle is over, and shoot the wounded."

On September 20, the *Fall River Herald News* called for Barney's immediate resignation. In the fall of 1988, the newspaper had endorsed him for reelection as "a lawmaker of high responsibility, keeping an equal eye on national policy and [constituent] interests of the Fourth Congressional District, who has endeared himself to area voters by frequent visits here." The September editorial focuses on Barney's admission that he had hired male prostitutes on several occasions. It reads: "Prostitution, however, whether of males or females, is degrading to the person and destructive to the social order . . . and it is a particularly unseemly recourse for a congressman who pledges to uphold the laws of the land and the dignity of the House of Representatives. . . . And in the course of a review [by the ethics committee] how many more revelations will Barney Frank be obliged to counter or accede to? Why should he be sacrificed to further humiliation—or the hypocrisy of human nature?"

Barney was deeply concerned about whether he could be an effective legislator again. In September, he gave an interview to *Newsweek*, which ran a cover story on the scandal in the September 25, 1989, issue titled "Barney Frank's Story." "If I am hurting the values I'm interested in conveying, then I wouldn't continue," he told *Newsweek*.

Even liberal allies and friends, such as the columnist Mark Shields, joined the clamor for Barney to step down. The *Boston Globe* columnist Ellen Goodman, who lived in the Fourth District, described the scandal as a political sea disaster: "Steve Gobie, a hooker at the helm, opens up a leak the size of the hole in the Valdez and pours oil, 100 percent crude, over Frank's reputation." She concluded, "And so now you want to tell him, Barney, it won't wash. Give it up." "Ellen Goodman's column, elegant and articulate, really hurt," Cahn said. "How could she come to those conclusions so quickly?"

Some House Democrats said privately that they hoped Barney would step down quietly. The Democratic strategist Bob Beckel predicted that he wouldn't last much longer. The articles in the *Washington Times* continued with headlines such as "Embarrassed Leaders Want Frank to Go," "Outrage Grows in Mass.," "Tide Is Rolling against Frank," and "Democratic Leaders Desert Frank." "It's looking worse every day," Barney's close friend Joe Moakley said. "It's Chinese torture, drop by drop by drop."

Barney was on the ropes. His political career appeared to be over. Potential candidates from both parties were waiting to run for his congressional seat should he resign or be expelled from the House. Democratic state legislator Lois Pines was reportedly raising money to run for the seat. Bush White House officials urged the television personality Bill O'Reilly to run for the seat, and he considered the idea. Republicans Avi Nelson, a radio and television analyst, Newton mayor Ted Mann, state senator David Locke of Sherborn, and state representatives Robert Marsh of Wellesley and Kevin Poirier of North Attleboro were reportedly considering a run for the House seat. But none of these potential candidates was ready to declare for the seat while Barney was still occupying it.

The events took a toll on Barney. "I wasn't functional," he recalled, describing that period in his life. Cahn said of him, "an energetic, highly verbal, and aggressive member basically shut down." He added, "Barney did not come into the office with the same regularity. He felt morose and uncomfortable. When he came to work he stayed in his office with the door shut. He would dictate a few letters. He was no longer talking to the press, which was part of the shutting down process." A month after the scandal broke, Barney was still in a funk. "After I returned from vacation I went to see Barney and he was clearly battered and shaken," Amy Isaacs recalled.

Vic Basile, Eric Rosenthal, and Tim McFeeley, leaders of gay rights organizations, went to visit Barney at his Capitol Hill apartment. "Barney was always so self-sufficient. It was the first time that I had seen him vulnerable. There is a soft side to him, a soft underbelly. It was the first time I ever felt needed by him," Basile recalled. According to Basile, at one point Barney broke down and really started to cry. "He cried so hard he lost a contact lens and we were all down on the floor looking for the lens. I don't think we ever found it." "Barney was a different person that fall," McFeeley said. "He was tortured and tormented, not as much about the sex stuff but being so stupid, so vulnerable, that such a scum bag could jeopardize his public service and his career. He felt such shame in being so stupid."

Barney fell into despair. It upset him to be told by his sister Ann that people didn't believe him because they couldn't believe that someone so smart would not have known more. Family, friends, and House colleagues, worried about his depressed state of mind, persuaded him to get the help of a psychiatrist, whom he did see briefly for clinical depression and who recommended an antidepressant medication.

Barney had supporters, among them Speaker Tom Foley, who said, "There is no more able, articulate and effective member of the House of Representatives than Barney Frank. He has provided outstanding service to his constituency and the nation and I am absolutely confident that he will continue to do so long after this matter is forgotten." California representative Barbara Boxer pointed out that what Barney did was "human and vulnerable—not corrupt." Margaret Carlson wrote in *Time*, "On a scale of 1 to HUD, Frank's transgression is a low single digit: there is no suggestion that he used his public office for personal gain." But she warned that in the eyes of some, "private failings are far more serious: they go to a leader's judgment and character." Ronald Brown, then chairman of the Democratic National Committee, urged him not to resign, and groups such as the Council for a Livable World publicly backed him: "To be blunt, even a Barney Frank, whose effectiveness in Congress is somewhat diminished this year, still ranks among the most effective members of the U.S. Congress."

Although Barney thought that he was finished politically, he never wavered in his determination not to resign from Congress. "I knew I had done something stupid—and wrong—in engaging Gobie and keeping him around and getting involved with him to the extent I did. As low as I got, I did not want to quit because the ethics committee was the only forum in which I could prove that most of what Gobie accused me of—letting him run prostitution in my apartment, among other things—was bullshit. If I resigned from Congress, the ethics committee would have lost jurisdiction and ended the proceedings," he explained. "It also would have looked like I was afraid of [Gobie] and would have confirmed in people's minds the set of lies told by Gobie."

Gobie made his first charges in late August. By mid-October, Barney had gone from being really depressed to being angry. He was angry, for example, that people assumed that Gobie was running a male prostitution ring out of his apartment, when he had always said it was a female prostitution ring.

Finally, battered and hurt, he rose slowly to his feet to continue the fight. "I screwed up in my personal life. I have an obligation to show people this was part of my personal life and did not affect my public judgment," he said.

For the six weeks after Congress returned from recess in September, Barney kept an uncharacteristically low profile in the House to keep from bringing further attention to himself. In addition, he refrained from speaking out on public issues to avoid inadvertently doing damage by association to causes that he cared about—low-income housing, the plight of the poor, and the State of Israel.

The first subcommittee hearing on the HUD scandal after the August recess was scheduled for September 15, with former HUD secretary Sam Pierce as the witness. The night before the hearing, attorneys for Pierce informed the subcommittee that Pierce was reneging on his agreement to appear voluntarily the next day. At the hearing, Chairman Lantos announced that the subcommittee would be voting to subpoena Pierce. Barney arrived for the September 15 hearing, and Lantos greeted him warmly. The strain and worry that Barney had been under showed on his face. He spoke softly and his mood was somber. Some people were surprised that he was present at the hearing. The conservative columnist Patrick Buchanan had said, "Frank has no hope of attacking the mismanagement at HUD when he himself couldn't spot a whorehouse in his own basement."

Pierce subsequently appeared before the subcommittee, under subpoena, at a hearing on September 26, and Barney was there. When Pierce refused to testify, invoking his Fifth Amendment right and citing an accusatory atmosphere at the subcommittee, Barney got in a gibe. "The Fifth Amendment does not say that the atmosphere is too tense and therefore I will not testify," he said.

Gradually Barney began to increase his visibility, taking part in floor debates and participating in committee hearings. But at first he remained low-key and cautious. On October 18, he spoke on the House floor against a Republican motion to instruct conferees for the 1990 reconciliation bill to strip from the bill the child-care provisions championed by the Democrats. A week later, he was back on the floor discussing legislation that came out of the Judiciary Subcommittee on Administrative Law, which he chaired.

By late October, when several members asked Barney to participate in a debate in defense of the Legal Services Corporation, he was beginning to seem more like his old self. On Tuesday, November 7, he organized a special order, with fifteen Democrats participating, on budget priorities and sequestration. On Wednesday, the administrative law subcommittee concluded hearings on a bill to compensate uranium miners and other westerners who claimed to have been injured by government nuclear testing in Utah in the 1950s and 1960s. On Thursday, he spoke on the House floor on the Defense Department appropriation conference report.

That same day, Barney played a pivotal behind-the-scenes role in fashioning a compromise and moving the HUD reform bill, containing management reforms and safeguards at HUD, out of the Banking Committee. Many Democrats on the committee and particularly its housing subcommittee wanted to hold the HUD reform package hostage to a broad, major housing authorization bill. Barney was influential in persuading Democratic members to report the HUD reform package as a separate piece of legislation. "The alternative is for Congress to be accused of having uncovered a scandal and not passing legislation to address it," he argued to his Democratic colleagues. *Congressional Quarterly* recognized Barney's central role in persuading the Democrats to accede to the Republicans on the HUD reform measure and noted that his influence over his colleagues "seemed as strong as ever."

Barney needed legal counsel for the ethics panel investigation, and he had to raise money for a legal defense fund. In late October, he hired Stephen Sachs, a former Maryland attorney general and U.S. attorney, from the law firm of Wilmer, Cutler, and Pickering, to represent him before the House ethics committee. While Sachs was a highly competent attorney, he had not previously handled any cases before the ethics panel.

Many observers were surprised that he had not retained his friend Stanley Brand to defend him. Brand, a well-respected white-collar criminal defense attorney, had served as House general counsel for seven years under Speaker Tip O'Neill. He was extremely knowledgeable about House rules and precedents and had appeared before the ethics panel more often than any other lawyer. Brand's high-profile clients had included Democratic whip Tony Coelho, Democratic members of Congress Dan Daniel of Virginia, Jim Weaver of Oregon, Austin Murphy of Pennsylvania, and Mario Biaggi of New York. But Barney believed that hiring Brand sent the signal "member in trouble" and that Sachs would bring a fresh perspective. "At the time," Brand recalled, "I thought it was odd. As I have gotten older, I realize that Barney may have played that right in the sense that at some point he didn't have a criminal problem but simply a political electability problem. He didn't have a cascading number of issues nor the kind of collateral damage such as a grand jury that other members [that I represented] before the ethics committee typically had."

Barney became a target for the conservative right. The Conservative Caucus, a group chaired by Howard Phillips, ran a full page ad in the *Washington Times* on January 30, 1990. The ad was in the form of a petition urging Jay Stephens, the U.S. attorney for the District of Columbia, to initiate criminal action against Barney Frank. The ad was boldly headlined: ATTENTION: U.S. ATTORNEY JAY STEPHENS — YOU'VE PROSECUTED D.C.'S #1 BLACK HETEROSEXUAL, MARION BARRY. NOW WILL YOU PROSECUTE THE WHITE HOMOSEXUAL CONGRESSMAN BARNEY FRANK? The petition suggested that Barney had engaged in various forms of criminal behavior under D.C. law, including sodomy, keeping a bawdy or disorderly house, and making a lewd, obscene, or indecent sexual proposal and may also have violated federal mail-fraud statutes based on the letter he sent to Gobie's probation officer in Virginia. It called Barney a hypocrite because "he has self-righteously ranted and raved about the ethical standards of conservative leaders and elected officials" and "he has accused decent men and women of sleazy behavior" while "his perverse ethical perspective has blinded him to his own faults."

Illinois Democrat Gus Savage, who was found by the ethics committee to have made sexual advances toward a Peace Corps volunteer during a trip to Zaire, attacked Barney in a House floor speech on February 2, 1990, for being one of the three members, along with Patricia Schroeder of Colorado and Matthew McHugh of New York, who had filed an ethics complaint against him. "Believe it or not," Savage said, "among these self-appointed guardians of personal morality was one who since has admitted keeping and prostituting a homosexual."

Even during the midst of the debilitating scandal, people who knew Congress still recognized Barney's talent and intellect as a legislator. On March 5, 1990, *Roll Call*, the newspaper of Capitol Hill, reported the results of its survey of congressional observers in compiling a list of the twenty smartest members of Congress. *Roll Call* defined "smart" as raw brainpower, the ability to digest, process, and use information quickly and without much help from staff. Barney Frank was the number-one vote getter in the poll by a considerable margin. The article noted that what Barney Frank may lack in common sense he more than makes up for in sheer brainpower and quick-mindedness. And, it said, "He can reduce a blowhard bureaucrat to rubble from 30 paces with just a few well-chosen arguments."

A long-awaited and much-hyped article based on an exclusive tell-all interview with Steve Gobie, for which he reportedly received fifty thousand dollars, appeared in the March 1990 issue of *Penthouse*. The promo above the title of the magazine cover read: "Exposed: Washington's Biggest Sex Scandal." One of the other teasers on the cover of the magazine touted: "Stocks & Bondage: The Women of Wall Street." Both articles turned out to be duds. "Stocks & Bondage" was no more than a satire with caricature drawings.

The article, written by Rudy Maxa, who had broken the Wayne Hays–Elizabeth Ray sex scandal in 1976, was titled "Washington's 'Mayflower Madam.'" It described a nocturnal tour that Gobie had escorted Maxa on of the some of the seedy nightspots in downtown Washington, secretly frequented by powerful gay Washingtonians. But it contained few new revelations about Barney other than Gobie's allegation that Barney lusted after Rep. Joseph Kennedy. Barney dismissed the article as "sleaze" and called the allegations "a vicious, crazy set of lies." As usual, William Dannemeyer inserted the most provocative parts of the article in the *Congressional Record*.

Barney initially considered not running for reelection. He feared that if he were the Democratic nominee, the Republicans could win the seat. When Barney told Herb Moses that he wasn't going to seek reelection, Herb urged him to run. When he told his mother, she said, "Oh, you're running for reelection. You're not going to quit because the *Boston Globe* said so." "I spoke to him like he was ten years old," Elsie said later.

Barney kept flip-flopping and finally waited until he was convinced that he would not lose the seat for the Democrats and would not damage progressive causes before deciding to run for reelection.

In March 1990, he phoned Dottie Reichard from Washington and told her that he had made up his mind and had decided to run. But when she picked him up at the airport to drive him to a meeting with his top staff, he said, "I just can't do it. I am not going to run." Reichard recalled that he "looked like a sad sack," but she just said, "Let's talk about it at the meeting."

John Marttila, Tom Kiley, Jim Segel, and Dan Payne were all present at the meeting. By the time it was over, Barney had agreed to poll the district to help him determine whether or not to run. Kiley agreed to draft the poll questions for Barney's approval. Two days later, when he faxed the questions, Barney rejected them. "I don't want to ask people these questions," he said. But Kiley and Reichard convinced him that if he wanted to know the truth, he would have to ask the questions. He relented and gave the go-ahead.

"The results of the poll were unbelievable," Reichard said. They revealed that Barney's constituents didn't care about his sex life. All they knew was that he provided good constituent service and that's what counted. They believed that he had behaved stupidly but they thought he should run. "In a poll match-up with a mythical Mr. Smith, a married Republican with two kids, I even beat him, the perfect candidate, by 55 to 45 percent," Barney said.

The strong support for Barney in the poll was not limited to liberal Newton and Brookline but extended to Fall River, where the largely Portuguese community stood by him. "The people in Fall River were disappointed, angry and didn't like what happened but got beyond that and were willing to forgive him," Mayor Viveiros said. "They understood that having Barney Frank as our congressman was in their own best interest."

Several of Barney's advisers had in the back of their minds the precedent of Gerry Studds, the Massachusetts congressman who had easily won reelection after being censured by the House in July 1983 for admittedly having a sexual relationship a decade earlier with an underage male page and for making sexual advances to two other male pages.

The Committee on Standards of Official Conduct, a bipartisan panel consisting of an even number of Democrats and Republicans, began its preliminary inquiry on September 12, regarding "assertions relating to the conduct of Representative Barney Frank in connection with his employment of a personal assistant." Committee member Chester Atkins, a Democrat who represented the adjoining Fifth District in Massachusetts and was a friend of Barney's, recused himself from the inquiry. He was replaced by Democrat Louis Stokes of Ohio, a former chairman of the ethics panel.

Stephen Gobie testified under subpoena before the ethics panel on December 6 and did not come across as very credible. When Gobie was questioned about prostitution activities involving third parties taking place at Barney Frank's apartment, he was evasive and nonresponsive: "I run an escort service, sir. . . . I sold time with escorts on an hourly basis with a fee attached. Whatever happens during those encounters, . . . whether there was sexual activity or not involved, that is not something I'm privy to. I ran an escort service. Plain and simple."

"Gobie got in trouble by making up too much and some were obvious lies," Barney said. Barney also pointed out that Gobie made the mistake of getting too specific and that is the main reason he was discredited. "He would say that on such and such date I did something. They would check and I was in Massachusetts with four hundred people that day. He overembellished and that became rebuttable."

For example, during his testimony, to support his claim that Barney was aware of the activities taking place in his apartment, Gobie said, "When his landlord discovered the fact I was doing this, accidentally an associate of mine came for a job interview one day and asked the landlord where do I go for the interviews for escort and modeling jobs. The landlord almost fell off the ladder he was working on outside, and the landlord read the riot act to Congressman Frank when he came back Monday." The landlord, Colonel James Daugherty, denied under oath that the event ever took place.

Gobie's claim that he had arranged to have phone calls from two different escort service telephone numbers forwarded to Barney's apartment from January until approximately August 1987 were contradicted by C & P Telephone Company records that the committee subpoenaed. The records indicated that call forwarding was provided for only one phone number and for only six weeks, from January through February 13, 1987.

Barney cooperated fully with the ethics committee and appeared before the panel on December 11, accompanied by his attorneys, Stephen Sachs and Lloyd Cutler. He said: "I want to express my very deep regret and apology to you as my colleagues. . . . I did not handle the pressures of having a public life, of being a closeted gay man, nearly as well as I should have. I do think I managed to confine most of the damage to myself. But when you are in a public position, inevitably something spills over. . . . I don't deny that I did things I shouldn't have done. I got accused of a lot more. I appreciate the chance for trying to differentiate them."

Ralph Lotkin, the ethics committee's chief counsel from 1985 to 1990, recalled in a 1998 interview with *Capital Style*, "I think Barney Frank ranks high on the list, if not at the top of the list, as one of those members who found himself in an extremely uncomfortable situation and handled himself with dignity and aplomb, and I think helped himself incredibly by accepting the errors of his ways."

Lotkin explained in an interview for this book in October 2004, "Based on my experience at the committee, given the potential that many members could find themselves in an adversarial or potentially confrontational environment, some members will go on the offensive, which sometimes didn't make any sense since they were the ones who had to explain their action. In the sixteen or so cases that I investigated or prosecuted [at the ethics committee], there was normally a tension. There wasn't [that] tension [with Congressman Frank]." Lotkin described how Frank interacted with the committee: "Congressman Frank never adopted any of that type of hostility or aggression or intellectual disingenuousness. Congressman Frank was just straightforward and honest. His answers did not give pause in terms of the integrity or candor or accuracy of his responses. I think that did play a large role in terms of how the committee received the congressman's explanation and clarification of his conduct."

Barney clearly and unequivocally denied the validity of Gobie's assertions. "Absolutely not," he said when asked whether he had any conversation during which Gobie notified him or said something that would have made him suspicious that Gobie was engaging in escort or prostitution activities in his apartment. When questioned about Gobie's accusation that the two of them had sex in the House gym, Barney replied without equivocation, "I have never had sex with anyone in the gym nor have I heard of other people doing it. That is the craziest notion."

Barney's landlady, Mary Jo Daugherty, who lived in the house above his basement apartment, corroborated his account that he had no knowledge of Gobie's activities in his apartment until August 1987 when she informed him of her suspicions. She said she phoned Barney, who was on vacation, and told him something was going on in the apartment that looked like a hooker ring. Barney was upset, said he was sorry about it, thanked her for calling, and assured her that Gobie would not be back on the property.

Daugherty testified that none of the activities giving rise to her suspicions occurred when Barney was present. In her view, Gobie's assertions that he used the apartment for prostitution with Barney's knowledge were "obvious lies." "It is my strong belief, based on my knowledge of both Congressman Frank and Mr. Gobie, that Mr. Gobie took advantage of Congressman Frank and had begun to misuse the apartment without Congressman Frank's knowledge or permission," she stated in a sworn affidavit. Barney's failure to detect what Gobie was doing in his apartment is consistent with the fact that in his personal life he often doesn't pay attention to details and often misses clues.

Patty Hamel was the only member of Barney's staff called to testify before the ethics panel. "Gobie lied about me and I know he lied about Barney," she said. "This was a guy Barney, who has a heart of gold, was trying to help."

The ethics committee reviewed all of the newspaper coverage that Gobie's story had generated and followed up with the people involved. On May 10, the committee interviewed a young woman identified in a *Washington Times* story as a prostitute who worked for Gobie and who stated in the article that Rep. Frank knew prostitutes were using his Capitol Hill apartment as a bordello. Under oath, this woman testified that her personal knowledge of prostitution activities in Rep. Frank's apartment was limited to a brief period, from June 17 through July 31, 1987. She stated that only once during that period did she have a brief phone conversation with a man whom she believed was Rep. Barney Frank, because she recognized the voice. The caller did not identify himself as such and she had no recollection of ever seeing or hearing the congressman on radio or television. That brief phone conversation did not involve any expression of knowledge about sexual activity nor did she volunteer any. In addition, she stated that she was unaware of any conversation during which Gobie told the congressman about his illegal activities in the apartment. The woman denied telling the reporter that she spoke with Rep. Frank "two or three times a week" and maintained that she had told the reporter exactly what she told the committee.

Thus, in numerous instances, where an assertion made by Gobie, either publicly or during his appearance before the ethics panel, was investigated for accuracy, Gobie's claim was contradicted or refuted by third-party sworn testimony, documentary evidence, or other evidence provided by Gobie himself.

The ethics committee spent almost ten months investigating Barney's relationship with Gobie and whether he had misused his office or condoned illegal activities. There had been thirty hours of depositions. The ethics committee found most of Gobie's claims to be baseless. The panel rejected the most serious allegations, including Gobie's assertion that Rep. Frank was aware that he ran a prostitution service out of his Capitol Hill apartment. The committee found that Rep. Frank "did not have either prior or concomitant knowledge of prostitution activities involving third parties alleged to have taken place in his apartment." Nor did the committee find any truth in Gobie's accusation that Rep. Frank had engaged in sexual activities in the House gymnasium. The committee found no basis to support Gobie's claim that the congressman had attempted to pressure his probation officer or his court-ordered psychosexual therapist when he contacted them. Both expressly denied under oath that Rep. Frank had attempted to pressure them or to intimidate them in any way regarding Gobie's probation.

The committee ultimately dismissed all of the allegations of wrongdoing except for two minor actions—sending a misleading memo to Gobie's parole officer and fixing several parking tickets on Gobie's behalf. The first related to an April 16, 1986, memo containing misleading statements that Barney had written on congressional letterhead to an attorney who represented Gobie in the probation proceeding. In that memo Barney was not totally candid in describing the circumstances under which he came to meet Gobie (I met Steve about two years ago "through mutual friends") or Gobie's activities while on probation (with one apparent exception, marijuana use, he has been "scrupulous about meeting his probation requirement"). This memo was subsequently sent by Gobie's attorney to the commonwealth attorney for the City of Alexandria, Virginia. Neither Barney nor anyone on his congressional staff ever contacted the commonwealth attorney on Gobie's behalf. The commonwealth attorney told the committee that the memorandum had no bearing on the probation decision involving Gobie nor did it lead him to believe that he was being pressured. Gobie's probation was in fact extended. The committee, however, concluded that Rep. Frank should have reasonably anticipated that this memo containing misleading statements might be communicated to law enforcement officials having a role in Gobie's probation and could be perceived as an attempt to use political influence to affect the outcome of the administration of Gobie's probation.

The second related to Barney Frank's action in connection with thirty-three parking tickets incurred by him or by Gobie in the District of Columbia at times when the car was being used for personal activities rather than official business. These parking tickets had been administratively dismissed or waived under the congressional perk that allows members of Congress to park their vehicles in any available curb space while on official business. Only nine of the thirty-three parking tickets that were erroneously waived had been done at Barney's express request.

Under the rules and precedents of the House and the Committee on Standards of Official Conduct, the panel was authorized to propose any form of punishment it deemed appropriate under the circumstances. For many years, the only vehicle the committee had used was going to the House floor for a reprimand, censure, or expulsion. During Chairman Julian Dixon's tenure, however, the committee had considered and adopted, at the suggestion of its chief counsel, Ralph Lotkin, an alternative penalty that did not require floor action—a letter of reproval. According to Lotkin, a certain type or level of conduct should not require a call of the 435 members of the House and an hour or more of debate. The term *letter of reproval* was broad enough to encompass petty offenses and actions that may have emanated from an administrative oversight or stupidity. Lotkin described the letter of reproval as "an attempt to be firm ethically and compassionate to the circumstances." The approach appears to have been warmly received by members, the press, and the public. The ethics committee under Dixon's leadership had issued letters of reproval in several earlier cases.

The twelve-member ethics committee was divided for several weeks over a penalty. Most Democrats on the committee, including Dixon, favored a letter of reproval, which would have required no further action by the full House. A few Republicans on the committee were undecided. They tried to be careful and thoughtful in their deliberations. Yet they had no frame of reference, asking themselves, "How could it happen, prostitution taking place in his apartment and he did not know about it?" Other Republicans on the panel, including Rep. Larry Craig of Idaho, held steadfast for a more serious sanction. "I had heard rumors that Craig was gay but he had denied it," Barney said. As a Senator in 2007, Craig was arrested by an undercover police officer and charged with lewd conduct in a men's bathroom at the Minneapolis airport and pleaded guilty to disorderly conduct.

Tom Oliphant reported in the *Boston Globe* that Chairman Dixon decided that a recommendation of reprimand by a united, unanimous panel was more advantageous than a divided 9–3 panel vote in favor of a letter of reproval. "The reprimand was a function more of the politics of the House than the substantive merits of the case," he said. "Factually it was simple. He booted the guy out after he found out what was going on in the apartment. After that, it was just parking tickets and homosexuality. I am positive that if you took the homosexuality out of it, the committee would have gone back to a letter of reproval."

Dixon hoped that the panel's unanimous recommendation for the harsher punishment of reprimand might avoid a divisive floor fight in which the Republicans could push for a tougher penalty. With the mid-term congressional elections coming up that fall, the unanimous committee recommendation for reprimand also provided cover and made it less risky for Democrats to vote against motions for harsher penalties. Dixon did not want to give the Republicans ammunition and a battle cry in the upcoming congressional elections. He wanted something that would end the matter definitively. It was also well known by then that Barney was not in any trouble in his district with respect to reelection.

On July 19, the ethics committee found, based on the thirty-three parking tickets and the misleading 1986 memorandum in support of ending Gobie's probation, that Barney Frank's conduct reflected discredit on the House in violation of House rule XLIII, Clause 1, and unanimously recommended that he be reprimanded by the House. A reprimand is the lowest level of official sanction that the full House can apply.

Roll Call argued in a July 23 editorial that a reprimand was far too harsh a penalty for fixing a few parking tickets and being the source of a harmless though misleading memo. The editorial advocated that a letter of reproval was the appropriate penalty in Barney Frank's case and urged House members to reject the committee's recommendation. It argued that, because of the decisions rendered by the panel on other recent charges of misconduct, the penalty recommended by the committee was excessive. It pointed out that a year earlier the ethics committee had sent a simple letter of reproval to Democrat Jim Bates of California, who had in repeated incidents sexually harassed female members of his staff. Democrat Gus Savage didn't get even a reproval letter for his improper conduct with a Peace Corps worker. The editorial facetiously suggested that if members of the House decide to go along with the committee's recommendation, they should "insist that the [General Accounting Office] perform two audits, one of the records of the Sergeant at Arms to find out whether any other traffic tickets have been improperly fixed and one of the records of every Representative to ferret out any slightly misleading memos that might benefit friends or acquaintances."

Committee chief counsel Lotkin candidly remarked during an October 2004 interview, "I personally believed a letter of reproval would have been a more than adequate response . . . to the improprieties of the parking ticket and the [congressional] letterhead. Neither of those, separate or together, in my personal view after the fact, necessitated going to the floor of the House."

Barney did not contest the finding by the ethics committee that his conduct in improperly fixing thirty-three parking tickets and writing a misleading memo on behalf of Gobie reflected discredit on the House. "I was sloppy with the parking tickets," he conceded. He accepted the committee's recommendation for a reprimand. He did so to make it easier politically for his Democratic colleagues, with an eye on the November election, to argue that they simply supported the committee's recommendation. "I felt guilty about screwing up and I didn't want it to be used against everybody," he explained. Barney did not believe that a reprimand was the appropriate penalty, but he accepted it because he did not want to hurt Democratic members in the process. Steny Hoyer of Maryland remembered Barney's saying at a Democratic whip meeting, "I don't want anyone but me to take a hit for this. It's my screw-up and I'm sorry."

Several House members suggested to Barney that he was hardly the only one to share his parking-ticket privileges with others or to have written a slightly misleading letter on congressional stationery for the benefit of a friend, admitting, "There but for the grace of God go I." Pity the House member who writes a college or law school recommendation on congressional letterhead without revealing that the student's parents were longtime campaign contributors, they contended. But Barney did not want to seek shelter in the others-do-it line of defense. "That is one of the reasons why I lost some respect for Dan Rostenkowski [in the 1994 House post office scandal] when he said that everybody does it," Barney said.

Barney told Democrat Liz Patterson of South Carolina, who was facing a tough reelection battle, to vote for censure because he didn't want her to suffer politically for his mistake. She expressed her appreciation for his being so understanding. But when the time came, she could not bring herself to support Newt Gingrich's motion for censure and instead voted for reprimand.

Democratic majority leader Richard Gephardt organized an informal whip count on Barney's behalf. Sam Gejdenson told Gephardt, "Be careful when you are polling our members, just remember one thing, some of them will lie."

On July 26, the House of Representatives considered what action to take against Barney Frank. The telephones in the House offices nearly stopped ringing. It was clear that the men and women on Capitol Hill were totally absorbed by the debate. The raucous and acrimonious debate lasted nearly four hours and featured blistering attacks from two gay-bashing members, William Dannemeyer and Robert Dornan, who wanted Barney expelled from the House. At times lawmakers shouted at each other. Partisan attacks were greeted with supportive applause and occasional hissing from the other side of the chamber.

Normally, the ethics committee would present its report and evidence first. Dannemeyer, however, insisted on going first. The committee struck an agreement with him and Dornan, allowing them to go first to present their case for expulsion. There would be an hour of debate followed by a roll call vote on the expulsion motion.

Ralph Lotkin defended that agreement: "Dannemeyer represented a fringe in the House and that fringe had a right to its voice but not to dominate the thought processes of the House. It was better not to give them more time in the limelight. Let them spew their thoughts and get them off the stage." Lotkin added, "[The agreement] was an effort to try and bring the matter to a rational conclusion while dealing, in my judgment, with people who had been irrational if not clearly mean spirited, in terms of manufacturing under the guise of fact, so-called leaks which weren't leaks, but they were manufactured to have them printed in the *Washington Times*, which was clearly an instrument of Dannemeyer and Dornan. The approach [the committee took] was a way to diffuse that and bring the matter to a sensible end."

The debate began with Dannemeyer offering a privileged resolution to expel Barney Frank from the House. His assertion that he took no enjoyment in doing so rang hollow. As one observer described Dannemeyer, "He was a homophobe. It didn't really matter what Barney Frank did or didn't do. He wanted to rid the House of anybody who wasn't a heterosexual."

Over the years, Dannemeyer had often been stung by Barney's zingers. For example, on November 1, 1985, Dannemeyer demanded an up or down vote on the Gramm–Rudman deficit reduction bill, criticizing Speaker O'Neill for not giving Republicans a vote. Barney asked Dannemeyer, "Why, when the minority had it within their control to frame an instruction motion to the conferees after Gramm–Rudman first passed the Senate, they did not do that? They are now clamoring for a vote. The minority had it within its power to offer an instruction, and could have instructed on Gramm–Rudman and they decided not to." Dannemeyer responded angrily, "Would you like the answer? I may be dense but I am not dumb, you do not have to repeat it again." Barney, with a sheepish grin and a twinkle in his eye, countered, "I hope the gentleman is not asking me that."

Expelling a member from the House is the most serious punishment possible and has occurred only four times in the nation's history. Three House members were expelled for rebellion and treason in 1861 and a fourth, Democrat Michael Myers of Pennsylvania, who was videotaped during the Abscam scandal, was expelled for corruption in 1980.

Dannemeyer declared to his colleagues: "We must stand and affirm the existence of standards in our society, because to put this issue in perspective, what is going on in America is a cultural war. The Judeo-Christian ethic on which this nation was founded says very clearly that there are fixed standards which God gave to man to govern people in our society." He accused the ethics committee members of a whitewash, referring to their report as "a brief prepared for the benefit of Mr. Frank" and not "an objective analysis of the evidence."

Dannemeyer charged that Barney knew that Gobie was running a prostitution business out of his apartment. He recounted assorted allegations against Barney and launched into his analysis of the evidence that he felt proved that Barney "knowingly condoned a house of prostitution being run out of his residence."

Julian Dixon, the normally mild-mannered Democratic chairman of the ethics committee, was incensed by Dannemeyer's charges and lashed out in a booming voice, "You have just heard one of the most edited, selective garbage that has ever been put forth, in my opinion, in this House," he said. The Democratic side of the chamber broke out in applause.

Dixon was outraged that Dannemeyer would stand in the well of the House and claim that he did not come with any predisposed disposition on this case. He accused Dannemeyer of having arrived at his conclusions months before the committee released its report. He pointed out that back on January 23, several months before the committee had concluded its investigation, Dannemeyer had promised to introduce the expulsion motion after the committee had issued its report. "Did he have any information at that time?" Dixon asked. "He had information on Congressman Frank's lifestyle. That is the only information he had at that time."

"I am not going to attempt to refute every garbage statement made, but I am going to go through a brief analysis for you," Dixon said. He pointed out that

Dannemeyer had relied on a statement quoted in a *Washington Times* article to charge that Barney and Gobie were present at a dinner party when the operation of an escort service was discussed. "That is absolutely not true," Dixon shouted. The person who was supposedly quoted had been interviewed by the committee and had completely refuted the *Washington Times* story.

"Follow along, Mr. Dannemeyer, on page 49 of the report, the entire sentence," Dixon said. "Look at it Mr. Dannemeyer! It's on page 49." Dixon read the sentence: "The witness specifically took issue with the disputed accuracy of the May 1, 1990 news article with respect to the statement that on one dinner occasion in which Representative Frank and Mr. Gobie were present the operations of the Saxons escort service were discussed."

Dixon also insisted that Dannemeyer "please listen" and read along with him to refute his claim that Barney had successfully influenced probation officers on behalf of Gobie. He also pointed out that the psychosexual therapist said that Barney's call to her "was completely appropriate in every way." Dixon read from the therapist's testimony: "He asked nothing of me that was in any way inappropriate. I discerned no attempt to influence me in my treatment of Mr. Gobie or in my contacts with the Probation Department. His inquiry was like many calls from employers of clients of mine."

Dixon concluded: "Can you fairly say that Mr. Frank successfully influenced the people that were supervising Mr. Gobie? That is not fair, Mr. Dannemeyer."

Robert Dornan, a combative, controversial, and often nasty right-winger, nicknamed "B1 Bob" for his zealous support of the B1 bomber, spoke in support of Dannemeyer's expulsion motion. He, like Dannemeyer, had often been the target of Barney's wit and sarcasm.

In November 1982, Dornan had introduced an amendment to prevent the Internal Revenue Service from going after the tax-exempt status of Bob Jones University. During the debate, he attacked the IRS for giving "a witches' coven of lesbians" in Massachusetts a tax-exempt status. Barney had responded: "I never thought I would be privileged to be present on the floor when a genuine witch hunt was in progress. I would say, based on my experience, racial discrimination and bigotry are doing a lot more harm in America today than witches. I congratulate the IRS on its priority in going after the bigots."

In June 1987, Dornan offered an amendment on the House floor to recognize a state of belligerency in the republic of Nicaragua. Barney remarked, "I do not think the gentleman from California needs a declaration of a state of belligerency since, when we debate foreign policy, he is in a permanent state of one."

This was payback time for Bob Dornan and he was relishing it. He pronounced to the House membership that Barney Frank should be expelled. "I don't care about the details. The devil is in the details. That is for you lawyers," he maintained. Dornan asserted that such conduct would have destroyed the careers of other professionals—a high school principal, a business leader, or a broadcaster would have lost his job after such a scandal. He concluded, "I will vote for expelling because [Barney Frank] didn't have the honor and decency to resign." As Dornan was leaving the well, he turned to Barney and shouted, "Finis, finished, done. Out the door, Barney."

Louisiana Republican Clyde Holloway also spoke in support of the resolution for expulsion. "I am here to say that Frank has admitted enough to me to say that, as a person who believes in the Christian ethics of this nation, . . . if you are willing to let [Barney Frank] get by with this, if you are willing to accept this, what will we accept next?"

Several GOP members of the ethics committee opposed the Republican-led efforts to expel or censure Barney and argued during the debate that expulsion and censure were inappropriately strong punishments for his transgressions. They implored their colleagues to "forgive the sinner and condemn the sin."

Ethics committee chairman Dixon and the ranking Republican on the committee, John Myers from Indiana, then introduced the committee report and defended the committee's recommendation of a reprimand. Many of the ethics committee members spoke to explain their positions. Perhaps the most heartfelt statement was made by Republican Fred Grandy from Iowa, who had played Burl "Gopher" Smith on the ABC television series *The Love Boat*. "We are here to prosecute not persecute," Grandy argued. "And we do not enshrine and enhance traditional values by damning individuals whose lifestyles differ from our own." He added that Dannemeyer was not qualified "to sit on some Olympian council that passes down moral dictate" and said in conclusion, "This committee has given [Barney Frank] a fair trial. It will give him a fair verdict. I ask Members to do the same and support the reprimand."

Newt Gingrich, the Republican whip and a moral crusader, was the point man in the effort to push for the more serious punishment of censure. Under censure the offending lawmaker is stripped of committee chairmanships for the rest of that Congress and is compelled to stand in the well of the chamber and face his colleagues as the charges against him are read. A year earlier, Gingrich had told *USA Today Weekend*, "You're not going to get a Congress of saints. You don't want a Congress of saints. All of us have had moments in our lives that we're glad weren't videotaped and shown to our mothers. Human beings have weaknesses and do dumb things."

Gingrich, who six months earlier had himself been under investigation by the ethics committee and had received a fairly critical letter from the committee stating, among other things, "You were remiss in your oversight and administration of your Congressional office," rose to offer a motion for censure. Many

Republicans would have preferred that someone other than Gingrich offer the censure motion because of Gingrich's own ethical lapses and because of his public role in precipitating the ethics investigation of former Speaker Jim Wright that led to Wright's resignation. The Republicans, however, could not persuade another member to offer a motion for censure. Gingrich was motivated solely by partisan brinksmanship. He sought to take political advantage of the situation and hoped to make the Democrats' votes against censure an issue in the November election. Gingrich made an impassioned appeal for censure. "We are not here today simply to deal with Mr. Frank. We are here to repair the integrity of the United States House of Representatives," he declared.

Throughout the long debate, Barney sat midway in the Democratic side of the House chamber, his hands clasped. Sympathetic colleagues sat in the seats surrounding him, offering comfort and support. At times he chatted with these members or others who momentarily came by to shake hands or pat him on the shoulder, but most of the time he sat pensively in silence. Doug Cahn sat in the rear of the chamber next to Ed Markey and observed the proceedings. It was the first time in almost ten years on Barney's staff that he had ever been on the House floor. Dottie Reichard and the district office staff watched the proceedings on C-SPAN. "I don't know how poor Barney sat through all that on the House floor," Reichard said.

When Barney rose to speak, over four hundred members were in their seats in the House chamber. Members who had been milling about the House floor, walking in and out of the chamber, and talking with colleagues all sat down. Barney, appearing obviously pained, walked solemnly down the aisle. The swagger in his step was missing. There was silence in the chamber as he approached the microphone to speak. Standing in the well of the House, he was subdued and somber as he looked out at his colleagues and began to address them as well as a national television audience on C-SPAN. He spoke in an uncharacteristic quavering voice and the words drifted out slowly. He did not rely on any notes.

"Mr. Speaker, I am not here today to join this debate in the normal sense," he began. "I am here to offer an apology, and an explanation that is not meant to detract from the apology because I am here to apologize to my colleagues, to the institution, and those around me. . . . I want to say here that these mistakes were mine; they were not mistakes of my colleagues, of my staff, or of my family. To the extent anyone close to me had some sense of what I was doing, they tried to get me to stop it. It was all mine. I made some mistakes. I made mistakes which included, in a couple of cases, misrepresenting facts." He continued, "I think members will agree that I have always had a reputation for honesty—not always tact or tolerance, but honesty. There was in my life a central element of dishonesty for about 40 years, no 34. And it had to do with my privacy and my private life."

Barney stated that he had no quarrel with the ethics panel's unanimous recommendation that he be reprimanded. He admitted that to conceal his homosexuality he made misrepresentations about his relationship with Gobie. Barney
concluded his remarks by saying, "I should have known better. I now do, but
it's a little too late."

The House voted 38 to 390 to reject Dannemeyer's motion to expel. Barney voted "present," as did Gus Savage and Donald E. "Buz" ("I didn't know
she was only 16 years old") Lukens from Ohio, two members embroiled in sex
scandals of their own. Two conservative Democrats from Texas, Bill Sarpalius
and Ralph Hall, joined with thirty-six Republicans in voting to expel Barney
Frank, although both subsequently apologized to him for voting for expulsion.
Sarpalius, a freshman facing a tough reelection battle, explained to the *New York
Times*: "It's nothing against Barney Frank personally, but I'm accountable to the
people that elected me. . . . What people objected to more than anything was his
lifestyle. That was what was unacceptable."

The thirty Republicans who voted for expulsion included future Speaker Dennis Hastert and Bob Livingston from Louisiana, who in 1998 was on the eve of
being elected Speaker when disclosures of marital infidelity prompted him to
resign from Congress. Barney was surprised and disappointed that Chalmers
Wylie of Ohio, the ranking Republican on the Banking Committee, someone
with whom he had worked closely on housing legislation over the years, voted for expulsion. A few days later, Barney told Joseph Ventrone, a Republican
staffer on the Banking Committee, "I am very disappointed with your boss. I
worked with him." "Congressman, you have to understand. It was his strong,
domineering wife, Marjorie, a devout Catholic with strong views about homosexuality, that basically told him to vote that way," Ventrone explained.

Republican Jim Lightfoot of Iowa, who had served on the Employment and
Housing subcommittee as a freshman in 1985–86, voted for expulsion. In November 1985, Barney had helped Lightfoot by agreeing to hold a field hearing in Lightfoot's district, in Council Bluffs, Iowa, to examine the role of the
Job Training Partnership Act, legislation geared primarily to retraining factory
workers, in meeting the retraining needs of farmers. Many Democrats in Congress, as well as the Democratic Congressional Campaign Committee, were angered that Barney held the hearing. Lightfoot's House seat was vulnerable and
the favorable publicity from the local hearing, as well as Barney's complimentary
comments about Lightfoot, helped to enhance his reelectability. Barney said
recently of Jim Lightfoot: "He turned out to be this hyper-fundamentalist type
of guy."

After the motion to expel had been voted down, Dixon ended the debate by
urging his colleagues to follow the unanimous, bipartisan recommendation of
the ethics committee that had examined the case for almost a year and simply

vote for the reprimand. "If you have any doubt, you owe it to this institution, and I dare say the members of the committee, to accept their judgment. . . . There has not been anything that has come up here on this floor today that has not been discussed and examined in our committee," he said. In a voice full of drama, he declared, "We cannot restore the dignity of this House by voting for censure. This man has suffered—rightfully so. We gain nothing by piling on." Dixon concluded by asking his colleagues: "33 parking tickets and one memo that admittedly has wrong material in it . . . and he has come here and apologized for that and explained why it happened. . . .'Is that worth a censure'?"

The House voted, mostly along party lines, to reject Gingrich's censure motion, 141 to 287, with 12 Democrats voting in favor of censure, and 46 Republicans voting against. Three Republicans on the ethics panel, James Hansen of Utah, Thomas Petri of Wisconsin, and Larry Craig of Idaho, voted to hike the penalty to censure, contrary to their committee report.

The House then voted 408 to 18 to accept the ethics panel's recommendation for a reprimand. Eleven conservative Republicans who favored more severe discipline and had earlier voted for expulsion and seven liberal Democrats (Black Caucus members Bill Clay, Mervyn Dymally, and Craig Washington, as well as Nancy Pelosi, Henry Waxman, Sidney Yates, and Bob Mrazek) who believed that a reprimand was too stiff a penalty voted against the reprimand.

The House vote was more than anything a political decision made with an eye to how voters would react. Many Democrats voted for a reprimand because it was a defensible middle ground and they feared that a lesser penalty might be considered no more than a slap on the wrist and hurt them politically in the November election.

As Doug Cahn was leaving the House floor, he was given the big roll of paper on which the votes are recorded. He carried it back to the office as a sort of memento.

Following the reprimand, Barney answered a few questions posed by reporters who had gathered outside the House chamber. He stated that there seemed to be a vendetta against him and cited Dannemeyer's history of disparaging homosexuals. "There is something about homosexuality that sets Mr. Dannemeyer to vibrating. I don't know what it is," he said. Barney was feisty and rebuffed efforts by reporters to elicit his inner thoughts about the proceeding. When a reporter said he was "curious" about what Barney was thinking while Dannemeyer was trying to expel him, Barney responded, "You will remain so." Asked whether he would become a major political issue in the November House elections, Barney said, "It is not my impression that I am on the top of people's minds across the country."

Barney returned to his office suite, where he entered his inner office, closed the door, and reflected. The eleven-month ordeal had finally come to an end. "I had long come to terms that I did something I shouldn't have done. What I was looking for was having it clearly established that was all I did. As I sat alone in my office, I was glad that I had established the truth," he said.

Shortly thereafter, Barney and Herb Moses flew to Massachusetts, where Barney held a press conference at the Newton Community Service Center, the same venue where he had spoken the morning the *Washington Times* story broke. He was much more relaxed this time. "This is not a moment of self congratulations for me," he began. "Having been accused of a couple of dumb things, one careless one and four outrageous ones, I got it down to one dumb one and one careless. . . . These were not mistakes made by my staff, by my co-workers, by other members of the House, by anybody else but me. I have 100 percent responsibility for this," he declared.

He had been reprimanded by the House for writing a misleading letter that he never actually sent to probation officials to help end Gobie's probation and for thirty-three unpaid parking tickets that had improperly been waived. Barney argued that the only parts of the letter that were incorrect were his attempts to conceal his homosexuality. With respect to the parking tickets, he said, "The D.C. Police must have doubted that a dented 1983 Chevrolet Chevette belonged to a congressman."

Several days later, Barney wrote a letter to friends and longtime supporters in which he said: "The past ten months have been difficult, in part because of my own errors and in part because of inaccurate and distorted efforts to capitalize on these errors. I do feel now that I have been able to sort out the truth from the fiction in the things that have been brought forward."

Reflecting on that discipline more than fifteen years later, Barney pointed out that he had filed a bill in the Massachusetts legislature in 1974 to provide for an independent prosecutor rather than an in-house ethics investigation because it is a mistake to have legislators judge each other when they also have to work together. "It is hard to be colleagues 360 days a year and then for 5 days to step back and be a judge," he said. "People say that an in-house ethics committee is too soft on each other but given the nature of things I would have been better off if it weren't members of Congress [judging me]. I would have gotten less of a punishment if there weren't the political element."

A week after the House reprimand, Barney was back in action as the House was debating the campaign finance bill. As a result of an apparent mix-up among Democrats, the House inadvertently adopted by voice vote a liberal Democratic package, including public financing of House campaigns, one that the leadership had no intention of passing. This caused confusion on the House floor as the Democratic leadership scrambled to find a procedural way to reverse the vote. The Republicans were gleeful and attempted to bait the testy Democrats. Mickey Edwards of Oklahoma needled Barney, saying, "I'm sorry that the gen-

tleman finds this all such a strain." Barney, reflecting on the events of the prior
week and the past year, replied, "I feel no strain at all right now," and pointed
out that "[Edwards] misapprehends the rules."

On October 7, Robert Michel, the Republican leader, had urged House members to pass a bill containing higher gasoline taxes and other tax increases. Ten
days later, Michel spoke forcefully on the House floor against any tax increases.
Barney could not pass up the opportunity to needle the Republican leader. On
October 17, Barney told his colleagues, "I heard the Republican leader yesterday
speak strongly against any tax increases, and that causes me some concern about
the security of this House because 10 days ago a person purporting to be the
Republican leader stood here and urged this House to pass a tax increase. He
said it was urgent that we do that." Barney noted that he had not been on the
House floor ten days earlier but had read it in the *Congressional Record*.

Henry Hyde rose from his seat and said that the reason the gentleman from
Massachusetts wasn't around and had not heard Republican leader Michel speak
ten days earlier was that he was "in the gymnasium doing whatever he does
in the gymnasium." Barney was surprised and upset by Hyde's comment. Ron
Dellums from California voiced objection to Hyde's remark and moved that it
be stricken from the *Record*.

Hyde later explained why he reacted in that fashion, so out of character for
him: "I respected Bob Michel and took umbrage at what Barney said. I thought
it was unfair and invited a response in kind." Hyde immediately realized that
he was out of line and that what he had said "really was personally offensive to
Barney and improper." He added: "I apologized to him as quickly as I could. He
had the good grace to accept my apology."

Barney's campaign reelection ads in the fall of 1990 dealt with the matter
squarely. A sixty-second radio ad called "Montage" included snippets of people's
comments about Barney: "He is stupid in his personal life." "People like to focus
on the bad things." "He made some big mistakes." "He should not be in the
position he is holding right now." "To me it makes no difference." "I don't know
that it has affected his ability to do good in Congress for us." "I think his record
is far more important than anything." "If he's done his job right they ought to
just leave him alone." "Sure he'll get my vote and all my friends' votes." The ad
concluded with the comment: "Barney is the best congressman we have had in
this district. Keep him in there."

At a debate before the general election, the GOP candidate, forty-seven-year-
old John Soto of Attleboro, who was not the smartest person in the district,
boasted that he had taken an AIDS test and passed. Barney, in a bemused tone
of voice, remarked that it was probably one of the few tests he ever passed.
Soto challenged Barney to do the same and publicly reveal the results. Barney,

with a flair for the rejoinder, fired back that he would do so if Soto agreed to take an I.Q. test and publicly reveal the results. Later in the debate, when Soto confronted Barney about why he had not served in Vietnam, Barney answered, "Well, I'm glad that you agree with me that gay people should serve in the military."

On October 29, the *Boston Globe* endorsed Barney Frank for another term in Congress, saying: "This is the same newspaper that advised Frank on September 17, 1989, to call it quits after the House [ethics committee] announced an investigation into his hiring of a prostitute. . . . We thought the revelation of squalor in his private life would hamper his effectiveness beyond repair. We were wrong. Frank ignored our advice and announced for reelection. He has been stronger and more articulate than we thought. The Republican Party evidently agrees because it failed to produce a strong candidate in the district. . . . We foresee a long and fruitful career for Barney Frank and commend him to voters of the 4th Congressional District."

Barney easily won reelection, with 66 percent of the vote. The day after the election, when a reporter asked Barney whether he thought that his large margin of victory meant that the Gobie scandal had finally been put to rest, he replied, "Probably not, because people like you will continue to keep asking about it."

According to former House general counsel Stan Brand, few House members survive ethics problems and get reelected. "Usually," he said, "as they say in sports, it is a career-ending injury." Barney was a sex scandal survivor in large part because of the abundance of goodwill that he had generated over many years among his House colleagues. His survival can be attributed partly to strategy and luck. He told the truth rather than attempting to stonewall, he was contrite, and he admitted his mistakes. Also, he was fortunate that the sex scandal erupted in August 1989 rather than closer to the 1990 election. Time was on his side and he spent a great deal of time in his district

Barney did not face a serious challenger in his bid for reelection. First-tier candidates, both Democrats and Republicans, were hesitant to challenge him. The ultraconservative Soto, a lawyer and accountant with New England Telephone, was one of the weakest opponents he ever faced. Soto, who was relatively unknown in the district, had lukewarm Republican Party support and spent only thirty-two thousand dollars on his campaign. Also, Barney represented a liberal and forgiving district that remained faithful to him.

On Saturday evening, November 17, five days before Thanksgiving, Barney suffered a mild heart attack. He had been working out at a health club in the Back Bay neighborhood in Boston when he felt some chest pains after exercising on a stationary bike. "At first I thought it was indigestion. I took some Tums but it didn't help. So I jumped in a taxi and went to Beth Israel Hospital. I told the staff at the hospital, 'I'm fifty years old with a history of heart condition in my family.'" Barney's heart attack was due to a blockage in a coronary artery and he underwent an angioplasty, a procedure in which a balloon-tipped catheter is inserted in an artery and inflated with air to expand the blocked area. Before being taken into the operating room, he phoned his mother, his siblings, and Herb.

"I'm sure that the heart attack was related to the stress and anxiety caused by the Gobie scandal," Barney explained. "The adrenalin had gone. The Gobie thing had ended with my reelection to Congress eleven days earlier."

17

A Frank Compromise on
Gays in the Military

DURING THE ADMINISTRATION of President Ronald Reagan, the long-standing ban on homosexuals serving in the military began to be aggressively enforced as thousands of gay men and lesbians were discharged from the armed forces. On July 31, 1991, Secretary of Defense Dick Cheney appeared at a House Budget Committee hearing to discuss defense policy in the post–Cold War era. Barney's final question to Secretary Cheney concerned the issue of gays and lesbians serving in the military. Cheney acknowledged that the argument for excluding gays from serving in the military because they are security risks was "an old chestnut." He also stated that the policy that had been in place for many years in the Defense Department was based on the proposition that a gay life-style is incompatible with military service.

Barney pointed out that the claim that there is something somehow inherently incompatible is just like the arguments that were used to segregate racial minorities and to greatly limit women. "What is the incompatibility?" he asked.

"I have not spent a lot of time on the issue. It is a policy I inherited as Secretary. I think there have been occasions when it has not been administered in a fair fashion. But the basic fundamental policy today has been that a gay lifestyle is incompatible with military service," Cheney responded.

"If all you can say in favor of something is that it is inherited, maybe the time has come for you to take another look at it," Barney suggested.

In mid-October 1991, Bill Clinton, then a candidate for the Democratic nomination for president, met with a group of gay and lesbian activists in Los Angeles and pledged, as an indicator of his commitment to gay rights, that as president he would issue an executive order to lift the ban on gays and lesbians serving in the military. He repeated that pledge publicly later that month when he spoke at Harvard University. However, the exclusion of gays from military service was not a central issue in the campaign.

Barney brought up the topic again on February 5, 1992, when Secretary Cheney and Colin Powell, the chairman of the Joint Chiefs of Staff, appeared at a House Budget Committee hearing to review the Defense Department's fiscal year 1993 budget request. Powell recounts what happened in his memoir, *My American Journey*. First Barney turned to Cheney and said, "When the Secretary was here last time, he said that the security argument was not part of the reason for keeping gay men and lesbians out of the military." Then, Powell reports, "Frank then turned to me. 'Are we to some extent dealing here with a prejudice that a majority has against a group of people?' he asked. And was this prejudice 'a valid reason for telling gay and lesbian people they are not wanted in the armed forces?' There it was, out in the open, the hottest social potato tossed to the Pentagon in a generation."

Powell agreed with Cheney that the security-risk argument was not a reason to keep homosexuals from serving in the military, nor was it a matter of performance on the part of homosexuals. Rather, he stated, in his judgment and that of the Joint Chiefs, it would be "prejudicial to good order and discipline" to try to integrate "individuals who favor a homosexual lifestyle" in the current military structure, where there is no privacy.

On April 4, 1992, a few days before the important New York presidential primary, Democratic candidate Bill Clinton met with a large group of AIDS activists at his Manhattan hotel suite. Before the meeting he was briefed by Barney and David Mixner, a gay activist and friend of the candidate's. Barney discussed most of the substantive issues during the briefing session. With the support of the gay and lesbian community, Clinton handily won the New York primary.

On November 12, president-elect Clinton, at his first press conference, held in Little Rock, Arkansas, was asked by a reporter about his reaction to a federal court decision in California in the *Keith Meinhold* case ruling that the ban on gays in the military was unconstitutional. Clinton reaffirmed that he would follow through on his campaign promise to end the ban on gays in the military early in his administration.

Three days later, Democratic senator Sam Nunn of Georgia, the chairman of the Senate Armed Services Committee, appearing on *Face the Nation*, voiced his opposition to lifting the ban on gays in the military and called on the president-elect to refer the issue to Congress. On another Sunday morning talk show, Senate Republican leader Robert Dole voiced similar resistance to ending the ban. These appearances were followed by aggressive grass-roots lobbying by the religious right and veterans groups. Military leaders opposed lifting the ban and lobbied hard behind closed doors.

It was difficult, however, to get gay and lesbian groups to come together and fight the ban on gays in the military. "Many gays on the left are not fond of the military and very judgmental about gays who go into the military," Robert Raben, Barney's legislative counsel from 1993 to 1999, said. With the new president fighting Congress and the military establishment on behalf of gay and lesbian Americans, "it was almost impossible to believe at that time that we could lose," Tim McFeeley said. Barney urged caution, fearing that the gay community was going to lose this battle in Congress.

Barney likened the arguments that were being made in 1993 for banning gays from the military with those that were made in 1948 for imposing racial segregation in the military. Describing how the attitude toward both groups was expressed, he said, "It is not that these are bad people. In fact, they would be very well behaved and capable. But there is a dislike of them among the majority that would make their presence disruptive and therefore they should be excluded."

When a federal judge in California ruled that the ban on gays in the military was unconstitutional, President Clinton had to react. "He couldn't wait," Barney said. "It would have been better if he could have waited."

President Clinton's initial plan to lift the ban was to implement it in two stages, to put the policy in effect and to see how it worked. The first stage would be to stop the practice of asking recruits about their sexual orientation and to end the practice of prosecuting and expelling gay soldiers. Then, six months later and after consultation with military officials, the president would lift the ban.

On January 24, 1993, the Sunday after the inauguration, Les Aspin, the new secretary of defense, appeared on *Face the Nation*, where he was asked about lifting the ban on gays in the military. Aspin acknowledged that the administration did not have the votes in Congress, that fewer than thirty senators would support lifting the ban.

On Thursday afternoon, January 28, Barney received a telephone call from Morton Halperin, an assistant to the secretary of defense. Halperin told him that Senator Nunn was demanding significant concessions that the president felt he had to make. It was clear to the White House that Senator Nunn had enough votes on the committee to interfere with the president's effort to lift the ban and that together with the Republicans, Nunn had the votes to codify the ban into federal law. Senator Dole had threatened to attach an amendment codifying the ban to the Family and Medical Leave Act, the Clinton administration's top domestic legislative priority, which was expected to be taken up on the Senate floor the following week.

The next day, President Clinton announced a cooling-off period until July 15 to resolve the issue of gays in the military. He put the best spin on it, calling it "a dramatic step forward." During this six-month period recruiters would stop their practice of asking potential enlistees about their sexual orientation. Cases against gays and lesbians in the military based on their sexual conduct would

continue, including discharge. Cases against soldiers based on their acknowledged homosexuality would also continue, but their discharge would be suspended until the policy was resolved. During the six-month cooling-off period,
the secretary of defense would examine key issues, such as the impact lifting the
ban would have on privacy, maintaining morale, and efficiency and discipline
in the armed forces, and Congress would hold public hearings on the subject.
Referring to ending the ban, President Clinton said that between then and July,
"I don't expect to change my position."

"I'm disappointed. Not in Clinton, but in the reality," Barney told the *Boston
Globe*. "I'm sorry that the president couldn't deliver more. He's been committed and honorable. I didn't realize how intent Sen. Nunn is in perpetuating
discrimination." He added, "The fact is Bill Clinton did his best. . . . It is now
up to the gay community. I've begged people to organize; but the 'antis' got
there first." "Not only had we failed to anticipate and combat the opposition to
Clinton's initiative to lift the ban but at that time we didn't recognize that we
had already lost the debate," Tim McFeeley later wrote.

The six-month cooling-off period was a crucial victory for Nunn, the Republicans, and the Joint Chiefs of Staff. Senator Nunn promptly scheduled hearings
on the ban. "Senator Nunn was jealous of Bill Clinton and jumped on the issue and so we had a bad political situation," Barney said. He described Nunn
as "a bona fide bigot, a man who has shown very little zeal in his career other
than when he was leading the charge against gays and lesbians in the military."
He pointed out that Nunn acknowledged that early in his career he fired two
men who were gay because he said they could be security risks. In a newspaper
interview at the time, Barney charged that Senator Nunn was obsessed with
what happened "in other people's bedrooms." Senator Nunn responded to that
criticism on NBC's *Meet the Press*: "I appreciate Representative Frank trying
to enhance my dull image, but in terms of the obsession with sex, I'm not in
Barney's league."

In early February, the ad hoc organization Campaign for Military Service was
formed, led by Tom Stoddard, the former executive director of the Lambda
Legal Defense Fund, and financed by Hollywood executives David Geffen and
Barry Diller, to mobilize public support and lobby to lift the ban. When that
and other gay and lesbian groups finally began to lobby, Barney was critical of
some of their efforts. He pointed out that having petitions signed by thousands
of people is an ineffective lobbying instrument. McFeeley agreed that the tactics
were wrong. "We didn't have political strength. This is a democracy. You have
to win over a majority," he said.

On April 16, President Clinton became the first president to officially meet
with representatives of gay and lesbian organizations in the Oval Office. At
this historic meeting with eight leaders of the gay and lesbian community, the

president, with tears in his eyes, declared unequivocally his intention to sign the executive order lifting the ban on July 15 as promised. "Clinton went out of his way to assure us not to worry." McFeeley, who attended the meeting, said. "He was totally convincing. I think he convinced himself. It brought tears to our eyes."

On April 25, hundreds of thousands of gays and lesbians participated in the March on Washington for Lesbian, Gay and Bi Equal Rights and Liberation. Barney was disappointed. "Everybody came to Washington and talked to each other, and said how wonderful we were, and nobody did any lobbying," he said. Furthermore, although gays in the military was a principal issue on the agenda, Barney saw no evidence that any significant number of the marchers had bothered to talk with their senators or representatives on the issue. He also decried the fact that the marchers had no sense of public relations. "I remember there were ten gays who were about to be kicked out of the military and the idea was for them to appear at the rally in their military uniforms and be cheered by the crowd. Someone decided let's have some fun and the ten servicemen started doing a kind of can-can kick line. I reacted angrily and went over and said, 'Stop it, for God's sake. It's bad for television. Someone said I was acting ridiculous for getting so upset over something like this." As McFeeley pointed out, "More people donned the trendy Lift-the-ban dog tags and danced until dawn than ever lifted a pen to write their congressmen."

Barney contrasted the cultural self-expression of those who marched on Washington on April 25, 1993, with the disciplined conventional political performance by those who marched on Washington for the civil rights of blacks in 1963. At the gay and lesbian march, he said, "a crude comedian, Lea Delaria, said how she would like to have sex with Hillary Clinton. If Redd Foxx had gotten up during the [civil rights] march and speculated about having sex with Jacqueline Kennedy, he would have been thrown into the Reflecting Pool, after the water was drained."

Marches in Washington, Barney pointed out, have no political impact on the elected officials, and for that reason they are a waste of time. "Twenty-five years ago, our need was for visibility. We didn't know who each other were. The world didn't know we were here. Once you get behind the simple desire for visibility, political marches do you zero good. Politicians are simply not influenced by them. No politician cares that there are a hundred people, a thousand people, a million people out there—unless he hears from some part of those people," he said.

The gay community "did the worst job of political lobbying on an important issue that I have ever seen," Barney said. He added, "I was frustrated as hell at not being able to get people to do anything." He pointed out that the people in the gay and lesbian community had plenty of energy but they wasted all their energy by participating in a march, believing it to be a form of political action. As a result, they didn't do the things that are important. "It's kind of like, 'Well, I gave at the office.' I say to people, 'Look, I don't mean to be rude. I hope you're having a nice time in Washington. But please do not think that you have advanced our political agenda one iota. If you want to advance our political agenda, then you've got to vote,'" he said.

"The notion that you just lash out is crazy. They are still fighting their battle the Stokely Carmichael way, still singing, singing, stomping their feet," Barney said. "A lot of their political activity is just feel good activity. They have the notion that Martin Luther King and the rest of the gang just let it all hang out and that the civil rights movement was just a series of spontaneous outbursts. But it was in fact a series of strategic decisions." During the 1963 civil rights March on Washington, John Lewis was asked to edit and tone down his speech because it was too radical. Lewis complied with the request because he realized that they all had to stay together.

In Barney's view, American society functions politically according to who gets organized and who gets out the vote and defends themselves. He sees the National Rifle Association (NRA) and the American Association of Retired Persons (AARP) as two groups who are very effective in influencing government and lobbying members of Congress. "The NRA doesn't have marches. They don't have demonstrations. They don't shoot their guns in the air. It's just good, straight democracy. The AARP doesn't have shuffles. They just write to us and call us and tell us that they're there," he said.

When the gay activists came to Washington, they formed a ring in a human chain around the Capitol and then turned their backs and held hands. It was a gesture, according to Barney, that had "zero impact on public policy." In a speech on the House floor he wondered how you could literally form a human chain around the Capitol and then turn your back on the Capitol without letting go of the chain. He had fun pantomiming and putting himself through contortions trying to figure that out.

Barney explained to *New York Times* reporter Claudia Dreifus: "Direct action, as a political tactic, is second choice. The first choice is to exercise political power, to scare them into voting the right way. Direct action is what you do when you have no power. Blacks in the South had to use direct action until they got a voting rights act."

While the gay community was busy participating in marches and parades and making speeches to each other, the right wing was flooding congressional offices with letters and phone calls demanding that members of Congress vote against lifting the ban on gays serving in the military.

It became clear to Barney that if it was going to be all or nothing, the gay community was going to get nothing. His political instincts and conversations with other members convinced him that support for lifting the ban was slipping fast. There was just no way that they would be successful in getting a majority in Congress to support lifting the ban in the face of the vehement opposition by the popular and well-respected General Colin Powell and the Joint Chiefs of Staff.

Barney saw support in Congress solidifying behind "Don't ask, don't tell," a proposal being touted by Senator Nunn as a compromise, permitting gays to serve in the military as long as they didn't reveal their sexual orientation, a proposal Barney considered to be meaningless. "I saw a compromise coming and I saw that compromise being negotiated without any of us. You can't be part of the compromise if you are not willing to compromise," he said in a June 1993 interview with the political science professor David Rayside. Waiting too long, particularly on controversial issues, Barney believes, risks backing other politicians into declaring their opposition publicly and reduces the room to maneuver.

Recognizing that the gay community was not going to win and that there needed to be some workable compromise, Barney tried to get a better deal. On May 18, he proposed an alternative to "Don't ask, don't tell" based on political reality, a sort of "Don't ask, don't tell, don't listen, and don't investigate" policy. Under his plan, gays in the armed forces would be allowed to be open about their sexual orientation and live an openly gay life when off-duty and off-base without fear of punishment or reprisal, but not while on duty. He believed that this proposal permitting gays to serve in the military would substantially improve their lives in the military by reducing the likelihood of discharge. At the same time he hoped that by increasing familiarity with gays and lesbians in the military, it would overcome the skepticism of military officials and ultimately bring about greater tolerance.

The Frank compromise was abruptly rejected by both camps. Senator Nunn reacted harshly and negatively to the proposal. It was unacceptable to conservatives and military officials. Some gay leaders criticized the proposal as capitulation. Gerry Studds criticized his friend and colleague for "prematurely raising the white flag." Barney was vilified by the gay community. Many gay and lesbian groups called it a sellout and were angry at him for proposing a compromise that would result in only a gradual integration of gays in the military.

Barney was taken aback by the attacks from his friends. Politicians get a lot of undeserved credit for standing up to their enemies. But that's easy, Barney says, and generally profitable. The hard thing to do is to stand up to your friends when you think they are wrong. "You tend to be madder at your friends than at your enemies because you don't expect anything from your enemies," Robert

Raben, Barney's legislative counsel, said. "It was one of the few times I saw Barney emotional, very upset, and genuinely frustrated, angry, and sad at the whole situation."

"If the attitude among feminists had been that women must be fully integrated into the military, there would be no women there other than typists," Barney contended. One radical gay group, Queer Nation, staged a protest outside his congressional office and the group referred to him as "Uncle Barney," not as a term of endearment but rather a variation of the label "Uncle Tom" used among blacks during the civil rights movement. President Clinton, however, was supportive and phoned Barney to express his gratitude.

On July 19, President Clinton announced a policy on "an issue that has divided our military and out nation" that largely mirrored Senator Nunn's "Don't ask, don't tell" proposal. Although the practice would be not to ask recruits about sexual orientation in the enlistment process, servicemen and women could not engage in homosexual conduct at any time, from the day they joined the service until the day they were discharged. An open statement by a service member that he or she is gay would create a rebuttable presumption that he or she intends to engage in such prohibited conduct and could result in discharge. While President Clinton called the new policy "a substantial advance" and "an honorable compromise," he recognized that it was not a perfect solution and would not please everyone.

That evening, Barney appeared on the *MacNeil/Lehrer NewsHour* and criticized the new policy but not President Clinton, who, he said, "did the best he could in the face of political opposition and bigotry." The compromise was not acceptable to him because it fell short of what was necessary. The problem was, he said, "any place, any time, you express your sexuality, you can get kicked out."

On July 23, the Senate Armed Services Committee voted 17 to 5 in favor of Nunn's policy on gays in the military, and the full Senate voted to codify Nunn's "Don't ask, don't tell" policy as part of the Defense authorization bill. The Nunn provision included the following: "The presence in the armed forces of persons who demonstrate a propensity to engage in homosexual acts would create an unacceptable risk" to military standards and morale. Senator Barbara Boxer introduced an amendment to strike the Nunn provision from the bill and to leave the issue of gays in the military to the president to decide. It failed by a vote of 33 to 63.

Gay and lesbian activists wanted a vote in the House on an amendment to remove Senator Nunn's "Don't ask, don't tell" language and leave the issue to the president's discretion. Even though the amendment was certain to lose, the goal was to force supporters and opponents on the record and to show that there was considerable support in Congress for lifting the ban. Many Democratic members did not want such a vote and pressured the leadership. Barney, however, lobbied the Democratic leadership to allow the vote. "This is very, very important to me. I have campaigned for colleagues and made the argument that there is a real difference between the parties on this issue," he told the leadership. "They would have risked alienating me and losing my support on a whole range of other matters, and I made that very explicit." On September 28, Massachusetts Democrat Martin Meehan offered an amendment to the Defense authorization bill that did not lift the ban and made no judgment about the wisdom of gays serving in the military but simply left the issue to the president. It was defeated in the House by a vote of 169 to 264.

Ike Skelton of Missouri then offered another amendment that contained the language already in the bill. Barney urged members to vote against the amendment, explaining the seemingly complicated parliamentary situation: "It is an amendment to put into the bill the language that is already there. So you can defeat it and have the language that is in there, or pass it and have the language that is in there." He argued that the policy that House members were being asked to approve was that if an individual comes into the military and puts on the uniform and abides by every rule of conduct while on duty, and then off the base, on his or her own time, in the privacy of his or her home, discreetly and consensually expresses love for another individual that some House members did not approve of, they punish that person by degrading him or her and kicking that person out of the armed services of the United States, no matter how patriotic or how committed to this country he or she is.

Barney was disappointed by the end result. "Clinton lost on gays in the military," he said. Barney sees the implementation of "Don't ask, don't tell" as a blot on Clinton's record, the one place where he failed the gay community. Because Clinton did not serve in the military in Vietnam, "the one area of public policy where he almost always caved is the military." Barney is critical of President Clinton for allowing the military to make a mockery of "Don't ask, don't tell." When the military cracked down on gays and lesbians, Clinton, he said, was "too afraid of them to protect people."

In Barney's view, however, President Clinton's approach to gay and lesbian rights during his presidency is of historic importance. "Bill Clinton's role in advancing fair treatment for gays and lesbians is at least equal to and I think better than John Kennedy's in pushing the civil rights agenda. Neither one had perfection but was enormously important in the context of his time," he said.

Clinton's achievement, for example, in doing away with the anti-gay security clearance restrictions that were implemented in 1954 by an executive order signed by President Dwight Eisenhower didn't get the attention it deserved. In 1950, a Senate committee run by the Democrats had passed a resolution that said you cannot have homosexuals in government, on the grounds not just that they pose a security risk but that they are morally weak. That resolution, Barney pointed out, ushered in "forty-five years of entrenched bigotry against gays and lesbians, impugning our reliability, our patriotism and our honesty" that was abolished by an executive order President Clinton signed in 1995 and made stick. In his apartment in Washington, Barney keeps a copy of that 1950 resolution in a frame side-by-side with the 1995 executive order issued by President Clinton.

Barney looks at the progress made since 1954, when President Eisenhower issued an executive order that said if you were gay you couldn't get a security clearance. In June 2000, the Central Intelligence Agency director George Tenet welcomed Barney as the speaker at the celebration of gay pride day at the CIA, an event attended by about sixty CIA employees. In his remarks, Barney made reference to his longstanding efforts in Congress to cut the CIA's budget and have it declassified. "Let me be clear. I've not only been trying to cut your budget, I've been trying to out your budget," he said.

18

The Most Hated Man in Gingrichdom

SOON AFTER HIS FIRST ELECTION to Congress in 1980, Barney found himself frequently paired with Republican Newt Gingrich of Georgia on political talk shows and issue debates on news programs. Although the two men were polar opposites ideologically, there were several similarities. They were about the same age (Gingrich was born in 1943, Barney in 1940); they were elected to Congress about the same time (Gingrich in 1978, Barney in 1980); they both represented fairly diverse suburban districts near big cities (Atlanta and Boston), with more voting freedom than many of their colleagues; and neither was shy about criticizing his party's leaders when appropriate.

Newt Gingrich is a right-wing intellectual with a sense of history. He has a master's degree and a Ph.D. in modern European history from Tulane University, and he was a college professor in Georgia for eight years before being elected to the Congress. Gingrich was one of the more articulate members of Congress. He was outspoken, ambitious, and pugnacious, and he enjoyed a good fight. He was a good sparring partner for Barney.

At first, there was a certain level of camaraderie and rapport between these intellectual warriors from the right and left. That was before Gingrich began to think of himself as a revolutionary and decided to declare war on Democrats.

A House debate on April 23, 1987, sparked a clash between Barney and Newt Gingrich. When a GOP member blamed liberals for handcuffing President Ronald Reagan in his efforts to negotiate an arms control agreement with the Russians, Barney accused the Republicans of arguing both sides. "You are telling us 'don't interfere with Ronald Reagan, he is on the eve of an agreement.' If he is on the eve of an agreement, he must live in the Land of the Midnight Sun because this man has been on the eve of that agreement since sometime in 1982." He pointed out that, on one hand, the Republicans were mad at the liberals for stopping them from having an agreement, and, on the other hand, they are mad at their own side because they might have an agreement. "Pick an argument," he said, "and make it."

Newt Gingrich jumped in. "On the one hand you are glad Reagan is negotiating, and on the other hand you distrust him so much you want to cripple him with legislation. It is fundamentally wrong for the U.S. House of Representatives to cripple its own government while going into negotiations," he said, inspiring Barney to say, "The gentleman from Georgia equates legislating national security with crippling the president, a bizarre notion."

"I want to respond to my good friend, who is very, very bright and very, very able, but I think he was being a little too cute," Gingrich said. "I just think it is incredibly dangerous in the modern age for the U.S. House to write foreign policy into law. . . . If you read the Federalist Papers, if you read the debate in the 1790s among the Founding Fathers, they were very, very vehement that the No. 1 lesson of the Articles of Confederation was not to allow the legislative branch to directly involve itself in foreign policy."

"I gather that I must have misunderstood. I assumed that [Mr. Gingrich] was one of those who had fought the Panama Canal Treaty. I must have been wrong. He must have been one of those who thought that even if they disagreed with President Carter's position, the House has no right to try to take a position on that specific," Barney countered.

Following the Democrats' crushing defeat in the 1994 midterm elections, the Republicans took control of the House of Representatives in January 1995 for the first time in forty years. When Gingrich was elected Speaker, the Democratic leadership asked Barney to take on the job of engaging the Republicans, in a parliamentary way, and he became the Democrats' point person in floor fights against the GOP majority. He would have preferred to make public policy. But because of the Democrats' recent losses, they were now the backbenchers with the ultimate goal of winning back the voters. At the time, he said, "My job is to shine the light on those things that the Republicans would just as soon do in the dark." He also told the *Boston Globe*: "We want to make sure that votes are taken on every issue, no matter how controversial they may be. We want the Republicans to take responsibility for everything they do." "I'm used to being in the minority. I'm a left-handed gay Jew," he told the *New York Times Magazine*. "Being in the minority allowed him to be the unfettered Barney Frank," Ed Markey said. He would prowl the floor of the House, waiting to pounce on any unsuspecting Republican speaker.

Barney became a thorn in Newt Gingrich's side from the moment Gingrich became Speaker. In the film *Rambo III*, which takes place in Soviet-invaded Afghanistan, John Rambo, played by Sylvester Stallone, is questioned by the Soviets, "Who are you?" "I am your worst nightmare," Rambo famously responds.

Similarly, Barney was Speaker Gingrich's constant nemesis—his worst nightmare. In an article published February 25 in the *New Republic*, Weston Kosova referred to Barney as "the most hated man in Gingrichdom." In a story published March 6 in the *New Republic*, under the title "Frank Incensed," Kosova wrote, "Minority Leader Richard Gephardt and Minority Whip David Bonior may have the lofty titles, but Frank has stepped in as the true leader of the opposition."

Barney started tormenting Newt Gingrich and his right-wing band from the opening bell of the 104th Congress on Wednesday, January 4, 1995. He spent most of the fourteen-hour session on the House floor jousting with a series of Republicans. Matt Salmon, a freshman GOP member from Arizona, remarked to Barney during the debate, "I am impressed. You are even better in person than you are on C-SPAN."

As the GOP rhetoric grew louder about the need to open up committee meetings to public view, two Republicans weighed in. Frank Cremeans, a freshman from Ohio, asserted, "No longer will House business be allowed to take place behind locked and closed doors." Jan Christensen from Nebraska declared, "The days of the smoke-filled room and closed doors are over. It's time to open the doors, throw open the windows, and let the glorious light of representative democracy shine in."

"I am all for this," Barney responded. "I was not aware that there were many meetings that were not open. Most of the members I know generally try to get the press to come to their meetings rather than keep them away." He pointed out, however, that there are political organizations controlled by members of this House that are not open. "What better way to tell the people of GOPAC [Gingrich's political action committee] that they should be open than for us to follow that same rule?" Barney observed, eliciting from Republican Bill Thomas of California the warning, "The gentleman skates very nicely on thin ice."

Barney's time to speak on the floor had expired. "I would ask for an additional thirty seconds, since I yielded to Tanya Harding over there," he said.

Then Barney challenged the notion that the Republicans were bringing in change in the way business was conducted. "In my experience I have seen very few, in fact, no closed meetings," he said. He described that famous device known as the elephant stick: "The elephant stick is a stick that a man carries around Dupont Circle, and people say, 'What are you doing with that stick?' And the answer is, 'Well, it is to keep away all the elephants.' They say, 'Well, there aren't any elephants at Dupont Circle.' Then [the man] says, 'My stick works.'" Barney accused the Republicans "of banishing nonexistent elephants at a fast and furious pace." "If they want to take credit for it, that is fine," he said. "But I have to tell you that these closed meetings they talk about are widely a figment of their imagination."

As the debate continued into the late evening of the opening day, during which Speaker Gingrich and the Republicans had pledged to pass an entire package of House reforms, Barney commented on the House floor: "There has been a great deal of discussion of history tonight, so let us quote Karl Marx: 'History repeats itself; the first time as history and the second time as farce.' Farce is what we are getting tonight. It is from the 18th Brumaire of Louis Napoleon."

During the debate on the Congressional Accountability Act, Barney continued to needle the Republicans. "We are in favor of [the Congressional Accountability Act]. Most of us worked hard for it. We passed it last year. It was bipartisan. Why are you rushing this through on a totally closed rule? " Barney chided the Republicans, "You told us you would be family friendly. You forgot to tell us it would be *The Addams Family*, because we will be doing it at 3 o'clock in the morning."

"Let me tell you from experience," he said, "when you are in the majority, sometimes inevitably you got to defend some dumb things. But in one day you've been dumber than we were in two years. . . . Why not wait until tomorrow? [Why not] go home for the night, and come back tomorrow and then act on the bill in the sunshine, not at two o'clock in the morning? Do you want to hide the debate on [allowing members to use federally funded frequent flyer miles for personal use]?" He added, "You are rushing it through, because the Republicans promised it would be done on the first day. It will be after midnight. Now you are even fooling with the clock. Be sensible. . . . Do it tomorrow, and do not exempt yourself from the most important law of all, common sense."

As the debate dragged on and the clock struck midnight, Barney emerged from the Democratic cloakroom and shouted, "Mr. Speaker, I have a parliamentary inquiry. Will the Speaker tell me if it is his ruling that it is still Wednesday? I just want to know what day it is. I was told we have to do [all] this on the first day."

When another hour passed, Barney remarked, "What we have got is this silly insistence of rushing this bill through with no amendments at one o'clock in the morning, when we are going to take ten days off and do absolutely nothing so that the Republicans can take something that was passed under Democratic leadership last year and claim authorship to it. They are lucky that one particular bill does not apply to Congress, the copyright laws, because if it did, this example of intellectual theft and attempted partisan piracy would be ruled illegal."

Several days later, Barney and Chuck Schumer led an outcry by House Democrats over Speaker Gingrich's appointment of Christina Jeffrey to the job of historian of the House of Representatives, forcing Gingrich to fire her. Barney called the appointment of Jeffrey, an assistant professor of political science and one-time teaching colleague of Gingrich's at Kennesaw State University in Marietta, Georgia, "outrageous" and described her as having an "offensive nutsy streak."

In 1986–87, Christina Jeffrey (under her maiden name, Christina Price) headed a school curriculum review panel for the Department of Education that turned down a seventy-thousand-dollar grant proposal submitted by Facing History and Ourselves, a Brookline, Massachusetts, foundation, to distribute a course on the Holocaust and hate crimes aimed at middle-school students. Jeffrey rejected the funding application because the curriculum did not present the Nazi point of view. In her evaluation she wrote: "The program gives no evidence of balance or objectivity. The Nazi point of view, however unpopular, is still a point of view, and it is not presented, nor is that of the Ku Klux Klan." At the time, Barney characterized Jeffrey's evaluation as "wacko."

One of the rules changes that the Republicans passed on the opening day of the session was to require a substantially verbatim transcript of the House proceedings in the *Congressional Record*, including rulings of the chair. Only technical, grammatical, and typographical corrections could be made by legislators.

On Wednesday, January 18, Democrat Carrie Meek of Florida took to the House floor to raise questions about the lucrative book deal the Speaker had negotiated with the publisher Rupert Murdock, contending that there was a perception of impropriety and a potential conflict of interest. Meek stated that although Speaker Gingrich, in response to criticism, may have given up the $4.5 million book advance, he stood to gain that amount and much more in sales. "That is a whole lot of dust where I come from," Meek said. Bob Walker moved to have Meek's words stricken from the record. Cliff Stearns, the Speaker pro tem, ruled that Meek was out of order and that her words be stricken, stating that "innuendo and personal references to the Speaker's personal conduct are not in order." He also ruled that "a higher level of respect is due to the Speaker."

Overnight, the House parliamentarian changed two words spoken by Stearns. In the first comment, "personal" references were changed to "critical" references. In Stearns's second comment, a "higher" level of respect was changed to a "proper" level of respect. The parliamentarian made these changes in the belief that the new rules could be stretched to make sure that Stearns's ruling did not overstep his authority and that it was consistent with the customs and precedents of the House.

Barney noticed the changes that had been made in Stearns's ruling as Speaker pro tem and found them to be substantive rather than technical, grammatical, or typographical. The next day, he made a point of order on the House floor and charged that it was a violation of the new Republican-passed House rule.

The Speaker pro tem initially ruled that the issue was going to be examined in consultation with the parliamentarian. "I am all in favor of conversation, but I am surprised that a new rule as part of the Contract with America is breached and has as its remedy a conversation by the Speaker with the parliamentarian," Barney replied.

In response to a parliamentary inquiry by John Dingell, the presiding officer ruled that the changes that had been made in Stearns's comments were technical and not substantive. Barney was puzzled by that ruling. He asked whether, if the ruling meant that "personal" and "critical" are the same thing with respect to the Speaker, did the chair's ruling mean that "any personal references to the Speaker will inevitably be critical?"

In early January, Barney publicly described Speaker Gingrich as "the meanest and most destructive political figure I have seen." According to Barney, since the late 1980s, Gingrich had been very successful in his quest to destroy bipartisan cooperation, asserting to his GOP colleagues that bipartisanship is a bad thing, and that the Democrats are not honorable people with whom they disagree but evil, immoral, corrupt, treasonous people who must be destroyed. Gingrich had come to power by savaging the House and its Democratic Speaker. "Gingrich was motivated primarily by a lust for power, unhindered by any great principle, and willing to degrade other individuals in the course of it," Barney said. He referred to Gingrich as "a total opportunist," "vicious," and "unprincipled" and "the thinnest-skinned character assassin I ever met," a man skilled at throwing punches but who could not take a punch. "In boxing parlance, Newt is a 'bleeder.'" Then he added, "Early in 1995, I forget exactly what I said, it was some criticism of his tactics. Newt's response was, 'Oh, how terrible!' He was moaning, almost weeping. He was just supersensitive. I was struck by how damaged he was. That just encouraged me to keep going after him."

"You had Newt Gingrich, a pseudo-psychotic leader who was a smart man but unprincipled dealing with a man who was smarter and principled. Their philosophies were inevitably going to contradict. Barney called him on his inconsistencies," former representative Tom Downey said.

In a speech to the Republican National Committee on Friday, January 20, Speaker Gingrich singled out Barney Frank and Democratic whip David Bonior of Michigan as the GOP's most persistent Democratic nemeses. "Barney Frank hates me," Gingrich said, giving as a reason a grudge he believed that Barney bore against him because of his unsuccessful move on the House floor in August 1990 to have Barney censured for ethics violations. Barney's genuine dislike for Gingrich was unrelated to that effort.

Barney's persistent criticism and needling of House Republicans started to get to them. On Friday morning, January 27, during an interview with several radio correspondents, House majority leader Dick Armey of Texas was asked about the difference between his upcoming book (*Revolution: A Strategy for the Rebirth of Freedom*), for which he took no advance and planned to donate all profits to charity, and Speaker Newt Gingrich's book deal that had generated so much controversy because of the $4.5 million advance. Armey responded, "Newt's a very patient fellow. And Newt is always able to handle a harangue going on around him better than I am. I like peace and quiet. And I don't need to listen to 'Barney Fag'—Barney Frank haranguing in my ear because I made a few dollars off a book I worked on. I just don't need to listen to it."

Initially, Armey denied uttering the slur. But when confronted with a recording of his words, Armey apologized, calling it an unintentional mispronunciation of a colleague's name in a way that sounded like a slur. Armey remarked to reporters that he had trouble with his alliteration, saying he had not yet had his coffee. "I don't use the word in personal conversation. I would not use such an expression," he maintained. Armey also apologized to Barney during a brief private conversation on the House floor, saying he had stumbled over his name.

Armey then spoke about the episode on the House floor and criticized the media for playing the tape on the air and turning the incident into a firestorm. In a rambling speech he remarked, "This was nothing more than the unintentional mispronunciation of another person's name that sounded like something it was not. There is no room in public discourse for such hateful language, and I condemn the use of such slurs." The Texas lawmaker lashed out at the press. "I simply mispronounced a name and do not need any psychoanalysis about my subliminals or about my Freudian predilections. . . . Can we not get back to real issues? Cannot the press report real events?" he asked.

Barney listened to the recording to make sure that Armey had uttered that remark. He thought about it for a while before deciding how best to respond. He then held a press conference, and speaking on behalf of the millions of gay people who face and feel prejudice like that expressed by Armey all the time, he responded aggressively to what he called an outrageous example of bigotry. "There are people in the right wing of the Republican party who have said to Dick Armey and others—why do you let a fag like that give you this grief," he said. He rejected Armey's claim that the slur was simply a mispronunciation of his name. "There are many ways to mispronounce my name. That one is the least common," he said. "I turned to my one expert, my mother, who reports that in the fifty-nine years since she married my father, no one has ever called her 'Elsie Fag.'" He added, "I don't think Armey intended to say it. He blurted out what he was thinking. I don't think it was on the tip of his tongue but it must have been floating in the back of his mind. Things can't slip out if they weren't first in there."

Barney believed, however, that Armey's feeling the need to lie about the slur was a sign he considered it a bad thing to do. It showed how the political climate toward gays in this country had changed.

Steve Gunderson, a gay Republican from Wisconsin, defended the majority leader: "Dick Armey does not have a malicious bone in his body." Barney responded, "He may not have a malicious bone in his body but he did have a malicious thought in his heart."

The next day, in a previously scheduled speech to the Consortium for Psychotherapy in Boston, Barney discussed Armey's claim that the slur was a mispronunciation. He told the audience of psychotherapists that the majority leader was straining credibility "by suggesting that professionally you could all be replaced by speech therapists." He discussed his relationship with Armey and other bigoted legislators: "We have a rule around here that you're not supposed to take things personally, but I take personal things personally. I do not say, 'Oh well, that's just politics' when people make personally bigoted remarks." Although Barney had worked with Armey in some areas before the "Barney Fag" incident, they did not have any kind of working relationship or personal dealings after it. However, when the *Washington Post* subsequently misidentified Armey as Barney Frank in a photo caption, Barney could not resist approaching Armey on the House floor and asking, "Which one of us is going to sue?"

In a letter to campaign contributors, Barney mentioned that the Democratic political consultant James Carville had criticized Dick Armey for the "Barney Fag" utterance and in the process referred to him as "Barney Fife." "Mr. Carville, who is a friend, explained that he obviously was thinking about the *Andy Griffith Show* when he referred to me in that way and he contrasted what I made him think about with what Mr. Armey thinks about when I am the subject," Barney wrote. "I await the next variations of my name—Barney Google, Barney Rubble, or Barney the Dinosaur, depending on the generation of the speaker." He pointed out to the contributors, however, that "people have gotten my name right where it is most important—as the payee on the checks."

As if to prove Barney's contention that Armey had said what he was thinking, five years later, at the Republican national convention in Philadelphia, at a late-night party with a small group of journalists, Armey made another disparaging, anti-gay remark about Barney. Humor columnist Dave Barry of the *Miami Herald* asked him whether he was Dick Armey. He replied, "Yes, I am Dick Armey, and if there was a dick army, Barney Frank would want to join up."

"It's a fairly gratuitous reference to my being gay, pulled out of nowhere," Barney commented at the time. "What kind of crude, silly, juvenile jibe is this for a national politician to be making?" He pointed out that the comment by Armey, one of the top leaders in the Republican Party, was ironic in the light of the message of tolerance and inclusiveness the Republican Party tried to convey at their convention. "The problem is Dick Armey really represents the Republican Party, not the show they had." A reporter asked whether he was seeking an apology from Armey. "I'm trying to think of what I would be less interested in than an apology from Dick Armey—maybe the lyrics to the national anthem of Bhutan," Barney replied.

According to Barney, Gingrich took advantage of public anger with the Democrats to win in 1994. But he and the other Republicans did themselves a disservice by preselecting the items in the Contract with America because they were very popular. "With any group, as you begin to succeed you get through the more popular parts of the agenda and you get to the less popular parts that you care about but have more resistance," Barney said.

Squaring off against GOP whip Tom DeLay on CNN's *Inside Politics* on February 23, about the first fifty days of Republican control of the 104th Congress, Barney showed that he was not impressed. "They are keeping promises and made easy ones to keep. They put quantity ahead of quality of thought," he argued. He compared the Republicans to "kids who go to school and say, 'Teacher, here's the deal—you can judge me on arithmetic but not division, only multiplication and addition; history, I just want to do American, none of this European stuff.'"

When Barney thinks of Newt Gingrich, he thinks of Broadway show tunes. He suggested that Gingrich's theme song should be "Show Me," the song from *My Fair Lady*: "The song begins, 'Don't talk of love, show me.' With Gingrich the song goes, 'Don't talk of ideas, have one.' See, Gingrich has no ideas. The quality of the thought is third rate. Literally, there is no substantive issue on which anyone regards him as an authority."

"The Republicans have achieved nothing except a shutdown of the government. Legislatively there have been minimal changes in public policy," Barney later argued. He also said, "All in all, this was not a successful revolution. It was an attempted revolution. They seized the palace and shut down the government, but only for a while. They used the shutdown to coerce the president to go along with the revolution. He wouldn't do it, so now they are going to try some other way." With respect to the federal government shutdown, he pointed out that the public didn't like it and it really backfired on Gingrich, who now regrets that it happened. "Well, I'm sure Mussolini, if we could ask him, would regret World War II. I mean, people often regret fiascoes. But that doesn't mean that they have any change of heart, morally," Barney said.

Barney described Gingrich's performance as Speaker as "awful," pointing out that it is hard to make yourself that unpopular as Speaker of the House, that nobody else has been able to do it. "He has a penchant for saying really dumb things," Barney said. "He has also run the place badly and shabbily." In a *Playboy* interview, Barney said: "Newt represented the worst trends in American politics. He more than anyone else brought in the negativism. But it ultimately consumed him, which was extremely satisfying."

In contrast to his combative relationship with Gingrich and despite differences of opinion on most substantive issues, Barney enjoyed a special relationship with Sonny Bono, the one-time pop entertainer turned Republican congressman from California. "Barney thrives on intellectual engagement and didn't have high expectations for that relationship. He was genuinely surprised at how much he liked Sonny and how well they got along," Robert Raben said.

The first time they met, shortly after Bono's election to the House in 1994, Bono, a star-struck fan, told Barney, "I've been watching you a lot on C-SPAN. I like the way you handle yourself. I want to be just like you." Barney was taken aback by Bono's comments. It was one of the rare times when he didn't know how to respond.

According to Bono's widow, Rep. Mary Bono, "Sonny was always great in recognizing talent in others—political talent, comedic talent, certainly dramatic and theatrical talent. That was one of his strong points in life. He truly saw in Barney incredible talent. What he enjoyed and admired about Barney was his wit, timing, ability, political cunning, and savvy."

Every January the Washington Press Club Foundation holds a dinner to welcome the members of Congress. It has come to symbolize the start of a new session in Congress. On Wednesday evening, January 25, 1995, the ballroom of the Grand Hyatt Hotel, several blocks from the Capitol, was filled with politicians, the press, diplomats, and lobbyists for the fifty-first annual Washington Press Club Foundation dinner. Four legislators from the newly elected class of 1994 were invited to address the crowd and to be funny.

Sonny Bono was the closing act. He followed Texas senator Kay Bailey Hutchinson, who had left the crowd tired, restless, and eager to go home. "Sonny took Washington by storm. He got up and did this great routine, it was free flowing, a lot of shtick," Barney recalled. "He even made fun of Bob Dornan. That's when he and I bonded."

The fifty-nine-year-old Bono delivered a twenty-minute rambling, spontaneous monologue about his first three weeks in Congress and observations about his colleagues that brought down the house in the packed ballroom. He poked fun at Gingrich, Democratic whip David Bonior, Texas senator and presidential hopeful Phil Gramm, and others. "I heard Phil Gramm tell a crowd, 'You can't eat corn if you ain't a pig,'" Bono said. He turned to his wife and asked, "What the hell does that mean?"

Earlier that day, an out-of-control Bob Dornan had accused President Clinton of "avoiding the draft three times in putting teenagers in his place" and of "giving aid and comfort to the enemy during the Vietnam War" by demonstrating against the war while a student at Oxford. Bono described Dornan hyper-ventilating on the House floor, saying that he was ready "to eat the podium." "I said Bob, why did you do that? He said, 'I'll be on C-SPAN every hour. So who cares?'" Bono added, "Dornan doesn't care when you talk to him, what you say, or why you're saying it or even if you're there. I've never seen anything like it."

"The guy is amazing," Bono said about Barney. "He can fly from one mike to another mike, shouting, 'Mr. Speaker, point of order, point of order.' I go wow, I'm impressed by this guy." He said that Barney did "the best Shecky Greene I've ever heard." Looking at Barney in the audience, he concluded, "I'm going to keep watching you, if you don't mind, because you're the best I've ever seen. I haven't figured out what the hell you do, but it's good."

When Bono was asked in an interview after his first year in the House which members of Congress impressed him most, he began with Barney Frank.

At a Banking Committee hearing in February 1996, Barney was critical of the Republicans for attacking the secretary of the Treasury for saying we should not shut down the government, and then for keeping the government open by skirting the debt limit and avoiding a government default by transferring retirement funds. "Singing is not one of the 2,477 things I do best," Barney acknowledged. In the second grade, his teacher, Mrs. Doyle, told him simply to move his lips while the rest of the class sang "My Old Kentucky Home." Therefore, Barney prefers to speak-sing songs like Rex Harrison and would try to "mumble the song with minimal damage to people's aural sensibility." "If I could sing better I would sing for spite the old song 'First you say you do, and then you don't; you say you will, and then you won't,'" he told his committee colleagues.

Bono, who knew a little something about singing having performed as half of the pop duo Sonny and Cher, said to Barney, "If you're ever going to go on the road as a singer, OK, I'll go with you, but after hearing you sing, you have to take the harmony."

"I think someone once said that to you, too," Barney retorted.

"You always got to get in the last word, don't you?" Bono replied.

Yet there was a serious side to the friendship between Barney and Sonny Bono. In June 1996, during the Judiciary Committee markup of the Defense of Marriage Act, Barney introduced an amendment to delete the provision that prevents gay spouses from claiming benefits under Social Security or other federal programs, arguing that it was a question of states' rights. Bono turned to Barney and said apologetically, "I'm not homophobic," noting his love for his daughter, Chastity, a lesbian. "I simply can't handle it yet, Barney. I wish I was ready, but I can't tell my son it is OK." Barney answered that he and other gays were seeking tolerance and fair treatment, not approval. "I can't go as far as you deserve, and I'm sorry," Bono responded.

Barney enjoyed serving with Bono on the Judiciary Committee and exchanging banter and little friendly jabs that grew out of their respect for each other's abilities. Bono often presented himself as not very well educated, but that was part of his shtick. One day when Bono was preparing to question a witness at a hearing, Barney interrupted for a moment, turned to the witness, and said, "Let me caution you. He's going to pull that 'aw-shucks' routine on you. But don't believe that for a minute because you're in big trouble with this guy."

Barney recognized that Sonny Bono was often underestimated. He told the *New York Times* writer Claudia Dreifus during a 1996 interview, "[Sonny] has a better understanding of the dynamics of Congress than almost anybody else. He is not a great student of the substance of the issues, but he understands the craft of politics. He is an analyst. What I have seen of Sonny is that instinctive understanding of how audiences will receive certain things."

Mary Bono concurred with that assessment. "Sonny's experience before a live audience and ability to read an audience was a great asset for him as a politician. He knew what an audience was thinking, feeling, and wanting, and he knew the point when the audience was tired and didn't want to hear any more," she said. "Sonny truly understood the theater of politics. There is no one in Congress who understands it or performs it as well as Barney. Sonny was a consummate showman and entertainer and so is Barney. That is what Sonny enjoyed so much about Barney."

On occasion, Sonny and Mary Bono and Barney and Herb Moses got together socially. Recalling an evening when the four of them had dinner with the director John Waters (Sonny Bono had starred in Waters's 1988 film *Hairspray*, a comedy satire about integration and a teen dance competition in 1962 Baltimore) at an Italian restaurant in downtown Washington, Mary Bono said, "We all just had a great time that evening. John loved it. It was perfectly comfortable for Sonny and me to be out with Barney and his partner."

When Sonny Bono died in a skiing accident in January 1998, Barney was deeply saddened. "I valued him not only as a colleague but as a friend," he said. Mary Bono fondly recalled how quickly Barney reached out to her, how warm he was to her when she was first elected to her husband's former seat in the House.

In early 1998, Herb Moses left his job with Fannie Mae to run a pottery studio. In June 1998, Barney and Herb broke up after a relationship of almost eleven years. It was especially difficult for Barney, who thought that he had found a life partner. But Herb wanted to settle down and have a family. When Herb decided to leave, he told Barney, "I love you but I can't continue to live like this." Politics takes its toll on marriages and relationships. It leaves little free time for couples to spend together. Barney understood why Herb left. "It's hard enough to be a political spouse, particularly a same-sex political spouse and to be the only one," Barney said.

Shortly after they split up, Joe Martin, Barney's former legislative aide, talked with Herb at lunch about the breakup. "I was tired of going to receptions and parties where people wanted to give all of their attention to Barney and ignored me," Herb told Martin. Martin feels that Herb was naïve not to understand that that was inevitable, since Barney is the politician and a very important political figure. He suspects that what Herb went through is common to congressional spouses, which is essentially what he was. "I think on some level, maybe Herb forgot that," Martin said. He recalled an event a year or two earlier that he had attended with Barney and Herb. He was off to the side talking with Herb and they were speaking admirably about Barney when Herb remarked, "You know, I would like to be Barney Frank." Martin pointed out to Herb that that was the big difference between them, "I admire Barney but I have no desire to be Barney."

When the news came out that Barney and Herb had split up, the *Boston Globe* ran a front-page story about it on July 3, 1998, under the headline "Frank Breakup Ends an Era in Gay Politics." After reading the headline Barney asked the editors at the newspaper, "Gee, did I ruin it for everybody?" The response was, "No, we simply meant that you two were the first." The article refers to them as "pioneers in national politics, an openly gay member of Congress and his male lover." "For nearly 11 years, Rep. Barney Frank and his partner, Herb Moses, were the capital's most prominent and influential homosexual couple. They changed the way gays and lesbians are treated in Congress, in Washington society, and in the public eye." Barney refused to comment for the article on the reason for the split, declaring, "It's nobody's business." "It's an unhappy part of life's experiences" but "the breakup doesn't undo any of the positive effects," he remarked. Barney joked that he told Herb that he would "take custody of annoying questions from reporters about the breakup," adding that Herb was a private citizen again and didn't have to answer them anymore. Barney commented to a friend at the time, "At least he didn't leave me for a younger man."

The breakup was listed in *Time* magazine's July 13, 1998, issue under Milestones: "Separating—Massachusetts Congressman Barney Frank, 58, and his partner of more than 10 years, Herb Moses, 41, formerly an executive at the Federal National Mortgage Association."

The separation was amicable and the two remain friends to some extent. Herb now has the family he has always wanted. According to Barney, Herb is living with "a nice fellow" in Orange County, California, and they have adopted children.

19

Defending the President against Impeachment

In late July 1994, Barney became involved in the investigation of Whitewater as a member of the Banking Committee and began defending President Bill Clinton against accusations relating to the failed Arkansas real estate venture. "Robert Fiske, Kenneth Starr, and Jay Stephens have investigated all of this and have come up with no misdeeds against the Clintons. . . . With all the investigating . . . no one has yet brought forth any accusation against either President Clinton or Hillary regarding any violation of the law or misuse of public funds regarding Whitewater," Barney said. He referred to the hearings as "allegations in search of proof."

Prior to the Whitewater hearings, Barney had been asked by Bristol Community College in Fall River to help get Secretary of Labor Robert Reich to speak at the college. He made the request and Secretary Reich committed to appear at the college. It was a major event for the small college and they invested a great deal of time and energy publicizing the event. Two days before the Friday event, Reich's staff informed the college that the secretary had a conflict that day and would not be able to attend. An upset college administrator contacted Barney's office and asked what the school should do at this late date. "Reich broke his word. There was no good reason why he couldn't come," recalled Barney.

An angry Barney phoned the White House and told presidential adviser George Stephanopoulos that he would not be able to attend the Whitewater hearing the next day because he was "busy having to deal with the damage caused by Reich not speaking at the college." Stephanopoulos asked him to hold for a moment. When Stephanopoulos returned to the line he told Barney that Secretary Reich would be speaking at the college on Friday as scheduled and that Barney would have the time to attend the Whitewater hearing the next day.

Barney also defended the president against charges related to incidents that became known as "Filegate" and "Travelgate" and against other attacks by the Republicans that he believed were unfounded. Referring to the FBI files of several hundred Republicans that were obtained by the White House's Office of Personnel Security, Barney said, "Clearly the White House erred in having those files, but again all the evidence seems to suggest it was an honest error, not one instance of anyone—a reporter or anyone else—alleging they were given negative information about any political opponent of the president based on the FBI files." Referring to the firing of employees in the White House Travel Office, he said, "I do not think the White House had a justification for firing them. . . . They were guilty of hasty overreacting and unfairness to individuals but did not act illegally."

At a Judiciary Committee hearing in October 1997, Barney defended Attorney General Janet Reno's decision not to appoint an independent counsel to investigate a litany of events involving President Clinton that committee Republicans had urged her to investigate. He dissected the letter the Republicans had sent to the attorney general. "They want a criminal investigation for bribery because the president designated land in Utah for a monument, something which environmentalists were very for, and this stopped coal mining there and he may have done this as a favor to the Lippo Group [which has coal in Indonesia]." Barney called the suggestion that the Utah monument was really a Lippo plot "one of the silliest things I have ever heard advanced in 18 years." He advised Attorney General Reno, "Don't spend too much time on the Utah connection. Leave that to the movies."

A second charge Barney took issue with involved Vice President Al Gore, who called some people to ask for money. One of the people he called said he felt pressure to contribute because he has so much business that touches on federal government telecommunications, tax policy, and regulations. "Among the things we cannot do is to accuse each other of being hypocritical, so I will not do that," Barney said. "But for members of Congress who have authority over telecommunications, tax policy, and regulations, and almost all of whom, in my experience, regularly call people up and ask them for money, to say the vice president ought to be criminally investigated simply because he called somebody and an anonymous person said 'gee, I felt pressured,' if everybody who one of us called and didn't want us to call them triggered an indictment, you could just put bars outside and lock us all up."

Barney summarized the allegations: "The vice president called me up, I felt pressured, indict him. The president decided to protect land in Utah and there is coal in Indonesia, indict him." Later, on the *FOX on Politics* program, November 15, 1997, he was even more direct. "None of the allegations in the Republican letter, and I assume they gave it their best shot, rise to the level of a crime. Let me use a technical term—those are stupid," he said.

Barney sympathized with the president and the first lady. "When the Bill Clinton issue came along, I knew from experience what it was like to have political enemies mad at you for other reasons magnify something you had admittedly done wrong to try to destroy you," he explained.

At the same time, the Massachusetts liberal disagreed with the president on budget priorities and domestic policy. He took issue with Clinton's saying in January 1996 in his State of the Union speech that the era of big government is over, charging that the president "curried favor with the right by buying into the term 'era of big government.'" I don't know when the era of big government was. I guess I was absent that day. The notion that we ever had a situation where the government was so overreaching that it was interfering with our ability to function in a society was wrong. It was a cheap shot that Bill Clinton took at his own side," he said.

In the summer of 1996, when President Clinton signed a welfare law that Barney believed was draconian, he told *USA Today* that the president had "traded the poor people for two more points in the polls." In May 1997, Barney and several House Democrats sent a letter to the president expressing their belief that the balanced budget agreement shortchanged social programs and provided unfair tax breaks. The letter accused the president of betraying party principles. Later, a reporter from the *New York Times* asked what response he had received from the White House to the letter. Barney replied, "We didn't receive an answer, probably because we addressed the letter to the Democratic President of the United States and it came back 'addressee unknown.'"

According to Barney, the biggest mistake Bill Clinton made was to sign off in 1997 on what he called "that terrible Balanced Budget Act, which basically cut Medicare so that you could have a capital gains tax cut." Barney feels that cutting Medicare was unnecessary, because the budget deficit was declining for other reasons, and there was no political justification for the cuts, because Clinton could not run again.

Looking back at the Clinton presidency, Barney concluded that on the whole Bill Clinton was a very good president, though not as good as he could have been. "The presidency for me is a place where you fight to get values implemented that makes the society better. That is the perspective I bring to rating Bill Clinton," he said. "Bill Clinton started out with a policy more liberal than he could get through Congress. His set values were more to the left than were prevailing in the country when he took over. In 1993, President Clinton put through one of the best tax packages in the history of the country. It made the tax code more progressive. It demonstrated that the Democrats could be fiscally responsible, i.e., reduce the deficit, while preserving government programs. However, in late 1993, President Clinton found that he had overreached and had to be more careful how he did it. He sensibly pulled back. What played out was a struggle on how far he could move the country. I don't fault him for that at all."

Barney feels, however, that Clinton became too enamored of "this notion of centrism" and that he continued to be a centrist when there was no longer any political need for it. During the last couple of years of his presidency, he did not stick to his goals. "President Clinton had a failure of nerve at the end," Barney said.

Barney became one of the most outspoken critics of independent counsel Kenneth Starr. In his opinion, Starr should never have been appointed as independent counsel because of discussions that Starr had in 1994 with Gilbert Davis, the attorney for Paula Jones, the woman who charged Clinton with sexual harassment when he was governor of Arkansas, while Starr was acting as an unpaid counsel to Jones's legal team.

In February 1998, Barney was outraged by Starr's action in summoning senior White House aide Sidney Blumenthal, a former *Washington Post* reporter, who twenty years earlier had covered Barney in the state legislature as a reporter for the *Real Paper* in Boston, to answer questions before a grand jury about contacts he had had with the press about Starr and his staff. Barney was so angered by what he saw as Starr's assault on the First Amendment that he issued a press release headlined, "Frank Risks Subpoena by Criticizing Starr." The press release reads: "There are only two possible explanations for the bizarre decision by Kenneth Starr to summon some of his critics before a grand jury to answer for their impertinence in speaking ill of him. . . . One, he has misread the Independent Counsel statute and believes that it supersedes not only the Justice Department but also the First Amendment, . . . which has heretofore been thought to protect people from official sanction for criticizing public officials in conversations with the press. Two, he has become delusional and is under the impression that he is a hamburger, the United States is the state of Texas, and Sidney Blumenthal is Oprah Winfrey." The second explanation referred to a comment Oprah Winfrey made to her television audience during an April 1996 segment on mad cow disease. When Winfrey said that concern over the disease "has just stopped me cold from eating another burger," beef prices plummeted. In a speech in his district, Barney reiterated his reference to Kenneth Starr as a hamburger, adding, "I think Kenneth Starr is acting like a piece of meat—rump of horse."

Barney had risen in seniority to become the second-ranking Democrat on the Judiciary Committee behind John Conyers, the only remaining panel member from the 1974 impeachment proceedings against President Richard Nixon. In March 1998, as the seeds for an impeachment inquiry began to take root, press attention began to focus on Barney. Paul Gigot wrote in the *Wall Street Journal* on March 20: "The man at the crossroads of all this is Barney Frank, who this year might be the most powerful Democrat in Washington. He sits on the House Judiciary Committee, which will assess any report by Kenneth Starr. His sister is White House spin-cyclist Ann Lewis, so he doesn't hurt for access. He has the credibility to rally other liberals and the verbal skill and meanness to dominate any impeachment hearing."

On *Face the Nation* on March 22, the moderator, Bob Schieffer, asked Barney about Dick Armey's comment that some Republicans favor having a small group of members go and talk to Kenneth Starr rather than having it done by the Judiciary Committee because some Democrats on the committee would turn it into a partisan food fight. "Of all the people I am willing to accept instruction in political decorum from, Dick Armey, is, to be honest, quite low on the list," Barney responded. He rejected the idea of "sending a little posse to see Kenneth Starr."

On March 25, the House Republicans approved, over Democratic objections, a $1.3 million supplemental appropriation for the Judiciary Committee to investigate President Clinton. According to several Democrats, they were less concerned about Judiciary Committee chairman Henry Hyde than about Speaker Newt Gingrich, who was playing a prominent behind-the-scenes role in orchestrating the Republicans' planning for an impeachment inquiry. That is, according to Barney, they were "more concerned about Dr. Jekyll than Hyde." Later, when Speaker Gingrich directed House Republicans to maintain decorum in speaking about President Clinton's problems, Barney retorted. "Having Newt Gingrich issue rules on decorum is like Mike Tyson reissuing the Marquis of Queensbury rules."

Barney continued to be sharply critical of the independent counsel, telling reporters that Kenneth Starr had been pursuing Clinton since "shortly after my bar mitzvah." On *Meet the Press* on July 12, Barney suggested that people read *Moby Dick* to understand the investigation. "Kenneth Starr has become Captain Ahab. He is so determined to bring down the white whale that he is going to keep going and going," he said. Barney also likened Starr to Inspector Clouseau, the bumbling police officer played by Peter Sellers in the Pink Panther movie series. "No one has investigated so much and come up with so little."

Barney became the point person and the dominant player on the Democratic side of the committee table in defending President Clinton at the impeachment hearings, which focused on a consensual sexual affair the president had with the White House intern Monica Lewinsky that he then lied about. "The challenge in this sort of debate," Barney said, "is to use humor to try to show in some ways these people are ridiculous, but not to the point where people forget that it's very serious."

Barney felt he was in a good position to help defend the president. "At first," he said, "I thought the fact that I had been involved in a sex scandal of my own would make me almost ineligible to take a leading role here. But as it evolved, it turned out that precisely because I had been through it, I couldn't be scared by it, I couldn't be damaged by it. From the outset, I was just less afraid of this whole thing and more willing to take it on, knowing that you could defeat this kind of thing. . . . Defending someone who had violated conventional sexual morality was not a problem for me. People for whom [what Clinton did sexually] was a big deal weren't my supporters anyway. I lost those people a long time ago."

"Barney approached the impeachment hearings with intellectual thoroughness and he figured out right away what were the substantive legal issues and how to approach them," Robert Raben, his legislative counsel, said. "Once that happened he was very impatient when others couldn't keep up with him. Barney did the primary research himself. He did not rely on me to synthesize it or say here is the import. We did it parallel. He read it. I read it. He had questions. I had questions," Raben explained. "Barney homed in on what he considered the weak spots in the impeachment. He talked to some people that he had grown to respect out in the world to get their thoughts on what he thought was in play."

The conservative Henry Hyde, the Judiciary Committee chairman conducting the impeachment hearings, and the liberal Barney Frank, who served as President Clinton's leading advocate, went head to head, clashing daily on a national stage. The two lawmakers admired and respected each other. Barney, who believed that Hyde was one of the fairest members in Congress, explained to Sally Quinn of the *Washington Post* why Hyde was held in such high regard by his colleagues: "He is a man of considerable personal decency. I don't think he is a guy who glories in other people's misery, even if he doesn't like the other people. The thing I like about Henry Hyde is that he didn't come here to head a posse. He came here to make public policy. He's good at what he does. . . . He's the kind of guy who likes the legislative process and understands it." Hyde said of Barney: He "overwhelms you with rapid rhetoric, but there is usually substance behind it. He's a fearsome adversary who appears to enjoy his work. He's quick, he's sharp, and he's effective. Basically, Barney is a lot of fun. . . . Barney and I have totally opposite points of view but we have become friends over the years and I admire his talent, seriousness, and ability."

When revelations surfaced in the press in September 1998 that Hyde, who was married, had had a multiyear affair with a married woman thirty years earlier, a reporter asked Barney whether Hyde's adultery was relevant to his role as chairman of the committee conducting an impeachment process. "No. But it might have been relevant when he was supporting the Defense of Marriage Act," he replied.

When Barney's white-haired mother, Elsie, attended one of the Judiciary Committee impeachment hearings, he introduced her to the white-haired committee chairman. At the start of the hearing, Hyde graciously announced, "With the permission of the gentleman from Massachusetts, I'd like to introduce Elsie Frank, Barney Frank's mother" and Elsie rose from her seat. At that day's hearing there was much graphic testimony regarding the relationship between Bill Clinton and Monica Lewinsky. Barney whispered to Democratic colleague Maxine Waters, "I never thought that I would be sitting around talking about oral sex in front of my mother." A few days later, when Barney was a guest on NBC's *Conan O'Brien Show*, the Harvard-educated comedian asked about this meeting between his mom and Henry Hyde. Barney joked, "I thought it would be useful for them to meet to see if they were compatible in case either one of them needed a hair transplant."

Barney was the most visible Democrat on the Judiciary Committee during the media frenzy. He made the requisite network television appearances because nobody else wanted to. "It wasn't because they had a meeting of all the television people and they said 'Let's get Frank, he's the best.' It was 'Who can we get?' She won't do it. He's sick. He's getting his hair done. Well, get Frank," he explained. He did dozens of television and radio interviews, often being asked the same questions, which he found boring. Nonetheless, he persevered. "You can be bored but you can't afford to be boring. You have to recognize that each of these media appearances is a brand new thing for the people watching it," he said. "Frankly, it can be a strain. It is not my natural personality to go about being cheerful all the time, but if the issue is important enough, personal considerations have to temporarily get put aside."

Barney appeared with the Senate Judiciary Committee chairman Orrin Hatch on *Meet the Press* on August 16, 1998, the day before President Clinton was to testify before Kenneth Starr's grand jury. Tim Russert, the program moderator, began with the observation that Barney Frank "has been one of the most ardent defenders of President Clinton." Russert noted that according to reports by NBC News and the Associated Press, the president "told his advisers and his lawyers that he had a sexual relationship with Monica Lewinsky and is going to testify to that." He then asked Barney, "Do you feel used?" Barney replied, "No, I don't feel used at all. And I never claimed to know the truth of what happened. . . . Kenneth Starr was appointed more than four years ago, long before you and I had heard of Monica Lewinsky. At least me, I can't speak for you. You learn to be cautious. . . . I'm proud of my role in defending the president against what now, I think, turn out to have been inaccurate accusations about Whitewater. As to the Monica Lewinsky affair, I never claimed to know one way or the other."

Russert continued on the path of trying to analyze the president's grand jury testimony in advance of his appearance. "The president said he would testify completely and truthfully. And now we have his aides and his advisers telling the media he acknowledged to us that he had sex with Monica Lewinsky. And then they write, 'The advisers caution the president could still change his strategy in the hours before his testimony.' How can you change a strategy if you have pledged to tell the truth?" Russert asked. "I don't know," Barney replied. "Tim, if you thought you were getting a member of the Psychic Friends Network, someone misled you. I don't know what he's going to do. I have the same inferences you do. . . . I guess I don't understand why there is a need to do that particular analysis today. Couldn't we do it Tuesday or Wednesday? I mean, why analyze the testimony before he gave it?"

"Do you believe if the president acknowledges that he had sex with a White House intern that would be reckless behavior?" Russert asked. "I would have to look at the whole context. It would be a lack of responsibility. As to reckless, I would have to know more about the circumstances, frankly, than I want to know," Barney responded.

Barney believes that Clinton, like a lot of other people, got in serious trouble more because of the cover-up than because of the act itself. "I learned that lesson in 1989," he said. "When someone is hit with many accusations, it is important for him or her to admit quickly what did—and did not—happen. Otherwise, all the charges tend to blur together. I did that up front. The only way to expose the lies is to acknowledge the truth."

Although Barney was sympathetic to the president and one of his staunchest defenders at the impeachment hearings, he was critical of Clinton's tactics and actions. "The president behaved quite wrongly," he said. "He should not have had sex with Ms. Lewinsky, and he certainly should not have lied about it to the public and played the misleading and intellectually dishonest legal games he played regarding it in the Paula Jones deposition, and to some extent in the grand jury testimony."

In Barney's view, the president should have apologized early on. "First, he did something wrong. He was president of the United States and owed the country a genuine apology. Second, we were still assuming that there was some rationality on the GOP side and thought that an apology of the right sort could put an end to what was not really in the country's interest." He believed that the president should have said something along the lines of "I was very embarrassed by this; I knew what I did was wrong; I knew it was shameful; and I very much wanted not to admit it. So I went into that deposition trying hard as I could to conceal the truth without lying, and now that I think back on it, I may not have been fully successful." According to Barney, even in President Clinton's address to the nation on August 17, 1998, the day he testified before Kenneth Starr's grand jury, the president missed a chance to level with the American public. "I think he over lied about it. He should not have gone on television and said 'I never had sexual relations with that woman, Ms. Lewinsky.' If I were he, I wouldn't have said 'my answers were technically accurate,'" Barney explained. "Bill Clinton lies by being technically accurate. I wish he would stop it. I wish he would learn that 'I didn't inhale,' 'No, I didn't do it by standing on one leg on Thursday,' is just not worthy of him and everyone sees through it. He is not fourteen anymore trying to outsmart the principal."

Barney contended that Clinton was entitled to fairness but not to indignation on his behalf. "He screwed up. He's not a purely innocent person having suddenly been mugged. The guy's done something he shouldn't have done and he should have known better." He maintained that Clinton's actions were wrong and that he deserved to be punished. "Nobody is going to forgive and forget but not impeaching is not the same thing as forgiving." He argued that Clinton did not do anything that came close to the threshold for impeachment, that Clinton's admission of inappropriate consensual sex with Monica Lewinsky did not constitute an impeachable offense, even though he took steps to conceal it.

Barney believes that impeachment is not a regular way to discipline elected officials. That, he says, is what elections are for. "The normal sanction for the kind of irresponsible behavior and terrible judgment that Bill Clinton has shown is that you get defeated in the next election. That's the ultimate penalty that a politician pays." But, he added, "what we are looking for now is the constitutional equivalent of a good kick in the ass."

Since the president was constitutionally prohibited from seeking a third term, Barney took the view that President Clinton deserved censure. Throughout the impeachment proceedings he urged the Republicans to settle for censuring the president. He strongly disagreed with those who were dismissive of censure, who contended that censure is somehow a triviality and would mean nothing to the president. "The notion that Bill Clinton doesn't care what people think about him is nonsensical. Of course he does. He cares about what history says about him. I've never heard anyone suggest before that when the House or Senate censures or reprimands someone it's irrelevant," he said.

To his Judiciary Committee colleagues he said: "I would tell you that having been reprimanded by this House of Representatives, where I am proud to serve, was no triviality. It was a very sad moment for me. It is something that I will always have to live with. It is something that, when people write about me, they still write about. It is not something that's a matter of pride. I wish I could go back and undo it." Furthermore, he said, pointing out that the Republican arguments against censure were inconsistent: "They maintain that censure would cripple future presidents because it can be used so easily. On the other hand it doesn't mean anything. But how can something that doesn't mean anything cripple future presidents?"

On August 19, on the *NewsHour with Jim Lehrer*, Barney and GOP senator John Ashcroft of Missouri debated the issue of whether President Clinton should resign. Ashcroft argued that President Clinton had disgraced the office, broken the trust of the American people in the office, and damaged his capacity to operate domestically and internationally.

Barney countered: "I think there is confusion here between the types of systems we have. What Bill Clinton has done, clearly, is to his discredit. . . . But we don't have a parliamentary system. We have a constitutional system. We say when you get elected, you get elected for a fixed term. In parliamentary systems, you lose confidence, there's a way to deal with that. That's not in our system and there's no reason for it to be. In fact, it would be much more disruptive to have a resignation."

He called Ashcroft's reasoning circular and argued: "He says he has to resign because he's incapacitated. Well, Senator Ashcroft, as is his right, is trying mightily to incapacitate him, but I don't think it happens. The fact is that the president continues to have a lot of support from the public on the public policies, and I think there's no sign whatsoever that he hasn't continued to function effectively as president, including in foreign policy."

On September 11, independent counsel Starr submitted a report and other materials to the House of Representatives that in his opinion provided substantial and credible evidence that might constitute grounds for impeachment of President Clinton.

On September 18, the Judiciary Committee voted behind closed doors to release to the public the four-hour videotape and transcript of President Clinton's grand jury testimony. Chairman Hyde told the press after the meeting: "We had a vigorous and spirited debate, but it was civil. I would say that the spirit of bipartisanship is still alive and flourishing." The Democrats called this action, forced through by a Republican majority, unfair and designed to embarrass the president. Barney told the press gathered outside the hearing room, "If this is bipartisanship, then the Taliban win a medal for religious tolerance." On another occasion he referred to the Republicans rush to impeachment as "unilateral bipartisanship."

"The low point was when the House voted in September to release the Starr material. Three hundred sixty members of the House, including the great majority of the Democrats, voted with all the Republicans. Everybody thought it would kill Bill Clinton. Everybody expected nasty, salacious stuff. That was the low point because I thought he might be thrown out of office—a terrible victory for the right wing," Barney explained in a July 1999 *Playboy* interview.

Barney drew a comparison between the Republican effort to impeach Bill Clinton and the 1955 Alfred Hitchcock film *The Trouble with Harry*, in which a body is found that many people assume is that of a murder victim, though it turns out that the person died of natural causes. In an effort to protect the presumed murderer, someone buries the body and then people keep digging it up and reburying it. "It was the same with impeachment," Barney said. "The Republicans kept burying the body and then had to dig it up because the right wing insisted that they keep going. We kept assuming that it was buried and it kept getting exhumed and put back again."

In September, President Clinton, in an effort to shore up the team that would be defending him against impeachment, appointed Gregory Craig, a partner at the law firm of Williams & Connolly, as assistant to the president and special counsel in the White House. Craig, an Allard Lowenstein protégé, had been friends with Barney for over thirty years, beginning when Craig was a seventeen-year-old freshman at Harvard. Craig believes that because of their longtime friendship, Barney felt comfortable talking to him honestly about various committee members and issues. "Barney's political antennae were excellent. He was a constant resource of good advice on how to deal with various Democratic members of the committee," Craig said, adding that the entire team defending the president felt the same way. "If someone said Barney thought we should do it this way, that was huge."

On October 5, the Judiciary Committee began debate on a Republican proposal for an open-ended impeachment investigation. Barney reflected on the motive for an open-ended inquiry: "There is a fear on the part of many who want to destroy Bill Clinton, who didn't like the '92 election, who didn't like the '96 election, and would like to undo it, that the matters in the Starr referral do not carry enough to justify an impeachment." He concluded, "I don't think much of the job [Starr's] done, but . . . let's look at what Mr. Starr charged the president with and decide."

As a member of the Judiciary Committee, Barney was a team player, despite the Democrats' being in the minority on the committee. But away from the television cameras, he was deeply frustrated that he had not been able to cut a deal with the Republicans on the committee. "The Republicans on the Judiciary Committee were told that their political futures would be jeopardized if they compromised, so who were we going to negotiate with?" he asked.

Barney also had to deal with disparate points of view among the Democrats on the committee that came out in their caucus meetings. In an effort to find common ground, according to Abbe Lowell, the Democratic chief investigative counsel, Barney "in his inimitable way" used "a dash of bravado, a dash of humor, a dash of deprecation, and some brilliance." Lowell explained that it was often Barney's comments on strategy that "stopped everybody in their tracks" and caused committee Democrats to reassess their positions and coalesce around a consensus. For example, some Democrats on the committee argued for an expanded impeachment hearing that would include witnesses in support of President Clinton, but Barney resisted, saying, "When your opponent is busy committing suicide, you get out of his way."

"It was Barney who said let the Republicans steer this ship, they will crash it on the rocks," Lowell recalled. "He figured out that it didn't make sense to try to engage the Republicans in a rational middle ground because their excesses would undermine their credibility. His view was let it play out because they can't help themselves and they will self-destruct and that is exactly what happened. . . . Barney was stifled at every juncture by the Republicans who asserted their majority power. The Republicans wouldn't even pretend to make it a fair process," he said. When the Republicans on the committee veered away from calling any witnesses, Barney was incredulous. "What are we going to do at this hearing, play cards?" he asked.

One day that fall, Barney was in New York City and met his former college roommate, Charles Halpern, for lunch. At the time Halpern and his wife were living in the Upper West Side near Broadway. "As I walked along Broadway with Barney, it was extraordinary. It was like being with a rock star. Heads would swivel as he walked by," Halpern said. While they sat eating at an outdoor café, Halpern added, "people would stop at our table and tell Barney what an inspiring figure he is, and how much they admire his courage, wit, and effectiveness."

"I remember my kids, the three Lowenstein children, each phoning me during the impeachment hearings and saying how wonderful Barney Frank is," Jenny Lowenstein Littlefield recalled. "He was a great hero to them because of what he did and what he was saying. These kids are very picky as to who is a hero."

Barney was in frequent contact with his sister Ann Lewis, the White House communications director. The press was eager to know about communications between the siblings during the impeachment proceeding. "There was a time," he told reporters, "when my sister forced me to look away from sexual impropriety. It was in 1946 when she took me to the movies to see *Gone with the Wind*. She made me hide my eyes when Scarlett was riding over the bridge [during the rape scene]."

Perhaps Barney's strongest legal argument on behalf of the president concerned the right to privacy. In this country almost anybody can sue anybody else. Once you are sued, you are then subject to unlimited discovery even about matters that are not relevant to the private lawsuit. Barney considers it an erosion of privacy to allow anyone who files a lawsuit to compel the president, or anyone else, to answer under oath, under penalty of punishment, questions about intimate details of his or her life that are peripheral to the lawsuit. In Barney's legal opinion, the clearly consensual relationship that the president had with Monica Lewinsky was irrelevant in every way to the allegation of harassment in the Paula Jones case. Therefore, the seriousness of Clinton's lies at his January 17 deposition in the Paula Jones lawsuit was mitigated by the unwarranted intrusiveness of the laws under which he was questioned.

Barney also made the case that perjury is rampant and that thousands of police officers lie under oath every year. Barney recalled, "I had one Republican member tell me privately, 'I'm a divorce lawyer and all my life I've been telling people to lie about their sex lives. How can I go after Clinton about this?'"

The impeachment of Bill Clinton, according to Barney, was "an effort by the right wing to destroy a man whose political success was making them almost a little bit crazy." Before the television cameras outside the Judiciary Committee hearing room, he accused the Republicans of playing partisan politics. "The Republicans don't want justice. They want to take down a popular Democratic president," he asserted. "They weren't just trying to impeach Bill Clinton. They were trying to drive a stake through his heart."

When an anonymous group placed a stack of reprints of the September 25, 1989, *Newsweek* cover story about Barney's own sex scandal on the press table at the impeachment hearings in an effort to discredit and embarrass him and thus to diminish his effectiveness, Barney said he was not surprised and that actually he was "kind of encouraged by it." "It is flattering when people for whom you have so little respect treat you as one of their major enemies. I think that gives you some bragging rights," he said.

Barney described his tactic of making numerous references during the impeachment proceedings to his sexual orientation and his own experience with a sex scandal as "a little bit of expiation." It was, he said, "one more way of saying, 'I know that I screwed up.'"

"The president was understandably embarrassed. He had private sexual activity that he wanted to conceal, and he lied about it, and that is a subject, as an expert on which, I fully understand," he remarked. "I am a little bit bemused by people denouncing [President Clinton] for lying about private sex, because they denounced me for telling the truth about it."

Asked by a reporter to comment on the Starr report, he replied, "Too much reading about heterosexual sex." At a press conference he compared the Republicans to the Red Queen in Alice in Wonderland, whose philosophy was sentence first, trial afterward. When he was informed by reporters that the character he was thinking of was the Queen of Hearts, he quipped, "It's very embarrassing for a gay man to get his Queens wrong."

Horatio Sanz played Barney Frank, without distinction, in two 1998 *Saturday Night Live* skits about the Judiciary Committee impeachment hearings with Will Ferrell as Henry Hyde. "I was really pissed that the guy who played me on *Saturday Night Live* was way too fat and ugly," Barney had complained to Democratic colleagues. "But then I saw that Maxine [Waters] was played by a guy [Tracy Morgan] who was even uglier, so I realized she had the bigger complaint." But it was not all Sanz's fault that he didn't succeed. Barney's spontaneous remarks at the impeachment hearings were funnier than the lines scripted for Sanz by the writers at *Saturday Night Live*. For example, Barney said, "It's hard to give exculpatory evidence when one ground for the perjury in the grand jury is that the president remembers the sex, which he acknowledged, as having begun in February of '96 and Ms. Lewinsky says it began in November of '95. What is the exculpatory evidence he is going to bring in? A February calendar saying 'Oh my God! Monica and I finally did it today.'"

Barney believed that the Republican leadership was in a quandary in designing an exit strategy for the impeachment process. "They don't know whether to bring it to an end or expand it and they clearly are not happy. They thought they had a horse they could ride all the way but now they don't know whether to shoot it or sell it to the dog food factory," he explained.

On November 19, during the morning session, independent counsel Kenneth Starr gave what amounted to a summary of the contents of his report in an uninterrupted two-hour presentation to the members of the Judiciary Committee. Barney had strongly opposed allowing Starr to testify as a witness, arguing that it was ridiculous to have the prosecutor come before the committee and restate what was written in the report as if he had any first-hand knowledge. Abbe Lowell, who would be the first Democrat to cross-examine Starr, paid close attention to Starr's remarks and began anxiously preparing his questions. Barney relieved some of the tension when he leaned over and said to him, "I will give you a dollar for every time you use one of the actual sexual terms and stop talking about them in euphemisms."

After about fifteen minutes of listening to Starr slowly read his fifty-eight-page statement uninterrupted, Barney became restless, turned to his counsel Robert Raben, who was sitting behind him, and informed him that he was going to the House gym to work out. He quietly slipped out of the hearing room and suddenly Raben found himself with an unobstructed center court view of Starr's plodding two-hour marathon presentation. Barney rode an exercise bike while reading the newspaper and listening to Starr's testimony on the television set up there. He was multi-tasking. "He is what Jews call *shpilkos*. He is incapable of doing only one thing. He must be doing several things at once," Raben said.

Asked by reporters during the lunch break about his absence, Barney explained that he'd already read everything Starr said, that his presentation in the hearing room was simply a streamlined version of his 454-page impeachment report. As for Starr's performance that morning, he told the reporters, "I would say Mr. Starr reads well and talks slow. What can I tell you?"

Kenneth Starr appeared confident as he sat down at the witness table after the lunch break to answer questions from committee counsel and members. As a former solicitor general, Starr was experienced in fielding questions from the Supreme Court Justices. He had prepared for the hearing the same way he prepared for oral arguments before courts, by having his associates pepper him with questions that would likely be asked, as well as some that were not likely.

The rules in Congress were different, though, and Starr adapted his strategy accordingly. Each committee member had five minutes to question the slow-talking Starr. During his preparation Starr was advised to follow the maxim of basketball and football coaches whose teams are leading in the fourth quarter and tell their players "to use the clock." Starr was told to take his time in responding to a question. The more time that he consumed responding to a hostile question posed by a committee Democrat, the fewer questions that member could ask. He was advised to remember when being grilled by Barney Frank or Chuck Schumer that when their five minutes expired, he wouldn't have to worry about them again for several hours until the next round of questions.

During an oral argument before the Supreme Court, an attorney should not equivocate and should respond fully and directly to any question posed by one of the Justices. But it was different when Starr appeared before the Judiciary Committee. There, dodge ball was the game of choice as Starr used equivocation and evasiveness to handle unfriendly questions.

Barney was at his best when confronting Kenneth Starr. Five minutes is not enough time for a member to get into an extensive debate about issues with the witness. He wisely wasted none of his allotted time by making a speech and instead proceeded directly to badger Starr and put him on the spot. Barney's first concern was the finding by district court judge Norma Holloway Johnson that in twenty-four instances information undermining the president had been leaked to the press during the investigation, in violation of grand jury rules.

"Mr. Starr," Barney began, "are you aware of any member of your staff who in fact was guilty of what Judge Johnson has found to be a prima facie violation?"

"Well, with all respect, I think that is an unfair question and the reason I do— " Starr said, bristling.

"Then I'll withdraw it. Mr. Starr, you're the expert on unfair questions! If you're telling me it's an unfair question, I'll withdraw it," Barney said. He rephrased the question. "Did anybody in your staff give out that information on any of those 24 instances?"

"There are a couple of instances where we issued a press release— But may I say this? I am operating under a sealed litigation proceeding," Starr responded.

Barney pointed out that the proceeding was sealed at Starr's request and that therefore he could waive it. "If you didn't do any of the leaking, why don't you just tell us if it's wrong factually? On the other hand, if you're going to say 'Well, you successfully got the Circuit Court to seal it,' I suppose I can't do much."

During Starr's two-hour opening presentation that morning, he had mentioned in passing that he found no evidence of impeachable offenses in connection with Travelgate and Filegate. Barney proceeded to follow up on that issue.

"You say on page 47 of the testimony that 'Our investigation which has been thorough found no evidence than anyone higher than Mr. Livingstone or Mr. Marceca was involved.' When did your investigation determine that?" he asked Starr.

"Well, under 595(c)— " Starr began.

Barney would allow no filibustering. "It's a simple factual question," he said. "When did you determine that?"

"We determined that some months ago," Starr replied.

"OK. Well before the election. When did you determine with regard to the Travel Office that the President was not involved?" Barney asked.

"We have— "

"Factual, Mr. Starr. When?" Barney said, cutting him off.

"It is not a date certain. We have no information with respect to— "

"I'll take a date ambiguous. Give me an approximate," Barney said, causing laughter in the crowded hearing room, even by some GOP members.

"As of the date of this reporting, we do not have any information that the President is involved," Starr replied

Barney started to dissect Starr's response. "Let me just say here is what disturbs me greatly. You filed the report about Lewinsky before the [November 1998] election. You tell us that months ago you concluded that the President was not involved in the FBI files, and you've never had any evidence he was involved in the Travel Office. Yet now several weeks after the election is the first time you are saying that. . . . Why did you withhold that before the election when you were sending us a referral with a lot of negative stuff about the President, and only now you give us this exoneration of the President several weeks after the election?" he asked.

"Well again, there is a process question. What we provided you in the referral is substantial and credible information of possible potential offenses. The silence with respect to anything else means necessarily that we had not concluded— " Starr answered.

"In other words, [you] don't have anything to say unless you have something bad to say," Barney asserted.

"Barney went right to the heart, right to the core, in his questioning of Starr to show that this is an unfair process that was skewed from the beginning," Lowell said. "Barney pointed out that over many years the president had been reviewed for Travelgate, Whitewater, Personnelgate, every gate imaginable, and the only thing Starr was coming forward with was Monica Lewinsky and had failed to tell anybody on the planet that he had closed the book on all these other things. Doesn't that say it all?"

Later that afternoon, Democrat Robert Wexler of Florida asked the independent counsel: "Did your agents or did they not threaten Ms. Lewinsky with 27 years of prison if she contacted her attorney? It's either yes or no. Not the legality." When Starr responded, "I would have to conduct an interview with my agents to know what the position of the office is," Barney shouted out to Wexler and everyone else in the hearing room, "The answer was yes."

Once Starr confirmed there was nothing to any of the charges involving the FBI files or the firings in the Travel Office, the Republicans, Barney observed, had "a real problem." When all the investigations began, the Republicans had assumed they were speaking for public opinion. But after the November 1998 election, it became clear that the public was not in tune with Republican thinking. The public, Barney said, "did not support canceling our presidential election because of this relatively minor issue. The Republicans had to try to persuade America that a president should be thrown out of office because of what happened between him and Lewinsky. They had to try to magnify the importance of this charge and I don't think it went over very well. . . . We weren't defending Bill Clinton's personal sexual behavior. We were defending important democratic principles and the right of the public to decide what the structures of government would be."

That evening, following twelve hours of testimony by Kenneth Starr, the Judiciary Committee voted along party lines in a closed-door session to issue new subpoenas for Katherine Willey and her attorney; Robert Bennett, President Clinton's attorney in the Paula Jones case; and the Democratic contributor Nathan Landow. Barney was optimistic, believing that the new subpoenas would come as "bad news" to the angriest Clinton haters. "Hope springs eternal in the breasts of the right wing, but I think it is less and less likely that we are going to come up with anything," he said.

To Barney, the hearings were nothing more than "a partisan food fight." He often reminded the Democratic chief counsel Abbe Lowell during the proceeding to stop trying to pretend that the Republican's case against the president was legitimate and trying to put it in its constitutional context. "No one on the committee was more instrumental in terms of me getting it right than Barney," Lowell recalled. "He was on my butt all the time. He pressed me. He made me better. He didn't accept a superficial analysis. He was relentless but inspiring. It was a good thing that I knew and appreciated him because I might have taken it wrong and gotten discouraged," he said.

On December 1, the Judiciary Committee held a hearing on the "consequences of perjury and related crimes." Barney questioned why the committee at this time was holding what Chairman Hyde had described in his opening remarks as a general oversight hearing. "I guess it is kind of a dead time . . . and oversight on perjury in general just happened to fill an empty agenda."

The first witnesses were a women's basketball coach and a physician, both of whom had pleaded guilty to perjury charges for giving false testimony about a sexual relationship during a civil case. Barney pointed out that these witnesses were accused of perjury on matters that were central to the case at issue. In the Paula Jones situation, however, the questions put to the president before a grand jury, for which he was being accused of perjury, were "entirely peripheral, ultimately ruled not to be directly relevant."

Barney asked Henry Hyde, "Are you saying that if you were a prosecutor, you would prosecute the President for having [said in August 1998] that the sexual activity began in February of 1996 rather than November of 1995? That is one of the three counts of perjury to the grand jury that Kenneth Starr has put forward."

"I would rather not answer that. It does not strike me as a terribly serious count," Hyde replied.

Later Hyde complained that he was being browbeaten by the Democrats on the panel for trying to do his job, "and it is not an easy job," he said. But when Barney said, "Thank you, Mr. Chairman. I promise not to browbeat you in my response and I apologize for the stress that you— " Hyde interrupted and said, "Oh! Go ahead. Why should you be different?"

After the laughter had subsided, Barney replied, "I don't know why I am different, Mr. Chairman, but I just am."

The committee then heard testimony from a panel of witnesses, including Admiral Leon Edney, a retired former vice chief of naval operations. Edney suggested that if the president were not impeached for perjury, it would undermine morale in the military and lead to an outbreak of lying in the military. The admiral asserted that this would "undermine the trust and confidence so essential to good order and discipline as well as mission success."

Barney jumped in. "Admiral, in December of 1992, George Bush, the outgoing president, pardoned Caspar Weinberger, who had been Secretary of Defense for I think, six years during the Reagan administration. Weinberger was indicted on four counts, including two counts of perjury. I guess the question is, when George Bush pardoned Caspar Weinberger was he saying to the military, 'Look, he's not going to be held accountable,' and did that have a bad effect to pardon someone before he was even tried but was indicted?" he asked.

"There was no proof on whether or not Caspar Weinberger committed— " Admiral Edney started to say.

"Of course there was no proof because it didn't go to trial. There couldn't be proof. George Bush made it proof-proof. That is the problem. So if we don't move to impeach President Clinton there won't be any proof either. They are on the same footing. My guess is this doesn't have a big effect on morale in either case," Barney contended.

"One of the differences is the Weinberger case involves the execution of foreign policy which is much more complex to understand," the admiral responded.

"The charge was lying and not remembering. It wasn't some complex question about name six Ayatollahs. It was not a foreign policy test. It was, 'Do you remember? No, I don't remember.' 'It happened last week. Do you know of any such things?' They were on his desk," Barney retorted.

On December 10, the Judiciary Committee began a debate on whether to vote articles of impeachment against President Clinton. In Barney's view, the Republicans looked at Kenneth Starr's three charges and said "Whoa!—we can't defend these" and so they obfuscated and dressed them up. Barney summed up the case against the president after more than five years of investigations of Whitewater, the FBI files, and the Travel Office by every possible investigative tool of the federal government—congressional committees, the FBI, and independent counsel. "We have the following charge against Bill Clinton: He had a private consensual sexual affair and lied about it," he said.

Barney called Republican chief investigative counsel David Schippers's invocation of unnamed and unspecified further crimes by the president that he claimed he was still investigating and his statement that there is more out there "irresponsible." "Why do people say there is more out there?" he asked. "Responsible people don't like to be in the position of making empty threats like that. It is not fair for anybody to say, particularly after five years and more of multiple investigations, oh, but there may be more out there."

Barney ridiculed Schippers's plea that members not be cajoled into considering each event in isolation or separately. "What Mr. Schippers is saying is, please believe that I have a whole that is greater than the sum of the parts, because they understand that the sum of the parts is not impeachable. The sum of the parts is and the whole is that Bill Clinton gave into a sexual affair that he shouldn't have had and shouldn't have lied about it. That is it," he said.

Barney examined the charge that the president committed perjury in the grand jury when he acknowledged an inappropriate sexual affair and that there was sexual contact between Monica Lewinsky and himself, concluding that he "shortchanged us on the details." "The President stands charged with being insufficiently graphic. He did not talk about what he did in reciprocation, and that is not a basis for impeachment," he said. He further explained, "The reasons for impeaching the President on grand jury testimony are what he touched and when he touched it. Ms. Lewinsky claimed that the President touched her in certain places, and that he did it in November and not in February. When he admitted to her performing sex on him, he did not tell us that he touched her in return, and for that we are going to undo two Presidential elections."

Barney poked fun at the way the articles of impeachment were drafted, listing four general categories without any specificity and without saying which ones the Republicans stand behind. "The President stands accused of committing perjury with regard to I, II, III or IV or more. You have taken an article of impeachment and made it a multiple choice test," he asserted. "Shouldn't [there] be a V, all of the above?" "Here is what it will say: 'The President provided perjurious, false, and misleading testimony to the grand jury concerning one or more of the following.' So maybe it was I or maybe it was II, and maybe it was III, maybe it was III and IV, maybe it was I, II, and IV." He continued, "Is this a shell game? Under which pea is the impeachment? Is it under number I, or is it number II, or maybe it is under III and II . . . ? I hope this doesn't go anywhere, but I am almost intrigued here. I want to see Chief Justice Rehnquist sitting there while the Senate is trying to guess under which pea you have concealed the impeachment."

Barney contended that impeachment is not a criminal proceeding or a strictly judicial proceeding. It is a political proceeding in the broadest sense of the word. "Those who say there should be no political element fly in the face of the Founding Fathers," he argued. "The people who wrote the constitution had choices. They could have put impeachment in the hands of the courts. They decided and they were very good politicians themselves, they kind of invented democratic politics in the world and they decided that this would be in a combined legal-political context. They were certainly smart enough to know that if you didn't want public opinion and politics to have any influence at all, you wouldn't ask [535] politicians to decide something."

He maintained that politics ought to be part of the process. "We are talking here about democracy, about whether or not an act of misbehavior was so grievous as to justify overturning the most solemn decision ever made by the American people, a presidential election." He concluded, "We're not debating whether or not this was right or wrong. It was wrong. But is it so wrong, so outrageous, that it must be overturned? . . . Censure is the appropriate response, and I hope the Republican leadership will not allow partisanship to keep the American people from seeing the decision they want."

When tempers started to flare between conservative Republicans and liberal Democrats on the committee, Barney sought recognition from Chairman

Hyde. A tired and exasperated Hyde said, "I swing to the gentleman from Massachusetts." To which Barney replied, "I appreciate your swinging my way."

Hyde compared the panel's role to that of a grand jury in a criminal case. He quoted Democrat Barbara Jordan, who said, when she voted for the impeachment of President Nixon in 1974, "The House accuses and the Senate judges." Hyde told the panel members that they could vote for impeachment even if they were not in favor of getting rid of the president. "If we vote these articles of impeachment, we are not throwing him out of office," he said.

Barney strongly disagreed. "We are beginning the process of throwing the President out of office . . . [and] undoing the last election. To suggest otherwise degrades the constitutional process." He explained: "Impeachment is the most solemn duty of the House of Representatives, after declaring war; impeachment is the absolute essential first step for canceling an election and throwing an elected President out of office." He pointed out that the impeachment resolution does not say "Hey, Senate, what do you think?" The resolution says "Kick him out." "What we now have people trying to do is to have their cake and eat it too; to impeach the president and begin the process of expelling him while denying that is what they are doing," he said.

Barney added, "In effect, what we are having people say is, we are going through the anguish, we're grunting and groaning and fighting, but don't worry, the outcome is fixed. I do not think it serves the Constitution, maybe it is the influence of Jesse Ventura, to treat impeachment as if it is professional wrestling; to tell people that all of this energy and all of this stress . . . in fact, don't worry about it, because we all know in the end it's not going to go anywhere."

Barney pointed out that Hyde was in effect making the Democrats' argument for censure. The suggestion that the committee vote for something that is critical of the president because it won't lead to his being thrown out of office, he said, is censure, not impeachment.

Barney knew that the Democrats would have a hard time getting a censure vote on the House floor. "In the House we have a rule that an amendment has to be germane to a bill," he said, adding, "In the Senate they think 'germane' is Michael Jackson's brother."

Barney pointed out that though Hyde, as the chairman of the Judiciary Committee, was under tremendous pressure from the right wing to go forward, procedurally, he had been fair. The Republican leadership, not Henry Hyde, he said, was "calling the shots" and the underlying strategy of the hearings was "very unfair." Hyde, he added, "doesn't enjoy this because his reputation is taking a hit." Barney, however, did offer some criticism of Hyde. "In the end Henry fell victim to *The Bridge over the River Kwai* syndrome. He just had to build the bridge. When impeachment got to the Senate, he became furious. It was like he was transformed. He was out for blood and became part of the pack."

In Barney's opinion, it turned out that the right wing was stronger than Hyde thought and the moderate Republicans weaker. "Here is what happened in the Judiciary Committee. Henry Hyde said we can't just impeach him over sex but the right wing of the party said, 'Oh, yes you can.'"

Barney's stalwart defense of Bill Clinton was serious and substantive. He was able to outthink and outmaneuver the Republicans. His insightful arguments, combative style, and ready wit won him accolades in the press. Sally Quinn of the *Washington Post* described Barney's performance at the impeachment hearings: "In defense of the president at the House Judiciary Committee hearings, Frank put on a tour de force—interjecting procedural questions, leaping on points of order, deftly zinging an opponent, cracking jokes when the atmosphere became particularly poisonous. Known throughout Congress for his ability to simplify the issues, Frank characterized the proceedings against the president as an issue of 'what did he touch and when did he touch it?'"

Greg Craig, from the president's defense team, said that what impressed him most about Barney was that he was "indefatigable." "He sat at those committee hearings forever and never gave up a minute of his time. He was constantly there defending the president, not his conduct so much as the notion that whatever he has done does not rise to the level of an impeachable offense. He was inexhaustible and relentless." William Delahunt, a Democratic member of the Judiciary Committee, called Barney "the core of the impeachment hearings."

Even Bob Barr, who, as a conservative Republican member of the committee, regularly battled with Barney at the impeachment hearings, told the *Boston Globe* in 2005: "Some of the members on that committee were just loud. Others just talked and talked. What makes Barney stronger than them, and more formidable, is that there is substance behind what he's saying. He has the credibility. When he says something, you can take to the bank that he knows his stuff."

President Clinton was very grateful for Barney's efforts on his behalf. After the committee impeachment hearings had ended, he phoned Barney from Israel to thank him for his hard work and skillful defense. A freshman Democrat called to thank Barney for taking such an aggressive stand on behalf of the president, saying that absent such a vigorous and convincing defense he and other freshman Democrats would be facing uphill battles for reelection. Several years later, when *Let's Get Frank*, a documentary by Bart Everly that looks at the Bill Clinton impeachment hearings by the House Judiciary Committee through the eyes of Barney Frank, opened in New York City on July 14, 2004, the film received a favorable review in the *New York Times*. A few days later, Barney received a handwritten note from Bill Clinton that said: "I just read the review of *Let's Get Frank* in the *New York Times* and it reminded me of how great you were when I was going through hell. I will always remember that."

During the December 18 debate in the House on the Articles of Impeachment, Barney referred to the proceeding as a "historically tragic case of selective moralizing." He recalled that when George Bush, as the newly elected president, pardoned Ronald Reagan's secretary of defense, Caspar Weinberger, who had been indicted for perjury by an independent counsel, Republicans applauded the action. And when Speaker Newt Gingrich was found to have made false statements in an official proceeding to the House ethics committee, he was reprimanded and simultaneously reelected Speaker with the overwhelming vote of the Republicans. Then Barney pointed out that a large number of the voters believed censure was appropriate. "While we have the right not to vote for something just because there is overwhelming public support, in a democracy we have no right not to vote on it."

On December 20, Barney argued that the House's rejection of one of the Articles of Impeachment alleging perjury substantially weakened the case against the president in the Senate, pointing out that the only perjury count approved by the House concerned Clinton's statements to a grand jury about when the affair with Monica Lewinsky began and where he touched her. "They want to throw the president of the United States out because he was off by two months and by two organs," he said.

During an interview with *Rolling Stone* in December 1999, Barney was asked to explain what happened between Thanksgiving, when he predicted that impeachment was dead, to just before Christmas, when the House passed the Articles of Impeachment. "Well, resurrection came at Christmas this year, instead of at Easter. The right wing simply showed a dominance over the Republican Party that exceeded all expectation," he said.

What started out as an effort by the Republicans to destroy President Clinton ended up with the Republicans destroying themselves. After the impeachment proceedings, Barney was able to joke, "I always thought that having a sex scandal and a reprimand would hold back your career. Now I don't know whether I should run for president or Speaker."

On July 30, 1999, Barney underwent quadruple coronary bypass surgery at Bethesda Naval Medical Hospital. His doctors had recommended the surgery after he had experienced some mild discomfort. The day before the heart surgery, he sparred on the House floor with Ernest Istook, a conservative Republican from Oklahoma. He later explained to *Roll Call*, "Yelling at Ernie Istook is, in fact, medically indicated. It's in Black's [medical] dictionary."

Despite the humor and the public face that he projected the day before the surgery, he was terrified by the prospect of coronary bypass surgery because of his father's early death from a heart attack. Friends pointed out that he was fortunate because such medical procedures did not exist in his father's day.

After recovering from the heart surgery, he remarked, "I had my first heart attack after I was involved in my own set of accusations, so maybe there is a correlation between sex-related scandals and heart attacks—in which case I hope everybody will behave. It gives the phrase 'affairs of the heart' a new meaning."

When President Clinton had heart surgery in 2004, Barney sent him a note stating, "I don't want to tell you that I'm better than you because I had one more bypass." Clinton responded, "Barney, I always follow your lead."

In the fall of 1999, the Bayonne Jewish Community Center selected Barney Frank, who had shone in the national limelight defending President Clinton during the impeachment hearings, as its person of the year. On Sunday evening, October 31, as a few children, many in costume and some wearing just masks, finished trick-or-treating among the two-family houses that predominate in Bayonne, well-dressed adults were entering the doors of the Jewish Community Center. The forty-five-year-old building, once grand and ahead of its time, was showing its age and seemed small by modern standards.

Barney was being honored at the Jewish Center's forty-seventh Sustaining Dinner, the proceeds from which would be used to help fund the center's many programs and services. It was a celebratory homecoming and a special evening for Barney. About 150 people attended, including Barney's eighty-seven-year-old mother, Elsie, his Aunt Fanny, who was then ninety-eight, several other relatives, Rep. Robert Menendez (currently a New Jersey senator) from Hoboken, whose congressional district included Bayonne, Joseph Doria Jr., the mayor of Bayonne, and other local dignitaries. Barney declared it "a lovely event," noting how friendly everyone was, how cozy and intimate ("so *heymish*").

The dinner was held in the social hall of the building that had meant so much to Samuel Frank because he had helped raise money for its construction, the same room that had not been completed in time for Barney's bar mitzvah party. Forty-six-years later, Barney finally got to have a party in his honor in that room. In the dinner program there was one ad that caught Barney's eyes. It read: "Barney, Come home and be our U.S. Senator. Uncle Abe, Aunt Dot, Cousins Renee, Dare, and Jason Golush."

20

The Gay Washington Monument

BARNEY FRANK'S CAREER as a legislator has paralleled the history of the gay rights movement. Barney was elected to the Massachusetts state legislature in 1973, three years after a police raid on the Stonewall Inn, a gay bar in Greenwich Village, touched off what became known as the Stonewall riots, an episode that brought the gay community out of the closet and into the streets and marked the beginning of the gay rights movement. Today, Barney is the most prominent openly gay politician in the United States. He has been a pioneer in the fight for fair treatment for gays and lesbians since 1973, when, as a freshman legislator, he introduced the first gay rights legislation in the history of Massachusetts—bills to outlaw discrimination against gays in employment and housing and to repeal the sodomy laws. His voluntarily revealing in 1987, as a fourth-term congressman, that he is gay marked a milestone on the road to the acceptance of gays in national politics. Vic Basile has called Barney's contribution to the gay rights movement "enormous and unparalleled."

Barney has become a hero and a role model for the gay and lesbian community. Among his admirers is Robert Raben, who began his career as Barney's legislative counsel. "I got to see an openly gay man who was also a respected policy maker, politician, and substantive leader. He could be all of that in a way that really was admirable and for a young person who was thinking of coming out, it was psychologically life saving," Raben said. The actor Nathan Lane credits Barney with helping to shatter stereotypes about gays. At a meeting of a gay rights organization in the Hamptons, Lane introduced Barney to the audience and said that he was grateful to Barney, who was responsible for his latest role playing a gay congressman in the short-lived 2003 television series *Charlie Lawrence*. Lane offered to speak to Mel Brooks about casting Barney in the role of Max Bialystock when *The Producers*, Brooks's smash Broadway show, comes to Washington. Barney responded, "I'm sorry, but playing a loud, pushy Jew is too much of a stretch for me." The late rock star Frank Zappa, a C-SPAN junkie, called Barney "one of the most impressive guys in Congress" and "a great model for young gay men."

"He has played a tremendous role in advancing the public respectability of gay people not only by his aggressive actions in Congress on behalf of gay causes but also when he is talking on television about housing policy, defense, or this or that and gay people see him and he serves as a gay role model that we never had growing up," Hastings Wyman, a gay man and one of Barney's roommates at Harvard, said. The gay activist and political strategist David Mixner wrote in his memoir *Stranger among Friends*: "No one understands Congress better than Barney Frank. There is no doubt in my mind that he will go down in history as one of the most effective and powerful of all congressional leaders. Despite our differences, he is a source of great pride to many of us in the [gay] community." In an interview published in March 2003, *MetroWeekly*, a Washington, D.C., gay and lesbian magazine, refers to Barney as the "gay Washington monument."

In that interview, Barney was asked to comment on his legacy as it relates to the gay community. He was modest in his response: "People have done more for me than I've done for them. That's one of the things about politics. There's a great disproportion in rewards versus output. An awful lot of people have worked very hard on my behalf and I get to reap much of the reward. So I really feel much more indebted than not. But I do think I was one of those who showed that you could come out and prosper."

In 1996, Bob Barr, a thrice-married, conservative Republican from Georgia, introduced a bill titled the Defense of Marriage Act, or DOMA. The bill established a first-ever federal definition of marriage as a union between a man and a woman for purposes of federal spousal benefits under Social Security, Medicare, and other federal programs, as well as immigration law. Enactment of the bill would prevent gay couples from receiving federal benefits in the event an individual state permits same-sex marriage. The bill also provided that states may refuse to recognize the validity of any same-sex marriage legally sanctioned in other states in the future.

Barr and other conservatives maintained that the bill was designed to preempt a court decision that could lead Hawaii to become the first state to grant same-sex couples the right to marry. "They made this bullshit argument that they had to do it because the Hawaiian court was about to act. That is why a Supreme Court decision in Hawaii from 1993 which will not be made final probably until 1998 comes up in 1996," Barney contended. In fact, the Hawaii Supreme Court did not act until two years later and its decision was later overturned by referendum.

Privately, Barney thought that the gay and lesbian community and their lawyers had made a tactical mistake in the Hawaii case. He believed that the position of the gay rights groups should have been to protect the right of Hawaii to recognize same-sex marriage and to try to win federal recognition of that right. Instead the plaintiffs argued that if Hawaii granted same-sex couples the right to marry, every other state in the country was bound to recognize those marriages. In Barney's opinion, that argument was legally dubious and certainly not politically sustainable.

Many House Democrats believed the Defense of Marriage bill was a politically motivated effort to deal with a nonexistent problem and was simply a cynical ploy by Republicans to fuel anti-gay sentiments among voters in advance of the November 1996 election. Pat Schroeder, who called the bill an outrage, said, "If you think there isn't enough hate and polarization in America, you're going to love this bill." Barney called it a "defense against a non-attack." "This is not the defense of marriage, but the defense of the Republican ticket," he said. "The bill was so titled so that its sponsors could argue not that they were seeking to prevent lesbian or gay couples from formalizing their relationship, but rather that they were protecting heterosexual marriage against the terrible influence that would emanate from same-sex marriage."

Barney was angry that House Speaker Newt Gingrich and his fellow Republicans brought up the bill for a vote. It was hypocritical in the eyes of many that Gingrich, who would soon be divorcing his second wife and embarking on a third marriage to a young Hill staffer with whom he was having an affair, would laud a bill labeled "Defense of Marriage." The emotional floor debate in the House began well past midnight on July 11, 1996.

Opponents of the bill included Patrick Kennedy of Rhode Island, who called marriage "a basic human right," arguing that "love and commitment are essential pillars of marriage" and "they are qualities that do not discriminate on account of gender." Cardiss Collins, an Illinois Democrat, said that the bill should really be called "The Republican Offense on People Who Are Different" because it is nothing more than blatant homophobic gay-bashing.

Steve Largent, an Oklahoma Republican and former professional football star wide receiver, set the tone of the debate by proponents of the bill.

> This is not about equal rights. We have equal rights. Homosexuals have the same rights as I do. They have the ability to marry right now, today. However, when they get married, they must marry a person of the opposite sex, the same as me. . . .
>
> There is . . . a radical element, a homosexual agenda that wants to redefine what marriage is. They want to say that a marriage not only is one man and one woman but it is two men or it is two women. What logical reason is there to keep us from stopping expansion of that definition to include three people or an adult and a child, or any other odd combination that we want to have? There really is no logical reason why we could not include polygamy or any

other definition to say, as long as these are consenting human beings, and it does not even have to be limited to human beings, by the way. I mean it could be anything.

Americans who were still up at that hour of the morning heard an eloquent speech by John Lewis of Georgia, who had fought courageously against racial discrimination at Martin Luther King's side. Lewis invoked the civil rights struggles of the 1950s and 1960s and called gay rights the final chapter in the history of civil rights.

This is a mean bill. It is cruel. This bill seeks to divide our nation, turn Americans against Americans, and sow the seeds of fear, hatred and intolerance. . . . You cannot tell people they cannot fall in love. Dr. Martin Luther King Jr. used to say when people talked about interracial marriage and I quote, "Races do not fall in love and get married. Individuals fall in love and get married." Why do you not want your fellow men and women, your fellow Americans to be happy? Why do you attack them? Why do you want to destroy the love they hold in their hearts? . . . We are talking about human beings, people like you, people who want to get married, buy a house, and spend their lives with the one they love. They have done no wrong.

Lewis concluded:

I have fought too hard and too long against discrimination based on race and color not to stand up against discrimination based on sexual orientation. I have known racism. I have known bigotry. This bill stinks of the same fear, hatred and intolerance. It should not be called the Defense of Marriage Act. It should be called the defense of mean-spirited bigots act.

The debate continued the next day and was laced with gay-baiting barbs and biblical references by supporters of the bill. Bob Barr stated, "As Rome burned, Nero fiddled, and that is exactly what [those on the other side] would have us do. We ain't going to be fooled." He declared, "The very foundations of our society are in danger of being burned. The flames of hedonism, the flames of narcissism, the flames of self-centered morality are licking at the very foundations of our society, the family unit."

Barney spoke against the bill with passion and wit. He argued that it was silly to claim that gay relationships threaten traditional marriage and that if you allow same-sex marriage in Hawaii, five thousand miles away, the marital bonds will crumble. "I find it implausible that two men deciding to commit themselves to each other threaten the marriage of people a couple of blocks away. I find it bizarre, even by the standards that my Republican colleagues are using for this political argument here, to tell me that two women falling in love in Hawaii, as far away as you can get and still be within the United States, threaten the marriage of people in other states." He asked, "Is there some emanation that is given off that ruins it for you? Gee, Hawaii is pretty far away. Will not the ocean stop it? Are those waves that undercut your marriage?"

He challenged several GOP members: "How does the fact that I love another man and live in a committed relationship with him threaten your marriage? Are your relations with your spouses of such fragility that the fact that I have a committed, loving relationship with another man jeopardizes them? Do you think people are going to learn that Herb and I live together . . . and they are going to leave their wives? I find satisfaction in committing myself and being responsible for another human being who happens to be a man and this threatens you. My God, what do you do when the lights go out? Sit with the covers over your heads?"

When Steve Largent responded that Barney's relationship with another man did not threaten his marriage but that it threatened the institution of marriage, Barney said, "That argument ought to be made by someone in an institution."

He continued to attack Largent's statement. "That of course baffles me some," he said. "Institutions do not marry. They may merge, but they do not marry. And no one who understands human nature thinks that allowing two other people who love each other interferes."

Proponents argued that the bill was necessary to keep other states from being obligated to recognize Hawaiian same-sex marriages should Hawaii decide to give same-sex couples the right to marry in that state. According to Barney, most of the bill's sponsors believed that the states already had a right to refuse to recognize same-sex marriages from other states. States are free to reject marriages approved by other states that violate public policy, such as marriages that are incestuous or polygamous, that involve minors, or that are based on common law. The bill, he asserted, was nothing more than "a declaration that the states have the rights that they already have coming a few months before the presidential election."

Barney offered an amendment aimed at the second section of the bill, the part that attacked states rights by saying that if Hawaii or any other state decides to allow same-sex marriage by whatever means, the federal government will substantially overrule that decision and declare that such a union is not a marriage as far as federal law is concerned and it will have no federal tax benefits or pension benefits. His amendment would uphold state autonomy by providing that if the State of Hawaii decides to allow gay marriage, the federal government would treat marriages that Hawaii validates the same as it treats others and recognize them.

Anticipating some of the arguments raised by the Republicans during the debate to support their claim that the state action in Hawaii could be based simply on "three activist judges" upholding same-sex marriage, Barney was ready with a second amendment that provided that if a state makes a democratic decision to allow gay marriages—by involvement of its electorate either directly in a referendum or through its legislature or by a legislative decision to allow a court decision to stand after enough time has gone by—the federal government will treat that state as it treats anybody else and honor that democratic decision.

Acknowledging the "consummate cleverness" of its proponent, Bob Barr called the Frank amendment "a killer amendment." "It may be sugar coated, it may have a silencer on it, but the effect is just as deadly," he said.

Barney thanked Barr "for the reference to my consummate cleverness," adding, "There are circles in which I will have to explain away having received that compliment from him, but I am willing to take on that burden."

Before the vote, Barney suggested to Democrat Samuel Gejdenson, who had been involved in several extremely close elections, that it would not be good for his political future to vote against the Republican bill. "I'm not voting for them. I am voting for me," Gejdenson replied. He was narrowly defeated for reelection in 2000.

The Frank amendment was defeated by a vote of 103 to 311. The Defense of Marriage bill passed the House 342 to 67 and was overwhelmingly approved by the Senate. The legislation was signed into law by President Bill Clinton in private and without comment at 12:50 a.m. on Saturday, September 21. Barney was not surprised that the president signed the bill. He recognized the political expediency of Bill Clinton's and Al Gore's unwillingness to take on very serious political damage three months before an election and said that he was not disappointed because both men had "been good" on every other gay rights issue. Besides, he didn't want his friends to commit what would have amounted to political suicide.

"At last count," Barney wrote in 2000, "five of the House members who voted to deprive us of the right to marry so as to protect the sanctity of heterosexual marriage have been shown to have engaged in adulterous affairs. . . . They claim that my ability to marry another man somehow jeopardizes heterosexual marriage. Then they go out and cheat on their wives and commit adultery. That doesn't jeopardize heterosexual marriage?"

In early September 1998, California Republican Randy "Duke" Cunningham, a decorated Vietnam War–era navy combat pilot, made a crude reference to Barney's homosexuality during an event with constituents in San Diego. In discussing the recent surgery he had had to remove a cancerous prostate gland, Cunningham said that the rectal procedure he had undergone was "just not normal, unless maybe you're Barney Frank."

When asked by reporters to comment, Barney said, "He was talking about rectal surgery he had, and that is the context in which it came up. I'm afraid that

in the course of that [procedure], he may have suffered a little slight brain damage. That's my comment." He dismissed Cunningham's insult as coming from a
man not well respected in Congress.

Later when reporters asked Barney whether he had received an apology from
Cunningham, he replied, "I haven't heard from him. I'm not particularly interested. Having Duke Cunningham say something dumb about you is kind of on
the level of finding out that your shoelaces are untied."

In November 2005, Cunningham pleaded guilty to federal charges of conspir-
acy to commit bribery and tax evasion for accepting $2.4 million in bribes from
defense contractors and others, and he resigned from Congress in disgrace.

Barney relishes answering letters from cranks and bigots. When one person living outside his district sent Barney three long handwritten letters in
one week filled with antiliberal, anti-gay, and anti-Semitic tirades, Barney responded simply, "I'm sorry you've run out of medication before you ran out
of paper." When this same individual sent him a new seven-page rant, Barney
replied: "I was surprised to find an absence of explicit anti-Semitism this time.
Was a page missing?"

In the early evening of October 14, 1998, five thousand people, including
a dozen members of Congress and some Hollywood celebrities, gathered on
the steps of the U.S. Capitol, where they held a somber and emotion-laden
candlelight vigil for Matthew Shepard, the twenty-one-year-old University of
Wyoming student who several days earlier had been beaten nearly to death by
two young men consumed with hatred. They had tied him to a fence and left
him in near-freezing temperatures to die alone. Shepard's brutal murder, much
like the horrific death forty years earlier of Emmett Till, stirred the conscience
of the nation.

Ellen DeGeneres and her partner, Anne Heche, spoke, as did Ellen's mother, Betty, who read the Twenty-third Psalm. Then Senator Edward Kennedy,
House Democratic leader Richard Gephardt, former Wyoming senator Alan
Simpson, and Representative John Lewis addressed the crowd. Friends of Matthew Shepard's and the directors of several gay and lesbian advocacy groups also
gave short speeches.

When Barney was introduced and stepped to the microphone, he was greeted
with thunderous applause from the crowd. It was a welcome that no other politician received that evening, a spontaneous salute and tribute to one of the gay
and lesbian community's most respected leaders. Barney was deeply moved. "It
made me realize that I am very important to these people," he recalled. "There
were so few of us." By that time, he said, with regard to other members of
Congress who were also gay, Democrat Gerry Studds of Massachusetts and Republican Steve Gunderson of Wisconsin were no longer in the House, Democrat Tammy Baldwin of Wisconsin had not yet been elected, and Jim Kolbe of

Arizona was restrained in his support of gay rights by his being a Republican. The applause was a reminder to Barney of how much of a burden it was to be a leader, "not in the negative sense, but what a heavy load to carry."

Barney is not an orator on the level of Mario Cuomo or Barack Obama. But that evening Barney gave a passionate and riveting speech in which he told the crowd:

> It could have been me. Had I, alone and unarmed, confronted these two thugs, I could have been subjected to the same brutalization that Mr. Shepard was in Wyoming, because his crime was to be a gay man. . . . Sadly, the vicious, cowardly thugs who murdered him were only a few years out of high school. We know that young gay and lesbian students are often subjected to mistreatment and torment. We know and we have told the world again and again that that kind of abuse and ridicule becomes physical assault and can lead to this kind of murder. . . . The right wing has been much too successful in interfering with what we have a great need for—programs that protect the younger Matthew Shepards from the violence that ultimately took his life and from the viciousness and hatred that perverted those people to the point where they dehumanized themselves and him.

Four years earlier, on March 24, 1994, Barney had spoken emotionally against an amendment to the Improving America's School Act that would have cut off all federal funding to schools in Los Angeles and New York because the schools had provided sexual-orientation counseling programs. The amendment's sponsors had argued that by providing sexual-orientation counseling, the schools were promoting homosexuality. "How would you promote homosexuality, like have a jingle?" Barney asked. "I have yet to meet anyone, straight or gay, who has any idea about how one would promote homosexuality. . . . If you gave me a million dollars and told me to promote homosexuality I wouldn't know how to do it. Do I hire Don King?" he asked.

He continued: "I suppose if we have a sixteen- or a seventeen-year-old whose feelings are homosexual and cannot turn them off, like a water faucet, despite the shallowness of the understanding that some people in here have of human nature. If we take that kid who has been abused and who has been picked on and put him in a more supportive environment, then we lose our money. How do we dare support that kid? How dare we tell her she is not worthless?" The amendment was defeated.

The day after the vigil at the U.S. Capitol for Matthew Shepard, Barney spoke on the House floor about the need to add a provision to the federal hate crimes legislation that would encompass cases like that of Matthew Shepard.

> I hope that one of the things that will come out of this terrible, terrible murder will be a cessation of those trying to prevent schools from trying to prevent this. . . . We talk about teaching values. But when some talk about teaching

the value of tolerance, when some talk about condemning violence based on someone's basic characteristics, we are told we cannot do that. We have been told that we cannot let a school teach acceptance of the gay lifestyle. . . . What does nonacceptance mean? If acceptance is interpreted to mean approval, I and others do not care. There are bigots in this world whose approval holds no charms for me. But when nonacceptance means not accepting someone's right to live, we have a serious problem.

If the two murderers who so brutally beat Mr. Shepard to death and left him in this situation ultimately to die, if they had been in a school system where people had taught that gay men and lesbians were human beings with a right to live, maybe this would not have happened.

Barney started dating Sergio Pombo, a thirty-four-year-old native Colombian, during the Clinton impeachment hearings, and the two maintained an intimate relationship until 2005.

Sergio Pombo was born in Barranquilla, Colombia. His father, a lawyer and intellectual from a well-bred family, had died at age thirty-seven from a heart condition. Sergio's mother was a passionate, self-educated, and business-minded woman. Sergio studied with the Jesuits in Colombia and garnered their support to study at Georgetown University, a Jesuit school in Washington, D.C., beginning in 1985. As an undergraduate, he majored in business and later earned an MBA in international finance from American University. After graduation he was hired by the World Bank to work for the International Finance Corporation, which supports and invests in private-sector family companies in poor countries that have growth potential.

From 1994 to 1998, Sergio worked in London, on loan from the World Bank to the European Bank. In late 1996, he met Barney for the first time when he returned to Washington briefly to attend a meeting at the World Bank and a friend of his, a vice president at the World Bank who was openly gay, invited him to attend a dinner party at his home. Barney was there with his partner, Herb Moses. "We had a good conversation about many things," Sergio, who had never followed Barney's career, recalled. "My first impression of Barney was that he came across as rude but also very knowledgeable about so many issues."

The assignment in London ended in early 1998 and Sergio returned to Washington to work at the World Bank. One day, while walking from his home to the gym to work out, he ran into Barney on the street. "We looked at each other. He looked at me. I looked at him. Finally, I went up to him and said, 'You probably don't remember me. I met you a few years ago at dinner. I work for the World Bank,'" Sergio said. The two started talking. Barney suggested that they meet for coffee some time. Sergio agreed and gave him his business card. Shortly thereafter, the two men got together for coffee and then one night went out to dinner. That is how the relationship started.

Barney's relationship with Sergio was very different from what he had had with Herb Moses. Unlike Herb, Sergio is an independent man with a rich professional life of his own. From the start Sergio recognized that Barney had a demanding job but he made it clear to Barney that he too had a job and a life as well. While they were still together he explained the relationship: "We spend time with each other, we care about each other, but we have in many ways different responsibilities. He travels a lot and so do I. I have a job that keeps me traveling to other countries. While we talk to each other on the phone every day, sometimes we don't see each other for two weeks because we are on different continents. I don't think that is negative." Sergio added, "We accept that and that has been enriching as opposed to devaluing our relationship. We enjoy our time together even more." One difference he pointed out, however, was that whereas Barney was very comfortable and eager to be around people, he needed time "to be alone, to disconnect from the outer world."

Sergio's initial concern about dating someone significantly older than he and someone who was a public personality was soon eased as he began hanging out more with Barney. "He really doesn't take himself seriously. He always cracks a joke. He has a profound intellectual honesty," Sergio said. "I love his wit. He makes me laugh. It keeps our relationship growing and very young."

Sergio realized early on that he was gay. But, he said, "because of my education, and maybe because of the expectations of my mother, my family, then the Jesuits, and then friends, I was willing to let go of that part of my life to actually concentrate on the positive part of my life—being a good student, a good son, a good member of my family." He added, "I was hiding that part of my life, suppressing it, growing up lonely in many ways but with a lot of people who wanted to be my friend."

He described his undergraduate years at Georgetown University as "being pretty sad as my gayness was coming to a head." He dated women but couldn't fully connect with them and feel like a normal person. "In several instances, friends of mine told me they were gay, and I basically didn't call them anymore. That is how afraid I was of being associated with gays, and so afraid of myself," Sergio explained. "Now that I am comfortable with being gay, I have gone back to them and apologized and they are good friends of mine." He found a more relaxed campus environment at American University, where he saw openly gay people for the first time.

Barney invited Sergio to attend the White House Christmas Party for members of Congress in December 1998. Sergio was hesitant to go because he had not come out to colleagues at work or to his family yet. But he changed his mind and went, after Barney assured him that the press was never invited to this event.

"All of the members and their spouses were friendly and nice to me," Sergio recalled. Although he was hesitant and somewhat anxious about meeting the president, Sergio found him very personable. "Bill Clinton is just incredible when it comes to making people feel comfortable. He does it with body motions and with his eyes," Sergio said. "Soon we are talking about Colombia and his relationship with the president of Colombia. It was fantastic. Imagine me, a guy from Colombia, meeting and talking with the president of the United States about Colombia." Barney and Sergio were invited to several dinners at the White House by the Clintons, including a state dinner in 1999. That was the first state dinner Barney had ever been invited to during almost twenty years in Congress.

Sergio accompanied Barney to the 2000 Democratic Convention in Los Angeles. Although he had been dating Barney for almost two years at the time, he had not come out publicly. He was comfortable with his anonymity. He walked with Barney to the convention stage, where Barney was set to give a short speech to the delegates. The gatekeeper, who knew Barney said, "Why don't you take him with you on stage?" Barney looked at Sergio and asked, "What do you think?" There wasn't enough time for Sergio to think about the ramifications. Barney had already been announced as the next speaker. Sergio had to act quickly and he walked onto the convention stage with Barney and stood to the side while Barney addressed the delegates.

After Barney's speech, the two men embraced on stage as cameras flashed. "It was the first time I was in public with Barney," Sergio explained. The photo of the two men hugging after the speech with a frontal shot of Sergio smiling happily appeared in the *Washington Post* on August 18, 2000, and in several other newspapers across the country. The caption referred to Sergio Pombo by name. The photograph was picked up by the international wire services and was published in newspapers in Colombia, Brazil, and all over South America.

Sergio's family saw the photo in a newspaper in Colombia before he had an opportunity to explain. Now that his sexuality was suddenly out in the open, Sergio felt compelled to travel to Colombia to talk with his family, something, he said, "I should have done earlier." He had been hiding his sexuality for almost thirty years. "It was very painful, but after a week everything was fine," he said.

Sergio was fearful for his job at the World Bank. Some of his friends and colleagues at the bank knew that he was gay but most did not. Barney was very supportive, telling him that everything would be fine, that is would be the best thing that ever happened to him. "That turned out to be true. It was incredible," Sergio said. He reported that a couple of people were nasty to him, but by and large most people at the World Bank reacted positively and were supportive.

Being part of a gay couple was something fairly new to Sergio, who was once in a relationship that lasted for about eighteen months. "Then for about ten years I was not doing anything. Barney was the second serious boyfriend or partner that I had in my life," he said. They loved each other and enjoyed poking fun at each other. When they discussed politics and disagreed, Sergio called Barney a leftist and Barney called him a Republican, telling him that he didn't matter since, as a noncitizen, he could not vote.

When Barney went to visit Sergio's mother in Colombia, the two men stayed together in a hotel. They invited Sergio's mother and other family members, none of whom spoke English, to the hotel for dinner. Everything was all smiles. "It is so wonderful when you meet your in-laws and basically you cannot talk to them," Barney later commented.

When Barney traveled out of the country to official events, the State Department in the Bush administration generally made sure that Sergio was invited. "The United States Embassy goes out of its way to treat us nice like other couples," Sergio said.

There was an incident, however, in Israel in 2003. About an hour before a reception hosted by Prime Minister Ariel Sharon, Barney answered a telephone call in his hotel room. When he heard that Sergio could not attend the reception with him, he shouted into the phone, "Then tell the prime minister if Sergio doesn't go, I'm not going either." Sergio remembers that Barney was so upset he was shaking. He took off his clothes, got into bed, and said, "Screw 'em, if we're not good enough for them, I'm not going." Barney's general rule was, "We need to be treated like anyone else. I am not going to accept anything less."

When the U.S. ambassador to Israel called and apologized, saying there had been changes in the plans and they were outside of his control, Barney said he understood but that he would not go. Only when Prime Minister Sharon's office called to inform Barney that all the spouses had been uninvited and Sergio urged him to attend, did he agree to go.

At a White House picnic, Barney and Sergio sat down at a table in front of Senator Jesse Helms, with whom in Barney's words, "I am sometimes aligned on critical issues such as adjournment *sine die* and when to take a Fourth of July recess." During a television interview in 1989, Dick Cavett asked Barney how he thought Senator Helms would deal with a particular situation. "Dick, I have a fairly strong ego and will assay explanation of a lot of things," Barney responded, "but explaining the workings of Jesse Helms's mind is one of those things which I think is beyond rational discourse." At the time of the White House picnic Senator Helms was in ill health. "Members of Congress, Democrats and Republicans, would come up to us and suggest that we kiss in order to give the SOB a heart attack," recalled Sergio.

Barney and Sergio split up in late March 2005. "He really didn't like politics, and I didn't like a lot of what he did," Barney explained. "The personal bond couldn't outlast a real divergence of interests. He was more cultured. He did me a favor by coming to the Democratic convention in Boston." The two men remain close friends.

Barney has seen significant changes in the gay community since he first took public office. In an interview with the author Keith Boykin, he said: "Thirty years ago, only a very small number of gay men and lesbians would acknowledge their sexual orientation to others. Today, I believe that a majority of gays and lesbians have told at least some straight people that they are gay. . . . The more gays come out, the more people realize the stereotypes are baseless." He noted that as more people came out of the closet, "ten of millions of Americans have learned that their relatives, their clients, their teammates, their bosses, their friends, a whole lot of people they deal with are gay and lesbian."

In those three decades, the opposition to equal rights for gays has changed. In a speech at Georgetown University in October 2001, Barney explained that when he introduced the first gay rights bill in the Massachusetts legislature in 1973, the opposition to the bill was very explicitly based on prejudice. "Today, the opposition disguises itself," he said. Where once "homosexuality was the love that dare not speak its name," now anti-gay prejudice "dare not speak its name" and those who are opposed to gay rights are in the minority. In Congress, Barney said, anti-gay legislators fight against antidiscrimination bills by saying, "We're not opposed to antidiscrimination, but we don't want to give these people 'special rights.'"

Barney thinks that the gay rights movement has brought about the most fundamental change of any political or social cause in the past thirty years. While he is proud of the enormous progress made and the substantial decline in prejudice against gays and lesbians, he believes that there is still a considerable distance gays and lesbians must go before they are treated equally. "As we acknowledge who we are, it turns out there's really nothing to the stereotypes. We're just pretty much like everybody else. And the average American has learned that he isn't homophobic, he just thought he was supposed to be," he explained.

Barney travels across the country in support of gay causes and speaks regularly to state chapters of the National Stonewall Democrats and other gay and lesbian organizations. According to Hastings Wyman, Barney often makes appearances in areas where gays are not widely accepted, such as North Carolina and South Carolina, where his presence is particularly uplifting to people. He tries to energize gays and lesbians to get out the vote and be active politically. He compares not voting to being a vegetarian and going to a butcher. "We go to courts to try to win rights and then having won them we have to defend them in the political process if we are to maintain them," he tells the gay community. In his view, the strength of the religious right-wing of the Republican Party is that they are able to turn out the vote on Election Day. "There will be two groups of people over the weekend that care a lot about gay rights," he tells them. "On Saturday night they'll be gathered in bars and houses and theaters and having a good time. On Sunday morning they'll be gathered in front of churches. One group will be strongly pro-gay and the other will be strongly anti-gay. But the Sunday-morning crowd votes and the Saturday-night crowd do not."

On July 19, 2003, Barney addressed the Delaware Stonewall Democrats at an event attended by over three hundred people. He was introduced by Delaware governor Ruth Ann Minner, who said, "I could stand here and use a thousand words and it would not begin to describe Barney Frank. It isn't what you say, it's what you do and he has done what he said he would do." When it was his turn to speak, Barney said: "To be here with the governor and state party chair is really remarkable. I grew up in a time of total homophobia and yes, while there is less prejudice today, there shouldn't be any. People are still being fired and teenagers are still being harassed for who they are."

He accused the Republican Party of distorting the issue of whether gays should legally marry. "They say it will totally destroy the traditional family." Using a vintage V-8 commercial to lampoon the idea, he said, "I can see it now. The headlines read: 'Gays allowed to marry' and married men everywhere are gonna smack themselves on the head and say, 'Wow, I could have married a man!'"

He told the group in Delaware, "We can win this thing democratically but it requires getting out there talking to people. I refer to this as cruising for equal rights."

Barney is continually strategizing and thinking of issues in pragmatic terms. The volatile issue of same-sex marriage is no exception. "I care deeply about this issue. But the more deeply I care, the more sensible I have to be in achieving it," he explained. He believes that while public sympathy for gays and lesbians has steadily increased there are still enough doubts and enough voters who are uneasy about gay marriage that he would have preferred that the push for same-sex marriage not come up so early.

He considers same-sex marriage a matter of basic rights. "You don't want to call it marriage? If that makes you feel better, you can call it whatever you want. I object to the denial of benefits to people who pay taxes on an equal basis," he told Chris Matthews on the television program *Hardball* on July 31, 2003. During the House debate on a bill denouncing same-sex marriage, Barney said, "If it bothers people, turn your head."

On November 18, 2003, the Massachusetts Supreme Court ruled that the state failed to identify any constitutionally adequate reason to deny gay adults the same constitutional rights all other citizens have. Barney appeared that day on CNN's *Crossfire* to debate the issue with Rev. Jerry Falwell, the founder and chancellor of Liberty University. Barney pointed out that a lot of fears had been stirred up in Massachusetts by forecasts of chaos and disruption and he predicted that after the ruling had been in effect for a couple of years, all of those forecasts would have been proven meaningless, as similar ones were in Vermont, which passed a law recognizing civil unions between two people of the same sex.

When Robert Novak started in, saying, "Congressman Frank, we are not talking about love— " Barney, clearly angry, interrupted. "What do you mean we are not talking about love? What do you think gay marriage is—a corporate merger?" he said.

Barney continued, "I am really struck by your insisting that we should separate love and marriage. If I could sing, I would sing the song about a horse and carriage, but I got a lousy voice. We are talking about love. We are talking about two people in love. . . . All of the arguments that we are hearing against marriage today from Mr. Falwell, yourself, and others, we heard against civil unions [in Vermont]. This notion, civil unions only looked good to you people by comparison to marriage. You are using that as a stick to beat marriage with."

"It is wrong for the culture, for the nation, for the state to endorse moral perversion," Falwell said. "We should not reward that with the privileges and benefits of marriage which has been for six thousand years of recorded history the only unit, a man legally married to a woman, and it is going to be that way a thousand years from now."

The heated debate between Barney Frank and Jerry Falwell on gay marriage continued the next morning on the *CBS Early Show*. Like two boxers who keep slugging it out after the final bell, the two men continued battling after the moderator, Harry Smith, thanked them and said the debate was over. Smith announced that the final word belonged to Congressman Frank. However, when Barney finished his remarks, Falwell, appearing on the split television screen, responded: "Barney, I want to see our children and our children's children guaranteed that a family forever is one man married to one woman, period."

"Who does it hurt if two people who are in love want to make themselves legally responsible for each other?" Barney asked.

"I have to pay taxes to support people like you living together in a relationship and I am opposed to it," Falwell said.

"I pay taxes for you and it bothers me as much as I bother you," Barney replied angrily. He asserted, "What Jerry Falwell is now saying is that Massachusetts should be overridden by the federal government. He is not prepared to abide by a constitutional referendum."

On February 4, 2004, the Massachusetts Supreme Judicial Court, in a 4-to-3 decision (six of the seven justices had been appointed by Republican governors), ruled that under their interpretation of the state constitution, only full marriage rights for same-sex couples, not civil unions, pass constitutional muster. "Civil unions rather than full marriage rights would relegate same-sex couples to a different status," the court said. "The history of our nation has demonstrated that separate is seldom, if ever, equal." The court cleared the way for gay and lesbian couples to marry by ordering state officials to begin issuing marriage licenses to same-sex couples by May 17, 2004.

The next morning, Barney debated the commentator and former 2000 presidential candidate Patrick Buchanan on the issue of gay marriage on the *Today Show*. Barney pointed out that Dick Cheney, at the October 2000 vice presidential debate with Joe Lieberman, had acknowledged that marriage is a matter that has always been left up to the states and said he didn't think there should necessarily be a federal policy in this area. During that debate Cheney stated: "The fact of the matter is we live in a free society, and freedom means freedom for everybody. . . . And I think that means that people should be free to enter into any kind of relationship they want to enter into. It's really no one else's business in terms of trying to regulate or prohibit behavior in that regard. . . . I think different states are likely to come to different conclusions, and that's appropriate. I don't think there should necessarily be a federal policy in this area." As Barney sees it, Cheney recognized that states may come to different conclusions and that this is a good thing.

In the debate with Buchanan, Barney predicted that same-sex marriage in Massachusetts would not in any way affect traditional marriage. "If you are a heterosexual man in love with a heterosexual woman, the fact that you are now given an option that has absolutely no appeal to you, won't affect your marriage. Two women in love across the street will have no impact on your marriage," he said.

When Buchanan attacked the "activist judges," Barney asked, "Don't you have to uphold the law? If you have to uphold the law, can you at the same time denounce activist judges? What are judges—pirates?"

Buchanan blasted the court's ruling on gay marriage as "an absurdity" and referred to a "bevy of blushing June brides in beards in Provincetown." When Katie Couric asked Pat Buchanan, "Do you really think you speak for all Americans?" Barney interjected, "Five hundred thousand in the last election."

Barney considered the Massachusetts court decision a national model for orderly, legal protection of gay marriage. During the first year after same-sex marriage became legal in Massachusetts, 6,100 same-sex couples were married.

The Massachusetts court ruling was the catalyst for San Francisco mayor Gavin Newsom's decision in February 2004 to challenge California law by issuing marriage licenses for gay and lesbian couples. Barney is an astute judge of what to push for and when. He went against the flow and criticized Newsom's decision, calling the mayor's action "a well-intentioned mistake." At the time he said, "In San Francisco they are kind of testing the law by breaking it." "Whether publicity in and of itself is good depends on how the population is feeling," he explained. "During the civil rights struggle people across the country were overwhelmingly in favor of blacks eating at lunch counters. However, people today are not overwhelmingly in favor of gay rights and same-sex marriage."

Barney called the wave of same-sex marriages in San Francisco that followed the announcement of Mayor Newsom's decision "a spectacle" and "political hoopla with no political gain." He referred to them as "pretend marriages" and said that they were "a distraction" that could damage efforts by gay rights advocates defending the recent Massachusetts court ruling. They were arguing at the time with Governor Mitt Romney, who was threatening not to follow the law. "We said, 'What are you, George Wallace?' You can't do that. You can't have civil disobedience," Barney said. Having Newsom not following the law totally undercut that argument.

"There were no mass marriages in Massachusetts. It was not a social cause. It was human beings in love," Barney said. Newsom's action, however, inspired government officials in New Paltz, New York, and in Oregon to take similar actions and, Barney said, "It looked like it was out of control." The marriages in San Francisco, he contended, were not legal and accomplished only one thing. They increased support for President George W. Bush's proposed constitutional amendment that would limit marriage to a union between a man and a woman.

"Barney saw that much earlier than the rest of us," Vic Basile said. The over four thousand gay marriages that took place in San Francisco were subsequently voided by the California state supreme court.

Barney was saying out loud something that many other gay leaders thought privately about the events in San Francisco. Others in the gay community, however, criticized Barney for "thinking too strategically." In a *Washington Post* interview in March 2004, he reiterated his belief that the hardest thing to do in politics is to criticize your friends. "When you're engaged in a political fight, if you're doing something that really, really, really makes you feel good, then it's probably not the best tactic," he said.

As deeply as Barney is committed to gay rights, his primary interest is in the success of the Democratic Party, and if ensuring that success requires making compromises on certain issues to elect a majority of Democrats in more conservative areas, he is willing to do that. In 2004 he understood that every photograph of gays getting married on the steps of City Hall in San Francisco in defiance of state law cost the Democrats votes in the South.

"People who are opposed to gay marriage fall into two categories," he explained. "There are the militants who are driving the opposition to same-sex marriage because they do not like the idea that there are any gay or lesbian people at all. If they hate the idea that there is even one of us, they are made crazy by the notion of two of us hanging around. Basically, if you don't like one, you don't like two. It's geometric. The larger percentage are people who are generally supportive of equal rights, as they have been in Massachusetts, but they hear these predictions that legalized gay marriage is going to be socially disruptive and they figure, 'Why take the risk?'"

Barney wants to see experiments with gay marriages and civil unions go forward in the states. He believes that such experiments will eventually persuade moderate opponents of gay marriage that it does not in fact threaten heterosexual marriage, and that as a result opposition will gradually ebb. He predicts that within his lifetime, the issue of gay marriage will become a nonissue, much like the issue of civil unions.

On March 23, 2004, Barney appeared as a witness before a Senate Judiciary subcommittee at a hearing on the Federal Marriage Amendment to the Constitution that would bar same-sex marriages by defining marriage as a union between a man and a woman. Referring to his personal life and sexual orientation, Barney told the committee in an emotional testimony: "Imitation is the sincerest form of flattery. What you have with marriage, we admire it, we would like to be able to share it." He asked the subcommittee members, "When I go home from today's work and I choose because of my nature to associate with another man, how is that a problem for you? How does that hurt you? . . . If people decide to allow it, you who do the constitutional amendment will cancel the rights of the people of Massachusetts and I do not think that is an appropriate response to make here. And certainly not to the threat that millions of people are threatening to commit love."

Two years later, Barney reflected that in 2004 the political climate in Massachusetts was against same-sex marriage and that if a referendum had been held back then, same-sex marriage would have lost. By 2006, he thought such a referendum would pass. "What we expected to be the case has proved true. The existence of same-sex marriage has had no impact on any heterosexuals—except some who live next door to a couple of lesbians and had to buy them a wedding present," he joked. "The fears that people have in anticipation disappear in reality. It never is as terribly disruptive as people expect. Once the reality is there, it changes public opinion."

Barney has continued to focus on what is attainable in terms of gay rights legislation based on political reality. In the fall of 2007, he decided to delete transgender individuals from the Employment Non-Discrimination Act so that this bill providing that people should not be denied jobs because of their sexual orientation would have enough votes to pass the House. Some leaders in the

gay community called it a sellout, charging that Congress has to do it all together in one bill. "The public reaction to transgender is like the reaction to
gays thirty-five years ago. It is too freaky to people," Barney explained. "I am
confident that the average gay and lesbian person believes that you do not kill
the bill over it."

21

Talking Frankly and Not Beating around the Bush

BARNEY TOOK THE 2000 presidential election results in stride. Speaking at an ADA counter-inaugural ball and fund-raiser, he told the gathering, "John Ashcroft went to the world capital of bigotry, Bob Jones University, and accepted an honorary degree. They gave him a hood and it was white and it had eye holes in it." He also said that he hoped that Ralph Nader, who played the role of spoiler in the election, and Gale Norton, who favored opening up more federal lands for oil drilling and logging and was President George W. Bush's choice for secretary of the interior, would "live happily ever after."

As president, George W. Bush had a nickname for most politicians. He called Barney "Sabretooth." In early 2001, when the newly elected president met with House Democrats, he faced several tough questions from members. After the session, a relieved President Bush approached Barney and thanked him for not asking any questions.

Although Barney and President Bush disagreed on most substantive issues, they had a good personal rapport and enjoyed one-on-one banter. The first time that Barney and his partner Sergio Pombo went to the Bush White House was for the annual Christmas party for members of Congress. A large model of the White House made out of gingerbread sat in the hallway and Barney noticed a small sign on it that read, "Beware of Barney." When they entered the reception area and were greeted by President and Mrs. Bush, Barney said to the president, "By the way, I didn't take offense at that sign on the gingerbread White House that said, 'Beware of Barney.'" "So long as you don't do what Barney does in the White House," the president replied, referring to his Scottish terrier. "What is that?" Barney asked. "He pisses all over the place," the president said. "Mr. President," Barney responded, "how about if I just piss on some of your legislation?" "You could tell that the president wanted to respond but couldn't come up with a smart retort," Sergio recalled.

In the final year of his presidency, on Monday evening, January 28, 2008, before delivering his last State of the Union address, President Bush walked up to Barney, who was talking on his cell phone in the Speaker's lobby near the House chamber, patted him on the shoulder, leaned over, and remarked, "Tell him I said hello." After the speech, Barney found the president in Statutory Hall and told him, "Mr. President, the person I was talking to when you said to say hello was my boyfriend." "Well," President Bush said, "I hope you said how open-minded I am."

During the first term of Bush's presidency, Barney disagreed with the suggestion by some Democrats that Bush was incompetent. "He is very good at what he does, sometimes too good on the political side, from my standpoint. He is very clever politically," Barney said. He views Bush's presidency as a very conservative, right-wing administration, one that makes his father's administration seem quite moderate by comparison. He has referred to George W. Bush as "the heir of Ronald Reagan."

One of the things people have to understand with politicians, Barney says, is that you should not confuse amiability with a lack of ideological fervor. Someone who is personally pleasant is not necessarily someone who is ideologically moderate. Personality and ideology are unrelated. He described President Bush as "a very amicable man who is uniformly pleasant company, it would appear to be most of the time" but he followed a "very, very right-wing course." On virtually every issue, the budget, the environment, the rights of working people, in Barney's view, the Bush administration was about as far to the right as it could go within the current framework of U.S. politics. Bush believed that the most effective way to reduce the level of government activity was to reduce government revenues. Barney called this restriction of government spending "starving the beast."

He believes that President Bush was unable to grasp the reality of the nation's economy and subsequently the war in Iraq. Rather than the boy who cried wolf, he said, George Bush was the reverse. He claimed that there was nothing wrong when there was. He was "the boy who cried, 'Nice doggie.'"

In the fall of 2001, Barney voted against the Patriot Act, an antiterrorism bill that granted the police more surveillance power and sharply curtailed Americans' privacy. The administration had quickly patched together this "antiterrorist" legislation from a wish list compiled by law enforcement officials, including many provisions Congress had refused to act on in the past, and clandestinely stampeded it through Congress, allowing little opportunity for public debate. Barney told his House colleagues, "This bill, ironically, which has been given all of these high-flying acronyms—it is the Patriot bill, it is the USA bill, it is the stand-up-and-sing-the-Star-Spangled-Banner bill—has been debated in the most undemocratic way possible, and it is not worthy of this institution." He disagreed with the awkward title given to the bill in order to create the acronym PATRIOT. "Only my strong commitment to freedom of expression in general keeps me from filing legislation to ban the use of acronyms in legislative work. But invoking *patriot* in the context of this bill gives the unfortunate impression that those who disagree with it are not patriots."

Barney voted against the Iraq Resolution, passed by the House by a vote of 296 to 133, to delegate to President Bush the sole decision-making authority, without further congressional debate, to wage war against Iraq. He spoke out against the Bush administration's rush to war with Iraq, calling it "an unnecessary war." He saw a significant distinction between states that are oppressive and poorly run and those that are a danger to the United States. He didn't buy the administration's justification that Iraq posed an immediate threat to the United States.

He was critical of the Bush administration for misleading the American public about evidence of weapons of mass destruction in Iraq. "This is an administration that argued, in part, that the weapons of mass destruction were a major reason to go to war. . . . [Now] we are getting from [the administration] bait and switch," Barney said on the House floor on June 25, 2003. "Let us go to war because of weapons of mass destruction, and now it is because, well, [Saddam Hussein] was a terrible man. Yes, he was a terrible man. Terrible people are killing people in the Congo. Terrible people run Liberia. Terrible people run Burma. If, in fact, we are going to become the ones that go to the rescue of people misused and abused by their government, there are a lot more that we can go to."

He took issue with those who compared Saddam Hussein to Hitler. "While Hitler had been appeased, Saddam Hussein had been effectively contained," he explained. "Hitler was left alone to go into the Rhineland and then to Czechoslovakia. … and he was allowed to get stronger and stronger. From the day Saddam Hussein marched into Kuwait, he was weakened. With sanctions and overflights, there was a great difference between the way the world treated Saddam Hussein and Hitler." "We have been flying over and spying on him," he added. "What I take from Colin Powell's speech to the U.N. Security Council is that when Saddam Hussein sneezes, we know it. I mean look at the degree of electronic penetration we have. So I do not think he's in the position of doing anything bad, even though he would like to." The Bush administration tried to establish a link between Saddam Hussein and Osama bin Laden and al Qaeda. Barney, however, was unconvinced that such a link existed. "Osama bin Laden is an extremely fanatical Muslim, and until a few years ago I was a better Muslim than Hussein."

For almost thirty years, people have been coming to see Barney in his office to ask for things. Taped to the door leading to Barney's inner office is a piece of paper with the printed words from George Washington's *Rules of Civility and Decent Behavior*:

> 88th
> Be not tedious in Discussion,
> make not many Digressions,
> nor repeat often the same manner of Discourse.

Barney lives by this rule and expects others to. In the late 1980s Richard Goldstein, Barney's first legislative assistant, who had since joined a law firm, came to Barney's office with a name partner, Chuck Edson, to lobby him. They asked Barney to talk to Rep. Chuck Schumer about a particular issue, and Barney said, "Okay, I will talk to Schumer." When Edson followed up with, "Thank you, it would be great if you spoke to Chuck Schumer," Barney exploded. "I just told you I would. You don't have to repeat yourself," he said and proceeded to lambast Edson for three or four minutes for having confirmed and repeated something for three seconds. After Edson and Goldstein left Barney's office and were in the hallway, Edson turned to Goldstein and said, "Next time you lobby him by yourself."

Lester Hyman, an attorney and friend of Barney's who was the chairman of the Democratic Party in Massachusetts from 1967 to 1969, was representing the Massachusetts Broadcasters Association and set up a meeting between Barney and representatives of the radio stations that belonged to the association. The leader of the group began by telling Barney about the legislation they were seeking. Before he could explain why they needed it, Barney interrupted. "I'm for the bill," he said. When the group leader attempted to continue with the explanation, Barney interrupted again. "You don't have to persuade me," he said. "I don't care why you need it." The key to communicating with Barney, Hyman concluded, is to tell him something he doesn't already know.

In 1998 the Judiciary Subcommittee on Courts and Intellectual Property was scheduled to mark up a patent reform bill. Recognizing that the higher-education community had an interest in this patent legislation, Barney invited Kevin Casey, the director of government relations from Harvard University, and Terry Crowley, Casey's counterpart from MIT, to a meeting to discuss the legislation and "to tell me what you need in this bill." It was a highly technical bill designed to harmonize U.S. patent provisions with international patent law, to create a prior user right, and to deal with the issue of reverse engineering in software technology, among other things.

The two college government relations directors came to the meeting in Barney's office armed with their respective patent and technology experts. "I knew enough then that if you were going to a meeting with Barney you needed to have people who knew what they were talking about," Casey said. They went through the bill section by section. With each problem that the experts raised in the bill, and they were often quite technical, Barney would say, "I got it, get me some language on that" (for an amendment) or he would say, "I don't agree with that" and explain why. After a brief debate on the merits, they would move on to the next issue. "It was a classic meeting," Casey recalled. "We just sat there and watched this volleying tennis match between Congressman Frank and our two experts, going back and forth right through the bill. It was a mesmerizing performance and a prime example of his intellect and command of the issues."

The Harvard and MIT experts subsequently drafted about half a dozen amendments to the bill, ran them by some of their educational colleagues across the country, and delivered them to Barney. Casey was impressed to learn that Barney got every one of those amendments into the bill that came out of committee to the House floor.

In early 2000, Amy Isaacs, the executive director of ADA, tried to get the Democratic leadership in the House to focus on the dangers of Ralph Nader and the Green Party. She went to lobby Barney to set up a meeting with Democratic leader Richard Gephardt about Nader. She was accompanied by an associate who didn't know Barney at all. They met with Barney for all of about three minutes. As they were leaving Barney's office, the associate proclaimed that the meeting was a waste of time. "Just wait," Isaacs told him. Within a week they had their meeting in the Capitol with Gephardt and nine Democratic members of Congress about the dangers of Ralph Nader. "Barney understood exactly what we were talking about, he was the rainmaker, he made the meeting happen," Isaacs said. "Barney didn't feel it was necessary socially to continue meeting with us for more than three minutes. This other guy didn't understand it."

There is a sense of humility in Barney Frank. When you enter his district office in Newton, the first photograph you see on the wall in the reception area is of Father Robert Drinan, who represented the district in Congress from 1971 to 1980. It is a tribute and it shows the degree of respect Barney has for the man whose career in the House was cut short by papal edict.

Barney remains immensely popular in the Fourth District. Jerry Grossman, the longtime liberal activist who had drafted the reluctant Drinan to run for Congress in 1970, has a much higher opinion of Barney today than he did in 1980. In November 2004, the eighty-eight-year-old Grossman declared, "Barney Frank is a worthy successor to Drinan." He is highly visible, attentive, and responsive to local issues, and readily accessible to his constituents. He still spends considerable time in every city, town, and hamlet in the district. He works hard on constituent matters whether it is in securing federal funds to build a new drawbridge connecting the city of Fall River to the town of Somerset, the second largest construction project in Massachusetts, or getting the owner of a large pig farm in Rhode Island to take steps to reduce the odors that cause serious problems for residents of Westport and Fall River.

Barney has been praised for spending time in his district dealing with local issues that other members with his seniority wouldn't bother with. His philosophy is to be proactive. "He always wants to make sure that he has some kind of an early warning system, to know if something is going on that he needs to pay attention to," Dan Payne, his media adviser, said.

The basic rule in Barney's Washington office is that if a constituent walks through the door to see the congressman, the constituent gets in first no matter who else is waiting. "Over the years there have many notable heavy hitters sitting on the couch in the reception area waiting to see Barney when some constituent from Fall River stopped by unexpectedly, and the constituent has always gone first," a staff aide said.

During his early years in Congress, Barney would often take a turn answering the telephone during lunch time. "Congressman Frank's office," he would tell the caller. "You're talking to him," would often be the next line. When the caller didn't believe he was actually speaking with the congressman, Barney would hang up. The person would call back and Barney would answer the phone with the words, "What do you want now?"

He still reads constituent letters regularly. One staff assistant remembers Barney reading a letter from a blue-collar constituent and telling the assistant that he wanted to speak to the man right away. "The guy was shocked that the Washington office was phoning him and in total disbelief when I told him that Barney Frank wanted to speak with him," the staff assistant said. That doesn't happen in many offices on Capitol Hill.

The redistricting following the 2000 census did not have a significant impact on the Fourth District, which continues to be a safe Democratic seat. Most of the residents in Fall River were shifted into the adjoining district, and Taunton and New Bedford, the largest fishing port on the East Coast, were added to the Fourth District. "We didn't want to lose him," Carlton Viveiros, the former mayor of Fall River, said. "I'm comfortable in saying that the vast majority of Fall River residents would have preferred that he stay here, not taking anything away from the current congressman [Jim McGovern]." When New Bedford became part of his district, Barney began fighting for fishing-boat owners against unfair IRS rules and harsh fishing regulations. Many of the residents of New Bedford, like Fall River, are of Portuguese descent. Barney was successful in getting Portugal added to the list of countries for which the United States does not require visas for visitors. This and other legislative efforts on behalf of Portugal earned him the Order of Prince Henry (named after Prince Henry the Navigator), the highest medal that the government of Portugal gives to foreigners for services to Portugal. He regularly visits the Azores, an autonomous Portuguese island chain. Not one for pomp and circumstance, Barney once got off the plane and walked into an official greeting by local government officials wearing sweat pants and a sweatshirt.

Barney was first elected to Congress in 1980 with 52 percent of the vote. In 1982, he won reelection against Margaret Heckler with 60 percent of the vote. He has not faced a difficult campaign challenge since the Heckler race and has been reelected consistently by wide margins. His lowest vote total since the Heckler race came in 1990, on the heels of the Gobie sex scandal, when GOP political novice John Soto held him to 66 percent of the vote. He has won reelection by larger margins against Republican opponents ever since. In 1992, he easily defeated Edward McCormick, receiving 68 percent of the vote. He ran unopposed in 1994. In 1996, he was reelected with 72 percent of the vote against Jonathan Raymond, and he then ran unopposed in 1998. He won easily in 2000 with 75 percent of the vote against Martin Travis, and he ran unopposed for reelection again in 2002.

In the 2004 election, Chuck Morse, a conservative forty-seven-year-old businessman and radio talk-show host, challenged Barney, whom he called "out of place" and "the last gasp of limousine liberalism." Two years earlier Morse had published a book of his collected columns titled *Why I Am a Right-Wing Extremist*. In the book Morse praises the late Senator Joseph McCarthy and expresses the view that McCarthy was unfairly criticized. He says of Barney: "Frank, a self-described homosexual, exhibits the type of aggressive male behavior that is perhaps enhanced by a life without the civilizing influence of a woman." In the next sentence, he compares gay activists to Nazis.

Morse, who is Jewish and a native of Brookline, retained some name recognition from his Boston radio talk show *Morse Code* and from a local cable television program. But he missed the deadline under Massachusetts law for changing his party registration from Democrat to Republican to be able to run as a Republican in the congressional election, relegating him to running as an Independent.

In March 2004, Morse sent a fund-raising appeal to about 250,000 conservatives, mostly outside the Fourth District, including members of several ultra-conservative evangelical Christian groups, such as the Christian Response, to raise money to fight "the gay menace." He referred to Barney in the letter as "the most outspoken proponent of gay marriage in America" and "perhaps the most well-known and notorious gay rights activist in America" and concluded by saying, "Never has there been a better chance to throw Barney Frank out of office!"

Morse faced a tough battle to unseat the popular incumbent, who was nearly untouchable by any opponent in the Fourth District. Barney, however, did not take the challenge by Morse lightly and expended time and effort to confront him and his tactics. In a 2004 campaign fund-raising appeal that coincided with his sixty-fourth birthday, Barney borrowed from a song by Paul McCartney, asking "Will you still need me, / Will you still feed me, / Now I'm sixty-four?"

In keeping with his practice in campaigns over the years, Barney agreed to a series of debates with his opponent. As an officeholder, he believes it is his civic duty to accept such invitations. During one of these debates, Morse's constant recanting of reported press statements of his position on various issues drove Barney to announce, "He's become a serial untruth teller." At their debate in New Bedford, Morse charged that legislation Barney had sponsored in 1990 enabled the 9/11 hijackers to enter the United States. Barney refuted Morse's absurd charge and dismissed it as "the local version of the Swift Boat Veterans for Truth." Barney soundly defeated Morse in the general election with 80 percent of the vote.

Barney is a career politician. He opposes term limits and does not believe that elected representatives should come to Congress, take care of the business of government, and then after a time, like Cincinnatus, the Roman dictator, return home to their fields. In 1995, during the Judiciary Committee debate on a term-limit bill sponsored by Republican Bill McCollum of Florida that provided for a twelve-year limit, Barney proposed an amendment to apply the limits retroactively. "If in fact this is such a good idea, and if in fact too many elections have a negative influence, I can see no reason whatsoever for putting this off," he said. His amendment was rejected in committee by a vote of 15 to 20. When the bill came to the House floor for a vote, he spoke out against the bill and its hypocrisy, calling the issue one with "a lot of lip service and no teeth." "Never have so many voted yes but prayed for a no vote," he said.

In 2000, Barney remarked that he hoped to serve in the House another fifteen years or so. "I'd rather be here than anywhere else. There isn't anything I'd rather do," he said. "Barney is a pit bull and can stay in the ring with these guys," the former representative Michael Harrington said, referring to the Republican leaders. "He brings skills and credibility to that role." Cragg Hines of the *Houston Chronicle* said, "It's a good thing that the Democrats have someone like Barney Frank in the House. Without Barney, the House would be an awfully dull place."

In 2004 Barney said, "I am not in politics to win but I am in politics to affect public policy and I want to have a good debate." A decade of Republican control of the House, however, made him restless. He became frustrated by the absence of thoughtful debate in the House under Republican control. "There is an inverse relationship—the less important the legislation the more open-handed the Rules Committee will be in letting us discuss it," he remarked. He described the new system to E. J. Dionne Jr. of the *Washington Post*: "I don't mean to sound alarmist, but this is the end of parliamentary democracy as we have known it. [It is] 'plebiscitary democracy' in which leaders of the House have imposed such a strong sense of party discipline that they will ultimately pass whatever legislation they bring to the floor."

The Republican leadership ruled with an iron fist and were not prepared to allow GOP members to vote contrary to the leadership position if their vote mattered. "It was no accident that Tom DeLay was known as 'The Hammer,'" Barney said. On those rare occasions when a bipartisan coalition voted against the position of the leadership, the Republican leadership bent and subverted the House rules by holding fifteen-minute roll-call votes open, sometimes for three hours, to change as many votes as they needed to reverse the outcome—doing so by pressuring, intimidating, and effectively twisting the arms of Republicans to switch their votes. "There are no rules now," Rep. Pat Schroeder said. "The rules are [the Republicans] win and till they win the rules will be changed."

The most egregious example of the new Republican order, according to Barney, came in November 2003 on the Medicare prescription drug bill, which passed narrowly only after Republican leaders held the vote open for nearly three hours when it appeared that the Republican side had lost. By 6:00 a.m. Barney was irritated and exhausted. The Republican leadership had finally prevailed and enough Republicans had changed their votes to pass the measure. When he asked for a motion to reconsider, the Speaker pro tem reminded him that such a motion could be entered only by someone who voted on the prevailing side. "After all the razzle-dazzle, exactly what was the prevailing side?" Barney inquired.

The same thing happened again on July 8, 2004, when a bipartisan House majority (twenty Republicans joining with most of the Democrats) voted in favor of an amendment to an appropriations bill offered by Independent Bernie Sanders of Vermont to block a controversial provision of the Patriot Act and restore the civil liberties of people who go to a library or a bookstore. The GOP leadership held the vote open for more than thirty minutes in an effort to reverse the outcome.

The next day, on the House floor, Barney voiced his strong feelings about that "degrading spectacle" that undermines democracy. "It was particularly ironic that the Republican leadership chose to use extremely undemocratic tactics because there was a fear that democracy might break out," he said. He spoke about this nation's efforts to help the people of Iraq understand democracy. "We want them to be open. We want them to fully engage debate, not to suppress dissention. . . .

I hope you will convey to any Iraqis who might be watching the proceedings of this House on television with regard to democracy, if they see what we are doing, please do not try this at home." He pointed out that the delay in tallying the votes was not for the convenience of and to accommodate members so they could vote. Instead, he said it was a very particular form of delay carried out at the behest of the majority leader, Tom DeLay: "a 'DeLay-delay.'" The purpose of "this kind of 'delay squared'" he said, "is to allow members of the Republican leadership to press members of the Republican Party who have voted one way to now abandon that position lest the way they voted prevail."

The House ethics committee subsequently admonished DeLay for his conduct on three occasions, including his action of offering to endorse retiring member Nick Smith's son in the GOP primary to succeed him if Smith agreed to vote yes on the bill to add a prescription drug benefit under Medicare. DeLay complained about being rebuked by the ethics committee. As a result, the Republican leadership decided "to punish the ethics committee" by firing the Republican chairman, Joel Hefley from Colorado, and purging several independent-minded Republicans from the panel and replacing them with DeLay loyalists.

Appearing on *Meet the Press* on April 17, 2005, Barney told Tim Russert: "Let me be straightforward: fifteen years ago, I had a problem because I behaved inappropriately and the ethics committee stepped in. Newt Gingrich had a problem . . . and the ethics committee stepped in." "The difference between us and Mr. DeLay," he explained, is that "we changed our behavior. Mr. DeLay changed the ethics committee."

In May 2005, Democratic National Committee chairman Howard Dean remarked, "Tom DeLay ought to go back to Houston, where he can serve his jail sentence." Although Barney was probably the most vocal critic in Congress of the way Tom DeLay ran the House, he nevertheless came to DeLay's defense and publicly condemned Dean's remark in a guest appearance on *The O'Reilly Factor* on May 17, 2005. "To say that [Delay is] a criminal, at this point there's no basis for that. He hasn't been indicted. And yes, I thought it was a very unfair and inappropriate thing to do," he said. He then explained to O'Reilly: "Most of the time I'm going to agree with the Democrats and disagree with the Republicans. But on those occasions when I do strongly disagree with the Democrats and I don't say anything, I think I forfeit my right to have people pay attention to me when I say the things that I don't like about what Republicans are saying."

Barney was the senior Democrat on the Financial Services Committee. "It used to be the Committee on Banking and Urban Affairs until conservative political correctness banished the phrase 'urban affairs' from the title," he explained. During that period he got along remarkably well with the more conservative committee chairman, Michael Oxley of Ohio, and because of that strong personal relationship he was considered to be among the most effective ranking committee members in the House. As Barney sees it, in some ways it is much tougher being the ranking minority member than heading the committee. "As the ranking member you are constantly making choices. My view is that you have an obligation to get things done. If you can't get things done then you make the best political statement," he said in July 2008. "When I was in the minority, I didn't think that I would get much done in housing, so I made a political statement." The toughest situation, especially if you are in the minority, Barney feels, is to decide at what point you are compromising too much. "That is the most agonizing choice. Are you compromising too much or at some point are you better off with nothing?"

As the ranking Democrat on the Financial Services Committee, Barney often had an opportunity to verbally spar with Federal Reserve Board chairman Alan Greenspan. In 2001, Greenspan had supported President Bush's tax cuts and then three years later proclaimed that the government could not afford to meet Social Security commitments. "Sometimes mixed metaphors say it best," Barney remarked. "Greenspan's call for significant reductions in Social Security can best be described as a case of the fox in the chicken coop crying wolf. He is greatly exaggerating the dimensions of a problem that he helped create."

In 2004, Barney's eyes began to stray to "the other body." In 1984, he had told the *Boston Globe*, "I don't have the posture to be a senator." In his twenty-fifth-year Harvard reunion book, he wrote, on the subject of being a member of Congress, "It's a job I enjoy tremendously and felt very lucky to have it and hope to keep it for 30 years or so." In 1987, when asked by *Roll Call* whether he wanted to be a senator someday, Barney responded, "Hardly. I've been over to the Senate and there are two guys sitting around talking and a few guys playing cards. Nobody's listening; nobody's working most of the time. I'd be very stressed."

In early 2004, however, almost twenty-four years after being elected to Congress, he was ready to leave the schoolyard-brawl atmosphere of the House and move on to the pomp of the more formal and dignified U.S. Senate. He was eager to master the rules and procedures of the Senate, to perform his shtick on a more elegant stage, and to joust with the reigning lords, ladies, and knights of the Senate. "Could you see Barney in the Senate raising hell with the Republicans who then controlled the Senate? It would be worth the price of admission," one veteran Massachusetts politician said.

Barney was one of the earliest supporters of John Kerry in the crowded Democratic primary field for president. He considered Kerry to be the most electable Democrat because of his background as a decorated Vietnam War veteran and a tough prosecutor. "It is hard to demonize as an irresponsible leftist a man who has locked up criminals and shot Communists," he said. In 2003, a conservative group posed the following on its Web site: "Question—What could possibly be worse than President John Kerry? Answer—Senator Barney Frank."

Senator Kerry's presidential candidacy created an unusual political situation in the Bay State. The Democratic-controlled state legislature took the power of appointing an interim senator away from Republican governor Mitt Romney by passing legislation mandating that an election be held within 160 days after a senator declares an intention to vacate the seat. This meant that if Kerry won the presidency, there would be a special election for an open Senate seat in early 2005. That would have allowed current House members to run without having to give up their House seats. There likely would have been a Democratic ballot stampede and the field of candidates, in addition to Barney Frank, most likely would have included Ed Markey, the senior member of the Massachusetts congressional delegation, with just under three million dollars in his campaign bank, Martin Meehan from Lowell, with over four million dollars, and Middlesex district attorney Martha Coakley.

Anticipating that Kerry might win the presidency, Barney started laying the foundation for a run for the Senate and actually launched a preemptive shadow Senate race. Part of the preparation involved a furious effort to quickly raise campaign funds for a potential Senate race. He purchased $350,000 of television ad time, mostly on Boston TV stations, to air in eastern Massachusetts, for a congressional race in which his opponent, Chuck Morse, had no real chance of winning. He had not made a television campaign ad since the 1982 contest against Heckler. "The idea was to present Barney as someone with national stature who has stood up to powerful people," Dan Payne said. In a commercial titled "Stood Against," the announcer says that Barney stood up to President Bush and Vice President Cheney's rush to war in Iraq and opposed Attorney General John Ashcroft's Patriot Act. The tag line is "Barney Frank, who else?" After the commercial started airing, Barney's sister Doris, an administrator at Brandeis University, had people coming up to her and saying, "Who else?"

At the end of each of these commercials, Barney pokes fun at the new election requirement that candidates verbally approve their ads, the "own your own commercial" rule. He looks at the camera and says, "I'm Barney Frank, and I authorized this message." Then he shrugs and adds, "Who else would?" He used different variations at the end of each commercial, such as "I'm Barney Frank, and I approved this message. Isn't that a surprise?" or "I'm Barney Frank and I authorized this message. I can't imagine who else would." According to Payne the device worked well for Barney because he has an established persona as a wit.

Former representative Tom Downey explained to Barney, "If you are going to run for the Senate, you gotta be nice to people." Barney replied, "I can be nice to people." A few weeks later, Barney called Downey "to say he had been nice to someone that day."

The Frank family was ready and eager for a Senate campaign. "I'm alive and ready to do another television campaign ad," Elsie Frank said in May 2004. She was ninety-one. Doris was set to act as treasurer and handle the financial record-keeping for a Senate campaign. Everyone was preparing to tap the Jewish, liberal, and gay communities for a campaign war chest and eager to see how Barney would do in a statewide race. David was ready to take a leave of absence from his job with a public relations firm in Washington to help manage his brother's Senate campaign. And Ann, who received high marks for assisting Hillary Clinton in her successful Senate campaign in New York in 2000, would certainly be involved in Barney's Senate race in some capacity.

Celinda Lake, a national Democratic pollster and campaign consultant, did some surveys for Barney for the potential Senate race. "We were a bit surprised by how popular he was statewide and how he had gotten entrenched over the years with a wider audience across the state," Dan Payne said. "He had a 76-to-11 favorable-to-unfavorable rating and a huge lead over all the other candidates. Ed Markey and Martin Meehan were in single digits." According to Payne, while the people polled didn't always agree with Barney on the issues, they liked the fact that he is smart and funny and stands up and says what is on his mind.

Had John Kerry won the presidency, Barney would have won the Senate race in 2005 "walking away, no question about it," Philip Johnston, the Massachusetts Democratic Party chairman from 2002 to 2007, said. "I know that state inside and out and he would have been the senator." Former lieutenant governor Tommy O'Neill agrees wholeheartedly.

Although Barney had a big lead in the polling numbers, Markey and Meehan both had large campaign war chests to use to close the gap. Senate races in Massachusetts tend to be expensive. It wasn't as easy as Barney thought it would be to raise funds for a Senate campaign. Fund-raising requires a lot of hard work and time on the road. Barney hadn't had a tough election fight since 1982 and he does not enjoy campaigning. "It depended on whether Barney had the hunger in his belly to campaign hard for the Senate seat," Jim Segel, Barney's campaign manager during his first race for Congress in 1980, said.

Barney does not like to read prepared speeches because in his opinion he doesn't do very well. He was a speaker at the 2000 and 2004 Democratic National Conventions. When organizers at the 2004 convention insisted that he submit a text of his speech in advance, he scribbled down something on paper. Told by his staff that he was supposed to give the speech that he had submitted, he remarked, "C-SPAN is covering the speech. I'm there. What are [the convention organizers] going to do? Is there a trap door on the stage?" Instead of delivering the prepared speech he spoke extemporaneously to the convention delegates and the national television audience.

Speaking on behalf of the National Stonewall Democrats on the last day of the convention, he told the delegates: "When Ralph Nader tells us there is no significant difference between the parties, he trivializes our lives. Among the differences between the parties of overpowering significance are the issues of gay and lesbians to be treated fairly. . . . We believe we should be able to fight for our country. We believe employment should be based on performance, not sexual orientation. We believe that a fifteen-year-old who is different sexually ought to be able to go to his high school without being beaten up."

The third and final presidential debate between President Bush and Democratic candidate John Kerry was scheduled for October 13, 2004, at Arizona State University in Tempe. Kerry prepared for this debate that was to focus on domestic issues by discussing the economy, job losses, the nation's housing problems, and other domestic matters with Barney at a hotel in Santa Fe, New Mexico. Barney explained to the *Boston Globe* that as a member of the minority party in the House he is used to Republicans' limiting the speaking time for Democrats. "House members learn to talk in two-to-three-minute sound bites. You get to understand. Don't make too many points, and try to be substantive."

Barney went out to New Mexico to assist with debate practice at the suggestion of several colleagues, including Senator Ted Kennedy. Barney feels he wasn't much help. "I had a few things to suggest, and one or two he paid attention to. It was not a very useful thing. Kerry had this coterie around him. It's a classic example of staff resisting, feeling threatened, many of whom resented that I was there," he said. John Kerry disagrees. "I thought from my perspective he was enormously helpful. Barney in fact did help me think about a couple of things with some clarity. There is no one better," he said. Gregory Craig, who played George W. Bush in the mock debate with Kerry, said that Barney sat through the whole day of debate preparation and had some good ideas and good thoughts. "When Barney spoke," Craig said, "John Kerry listened to him, no question about that. He had enormous impact when he wanted to, but he wasn't the critical person in that room."

The November 2004 election turned out to be a disappointment for liberals and gay rights advocates. The Democratic Party lost five Senate seats in the South. The issue of gay marriage proved to be widely unpopular as voters in eleven states approved constitutional amendments banning same-sex marriages. "To those voters who are devastated by the election, who feel discredited, marginalized, ostracized, and humiliated by what their fellow Americans did to them on November 2," Barney's advice was, "Get over it." "The challenge," he said, "is to move from despair to strategy." He pointed out that John Kerry had won more votes than the Republican candidate for president did in 1992, 1996, and 2000. He was convinced that the 2004 election results were due to the Republicans' successful manipulation of the American public's fear and anger after the events of September 11, 2001.

At a time when liberalism appeared to be heading into exile, Barney did not waver. He remained committed to everything he has always stood for. He was not about to surrender to red-state values. "[The Republicans] govern by the simple view that all we need to achieve the good life is to take all restraints off capital—do not tax it, do not subject its owners to regulation, do not make them deal with labor unions, or worry about the environment," he said.

As Barney sees it, the right-wing Republicans want an intrusive government because they want to tell a woman what to do in a difficult pregnancy, they want to tell us with whom we can be physically intimate and under what circumstances, and they want to tell us what we should watch on television and when we should pray. "Republicans," he said, "have put extraordinary energy into using the mechanism of government to impose their own particular views on others and to achieve the spiritual ends to which they are personally committed, to make you more religious than you are." He told a predominantly Jewish audience in Massachusetts: "There's going to be more pressure for prayer in school—and I don't think it's going to be the *Sh'ma*. . . . I have not found too many Orthodox Jews who are in favor of prayer in the schools for a very simple reason. Few Jews expect school prayer to be conducted in Hebrew."

The Bush administration misread the 2004 election results as an endorsement of the right-wing agenda, economically and socially. President Bush's first proposal was to privatize Social Security by creating private investment accounts. According to Barney, this proposal was based on the Bush administration's misperception that the American public agreed that the free market system is wonderful and that government sucks. Their message was: "Have we got a deal for young people, a chance to get away from government which is so dumb and incompetent? We are going to allow you to take the money and instead of putting this money in a guaranteed system which is going to pay you a certain amount of money when you are old, no matter what, we are going to allow you to take the money and go into the stock market. Aren't you lucky?" But, Barney said, "When offered this choice of getting away from this old socialist government system of Social Security, where everyone gets the same amount of money, where there is no chance to shine, no initiative, no recognition, it was overwhelmingly unpopular. The American public did not buy into the notion that the private sector is always better than the public side." All along, the Democrats resisted and contended that privatizing Social Security was a terrible idea. According to Barney, Bush's proposal to privatize Social Security completely collapsed "to the point where if you said a Republican was for George Bush's Social Security proposal, he would call you a liar."

When Barney arrived in Washington on Saturday, March 19, 2005, he received a message that the House would be in session the next day, Palm Sunday, to deal with issues in the Terri Schiavo case. There was a midnight debate in the House on emergency legislation that had been approved without objection by the Senate to allow the parents of Terri Schiavo to seek *de novo* review in the U.S. District Court for the Middle District of Florida of their daughter's constitutional right to life and to request that the feeding tube that was keeping her alive be reinserted to keep the brain-damaged woman alive.

At the start of the debate, James Sensenbrenner of Wisconsin, the chairman of the Judiciary Committee and the Republican floor manager of the bill, said the battle to defend the preciousness of life is "not only Terri's fight, but it is America's fight." Sensenbrenner maintained that it was not a private bill.

Barney disagreed. As the floor manager for the opponents of the bill, he said: "Perhaps in the technical and irrelevant terms of the House calendar it is not a private bill. In fact it is a very private bill. It is so private that it only deals with the Schiavo case and her parents." "Section 7 of the bill specifically provides that 'Nothing in this Act shall constitute a precedent with respect to future legislation.' If this is such a good idea, why go to such pains, those of you who wrote the bill, to say it should not be a precedent?" he asked. "Anyone who thinks it will not be a precedent, of course, is not paying attention. What you will do . . . is invite every family dispute of this terrible, painful, heartrending nature to come to the Congress."

When several GOP members made specific medical arguments during the debate, challenging the diagnosis of Terri Schiavo's condition as persisting in a vegetative state, Barney warned his colleagues that elected lawmakers are ill-equipped to accurately diagnose her condition and make medical decisions. "The caption tonight ought to be: 'We're not doctors—we just play them on C-SPAN.'"

"Does she or does she not have brain function? Does she or does she not respond? Nobody in here has any way of knowing. What we have are members choosing a side based on their ideologies," he explained. "We had the eminent Dr. Frist looking at it on television and making his diagnosis. We have people making specific judgments about her medical condition. I do not know her medical condition. But neither do any of you." He contended that because the majority, for ideological reasons, does not like the decision of the Florida courts, we now have a new principle—"the Congress of the United States acting as the 'super Supreme Court of Florida.'" "Talk about forum shopping," he said. "This is the grandparent of all forum shops. We dislike what the courts in Florida have done, so we cancel their decision and we send it elsewhere."

After almost three hours of debate on the bill, majority leader Tom DeLay told his colleagues: "The legal and political issues may be complicated, but the moral ones are not. A young woman in Florida is being dehydrated and starved to death. For fifty-eight long hours, her mouth has been parched and her hunger pangs have been throbbing. If we do not act, she will die of thirst. . . . No more words, Mr. Speaker. She is waiting. The members are here. The hour has come."

The House passed the bill by an overwhelming vote of 203 to 58, with most Republicans supporting the bill and a narrow majority of Democrats voting against the measure.

"We overruled all of the decisions of all the courts in Florida and remanded it to the federal courts with instructions on how to decide the matter, including ignoring the rules of standing," Barney said. In pure legal terms, Congress basically conferred standing on Terry Schiavo's parents to intervene. Of the twenty-four federal judges who ruled on the issue, twenty-three, according to Barney, said, "You must be kidding." "One of them said 'I'll hear further argument.' Nobody said [Schiavo's parents had standing] and that included [Justices] Scalia and Thomas."

When the Republicans first came up with the proposal to keep Schiavo alive over the objections of her husband, the Republican leadership thought that it would be overwhelmingly popular because people would be sympathetic with Schiavo's parents and want to keep her alive. Many Democrats felt pressured to vote for the bill because they thought it would be popular back home in their districts. "That evening," Barney recalled, "at least eight Democrats came up to me and said that they didn't like the bill but were afraid not to vote for it."

What happened, however, was that the public was on the other side and reacted angrily to the bill. "The American public was furious," Barney said. "A lot of people who themselves had to make those types of anguishing decisions regarding the end of life of someone they loved took this as a criticism of their decision."

The Democrats in the Senate did not want to vote on the Schiavo legislation and the Senate had passed the bill unanimously. "The Senate is a wonderful place," Barney said. "As public opinion made itself clear, we now have apparently a majority of the Senate being on record as being opposed to the bill that they passed unanimously."

The week after the fight over Terry Schiavo, Barney received the kind of response from the public that he had last received during the Clinton impeachment hearings. "Strangers stopped me on the street and said not just that they agreed with me but thanked me and said, 'These crazy people [the Republicans] are coming after me and they can't be allowed to do this.'" Thus, according to Barney, in the two major issues after the 2004 election, one economic and one social, the American public did not agree with President George W. Bush and the Republicans.

In some ways Barney is old-fashioned. For many years, he resisted pleas from his staff to carry a cell phone. "I don't know CPR, and I can't make bail, so I'm of no use in an emergency," he said. Finally, in 2007 he began using a cell phone to communicate with his staff and a few select others. "He has lost a bunch of cell phones," one staff aide commented.

He advises his office staff to stay away from e-mail because he doesn't believe it is secret. "There are more people who get in trouble because of e-mails," he said. Barney tells everyone that works for him something that he learned in Boston in 1968 when he was Mayor Kevin White's chief of staff. It is the same advice that the legendary Boston political boss Martin Lomasney had given to his followers a century earlier: "Never write when you can talk, never talk when you can nod, and never nod when you can wink." He would place that message next to every e-mail keyboard.

Even in the minority during the Bush administration he was influential behind the scenes. In two court cases involving antidiscrimination claims brought by former employees against members of Congress, the members involved cited the speech-and-debate protection that they enjoy under the Constitution. They contended that nothing in the Congressional Accountability Act, passed by Congress in 1995 to outlaw discrimination against congressional employees, could overcome that protection.

Barney traced the speech-and-debate provision in the Constitution and the protection given members from, for example, being arrested on the way to work or from being sued in court for something they said on the floor, to the Elizabethan era in Great Britain. Members of the House of Commons wanted to be independent of Queen Elizabeth I and King James I. The monarchs would interfere with Parliament by preventing the House of Commons from assembling or by penalizing members for what they said in the House.

"The provision [in the Constitution] that says members of Congress cannot be arrested except for high crimes or misdemeanors, a phrase I must say I never understood why it is a high crime and misdemeanor. Seems to me it should have been a crime and a high misdemeanor, but I think even James Madison probably felt tired at two o'clock in the morning," Barney said. "He was doing a little drafting and made a little mistake, and he did not have the staff to do technical and conforming changes the way we do."

Barney argued persuasively that the speech-and-debate clause should be construed narrowly, and that in such circumstances any conflict between the antidiscrimination provisions of the Congressional Accountability Act and the speech-and-debate clause should be resolved in support of antidiscrimination law. In his view, dismissing an employee for discriminatory reasons has little to do with a member's legislative function.

The so-called Bipartisan Legal Advisory Committee, consisting of the speaker, the majority leader, the majority whip, the minority leader, and the minority whip, was considering whether to have the House counsel file an amicus brief in these two cases as a matter of institutional concern. Barney persuaded the Democratic leadership not to do so, even though one of the members charged with discrimination was a Democrat, Eddie Bernice Johnson of Texas, because it would undercut and infringe upon the Congressional Accountability Act. Based on Barney's arguments, the Democratic leadership chose not to participate in the filing of an amicus brief and the Republicans had to do it on their own and it was viewed as a partisan brief.

Barney took the same position regarding the speech-and-debate clause when the FBI, armed with a warrant issued by a judge, searched the office of Democrat William Jefferson of Louisiana. While the bipartisan House leadership sharply criticized the FBI's search of Jefferson's office, Barney believed that the congressional leadership overreacted and spoke out in support of the FBI search. Brian Unger asked Barney on MSNBC's *Countdown* on May 30, 2006, whether there was any irony in many House Republicans approving of warrantless wiretapping of average citizens but taking a different position when it comes to the warranted search of a congressman's office. Barney responded, "I would say there is more irony here than in the collected works of George Bernard Shaw." He added, "This was not an imprudently granted warrant. And the notion that we would object when a search is conducted of one of our offices pursuant to a warrant, when [members] don't object when there are searches without warrants of average citizens, yes, that's pretty ironic."

Barney believes that it is right under the speech-and-debate clause that members not be subjected to libel and slander laws in order for there to be free debate. However, in his view, it is inappropriate to interpret the speech-and-debate clause to give members of Congress special legal protections, superior to those of the average citizen, for searching their offices. "It's the speech-and-debate clause. And I got to tell you, my office has never made a speech," he told Unger.

On July 11, 2006, during the debate in the House on a bill to ban most gambling on the Internet, Barney stood at the podium and skillfully poked holes in the various arguments advanced by the proponents of the legislation. One congressman argued that gambling on the Internet does not add to the gross domestic product or make America competitive. "Has it become the role of this Congress to prohibit any activity that an adult wants to engage in voluntarily if it doesn't add to the GDP or make us more competitive? What kind of sociocultural authoritarianism are we advocating here?" he asked. "If an adult in this country, with his or her own money, wants to engage in an activity that harms no one, how dare we prohibit it because it doesn't add to the GDP or it has no macroeconomic benefit."

Another House member argued that the legislation was necessary because college students abuse Internet gambling and some have become addicted to online poker. "We should try to diminish abuse," Barney suggested. "But if we were to outlaw for adults everything that college students abuse, we would all just sit at home and do nothing." He pointed out that credit card abuse among students is a more serious problem than gambling and yet we don't ban credit cards for them.

Barney acknowledged that there is a practice around today that people do in excess, which causes a lot of problems, damages families, and causes people to lose their jobs and get in debt. "It is called drinking," he said. "Are we going back to prohibition? Prohibition didn't work for alcohol. It won't work for gambling," he argued. He maintained that the sensible thing is to try to deal with the abuse, not outlaw it.

As Barney sees it, the value of gambling is that some people enjoy doing it. We should therefore allow them to do it. But some people don't like gambling. "Well, fine," Barney said, "then don't do it. But don't prohibit other individuals from engaging in it," he urged.

Two days later, on July 13, Barney gave a lengthy discourse, without any notes, on the House floor about the Bush presidency. David Broder of the *Washington Post* wrote a column about Barney's talk, calling it an important speech that deserves more attention. The problem, Barney said, was that President Bush believed in a "plebiscitary presidency" in which the election makes the occupant of the White House the "decider" of national policy, adding that *decider* "is not a word that you will find often in American history." "This is an administration that believes that democracy consists essentially of electing a president every four years and subsequently entrusting to that president almost all of the important decisions," he said. "You elect [the president] and then get out of [his] way; and checks and balances and congressional oversight and media scrutiny, these are all interferences."

He questioned the president's authority to ignore a law like the Foreign Intelligence Surveillance Act that had been enacted in a constitutional manner and sets out a method for wiretapping and eavesdropping in cases involving foreign threats to the United States. "Presidents have a right to assert unconstitutionality but they do not have a right to ignore the law in secret," he argued.

Some supporters of the president contended that the president's authority to ignore a law derives from the vesting clause of the Constitution. "I thought gee, that is a pretty important clause apparently; it gives him all that power. How come I do not remember it better? So I went and looked it up," Barney said. "It says 'the executive power shall be vested in a President of the United States of America.' That is it. From those words the president and his defenders draw the conclusion that the president can ignore a duly enacted law of Congress if he thinks it should be done in a different way."

He pointed out that the Bush administration considered checks and balances to be a hindrance to effective governance. "Congress is supposed to be part of the constitutional mandate for collaboration. It does not come from Miss Manners; it comes from the Constitution. It is not a courtesy; it is a requirement of collaborative government," he said. "Shutting out the Congress means that you think you are perfect. But the problem of shutting Congress out is that you don't get that input that allows you to exercise powers in a reasonable way."

Barney pointed out that if the president doesn't like a bill he can veto it. But what Bush did was to pick and choose, as though the legislation "is a supermarket." "He walks in, he takes some from here, some from there, he discards what he doesn't like. That is not appropriate."

On August 24, 2006, Barney squared off against the outspoken conservative pundit and author Ann Coulter on CNBC's *Kudlow and Company* about the economy, immigration, and terrorism. Asked by the host, Larry Kudlow, to comment on Ann Coulter's remark that she wishes we could come up with a way to tax only rich liberals, Barney observed, "It has no more logical content than the rest of what Ms. Coulter has said." When Coulter interrupted that she had been about to say nice things about him, Barney responded, "If you said nice things about me, it would take me months to recover with everybody I care about. Please don't ever do that. I know you can be very nasty but saying something nice about me would be even for you a new low."

At the end of the program, an exasperated Ann Coulter asked Kudlow, "Am I ever going to go on with a Democrat who doesn't personally attack me the whole time and then call me nasty?" Barney replied, "Ann Coulter complaining that other people are being nasty is real chutzpa."

In the fall of 2006, running unopposed for reelection to the House, Barney traveled across the country campaigning nonstop for Democratic candidates in an effort to help the Democratic Party win back the House after twelve years of Republican control. In one of these campaign stops, he appeared at a fund-raiser in Palm Springs, California, for David Roth, the Democrat trying to unseat the Republican incumbent, Mary Bono. Bono had urged Barney not to come into her district to campaign against her. It was not an easy choice for him since she had been a friend for more than ten years. But he chose to put the Democratic Party ahead of personal friendship. He explained to Bono that it was not personal, that he was not going to say bad things about her, but that he was supporting Democratic candidates. He recounted the story from his 1982 campaign when Margaret Heckler was furious at Tip O'Neill for campaigning for Barney, and Tip explained to her that even if his own brother were running as a Republican he would campaign against him. According to Barney, he would have campaigned for the Democratic candidate even if the incumbent had been Sonny Bono.

On the campaign trail, Vice President Dick Cheney warned voters that if the Democrats take control of the House, liberals such as Representative Barney Frank of Massachusetts would become chairmen of powerful House committees "and I don't need to tell you what kind of legislation would come." "[The vice president] doesn't think any legislator should be making policy, members of Congress, conservative or liberal, given his view of the Constitution. So I wasn't too upset," Barney said.

Rep. John Hostetler warned voters in a campaign ad in Indiana that if the Democrats win the House, Speaker Nancy Pelosi would allow Barney Frank to advance a radical homosexual agenda. Hostetler was defeated in his bid for reelection. "That apparently left some people expecting me to produce a radical homosexual agenda, and I don't have one. I felt inadequate," Barney said. "I do think we should allow gays and lesbians to serve in the military, get married, and have a job but, by tradition of radical standards, being in the military, working for a living, and getting married are not the stuff of radicalism. So I'm still looking for a way to satisfy that demand."

22

A Committee Chairman at Last

AFTER TWELVE YEARS of being in the minority, the Democrats finally regained control of the House following the 2006 elections, and Barney Frank became a House committee chairman at last. It had been a long time coming. According to Robert Kaiser, the associate editor of the *Washington Post* and a friend from NSA days, every two years since as early as 1996, with unwavering optimism, Barney had expected the Democrats to take back control of the House because he believed they were on the right side of almost every issue. "I think to the present day he doesn't really want to acknowledge the Democrats' role in how things went south," Kaiser said after the elections. Barney was always "too optimistic, too certain." "It has been hard for him." Becoming a committee chairman, he added, "is really a big thing" for Barney.

Barney became chairman of the Committee on Financial Services, which has legislative jurisdiction over affordable housing programs, one of his passions, as well as insurance, banking, and the securities industry "in all of its recent, exotic transmogrifications," as Barney described it. The committee also oversees the Federal Reserve System and international financial institutions, such as the World Bank and International Monetary Fund, as well as the economic reports mandated by the 1978 Humphrey–Hawkins Full Employment Act.

Barney had always assumed that if he stayed in Congress long enough he would become chairman of the Judiciary Committee, since he was the second most senior Democrat after John Conyers, who was in his seventies. He did not expect to become chairman of the Financial Services Committee. There he was behind Chuck Schumer, who was ten years younger than he, and also behind John LaFalce and Bruce Vento, who were about his age. But in 1999 Schumer was elected to the Senate, in 2000 Vento died of cancer, and LaFalce, who had been the ranking Democrat on Financial Services, did not seek reelection in 2002 because of the redistricting changes the New York legislature made following the 2000 census.

The day after the 2006 election, in a speech to business leaders in Boston, Barney proposed a "grand bargain" to ameliorate some of the tensions between business and labor and make the system better for both. He called on the business community to increase the wages of its workers, stop busting labor unions, and support universal health insurance in return for the passage of legislation to break the gridlock on trade, immigration, deregulation, and foreign direct investment, and other economic legislation that business believes contributes to growth. It was an attempt to convey to the business community that while he was supportive of many of the things that business believes are necessary to take advantage of the efficiencies of globalization, unless business worked with Congress to make sure that some of the benefits go to the people who get hurt, the business community was going to be stymied legislatively. Barney was subsequently disappointed that business in general and the Bush administration in particular showed little interest in supporting this "grand bargain." However, after two years at the helm of the Financial Services Committee, and after earning the respect and trust of the business community, he is hopeful that they will reconsider this "grand bargain" during the 111th Congress.

After the 2006 election, he recognized a need to be circumspect with his witticisms because what he said as the chairman of the Financial Services Committee might have an effect on the financial markets. However, that was easier said than done. When the Securities and Exchange Commission changed its rules to loosen the reporting requirements for executive compensation just before Christmas 2006, Barney joked, "I didn't even know they had a chimney at the SEC."

"When Barney was first put on the Banking Committee in 1981, there was a great deal of trepidation among the bankers in Massachusetts about having a liberal Democrat on that committee," Richard Goldstein, a former legislative assistant, recalled. "Soon the bankers came to love him. The bankers urged, 'Deregulate us,' 'Let us compete.'" Barney, he said, supported the philosophy of deregulation. "He is a liberal who understands business." Unlike many liberals, Barney believes that deregulation of industry is often good, even if it eliminates weaker competitors. "Supermarket chains do better for the consumer than the corner grocery. Ma and Pa—I'm all for the concept, but they're inflationary," he observed.

In Barney's view, it is unfortunate that the term *regulate* is used to cover two different phenomena. In most cases, he opposes regulation that displaces the market by trying to set prices, regulate entry, or allocate resources. That, he says, is almost always a mistake, whether it is in trucking, the airlines, or agriculture. However, he also believes that there are some regulations that are needed because there is nothing in the free market system, for example, that is going to clean up the environment or protect the health of workers in a factory. "The free enterprise system doesn't pretend to do these things. If you want to protect the health and safety of workers, the government has to set the rules," he said.

Barney has long been a supporter of the free market system. In August 1987, he opposed a banking bill because it involved some reregulation in the bank–nonbank limitation that many of the major financial institutions themselves had asked for. "We have a lot of business people in this country that joined some of my Republican colleagues in being very great supporters of free enterprise and competition in general, but not being too crazy about it in particular," he said. "The vaunted American preference for free enterprise turns out to be something of a spectator sport. A lot of business people like to watch other people engage in competition, but not engage in it themselves."

He agrees with conservatives that a free market is a necessary condition for a prosperous America, but also believes that capitalism must be compatible with concerns for fairness. The capitalist system, as he sees it, is built on inequality in that people are unequally rewarded, which is not a bad thing. "If people who make better judgments where to put resources, if people who better understand what the market wants, and if people who work hard and come up with better ideas don't get unequally rewarded, then the capitalist system doesn't work," he said. "However, left entirely to its own devices, the free market will produce more inequality than is either socially healthy or economically necessary for the efficient functioning of the system." Thus, he believes, the role of government should be to diminish that inequality where it's not socially healthy without getting to the point of losing market efficiency. It is the job of those with public policy responsibility to formulate rules that allow the capitalist system to function, which it does by creating incentives that allow for the necessary level of inequality but do not allow that inequality to become too great.

According to Barney, we cannot have economic growth without paying attention to how that growth is shared. "Workers are angry because their real wages have eroded as the gross national product has risen," he said. He often cites former Federal Reserve Board chairman Alan Greenspan's testimony to the Financial Services Committee that the great majority of people, particularly working families, have not shared in the increased gains of economic growth. Toward the end of the Bush administration, he pointed out that 95 percent of workers in the United States had had no increase in their income after inflation in the preceding six years, despite claims by the Bush administration to the contrary. Borrowing a line from the Marx brothers, he asked, "Who are you going to believe—me or your wallet?" He would reduce that inequality by raising the minimum wage, expanding unionization, and providing public-sector programs that help people go to college.

His least favorite metaphor is the one first used by President John Kennedy, that "a rising tide lifts all boats." In Barney's view, although John Kennedy said many profound and useful things, that was not one of them. Barney strongly disagrees with the concept that a steady increase in the overall gross national product will make everyone better off, so that there will be no real need for governmental activity aimed at people who are in economic need. If you extend the metaphor, he points out, you have to consider the people who don't even have a boat because they can't afford one and are standing on tiptoe in the water. "For them a rising tide is not a cause for jubilation." According to Barney, the liberal position ought to be very clear: "We are supportive of the free enterprise system and want to stimulate it, but we don't think it lifts all the boats; a booming GNP is a necessary but not a sufficient condition."

Barney loves being chairman of the Financial Services Committee. He once said the job makes him feel "like a kid in a candy store, assuming they still have candy stores." In early 2007, he declared publicly that he would not give up the chairmanship of the Financial Services Committee to run for the Senate should John Kerry decide not to seek reelection in 2008. "That's a lot to give up to become a freshman senator. There is more ego but less public policy impact in being a senator," he said. "Finally, at age sixty-seven I get to do something as chairman. It is a whole new chapter. My best legislative work is now." "I am an overnight sensation at age sixty-seven," he told the television interviewer Charlie Rose in November 2007.

Earlier that year he said, "For the first time in my life I have more power than knowledge in some areas." "In housing I have an agenda. On the economy, macro-economics, poverty, inequality, I know what I want to do. But in the securities area, I am not sure what to do about hedge funds and other exotic market instruments. That's daunting."

It has been an exciting and challenging first two years for Barney. He became chairman of the Financial Services Committee at a time when the subject areas within its jurisdiction were among the most critical facing the nation. According to Barney, he has been working harder at this new job than at any other time since his first years as executive assistant to Boston mayor Kevin White, when he was often in his City Hall office seven days a week, for up to sixteen hours. "I now know a very great deal about those things that are in the jurisdiction of my committee, and less about almost everything else than I have ever known in my life," he said.

Just as in 1981 when he was first appointed to the Banking Committee and the business community assumed that he would be antibusiness, the assumption that as chairman he would be antibusiness has been proven incorrect. "He has a real zeal for bringing legislation out of the committee," Dennis Shaul, a senior committee aide and a longtime friend of Barney's, said. The committee under Barney's leadership was remarkably productive during 2007, passing with bipartisan support a steady stream of legislation, ranging from bills to restrict subprime mortgages, to those that tighten federal review of foreign takeovers of U.S. companies, and others that extend the federal terrorism insurance program. Some of these bills had languished in committee for years before Barney took over the chairmanship.

The Mortgage Reform and Anti-Predatory Lending Act, the first legislative response to the crisis in subprime mortgages (loans offered to borrowers with spotty or weak credit histories) that addresses the problem of irresponsible lending, passed the House on November 15, 2007, by a vote of 291 to 127. The bill, sponsored by Barney, reins in abusive practices by lenders and establishes minimum standards for borrowers to be able to repay loans. In Barney's view, regulation has to keep up with innovation. The regulation contained in this bill, he contends, is market sensitive and not disruptive, and this kind of regulation improves the quality of the market and enhances the market. "Regulation didn't kill the secondary subprime mortgage market, excesses killed it," he said. "Regulation that gives investors some assurance that when they go into the market they are going to be buying things that have some reality to them is a pro-market thing."

From the time he took over the chairmanship of the committee, Barney has had the overarching legislative goal of making affordable housing available to low-income families. Early on, together with Maxine Waters, he began drafting legislation to deal with the tremendous deficit in affordable housing in many parts of the country. One such measure would establish the National Affordable Housing Trust Fund to provide for the construction, rehabilitation, and preservation of decent, safe, and affordable housing for low-income families.

Barney and Waters were among the first to recognize the importance of helping cities and local governments deal with the problem of surplus foreclosed properties and avoid the blight resulting from large-scale foreclosures, abandoned homes, and deteriorating neighborhoods. The idea of buying up the foreclosed surplus properties to use as affordable housing was essentially Barney's. "I thought about when the Resolution Trust Corporation bought up properties during the savings-and-loan crisis [in the 1980s] and we put in a rule that some of those properties be sold at a low cost." It was originally drafted as a stand-alone bill and the strategy was to tee up the legislation and have it ready for when a Democratic administration came along.

Barney was the chief architect of the Housing and Economic Recovery Act of 2008. He set out to craft a package that combined the priority items of the Bush administration and the Republicans, such as modernizing the Federal Housing

Administration (FHA) and reining in government-sponsored enterprises Fannie Mae and Freddie Mac by providing a new regulator and tighter controls, with Democratic agenda items. This package gave him a good vehicle to move the affordable housing measures. "We figured [the administration] would need us and we put it all on the train," he explained. According to Barney, the art of the deal is to try to have legislation that more people want than hate. You have something that a lot of people want, it has some things they don't like, and very few things they absolutely can't stand. "In the end," he said, "you throw out the things they can't stand and do the deal."

In the face of an economic perfect storm, with crashing home prices, a flood of home foreclosures, banks teetering on collapse under the weight of enormous losses from worthless mortgages, the faltering economy on the brink of a national recession and threatening the stability of the global financial system, Barney had a responsibility to act. He aggressively responded to the crisis by crafting legislation to stem foreclosures and provide stability to the housing and financial markets.

The foreclosure rescue plan was designed to help the hundreds of thousands of homeowners who are at risk of foreclosure because sharp increases in rates on their mortgage obligations combined with plummeting housing prices have caused their mortgage obligations to now exceed the current value of their homes. The rescue plan will allow them to refinance with affordable loans that are backed by the FHA and based on current home value.

He takes offense at criticism that banks such as Credit Suisse and Bank of America and other lenders were included in the discussion and had a role in drafting parts of the bill. "We can't abrogate contracts and we can't force the banks and other mortgage holders to abrogate contracts. We have to induce them to do it voluntarily. So we talked to them and they were players at the table," he explained. "Besides, I thought of [the plan] because it is the only logical thing to do."

Barney spent a great deal of his time on the politics of moving the legislation, which he described as "complicated." Referring to a bloc of forty-seven fiscally conservative Democrats who advocate pay-as-you-go budgeting, that is, any new spending must be offset by tax increases or spending cuts elsewhere, he said, "The 'Blue Dogs' objected if we didn't pay for it, and the Ways and Means Committee complained about having to pay for it and give up some of the tax [offsets] that they wanted for other purposes." The Congressional Black Caucus wanted to be involved as well.

Barney was the lead House negotiator and, together with Senate Banking Committee chairman Christopher Dodd (and sometimes also the panel's senior Republican, Richard Shelby), and Treasury secretary Henry Paulson Jr., he hammered out the final legislative package.

According to Barney, neither he nor Paulson, who became Treasury secretary in June 2006, expected their working relationship to be as productive as it was. "As we began talking, it turned out we got along well, we could communicate, and get things done," Barney said. He has a high regard for Paulson, who, he said, proved to be invaluable for his ability to move President Bush and persuade the president to do things he would otherwise have resisted.

Dealing with the Senate, however, and bridging the divide between the House and the Senate became frustrating for Barney. But he remained optimistic. Republican Jim Bunning from Kentucky led the fight in the Senate to defeat the legislation. When a reporter asked Barney whether he thought that Bunning would be successful in stopping the bill, he replied, "He will get slightly more votes than his lifetime E.R.A. and he was a pretty good pitcher in the major leagues and so that is not a very large number."

With an eye toward compromise, Barney made several changes in the bill to accommodate White House concerns, dropping a provision that would have established an auction process through which lenders could transfer mortgages in bulk to FHA insurance, and adopting a provision that bars homeowners who lied about their income or key information from obtaining FHA assistance.

One of the great strengths that Barney had in the negotiating process was an overwhelmingly unified Democratic Caucus. In the fall of 2002, Barney had started preparing for his role as the ranking Democrat on the Financial Services Committee by reading Robert Caro's *The Years of Lyndon Johnson* to learn from Johnson's experience as Democratic leader in the Senate. "It helped me establish a relationship with other members," he said. In Barney's view, as committee chairman, you appear to people on the outside as more powerful than you are. What you get as chairman is the ability to put coalitions together. The House is an extremely diverse body. There are coalitions and caucuses based on issues and others based on age, race, gender, ethnicity, geography, and political philosophy. "The most important thing was to have the thirty-six Democratic members of the Financial Services Committee solidly behind me," he explained. That group, a microcosm of the Democratic Caucus, included some popular Blue Dogs and several leaders of the Black Caucus. "I kept them informed, and by making this a committee project, having my members proud of it and involved with it, I had all these allies in the Democratic Caucus." In addition, Speaker Nancy Pelosi was very supportive of what he was doing.

During the negotiations Barney had more freedom to act than the other negotiators. "In some ways negotiating is tougher when you have more freedom," he said. "You sort of invent restraints on yourself." "Dodd would say, 'I can't get Shelby to go along with that.' Paulson would say, 'I have to deal with the White House.' I didn't have anyone," Barney explained. He called it "the Geraldine factor," after the character portrayed by the comedian Flip Wilson who always excused her behavior by claiming, "The devil made me do it." "I needed a devil," Barney said. When Speaker Pelosi asked how he handled this problem during negotiations, he responded, "I blamed you, the Blue Dogs, or the Black Caucus, depending on the issue."

The $3.9 billion in funding, provided in the form of community development block grants (CDBGs) to help localities hardest hit by the housing crisis buy and rehabilitate foreclosed properties, posed a dilemma for Barney. "We always had this problem in the House of paying for the program because of the 'Blue Dogs,'" he said. "We thought maybe it would go in a second stimulus package." Then the Senate included this provision in their housing recovery bill, and that caused problems. The Bush administration threatened to veto the bill. Barney wanted to add the CDBG funding to the bill but felt bound to some extent by his agreement with Paulson. He believed that adding the CDBGs would have escalated the conflict, and either it would have been a deal breaker or it would have caused the president to veto the entire legislation. He recognized that Secretary Paulson had a very conservative administration telling him that they were willing to swallow the affordable housing trust fund but didn't want the CDBG funding on top of it. "There is too much that is important in this bill, and it has already been too long delayed by procedural problems in the Senate for us to risk the further delay involved in a veto," Barney said. In his pragmatic mind, getting a substantial part of something accomplished is far better than getting nothing done. "If you lose and you politicize it, what does that get you?" he asked. "It is not easy to lose and turn that into a win. People do it for emotional satisfaction."

Maxine Waters, the vice chair of the committee and a longtime ally, who had been constructive in moving this legislation, however, threatened, on behalf of the Black Caucus, to vote against the bill unless the CDBGs were included. "I don't know what Maxine would have done in the end," Barney said. "We were working to find a way to shift the funds to a must-pass spending bill. At the time I thought the best we could do was to get a firm commitment from the Speaker that it would go into a continuing resolution and we could survive a veto there."

Over the weekend of July 19, Treasury secretary Paulson asked for something new and far-reaching, standby authority for the Treasury to extend a line of credit for Fannie Mae and Freddie Mac and to purchase stock in the companies if needed. Privately, Barney believed that Paulson's request made public-policy sense and that it responded to the fears of the financial markets by providing reassurance of the mortgage giants' stability. Yet he also realized that this gave him an opening and provided some bargaining leverage.

When Barney arrived in his office on Monday, July 21, he found that the Republican leadership was denouncing Paulson's plan for a cash infusion for

Fannie Mae and Freddie Mac. This response had the effect of driving away any support for the bill by conservative Republicans. The Democratic left was also suspicious of Paulson's plan. Later that day, when Barney attended a meeting of the Democratic Caucus, it became clear to him that the bill could not pass without the funding for the CDBGs. Otherwise, they would risk losing as many as seventy Democratic votes.

After the Democratic Caucus meeting, Barney phoned Secretary Paulson and told him that the funding for the surplus properties had to be included in the bill. Paulson was upset and resisted. He reiterated the administration's substantive argument against the surplus properties program, calling it wasteful and asserting that it would help banks and lenders and not homeowners facing foreclosure. Referring to the effect of Paulson's action in adding the line of credit for Fannie Mae and Freddie Mac to the bill, Barney explained to the Treasury secretary: "I am not altering things. You raised the bet. I am seeing you but not raising you. I am calling you." It was clear to Barney that the bill would not pass without the CDBG funds needed to win the support of the Congressional Black Caucus. He asked whether Paulson could deliver the additional Republican votes needed to approve the legislation without the CDBG provision. Paulson could not and reluctantly agreed to the inclusion of the $3.9 billion in the bill.

The Housing and Economic Recovery Act was a complicated package. It provided FHA program modernization, and FHA mortgage rescue, the reform of Fannie Mae and Freddie Mac, and an affordable housing trust fund, a first-time home-buyer tax credit of up to seventy-five hundred dollars, and standby authority for the Treasury Department to extend a line of credit to Fannie Mae and Freddie Mac. Some members of Congress use charts mounted on large boards that are placed on easels on the House floor as visual aids in discussions of legislation. Barney never uses such charts. This one time, however, he had prepared a chart that he planned to use during the floor debate on the housing recovery bill. According to Barney, the mood wasn't quite right and he decided not to display it. The large display board showed a kitchen sink with a diagonal line through it.

On Wednesday, July 23, the House approved the legislation by a vote of 272 to 152. Forty-five Republicans supported the bill, many of them from districts that had been hard hit by foreclosures. "I would have liked to have gotten more Republican votes," Barney said. "Initially, I thought that we might get sixty Republican votes and was a little disappointed." According to some observers, Secretary Paulson did not do a good selling job when he appeared before the Republican Caucus on Tuesday, angering some GOP members. Barney rationalized that from the political standpoint of the Democrats it was the ideal number. "Too many Republicans in favor of the bill for the GOP to attack us from a demagogic populist position but not enough for them to take any credit for it," he said.

At the celebratory press conference after the House vote, Speaker Pelosi congratulated Chairman Barney Frank for doing such a wonderful job navigating the waters to pass the legislation. Barney recognized committee vice chair Maxine Waters and remarked, "This is one of the waters I had to navigate."

The Senate approved the legislation four days later. On Wednesday morning, July 30, despite misgivings and pleas from several House GOP leaders to veto the bill, President George W. Bush signed the bill into law in a private White House ceremony. As a result of the economic storm, Barney was able to get President Bush to agree to more of the legislation than he otherwise would have. From Barney's perspective, there were a number of good things in the bill and it didn't include anything that he hated. He maintains that it is the best low-cost housing bill in more than twenty years. He also made the broader point that liberals were responding in a way that validates the liberals' philosophy of regulation. It demonstrated that liberalism and understanding the financial system can go hand-in-hand.

In late August, several days before the Democratic convention in Denver, Barney was relaxing on vacation when Secretary Paulson phoned to caution him that they had examined the financial records at Fannie Mae and Freddie Mac and found more financial trouble than they had anticipated. Two weeks later, on Saturday, September 6, Barney was in Rep. Jerry McNerney's district in Stockton, California, one of the areas in the country hardest hit by foreclosures, chairing a field hearing of the Financial Services Committee on the effects of the foreclosure crisis on neighborhoods in California's Central Valley. During the hearing he received an urgent phone call from Paulson, informing him that the government was taking over Fannie Mae and Freddie Mac. "It seemed like it was needed for Freddie but not necessarily for Fannie. However, you couldn't do one without the other," Barney said.

On Thursday evening, October 2, the day before the House was scheduled to vote a second time on the seven-hundred-billion-dollar Emergency Economic Stabilization Act, Barney appeared as a guest on the television program *The O'Reilly Factor* to discuss the financial crisis. The host, Bill O'Reilly, began the segment by playing a July 14, 2008, video clip of Barney stating: "I think this is a case where Fannie and Freddie are fundamentally sound, that they are not in danger of going under. They're not the best investments these days from the long-term standpoint going back. I think they are in good shape going forward."

As Barney later described the exchange, "a ranting, vitriolically incoherent, finger-pointing Bill O'Reilly went out of control." The media pundit accused him of being responsible for the failure of Fannie Mae and Freddie Mac and for causing Americans to lose millions of dollars when the companies were taken over and called on him to step down as chairman of the Financial Services Committee.

Barney tried to defend himself. He said: "I became chairman of the committee on January 31, 2007. Less than two months later, I did what the Republicans hadn't been able to do in twelve years—get through the committee a tough bill [to regulate Fannie Mae and Freddie Mac]. And it passed the House in May. . . . Now from 1995 to 2006, when the Republicans controlled Congress and we were in the minority, we couldn't get that done. Although in 2005, Mike Oxley [then the Republican chairman of the Financial Services Committee] . . . did try to put a bill through to regulate Fannie Mae. I worked with him on it. As he told the *Financial Times*, he thought ideological rigidity in the Bush administration stopped that."

The exchange continued, growing more and more heated.

O'REILLY: All right, that's swell! But you still went out in July and said everything was great. And off that, a lot of people bought stock and lost everything they had.

BARNEY: That's wrong.

O'REILLY: Look, stop the B.S. here. Stop the crap! . . . Oh, none of this was your fault! Oh no. People lost millions of dollars. It wasn't your fault. Come on, you coward! Say the truth!"

BARNEY: What do you mean, coward? (*Barney looked stunned.*)

O'REILLY: You're a coward. You blame everybody else. You're a coward!

BARNEY: Bill, here's the problem with going on your show. You start ranting. And the only way to respond is almost to look as boorish as you. But here's the facts—

O'REILLY: Blame everybody else in the world and then call me boorish.

BARNEY: I'm not going to be bullied by your ranting. You can rant all you want, you're not going to shut me up! The problem was that we passed in 1994, in fact—

O'REILLY: Now we're back in 1994. This is bull. This is why Americans don't trust the government.

BARNEY: No, this is why your stupidity gets in the way of a rational discussion.

O'REILLY: At least [SEC chairman] Cox is man enough to say he screwed up. You're not.

BARNEY: Hey, Bill. This manliness stuff is very unbecoming from you. I don't see any—

O'REILLY: Cox is man enough to say he screwed up. You're not.

BARNEY: You think toughness is yelling and ranting and trying to bully. It's not going to work with me. The fact is in the very quote you played, I said it's not a good investment. I tried to get the regulations adopted.

O'REILLY: It is your fault.

BARNEY: . . . You don't listen at all, or maybe you are listening or you're too dumb to understand.

O'REILLY: No, you hit it. I'm too dumb. . . . (*Pointing his finger at Barney*) You're the brilliant guy who presided over the biggest financial collapse in federal history.

"O'Reilly thought that he had me nailed on Fannie and Freddie and the facts just don't support it," Barney said on December 4, recalling the intense exchange with Bill O'Reilly two months earlier. "It is hard to explain in a short period when [O'Reilly] is yelling."

Barney pointed out that the statement he had made on July 14 that O'Reilly had shown in a video clip was based on the fact that the Congress was poised to pass a bill that tightened regulatory control over Fannie Mae and Freddie Mac, in accordance with the Bush administration's wishes. Shortly thereafter, Secretary Paulson requested that the bill be amended to give the Treasury secretary two-hundred-billion-dollar standby credit-line authority for Fannie Mae and Freddie Mac. The bill passed by the House on July 23 included this authority. "We did think that would stabilize them," Barney said. "Paulson and Bernanke said give us this [legislation] and they are well capitalized." He added, "We were not encouraging people to buy their stock but we were hoping that people would buy their paper. You could buy their paper without risk because [the government] was standing by it." Barney acknowledged, "I underestimated the fear in the market. The market became irrationally depressed but that was after we had done all we could legislatively to fix it."

After the House passed the Emergency Economic Stabilization Act establishing the Troubled Asset Relief Program on Friday, October 3, Barney returned to his district and found that he had an electoral problem. A poll taken that weekend showed him to be weaker electorally than at any time since 1982. He was down to 55 percent from his usual 70 to 75 percent. Although he was not in any real danger of losing the election with the other 45 percent split three ways—17 percent for the Republican candidate, Earl Sholley of Norfolk, the owner of a flower shop and landscape business who had run unsuccessfully four times for the state Senate, 10 percent for the Independent candidate, Susan Allen, an educational consultant from Brookline, and 18 percent undecided—he was not taking any chances. Barney realized what had happened. The seven-hundred-billion-dollar financial rescue package, which many voters viewed as the taxpayers picking up the tab for failed investments by Wall Street firms, was overwhelmingly unpopular, and he had become the public face of the bail-out program. Also, he had been absent from his district for long periods doing committee work in Washington. For the first time in many years, he spent the month of October in his district campaigning for himself. He canceled a trip to California to do an Obama fund-raising event and several out-of-town trips to campaign for Democratic House candidates.

Barney became a target not just for Bill O'Reilly but for other GOP conservatives who tried to shift the focus away from the impact of deregulation to the Democrats and to liberals like him. They accused Barney of causing the financial crisis by protecting Fannie Mae and Freddie Mac, blamed him for the failure by Congress to act earlier, and contended that he was responsible for the subprime mortgage fiasco because of his support for efforts to promote homeownership by people who could not afford such loans. Earl Sholley, the right-wing GOP candidate running against Barney for Congress, started repeating the misinformation the Republican campaign apparatus in Washington was spreading. Sholley referred to Barney as "the chief architect of the mortgage meltdown" and nicknamed him "Barney Bailout." Barney responded aggressively to those accusations and defended his record in Congress. He pointed out that in 1994 when the Democrats still controlled Congress, they passed a bill giving the Federal Reserve Board chair the authority to restrict and prevent unregulated entities, such as mortgage brokers and finance companies, from making subprime mortgage loans. However, the Federal Reserve Board under chairman Alan Greenspan, a champion of deregulation and a firm believer that the markets know best, refused to use its power to regulate subprime mortgages. It was this authority that Bernanke used in 2007 to promulgate rules to prevent irresponsible subprime mortgage loans from being made in the future.

Barney argued that for twelve years, from 1995 to 2006, when the Republicans were in the majority and controlled Congress, not one bill to reform and increase regulatory control of Fannie Mae and Freddie Mac became law. While he supported a vigorous role for Fannie Mae and Freddie Mac in keeping housing affordable for low- and middle-income families, he did not thwart efforts to tighten regulatory control over these companies. He found the charge by his GOP opponent, Sholley, that he had singlehandedly blocked efforts over the years to reform Fannie Mae and Freddie Mac to be somewhat bizarre. And he was bemused by the suggestion that during the twelve years the Republicans were in power he somehow had a secret hold on Newt Gingrich and Tom De-Lay and they didn't do anything without his approval. "If I had the power to block things when I was in the minority, I wouldn't have started with Fannie Mae and Freddie Mac. I would have blocked the Iraq war, the Patriot Act, hundreds of billions of dollars in tax cuts to rich people, bills to weaken the Environmental Protection Agency, and a very flawed prescription [drug] program," he told the *Newton Tab* on October 6. In fact, in March 2007, just two months after becoming chairman of the Financial Services Committee, he moved a bill through the committee to regulate Fannie Mae and Freddie Mac. The House passed that bill in May, with all 223 Democrats voting for it and 103 Republicans voting against it.

"I was one of the politicians who said you are going too far with efforts to promote home ownership. I publicly opposed giving mortgages to unqualified borrowers because I believed that some families are better off renting," he said. He was pressing the Bush administration to do more rental rather than home ownership in support of his view that there is nothing wrong with some people being renters. In an op-ed column in the *Wall Street Journal*, Larry Lindsey, a former economic adviser to President George W. Bush, acknowledged the part Barney had played, calling him "the only politician I know who has argued that we need tighter rules that intentionally produce fewer homeowners and more renters."

Barney decided to go on the offensive by airing two television ads, something he had done only once since 1982, in 2004 as part of his shadow Senate campaign. The first thirty-second spot, created by his longtime media adviser Dan Payne and titled "Losing Control," begins with a clip of Bill O'Reilly ranting at Barney. The overhead caption reads: "The right wing is losing control of themselves over Barney Frank" while the announcer says, "For twelve years, the Republican majority refused to regulate the financial system. Last year Barney Frank became chairman of the House Financial Services Committee and started working on the subprime mortgage crisis, outrageous CEO compensation, and other Wall Street abuses. Now they're back—trying to stop Barney Frank." The announcer concludes, "Help Barney continue what he just started." At the end of the ad, Barney says on camera, "I'm Barney Frank. I approve this message and the chance to be on TV without interruption." Bill O'Reilly was so outraged by this ad that he aired it on his television program and used it to continue his attack on Barney. "O'Reilly took the bait," Barney observed at the time.

The second ad, titled "Elephants," begins with the announcer saying: "The Republicans are running scared from today's financial crisis. For twelve years they did the bidding of the financial giants that wanted no regulation. One man is taking them on and looking out for average people." Then, as a line of elephants performing in a circus appears on the screen, the announcer says, "Barney Frank wants these giant institutions brought into line." Barney has the last word: "I'm Barney Frank. I approve this message because it's time to end the circus on Wall Street."

In the closing days of the 2008 presidential campaign, GOP candidate John McCain in his stump speeches pointed to the dangers of unified control of government and charged Speaker Nancy Pelosi, Senate majority leader Harry Reid, and Financial Services Committee chairman Barney Frank with being "tax and spend Democrats." McCain took direct aim at Barney's call for a 25 percent reduction in defense spending, which had ballooned from $305 billion in fiscal year 2001 to $716 billion in fiscal year 2009.

After a month of constant campaigning in the district, Barney was able to regain much of his popularity and support and wound up with 68 percent of the vote in the November election. "I did well in Fall River and New Bedford and the traditional Democratic areas and perhaps a little better than expected in some Republican areas," he said. "The fall-off was in the middle America parts of the district."

Speaker Nancy Pelosi received only 72 percent of the vote in her San Francisco district in which she usually wins reelection with well over 80 percent of the vote. According to Barney, this outcome is an affirmation of the point that you really want people in leadership positions in the Congress who are not from marginal districts and have some votes to spare, because there are times when as a leader you have to do something that is unpopular in the short term.

In retrospect, Barney believes that the seven-hundred-billion-dollar financial bailout bill that he helped draft gave the Treasury secretary too much discretion in deciding how to use the rescue funds and which firms would get the money. He is angry that Secretary Paulson refused to spend any of the Troubled Asset Relief Program funds to help homeowners facing foreclosure. "When the program was passed by Congress we included very specific language to provide foreclosure relief," Barney said. The bill mandated that when the Treasury Department purchased troubled mortgage assets the Treasury secretary had to act to help borrowers stay in their homes and avoid foreclosures by exchanging high-cost loans for more affordable loans backed by the federal government. "It didn't occur to us that [Paulson] would shift entirely from buying up troubled assets to injecting capital directly into troubled financial institutions [by purchasing equity interests] and [attempt to] avoid doing anything to stem the rise of home foreclosures," he explained. He does not understand and has never received a good explanation from Paulson for why he shifted course, particularly after arguing so strongly how important it was for the government to buy these toxic assets and remove them from the banks' balance sheets. Also, he believes that Congress should have done more in the bill with respect to setting conditions for use of infused capital, such as requiring financial institutions to lend that money back out again. Although Barney generally admires Paulson, he believes that the Treasury secretary made a mistake by not leaning on banks to lend out that money in an effort to loosen the credit markets. Yet overall, he said, "We are better off than if we hadn't passed the bill." When asked whether he was disappointed that the financial crisis had consumed so much of his attention as committee chairman during the past two years, leaving him no time to focus on housing legislation, Barney replied, "We bootlegged every good housing bill into the Housing and Economic Recovery Act in July [2008]."

In many significant ways, Barney has not changed much in the past half a century. He remains unaffected by the trappings of office and the lure of the personal things that money can buy. When he arrived in Congress in 1981, he decided that the pension system for lawmakers was too generous and refused to join the plan, choosing instead to be part of the Social Security system like most other Americans. "Barney is a person that has no attachment to monetary, physical or personal wealth," his former boyfriend Sergio Pombo said. A former staff aide remarked, "Barney is probably the last person to ever be bought off because he is oblivious to material things." A congressman who has no interest in money, travel, golf outings, skyboxes, or lavish meals had to be lobbyist and influence peddler Jack Abramoff's worst nightmare. Barney recently explained to Daniel McGlinchey, a committee staff member, that the great thing in not caring about material things is that it gives you so much more freedom.

Barney still does the daily crossword puzzle, though now from time to time he finds himself in it as either a clue or an answer. He is more frequently recognized in public, and not just in Massachusetts and Washington. He has been portrayed on *Saturday Night Live* by Mark McKinney in a January 1995 sketch about Newt Gingrich's first day as House Speaker, by Horatio Sanz in the two 1998 skits about the Judiciary Committee impeachment hearings, and then by Alec Baldwin in a December 2005 skit about Barney as a guest on the *O'Reilly Factor*, a precursor to the O'Reilly tantrum in October 2008. In recent sketches about the financial crisis, Fred Armisen has played Barney. ("That guy is pretty versatile if he is doing me and Obama," Barney commented.)

"When you see Barney in the street today, he is exactly as he was thirty years ago and without missing a beat," Tommy O'Neill observed. "He can recall a conversation that he had with you twenty-five years ago, remembering what your argument was, and what point he was trying to make, and why his point was better."

He is still as smart, irreverent, and unpretentious as he was as a teenager in Bayonne, with the same sense of humor, the same charisma that draws friends, and the same obsession with politics. His political philosophy also remains the same. His friend Dennis Shaul sees a core of progressive politics in Barney that has not changed in the forty-five years they have known each other. That core, he said, "is not compromised by holding office." Another friend, Philip Johnston, said, "He is always conscious of what can be accomplished. His pragmatism is a constant and has never changed." He added, "Barney has always been consistent in his support for poor people and has never wavered." Barney relies on his values and instincts to determine what position to take on issues. One change his friends have seen is in his appearance. He is a lot neater now than he was thirty years ago.

Herb Gleason, who has known Barney since the late 1960s when they worked together for Boston mayor Kevin White, sees another change. "There is warmth now that was not obvious before," he said. Barney's longtime friend Mark Furstenberg sees other changes. "This is a particularly good time in his life. He is so much more comfortable, a more fulfilled person, more self-confident, much clearer what he wants to achieve," he said. In May 2008, Barney wrote a letter to past campaign contributors "simply to stay in touch" and with "no request whatsoever for money, praise, oral support or anything else."

His hair is thinner and graying in a distinguished way and he doesn't have the same energy he had twenty-five or thirty years ago. He has thickened around the neck and stomach and is continuously fighting to keep his weight down, yet, at sixty-nine, he looks more youthful than most men his age. The guy at the carnival would not guess his age within the requisite three years. He speaks a bit slower these days, at a speed better suited to normal ears.

For Barney Frank, in many ways "the best of times" is now. After twenty-eight years in Congress he is a seasoned legislator and a powerful and respected committee chairman. As he demonstrated in crafting the Housing and Economic Recovery Act, the seven-hundred-billion-dollar Emergency Economic Stabilization Act, and the fourteen-billion-dollar auto industry loan bill, negotiating with the Bush administration, and pressing and prodding House members to pass these bills (the auto industry rescue bill collapsed in the Senate), he is still at the top of his game as a lawmaker and as a deal-maker. He is at the center of measures by Congress to respond to the global financial meltdown, the most significant economic crisis since the Great Depression.

Barney's future in public life appears bright. He had no immediate interest in a cabinet position. "We are only partly there with affordable housing," he explained. "I want at least two years with President Obama and a solidly Democratic Senate so that we can get the federal government back in the housing business." Assuming that the housing legislation he is seeking would be in place within two years, the secretaryship of Housing and Urban Development would then be inviting to him ("I want to get people into housing") but not Treasury ("I don't want T-bill notes to be my major focus in life").

Barney has successfully blended his work life with a satisfying private life and in doing so has achieved greater happiness. He feels comfortable with who he is and he is no longer emotionally isolated. He is free to be himself. "I am what I am," he said, and quickly added, "sort of like Popeye." Toot! Toot!

Index